PAPER
LOSSES

PAPER LOSSES

A Modern Epic of Greed and Betrayal at America's Two Largest Newspaper Companies

Bryan Gruley

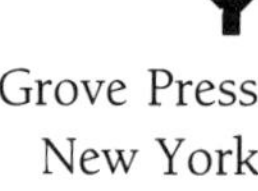

Grove Press
New York

Grove Press
841 Broadway
New York, NY 10003

Published simultaneously in Canada
Manufactured in the United States of America

Library of Congress Cataloging-in-Publication Data

Gruley, Bryan.
Paper losses / Bryan Gruley.
Includes bibliographical references and index.
ISBN 0-8021-1402-4
1. Detroit news. 2. Detroit free press. I. Title.
PN4899.D55N44 1993
071'.7434—dc20 93-6868

FIRST EDITION 1993
10 9 8 7 6 5 4 3 2 1

To Pamela Jean

Joel

Kaitlin

and Danielle

Contents

Cast of Characters

The Evening News Association

Peter B. Clark, chairman and president
Peter A. Kizer, executive vice-president, Broadcast Division
Edwin C. Frederickson, vice-president, finance
Jay Higgins, of Salomon Brothers

The *Detroit News*, circa 1984

Robert C. Nelson, publisher
Lionel Linder, editor
Benjamin J. Burns, executive editor
Richard J. McClennen, marketing director
Robert Kurzawa, circulation director

The Takeover Players

George Gillett, ENA shareholder
Ralph Booth II, of Booth American Company
John Booth II, of Booth American Company
Guerin Todd, ENA shareholder
Porter Bibb, of Ladenburg, Thalmann and Company
David McKearnan, of Donaldson, Lufkin and Jenrette
Robert Vlasic, of Cranbrook Educational Community
Norman Lear, Hollywood producer
A. Jerrold Perenchio, Hollywood producer
Robert Cahill, counsel to Lear and Perenchio

The *Detroit News,* circa 1986

Maurice L. "Moe" Hickey, publisher
Louis A. "Chip" Weil III, president
Robert H. Giles, executive editor
Christina Bradford, managing editor

The Gannett Company

Allen H. Neuharth, chairman and chief executive officer
John J. Curley, president
Douglas H. McCorkindale, vice-chairman
Lawrence J. Aldrich, senior legal counsel
John Stuart Smith, of Nixon, Hargrave, Devans and Doyle

Knight-Ridder, Inc.

Alvah H. Chapman, Jr., chairman and chief executive officer
James K. Batten, president
John C. Fontaine, general counsel
Robert F. Singleton, senior vice-president, finance
P. Anthony Ridder, president, Newspaper Division
Clark M. Clifford, of Clifford and Warnke
Philip A. Lacovara, of Hughes, Hubbard and Reed
Stephen M. Shapiro, of Mayer, Brown and Platt

The *Detroit Free Press*

David Lawrence, Jr., publisher
Jerome S. Tilis, president
Robert J. Hall, general manager
Heath J Meriwether, executive editor
Neal Shine, senior managing editor

The Unions

Louis Mleczko, president, Newspaper Guild Local 22
Donald Kummer, administrative officer, Newspaper Guild Local 22
Elton Schade, secretary-treasurer, Teamsters Local 372
Joel Wilson, president, Mailers Local 2040
Thomas Brennan, president, Graphic Communications Local 13
Eugene Driker, of Barris, Sott, Denn and Driker
Duane Ice, of Miller, Cohen, Martens and Ice

The Justice Department

Edwin Meese III, attorney general
William Bradford Reynolds, counselor to the attorney general
Frank Atkinson, deputy chief of staff
Michael Socarras, special assistant to Reynolds
William Levin, special assistant, Office of Legal Counsel
Morton Needelman, administrative law judge
Charles F. Rule, assistant attorney general, Antitrust Division
Seymour Dussman, attorney, Antitrust Division
Douglas Letter, attorney, appellate staff, Civil Division

Thomas W. Merrill, deputy solicitor general

Michigan Citizens for an Independent Press

State Senator John F. Kelly
W. Edward Wendover
Matthew Beer
William Schultz, of Public Citizen Litigation Group
David Vladeck, of Public Citizen Litigation Group

Others

William J. Keating, chief executive, Detroit Newspaper Agency
Michigan Governor James J. Blanchard
Warren E. Buffett
Jack Kent Cooke
Congressman John D. Dingell, Michigan
President Gerald R. Ford
Ralph Nader
President Richard M. Nixon
Detroit Mayor Coleman A. Young

Introduction

This is the story of two American newspapers and how they tried to kill each other.

They stood two blocks apart on West Lafayette Boulevard in downtown Detroit, separated by a bank, a saloon, and a gutted hotel. At one corner loomed the *Detroit News,* five square stories of imposing gray fortress, the paper of record for Detroit's hard hats and blue collars, who punched out from their factory jobs and grabbed a *News* to read over a beer before supper. The country's ninth-largest daily newspaper was Detroit's Old Gray Lady, plodding but thorough, lackluster but reliable, an unwavering sponsor of conservatism and restraint.

Two blocks east stood the *Detroit Free Press,* a fourteen-story tower reaching for the sky under a dazzling blue-and-yellow neon sign. The newspaper born here every night was known as the "Morning Friendly," breezy and unpredictable, beckoning its readers into the new day. The colorful pages of the *Free Press,* the tenth-largest daily in America, celebrated the young and the new, the daring and the untested, while offering a liberal voice of comfort to the downtrodden and dispossessed.

Between them, the *News* and the *Free Press* totaled daily circulation of more than 1.2 million. They vied for the hearts of readers and the wallets of advertisers in a gritty, workaday city teeming with stories of violent crime, seedy politics, big business, and professional sports. The natives truly loved their papers. Race riots, urban blight, population loss, and the decline of the auto industry did nothing to slake Detroiters' thirst for news of their troubled home. The *News* and the *Free Press* counted more readers per capita than any big daily in the country. Only New York and Chicago could boast as many as two such mighty papers.

Both more than a century old, the *Free Press* and the *News* thrived for decades, despite each paper's vigilant efforts to steal readers and advertisers from the other. The 1980s were a different story. For myriad sociological and economic reasons—not to mention fear, greed, and increasingly bitter rivalry—both papers began losing money. As the losses mounted into the tens of millions of dollars, their battle took on a deadly cast. The warriors were bloodied and barely standing, but they refused to fall, for the survivor would gain eternal life—a virtual monopoly of the $400 million Detroit market.

In 1986 they fashioned what appeared to be a truce. Allen H. Neuharth, chairman of Gannett Company, Inc., owner of the *News,* and Alvah H. Chapman, Jr., chairman of Knight-Ridder, Inc., owner of the *Free Press,* agreed to combine the newspapers' business functions—circulation, advertising, production, and promotion—while keeping separate news and editorial staffs. The peculiar result would be a joint operating agency, or JOA. The Detroit JOA would be the largest such combination in history. It would be a lucrative enterprise, promising Neuharth's Gannett, the nation's largest newspaper company, and Chapman's Knight-Ridder, the second largest, billions of dollars in profits over its hundred-year life.

Detroit was a fitting crossroads for Al Neuharth and Alvah Chapman, old rivals who had gotten to know each other in that very city twenty-six years before. The men and the companies they ran were as different as the *Free Press* and the *News.* Chapman was the quintessential Knight-Ridder executive—solid, workmanlike, nearly invisible, a well-to-do country gentleman whose father and grandfather had published newspapers in the Deep South. Chapman's Knight-Ridder was widely admired for running big-city papers that dominated the annual awarding of the coveted Pulitzer Prizes. Meanwhile, Gannett took the prize for making money. Neuharth was a street-smart hustler who had fled the anonymity of his South Dakota upbringing to become a latter-day press lord. He did it by building obscure Gannett into a vast network of cash-rich dailies in sleepy towns like the one Neuharth had left. Like its flamboyant leader, with his taste for limousines and luxury hotels, Gannett was bold and self-indulgent, a glitzy parvenu of the modern publishing elite.

By law, the armistice Neuharth and Chapman reached in Detroit had to be sanctioned by the federal government. On May 9, 1986, the companies filed an application seeking the endorsement of Attorney General Edwin Meese III. A prompt approval was not forthcoming, however. The case dragged on for nearly four years, wending its way to the highest court in the land. By then it was clear that the war between the *Free Press* and the *News*—and the rivalry between Neuharth and Chapman—was far from ended.

Both Detroit newspapers wrote about their pursuit of the JOA. As of August 1986, I was the reporter covering the story for the *News*. I did not regard it as a plum assignment. Personally, I took a cynical view, believing it next to impossible that the probusiness Reagan administration would deny a request by two large corporations. Professionally, I preferred that some other reporter cover the JOA; it didn't seem as sexy as the corporate takeovers I had been covering as a member of the *News*'s business staff. Also, I felt uncomfortable reporting on my employers and our loathed competitor, the *Free Press*.

By the time the JOA came before the U.S. Supreme Court in the autumn of 1989, I had a much different view of the story that had consumed three years of my life. Though still immersed in the legal, financial, and political minutiae of the publishers' quest, I began to believe the story of the Detroit JOA—or rather, the Great Detroit Newspaper War—was a watershed in the modern evolution of daily newspapers. The thirty-year battle between Detroit's dailies seemed to encapsulate the profound changes that had swept newspapering in the latter third of the twentieth century.

I wrote this book while I was a reporter for the *News* in Washington, D.C. Robert H. Giles, the *News*'s editor and publisher, granted me sixteen months' leave of absence, with full pay and benefits, while I researched and wrote much of the book. However, no one from the *News* or Gannett had any editorial control over my work. This is the first my bosses have seen of it.

Nevertheless, I am aware that some will perceive, at the very least, an appearance of a conflict of interest. To them I can only say that I have tried mightily to be fair and objective in telling this tale. But the reader also should know that I could not totally distance myself. I grew up in and have a great deal of affection for Detroit; my parents, who live there still, are lifelong *News* subscribers. I personally witnessed or otherwise experienced many of the occurrences that make up this narrative. I know a handful of the people I have written about—all minor characters—personally as well as professionally. Try as I might, I could not obliterate my personal feelings.

This is not a book about the impending death of the daily newspaper. Newspapers have undergone a vast, wrenching upheaval in the last thirty years, and they face enormous challenges to identify their role and find new sources of sustenance in a world of rampant illiteracy, fragmenting markets, sound-bite politics, and MTV. Nevertheless, newspapers will be around, in their familiar printed form, for decades to come. How they will thrive while carrying out their journalistic mission remains to be seen, but a few disturbing clues reside in the tale of the Detroit papers.

This book is a passage. Through its vessel, the Great Detroit Newspaper War, I have tried to sketch the grander scenarios that shaped the passing of an era: of families fighting to save their legacies from the voracious maw of the modern age; of once-mighty labor unions clawing for survival; of common people confronting the Goliaths of commerce; of newspapers struggling to honor their historic role as defenders of the public trust while serving new masters on Wall Street and Madison Avenue.

It is a tale of greed and venality, courage and nobility, hard truths and black lies. Above all, it is a story of our selfish unwillingness to let go of the past and confront the uncertainty of the future.

Part One

A Death in the Family

1

The Promise

Security at the *Detroit News* had been instructed to keep all non-*News* reporters and camera operators out of the building, especially anyone from the *Detroit Free Press.* So the curious camped outside on the sidewalk along West Lafayette Boulevard between Second and Third streets, hoping for a glimpse of whoever might be the new owner of the *Detroit News.*

It was August 29, 1985. The board of directors of the Evening News Association, the company that owned the *News,* had met the day before. There were rumors the directors had voted to sell their company, but no one who knew was talking. The bored reporters staking out the fortresslike *News* building had agreed among themselves that the buyer would be billionaire Jack Kent Cooke or Gannett Company, although they had not yet ruled out the New York Times Company. The reporters wished a buyer would show up soon so they could make their deadlines and go home.

Late that afternoon, a black stretch limousine drew up to the curb. The journalists crowded around as a short, trim man of sixty-two bounced out, flashing a brilliant smile. He wore a natty black sport jacket and gray slacks that accentuated his wavy silver hair. A fat diamond ring dominated his right hand and a slender bracelet of gold dangled from his left wrist. He grinned and winked at the reporters. He seemed to relish the attention.

"Hello, how are you?" he said charmingly. "Do you have your stories yet?" He enjoyed teasing them. The reporters shouted back, asking if his company would be buying the Evening News Association. In reply he gave them a sly smile and whisked through the revolving doors and into the front lobby of the *News.* One of his deputies told the guard at the reception desk that Allen H. Neuharth, chairman and chief executive of Gannett Company, had arrived.

The message was passed swiftly upstairs to the mezzanine, where Peter B. Clark, president of the Evening News Association, was waiting. Clark was expecting Neuharth, but he had thought the Gannett executive and his entourage would enter the side entrance to the building, where their cars could slip into a private garage without reporters spying who was inside. When he was told that Neuharth had come through the front door, Clark snapped.

"They can't come in here," he fumed. "I have to talk to my troops." Clark had wanted to address his employees before the news was out that Gannett had agreed to buy the Evening News Association. Now it was too late. Still, the outburst was uncharacteristic of Clark, a professorial man rarely given to displays of emotion. He would not remember it later. But perhaps it was then that Peter Clark finally realized, with strangers in his lobby and reporters rushing off to tell the world, that his anguished struggle to save his family's company was over.

For eight months Clark had played the role of embattled patriarch, bravely determined to rescue his great-grandfather's legacy from the clutches of the predators who would steal it. The legacy was the Evening News Association, or ENA, owner of five television and two radio stations; nine small newspapers in California and New Jersey; and the *Detroit News,* America's ninth-largest daily newspaper. For decades, the company had been controlled by a tight cadre of descendants of James E. Scripps, the penny-wise entrepreneur who founded the *News* in 1873.

Tall and fleshy-faced, with bushy eyebrows, spectacles, and a great shock of white-on-black hair, the fifty-six-year-old great-grandson of James Scripps had led the company since 1963; he was named publisher of the *News* the day John F. Kennedy was shot. Over the years it was Peter Clark who had sought to calm impatient young family members who, it seemed to Clark, cared less for the long-term preservation of Scripps's bequest than for what it might quickly yield in cash. It was Clark who had pushed the ENA to buy television stations and direct its gaze away from Detroit toward the Sunbelt, where the security of the future lay. It was Clark who had promised, time and again, that the *News* would triumph in its costly battle with the rival *Detroit Free Press.* And it was Clark who had painted a vision of the ENA as a powerful nationwide fleet of media properties, with the *News* as its proud flagship.

In the summer of 1985, Peter Clark's plans had tragically unraveled. The war with the *Free Press* had grown bloodier than ever; the *News* had lost more than $20 million in the first half of the 1980s. A handful of Scripps family shareholders, impatient with the *News*'s travails, turned against Clark. A trusted deputy betrayed him. ENA stock, once held almost exclusively by a few hundred family members, found its way into the hands of Wall Street traders. Speculators circled the ENA like vultures, coveting in particular its lucrative CBS affiliate in Washington, D.C. In July, a pair of wealthy Hollywood producers made a hostile takeover bid. Things got out of control then, happening so fast that Clark could not clutch tightly enough to keep the ENA from slipping through his fingers. Soon he had no choice but to seek a buyer of his own choosing, one that might sustain the bequest of James Scripps, that might even fulfill the splendid dreams Peter Clark once had had for the company.

The buyer was Gannett Company, owner of *USA Today* and eighty other dailies, forty nondailies, six television stations, fourteen radio stations, a weekly magazine, a polling firm, and a billboard operation. Gannett papers counted circulation of 4.7 million—more than 7 percent of the national total—collected $2 billion a year in revenue, and regularly posted some of the industry's highest profits. In twenty years Gannett had grown from an obscure regional group into the nation's largest chain. Much of Gannett's remarkable ascent was due to the impatient genius of its top executive, Al Neuharth.

Neuharth and his predecessor, Paul Miller, had built Gannett's empire on a foundation of small and midsized dailies in middle-American towns such as Chillicothe, Pensacola, Danville, Hattiesburg, and Port Huron. Facing little serious competition, the papers had posted remarkable profit margins, as high as forty cents on the dollar, while producing mostly unremarkable journalism. No one in the newspaper business questioned Gannett's financial prowess, and almost no one paid attention to its homey, small-town journalism. Then, in 1982, came *USA Today,* Neuharth's bold, irreverent attempt to make Gannett a leader in journalism as well as moneymaking. Though it lost incredible amounts of money and attracted the scorn of traditional journalists for its breezy approach to the news, gaudy, color-splashed *USA Today* made Al Neuharth a journalistic force, for better or worse, for the future of newspapering.

By 1985 he was the best-known American newspaperman of his time, by dint of the popularity of *USA Today,* his enormous ego, and his uncanny ability to draw attention to himself and his company. Neuharth delighted, for example, in the welter of brickbats tossed at *USA Today,* for they, more than anything, helped make his paper a household word. To Neuharth, there was no such thing as bad publicity. "Just spell my name right," he liked to say.

Neuharth had last been at the *News* in the early 1960s, when he was the number-two editor at the rival *Detroit Free Press.* Back then, he had walked from the *Free Press* building three blocks east on Lafayette Boulevard. Today, the limo had ferried him in comfort from the Westin Hotel in the shimmering glass towers of the Renaissance Center overlooking the Detroit River. A corporate jet was waiting to zip him back to Gannett's headquarters in suburban Washington. And his company was about to pay $717 million in cash for the ENA and the *Detroit News.*

Now he stood with Peter Clark at a makeshift lectern at the crotch of the *News*'s L-shaped, second-floor newsroom. The noisy, uncarpeted room was an anomaly of battered metal desks, unmatched chairs, and stacks of yellowing newspapers amid finely carved oaken walls and ceiling-high windows. Remove the computers and their unsightly tangles of wires, and the room would have looked as it had in 1961, when Clark first came to work at the paper.

The ENA president had calmed down. Looking stern and businesslike, he approached the lectern in white shirtsleeves and a navy blue tie flecked with white "ENA" insignias. Neuharth waited in the background to Clark's right. On one lapel he sported a brass pin with the word "News" etched across the numeral "1." Dozens of *News* reporters, editors, photographers, and clerks had abandoned their telephones and computers to form a thick circle around the two men.

The staff members had profoundly mixed feelings about Gannett taking over their newspaper. One was relief. They had been targets of a takeover for better than a month; it was good to know it was over and that the *News* would survive, one way or another. Their greatest fear had been that someone with no interest in journalism—those Hollywood producers, perhaps—would wrest control of the ENA merely to get WDVM-TV, the CBS affiliate in Washington. That might have meant the end for the *News,* because the paper would have been a nuisance to a buyer interested solely in money. After all, the battle with the *Free Press* was terribly expensive, and it did not look to be finished anytime soon.

The emergence of Gannett gave reason to hope. No longer would the *News* have to cower at the deep pockets of Knight-Ridder, Inc., the company from Miami that owned the *Free Press* and that was, behind Gannett, the country's second-largest newspaper publisher. Gannett had the money to make the *News* a better paper, hire more staff, maybe even challenge the *Free Press*'s dominance of the market for morning papers. But there was wariness, too. After all, Gannett had never run a paper the size of the *News.* The company had not had success competing against other dailies. Many *News* journalists considered *USA Today* a shallow paper that looked pretty while pandering to a generation of TV watchers. They knew that Gannett was the wealthiest newspaper chain for a reason: it kept a close watch on the bottom line, running highly profitable newspapers that, rightly or not, weren't known for producing first-rate journalism. No one could be sure if Gannett would be willing—or able—to fight the good fight in Detroit. Why had Gannett come to Detroit when so many other newspaper companies had taken a pass on bidding for the ENA? What did Neuharth, who had spent three years at the *Free Press* in the 1960s, want from the *News?* Would he care to spend the money, time, and energy it would take to win the papers' epic battle? Did winning even matter to him?

Neuharth had the answers they longed to hear.

Clark had made Neuharth's acquaintance in the early 1960s, when Neuharth was at the *Free Press.* Clark now introduced him as "a very tough editor, a very good guy, a very strong person, and a very honest person." The two men shook hands and Neuharth, a head shorter than Clark, addressed the anxious group.

He began by saying he empathized with the sadness and nostalgia the staff was no doubt feeling. Gannett was "fully aware of what James E. Scripps and his family members since then have accomplished here," Neuharth said. He called the ENA "the envy of many of us in the media . . . an extraordinary organization of splendid operations of newspapers and broadcast stations around the country." But, he said, recent events had shown again "that change is inevitable, whether it is universally wanted or not."

The merger of the ENA into Gannett, Neuharth said, would make both companies stronger. "This is a terribly exciting thing for us for two reasons," he said. "One, because of what I said about the ENA. We are a nationwide news and information company and the fact that Peter and the ENA associates have put together this organization in seven different states makes it a very wonderful fit for us."

Now he came to what his audience was waiting for.

"But more important for you in this room, the thing that really pleases us is the way the position of the *Detroit News* has been solidified as number one in this very, very attractive Michigan market. And you know that the fact is, the *News* is number one in every respect, no matter how you measure." He held up the first finger on his right hand. "You're number one in news content. You're number one in public service. You're number one in circulation. You're number one in advertising.

"Now, I can tell you of the importance of that, having worked down the street at number two for several years." Titters and a smattering of applause swept the room. Neuharth smiled. "So that number one position is something of which you should be extremely proud. And all of us ought to be willing to do whatever's necessary not only to maintain it, but to see that it is enhanced."

Neuharth produced some news clippings. They were, he said, his horoscopes for the day. In "the little paper down the street," as Neuharth called the *Free Press,* the horoscope for Aries read, "Make the best possible impression. Someone who can help your career is watching." That got a big laugh. "Well, that's true," Neuharth said. "Because you can help my career. We at Gannett can help your careers. That's what I think this is all about."

Neuharth turned to his *News* horoscope. "Funding," it said, "soon becomes available." There was more laughter. Neuharth glanced over at Clark. "Now, Peter, I think that's a way of saying that the Gannett check for $717 million will not bounce." He looked back to the staff gathered around him. "More importantly," he said, "I think that also says that we will have some money left over with which to fund the future—*fund the future*—of this great newspaper. For that opportunity, we thank you."

Laughter and applause washed over the room. Someone opened bottles of champagne. The people of the *News* had heard precisely what they wanted to hear: their paper was number one, it would forever be number one, and now it had a parent with the firepower to vanquish "the little paper down the street."

It all would have been such good news, if only what they were hearing had been the truth.

2

The Tin Box

When Peter Clark arrived in Detroit in 1961, he came a studious-looking professor in horn-rimmed glasses, a brush cut, and a dark suit with a skinny tie. He and his wife, Lianne, had left a splendid life in Connecticut, where Clark had been teaching in Yale's political science program. With their first child on the way and an uncertain future before them, the Clarks returned to Peter's birthplace, a tough, gritty town of auto factories and union halls that historian Robert Conot has called "the heart of American industry."

Into this heart plunged a young man who knew almost nothing of his new profession, newspapering, who as a youth had learned to love living in sunny California, and who had been warned against taking up with the family business. Clark came at the behest of Warren Booth, publisher of the *Detroit News* and president of the Evening News Association, who saw in the thirty-two-year-old a quick and penetrating intellect that would make easier his education in what was becoming a more difficult business.

Clark was one of several young Scripps descendants to have been interviewed by Booz Allen and Hamilton, a management consulting firm hired by Warren Booth to find candidates to succeed him and other aging ENA directors. The interviews had little to do with how newspapers ought to be run; instead they sought to gauge the prospects' intelligence and their attitudes toward the *News*. Clark, who was just beginning to savor the academic life, was not terribly interested in working at the *News*, but his background had prepared him well for the quizzing by Booz Allen.

Peter Bruce Clark was the great-grandson of James Scripps, founder of the *News* and the ENA. Peter's grandfather, Rex Brainerd Clark, had married Scripps's daughter Grace. Peter Clark was born an only child in Detroit and lived in the area until he was in high school, when his father, stricken with multiple sclerosis, moved the family to La Jolla, California. As a youngster, Clark listened intently as his parents chewed over their favorite topics: politics, government, and the family business, the *News*. In dinner-table chats about the troubled national economy, Roosevelt's New Deal, and a world at war, young Peter Clark was captivated by ideas of how a nation should be governed. He loved history and made sure each week to read the latest *Time* magazine, especially the articles on foreign affairs and the maps of faraway lands.

He also took an interest in the *News*, where his father, Rex Scripps Clark, had worked briefly in the classified advertising and photo departments in the 1930s. The elder Clark discouraged his son from taking too much interest, though. Rex Clark's own father had been a target of family scorn because in the 1920s he had committed the sin of borrowing against his ENA stock to invest in a posh hotel. Scrippses just didn't do that. They didn't borrow and they certainly didn't borrow against their ENA stock. "I hope you never get involved with the family firm," Peter Clark's father preached. "The family aspects would be difficult."

"I'm no fool," his son had concurred. "I would never be interested in that."

Still, Peter Clark couldn't help but feel close to the *News*. He would never forget the proud moment when, as a seven-year-old, he inherited 2,020 shares of ENA stock. He couldn't have known his stake would one day be worth millions, but personally owning a piece of the family treasure pleased him enormously.

He had no boyhood dreams of being a newspaperman, but he liked to hang around a local weekly, the *La Jolla Light*. Its big flatbed presses used an open fire to dry the printing ink. Sometimes the newsprint would catch fire, and Clark would help stamp it out. As a teen, he spent many hours at the knee of W. Steele "Doc" Gilmore, a former *News* editor of twenty years who had moved near the Clarks. Gilmore had strong feelings about keeping the ENA's increasingly far-flung family together. He lectured Clark that, if not properly tended, the family could easily fly apart.

Clark attended Pomona College near his La Jolla home, majoring in chemical engineering. Saturday nights in the lab became less appealing after he met the woman who would become his wife, Lianne Schroeder, and Clark changed his major to something that had long interested him, American government and economics. He took a course in newswriting—"just for the hell of it"—and sold ads for some campus publications. Still, he harbored no hankering to be a newspaperman.

He became Dr. Peter Clark upon earning his Ph.D. in American government from the University of Chicago, where he studied under renowned sociologist Edward Banfield. In 1959, at the age of thirty-one, he became an associate professor at Yale. Clark had it made. He was getting paid fifty-five hundred dollars a year to do exactly what he wanted to do. He and Lianne were expecting a child and enjoying a relatively carefree life. Their campus apartment in New Haven was just a short drive from the New England countryside and a train hop from the theaters and museums of New York City.

Then came a call from Warren Booth. Booth, a cousin of Clark's father, wanted Peter Clark to join the ENA board of directors. Clark had not forgotten his father's admonishments about getting involved in the family business, but he rationalized that a director, who didn't get involved in day-to-day matters, wasn't truly part of the business. All it would mean was going to Detroit once a month for a board meeting. He accepted.

A few months later Booth called again. The ENA's corporate secretary had died. Would Clark leave Yale to replace him? Clark balked. "I have a great job and a pregnant wife," he told Booth. The publisher called yet again to say the salary would be at least twenty-five thousand dollars. The Clarks packed their bags.

But not without some trepidation. Clark was genuinely concerned about the future of the *News*. After eight decades as Michigan's biggest daily, the *News* recently had slipped behind the *Detroit Free Press* in daily circulation, 482,850 to 480,673. The *News* had fallen behind briefly before, but the spring of 1960 marked the first time the *Free Press* had held the lead for an entire year. Clark envied the nimble, aggressive *Free Press,* which was expanding its circulation in outstate Michigan and making the paper more appealing to women and young people. The *Free Press* had the morning market to itself, while the *News* scrapped for afternoon readers with the *Detroit Times.* Knight Newspapers, which owned the *Free Press,* had recently sold the *Chicago Daily News,* and it seemed to Clark that Knight had since refocused all of its management energy on Detroit.

Next to the *Free Press,* the *News* was deadly dull, the Old Gray Lady of Detroit newspapering. While the *Free Press* was replacing its thirty-five-year-old presses, the *News* was still being printed on presses purchased in 1917. The old men who controlled the ENA board wouldn't buy new ones, because they refused to borrow money. The ENA either bought with cash or it didn't buy. Instead, the board reduced shareholder dividends and set aside the difference to buy a new plant and presses sometime in the future.

Clark worried about the company's attitude toward change. After the Clarks moved to Grosse Pointe, Clark asked why the *Free Press* was strong in the community. A *News* executive blithely dismissed the question. "That's out in the suburbs," he said. But middle-class Detroiters were moving to the suburbs in droves. The city's population had dropped by nearly two hundred thousand in the 1950s, while the suburbs had welcomed one million newcomers.

Detroit's economy also was unnerving. A glance at the *News*'s ad linage revealed how the ups and downs of the auto industry affected the local papers. The *News*'s ad volume tracked uncannily with employment at Chrysler Corporation, which had more city workers than either General Motors Corporation or Ford Motor Company. The Big Three had rebounded from a miserable sales year in 1958, but there were signs, however subtle, that their rule of the industry was vulnerable. By 1960, imports of foreign cars had zoomed to 445,000 from 57,000 in 1955, costing U.S. carmakers 50,000 jobs. Chrysler's payroll was halved in the latter part of the 1950s and, as auto suppliers closed or moved out of Detroit, the east side alone lost 71,000 jobs. By 1960, 78,000 Detroiters were out of work. Welfare payouts in the city had more than tripled in the 1950s. Clearly, the ENA would have to expand outside Detroit—perhaps even outside the industrial Midwest—to survive the lows of the car industry's roller-coaster economy.

Still, Detroit was friendly to newspapers. The metropolitan area was the country's fifth largest, with nearly four million people. Cyclicality aside, Detroit *was* home to three of the world's largest companies and a passel of other big concerns, like Burroughs, the business machine manufacturer, and Fruehauf Corporation, which dominated the market in truck trailers. Much of the time, the factories were churning out cars seven days a week and the downriver foundries were aglow with crimson heat long into the night.

The natives were skilled, hardworking people who owned homes and cars and spent $4.9 billion a year in the stores. Ten major chains operated nearly fifty department stores in the area, including five big anchors in downtown Detroit. Department stores were crucial to the newspapers' success; along with the five supermarket chains, they were the papers' biggest advertisers. Though the *News* had lost the circulation lead, it still carried more advertising than the *Free Press* or the *Times*, and its ad revenue was the highest. The *News* also owned a handsome circulation lead on Sundays, when the paper's huge ad volume made Sunday the most profitable day of the week.

It surely was gray, but the *News* still was Detroit's strongest paper, and still proudly carrying on the traditions established by Clark's great-grandfather —traditions of family ownership, of fierce independence, of unblinking journalism and service to the community. Peter Clark had been asked to help pass those traditions through another generation. As a college student and professor he had been captivated by theories of how organizations work. Now he had a chance to test those theories in an unforgiving classroom. How might he change the *News* so that it could thrive in a changing world, while honoring the memory of James Scripps? It would be a marvelous challenge. Clark had always felt grateful for the legacy that had enriched his family and made him proud to hail from Detroit. What better way to thank his great-grandfather than to follow in his storied footsteps.

James Edmund Scripps was born in London in 1835, son of a bookbinder and grandson of a newspaper publisher. His grandfather, William Armiger Scripps, had published the *London Daily Sun* and the *Literary Gazette*. James's family moved to the United States when he was nine, taking up on a farm in Rushville, Illinois.

As a young man Scripps took a job as a bookkeeper at a lumber company, where the rule was to save half the profits. He liked the rule so much that he adopted it as his own, setting aside half his salary as savings and sleeping in the company office to avoid paying rent. Scripps found the job boring, though, and left to work for a cousin, John Locke Scripps, one of three founders of the *Chicago Tribune*. There he learned of an opening as an editor at the *Detroit Daily Advertiser*. He moved to Detroit in 1859 and before long acquired a partnership in the paper, figuring prominently in its merger with the *Detroit Tribune*. The partnership permitted Scripps, who had vowed not to marry until he had a yearly income of a thousand dollars, to wed Harriet Messenger, his "Hattie." He settled into Detroit for the rest of his life.

Once a fur-trading mecca, the "City of the Strait" was a thriving hub of commerce along the Detroit River, exporting beef, butter, copper, whitefish, lumber, and hogs. Between 1860 and 1870, Detroit's population nearly doubled to eighty thousand as thousands of German, Irish, English, and Scottish immigrants came seeking work. The boom to come with the automobile was forty years off, but the city was fast becoming an industrial center. Manufacturing jobs increased nearly eightfold in the 1860s as Detroiters churned out iron products, tobacco, flour, feed, beer, shoes, furniture, and potbellied stoves. The center city, with its gaslights and brick streets, was home to most of the well-to-do, while the working classes scattered along the riverfront and to the outskirts, clustering in tenements plagued by lawlessness, pestilence, and infant death. It was a city of great impatience and great hope, run by machine politicians and the men who owned smoke-belching factories, utilities, breweries, and shipping yards.

The newspapers of Detroit, James Scripps felt, did not serve a good portion of the populace. The town's four papers were wide "blanket sheets" marked by turgid prose and a ponderous Victorian sensibility that catered to the social elite. None appealed to the workingman. A generation that had learned to read in the early public schools was coming of age, yet a third of Detroit's population did not read newspapers. Scripps aimed to court them with a "people's press" that would be cheap and physically easy to handle, a tabloid rather than a blanket sheet, with plenty of short, punchy stories of local and national news, nearer the practical interests of the commoner. He saw news being written "with the same freedom that would be allowed in conversation." It had to be concise because the average citizen had little time to read. An afternoon paper would be more convenient for the readers Scripps was seeking, many of whom would be at work in the mornings, when three of the other Detroit papers were published. And, unlike its competitors, Scripps's paper would be independent of any political party.

Scripps was no idealist, though. His ideas reflected business sense as much as journalistic reckoning. Smaller pages would reduce costs for ink and paper. The savings could be passed along to blue-collar workers, who were making but a dollar a day. Those who didn't yet read a paper might be able to afford one for a penny or two, instead of the nickel charged by the blanket sheets. Circulation would climb and sales of advertising, which Scripps saw as the key to financial success, would rise in turn. Scripps hadn't invented his ideas. He was just a newborn when James Gordon Bennett introduced the *New York Herald* as a smaller-page daily that vowed to be "the organ of no faction or coterie" and promised "brevity, variety, point, piquancy and cheapness." Scripps had noticed the trend spreading among eastern newspapers.

Still, hundreds of miles away in Civil War–era Detroit, the idea of a paper for the workingman was radical, and it met with little favor among Scripps's colleagues at the newly merged *Advertiser and Tribune*. Their paper was making money and they saw no reason to fix what didn't seem to be broken. Unable to sway his partners, Scripps finally resigned, but his ex-employer wound up helping him anyway. An Easter Sunday fire in 1873 destroyed the *Tribune*'s building. Scripps's share of the insurance proceeds was twenty thousand dollars, which would be the heart of his twenty-five-thousand-dollar stake in his new newspaper. One day he would buy the *Tribune* and fold it into his own "people's press"—the *Evening News.*

Scripps's paper first appeared on a Saturday, August 23, 1873. It sold for two cents—three cents cheaper than all of its rivals. In an editorial titled "Why I Started the *Evening News,*" Scripps vowed to "steer clear of the rut into which all my former associates and contemporaries have fallen. . . . Popularity and usefulness are our only aim, the wants of the great public our only criterion in the choice of matter for our columns."

The four-page paper contained more than a hundred brief news items, many consisting of just a sentence. The Spanish government was mounting a military force to fight the Carlist rebels. S. W. Walker and Company had won the contract for supplying Detroit city with coal. Charlie Horton's cow had given him a painful kick "near the waistband." The Boston Red Stockings had whipped the Detroit Empires, 37–4, in a game of baseball. Ads made up a tad more than half the paper, including three of the six columns on the front page.

The early days were a struggle. The first issue lost fifty to sixty dollars, and Scripps called it a "fiasco." He was so embarrassed that he stayed home from church the next day, lest he see someone he knew. On the third day of publishing he noted in his diary, "Advertising very slack and had hard work to get up matter enough to fill the sheet." Still, more and more people were buying the paper. But his printer, not surprisingly, was uncooperative. Lacking his own presses, Scripps had contracted printing to the *Detroit Free Press,* which could not—or would not—keep up with the growing demand for the *News.*

Scripps bought a small frame house and installed his own presses. Circulation rose, but Scripps was still losing fifty dollars a day. A wood dealer halted supplies and lenders threatened lawsuits. The publisher sought family help. He was joined in Detroit by half brother Edward, sister Ellen, and finally brother George, who sold the farm in Illinois and invested the proceeds, two thousand dollars, in the *News.* "Ours was already noted as being an eccentric family," Edward Wyllis Scripps later wrote, "and this proposed venture of ours—the starting of a two-cent paper—was supposed to be the climax of inherited insanity."

Their paper was born just before the outbreak of a countrywide financial panic, both a hindrance and a help. Advertisers weren't as keen to spend money, but readers were glad to try a cheaper paper. The *News*'s city circulation soon climbed to 8,000, more than any other Detroit paper. Jim Scripps kept a close eye on his costs, carrying a tin cashbox home each night to tally the day's receipts. To save money, reporters used both sides of a sheet of copy paper, and Scripps jotted editorials on used envelopes. The paper lost about $5,000 its first year, turning profitable its second. The *News* netted $9,275 in 1875, $12,800 in 1876, and $17,738 in 1877. In 1876, Scripps incorporated the Evening News Association with his siblings, George, Ellen, and Edward, and a cousin, John Sweeney.

As profits climbed, Scripps moved his company toward a Detroit monopoly, absorbing the *Daily Mirror* and the *Tribune.* He worked around the clock, reaching his desk around dawn so that he could oversee the makeup of the paper and its distribution to the newsboys. Afternoons he spent reporting and writing the next day's stories. Evenings were for counting cash. Before he retired each night, he knew how the *News* had fared that day, to the penny.

In the early days, Jim Scripps controlled virtually every word that went into the *News,* setting the paper on a radically different course from his competitors. Other Detroit papers had distinct political allegiances, often receiving financial backing from political parties. But Scripps, again with his eye on the masses, offered the *News* as champion of the common man. Fervently preaching reform, the *News* exposed political corruption, attacked the "corporationists" who ran the city's businesses, fought for the rights of labor, and lobbied for beautification and for municipal ownership of utilities. Detractors labeled the paper "sensationalist." Scripps knew that wasn't true—the *News* did not blare headlines or agitate for war—but he took it as a welcome sign that his paper had set itself apart.

The founder was a gangly, long-legged man of nearly six feet who sported bushy black whiskers and wore wire-rimmed glasses over his large, sad eyes. James Scripps was unassuming, almost studious, a lover of philosophy, art, and architecture, a philanthropist who would one day donate seventy thousand dollars to build a church. Awkward with people, whose names he had trouble remembering, he sought to maintain close personal control of his endeavors and occasionally rued the partnerships he had formed over the years. None caused him more trouble than the one with his brilliant, impetuous half brother, Edward Wyllis Scripps.

Nineteen years James's junior, E. W. Scripps had been a sickly child who was pampered by his older sisters. "My brother James," E.W. later wrote, "once told me that I was the most unpromising brat of a baby he ever knew!" His first real job at the *News* was as a six-dollar-a-week route collector. Clever, manipulative, and not much for hard work, the young E.W. took on additional routes and farmed them out to other boys, increasing his weekly pay to forty dollars, more than anyone else working at the *News.* With money and direction from his brothers James and George, he helped start the *Cleveland Press* in 1878 and the *St. Louis Chronicle* in 1880. A year later, the Scrippses took over the *Cincinnati Post.* The seeds of an empire were being sown, but James grew less and less interested in being part of it. He eventually withdrew from managing all but the Detroit paper, leaving E.W. to pursue his own daring ambitions.

Close on the heels of William Randolph Hearst and Joseph Pulitzer, E. W. Scripps strove to build a chain of many newspapers that would draw strength from each other by sharing their journalistic endeavors. Quite simply, E.W., who talked of becoming governor of Ohio and even president of the United States, believed more papers would mean more money, more influence, and more political power. E.W. fancied himself a "damned old crank" crusading for the working class; his papers advocated for labor organizing, and attacked those empowered by wealth, religion, government, or politics. His motto was, "Whatever is, is wrong." Building a chain also kept E.W.'s restless imagination busy; he was never as interested in running something as in starting or expanding it. "Scripps dreamed things, started things, picked lieutenants to finish them, gave them a free hand—and then turned his mind to new problems and experiments," wrote a biographer, Negley D. Cochran.

James Scripps did not share E.W.'s yen for expansion. Although James invested his money and valuable members of his *News* staff in the start-up of faraway papers, he was skeptical of so-called chain operations. Newspapers, Scripps believed, should answer first to their hometowns and could not properly do so if distracted by financial or other problems at a paper hundreds of miles away. James also could not keep close watch over such far-flung properties, which was uncomfortable for a man used to knowing daily how his business was faring.

In his dark, vested suits, James was the cautious model of maturity. A "fossil," thought E.W., himself a rakish redhead who wore flannel shirts and high boots and carried a flask of whiskey in his hip pocket. James considered his younger brother nothing more than "a junior enjoying patriarchal indulgence," in the words of historian Arthur Pound. They clashed over E.W.'s management of the Cincinnati and Cleveland papers, James wielding the whip hand of money and seniority, E.W. chafing at his brother's stubbornness. Eventually, though, James became convinced that E.W. had been "converted from one of those damned fools who believe that business is carried on for any other purpose than that of making money." When he fell ill in the late 1880s, James turned control of the *News* over to E.W.

While James was in Europe, believed to be dying, E.W. remade the *News* as he saw fit, breaking many of his brother's sacred rules. He borrowed money to buy printing presses. He raised the price of the paper. He added pages to fit more advertising. The debt hurt profits; a dividend was missed. Upon his return, James may well have felt that E.W. was trying to make the company so large that only E.W. could run it. James wanted mainly to run a solid, four-page paper that paid a regular dividend. E.W.'s *Detroit News* was not James's *Detroit News*. James fired E.W., handing control of the paper to his son-in-law, George Booth.

James's brother George Scripps died in 1900, leaving his one-third interest in the Evening News Association to E.W. Thus, when James died, E.W. would be in position to vie for control of the *News*. James would not stand for it. Years of litigation followed. Before he died in 1906, James agreed to swap his holdings in the Cincinnati, Cleveland, and St. Louis papers for the bulk of E.W.'s stock in the *News*. "Thus, at last," historian Pound wrote, "the notable family group which this eldest Scripps had gathered around him split apart, and each faction went its separate way."

From his seaside ranch in California, E.W. assembled a national empire of twenty-five newspapers, to be known as the Scripps-Howard chain, and helped launch one of the world's great news services, United Press International. James left the *Detroit News* in a thirty-year trust to be governed by his son, William, and sons-in-law George Booth and Edgar Whitcomb. In 1936, stock in the Evening News Association passed to forty-eight descendants of James Scripps. One of them was a schoolboy named Peter Clark.

One of the first things Peter Clark did as a director of the Evening News Association in 1960 was urge Warren Booth to buy the *Detroit Times*.

It was only natural. Newspapers had been buying out their competitors for decades. The *Detroit News* itself had absorbed several of its rivals, the last being the *Detroit Journal* in 1922. Only the very biggest American cities boasted competing papers; the two-newspaper town was becoming obsolete. Whereas in 1920 more than five hundred cities had more than one paper, forty years later only about seventy could make that claim. In many towns, papers had disappeared into the pocketbooks of their rivals, having been purchased and then closed. In some, a single owner published two papers.

Whether such monopolies were necessary was a matter of debate. The economics of newspapering, publishers argued, forced weaker papers out of business. Only the biggest and smartest could survive in a contest where everyone vied for the same prize, while the urge to dominate made it impractical to divvy things up so that everyone would have enough to live on. It also was true that in many towns, all competing papers were profitable. But a publisher could make more money if he didn't have rivals pressuring him to price low and spend a lot producing a competitive paper. As press critic A. J. Liebling noted, "That it is theoretically possible to make money by competition in the newspaper field is . . . immaterial, since there is a great deal more money to be made by *(a)* selling out and pocketing a capital gain; and *(b)* buying the other fellow out and then sweating the serfs."

And if one paper couldn't persuade a rival to sell, the two could always join forces under a joint operating agreement. In JOAs, which had been around since the 1930s, rivals agreed to stop competing and start making easier money by combining their printing, circulation, advertising, and other business functions. The merger reduced the papers' payroll and newsprint costs, but even better, it enabled them to jointly fix prices, an advantage the antitrust laws made unavailable to most other businesses. Newspapers had been allowed to skirt the law, and publishers saw it as a sort of unwritten rule that they should be permitted to continue in these lucrative arrangements. In return they kept alive the appearance, at least, of journalistic competition by maintaining the separate editorial products of papers that were otherwise joined as one. If some of those JOA papers were rather weak imitations of their former competitive selves, well, that was the way the business worked.

There was no chance of a JOA in Detroit in 1960, when three papers were locked in mortal battle. The leader was the *Free Press,* one of six dailies owned by brothers John and James Knight, which recently had captured the daily circulation lead the *Detroit News* had held since before the turn of the century. In a distant third was the *Detroit Times,* owned by the Hearst Corporation, the legacy of William Randolph Hearst and one of the nation's biggest newspaper chains.

The *Times* was struggling. Competing directly with the *News,* which also published in the afternoon, the *Times* had had relative strength in the city, where an exodus to the suburbs began in the 1950s. As daily circulation fell from 435,000 to 370,000, the *Times* started losing money. A forty-seven-day strike in 1955–56 cost it valuable ad linage. It suffered another blow in 1959, when the *News* introduced an innovative, easy-to-read guide to programs on television. The *News*'s TV guide siphoned more than 75,000 readers from the Sunday *Times.* In the latter half of the 1950s, the *Times* lost $10 million. In a bygone day, Hearst might have carried the paper on the strength of the other papers in its chain. No longer. The company had lost more than $2 million a year in 1958 and 1959. "We can't afford to penalize our good papers anymore," a Hearst executive told *Time* magazine. "With modern newspaper economics, you just can't tap a good paper to carry a dog." Hearst recently had rid itself of papers in Chicago and Pittsburgh. The next to go would be the *Detroit Times.*

But who would get it? A loser on its own, the *Times* nevertheless offered Detroit's other dailies a precious asset: hundreds of thousands of readers. Minus the *Times,* the rivalry boiled down to a head-to-head impasse between the *Free Press* and the *News.* In the fall of 1960, the *Free Press* led by about 2,000 papers a day. With the *Times*'s subscription lists, either paper could pass its rival by 300,000 copies a day—a lead that looked insurmountable. The *Times* was the spoiler. By dropping out of the race, the *Times* could decide it once and for all.

At the ENA, rumors were flying that Jack Knight was about to grab the *Times.* Knight and his brother had just sold the *Chicago Daily News* to one of their competitors, Marshall Field, Jr., for $24 million. Knight was expected to use that money to buy the *Times.* But Knight never spoke with the Hearst people, who had burned him on a previous deal. His best hope was that Warren Booth would be too timid to part with the millions of dollars required to buy the *Times.*

In fact, the ENA chief was not eager to make the deal. Booth was a savvy competitor, but he also embraced the conservatism of his ancestors. While other family-held companies—Hearst, Knight, Gannett, Newhouse, and of course Scripps-Howard—had been adding newspapers and even broadcast stations, the ENA basically had stood pat for decades. In 1920 it had started a commercial radio station, the nation's first, and later a Detroit TV station, but the company remained, in essence, the *Detroit News.* And though it had bought out newspaper rivals in the past, buying the *Times* would be, by comparison, an enormous undertaking. Booth abhorred borrowing money, and a $10 million cash outlay would amount to more than twice the ENA's 1960 profit of $4 million. Plans to build a new printing plant would have to be postponed.

Still, the alternatives were risky—perhaps fatally so. If the *News* did nothing, the *Free Press* would swamp it. The *News* could try to start selling papers in the morning, a market long owned by the *Free Press,* but that could cost more than buying the *Times.* Warren Booth liked to say, "We're going to keep our barnacles dry," meaning the ENA would run the *News* and the Detroit stations, make a nice profit, and stay out of debt. But Booth wasn't inflexible. "His first instinct was always to say no," recalled Martin Hayden, who was editor of the *News* at the time. Whatever the proposition, "He'd immediately say, 'That's ridiculous.' Then we'd discuss it and a day or so later he'd say, 'When are you going to do it?' "

Shortly after three o'clock on the chilly Monday morning of November 7, telegrams arrived at the homes of fourteen hundred unsuspecting *Times* employees. "It is with deep regret that the management of the *Detroit Times* must inform you of the termination of your services. . . . It is not necessary for you to report for further duty." The bleary-eyed reporters, editors, ad salesmen, and circulation workers stared in disbelief. The telegram said nothing about the *Times* being closed; many workers believed they alone had been fired, without warning or provocation. They must have stood in their foyers, shivering in their underwear, racking their brains for what they had said or done to get themselves fired. In the next few hours they learned the truth: the *Times* had closed and the *News* had paid $10 million for its physical assets—presses, some office equipment, and the prized subscription lists.

It was an ugly ending. The *Times* had taken its $10 million and walked away. "Why didn't they send the telegram collect?" one angry *Times* employee snapped. *Times* reporters and editors who were abruptly ordered to stop preparing Monday's edition left their newsroom a shambles of copy paper and empty whiskey bottles. Photographers urinated in the photo-developing soup. The *News* said it would hire no more than 10 percent of the *Times* payroll. Hundreds of loyal *Times* employees, some in their forties and fifties, suddenly were out of a job. Workers returning to gather belongings found padlocks on the doors of the *Times* building. Security guards ushered them to their desks and back out the door. Hearst had abandoned them, and the ENA was looking the other way. "People have the wrong idea about newspapers," one *Times* worker said. "They think that they are out only to serve the public. That's a laugh. A newspaper is a business and when it does not make money, it closes."

At the *Free Press,* executive editor Lee Hills wrote, "The death of a newspaper is to the readers like the passing of a close friend. We at the *Free Press* join *Times* readers in mourning the loss of the *Detroit Times.*" The grief passed quickly, though, because the *Free Press* had a job to do: steal *Times* readers from the *News.* It planned to do it by first going after the critical asset the *News* had so callously neglected: *Times* employees.

The *Free Press* aimed to get for free what the *News* had bought for $10 million. Led by Hills, a cool, calculating executive who had guided the paper to its newly won advantage, and a young newcomer named Al Neuharth, the *Free Press* within hours of the *Times* sale had hired dozens of the defunct paper's circulation employees. With many of those workers came the all-important newsboys, who knew *Times* subscribers and delivery routes intimately. The very first day, the *Free Press* produced 250,000 copies of an afternoon paper—dubbed the "Family Edition"—that mimicked the *Times* down to the pale green boxes atop page one. Green *Times* delivery trucks crowded the loading docks behind the *Free Press* building on West Lafayette Boulevard.

At the *News,* Booth was caught flat-footed. He had made no specific arrangements to obtain the subscription lists and just assumed *Times* circulation workers and newsboys would join the *News.* But those workers, feeling abused and cheated, were not about to simply transfer their loyalty to the *News* because some wealthy businessmen had signed a piece of paper. Quick as they heard the *Times* was gone, they collected their route books and threw them in their car trunks and hid them in their basements. "We were having a terrible time," recalled Joseph Speiser, a *News* circulation manager. Speiser and his colleagues couldn't get their hands on dozens of *Times* subscription lists. It soon became clear that the newspaper willing to pay would get them.

The Monday morning of the sale, Bob Kurzawa showed up at the dingy storefront where each day he passed out bundles of the *Times* to his crew of twenty newsboys. Someone from the *News* was there. "We won't be needing your services anymore," he said, flipping Kurzawa a sheet of paper that fell to the floor. It was a job application. Kurzawa would have to reapply for the job he had held for ten years. Kurzawa's boss from the *Times* showed up. "Don't worry," he told Kurzawa. "The *Free Press* is gonna hire us. Come back around three and get your kids to deliver the *Free Press.*"

At three o'clock, Kurzawa was standing in a parking lot across from his storefront station. With a wife and two young boys to support, he didn't care whom he worked for so long as he got a paycheck. As his carriers pedaled up on their bicycles, he waved them over. "I'm gonna work for the *Free Press* now and I want you guys to work for me," Kurzawa told them. The *News* worker summoned the police, who obligingly took Kurzawa to a nearby precinct. When they couldn't figure out what to charge him with, they returned him to the storefront, where the *News* worker was lecturing the newsboys from atop a stack of papers. As the police cruiser pulled up, the boys cheered. All but one scrambled off to join Kurzawa.

Now that he had his boys, Kurzawa had to make sure he would get paid. He went to the *Free Press,* where he got a runaround. "Don't worry," a *Free Press* worker told him. "You'll be taken care of." That wasn't good enough for Kurzawa, who hurried down Lafayette to the *News* building. There he waited in line to see Joe Speiser. Speiser asked his name and peered at a long, typewritten list. "You're hired," he said. Kurzawa was now working for his third newspaper that day.

He was assigned to a *News* station where *Times* newsboys had defected to the *Free Press.* He showed up on Wednesday afternoon, spotting a friend and former *Times*man named Lou Snell talking to the carriers in a parking lot behind the station. Kurzawa took him aside. "Look, Lou," he said, "the *Free Press* isn't guaranteeing anything, and I can tell you the *News* is gonna take care of me." Snell was unimpressed. But the mother of one of the newsboys, sitting in her car, overheard. She called over her son, who had the biggest route in the group, and told him to go with Kurzawa. Most of the other kids immediately followed. Snell panicked. He reached into his jacket and pulled out a pistol. "I'm gonna blow your brains out," he said, waving the gun at Kurzawa. "C'mon, Louie," Kurzawa pleaded, "I'm making a living just like you." Snell burst into tears and hurried off the lot.

It had always been a tough business. Things could get dicey when teenagers were making more money delivering two or three different papers than their fathers made working at the Chrysler plant. When newspapers tried to stop carriers from peddling a competitor's product, they often came up against an entire family. Circulation managers looked for "station captains" who could handle themselves in a scrape. "Those were some big kids around those substations, you had to knock some heads," recalled Speiser, who had honed his management skills boxing in the local Catholic Youth Organization.

Things got even tougher in November of 1960. The streets of Detroit were flooded with newspapers. To counter the *Free Press*'s guerrilla tactics, the *News* printed 400,000 extra copies a day and delivered them wherever a doorstep, a mailbox, or a newsstand could be found. It was not unusual for readers to find two or three editions of two different papers on their stoops. Mothers were pressured to order newsboy sons to work for one paper or the other. Delivery stations were looted. Bikes were vandalized. Bundles of newspapers were burned. On street corners across the city, fistfights broke out between newsboys delivering papers to the same homes. The Great Detroit Newspaper War had begun.

By 1963, when he became the fifth publisher of the *Detroit News,* one thing was abundantly clear to Peter Clark: to preserve his great-grandfather's legacy, he would have to change it.

That would not be easy. To the old men of the ENA board, change was anathema. "It was like you stepped back a hundred years, that's the way they thought," said Richard Wallace, a grandson of George Booth and one of several younger descendants who joined the board in the late 1950s and early 1960s. The way the older directors figured it, the *News* had provided well for ninety years—some $137 million in profits, $98 million of it paid in dependable monthly dividends—and, with the purchase of the *Times* assuring its franchise, the *News* would provide for ninety more. The *News* now had a comfortable daily circulation lead of 193,000 over the *Free Press.* The auto industry was perking up after a few rough years. Though the young fellow from Yale was talking about getting into TV and expanding elsewhere in the country, most of the ENA directors saw no need to go looking for trouble in other businesses or cities. They knew Detroit newspapering and intended to stick with it. They certainly weren't eager to invest their precious dividends in faraway TV stations or in newspapers that wouldn't get delivered to their doorsteps every day. And they certainly weren't going to borrow money. Never had, never would.

Clark wished he could have afforded such a simple outlook. It would have been nice to think the *News* would forever be Detroit's biggest paper, that its profitability would never falter, that newspapers would continue to command the attention of most Americans and by far the biggest share of the dollars spent by advertisers. It would have been nice, but it was impossible for a man as smart as Clark. The world was changing.

For one thing, Americans weren't the same kind of newspaper readers they once had been. It was no crisis, but as the United States shifted subtly to an economy founded more on services than heavy industry, workers found more time to read in the morning than the evening. Factory workers who punched a clock at dawn didn't have time for a morning paper, but their ranks were no longer growing as U.S. smokestack industries gave way to foreign competition. More people were buying papers, but a smaller percentage of the population was reading them. Television, though still a nascent competitor for news, was claiming an increasing share of advertising dollars.

The auto industry indeed looked healthier, but Clark knew it would slump again as surely as the Michigan winter would bring sleet. The population in the city, where the *News* was strongest, had continued to fall as middle-class whites moved to the suburbs, and there were hints as graphic as cross burnings that racial tensions were simmering. The *Free Press,* friskier than ever under Lee Hills, Al Neuharth, and a young star named Derick Daniels, chipped away at the *News*'s lead, lopping off 20,000 papers by 1966. Quietly, discreetly, in friendly chats with ENA directors and Warren Booth, who was still a powerful influence as chairman of the ENA board, Clark prodded and wheedled and lobbied for change.

It was an ironic mission. Though he had never known James Scripps, Clark admired his great-grandfather. Yet Clark's business philosophy veered closer to that of Scripps's expansionist brother, E.W., than to James's conservative credos. Clark envied Scripps-Howard, which owned eighteen newspapers and half a dozen healthy television and radio stations. If pressed, he had to admit that the ENA probably would have been stronger, more profitable, and more secure if it had borrowed a bit more of E.W.'s thinking.

In 1967, Clark won a small victory. On September 29, the ENA board unanimously adopted a plan calling for the acquisition of "promising business properties" in the newspaper and broadcasting fields. The plan came none too soon. In May of that year, the closing of a New York daily had become an omen for afternoon papers everywhere. The *World-Journal-Tribune,* an amalgam of three papers owned by Hearst, Scripps-Howard, and publisher Jock Whitney, had caved in under the crushing weight of $700,000-a-day losses. In Detroit that July, a race riot of burning, looting, and murder had ravaged the city, claiming forty-three lives and speeding the population exodus. On the heels of the riot came a crippling nine-month strike by workers at both newspapers. So the *News* and the *Free Press* were silent for much of 1968, a year that saw the election of Richard Nixon, the assassinations of Martin Luther King and Robert Kennedy, violence at the Democratic National Convention in Chicago, Michigan governor George Romney's unsuccessful presidential bid, and the Detroit Tigers' first pennant-winning season in twenty-three years. Both papers suffered, but the *News* took the brunt. "Not only did we have a strike, but we went back to a city that was quite different," Clark recalled. "Our readers lived somewhere else." By 1969, the *News*'s daily circulation had dropped by 83,000 papers; the 200,000-copy gap between the *News* and the *Free Press* had narrowed by more than half.

Events were playing into Clark's hands. The strike, the riot, the *Free Press*'s circulation surge—they all nudged the ENA toward change. Clark's plan, approved in 1967 but not yet acted on, called for $30 million of purchases over ten years in "regions or communities of substantial economic growth potential." It said the company would incur debt of as much as half of a property's purchase price. The board had committed to Clark's plan on paper, while recent history, however unfortunate, gave the board reason to make the plan reality.

Still, it was not easy. The younger directors were less hidebound than their predecessors, but they were hardly risk takers. "We were raised conservatively and thought conservatively from the time we were born," recalled director James Whitcomb, Jr., whose father had served on the board until his death in 1963. For the next thirteen years, every step, every purchase, every change would be a struggle for Peter Clark—a struggle with his board, a struggle with his top deputies, a struggle with shareholders who increasingly found reasons to criticize and second-guess him. And, in a way, it would be a struggle with himself.

By the mid-eighties, Peter Clark had spent twenty-five years in the newspaper business and barely two teaching on a college campus, but to many who knew him, it seemed his heart had never left the classroom. In the pit of his soul, they would say, Peter Clark was not a newspaperman or a businessman, but a professor.

He was remarkably bright, better read and schooled than many of his peers in the industry. His powers of recollection were legend; ENA directors could rely on Clark, fortunately or not, to remember what they had said at a meeting months ago. Edwin Wheeler, the ENA executive who tutored Clark in the business for two decades, thought his ever-curious pupil one of the smartest people he had ever met. John Whitney, a lifelong friend, said of Clark, "The guy is as smart as they come *without* being an intellectual."

Clark often astounded subordinates with his knowledge of weighty matters that had little to do with newspapering. When Ed Pfeiffer was managing ENA's CBS affiliate in Washington, he gave a reception for columnist Carl Rowan, who had recently hosted a program on the liberation of the African nation Zimbabwe from British colonial rule. Clark, who was in Washington, drove to the reception with Pfeiffer. Pfeiffer had done some homework on the subject and was feeling proud of himself when he asked Clark what he knew about it. For the next ten minutes Clark expounded on the leaders of Zimbabwe, what they stood for and which had the best chance of ascending to power. Pfeiffer was amazed: "He knew these guys backwards and forwards."

Clark's friends in the newspaper fraternity included Kay Graham of the *Washington Post* and Punch Sulzberger of the *New York Times,* but his closest pals were in academia. Clark might have been the only newspaper publisher ever to sit on panels evaluating curricula at Harvard, the University of Michigan, and the University of Chicago. His facile mind earned him invitations to chair the board of the Federal Reserve Bank of Chicago and advise the prestigious Woodrow Wilson International Center for Scholars at the Smithsonian Institution.

Yet even on his board of directors there were those who doubted Clark's ability to run a company. Directors Wallace, Dick Spitzley, and Warren Wilkinson all intimated that they could run ENA better than Clark. Wilkinson was a constant thorn in Clark's side. A Harvard graduate with a good head for figures and a penchant for speaking his mind, Wilkinson in the early 1960s had offered himself as a possible successor to Warren Booth. At nearly every board meeting Clark could expect Wilkinson to bring ENA financial numbers purporting to show that, when inflation was taken into account, the company was performing poorly.

His harshest critics said Clark was too smart for his own good. Impatient with people he considered his intellectual inferiors, Clark could be condescending and closed-minded. For instance, he seemed to talk down to Dick Spitzley, who, though he wasn't the brightest fellow in the company, still had more years on the ENA board and worked hard to stay close to family members, who felt Clark had fostered an icy distance. And though Clark would ask for questions and criticisms, it often seemed he didn't really want them. "He was a pretty dogmatic character," said director James Whitcomb, Jr. "He'd analyze the situation on his own and make his own judgment and he didn't like other people confusing it with their views." Discussions seemed to end quickly when someone disagreed with Clark. Peter Kizer, chief of the ENA's broadcast operations, called him "one of the great pouters of all time." Yet however stubborn he sometimes could be, Clark was hardly a person who through sheer force of will could compel others to embrace his ideas. Shy by nature, at a cocktail party he could usually be seen chatting with his glass against his mouth, as if he were trying to hide.

Clark enjoyed debating concepts, but he avoided the confrontations often necessary to making ideas reality. That wasn't a problem in the day-to-day management of the company; Clark always could assign one of his lieutenants to carry out his orders. But it *was* a problem in the shaping of the ENA's overall strategy, which fell to the board of directors. There Clark was more or less among equals, forced to reconcile the vast and varied interests of the ENA family. Each board member represented a different branch of the family tree. Each had the power, however subtle and unstated, to turn part of the family against Clark.

Keeping every board member happy was not easy, though, because they were such different individuals. Jim Whitcomb, Dick Wallace, and John Beresford ran their own businesses and were more inclined to support Clark's efforts to modernize the ENA. Wilkinson seemed to relish opposing Clark on nearly any proposal. Bill Revelle was a college professor who shared Clark's passion for journalism. None was keen on borrowing, but Dick Spitzley led the crusade against debt. In his wallet, Spitzley carried but one credit card, and he used it only when absolutely necessary.

The broader family was more inscrutable. Some wanted their stock to be liquid, so that the price would rise. Some wanted to keep the price low, to minimize estate taxes. Some were concerned only with the dividends. ENA insiders joked that the company actually was run by what they derisively called the "screamers"—a handful of stockholders' wives who agitated for bigger dividends so that they could buy furs, diamonds, and fancy cars. Some family members thought diversifying was smart; some thought the company ought to concentrate on Detroit. Older shareholders, though not all, tended to think owning a piece of a great newspaper was grand in itself. The *News* meant quite a bit less to younger shareholders, who were more concerned with the return on their investment—or inheritance, as was usually the case.

Clark had a vision for the ENA that his intellect told him was correct: preserve the company's foundation, the *News*, by growing in new businesses and geographical areas. But Clark had not forgotten his father's warnings about dealing with the family, nor Doc Gilmore's lectures about the family's tendency to fly apart. To pursue his vision while maintaining family cohesion, Clark sought—via the board of directors—the family's approval of every major step the ENA took. To Clark, that did not mean getting a majority to approve; it meant getting *everyone*. Diversification wouldn't be Clark's program; it would be *everyone's*. If he anticipated one or two directors opposing a potential acquisition, the board wouldn't be presented with it. He argued for his ideas, but backed off when sharp conflict arose. So, some things that should have gotten done—acquisitions, mainly—things that Clark himself believed should be done, did not get done. His detractors liked to call him stubborn, but Clark was not stubborn enough. In trying to appease the family, he gave it almost unlimited veto power.

Not surprisingly, his plans proceeded slowly. The ENA looked at a paper in Santa Barbara, California, but the board balked at the price, about $10 million. (Years later, when the paper was worth many times $10 million, ENA directors would recall with grim humor the one that got away in Santa Barbara.) In 1969, the company purchased TV stations in Mobile, Alabama, and Tucson, Arizona; in 1973, a group of small newspapers and a commercial printing firm in New Jersey; the next year, a small paper in Palm Springs, California, near Clark's old home. By 1980, the ENA had added another small California daily and TV stations in Oklahoma City; Austin, Texas; and Washington, D.C. The Washington deal was a swap. Fearing the federal government would outlaw ownership of two major media outlets in the same city, the ENA and the Washington Post Company traded local stations.

None of it came easily. "We were really in the minor leagues," recalled Edwin Wheeler, an ENA director and executive who spent forty-eight years with the company. Though it had almost no experience with acquisitions, the ENA did not seek the assistance of a media broker or an investment banker. Long-term bank debt remained taboo. "Some debt was acceptable," Wilkinson recalled, "but the minute we got it, we wanted to pay it off." Without borrowing, the ENA had to pay for acquisitions out of profits, but at least half of those were set aside to pay dividends. And as the 1970s wore on, more and more of the profits were being eaten up in the struggle with the *Free Press.* The number two paper closed fast in the 1970s, grabbing the daily circulation lead for one brief quarter in 1975.

The *News* struck back with a vengeance, led by the fiery Bob Nelson, Clark's top newspaper lieutenant and alter ego. Nelson was a gruff street fighter whose squat, jowly appearance earned him the nickname "Bulldog Bob," refined to "Junkyard Dog," which aptly described his competitive demeanor. He despised everything about the *Free Press,* from its yellow coin boxes on the streets of Detroit to its smug corporate owners in Miami. An engineer by training, he had joined the *News* in 1952 as a production manager, making his mark bending recalcitrant Pressmen and Teamsters to his will. Nelson proudly wore a "News #1" button on his jacket lapel and kept a stash handy for anyone he met, including the odd *Free Press* or Knight-Ridder executive. "Bury the *Free Press,"* he regularly exhorted his troops. As long as Bob Nelson had anything to say about it, the *Free Press* never again would go ahead—and stay ahead—of the *Detroit News.*

Nelson was named vice-president of the *News* in 1973, general manager in 1975. By the spring of 1976, the *News* had spent $42 million on a new printing plant in Sterling Heights, a suburb north of the city. The *News* started delivering papers to homes in the morning, going head-to-head in the *Free Press*'s franchise market. In 1982, the *News* added a $12 million plant in Lansing to speed delivery in outstate Michigan, also longtime *Free Press* territory. Meanwhile, Nelson held the daily price of his paper at fifteen cents, ignoring a five-cent hike by the *Free Press* in 1979.

Keeping the daily lead was crucial, Clark and Nelson believed. Advertisers spent more money in the market leader; increasingly, they were forgoing the second paper altogether. It was a killing disease that usually struck afternoon papers. Four big ones—in Philadelphia, Cleveland, Des Moines, and Minneapolis—had closed or been merged into morning papers in 1982 alone. Peter Clark and Bob Nelson intended to keep the *News* off that obituary page.

Their desire to stay on top became increasingly costly. The nation was in a deep recession. Detroit's Big Three automakers were being routed by the Japanese. People were fleeing Detroit in droves. The last big downtown retailer,

Hudson's, closed in 1983. In the first five years of the 1980s, the *News* lost $21 million. The *Free Press* was losing even more, but it had the deep pockets of Knight-Ridder, Inc. to carry it. With thirty newspapers, five TV stations, and operations in cable, business information services, and book publishing, Knight-Ridder posted revenue of $1.7 billion in 1984, more than five times the ENA. For 1984, the *Free Press*'s loss of $8.1 million would amount to 3 percent of Knight-Ridder's $255 million in operating profit, while the *News*'s deficit would represent 15 percent of the ENA's operating profit of $24 million. Indeed, after taxes and interest expense, there would have been no ENA profit if not for the success of its TV properties.

But Clark was not about to surrender to the *Free Press* and its Goliath-sized parent. The *News* had the all-important lead in daily circulation, a bigger lead on Sundays, a formidable 70 percent of the Sunday classified ad market, and 60 percent of Detroit's $260 million in advertising revenue. To maintain those advantages, Clark was willing to keep the *News*'s circulation price low and to discount its ad rates—even if it meant losing a lot of money. Nothing was more important to him than the survival of the *News*. "It was the first, the largest, the most important, the richest" single piece of the ENA, he would say. When family shareholders complained that the broadcast properties had carried the *News* in recent years, Clark would stiffly remind them that the *News*'s success had enabled the ENA to expand into TV in the first place. Besides, he argued, the paper had awesome moneymaking potential. In 1984, Detroit and its suburbs constituted a market worth at least $350 million in circulation and advertising revenue. If the *News* finally could subdue the *Free Press* and claim that market as its own, even a 10 percent profit margin, small by industry standards, would reap $35 million in profits, more than the combined profits of all the ENA's broadcast stations that year.

It seemed an insane way to do business. Huge yearly losses had become the price of victory in the Detroit newspaper war. The company that could carry them longer would prevail.

Alvah Chapman, the chairman and chief executive of Knight-Ridder, offered a seemingly sane solution. Privately, he proposed to Clark something called a joint operating agency, or JOA, between the *Free Press* and the *News*. Under a JOA, the papers would merge their business operations—circulation, advertising, production, promotion—while maintaining separate editorial staffs. The JOA would permit them to cut costs by eliminating duplicative workers and to increase revenues by fixing prices. It would end the suicidal rate cutting and assure both papers of a profitable future. Clark and Chapman secretly talked on a few occasions and exchanged letters, but they could not agree on the terms of a JOA. Clark insisted that the ENA control the venture, and that the *News* be allowed to retain enough morning circulation to remain Michigan's largest daily. Chapman disagreed; he thought Clark was bringing unnecessary sentiment to the bargaining table. The talks broke off. In a letter, Chapman chastised Clark for failing to compromise. "That is unfortunate, in my view, not only for Knight-Ridder but for the Evening News Association," he wrote. "And it may represent an error of historic proportions."

Alvah Chapman was a smart man, but he could not have known how quickly his prediction would prove true.

3

The Hornet's Nest

Young, blue-eyed Ralph Booth cast a bemused gaze at the picture of the shark hanging on the wall of Peter Clark's office. Clark, an avid scuba diver, cheerfully explained that a friend had photographed the eighteen-foot-long great white from the safety of a cage in the ocean south of Australia.

It was June of 1984, and Clark might have wished he had a cage to protect him from the predators circling the Evening News Association. Ralph Booth and his older brother, John, were two of them. The thirtyish Ivy Leaguers were great-nephews of George Gough Booth, who had married James Scripps's daughter Ellen. They ran Booth American Company, a group of radio and cable television properties with headquarters in Detroit. Lately they had been purchasing the few ENA shares they could find in the hope of accumulating enough to get a voice in the company's doings, maybe even a seat on the board.

Buying ENA shares was not easy. The company's 450,000-odd shares weren't even listed on a stock exchange, because they were held almost exclusively by Scripps's heirs—the families Scripps, Booth, Clark, Beresford, Revelle, Wallace, Whitcomb, and Wilkinson. Most investors never had heard of the Evening News Association. Because the stock was so thinly traded, sellers rarely surfaced and prospective buyers were scarce when on occasion a seller did arise. A shareholder wishing to sell might phone Richard Spitzley, the ENA's chummy corporate secretary, who would offer some chitchat and a promise to find a buyer. Usually he was of little help. Someone shopping for ENA shares might hire a Detroit stockbroker—as the Booth brothers did—to scavenge among family members for stock, but the search often was fruitless.

Deprived an open market, the shares had stagnated in value, and stockholders wishing to raise cash by selling shares could get little more than they would have five to ten years before. For decades, handsome dividend payments had compensated, but in recent years those had been reduced to reflect the growing losses at the *News*. The "extra" dividend, a once-a-year bonus that for many shareholders amounted to many thousands of dollars, had been eliminated. Those who lived comfortably off the dividends were irritated that their standard of living had been diminished. Those who needed cash to pay hefty estate taxes on inherited stock discovered that ENA shares weren't much more than handsomely embossed pieces of paper.

One solution was to offer to sell the ENA's stock publicly, to anyone willing to buy it. Clark had been talking about that prospect for years, while simultaneously putting it off. Going public raised the frightful specter of a takeover. Someone with no interest in journalism could gain control of the ENA and auction it off in pieces, like the estate of a dead millionaire. Clark couldn't tolerate the thought of the family business becoming chattel in the hands of greedy dealmakers and speculators. It troubled him even more that, once the ENA was out of family hands, there was no telling what might happen to the *News*.

Clark counseled patience. Until the *News* finally vanquished the *Free Press*, he told his shareholders, ENA stock would not command the price it ought to. Only after the *News* had prevailed would taking the company public be worthwhile. Clark had no doubt that the *News* would triumph, but it would take time.

Perhaps another five years.

Ralph Booth didn't care to wait that long, which was why he had asked to meet with Peter Clark. On this sticky Monday in June of 1984, Booth had come looking for the ENA mother lode: the 29,383 shares held by Cranbrook Educational Community. Cranbrook was an exclusive prep school that had been founded by the Booths' great-uncle. Lately its finances had fallen into disarray and the people who watched over the school had let it be known that its ENA endowment could be purchased, for the right price.

The rumblings were hardly good news to Clark, who had attended grade school at Cranbrook. The school was the ENA's single largest shareholder, owning 6.5 percent of the outstanding shares. That stake alone could give an unwelcome suitor enough of a position in the company to launch a takeover. At the very least it would force Clark and the ENA's directors to listen to an outsider who might not docilely bow to their conservative thinking.

Clark and Booth waited in Clark's modest office overlooking Lafayette Boulevard, making small talk, until Robert Vlasic arrived. Vlasic, a tall fifty-eight-year-old with snow white hair and a bow tie, was the chairman of Cranbrook's financial committee. He also knew something of family businesses, having run his father's successful Detroit pickle company before selling it to Campbell Soup Company for $33 million in 1978.

"So," Clark said after Vlasic had settled into a chair, "why are we here?"

Booth made his pitch. His company already owned several thousand ENA shares. Now Booth wanted to purchase half of Cranbrook's stake. He hoped the ENA would purchase the other half. This overture was friendly, Booth emphasized. The deal would give Booth American a respectable stake in the ENA while protecting the sizable Cranbrook holding from a less friendly buyer, Booth explained. He thought he could offer the ENA some needed expertise, particularly in the broadcast field.

Clark listened with a blank expression on his face. He had agreed to meet with Booth only as a courtesy, for it was highly unlikely that the ENA would find cause to do business with the Booth brothers. In the minds of Clark and several of his ENA directors, the young Booths were not to be trusted. Some ENA insiders didn't even regard them as family; after all, they were related to the Scrippses only through their great-uncle's marriage. In 1976, their father had nudged along the sale of another family enterprise, the Booth Newspapers of outstate Michigan, by selling his 10 percent share of the company's stock to newspaper mogul S. I. Newhouse. If that was how they showed their loyalty, Clark figured, he wanted nothing to do with them.

But Ralph and John Booth didn't consider themselves raiders. They simply wanted to grow their company. They had decided in the early 1980s to seek a strategic investment that would complement their business while offering a chance to expand. Their search ultimately took them three blocks from their downtown Detroit offices, to the ENA. The Booths figured they could work well with their relatives and both companies could prosper. They had no great desire to see the ENA delivered from family hands.

Yet they did think the ENA could be run better. While other media companies in the 1980s had been buying up TV stations in a genuine acquisition boom, the ENA had been sitting on its hands, preoccupied with its suicidal fight with the *Free Press.* To the Booths' chagrin, Clark and his deputies seemed to have no regular contact with Wall Street, no real presence in the broadcast market. Ralph's brother John had often told ENA director Warren Wilkinson,

"You guys consider yourselves a newspaper company with broadcast stations. You ought to consider yourself a broadcast company with a newspaper."

Advice like that would go unheeded, though, unless the brothers could get a foothold in the company. Cranbrook, a complex of schools and museums designed by famed Swedish architect Eliel Saarinen and nestled in the lush suburban countryside of Bloomfield Hills, was the solution—and the Booths were a solution of sorts for Cranbrook. The ENA wasn't earning what it should have been. Cranbrook's dividend was suffering. Facing cash shortages and pressing needs to renovate its sixty-year-old buildings, the school had had to borrow against its endowment.

Ralph Booth had lunched on a few occasions with Cranbrook president Dan Martin, who had hinted the school might be interested in selling its ENA stake. Martin had been nudged by a friend named Don Becker. Martin's wife was active with the Detroit Symphony Orchestra, of which Becker was a director. Becker also happened to be president of the *Detroit Free Press,* and he worried the newspaper war might go on forever if the ENA continued to own the *News.* Becker knew a few members of the ENA family, and whenever he bumped into one at a cocktail party or a concert he made sure to mention how poorly his or her investment had been faring, and how slim was the chance that the ENA would outlast Knight-Ridder. Martin, the school's president, was a favorite target.

Once the Booth brothers knew Cranbrook might sell, they didn't take long to decide they would be buyers. But they would not be dealing with schoolmarms. Bob Vlasic was a savvy businessman who had helped shape his father's company into a collection of diverse food interests that claimed more than a quarter of the U.S. pickle market. Two of his closest colleagues on the Cranbrook finance committee were F. Alan Smith, General Motors' top financial executive, and Edmund Carpenter, president of ITT Corporation and future CEO of General Signal Corporation. Vlasic also sought the advice of Cranbrook trustee William James, who oversaw cable TV for giant Capital Cities Communications.

Vlasic saw his duty as purely fiduciary: if the ENA assets weren't earning what they could have sitting in a savings account—and they weren't—they should be converted or moved into something that could earn more. But Vlasic couldn't seem to make Peter Clark understand that. Clark was always polite and glad to chat, but Vlasic couldn't get any useful information out of him.

Though Clark's profession was informing the public, he was fanatic about keeping the family business out of the public eye. He believed "confidentiality"—a word he preferred to "secrecy"—was a crucial advantage in the battle with the *Free Press.* If the *Free Press* didn't know exactly how the *News* was faring, it had little but speculation to use when plotting strategy or chatting up advertisers.* Once, when Clark learned that some sensitive ENA papers had surfaced at the *Free Press,* he ordered his home and those of several ENA executives swept for bugging devices. Desk locks were changed and executives were instructed never to leave even perfunctory documents lying around in their absence.

Publicly, the ENA was a sphinx. Because it lacked the five hundred shareholders that would have legally made it a public company, it was not required to disclose much information—and didn't. From the ENA's bare-bones annual report, an eight-page booklet printed on flimsy paper stock, a shareholder could learn how the entire company had performed, but nothing about an individual property or groups of properties. Even the largest shareholders couldn't confirm how much money the *News* was losing or how dependent the ENA was on its TV stations. On several occasions Bob Vlasic had asked Clark point-blank, "How bad are the losses at the *News?*" only to be told, "I'm sorry, I can't talk about that."

Despite that frustration, Vlasic was in no hurry to sell the Cranbrook stake. History preached caution. Cranbrook's trustees had been second-guessed for hastily selling its 8 percent stake in Booth Newspapers to Newhouse. Newhouse had paid $16 million, or $40 a share, for Cranbrook's 405,000 shares. Later, when a bidding contest opened with the Times Mirror Company, Newhouse upped the ante to $47 for each of the remaining Booth Newspapers shares. Jumping the gun had cost Cranbrook nearly $3 million. Vlasic wasn't about to make that mistake. He wasn't going to do anything but the best possible deal.

But who knew what that deal was? Lacking more information or an open market for the stock, it was nearly impossible to determine how much ENA shares were worth. In talks with Bill James and others who appraised media companies, Vlasic had been persuaded that ENA shares were worth quite a bit more than the $150 they had recently been fetching. But how was Cranbrook to boost the price—and therefore the yield on the dividend—without appearing ungrateful? The ENA endowment had been a gift. Scripps and Booth family members were intimately tied to the institution. ENA director

*Knight-Ridder, a public company whose shares were traded on the New York Stock Exchange, was more forthright with *Free Press* financial data.

Richard Wallace was a Cranbrook trustee who liked to remind fellow trustees that George Booth would not have appreciated seeing his gift used against the source of the gift itself. Cranbrook couldn't simply act as a cold-blooded shareholder. The ENA cache was sacrosanct.

Still, there were big bills to pay, so it wasn't so terrible for Cranbrook that Ralph Booth had called this meeting with Clark, even if it was going nowhere. Maybe the Booth brothers' interest would stimulate some action in the ENA stock. Maybe the suggestion that Cranbrook would sell might bolster the price. Maybe something would happen soon.

The meeting lasted just fifteen minutes. Clark listened to Booth and said, "Thank you very much." He wanted nothing to do with the Booth boys. If the ENA wanted to buy Cranbrook's ENA stock, Clark said, it could do so without the help of the Booths. Clark was betting Cranbrook would remain loyal to the ENA. In the meantime, he didn't need the Booth boys giving him advice.

The meeting over, Booth excused himself and asked Vlasic into an adjoining office, where he handed Cranbrook's representative a letter offering the school $170 a share for its holdings. Vlasic politely thanked the younger man and accepted the letter, while making no commitment whatsoever to selling the shares.

In the months that followed, the Booths gradually raised their bid to $270 a share. Clark got wind of the offers and into the bidding, making a series of complex proposals designed to increase the yield on the school's stock without severing its ties with the ENA. In a reverse form of greenmail—wherein a company pays a premium to rid itself of an unwanted shareholder—Clark was proposing, in effect, to pay Cranbrook a premium to *remain* a shareholder. Clark assumed the dickering was all quite confidential, but in fact other people—people who had little interest in newspapers—had begun to notice.

That was all the better for Cranbrook, all the worse for the ENA. The Booth brothers' pursuit of the Cranbrook stake was in vain, but by their very presence, the young entrepreneurs were frustrating Clark's attempt to secure the school's loyalty. Bob Vlasic, by raising the possibility of the school selling its stock, had nudged the ENA into dangerous waters.

He was waiting for the big money to come. And it would.

A company is considered to be "in play" when an unwelcome buyer makes an unsolicited bid that draws the attention of other potential buyers of all or part of the company. As prospective buyers multiply, the price of the company's stock rises. Shareholders become increasingly willing to make a profit by selling their shares, even before it is certain that the company will be bought. Wall Street is home to a bevy of short-term investors who will buy large chunks of those shares on the bet that they will reap a windfall when the company is finally sold. Those investors, known as arbitragers, don't care who owns the company as long as they get their profit. So, once it is "in play," a company usually finds it impossible to avoid being taken over, though it might be able to influence who ultimately gets it.

Rarely does a company put itself into play. But, in a way, that is just what the ENA unwittingly did on Pearl Harbor Day, 1984. On that day the ENA board decided for the first time in the company's history to make a formal tender offer to buy shares of the company from its stockholders. The so-called "self-tender," or "buyback," sought to purchase forty thousand shares, or about 8 percent of the ENA's outstanding stock, for $250 apiece.

The purpose was twofold: to give shareholders who were displeased with the company's performance a chance to sell their stock; and to rid the ENA of unwanted suitors, namely the Booth brothers and a Nashville investor named George Gillett, Jr.

Gillett had amassed a fortune in meat packing and in recent years had gone on a shopping spree for TV stations. Clark didn't know much about him, except that he was neither a family member nor a newspaperman, which was enough. Clark also didn't know that a few family members had contacted Gillett about buying the ENA. Clark's unfavorable impression of the investor was shaped during a surprise telephone call from Gillett in 1982. Gillett was in his private jet, circling above Detroit. Bad weather had prevented a landing, but Gillett had still hoped to speak with Clark about buying his company. Clark had told him the ENA was not for sale.

Since then Gillett, like the Booth boys, had been buying what shares he could find. Clark and the ENA directors hoped the buyback would make him go away. They assumed the most loyal family members would hold their stock. As director William Revelle later recalled, "I don't think anybody thought that waving dollar bills in front of people would make them sell out their family heritage."

But of course it did. When the offer expired December 27, the ENA had purchased 31,548 shares, many owned by shareholders who were loyal to Clark—including his own father, who sold his entire stake of 8,034 shares. Instead of weeding out unwanted buyers, the buyback strengthened the interlopers by diminishing the ranks of Clark loyalists among the stockholders. And it drew the attention of other prospective buyers. Shortly after the buyback ended, the Booths and others—Chicago investor Fred Eychaner, California media analyst Paul Kagan, New York media investment firm Henry Ansbacher, Inc.—were offering $300 a share and more. Sleepy ENA shareholders who had never seen prices like these woke up; more loyalists left the fold. Cranbrook—the pivotal holder—sat tight, though hardly out of loyalty. On Bob Vlasic's advice, the school had hired a Wall Street investment firm to appraise ENA stock. "It started to appear," Vlasic later recalled, "that the damn thing was in play."

To anyone sophisticated in the media business, $250 a share was a bargain for ENA stock. Even with the money-losing *Detroit News,* the company potentially was worth hundreds of dollars more per share. In the mid-1980s, the market for media properties was sizzling. Interest rates were low, the stock market was up, and junk bonds made borrowing a snap. More important, the Federal Communications Commission had raised the limit on the number of TV stations one company could own from seven to twelve. Suddenly, dozens of companies were trolling for TV stations. Wall Street had begun to assess TV properties as much for the sky-high prices they commanded as for day-to-day profitability. Stations that once sold for ten times their cash flow now could get as much as forty times. Any company with TV properties—especially stations in Top 10 markets such as Washington, D.C.—was a target.

At the same time, deregulators in the Reagan administration were clearing the way for hostile takeovers of media companies, once unheard of in the industry. In 1985 the takeover mania that had gripped so many businesses finally would engulf broadcasters and newspapers. A half-dozen media deals to be proposed in the first five months of 1985 would be worth $12 billion—more than quadruple the value of all the deals done in 1984. Capital Cities would merge with ABC in a friendly deal, marking the first time a network had been taken over. Fifty-six newspapers would change hands. Billionaire Jack Kent Cooke would make an unsuccessful hostile bid for Multimedia. General Electric would buy RCA Corporation, owner of NBC. Ted Turner would make an abortive run at CBS. Kohlberg Kravis Roberts, the Wall Street firm famous for leveraged buyouts, would rescue Storer Communications from a raid by Coniston Partners. Arbitrager Ivan Boesky, ex-Treasury Secretary William Simon, and Australian media baron Rupert Murdoch would enter the fray. Media was no longer a protected industry.

Peter Kizer, who ran the ENA's broadcast operations, had been preaching just that to Clark and company directors for two years. At industry meetings, Kizer had heard the ENA being bandied about as a takeover candidate, mostly because of the Washington station, which generated huge amounts of cash. At a golf outing in Oklahoma City in early 1984, Kizer told directors Dick Spitzley and Jim Whitcomb that the ENA's broadcast properties alone made the company worth $700 a share. They didn't believe him. "Find me somebody who'll pay seven hundred and I'll sell right now," Whitcomb had joked.*

Kizer repeatedly tried to persuade Peter Clark that the ENA was vulnerable, but Clark would have none of it. Instead he blithely instructed Kizer to lobby the FCC not to raise the limits on ownership of TV stations—despite overwhelming industry support for the change.

When they authorized the buyback, ENA stock was selling, however thinly, in the $200-a-share range. The directors considered setting their price as high as $300, but no higher. They had heard talk that ENA was worth quite a bit more but considered it irrelevant, reckoning that the appraised value of a *going* concern naturally would be lower than that of a company about to be bought and taken apart. Most of the nine ENA directors didn't think a takeover was remotely possible. As they told shareholders in a letter explaining the buyback, they owned or controlled a comfortable majority of the company's stock. Or at least they thought they did. In fact, among the shareholders whom the board counted as loyal were more than a few who had sold to outsiders in the past year. An informal analysis by the Booth brothers suggested that the board's "majority" might be illusory.

Nevertheless, on December 28 Peter Clark wrote shareholders that the buyback had been a success—even though the company had gotten only three of every four shares it wanted. Even though new predators were circling the ENA. "We believe that the recent flurry of activity in ENA stock has ended," Clark wrote. "We believe that the company enjoys a new and even more stable set of shareholder relationships."

The company indeed had a new set of shareholder relationships, but they were hardly stable. The buyback had worked like hitting a hornet's nest with a stick. As 1984 turned into 1985, the ENA's stock price inched up a few dollars at a time. Wall Street was abuzz with talk of the impending fall of a once-quiet little company called the Evening News Association. One of those buzzing was an investment banker named Porter Bibb.

His appointment arrived two hours late, but Guerin Todd was glad he had waited. He took an instant liking to Porter Bibb. The men both had attended

*Kizer's recollection. Whitcomb denied making this statement. Spitzley did not recall it but said Whitcomb might very well have made it.

Yale, Todd as a law student, Bibb as an undergrad. Todd, in fact, had roomed with the son of a senior partner at Bibb's New York investment firm, Ladenburg, Thalmann and Company, so he knew of its low-key profile. Todd and Bibb had never been formally introduced but vaguely recalled crossing paths many years before when Todd was a lawyer in the Pentagon and Bibb was a Washington reporter for *Newsweek*. They had something else in common on this Monday in February of 1985: the desire to wring money out of the Evening News Association.

Their meeting at the exclusive International Club in Washington had been prompted by yet another of the Detroit Booths, John McLaughlin Booth, the seventy-one-year-old grandson of George Booth, James Scripps's son-in-law. John M. Booth, stockbroker and ENA shareholder, had been the cranky, chattering bane of ENA officialdom for as long as anyone could remember. Booth thought—or so he said, in dozens of phone calls, letters, and meetings with Peter Clark and other ENA executives—that the company's shareholders were not getting their due. "You guys are thieves," he once told broadcast chief Peter Kizer. "You're stealing from us." He agitated for higher dividends, lobbied for a seat on the ENA board, and, in his booming voice, goaded Clark with questions at the yearly shareholder meetings. He thought the directors ran the ENA like a private club, viewing their attitude as: "To hell with the shareholders, *we* know best." Booth wanted them to take the ENA public. Over the years, Clark had put Booth off with assurances that going public was precisely what he hoped to do, when the time was right. But to Booth, the buyback was evidence to the contrary; he saw it as Clark and his director cronies making a lowball bid to procure enough shares to entrench themselves. In January of 1985 he warned Clark in a letter, "You cannot count on BLIND familial LOYALTY from . . . fifth, sixth, and even seventh generation shareholders as they develop minds and interests of their own."

Shortly after receiving that letter, Clark invited Booth to lunch with directors Dick Spitzley and Dick Wallace. Booth used the chance to press his demand that the ENA go public. As he had before, Clark made a polite plea for patience.

Booth, who didn't think Clark took him seriously, would not be put off. He already had found Guerin Todd in a Scripps family tree. Todd was a squat, priggish lawyer with a taste for fine wines and leisurely holidays along the French Riviera. He and his wife, Ann Wilkinson Todd, the sister of ENA director Warren Wilkinson, held more than ten thousand shares of ENA—enough, Booth figured, to give them some clout with the family. Yet, living in a suburb of Washington, D.C., they weren't so close to Clark that they were likely to be loyal. Ann, in fact, didn't get along with her brother. Todd sounded as if he might be inclined to stir things up. As Booth had learned in a few phone conversations, Todd was a loquacious fellow who believed in the power of words. "The pen," Todd quipped, "is mightier than the board." He had been a government lawyer, a private lawyer, and an investment banker, so he knew something of the legal and financial intrigues involved in a corporate confrontation.

Todd also was disenchanted with the management of the ENA. His son-in-law, a Harvard MBA, had told him his shares would be worth at least twice as much if the ENA or parts of it were sold. For Guerin and Ann Todd, that added up to millions of dollars. But they were phantom dollars unless Peter Clark and the ENA board found a way to bolster the stock. Todd was convinced Clark would never take the ENA public. The last thing Clark wanted, Todd believed, was to open the company to outsiders who might question his strategy or, God forbid, demand a halt to the *News*'s battle with the *Free Press.* In occasional letters to Clark, Todd had rooted for the *News,* but he also couldn't help but wonder how Clark expected to outlast Knight-Ridder.

As Todd saw it, Clark was on a crusade—to sustain the *News* at any cost—that was hurting the whole company. The buyback cemented Todd's thinking. A letter from Clark outlining the offer asserted that ENA directors and officers owned enough stock to control the company and, furthermore, they would be holding their shares. It sounded to Todd as if Clark and his pals had the arrogant notion that *they* alone owned the company. "There's something wrong here," Todd told his wife. "These guys want the shares back in their control."

John Booth put Todd together with Porter Bibb, a diminutive forty-seven-year-old who had worked on dozens of media mergers and acquisitions at the New York Times Company, Bankers Trust, and finally at Ladenburg, Thalmann. Bibb had arrived late for today's meeting because he was involved in the fractious infighting over the future of UPI, the financially strapped wire service founded by E. W. Scripps. Recently he also had been working with the dissident shareholders in the Des Moines Register and Tribune Company who would eventually help prod the Cowles family into selling its fine Iowa daily and a handful of other media properties.

He had been a bit player in other such skirmishes, which were just the latest episodes in the long-running decline of family-owned newspapers. Corporate owners were taking over. Since World War II, nearly two of every three family papers had joined corporate groups. Recent years had seen several big papers leave family hands, including the *Chicago Sun-Times* and the *Houston Post.* Some people, mostly journalists, bemoaned the trend on the theory that distant corporations would not attend as assiduously to the needs of local communities. That was debatable, but ultimately irrelevant to whether a paper would be sold. The more pertinent fact was that third- and fourth-generation descendants were more likely to view their newspapers as trust funds than family trusts. Money talked louder than journalism.

The ENA contest was an old story with new names. "You have basically dilettantes at the helm," Bibb told Todd, "and, ironically, one of the great editorial staffs in the country." Bibb thought the ENA was one of America's most poorly run media companies. He estimated that none of its TV stations, save the one in Washington, was posting the 30 to 40 percent profit margins that were standard in the industry. The *News* had to be losing close to a million dollars a year, he figured, with no saving JOA in sight. The ENA was wearing a big takeover bull's-eye. The managers were out of touch, the ill-advised buyback had roused shareholders, and the media market was hotter than ever.

"I think you guys have a good chance to sell this company," Bibb told Todd. At least, Bibb reckoned, they ought to be able to get enough shareholders squawking to make Clark do something—a recapitalization, an asset sale—to generate more dollars for the dissatisfied. They would need to assemble a critical mass of shareholders, representing perhaps 25 to 40 percent of the total shares. Of course, if something did transpire as a result, Bibb's firm would get a cut of the proceeds. And Todd, like lots of shareholders, would be richer than he ever imagined. "I think," he told Bibb, "we're on the same sort of wavelength." They ended their meeting with a friendly handshake.

Two days later, Todd wrote Clark a letter urging him to hire Bibb as an adviser. Bibb knew of other family-owned companies in which descendants of "a brilliant founder" had grown "vaguely restless and uneasy" with management, Todd wrote. Clark might find useful the "alternative responses" Bibb could offer.

"You surely have done a fine job against formidable odds," Todd wrote Clark. But there was also "the perception advanced by some stockholders that you are now a judge in your own cause, i.e., favoring one or another course and suppressing alternate possibilities for the purpose of buttressing preconceived notions."

Todd might as well have written to the *Free Press.* Clark could agree with at least two of Todd's conclusions, but he was not about to hire someone to sell his company out from under him. Friends at other newspapers had passed along disconcerting gossip about a fellow named Bibb quietly seeking buyers for the Evening News Association. In a cordial lunch with Todd at the private Detroit Club, Clark said no thanks to hiring the investment banker. But he had not heard the last of Guerin Todd and Porter Bibb.

Peter Kizer chose his words carefully. The ENA's executive vice-president for broadcast operations was addressing the company's annual meeting of shareholders on February 25, 1985, the same day Todd and Bibb, unbeknownst to anyone at the ENA, were meeting in Washington. Earlier on this raw winter Monday, Kizer had been instructed by Peter Clark to tell shareholders that the ENA was eagerly seeking acquisitions. Kizer had balked, believing the statement an obfuscation, if not an outright lie. The ENA hadn't acquired anything of note since the 1970s, and Clark had made it clear, at least in private, that future purchases were unlikely until the *News*'s fortunes improved. Still, Clark insisted that Kizer talk up acquisitions, arguing that the company had to appear strong in these dicey times. Just a week before, the *Free Press* had published a lengthy story detailing a "tug-of-war" between the ENA and outside speculators. The story used words like "breakup" and "takeover" and described the Booth and Scripps families as "pitted against each other" in a battle over the ENA's future. Worse, the *Free Press* reporter who wrote the story, Bernie Shellum, was sitting among the ENA shareholders today with a notebook and tape recorder. The company had to wear a brave face, Clark told Kizer; talk of buying new properties was part of it.*

Reluctantly, Kizer acquiesced. But his short speech wasn't quite as explicit as Clark might have hoped. Recent FCC rule changes, he told the ENA stockholders, represented "a long-term opportunity" for the company. He did not say the ENA was shopping for properties or would be buying anytime soon. He also did not say what he really thought—that those same FCC rule changes made the *ENA* an inviting target for nearly every acquisition-minded media company in the country. Kizer had been telling Clark that for months, but Clark didn't seem eager to listen. In recent weeks Kizer had begun to feel as if he were on a sinking ship that the captain refused to acknowledge was sinking.

Kizer didn't plan to go down with the ship.

He was a short, graying, ruddy-faced man of fifty-five who carried himself with the slightly exaggerated bravado of someone who wasn't quite sure of himself. He had come from a Detroit TV station in 1970 to run the ENA's

*Clark later insisted that he did not intend deception, but was honestly committed to further acquisition once the *News* was more financially stable.

Detroit radio station. The company had just embarked on Clark's broadcast acquisition program, and Kizer saw no one at the company with his depth of experience in the field. It was a tremendous opportunity, for most of Kizer's occasionally stormy tenure. By 1985, Kizer was running all the ENA's TV and radio stations. His $160,000-a-year salary made him one of the company's best-paid executives. He treated himself to perks that wouldn't have been dreamed of by any of the ENA's conservative bosses. While other executives flew coach, Kizer went first-class. While others hailed cabs, Kizer called a limo. His expense reports were legendary. "Kizer could [spend] three times a year what I could in expense accounts," Bob Nelson recalled. At the annual National Association of Broadcasters convention in Las Vegas, Kizer would book a two-level suite with a private pool and throw a bash with a live band, the fanciest food, and the best booze. Unlike most ENA executives, Kizer said so when he thought he deserved a raise. He even had his office redone to look more modern than those of his colleagues.

Kizer struck the old men of the ENA as typical of the new breed of broadcast executive, who had grown up in a go-go business that knew only ever-growing revenues, profits, and expense reports. Clark, though, almost despite himself, was taken by him. He liked Kizer's blunt style and admired his ability to sell. While Nelson and others carped about Kizer's spending habits and cavalier attitude toward ENA conventions, Clark looked the other way, telling himself that broadcast people were different from print people and, if the ENA wanted to be in the broadcast business, it would have to live with the Peter Kizers of the world.

In the 1980s, Kizer found it increasingly difficult to live with Clark and the ENA. His disenchantment stemmed largely from a retrenchment ordered by Clark in 1981. The nation was in recession, the auto industry was slumping badly, and the *News* had lost money for the first time since the strike of 1967–68. Clark called for a slowdown in spending at all ENA operations. Hiring was curtailed, budget increases were pared, and expansion projects were delayed, for newspaper and TV properties alike. As the *News*'s losses deepened, Kizer couldn't get money with which to join the broadcast buying spree or invest in cable TV or cellular technology, the waves of the future. Missed opportunities abounded.

Kizer would pitch this purchase or that, and Clark would show some interest, but nothing would get done. Meanwhile, Kizer's peers at other media companies were buying and growing new stations, increasing their salaries and bonuses. Kizer envied them. He wanted more than the ENA was about to give: more and bigger stations, a much larger salary, a sizable chunk of company stock. The latter was least likely, because the company had no program for sharing equity with executives who weren't members of the family. Stock options and the like, standard issue in most modern companies, were unheard of at the ENA.

By 1985 Kizer was angry and frustrated and not terribly loyal to Peter Clark. He focused his resentment on Clark because he blamed the ENA's troubles on Clark's seeming obsession with winning the newspaper war. Kizer felt Clark was plundering the moneymaking broadcast operations to funnel money to the *News,* which had lost $23,000 a day in 1984. While Kizer couldn't get $5 million for a much-needed renovation at the Washington TV station, the ENA's most profitable property, the company could find $12 million to build a new printing plant in Lansing and $17 million to upgrade the presses at the main plant near Detroit.

To Kizer, that wasn't only unfair, it was stupid, for the newspaper war seemed patently unwinnable. Kizer admired the *News*'s journalism, but he thought Bob Nelson and the others who ran the paper's business side were idiots. For example, he couldn't believe the market-leading *News* didn't take the lead in pricing. Its red ink was directly the result of its low newsstand price—fifteen cents—and its discounting of ad rates. Kizer's station managers occasionally sent him memos showing how the *News* could profit by raising prices; Kizer tossed them into the trash. "Hey," he told the managers, "that ain't gonna happen."

Kizer detested Bob Nelson, the *News*'s publisher and his counterpart at the head of the ENA's Newspaper Division. Nelson was everything Kizer loathed in a modern media executive—coarse, foulmouthed, stubborn, uncreative. He saw Nelson as a production expert who didn't know the first thing about selling papers and making money. And, besides Peter Clark, Nelson was the only ENA executive paid more than Kizer. Kizer called him "the Khrushchev of the *News*" for his repeated vows to "bury the *Free Press.*" That seemed an absurd objective to Kizer, who couldn't imagine Knight-Ridder letting the puny ENA push it around. Why not just agree to a JOA and make everybody happy? Why continue this masochistic war?

Kizer was fed up watching his part of the business—the ENA's lifeline—be treated like an unwanted stepchild. But he saw nothing changing. That was never clearer than at an ENA officers' meeting just prior to the 1985 shareholder meeting. Reviewing 1984, Clark said broadcast earnings hadn't been quite as good as they could have been. Kizer seethed. Clark later said he had intended no criticism, but all Kizer heard was that he wasn't doing a good job. And Clark had said it in front of Nelson. Screw this, Kizer thought. Why do I want to be here?

More than anyone at the ENA, Kizer believed a takeover was possible. That meant Clark's obsession with winning the newspaper war could drag the entire company into extinction—and with it Kizer's job, title, and six-figure salary. Though he wasn't delighted with his position at the ENA, at fifty-five, with a coronary bypass in his recent past, Kizer wasn't eager to go job hunting. He had his eyes open for his own personal white knight. If he assisted a buyer, he figured, he was more likely to survive a takeover. And he might even get the chance to build the ENA into a big-league broadcasting company.

Kizer didn't know it on February 25, 1985, but his prospective savior was sitting among the shareholders. Robert Cahill had come from Hollywood to listen to what Peter Clark, Peter Kizer, and the other ENA executives had to say. He listened carefully as Clark told his shareholders, "We believe you own a valuable stock. We believe that its value will greatly increase. We hope you will be with the company as it does."

After the meeting Cahill bumped into an old acquaintance, Lee Allan Smith, who managed the ENA's Oklahoma City TV station. A few days later Cahill called Smith to inquire about buying the company. Smith referred him to Peter Kizer.

The old man kept the conversation short, but it was long enough for Guerin Todd to hear what he wanted to hear.

Todd had come to Detroit in April of 1985 to have a talk with Warren Scripps Booth. Booth, ninety, a grandson of *Detroit News* founder James Scripps, was the retired chairman of the ENA and publisher of the *Detroit News*. "It is time to get out," Booth told Todd. They were alone in a sparsely furnished office in Bloomfield Hills, a well-to-do suburb north of Detroit. "It is time to sell."

Todd smiled. It *was* time to sell the ENA. He had met with Peter Clark more than once in recent weeks, and though their conversations were friendly, Todd came away thinking he had been talking to a wall. A European history buff who had lived in France, Todd liked to imagine Clark as a medieval king who isolated himself in a castle. A moat with drawbridges kept him safe from the taunts of villagers who actually owned the castle. Now Todd had come to ford the moat and crash the castle doors.

First he wanted the blessing of Warren Booth. The numerous Booths, especially Warren and his brother Henry, controlled considerable amounts of ENA stock that could be influential in a takeover fight. As well, Warren Booth's pedigree in the family and its business was impeccable. Booth had brought Peter Clark to Detroit and groomed him to lead the ENA. As far as Todd knew,

Booth had never spoken critically of Clark's reign. But now the old man was telling Todd it was time for that reign to end.

Booth spoke from behind a desk, where he had sat his long frame. He reminded Todd that he had been through a sale of family jewels before, when the group founded by his father, Booth Newspapers, was sold to the Newhouse newspaper chain for $305 million in 1976. The price had been right, and Booth gladly sold his sizable stake in the company. Todd started to recount a similar experience of his own. His family had sold a long-held electroplating company to American Can Company in the 1960s. Booth interrupted him. "You feel that our family is too numerous and too varied and losing interest," he told Todd. "That's what you were going to say."

"Well, yes, probably," Todd said.

Booth shook his head. In recent years, he had begun to worry about his estate and the need for liquidity in his ENA holdings. He did not want to leave his children an enormous estate tax bill. "The thing that must be remembered is there are many, many people who have no power," Booth said. "But there *are* shares of stock."

In other words, it was time, in Booth's view, for the stockholders to take control of their stock. Todd figured he had what he had come for. Booth said he did not have the energy to get involved in a shareholder uprising, but he would not stand in the way.

Todd smiled again. "I have lots of energy," he said.

Peter Kizer waited in the cavernous lobby of the Detroit Athletic Club. Under his left arm he clutched a plain manila envelope. He extended his right hand when his appointment, a tall Californian whom Kizer had never met, emerged from the polished oak and glass revolving doors, carrying a briefcase. His name was Robert Cahill.

The Detroit Athletic Club, for seventy years a private refuge for Detroit's corporate and civic elite, was a hushed enclave of lofty beamed ceilings, moody paneling, sprawling Oriental rugs, and walk-in fireplaces. Countless deals had been cut over club sandwiches in the casual elegance of the Grill Room, where Kizer and Cahill now chatted quietly in a leather booth. The two men vaguely knew each other, having talked at least twice by phone. Cahill was a balding lawyer who once had worked for the Federal Communications Commission. At first, Kizer didn't especially like him. Coming from glitzy Hollywood to grimy Detroit, Cahill seemed to think he was somehow better than Kizer. Kizer tried not to let it bother him. Working for Peter Clark, he had grown accustomed to condescension.

Besides, Cahill had some interesting things to say. He represented a wealthy group of people who wanted to buy the ENA. He didn't name names, but he assured Kizer his client had the wherewithal to complete a deal. Cahill didn't say why his client was interested, and Kizer didn't inquire. Cahill said his client preferred to buy companies with built-in management. That didn't mean Kizer was promised a job, but the hint was strong enough to satisfy him. What's more, Cahill said, his client liked to give top managers a piece of the action. Kizer assumed this meant he would get a nice chunk of stock if this buyer got the ENA. Cahill was getting more likable by the minute.

"I have something here I would like you to see," he said. He handed Kizer a typewritten document. "Could you give me an idea how accurate these are?"

Kizer was a little surprised at what he saw: specific estimates of 1984 revenue and profits for each of the ENA's various properties. None of the information was available to the public. Financial figures for the individual properties literally were kept under lock and key, in a safe on the mezzanine of the *News* building. Only ENA directors and a handful of executives, Kizer among them, saw the figures. Cahill probably hadn't seen the actual numbers, but he had concocted reasonably accurate guesses. "Your numbers are very close," Kizer said.

Cahill asked what Kizer thought the ENA was worth. Kizer said a thousand dollars a share wasn't unthinkable, on the strength of the radio and television stations alone.

"We're going to make an offer," Cahill said. "How should we go about it?"

"Go see Peter Clark," Kizer said.

Cahill frowned. Hadn't Clark made it clear he would under no circumstances entertain an offer for his company?

Indeed he had, Kizer replied. But only by making an offer would Cahill learn if Clark's position was shared by the ENA board. "That's a good idea," Cahill conceded.

Kizer pulled out the manila envelope he had brought. It contained a thin, legal-sized book with a brown vinyl cover, which Kizer had taken that morning from the safe at the *News*. It was his personal copy of the monthly financial report to the ENA board of directors, known as the "board book." In the closed cathedral of the ENA, the board book was the bible. A glance at it would tell a competitor, such as Knight-Ridder, whether the *News* was losing enough money to threaten the ENA's future. To someone plotting to buy the company, the book would supply specific data needed to calculate a price and persuade lenders to finance a purchase.

The few executives given copies of the board book were forbidden to show them to anyone, even sons and daughters who owned stock in the ENA. When the board books were disseminated every four weeks, they were hand-delivered where possible, and never sent through interoffice mail or left with secretaries. They were never left unattended where anyone could idly leaf through them. Executives were urged to return their copies to the safe before going home each night.

Kizer had broken that rule a few times so that he could work at home, but he had never risked toting the board book to something as social as a lunch. Indeed, he wasn't exactly sure why he had brought it. He hadn't really planned on giving it to Cahill. But now there seemed little point in not giving it to him. Cahill had the supposedly secret numbers, or at least close estimates. If Cahill had them, Kizer reasoned, others considering a purchase of the ENA must have them. He double-checked Cahill's estimates against the numbers in the board book. They were indeed close. He slipped the book back into the envelope and asked if he could keep the estimates Cahill had compiled. Sure, Cahill said.

"You may have this," Kizer said.

Reaching across the table, he offered the envelope containing the board book. Later, it would seem, in Kizer's recollection, that he had done it without thinking. He knew he might be viewed as a traitor, but Peter Kizer no longer cared. If the leak of the supposedly secret ENA numbers cost Clark his company, so be it.

The lunch was over. Cahill didn't open Kizer's gift until he was on a plane home to California. Kizer returned to his office. He didn't feel the need to discuss his lunch with anyone.

Kizer talked with Cahill again on the phone a few days later. Cahill revealed that he was working for A. Jerrold Perenchio, a Hollywood producer and promoter who had enjoyed a high degree of financial success. He didn't say that Perenchio's partner was Norman Lear, creator of *All in the Family.*

Kizer was eager to help. He mailed Cahill a copy of the ENA's confidential five-year financial forecast. Coupled with the board book, the forecast would help Perenchio persuade a lender to assist in a purchase of the ENA. In late May, Kizer and Cahill met at the Ritz-Carlton Hotel in New York. Cahill said Perenchio was preparing to seek financial backing for a bid.* Early in July, Cahill told Kizer over the phone that a tender offer might be forthcoming. That meant Perenchio planned to appeal directly to ENA shareholders, bypassing

*The record is unclear as to precisely when Kizer and Cahill met in New York. In court depositions, Kizer said the lunch was in late May, Cahill in early June.

Peter Clark and the board of directors. Kizer kept this to himself. Though he had never been promised a job, he assumed the new owners would hire him and give him stock in the company.

In mid-July, Kizer and Cahill dined at the Pine Lake Country Club near Detroit, where Kizer was a member. Cahill mentioned for the first time that Norman Lear also would be part of Perenchio's group. After that dinner, Kizer never heard from the Californian again.

Very soon, though, Peter Clark would.

In late April, ENA shareholders received a letter from something called the Shareholder Equity Evaluation Committee. The committee included Guerin Todd; John McLaughlin Booth; Todd's son-in-law, W. Earl McClure; Lloyd Marentette, whose wife owned 2,020 shares; and Marentette's son Danny, a professional horse trader who also owned ENA stock. Todd called them the "five prima donnas." Their two-page letter, signed by Todd, invited shareholders to pool their shares in the hope of pressuring the ENA to do something to improve the value of their holdings.

"A number of investors, speculators and other interested parties have been buying ENA stock recently, with reported recent prices in the $400-per-share range," Todd wrote. "Some believe the stock's value is considerably higher." ENA managers, he noted, refused to seek an independent appraisal of their company. "Misinformation or no information can be costly to individuals and charities owning the stock," he reminded them.

In the vague language of a corporate raider, Todd's missive said nothing about a takeover or a sale of the ENA, alluding instead to "exploring the options" and "concerted actions" the shareholders could take, "as appropriate."

Todd was an elusive character. For years he had been dropping Clark notes that were almost embarrassing in their effusive praise. In March of 1983 Todd wrote, "Congratulations . . . on the magnificent contest you are waging with Knight-Ridder." Later that year he applauded the *News*'s success in thwarting a *Free Press* circulation drive. "As in St. Louis," Todd wrote, "a newspaper . . . owned by a local area family can defeat a megabuck conglomerate owned by a holding company outside the circulation area. Great news!" In a handwritten note to corporate secretary and board member Dick Spitzley in December of 1984, Todd said he had told a stockbroker shopping for ENA shares that the company's management was "very successful" and that "shares will be worth about $500 each in 5 years!"

In the spring of 1985, though, Todd was telling Clark by phone and mail that the ENA had to take steps to help dissatisfied shareholders sell their stock at a fair price. Even those signals were mixed. On April 5 Todd wrote Clark to say that he and Mrs. Todd had "no interest in second-guessing your judgment and are quite satisfied to leave things alone." Three weeks later Todd wrote again: "Extensive discussions, initiated by others, have taken place in the past two weeks, persuading me to reverse my field and thus to move toward independent action." Clark didn't quite understand. It shouldn't have been a mystery, though. With the Booth brothers and other investors steadily accumulating shares, the price of ENA stock gradually was rising. Todd and his fellow dissidents were in position to get rich quickly.

From his elegant, three-story colonial amid the tony shops and restaurants of Old Town Alexandria, Virginia, Todd crafted a series of letters that poked whimsical fun at Peter Clark and the ENA board while seeking recruits to the dissident cause. In one letter, Todd wrote that Clark's many explanations for the ENA's failure to make its stock more liquid "can be condensed into [comedian] Eddie Murphy's famous two words: TRUST ME." Yet Todd maintained a genteel air, mailing Clark advance copies of the committee's letters between trips to French Polynesia, Tahiti, Paris, and the Sierra Nevadas.

The committee formed an alliance-at-arm's-length with the Cranbrook school. Porter Bibb stayed in close touch with David McKearnan of the Wall Street firm of Donaldson, Lufkin and Jenrette, which Cranbrook had hired to appraise the ENA. Donaldson, Lufkin's analysis valued the stock as high as $1,055 a share—assuming the company was sold off in pieces. The appraisal found its way into the hands of an assortment of prospective buyers, including Hollywood lawyer Robert Cahill, who discussed it with Kizer over lunch at the Ritz-Carlton. Bibb himself had approached Norman Lear, plus more than three dozen media companies.

Meanwhile, Todd and his wife were quietly selling small pieces of their goodly ENA stake. Each sale boosted the share price a bit, making it more attractive for other family members to sell their stock. In late May, Todd wrote shareholders that ENA shares were selling for as much as $650 apiece. At that price, family members who once refused to consider selling shares were softening. By June, Todd's dissident committee counted commitments from shareholders owning about 18 percent of the ENA's stock. Counting Cranbrook's stake, the dissidents could claim to represent a respectable 25 percent block. Stockholders with another 3 percent were considering joining the group.

On June 19, Todd and Donaldson, Lufkin's McKearnan met with Clark, Spitzley, Dick Wallace, ENA lawyer Harry Ruemenapp, and financial executive Ed Frederickson in the boardroom on the mezzanine of the *News* building. McKearnan outlined a smorgasbord of financial steps the company could take to mollify the dissidents, such as another buyback or sales of certain properties that would raise cash to buy out the group. Mainly, though, his presentation aimed to persuade Clark to hire McKearnan's firm to find a buyer for the ENA, for which the firm would earn a handsome fee. It was too late for that, though; Clark recently had hired Salomon Brothers, a respected and sizably larger Wall Street firm, to advise the ENA about its financial dealings.

Clark figured McKearnan and Todd had come to extract greenmail, which the ENA was not about to pay. Family members would have been furious—and, undoubtedly, lawsuits would have been filed—if the directors bought out a few selected shareholders at $500 or more a share. The meeting ended as it had begun, with Clark pitted against a burgeoning pool of unhappy shareholders. Later, Todd told *Metropolitan Detroit* magazine, "I couldn't help thinking he was rather like a big old walrus stuck out on an ice floe and watching the ice melt around him."

Peter Clark didn't think he was just floating along. He and the ENA board had taken a number of steps to try to appease family members and slow the momentum of Todd's dissident band. In April, Clark and Bob Nelson reluctantly raised the price of the *News*'s Sunday edition from fifty cents to seventy-five cents, following an earlier *Free Press* increase. Clark hoped the added revenue would show up soon on the company's bottom line. The board hiked the yearly dividend from $8.40 a share to $9.60, and in May declared a bonus dividend of $1.50. The directors also created, largely for the sake of appearance, a five-member "advisory committee" of younger shareholders to counsel the board about shareholder concerns. Clark made peace with Ralph and John Booth, who promised not to buy more than 5 percent of the ENA's stock—though they were prepared to *sell* their stake when the price was right.

Clark wrote shareholders to denounce Guerin Todd's committee, especially its suggestion that the ENA hire an investment firm to appraise the company. Todd's group, Clark wrote, obviously wanted to stimulate the sale of a large block of ENA stock, the sale of the entire company, or "worst of all," as Clark put it, "the dismemberment and piecemeal sale of ENA assets." He reiterated his commitment to the three-point plan he had outlined at the February stockholder meeting: pursue smart acquisitions, win the battle with the *Free Press,* and then take the ENA public.

He assured shareholders that broadcast chief Peter Kizer was working harder to expand the company. "Peter's extensive background in broadcasting and his experience with earlier ENA acquisitions will serve our expansion efforts well," Clark wrote. Of course there still were no immediate plans to buy new properties, and Clark knew nothing of Kizer's furtive dealings with the Hollywood group. With ironic prescience, Clark wrote, "The timing of the [Todd] proposal could hardly be worse."

Again he was pleading for patience, which put him at a decided disadvantage, for Todd held out the prospect of riches *now.* Knight-Ridder stepped up the pressure by announcing it would spend $22.8 million to expand the *Free Press*'s printing plant on the Detroit River. The expansion plan, in the works for better than a year, sent a clear signal that Knight-Ridder wasn't about to surrender anytime soon, and cast further doubt on Clark's strategy, which hinged on the *News* prevailing over the *Free Press* within five years. Clark's friends in Miami weren't doing him any favors.

There was little else to do, Clark thought, but wait and hope the family would hold together. Media analyst Paul Kagan seemed to sympathize with Clark. The ENA, he wrote in a June 10 newsletter, is "a textbook case of a well-run company pressured into a traumatic change by time, the course of events, fiduciary responsibility and the need for some investors to raise cash. The legacy of James Scripps . . . is not the issue here. While the integrity of a business enterprise must not be compromised, neither must its ultimate value." Kagan also argued that the ENA was worth an incredible $2,000 a share. He certainly hoped it was, for he owned a handsome cache of stock he had purchased at an average price of $325 a share.

As summer wore on, Clark maintained a brave front, but he was powerfully worried about his company's future. The words "breakup value" and "takeover" were appearing in print with increasing frequency. "There is no need to be rushed by an anxious few," Clark told shareholders in a letter July 1. "This company isn't for sale," he told the *Wall Street Journal* July 18. He believed he still had the loyalty of a majority of his shareholders. Little short of a big-dollar tender offer for the entire company, he felt, could wrench the ENA from family hands.

Clark believed he held a trump card: no one in the newspaper fraternity would make a hostile bid for the ENA. In that clubby circle, hostile deals just didn't happen. Indeed, Porter Bibb and David McKearnan had sounded out many of the country's biggest media concerns—Gannett, CBS, Times Mirror, Capital Cities, Hearst, Newhouse, the New York Times Company, Dow Jones—and though some were interested in the ENA, none were willing to go where they were not wanted. Maybe Clark could weather this storm after all.

Quoted in a lengthy *Free Press* story published July 21, he was in fighting trim. Danny Marentette of Todd's dissident group assailed Clark's strategy: "What it boils down to is whether the stockholders want to bet that the *News* can beat the *Free Press*. Would you want a major portion of your assets tied up in a gamble like that?" Clark didn't blink. "The Michigan marketplace," he declared, "can sustain two daily metros indefinitely into the future, and I think it will sustain them. I have no reason to believe that Knight-Ridder would change their posture with the *Free Press*, and I know we won't, so we're likely to both be here for an indefinite period. Indefinite means forever."

Forever would not be long for Peter Clark. The dominoes set up by Guerin Todd and Peter Kizer were about to fall.

4

White Knights

G. Barry Hubbard, the ENA's controller, walked into Peter Clark's office and dropped a thin document on his boss's desk. It was 8:50 on the morning of Monday, July 29, 1985.

"Have you seen this?" Hubbard asked.

Clark had not. The paper had been filed only moments earlier at the federal courthouse four blocks from the *News* building on West Lafayette Boulevard. It was a lawsuit entered by a company named L.P. Media, Inc., with an address on "Avenue of the Stars" in Los Angeles. L.P. Media wanted the court to bar the state of Michigan from enforcing a law that could keep the company from completing a hostile takeover of the ENA.

Peter Clark was thunderstruck. Quickly scanning the document, he saw that L.P. Media had begun a tender offer to buy all of the shares of ENA for $1,000 apiece in cash. The *L* in L.P. Media stood for Lear, the *P* for Perenchio. A gun had been at Clark's head for months. Guerin Todd had loaded it and Peter Kizer had cocked the hammer. Now a couple of Hollywood producers were going to pull the trigger.

As always, Clark kept his outward emotions in check, but inside he wanted to explode. Why the hell is Lear in this? he thought. What are they after? For the first time he caught himself thinking, This is real: We could lose the company. A palpable shock of horror gripped him as he imagined speculators rummaging through the sedate ENA offices like wreckers, selling lamps, desks, coatracks, pictures off the wall. Breakup, he kept thinking. Lear and Perenchio just wanted to break up the ENA, sell it off in pieces, make themselves a huge profit, and go their merry way, without a thought for what it would mean to the company's thirty-seven hundred employees or the communities they served.

Clark told his secretary to cancel everything on his schedule. He started making phone calls. He summoned the directors: Jim Whitcomb from Pittsburgh, John Beresford from Phoenix, Bill Revelle from Evanston, Illinois, the rest from Detroit. He caught Bob Nelson as he was heading out the door of his Bloomfield Hills home. "We're in trouble," Clark said. His mind was racing: At $1,000 a share, Lear and Perenchio were offering shareholders nearly seven times what their stock had been worth a year before, four times what their own company had offered just eight months before. Clark no longer could rely on the patience of the family, for now it was presented with a sky-high price and a ready and willing buyer.

Still, Clark thought this particular buyer might represent his best hope for rescuing the company. If the New York Times Company or Capital Cities had made the offer, he would have had little chance of dissuading shareholders from surrendering. But Clark believed—or at least hoped—that the ENA's 333 owners might deem Lear and Perenchio unworthy of the family heritage.

After all, Lear and Perenchio weren't journalists, but entertainers. Norman Lear was a onetime door-to-door salesman, press agent, and comedy writer who had invigorated the weary TV format of the sitcom by exploring taboo topics such as sex and racism. In the 1980s Lear had founded People for the American Way, a liberal foil for the archconservative Moral Majority. Clark thought the ENA family would think hard before handing Lear control of the *News*'s conservative editorial page. Jerry Perenchio was a talent agent whose company, Chartwell Artists, had represented megastars Marlon Brando, Andy Williams, Richard Burton, and Elton John, among others. He had emerged on the national scene in 1971 when he promoted the "Fight of Champions" between Muhammad Ali and Joe Frazier; that was followed by the infamous "Battle of the Sexes" tennis match pitting Bobby Riggs against Billie Jean King. More recently he had headed a group that bought Loews Corporation's national chain of theaters for an estimated $160 million. Perenchio was known in the industry as a shrewd negotiator gifted at divining the true value of a deal.

Lear and Perenchio had pledged to invest $62.5 million each in the ENA deal. No one doubted they had the money. But Clark doubted they had the desire to operate the *Detroit News*. He felt certain that the Hollywood producers coveted only the ENA's TV stations. Clark expected that the *News* would quickly be closed or sold or railroaded into a JOA that would relegate it to secondary status in Detroit.* Indeed, Lear and Perenchio's tender offer documents contemplated an ENA without the *News*. The family couldn't possibly sell to these greedy speculators, he thought. Even so, that did not guarantee that other, ostensibly more acceptable, suitors wouldn't soon surface in the guise of "white knights."

But Clark could fight only one fight at a time.

He called an impromptu meeting of his executive staff—Nelson, Frederickson, Spitzley, Wallace, and Peter Kizer. "We're going to fight this every way we know," he told them. Later that day Clark issued a public statement: "The Evening News Association is not for sale. We will vigorously oppose any takeover attempt and we expect to succeed."

The offer by Lear and Perenchio was scheduled to expire at midnight, Friday, August 23. For twenty-four years Clark had been struggling to hold the ENA together. Now he had just twenty-five days to keep it from flying apart.

That Monday morning, Bob Vlasic was on a putting green in Buffalo when he was called to a phone. Vlasic was waiting to tee off in a charity tournament with pro golfer Lee Trevino, who had done some commercials for Vlasic's food company.

The voice on the phone told Vlasic of the tender offer for the ENA. It was good news. Just like that, Cranbrook was $29 million richer. At $1,000 a share, the school could not afford to wait for Peter Clark's long-range plans to play out. Vlasic had been talking with Clark a good deal of late. The ENA had renewed its efforts to procure the Cranbrook stake by offering a combination of promissory notes and stock warrants priced quite a bit higher than the offers of the previous year. But the Lear-Perenchio offer was higher still, and it was in easy-to-count, easy-to-spend cash.

By law, Vlasic and his fellow trustees could not keep their shares from Lear and Perenchio simply because they didn't like the buyers. The only important qualification a suitor needed was the ability to pay. Then again, Vlasic was in no hurry to sell to the Hollywood people. Now that a tender offer had been launched, there certainly would be other buyers, with even more money. The next few weeks would be interesting.

*Lear, Perenchio, and their deputies, Cahill and Robin French, declined to be interviewed.

In Virginia, Guerin Todd was delighted to hear of the tender offer. What better evidence could there be of the dissidents' success? The Shareholder Equity Evaluation Committee had been prodding the family for just three months, and now the price of ENA stock had soared to $1,000 a share!

Todd wasn't so pleased to hear who had made the bid. The conservative Todd wasn't a fan of Norman Lear. Moreover, the tender offer was loaded with conditions that would allow Lear and Perenchio to abandon their offer without warning. But then, Todd didn't have to sell to Lear and Perenchio to reap a windfall. Lots of Wall Street traders would be happy to buy his stock and, betting that more bids were on the way, they would pay even more than $1,000 a share. Todd and his fellow dissidents couldn't help but make millions.

Peter Kizer went numb when he heard about the tender offer in the morning meeting with Clark and other ENA officials. Clark made no mention of anyone's furnishing information to the enemy. After the meeting, Kizer hurried to Ed Frederickson's office in search of a copy of the offer papers. On page 6 he found a brief notation that a "senior executive" of the ENA had supplied L.P. Media with information "which is not publicly available and has not been provided to the company's stockholders." The document said the unnamed executive had had "a number of conversations" with an unnamed L.P. Media official.

The jig was up.

Kizer had to fly to Washington that afternoon. A few minutes before he was to leave for the airport, Bill Saxton ducked his head into Kizer's office. By now, Clark was aware of the leak to Lear and Perenchio, and Saxton, a member of the ENA's law firm who frequently played golf with Kizer, was polling executives to see who was responsible.

"Hey, Pete, I gotta ask you this," Saxton said. "Were you the one who did this?"

"No," Kizer lied.

In Washington the next day, Kizer visited William Wetmore, a communications lawyer who counseled the ENA in regulatory matters. Kizer had planned to confess his betrayal to Wetmore and ask for advice, but somehow Wetmore already knew Kizer had been the source of the leak. He advised Kizer to come clean with Clark. Shortly after leaving Wetmore, Kizer placed a call to Clark's secretary and asked for a meeting on Wednesday afternoon.

War-gaming was a word Peter Clark frequently used to describe the endless plotting and strategizing he and his deputies did in their day-to-day combat with the *Free Press.* In the waning days of July 1985, its meaning was fraught with more immediate deadliness than ever before. After all, the fight with the *Free Press* had gone on for years and probably would last years more. The fight with Lear and Perenchio threatened to be swiftly fatal.

On Tuesday, July 30, Clark convened the ENA board of directors to "war-game" the company's response to the raid by L.P. Media. Clark had briefed them in a Monday conference call about the tender offer. They had unanimously agreed to resist. But how? Typically conservative, they had in the past eschewed adopting defensive measures that might now have helped to stave off the raiders or at least buy time to mount an effective defense. They had none of the golden parachutes or poison pills that other companies had eagerly installed in response to the merger mania that gripped corporate America in the early 1980s. As Clark would later put it, they were caught "bare-faced and flat-footed."

Prompted by Clark, the ENA directors mulled over what limited options they had. Their lawyers could seek to have Michigan's antitakeover statute enforced. That might delay the tender offer, giving the ENA more time to devise financial means of fighting it, and might even discourage Lear and Perenchio. The lawyers also could ask the Federal Communications Commission to block the takeover by questioning the moral character of buyers who would induce an insider—namely, Peter Kizer—to betray his employer. The FCC would have to approve the transfer of broadcast licenses from the ENA to L.P. Media. In the past the lengthy transfer process had discouraged hostile deals because it defeated the quick-strike strategy of a tender offer. Recently, though, billionaire investor Jack Kent Cooke had found a way around the rules. In his failed bid for Multimedia, Cooke had set up a third-party trustee who was to hold stock tendered until the FCC process was complete, when the shares would be transferred to the acquirer. L.P. Media had proposed a similar method, designating former Treasury Secretary G. William Miller as trustee.

Their best hope, the board members agreed, rested with the family's presumed distaste for Lear and Perenchio. But that hope, they knew, would diminish rapidly as Wall Street bid up the price of ENA stock. Indeed, family members were getting calls from stockbrokers asking if they would like to sell now, thus avoiding the risk that Lear and Perenchio might abandon their offer; the new offers were between $1,000 and $1,100 a share. Many simply couldn't afford to say no. Most of the ENA board members themselves stood to reap enormous windfalls. At $1,000 a share, Warren Wilkinson owned stock worth $11.5 million. Dick Wallace and his wife had nearly $8 million worth. Dick Spitzley's personal stake would bring $4.3 million. And Peter Clark stood to collect nearly $6 million.

As the board meeting was coming to a close, Edwin Wheeler, who had retired from the board but remained with the ENA as an adviser, leaned over to Bill Revelle and said, "We're dead."

"What do you mean?" said Revelle, who desperately wanted to keep the company in the family.

"Look at Spitzley, Wallace, and those other guys," said Wheeler, a non-family member who owned just twenty-five shares. "They'd all sell yesterday if they could."

Jay Higgins came to Detroit from Wall Street, ostensibly to help Peter Clark and the ENA board find a way to keep their company in family hands. The head of mergers and acquisitions at Salomon Brothers was a tall, athletic forty-year-old who smiled a lot and smoked a pungent cigar. Salomon had a sterling reputation for trading bonds and raising money for large corporations. It had less of a reputation as a player in the takeover game, nor was it known for its work with the media industry.

The ENA had hired the firm a few months before, largely on the advice of Ed Frederickson, an administrator who had scant experience with the New York investment community. Clark had wanted someone to prepare the company to go public, as well as to offer advice in case of a takeover attempt. Salomon was a good choice for the former, not so good for the latter. Had anyone at the ENA thought a takeover attempt imminent, the company might have chosen one of the other firms that had sought the company's business, such as First Boston Corporation, one of Wall Street's savviest takeover advisers.

Salomon's job was to find a way to enrich shareholders short of a sale of the entire company—essentially what Guerin Todd and Bob Vlasic had been urging for months. The ENA had several options, none terribly attractive: It could sell some properties for cash and borrow additional money to purchase big blocks of shares—such as Cranbrook's stake—at sizable premiums. It could split the company in half and swap the broadcast properties for stock in another media company. A group of ENA managers could buy the company with money borrowed against future profits—the ever-popular leveraged buyout. Salomon was to explore these and other alternatives with the help of computer analyses and the advice and Wall Street contacts of Jay Higgins.

Among Higgins's bigger deals were the defense of BankAmerica from a takeover and the leveraged buyout of Beatrice by Kohlberg Kravis Roberts. One of Higgins's last Detroit deals had been an embarrassment of sorts. In 1982 he was advising Bendix when it attempted a takeover of Martin Marietta that ultimately entangled United Technologies and Allied. Bendix chairman William Agee abruptly fired Higgins after deciding Higgins's advice was unsatisfactory. Salomon also did a lot of work for General Motors; Higgins had helped engineer the automaker's multibillion-dollar purchases of Hughes Aircraft and Ross Perot's Electronic Data Systems.

Salomon's presence made some of Clark's lieutenants edgy. Once the Lear-Perenchio offer was launched, the ENA agreed to a new arrangement with the firm that, instead of a fifty-thousand-dollar consulting fee, would pay Salomon a small percentage of the value of any transaction involving the ENA. Unfortunately for the ENA, that percentage would undoubtedly amount to millions of dollars—and in fact would get larger as *more* of the company was sold, not less. But it was a standard arrangement which the ENA had little choice but to accept. When Higgins strolled into the ENA offices one morning, Frederickson, a quiet, unassuming Clark devotee, wondered if by hiring Salomon the ENA hadn't sealed its fate. These guys, Frederickson thought, make their business *selling* companies.

In fact, Higgins thought the ENA was ripe for sale. He told Clark from the start that the tender offer meant the family's hold on the company might not be as permanent as the family would like. If the tender offer couldn't be quashed in the courts, the ENA would have to raise enough cash to divert shareholders from Lear and Perenchio. To raise the money, the company would either have to sell properties, borrow heavily, or do both.

Higgins worried that Clark and the ENA board weren't prepared to do much of anything—meaning Lear and Perenchio might walk away with the company for what Higgins considered the bargain price of $1,000 a share. "This guy Clark looked like he had printer's blood dripping from his ears," Higgins later said. "I was confident that there wasn't a price *with nine digits* that he wouldn't say, 'The company is not for sale.' It appeared that events were kind of overtaking him." Yet Higgins admired Clark. It was refreshing to meet a CEO who wasn't out for himself. Many a top executive in the throes of a takeover worried about protecting his job and his perks. If that was Clark's concern, Higgins didn't hear about it.

The two men had dined at the Detroit Club the evening Higgins arrived. Later, all Clark could remember was Higgins asking, "Do your directors really want to save the company?"

Yes, Clark was sure they did.

Higgins persisted. He wanted to know that the board was committed, because he believed an effort to rescue the ENA was likely to be futile. "Do your directors *really* want to save the company?" Again, Clark said he was sure.

Higgins pressed no further, but his queries hinted at a cruel reality: it no longer mattered much what Clark and his directors wanted.

When Peter Kizer walked into Peter Clark's office at 4:00 P.M. Wednesday, July 31, Clark rose to shake Kizer's hand. Clark always shook hands. ENA managers used to joke that if you ran into Clark in the hallway four times in a day, he would shake your hand each time. So Clark shook Kizer's hand on that Wednesday afternoon, even though he knew Kizer had stabbed him in the back.

Clark had known Kizer wasn't happy. Kizer had never been able to understand the importance of the *Detroit News* to the Evening News Association. Instead of remembering that the *News* had produced the money that bought the TV stations, Kizer chose to blame the *News* for the stations he didn't get. His anger, Clark thought, had finally overcome his ability to reason. How else to explain this suicidal act of treason, which would cost him his job and subject him to humiliation? Kizer would get nothing from Lear and Perenchio because, if Clark had his way, the Hollywood producers would not lay a finger on the ENA. Clark almost wished Kizer had simply left the company instead of choosing a path of vengeance and destruction. Perhaps, Clark thought, he should have seen it coming. He had indeed been shocked to read of the betrayal in the tender offer documents, but it didn't take him long to focus on Kizer as the culprit. Only Kizer, always the rebel, always the one flouting the unwritten rules of the staid ENA culture, had the gumption to try such a thing.

Kizer sat in a chair beside Clark's desk. "I've done a foolish thing," he said.

Clark's face was as blank as fresh newsprint. "Please tell me what you've done."

Kizer said he probably would have to resign. He had been the leak to Lear and Perenchio.

Clark heard an apology. Later, Kizer would insist that the "foolish" thing he had alluded to was not the leak of the secret financial information but having denied it to Bill Saxton. He remembered no apology and professed no remorse for his actions.

Clark asked Kizer to wait while he summoned lawyers Saxton and Harry Ruemenapp from the Detroit firm of Butzel Long. When they arrived, Kizer repeated his admission. Later, Clark and Ruemenapp would insist Kizer had apologized. Clark remembered Kizer explaining that he was certain Lear and Perenchio would succeed, and that he feared losing his job if he didn't help them. Ruemenapp would describe Kizer as "close to tears, if not in them. He was really broken. He was very sorry. He was very distraught." Curiously, Ruemenapp's partner, Saxton, didn't recall it that way at all. "He didn't express any remorse," Saxton said. "He didn't seem remorseful." Kizer himself remembered little. "I was at a point in my career which was unpleasant," he said, "and I wanted to get it over with."

Before the meeting ended, Clark suspended Kizer pending further disciplinary action. The next day the ENA board, meeting by conference call, took fifteen minutes to fire their executive vice-president of the Broadcast Division.

Kizer did not go quietly, though. He filed a wrongful-discharge lawsuit against Clark and the ENA. His lawyers argued that, in leaking the confidential information to Lear and Perenchio, Kizer merely was fulfilling his legal obligation to protect the interests of the ENA's shareholders. "I felt the company was in serious trouble and might get in more trouble, and a lot of the employees, especially those that I brought in, including myself, might be in jeopardy with the company," he testified in a deposition. "We had talked about it thousands of times. The answer kept being, we are going to do nothing different, nothing's going to change . . . and then over a five-year period, I decided that I should do something."

The *News* ran a front-page story on Kizer's firing. Clark was quoted saying the Kizer incident was "an outrageous example of broken trust and calls into question the business ethics and practices of the company involved in the takeover attempt." A few days later Salomon began distributing ENA financial data to companies interested in buying all or part of the company. The irony was not lost on Kizer's lawyers, who wryly noted that their client's "outrageous example of broken trust" apparently had become ENA board policy.

The tender offer was barely a day old when the calls started coming. It seemed every media company in the country wanted to be the white knight to rescue Clark's company from Lear and Perenchio.

One call came from former President Gerald R. Ford. "Hello, Peter, how's Lianne?" Ford asked. Clark had met Ford before—Ford had represented a western Michigan district in Congress for many years before replacing Richard M. Nixon in the White House—but it was hard to believe Ford knew Clark's wife's name. He imagined Ford talking with a three-by-five note card in hand.

"Hello, Mr. President," Clark said, "what can I do for you?"

Ford said he represented an investor group that was mulling a bid for the ENA. He mentioned a few names Clark didn't recognize, then one he did: George Gillett, that Nashville meat-packer with the private jet. Clark thanked Ford and referred him to Salomon Brothers.

Billionaire Jack Kent Cooke couldn't get Clark on the line, but he reached Michael W. R. Davis. Davis, a veteran Ford Motor Company public relations professional, had been hired by Clark to keep "misinformation" about the ENA out of the media. Cooke was best known as the owner of the Washington Redskins, but Davis, not a football fan, had never heard of him.

"What can I do for you, sir?" Davis said.

"Is it true that the ENA is in play?" Cooke asked.

"All I know is what I read in the papers."

"Well," Cooke said, "could you send me some of those clippings? Just send them to Jack Kent Cooke in Middleburg, Virginia." No address. No zip code.

Clark often was too busy to take suitors' calls, but he returned one from Allen Neuharth, the chairman and chief executive of Gannett. They had known each other since 1961, when Neuharth was right-hand man—some said hatchet man—to executive editor Lee Hills at the *Free Press.* The wiry little man had impressed Clark with his verve and aggressiveness. Clark was happy to see him leave the *Free Press* in 1963 to become general manager of a couple of Gannett dailies in Rochester, New York.

In some ways, Neuharth had since become the personification of Gannett. He had personally directed a good deal of Gannett's remarkable expansion, acquiring dozens of small and midsized dailies known more for profits than journalism. Recently the company's buying pattern had diverged with the acquisition of the *Des Moines Register,* a large paper by Gannett standards and one respected for journalism in the newspaper fraternity. As with the ENA, squabbling among family owners had made the *Register* vulnerable to a takeover.

"I was just calling as a friend," Neuharth told Clark. "Is there anything we can do to be helpful? Are you going to be able to work this out?"

"I think so," Clark said. He was trying not to show any emotion. "But it's a sticky situation. We're going to fight like hell to hold on to the Evening News."

Neuharth had respected Clark as a tough competitor in the early 1960s. After Neuharth went to Gannett, he was irritated to hear of smart acquisitions Clark had made that Neuharth's people hadn't even mentioned as prospects. Now Neuharth said he hoped Clark could hold things together. "Had I been fortunate enough to inherit a newspaper," Neuharth told him, "I would scratch and claw and fight like hell to keep it in the family. But, having failed that, I would want to very carefully pick my successor." It was clear whom Neuharth had in mind.

Neuharth mentioned that Jerry Perenchio had called Gannett seeking a partner, but Doug McCorkindale, the company's top financial person, had turned him away. Gannett doesn't do hostile deals, Neuharth told Clark. Gannett itself recently had evaded the clutches of Cincinnati investor Carl Lindner, who had bought a passel of Gannett stock and attempted to wrest control of the company through a proxy fight. "We will not buy a single share of your stock or make an offer without your invitation," Neuharth told Clark. "But if there is anything we can do to help . . ."

Clark couldn't think of anything just yet. He thanked Neuharth and hung up the phone.

At the urging of Jay Higgins, Clark allowed Salomon Brothers to speak privately with prospective bidders for all or part of the ENA. That did not mean, Clark insisted, that the ENA was for sale. "We aren't peddling the company," ENA spokesman Mike Davis told the *Wall Street Journal* on August 12. The ENA, he explained, merely was asking companies to estimate a sale price. It was a puzzling distinction. Salomon and other firms shopping the company moved cautiously, for fear that Clark might change his mind about any deal that had the *News* changing hands. "We never knew what Peter Clark was going to do," Mary Jo Zandy, a banker for Donaldson, Lufkin and Jenrette, later said. "He didn't want his company to be acquired."

Clark was as secretive as ever. When Gannett's accountants asked for more-specific financials to prepare a price estimate, Higgins had to tell them the ENA could not oblige because there had been leaks to the *Free Press*. The rationale was ludicrous; those numbers had come from Lear and Perenchio's tender documents. But Clark refused to budge. Even Davis, the ENA's official spokesman, couldn't get much information. Incredibly, he came to depend on the *Free Press* to tell him what was happening in his own company.

In that respect he was not alone. For months, hundreds of anxious employees of the *News* and ENA's Detroit radio and TV stations had been watching the *Free Press* for insights into their company's trials. Veteran *Free Press* business reporter Bernie Shellum had written story after story detailing the corporate intrigues and family bickering that afflicted the ENA. It wasn't easy to penetrate the ENA veil, but Shellum, a short, stocky man with a healthy sense of skepticism, had pieced the complex facts together from government records, court filings, family histories, and the furtive whispers of angry shareholders. The reporter saw unfolding before his eyes a grand, labyrinthian story of fear, greed, vengeance, and betrayal, and he could not let it go. "It even had a goddamn spy," Shellum later enthused. "Peter Kizer was like a gift from heaven."

Peter Clark thought Shellum a fine journalist, but he was skeptical of the *Free Press*'s motives. He and Lionel Linder, the *News*'s top editor, detected an undercurrent of glee in the *Free Press* coverage; they thought the *Free Press* was using its news columns to encourage a takeover. Indeed, the *Free Press* had been notably lax in its coverage of several similar stories, including the $2.5 billion hostile takeover of a revered Detroit company, American Natural Resources, and a nasty takeover scrape between a pair of Michigan's largest banks. The paper had a good deal more energy for the story of its competitor's travails. Publicity, of course, could only fan the takeover flames threatening the ENA, and the *Free Press* seemed determined to do so.

Guerin Todd, Porter Bibb, Earl McClure, and other ENA dissidents regularly tapped Shellum for information on their company's doings. Shareholders in Detroit were stuffing copies of Shellum's stories in Federal Express envelopes and sending them to shareholders across the country. Shellum didn't feel anyone at the *Free Press* was prodding him, but no one was standing in his way either. "I happen to be the kind of reporter who just hates to let go of a good story, and it *was* in [the *Free Press*'s] corporate interest," Shellum later said.

Meanwhile, the *News*'s coverage of the ENA had been almost nonexistent. *News* reporter Michael Schroeder had been assigned to the story in December of 1984 by his boss, business editor Andrew McGill. Schroeder, who had covered takeovers before, began reporting the ENA story with his usual diligence, but he found it surprisingly difficult to get anything in the paper. Every few days he would tell McGill what he had unearthed, and McGill would seem enthusiastic as he went to pitch the story to his superiors. When he returned, though, the message almost invariably was, "They don't want a story." Schroeder started wondering if he was being used as an intelligence agent for the ENA. He and McGill agreed that his byline would not appear on stories about the company. If he wasn't going to be able to cover the story freely, Schroeder said, he didn't want his name associated with it.

Unbeknownst to Schroeder, *News* editor Lionel Linder had ordered that ENA stories meet an unusually tough standard to get into the paper. Only the barest, hardest facts of actual events would be reported. No analysis, no opinions of experts or participants, no interpretation of events, however well founded, would be permitted. Facts would have to be checked and double-checked with ENA officials, a requirement that by itself constrained Schroeder's coverage, since no one at the ENA, including Clark and Bob Nelson, was eager to cooperate.

Indeed, Nelson complained to Linder that Schroeder was prying into corporate affairs. Schroeder was told to stop phoning ENA directors. The few stories he wrote were edited—first by McGill and then more closely by Linder, managing editor James Vesely, assistant managing editor James Gatti, and, occasionally, executive editor Benjamin Burns—to the point that Schroeder thought some were misleading. He felt certain he could equal the reporting of the *Free Press*'s Shellum, but the *News* had shackled him. It was humiliating.

Before the tender offer became public July 29, the *Free Press* had published at least three lengthy, detailed stories on the ENA's troubles. The *News,* which chased *Free Press* stories on a daily basis (just as the *Free Press* regularly chased the *News*), didn't even try to match them. When Lear and Perenchio launched their tender offer for Michigan's largest newspaper, the *Free Press,* appropriately, ran a story on the front page, with two accompanying sidebars. The *News* ran a single story, half the length of the lead *Free Press* piece, on the bottom of the business page, 5B. Of course the *News* story lacked a byline.

Then, suddenly, the *News* seemed to get interested. Between August 9 and August 13, the *News* published five front-page stories concerning the ENA takeover attempt. The stories were generally fair and balanced, but they never missed a chance to mention the supposedly unsavory character of Lear and Perenchio. Finally, albeit suspiciously, the *News* had begun to cover its own story. It was as if someone at the *News* or the ENA imagined that a few well-placed newspaper articles could dissuade the markets from doing their natural work, or could persuade shareholders to forgo the chance to become instant millionaires. Between the lines of those tortured stories could be read the desperation of Peter Clark.

Peter Clark was alone. It was nearing 11:00 P.M. in the Clarks' modest, gray-brick home in Grosse Pointe Farms. Lianne had gone to bed. Clark sat on a sofa in the family room. A chaotic batch of files and papers was spread on the cushions beside him. Clark had been reading and rereading them all evening. They kept telling him that he would have to give up his company.

More than three weeks had passed since Lear and Perenchio launched their unwanted bid for the ENA. Since then, virtually all of Clark's time and energy had been devoted to defending his company. There was little time to try to run it well, to think of operational strategy, to battle the *Free Press.* He seemed to spend most of every day in meetings and conference calls and more meetings with lawyers and investment bankers and a lot of other people who did not belong around the ENA or the *News.*

He couldn't help but feel naked. For decades the ENA had tended quietly to business and carefully kept its affairs shielded from public view in the hushed cluster of offices on the mezzanine of the *News* building. There was safety amid the smallish, Elizabethan offices, their leaded windows and walls of hand-carved paneling, their ceilings of delicately modeled plaster, the bronze bust of James E. Scripps, the paintings of Scripps, George Booth, Warren Booth, and William Scripps, the *News*'s third publisher. Clark felt as much at home there as he did in his own living room.

But now Clark and his company were visible for the world to see—in the *New York Times,* the *Wall Street Journal,* the *Washington Post, Newsweek, Business Week;* on the networks, the local radio stations; even in obscure trade magazines and newsletters. While he told reporter after reporter that the ENA intended to remain independent, Clark absorbed cheap shot after cheap shot from the people who opposed him. "Nineteenth-century relics" is how Guerin Todd described Clark and other ENA managers to *Business Week.* "These people," Todd said, "inherited their positions, but didn't inherit the genetic brilliance of the founder."

If the insults upset Clark, he did not show it. Especially before his reporters and editors—his "troops," as he called them—he maintained a brave countenance. One day, in the throes of the takeover fight, he bumped into reporter Richard Willing in the mezzanine washroom. "How goes the battle?" Clark asked cheerfully. It was one of his stock greetings. Still, Willing was amazed at Clark's even temper. "Gee, Mr. Clark," he said, "I'd kind of like to ask *you* that question." Clark just laughed. Could it be, Willing thought, that Clark did not appreciate the gravity of the situation? Was Clark so courageous—or stubborn—that he would not allow others to bear even the slightest burden of his ordeal?

Clark did not feel courageous late that August night, sitting alone in his family room with the remnants of his hopes to save the ENA strewn about him. As the gatekeeper of the Scripps bequest, he felt no bravery in opening the gate, however wealthy it stood to make him and his extended family. Had he been more courageous in the past, perhaps he would not have had to confront the hard reality of having to surrender the legacy. Had he borrowed more money, had he bought more newspapers and TV stations, maybe he would have been better able to satisfy the shareholders and keep the company in the family. Had he had the force of personality to stand up to the family members who mistrusted the future, to compel the reshaping of James Scripps's nineteenth-century enterprise into one that would thrive in the twenty-first century, perhaps the sad conclusions of this summer night could have been avoided.

But Clark had not chosen those paths, and now his choices had been narrowed to one. No one had hung on to the ENA as tightly as Clark, so no one but Clark could make the decision to let the company go. Of course, the board of directors would have to vote, but once Clark signaled it was time to sell, the directors would acquiesce. Clark was the last obstacle to the sale of the ENA. Now he decided it was time to step aside.

The sheets of paper scattered about him on the sofa contained the results of "Project Revere," Salomon Brothers' computer-generated analyses of alternatives to selling the ENA outright. Clark, Ed Frederickson, and Bill Revelle had chipped in their own analyses, suggestions, and observations. At first they had had great hopes for saving at least part of the company. They were seeking a way—through borrowing, selling properties, or a combination of the two—to raise enough cash to buy out enough shareholders so that Lear and Perenchio could not gain control of the company.

Each day, though, the amount of the required payoff had grown larger. Family members had been selling their stock to Wall Street traders dangling prices of $1,100 a share and higher. The price kept climbing. On August 19, Lear and Perenchio had formally raised their bid to $1,250 a share and extended the tender offer deadline to August 30. (Wall Street's Goldman, Sachs and Company, whose chairman, John Weinberg, was a Knight-Ridder director, would eventually push the price beyond $1,350 with its aggressive trading.) Each time the price rose, the ENA plan had to be reconfigured to incorporate more borrowing or additional property sales. Salomon Brothers could barely keep up. By the time the computer spit out a new projection, a rising price had made it obsolete.

When Clark reviewed the rescue effort that August night, prices were as high as $1,400 a share. At that level, the debt the ENA stood to absorb was crushing. The shareholders would never accept it. No dividends would be paid for years. Selling the TV stations, as Clark had contemplated, would put the *News* at great risk, for the ENA would have no other income with which to hedge the newspaper's huge losses and subsidize the war with the *Free Press*. The ENA had challenges pending in the courts and before the FCC, but Clark's lawyers were telling him those were unlikely to succeed.

The fate of the ENA wasn't entirely out of Peter Clark's hands. Clark knew he could not hold on to his company, but at least he might be able to control who would be its new owner. He'd be damned if it would be Lear and

Perenchio. Several reputable companies, including the New York Times Company, Capital Cities, Gannett, and the Tribune Company, were interested in buying at least part of the ENA—but only if invited. So, if Clark wanted his company to wind up in hands he considered friendly, he had to move quickly. He went to bed knowing exactly what he had to do.

At 10:00 A.M. on Thursday, August 22, the ENA board gathered in the oak-paneled conference room on the mezzanine of the *News* building. Ruemenapp reviewed the status of the legal proceedings and the sweetened offer from Lear and Perenchio. The directors moved to Spitzley's office adjoining the boardroom and, via conference call, listened as Jay Higgins told them that their plan to sell part of the company and keep the rest would not work. Around noon they returned to the boardroom. Clark took his place at the head of the twelve-foot-long, coffin-shaped table in the center of the room. On the wall behind him hung a portrait of snowy-headed James Scripps, wearing a three-piece charcoal suit, a bow tie, wire-rimmed glasses, and the hint of a smile.

As the board listened, Clark reviewed the remarkable ascent of the price of ENA shares. He listed properties that would have to be sold—"abandoned," as he put it—to raise enough money to keep the company. He spoke of borrowing tens of millions of dollars and how that would hurt the company's profits for years. He sketched myriad scenarios, all of them risky, debt-laden, possibly undoable. Each plan envisioned the *News* as the flagship of increasingly smaller versions of the ENA. Before the directors' eyes, the company was shrinking out of sight.

Normally, at the conclusion of such a report Clark would have offered a recommendation. Today he did not. Instead he said, "We're really being asked to earn our money today for the shareholders, because we're asking them on one hand to take this, this, and this, versus a cash payout right now.

"What do you believe we should do?"

Some questions followed: What might the *News* do to become profitable fast? Which shareholders might stay with the current management? Had the rising price precluded every possible alternative? Clark had no good answers. Finally someone said the board could no longer hope to hold on to the company at the prices being offered. One by one the others agreed. These people weren't about to try any leveraged buyout or complex restructuring. Those gimmicks were for another, younger generation. It was over. "Nobody *wanted* to sell out, emotionally," Warren Wilkinson later said. "We knew James Scripps wouldn't have wanted to sell out. But they offer you so much money, you can't *not* sell out, because you've got to do what's best for the shareholders."

There was no rancor, no sharp differences, only a collegial band of elderly gentlemen accepting the inevitable. Wilkinson, Dick Spitzley, and Dick Wallace had no doubts about the next step. Jim Whitcomb wondered if there was something the board had missed, but no one could help him. Bob Nelson, who had recently replaced Ed Wheeler on the board, did not want to give the *News* to someone who might lose the war with the *Free Press,* but he did not feel it was his place to oppose the family. Harry Ruemenapp, John Beresford, and Bill Revelle seemed most inclined to stay the course. Young Revelle—he was forty—made an impassioned pitch to save the *News,* arguing that a new owner, no doubt some corporate chain, would never bestow upon the *News* the special pride of ownership that made it a great newspaper. The directors appreciated the sentiment, but the arithmetic gave them no choice but to sell.

Finally, Peter Clark formally proposed that the ENA be put up for sale. "I think," he said, "the way this conversation has gone, we ought to vote on the question of disposing of the company to the highest bidder, intact or in pieces."

There was a brief silence. And then a vote: 9–0 in favor of auctioning the ENA. Consensus had been reached.

The auction of the Evening News Association began at five minutes past noon on Wednesday, August 28. By the time Clark and his fellow directors assembled in the high-ceilinged conference room on the second floor of the Detroit Club, a thin morning haze had lifted and a gaggle of reporters armed with notebooks and minicams had gathered beneath the shabby canvas canopy that extended from the club's entrance on Cass Avenue.

The Detroit Club, a stately redbrick building wrapped in ivy, was one of the downtown's two most prestigious private clubs, the Detroit Athletic Club being the other. Clark preferred the Detroit Club because it was just a five-minute walk from the *News.* Unlike the DAC, the Detroit Club boasted no squash courts or running track, but the food was reasonably good and the elegant surroundings, all hand-carved paneling and creaking hardwood floors, had the elite feel of the mezzanine in the *News* building. It was a place where it seemed one ought to whisper.

The ENA directors were ensconced in a spacious room from which, if they parted the flowered curtains, they could see the rear of the *Free Press* building and the yellow delivery trucks idled after their early runs. The board sat around a long, rectangular table, with Clark at the head. Standing nearby were Jay Higgins and John Schlesinger of Salomon Brothers. Lawyers were everywhere, whispering in each other's ears.

The roster of bidders was a bit disappointing: Edward Gaylord, an entrepreneur from Oklahoma City; Virginia billionaire Jack Kent Cooke; and Gannett Company. "We talked to the world," Higgins assured the board. Salomon had shopped the ENA to the New York Times Company, Times Mirror, CBS, the Tribune Company, Capital Cities, Dow Jones, Taft Broadcasting, legendary Omaha investor Warren Buffett, Detroit real estate magnate Alfred Taubman, and dozens of others. Several had expressed interest in buying pieces of the ENA, especially the Washington TV station, but only one big-name media operator, Gannett, was interested in all of it.

The ENA directors had hoped for more and bigger names, in part so they might be able to turn the *News* over to one of the nation's great newspaper companies, in part because they figured more bidders would produce a higher price. But they could not afford to wait. The legal barriers to the Lear-Perenchio bid had been swept away. The Sixth Circuit Court of Appeals in Cincinnati had barred Michigan's antitakeover law from being enforced. The FCC had approved the trust arrangement under which Lear and Perenchio would buy ENA stock. The board had to get a deal signed before midnight Friday, the deadline on the tender offer.

The first bidder to address the board was Jack Kent Cooke. The craggy owner of the Washington Redskins had amassed his billions in a plethora of different businesses, among them plastics, die-casting, real estate, ranching, broadcasting, and cable television. He introduced himself by saying, "None of you know me." That was fairly true, and it worked to Cooke's disadvantage. Several of the ENA directors, especially Bill Revelle, looked askance at Cooke, whom they viewed as a wheeler-dealer not far removed from the likes of Lear and Perenchio.

Cooke sought to allay those concerns by assuring the board he had no plans to change anything about the ENA. He appreciated the great tradition of the *Detroit News,* he said, and would honor its noble effort to win the newspaper war. He had no corporate staff, no corporate policy, no desire to interfere with the superb management of the ENA. "He was going to do everything, keep management in place, keep the directors in place, nothing would change except he would own it," director Harry Ruemenapp later recalled. "We looked on this with healthy skepticism." Warren Wilkinson hoped Cooke would be smart enough *not* to run the ENA as usual: "That was just the trouble."

Cooke's bid was impressive, though—at least on the surface. He offered $1,550 a share, or about $702 million. But there were catches. Only $1,000 a share would be paid in cash. The remainder would be in the form of debentures of uncertain worth. Cooke valued the notes at $662 a share, but in part their worth would be determined by how much the ENA received for selling some TV stations. In effect, he was asking nine people who despised borrowing to loan him a pile of money.

Cooke exited the Detroit Club through a pack of waiting reporters who did not at first recognize him. One reporter, guessing it might be Cooke, shouted, "Hey, why'd you trade 'Downtown' Charlie Brown?" Cooke turned, smiling, and started defending his recent trade of the Redskins' star pass receiver. A barrage of questions about the ENA bidding followed, but Cooke already had a foot in his limousine. "I'd like to talk about our quarterbacks this year," he said as he slammed the door.

Meanwhile, another limousine glided into the dreary parking lot behind the Detroit Club. The driver had been instructed to deliver his passengers there, where no reporters waited to badger them with questions they didn't care to answer just yet. They entered the club through the freight entrance, where they boarded a creaky wooden elevator that ferried them to the second floor. Jay Higgins passed word to Peter Clark at the head of the ENA directors' table that Al Neuharth had arrived.

The limousine was just one prop on the gaudy set on which Al Neuharth staged his life. His thirty-first-floor office, overlooking the Potomac River in suburban Washington, D.C., boasted gold-plated bathroom fixtures, snakeskin wallpaper, a bank of five TV screens arrayed before a desk of white onyx and brass, and a salmon-colored carpet that "you could lose a midget in," as one employee remarked. Neuharth recently had moved Gannett's headquarters from Rochester, New York, to a pair of crescent-shaped, glass-walled skyscrapers in Rosslyn, Virginia. One tower housed Gannett, the other *USA Today*.

Neuharth logged more than three hundred thousand miles a year in a sleek, $17 million Gulfstream IV jet, in which the upholstery, napkins, towels, soap bars, and even Neuharth's black-and-white slippers were emblazoned with the corporate logo, a white *G* superimposed on a globe. His San Simeon was a renovated log cabin on five hundred feet of oceanfront in Cocoa Beach, Florida. "Pumpkin Center," as Neuharth had dubbed it after a South Dakota country store, was outfitted with an indoor fountain and pool, tennis courts, a sauna, a hot tub, a high-technology security system, and an old ticker-tape machine in Neuharth's bathroom. He kept a $360,000-a-year suite in the Waldorf Towers in Manhattan, a $160,000-a-year suite at the Capital Hilton a few blocks from the White House, a ski hideaway in Lake Tahoe, and a 116-acre ranch in the Virginia horse country. Smiling Gannett minions attended to

Neuharth's every wish, ferrying him about, toting his luggage, keeping his hotel rooms stocked with boxes of large tissues, fresh fruit—minus grapes, per Neuharth's instructions—and a chilled bottle of pouilly-fuissé.

His garb ran to the garish, which was remarkable considering that he wore nothing but shades of black, gray, and white. Not many Fortune 500 CEOs were photographed in dazzling white sweat suits; Neuharth was. He and his second wife, Florida state senator Lori Wilson, once arrived at an industry convention in jumpsuits embroidered with the mastheads of Gannett papers. Neuharth attended another Gannett get-together in a loud black-and-white checkered jacket, a white shirt stitched with black, a black-and-white vest, a black-white-and-gray tie, black slacks, and gray sunglasses. The wife of a Gannett executive whispered to her husband, "Which family of the Mafia did you say he belongs to?" The wardrobe made traveling simpler, but also attracted attention—one of Neuharth's crucial needs. "I want recognition and high visibility," he once told an interviewer. "There have been times when I sought attention even though I knew it would mean criticism. I'd rather have people be critical of me than ignore me."

When visiting a Gannett city, he liked to have the mayor, a business leader, or a local college president meet him at the airport, whether or not they had business to do. When Neuharth was photographed with Gannett president John Curley, the taller Curley often sat so that he wouldn't dwarf his boss. Neuharth commissioned an enormous bronze bust of himself for display at *USA Today;* staffers called it the "Al head." Hearst and Pulitzer would have appreciated him. Neuharth was a throwback to the days of those press lords and, at the same time, a dashing, irreverent caricature of the corporate chief of the 1980s, a Donald Trump for the staid, stuffy newspaper industry.

And he performed, as Gannett's sterling financial results attested. The company had strung together seventy-one consecutive quarters in which profits increased. It had the highest profits and the second-highest revenues of any publicly traded newspaper company. For the preceding ten years Gannett had posted an average pretax profit margin of 24 percent, while Knight-Ridder, the New York Times Company, Times Mirror, the Tribune Company, and the Washington Post Company had averaged between 14 and 17 percent. Neuharth regularly won CEO-of-the-Year awards bestowed by finance-minded publications such as the *Wall Street Transcript* and the *Gallagher Report.* A story went around that Neuharth had been asked how to pronounce his company's name. "The emphasis," he supposedly said, "is on the net." Neuharth later claimed he never had said it—but wished he had.

He definitely was not ENA material.

The stylish sixty-one-year-old would have looked out of place at the Formica-topped corner table in the *News* cafeteria where Clark, Nelson, Spitzley, Wallace, and Frederickson ate lunch most days in their baggy white shirts and conservative ties. Neuharth wasn't much for chitchat and he disliked wearing ties. He couldn't have abided the Scripps family's inbred reluctance to borrow money and buy properties. When Neuharth wanted to buy, he bought; if it meant borrowing millions of dollars, so be it. Consensus, for which Clark strived, wasn't imperative for Neuharth. Bold steps, by their very nature, would have their naysayers. If Neuharth had waited for consensus, there might never have been a *USA Today,* and Gannett might still have been a sleepy regional operator unknown outside upstate New York.

Where Peter Clark was collegial and deliberate, Al Neuharth was dictatorial and impatient. Where Clark was brainy and analytical, Neuharth was street smart and decisive. Where Clark struggled to keep from losing, Neuharth strove mightily to win, be it a weekend tennis match or a multimillion-dollar bid for a newspaper. As one of Neuharth's associates once said, "Neuharth's the only man I know who would go after Moby Dick with a harpoon and a jar of tartar sauce."

Which was why the ENA directors were glad to see Neuharth walk into the conference room with his two top lieutenants, John Curley and Doug McCorkindale. They expected Neuharth to play to win. Just a few months back he had blown away the competition in a bidding contest for the *Des Moines Register,* offering $165 million to beat out runner-up Hearst by $35 million. The directors of the ENA did not want to give their company to Cooke, and they didn't expect much of a bid from Edward Gaylord. Surely Neuharth would save them from Cooke and the clutches of Lear and Perenchio. He would make them and their shareholders rich, and carry on the grand tradition of their forebears, the *Detroit News.*

Neuharth did not disappoint. As Clark introduced him, the directors reviewed a four-page letter, signed by McCorkindale, that spelled out Gannett's offer: $727 million in cash, or $1,605 a share. The offer was conditioned upon a number of minor legal and financial items to be negotiated later. Neuharth hadn't said a word and already the directors were feeling good about him. Cash was cash, after all. "You could see the dollar signs in their eyes," Bob Nelson recalled.

Earlier in the week in Seattle, the Gannett board had authorized Neuharth to pay up to $750 million for the ENA. At least one Gannett director had questioned the wisdom of investing in a city afflicted by crime, racial tension, and industrial decline, but Neuharth had assured his board that the *News* was not the most important part of the deal. "If it doesn't work, the rest of the package will," he recalled telling the board.

That wasn't what the ENA board wanted to hear, though, so Neuharth altered his tune a bit. The *Detroit News,* he said, was a "very important part" of the deal, and Gannett would run it successfully and certainly would not close it. He did not mention the possibility of a JOA with the *Free Press.* Like Cooke, he vowed to do everything he could to keep current ENA employees on the payroll. To assure that shareholders wouldn't tender their stock to Lear and Perenchio, he said Gannett would agree to "lockup options" that would require any other bidder for the ENA to sell the Washington TV station and the *News* to Gannett. He thanked the board for listening and slipped out the same way he had entered, with Curley and McCorkindale in tow.

Next the ENA board heard from Edward Gaylord's representative, William Wetmore, the lawyer who handled the ENA's Washington affairs. Gaylord was an Oklahoman who had made millions in newspapers and TV stations in the South and the Southwest. He had sold the ENA its Oklahoma City TV station in 1976, lending the company nearly half of the $22.8 million price. His absence today was not a good sign. Wetmore asked some questions and answered a few but said nothing about a bid. A few directors thought he was fishing. The Gaylord people "seemed to think because we bought the TV station from them that we would tell them what they ought to bid," Warren Wilkinson later recalled. If so, Gaylord was mistaken. Wetmore finally excused himself, leaving the directors scratching their heads in puzzlement.

Jay Higgins then informed the board that George Gillett had phoned in a bid of $1,410 a share, or $638 million, in cash. That put Gillett officially out of the running. There also had been talk that the Booth brothers might make an offer, but it never materialized.

The directors took a forty-five-minute break, returning at 2:45 P.M. Higgins reassured them that Gannett's all-cash offer was tops. By three o'clock they had instructed Higgins to begin formal negotiations with Gannett. Their final task was nearly complete.

Reporters were still camped at the Detroit Club's front entrance, having missed Neuharth entirely. Hoping to avoid them, Clark and a few other directors exited the rear and walked around the back of the *Free Press* building to West Lafayette Boulevard, where they turned westward to walk the three blocks to the *News.*

They might as well have turned eastward, toward the Manufacturers Bank building, for they all would soon be a great deal wealthier. When the ENA's negotiations with Gannett ended and Gannett agreed to pay $1,583 a share, or $717 million, Spitzley and his four children would gross more than $40 million. Wilkinson would get $18 million, Whitcomb $15 million, Wallace and wife $8 million. Clark's "ill-gotten gains," as he would half-jokingly call them, would be $9 million.

Cranbrook would add more than $46 million to its depleted coffers. The Booth brothers' company, which would prosper without its hoped-for link with the ENA, would gross some $30 million. George Gillett would need every penny of his $11 million take, for his empire would crumble beneath the weight of junk-bond debt in the years to come. Salomon Brothers would be paid $3.6 million for its services; Porter Bibb and Donaldson, Lufkin and Jenrette would get about $1 million each for assisting the dissident shareholders. Guerin and Ann Todd would pocket $11 million, some of which they would put down on a vacation home on the French Riviera. Peter Kizer would sell his one hundred ENA shares for about $160,000.

Now, as the ENA directors turned the corner at Washington Street and Lafayette, they found another throng of reporters waiting in front of the *Free Press.* The mob detained a few board members, but Clark pressed on, giving a thumbs-up sign as he passed. A TV reporter finally blocked his path in front of the old Fort Shelby Hotel one block from the *News.* A dilapidated hulk that was closed for good in 1975, the Fort Shelby had been Clark's home away from home when he was a young Yale professor commuting to Detroit for ENA board meetings.

James Scripps's home once had stood on that very spot.

The reporter thrust a microphone into Clark's face. "Mr. Clark," he said, "there are rumors going around that the Evening News Association has been sold."

"Oh, is that so?" Clark said, and he turned and walked away.

Part Two

The Great Detroit Newspaper War

5

Black Knight

Allen Harold Neuharth grew up in the dreary rural hamlets of Eureka and Alpena, South Dakota, a poor washwoman's son who wanted desperately to be rich and famous, a man of the world. While other teenaged boys were chasing girls and earning varsity letters, Neuharth was dreaming of wealth and power. Editing his high school paper, he used the pages to curry favor with friends and become a campus celebrity. "I felt like the most powerful kid in Alpena High," he would later write. "If having control of a newspaper could do that for me, I liked it."

Like a lot of ambitious young men, Neuharth was impatient. He wanted to be a newspaperman, but he could not bear the thought of slogging through years of nine-to-five days under some mercurial city editor. So, with a college friend, he struck out on his own. In 1952 they started a weekly newspaper that covered sports across South Dakota. *SoDak Sports* was a brash, innovative tabloid that got a lot of attention in the tiny burgs dotting the plains from Aberdeen to Rapid City. From a cramped office behind Sid's Liquor Store in Sioux Falls, Neuharth pilfered stories from the local dailies and spent weekends tooling between high school basketball games in his pale green Plymouth station wagon. Every Friday in the peach-colored pages of *SoDak Sports,* readers could find stories on fishing, hunting, football, golf, bowling, baseball, and softball from every corner of South Dakota.

After a year, *SoDak Sports*'s circulation was around 12,000, higher than Neuharth and his partner, Bill Porter, had expected. But the paper's dime-a-copy price didn't cover the cost of printing and distribution. Advertisers were few. *SoDak Sports* was losing money. The last issue of the paper appeared on newsstands just twenty-two months after the first. When they closed it for good, Neuharth and Porter were fifty thousand dollars in debt to family and friends who had chipped in to launch the venture. For perhaps the last time in his life, Neuharth was humiliated. He slunk off to Miami, where, with his wife, Loretta, and a newborn son, he started over as a ninety-five-dollar-a-week reporter for the *Miami Herald.*

He didn't stay humble long. Neuharth quickly convinced himself he was smarter and better at his work than the lot of reporters and editors at the daily *Herald.* Surely he *wanted* to succeed more than his contemporaries. Many were ambitious, of course, but how committed, how passionate could they have been without the lingering aftertaste of failure to intensify their desire for delicious success? How could they know, as Neuharth did so well, that humiliation would not destroy them? Neuharth no longer feared failure—therefore he could only succeed.

An all-out newspaper war was brewing in Detroit. It was November of 1960, and Lee Hills, executive editor of the *Detroit Free Press,* wanted Al Neuharth on the front line.

"I'll go anywhere you want me to," Hills's thirty-six-year-old charge said. "When?"

"Tomorrow morning."

Neuharth arrived in Detroit the day before the *Detroit News* bought the assets of the *Detroit Times* and swept past the *Detroit Free Press* to become the Motor City's biggest daily. Jack Knight, who had grown fond of the younger man, told him, "Kid, you've done all right in the softball league in Miami. Now we'll see how you can do in the hardball league in Detroit."

By now, Neuharth was a bona fide star in Knight Newspapers, the lucrative group of papers owned by Jack and James Knight. At the *Miami Herald,* he had risen from rewrite man to street reporter to Washington reporter to assistant city editor to city editor to executive city editor and finally to assistant managing editor, which gave him the run of the vast *Herald* newsroom. He had succeeded, in part, because he was good. As a writer, he was known for writing clean, crisp copy on tight deadlines. As a reporter, he had ferreted out a mail-order scam that prompted Congress to change postal regulations. As an editor, he had sought to leaven the *Herald*'s mix of hard-news stories with heartwarming, well-written features. Neuharth was talented enough that he could indulge his delight in toying with people he considered inferior. Sometimes that meant dawdling until fifteen minutes before deadline, then banging out a page-one story while the clock ticked and an editor grew panicky.

Still, it wasn't journalistic skill that set Neuharth apart but his peerless ambition and the focused, tireless, crafty, and at times ruthless way he pursued it. Promoted to city editor, he asked that the announcement be delayed for a few months while he toiled incognito on the city desk, gathering intelligence. A *Herald* reporter would later write of Neuharth: "Few who were there describe those early days without resorting to a cliché: He left the field littered with the dead." Envious peers changed his nickname from the "Wheatfield Kid" to the "Black Knight."

At the *Free Press,* Lee Hills installed Neuharth as the newsroom's number two, just above veteran managing editor Frank Angelo. The younger man played alter ego to Hills, a genteel executive who held himself above the more unpleasant duties of running a newsroom. Hills had conscripted Neuharth from Miami because he was an outsider, lacking the sentiment for tradition that made others reluctant to take the steps necessary to win the newspaper war. The *Free Press* staff was getting old and set in its ways. One of Neuharth's tasks was to prune it of dead wood. He became Hills's newsroom spy and the one who bore the bad news to editors or reporters who had outlived their usefulness, in Neuharth's opinion, and had to be given a less important assignment or nudged into early retirement.

Nearly every day Neuharth would descend one floor from his fourth-floor office to the city room, where he read the dispatches off the teletype machines. He looked almost comical standing there in his pastel shirts, constantly straightening his tie clasp, fussing with his shirttails, smoothing his jet black hair. He had yet to adopt an all-black-and-white wardrobe, but he fancied himself a sharp dresser, which alone would have distinguished him among newspapering's rumpled ranks.

He relished playing the heavy. When members of the Newspaper Guild complained that managers weren't adhering to contractual scheduling rules, Neuharth promised a remedy if reporters began coming to work at 9:30 A.M., the start specified in the contract. Every morning for the next two weeks, Neuharth stood at a newsroom entrance with a clipboard, noting the tardy arrivals. The scheduling complaints quickly died down.

The *Free Press*'s labor writer, Tom Nicholson, liked to gloat about the enormous overtime he accrued during auto industry contract talks. He would mark the passing of every hundred hours or so by buying drinks for his buddies. Neuharth was not amused. When Nicholson put in for several hundred hours of overtime during one bargaining round, he was told to see Neuharth. Neuharth curtly informed the reporter that he qualified only for the previous week's hours. "According to the contract," Neuharth said, "you're supposed to turn this in *every* week." Nicholson was furious, but technically Neuharth was right. Neuharth eventually credited the extra hours at straight pay instead of time and a half, and Nicholson didn't fool with overtime again.

Neuharth was attending a black-tie dinner one Saturday when a *Free Press* editor called to say that members of the printers' union had stopped producing the Sunday paper in a contract dispute. Moments later, Neuharth, in tuxedo, emerged from a freight elevator in the *Free Press* pressroom. Editors and managers almost never showed their faces in that hot, inky cavern. "You've finished reading your comic books," Neuharth snapped. "I know you're pissed off. I know you've got some problems. We're going to settle them if negotiations continue—but not if you don't put out the Sunday paper."

The printers returned to work.

Neuharth treasured his days at the *Free Press.* His newsroom role, however nefarious it appeared to the staff, suited him fine. "He would do almost anything, pay any price in criticism and ridicule, to get his way," Lee Hills later recalled. Neuharth didn't care what people thought of him—so long as they thought of him. Meanwhile, he enjoyed the jousts with the powerful union leaders, especially the Teamsters' Jimmy Hoffa. He loved the daily tussle for readers and advertisers. He was always learning; Hills encouraged him to dabble in circulation, production, and other *Free Press* business operations.

Early in his *Free Press* tenure Neuharth met another young Knight star named Alvah Chapman, Jr. Chapman was a financial and managerial whiz recently hired as James Knight's assistant at the *Miami Herald.* He had swiftly assumed responsibilities for other Knight papers as well. Chapman regularly commuted to Detroit to tend to business matters, one of which was to end the *Free Press*'s so-called Family Edition, the afternoon issue designed to attract former *Times* subscribers. By the spring of 1961 it was losing a hundred thousand dollars a month. Chapman worked closely with Neuharth; they often dined late at the swank London Chop House. Neuharth thought Chapman extremely bright and ambitious but a bit buttoned-down for his tastes. "He was so straight he made the very proper Hills look like a comedian," Neuharth later wrote. "Working with Chapman would have made me climb the walls."

Even more distressing was the prospect of working *for* Chapman. Neuharth's experience at the *Free Press* had intensified his desire to one day run an entire newspaper company, but it was beginning to look as if Knight

Newspapers was not going to be that company. One reason was Lee Hills, Jack Knight's close confidant and an obvious candidate to lead the company one day. Another was Alvah Chapman, whose career was hitched to the younger of the company's patriarchs, James Knight. Neuharth's path to the throne of Knight Newspapers appeared to be blocked.

So Neuharth left the *Free Press* in 1963 to join a little-known group of newspapers run by the Gannett Company from its headquarters in Rochester in upstate New York. At thirty-nine, Al Neuharth was again fleeing the establishment. He could have stayed with Knight Newspapers, enjoyed big-city life, collected a batch more promotions, a better salary, and perks, but he never would have been able to leave his own distinctive mark. "If you follow the pack," he once said, "you may do OK, but you won't do anything dramatically sensational." In Gannett, Neuharth found a company ripe to learn his definition of sensational.

If not for Paul Miller, the Gannett Company might not have been known at all outside the middling towns in which it owned daily newspapers. Gannett's top executive and president of the Associated Press in the 1960s, Miller stayed close to a network of chums and golf partners in the newspaper business. He enjoyed their company. And he liked their companies.

A tall, strapping ex-reporter who had traipsed the globe in search of stories, Miller wanted to build a big newspaper company—as big as or bigger than the few national chains that existed in the 1960s. Gannett wasn't exactly tiny in 1963; the company's sixteen dailies, three radio stations, and two television stations rang up annual revenues of $63 million. But its properties were in small to midsized towns like Ithaca, Utica, and Elmira, New York; Plainfield and Camden, New Jersey; and Danville, Illinois. Hardly anyone outside the newspaper fraternity had heard of Gannett. Its papers were widely viewed as mediocre products that made lots of money because they kept costs down and operated in markets with little or no competition.

Miller didn't think his papers' reputation was deserved, but their size made it difficult to compare them with the *New York Times* or the *Chicago Tribune*. It didn't trouble him much, though. Gannett was not about winning Pulitzer Prizes but managing profitable newspapers that quietly tended to the provincial concerns of the communities they called home. That was the legacy handed down by Frank Ernest Gannett, the businessman and journalist who had grown the company from a half-interest he purchased in the *Elmira Gazette* for twenty thousand dollars in 1906.

In his rimless glasses and three-piece suits, moonfaced Frank Gannett looked like a banker or an industrialist. He had loved newspapers since writing his first stories as a teen for the *Buffalo News,* but as a publisher, Gannett was less journalist than businessman. He gave his editors great autonomy, trusting they knew best how to serve their particular locale. It was said that Gannett papers were as local as the town pump. But autonomy did not extend to finances. The corporate staff in Rochester kept a vigilant watch over the budgets and balance sheets of each paper. Gannett expected his publishers to grow revenues and profits every year. The first person through the door of a new Gannett paper frequently was an auditor. "More failures come from faulty auditing," Gannett said, "than most people realize."

He was a prodigious buyer of newspapers in the 1920s and 1930s, though seldom did he shop in big cities where two or more giants were slugging it out. He distinguished himself, along with E. W. Scripps, as one of the first publishers to recognize the financial benefit in buying papers in smaller markets. By nature, Gannett was not a risk taker. He had been raised by his mother, Maria, a woman he adored, on aphorisms such as "God helps them that help themselves" and "Plough deep while sluggards sleep." Frank Gannett, who believed those saws, became the kind of man who saved the paper clips off of office correspondence. He valued hard work, thrift, and prudence. In the newspaper business, prudence meant investing in markets with no competition.

While Gannett's editorial pages extolled free enterprise and competition, monopoly became a central, if unstated, principle of his business dealings. He ventured into competitive markets—Rochester, New York, counted four dailies when he bought the *Times-Union* in 1918—but quickly consolidated by buying out rivals and merging competitive papers. In 1937 he resolved a classic two-city standoff with William Randolph Hearst by surrendering the morning and Sunday fields in Albany in return for Hearst's closing two papers in Rochester. With a wink and a nod, the millionaires handed each other lucrative monopolies.

When Gannett died in 1957, he left twenty-three daily papers, three television stations, and four radio stations, nearly all in his native New York State. He left the company in the control of the Frank E. Gannett Foundation, which he had founded in 1935. As his successor he named Paul Miller, an Oklahoman with big plans for the Gannett Company.

Many were wealthier, more famous, or more powerful, but few people in the newspaper business were better connected than Paul Miller. It was said that no one was on a first-name basis with more publishers. As chief diplomat for the Associated Press, Miller constantly barnstormed the country to hold publishers' hands and drum up new business for the wire service. He slapped a lot of backs, played a lot of golf, and told a lot of funny stories over drinks in the clubhouse. And, especially among the many aging patriarchs running family papers, he made a lot of friends.

They were good friends to have. In the 1960s and 1970s, many sought to sell their newspapers—not because they were losing money, but because the controlling families, now in their fourth or fifth generation, faced burdensome estate taxes and divisive squabbles over who would run the company in the future. Often the first person they called was Paul Miller, who was glad to lend a sympathetic ear and, in many cases, solve the families' problems by buying their papers.

Miller aimed to spread Frank Gannett's formula for prosperity across the nation. Though Miller hobnobbed with the people from Hearst, Knight, Scripps-Howard, Newhouse, and others of the newspaper elite, Gannett was too small and provincial to truly stand among them. And the company was not inclined to acquire the big-city dailies that would gain it a place in the club; those papers with their big unions and crosstown rivalries seemed terribly risky. On the other hand, Miller figured, Gannett could not be ignored if it owned more papers with more circulation than any other publisher.

The most important step Miller took toward achieving that goal was recruiting a young editor from the *Detroit Free Press* named Al Neuharth. Neuharth's ambition dwarfed even Miller's. "Big is good," Neuharth would say, and, at least in that sense, he wanted to make Gannett the best. He hadn't abandoned a promising career at Knight Newspapers to baby-sit a bunch of little dailies in the Northeast. If he was going to run Gannett—as he had every intention of doing—it was going to be the largest, most visible company in the U.S. newspaper industry. At Gannett, there were no Alvah Chapmans blocking his ascent. As it soon became clear at Gannett headquarters in Rochester, Al Neuharth was crown prince, and his kingdom would extend across the land.

Soon after he arrived, Neuharth started pitching a daring plan to launch a new daily in Cocoa Beach, Florida, where the fledgling U.S. space program was attracting people and money. The Knight brothers had laughed when he presented them with the idea in the 1950s. Gannett's financial bosses were skeptical too. After all, it was an age of newspaper consolidation, not creation. Gannett could find plenty of safe, moneymaking papers to buy without having to sink millions of dollars into a gamble.

Neuharth's fellow executives wondered if he had a death wish. He had the top job all sewn up; all he could do in Florida was lose it. But Paul Miller liked his protégé's idea. It *was* a risk, but for that very reason it would call attention to Gannett, and it might even make the big dollars Neuharth promised. Miller helped win over the board of directors, and Neuharth threw himself into the Cocoa project with the abandon of a man obsessed with his past—namely, the failure of *SoDak Sports.* He shuttled between Florida and Rochester, where he continued as general manager of Gannett's two flagship papers. He oversaw two weeks of dry production runs, trailing delivery trucks with a stopwatch in hand. He rewrote stories and headlines, worked elbow-to-elbow with typesetters, approved radio commercials, and made the dicey decision to raise *Cocoa Today*'s newsstand price to ten cents—from free—just a month after it was born in 1966. "Kid, you made your first and fatal mistake," Jim Knight chided Neuharth. "You can't sell that paper for full price. Too bad, 'cause I like you." Twenty-seven months later, *Cocoa Today* was profitable and growing. Neuharth had cemented his place as Paul Miller's heir apparent—and exorcised the demons of *SoDak Sports.*

Meanwhile, Miller took Gannett public. In October of 1967 the company sold five hundred thousand shares of common stock. Gannett was only the fourth newspaper company to go public, preceded by the Boston Herald-Traveler Corporation (later bought by Hearst), Dow Jones and Company, owner of the *Wall Street Journal,* and the Times Mirror Company, owner of the *Los Angeles Times.* Many others, including the Knight brothers, soon would follow. Going public offered growth-minded companies healthy infusions of money with which to buy newspapers, television and radio stations, and whatever else they fancied.

It also brought tremendous new responsibilities and pressures. Public companies had to subject their finances to the scrutiny of shareholders and Wall Street analysts, upon whom investors relied for advice on whether to buy or sell a stock. What showed up as profit or loss each quarter—never a crucial issue when finances were secret—suddenly mattered a great deal. Public companies had to concern themselves with far-flung shareholders as much as with readers, advertisers, and communities. As industry expert Leo Bogart has written, "An individual who is merely running a newspaper can let pride, ambition, conscience and loyalties counter the demands of his pocketbook. But one who is running three dailies, five weeklies, two television stations, and a handful of cable systems is bound to respond more as a businessman and less as a journalist."

Gannett's initial stock offering gave Miller $10 million to pursue his ambitions. First, Gannett bought Times Mirror's papers in San Bernardino, California. Neuharth, now an executive vice-president, pushed hard for the deal, which enabled Gannett to boast that it was a coast-to-coast company. Next came two papers in Florida. Then the Weil family's papers in Michigan, Idaho, Indiana, and Washington. Soon Gannett was in small towns in West Virginia, Hawaii, Vermont, Pennsylvania, Texas, Tennessee, and Guam. John Quinn, Gannett's young vice-president for news, joked that the company preferred towns that couldn't be reached by commercial airlines and had a single hotel with a leaky shower. He would never forget the sign proclaiming Rockford, Illinois, the screw capital of the world.

Gannett wisely used its publicly traded stock to, in effect, buy things without real money. Using stock instead of cash as tender, Gannett avoided borrowing, while shareholders of the acquired company avoided capital gains taxes. The stock stood to increase in value as long as the company grew and Wall Street took notice. The latter was a problem, for the investment community was not enamored of the newspaper industry. To New Yorkers, newspapers everywhere were like newspapers in New York, clunky operations with middling profit margins and labor headaches that made their financial performance annoyingly unpredictable. Wall Street took little note of the Gannetts of the world, quiet companies that ran small, high-profit papers with little unionized help.

They were missing a lot. Newspapering was a remarkably rich business, largely because it represented one of America's great unregulated monopolies. For decades, an unchallenged newspaper in a medium-sized town was virtually the sole comprehensive source of information, especially of the community proper. If it served its readers reasonably well, it was the only place a merchant could dependably reach the bulk of his or her market every day. That meant the newspaper could raise prices virtually at will. That newspaper, aggressively priced and attentively managed, could make from twenty to thirty cents of before-tax profit on every dollar of revenue, one of the largest profit margins of any U.S. industry. Very few businesses were in such a predictable position. People didn't need a new car, a new toothbrush, or a new refrigerator every day, but nearly everyone felt he needed a new newspaper. Almost everywhere, only one was available. "On the whole," *Forbes* magazine declared in 1969, "the newspaper industry has never been healthier, not even in the heyday of Joseph Pulitzer and William Randolph Hearst." One publisher, asked how much his newspaper was worth, replied, "How much do you think your wife is worth?"

In the late 1960s, Neuharth, Miller, and Jack Purcell, Gannett's top financial officer, set about introducing their business to the investment community. They visited stock analysts, had them up to Rochester, and flew them around the burgeoning Gannett empire, showing them the efficiently run printing plants and cost-cutting computer systems. When they journeyed to Wall Street, the Gannett people spent a lot of time talking about "how stuff was taking place west of the Hudson River," recalled Douglas McCorkindale, a financial and legal whiz Gannett recruited from the Wall Street law firm of Thacher, Proffitt and Wood. "It took Wall Street a long, long time to understand how good a business the media business is." After one frustrating session, a Gannett executive asked, "How do we go *un*public?"

Many of the analysts had watched fierce competition and union strife kill five New York dailies in the 1960s. They had to be told that Gannett didn't have many unionized employees. They had to be told that Gannett papers were installing computers before the big-city dailies. They had to be told that Gannett wasn't shy about raising prices, because readers would pay more for the only paper in town. They didn't talk much about journalism. "Wall Street didn't give a damn if we put out a good paper in Niagara Falls," Neuharth explained. "They just wanted to know if our profit increases would be in the 15 to 20 percent range."

They were exciting days. Neuharth and McCorkindale were having a ball, jetting around the country, buying papers, trying to get their profit margins up to 20, 25, 30 percent of revenues. "I knew every publisher, every department head, and maybe every number two department head in every one of our newspapers," recalled McCorkindale, who would one day be Gannett's number two executive. "It was great fun to put together the pieces so that the whole was better than all of the pieces."

The younger men of Gannett were taking over. Neuharth, named president of Gannett in 1970, was in on virtually every acquisition. He shaped the company's modern management structure, creating expert staffs to monitor each paper's sales, production, and financial performance. He cleaved Gannett's newspaper group into seven regions, each overseen by a president who answered to Neuharth. He installed a formal budgeting process requiring Gannett publishers to develop "profit plans" projecting revenues and expenses. The corporation refrained from setting profit goals for individual properties, but Gannett's overall aim, as it regularly informed Wall Street, was to increase profits each year by 15 percent. That could only be achieved if most of the company's papers embraced the same goal. So, while publishers could run their papers as they saw fit, someone nonetheless would be watching over their shoulders.

Paul Miller turned sixty-five; Neuharth hungered for the title of chief executive officer. He sent Miller suggestive memos, threatened to leave, and politely reminded his boss that, even if he stepped down as CEO, he would remain chairman of the board. But Gannett had no mandatory retirement age, and Miller saw no reason to surrender the reins. He was healthy and working hard and still had a few buddies who might like to sell some newspapers.

Neuharth was a persistent bully. In 1973 he finally snatched the CEO title by secretly lobbying board members to oust his boss. Miller remained as chairman, but Neuharth's and Miller's last years together were not always pleasant. Sixteen years later, when Paul Miller had been rendered speechless by a stroke, Neuharth would write of his old boss in deprecating tones, relating how he had "bested" Miller and, indeed, should have tried to remove him sooner so that Miller might have had more time to enjoy retirement.

In fourteen years, Paul Miller had added more than thirty newspapers to the Gannett stable and led the company into fourteen new states. In his last year as CEO, Gannett netted a profit of nearly $23.7 million on revenues of $288 million. Its stock was trading at record prices. And Gannett owned more dailies than any other U.S. publisher.

Something was missing, though. A *Wall Street Journal* headline summed it up in 1974: PROFITABLE THEY ARE, BUT GANNETT PAPERS FIND PRESTIGE ELUSIVE. The story quoted a Columbia University journalism professor complaining that Gannett managers "talk as if the business of journalism is business instead of journalism." As the company continued to gobble up new papers through the 1970s, it consistently won raves for its business prowess even as media critics panned its small-town brand of journalism. Gannett could not shake its image as a moneymaking machine that churned out, as onetime Gannett News Service Washington chief Jack Germond said, "a bunch of shitkicker papers." Even frothy *People* magazine needled Gannett for devoting "more space to church suppers than to in-depth reporting and enterprise."

It wasn't enough that Gannett bettered most papers it bought by plowing money into new equipment, more space for news, color reproduction, and other improvements. Miller found the criticism bewildering; after all, no one had bothered Frank Gannett about his papers' lack of distinction. "Some accounts could lead a reader to conclude that the Gannett company only lately sprang full-blown from nowhere into the now," Miller observed.

Try as he might, Neuharth couldn't ignore the carping. It genuinely bothered him, for not only did he believe his papers deserved more respect, he thought they served *their* readers better than the "Eastern establishment press," as he derisively called the bellwether papers in New York and Washington. "If you're doing a job for your readers in Boise, Idaho, or St. Cloud, Minnesota, how much difference does it make whether journalistic critics east of the Hudson or east of the Potomac applaud you for it?" he asked rhetorically.

Rather than shrink from the critics, though, Neuharth offered them a new target—*USA Today.*

Born in 1982, *USA Today* was the country's first national daily since the *National Observer* went belly-up in 1977. With its slick graphics, short stories, and breezy tone, Neuharth's multicolored baby sought to capture the fancy of the TV generation. They snapped it up; by June of 1984 the paper's daily circulation officially topped one million. Almost as gratifying to Neuharth was *USA Today*'s profound impact on newspapers across the country. While editors denounced *USA Today* as shallow, superficial, even cynical—"How stupid do they expect their readers to be?" asked *Publishers' Auxiliary,* a trade newspaper—they shamelessly stole from it. Newspapers everywhere started using bigger photographs, more color, and more charts and graphs to complement stories. Stories got shorter and snappier. Four-color weather maps became a staple. Sports sections got bigger and better to compete with *USA Today*'s late scores and statistical smorgasbord. Television news got more emphasis. Opinion page editors reconsidered the balance of their offerings, reflecting *USA Today*'s philosophy of presenting opinions on both sides of all issues. "I have never seen one newspaper have such a dramatic effect on the newspaper business," said Tom Holbein of Belden Associates, a newspaper research and marketing firm.

Many of Neuharth's peers grudgingly conceded he was, at the least, a marketing genius. But many also derided *USA Today* as typical of Gannett, a product that reduced journalism to a cynical search for the mass market's lowest common denominator. A comment by media critic and onetime *Washington Post* editor Ben Bagdikian typified the negative view. He said *USA Today* dealt "a serious blow to American journalists, since the paper represents the primacy of packagers and market analysts in a realm where the news judgment of reporters and editors has traditionally prevailed." Bagdikian and other critics complained that *USA Today* gave readers news they *wanted*—celebrity gossip, health tips, Horatio Alger business stories, gobs of sports statistics—at the expense of news people *needed.*

Neuharth shrugged it off. He appreciated the publicity—he figured readers would decide for themselves whether they liked *USA Today*—and anyway, he hadn't expected the newspaper establishment to comprehend his upstart creation. After all, he was adding readers. Most of the papers his critics glorified—indeed, most daily papers—had been *losing* readers for years. Since Neuharth's and Chapman's days at the *Free Press,* population growth had far outpaced growth in the circulation of the nation's 1,750 dailies. In 1960, nearly every household in the United States took at least one daily paper. By 1986, barely seven in ten did, and the number was declining. Even more frightening was the upcoming generation: fewer than half were regular readers.

There were lots of sociological and demographic reasons: People were spending more time playing. More women were working, shrinking a long-vital market, housewives. Increasing illiteracy was taking a toll. Television had grabbed a share of the market and made color, dynamism, and immediacy staples of the news. But newspapers themselves had to accept a great deal of the blame for their problems. More and more readers simply found them irrelevant, inaccessible, or just plain boring.

Neuharth found it incredible that so many who claimed to love newspapers could not see that readers were not getting what they wanted. Stories were too long and dull. Pages were too gray. The tone was too negative. Popular features and columns were shuffled randomly about the paper. Late sports scores didn't make the morning edition. Delivery was shoddy. The so-called great newspapers seemed increasingly out of touch with the concerns of common people. Editors and reporters preferred to dictate what people would read rather than give customers what they wanted. In Neuharth's view, journalists unwisely concerned themselves more with winning prizes than attracting readers. Readers attracted the advertisers, who brought in seventy-five to eighty cents of every dollar of revenue, which paid the bills—not least of which were the salaries of the journalists. You either had readers or you were out of business. Pulitzers wouldn't buy newsprint and ink.

USA Today sought to refocus the profession on its most vital constituency—the reader. And, in a way, Neuharth's newspaper challenged the popular notion that Gannett hungered more for profits than putting out good papers. By 1985, *USA Today*'s losses were in the hundreds of millions of dollars. It was money Neuharth could have used to invest in cable television, a promising new business, or to buy more cash-rich little dailies and TV stations. Instead, he gambled it on a venture that many in the establishment expected to fail. Of course Neuharth fully intended for *USA Today* to one day make Gannett untold amounts of money. But the "Nation's Newspaper" was a bid for respect as well as riches. Said Neuharth: "We wanted to break the newspaper establishment with something . . . and *become* the newspaper establishment."

There were trade-offs. Neuharth refused to let *USA Today*'s losses spoil Gannett's remarkable string of quarterly profit increases. So other Gannett papers had to take up the slack, by tightening budgets, reducing the space allotted for news, and raising prices on advertisers and subscribers. Star reporters and editors were "loaned" to *USA Today*—at their home papers' expense. Top editors at Gannett papers griped that their readers were paying a price for a newspaper they might not even read. As journalism scholar John K. Hartman wrote in *The USA Today Way, USA Today* was "the end-all and be-all of the Gannett corporate suite."

Even as Neuharth's name became familiar in households where Ben Bradlee and A. M. Rosenthal were unheard of, his critics continued to lambaste him. *USA Today,* they conveniently argued, was just a sop to Neuharth's gargantuan ego. He was wasting company resources to pursue his own vain dreams—and for what? A flashy product that, beyond the graphics and gimmicks, was little more than another Gannett paper, light and fluffy and no match for a truly great daily like the *Times* or the *Post.*

In the eyes of the establishment, Neuharth still had not proved he could play in the big leagues.

Then came the summer of 1985. Gannett bought the *Des Moines Register,* a paper revered by the newspaper establishment for its thorough coverage of Iowa and its serious heartland style of covering national politics. *Business Week* headlined a story, AL NEUHARTH WANTS IT ALL FOR GANNETT—EVEN RESPECT.

Next, Neuharth tried unsuccessfully to negotiate a merger with CBS. The talks broke down over who would run the new company. Neuharth would later fault himself for letting his ego get the best of him. "On reflection, I probably should admit to a slight case of egomania by the mid-1980s," he would write. "I lusted to add a few more jewels to my crown before hanging it on the fireplace mantel. That's when my ego went into overtime."

The chance to buy the Evening News Association arose. Neuharth was most familiar with the *News,* but other parts of the company appealed to him at least as much. The pearl was WDVM-TV, the CBS affiliate in Washington, D.C.; by itself it might have been worth $500 million. Some of the other TV stations also were attractive, and the two little California dailies were, as *News* publisher Bob Nelson put it, "licenses to print money."

The *News* was still in the fierce fight Neuharth had witnessed firsthand in the sixties, but it dominated most aspects of the market and, with Gannett's financial might, would have that much more ammunition to fire at the *Free Press.* Larry Miller, one of Gannett's top accountants, projected the *News* making a profit in a couple of years—though it wouldn't be nearly as high as at other Gannett papers. Profit margins, Miller noted, would improve handsomely if the *News* formed a joint operating agency with the *Free Press.* Anyway, Gannett would get the *News* at a bargain price. After backing out the values of the other ENA properties, analysts figured Gannett was getting the Detroit paper for $75 million to $150 million, less than the price of the *Des Moines Register,* which had less than half the *News*'s daily circulation.

More than just cold financial calculations figured in Neuharth's thinking, though. Although he would not admit to it—"We don't think with our glands," he told reporters—Doug McCorkindale and John Curley sensed an undercurrent of emotion. "He had deep feelings about Detroit," McCorkindale recalled. Neuharth would be returning to the city where he had first played "hardball," as Jack Knight called it in 1960. The two papers were playing it harder than ever now that both were losing money. Neuharth would be up against his old paper, the *Free Press,* and his old employer, Knight-Ridder. The head of Knight-Ridder happened to be Alvah Chapman, Jr., the straitlaced fellow who once obstructed Neuharth's path to the top of the Knight organization. Chapman's Knight-Ridder won Pulitzer Prizes with regularity and was admired by journalists everywhere. From his perch at Knight-Ridder headquarters in Miami, Chapman oversaw such prestigious big-city papers as the *Philadelphia Inquirer* and the *Miami Herald.* His company wasn't quite as big or profitable as Gannett, but it had something Neuharth and Gannett had failed to acquire: unstinting respect. Perhaps now Al Neuharth finally could gain the same measure of respect by beating Alvah Chapman and Knight-Ridder in Detroit—if that truly was what Neuharth had in mind.

On November 12, 1985, two and a half months after Gannett agreed to buy the Evening News Association, Al Neuharth addressed a packed house in the smoky, windowless Detroit Press Club a block away from the *News.* The DPC, once a main watering hole for *News* and *Free Press* reporters and editors, had fallen on difficult times as younger journalists shunned its gloomy ambience and annual dues in favor of other downtown spots. Tonight, though, rookies and veterans alike had come to hoist a few beers and query the man who would soon be running the *News.*

Neuharth stood at a table with *News* executive editor Benjamin Burns, editor Lionel Linder, and publisher Bob Nelson. As he spoke, Neuharth constantly fidgeted, cracking his knuckles, fiddling with his diamond ring, shifting his shoulders. "Because of Jack Knight and Peter Clark and others," he said, "being a newspaperperson in Detroit is probably the greatest journalism job in the U.S.A. There aren't enough journalists around the country who have an opportunity to enjoy or participate in that kind of head-to-head competition anymore." No one in the room was inclined to disagree. The journalists, some from the *Free Press,* some from the *News,* were proud to be fighting what they considered the country's last great newspaper war. Dailies competed in a few other cities—New York, Dallas, Houston, Denver, Chicago among them—but none of those skirmishes had the history of Detroit's clash, nor had those papers suffered such large financial losses. Detroit was easily the bloodiest battleground.

Neuharth, a veteran of the Detroit battle, knew exactly what his audience was thinking. "As long as we at Gannett have anything to do with it," he vowed, "Detroit is going to continue to be a two-newspaper town, and the number-one pin that I am wearing"—he glanced at his lapel—"and inheriting from ENA will stay on the lapel of all the *Detroit News* people."

Someone asked whether a joint operating agency was under consideration. Neuharth didn't flinch. He explained that such a quasi merger as a JOA would be allowed by the federal government if either of the papers could show that it was in danger of going out of business. "I have no idea whether a JOA will ever be a fact in Detroit," he continued. "There has been no discussion, no consideration, no conversations about it."

But, he added, "everything" was an option.

Next he was asked what he thought of a newspaper selling for fifteen cents, as the *News*'s daily edition did. Neuharth was one of the industry's most outspoken advocates of aggressive pricing. He launched into his standard hike-the-price spiel. "I delivered newspapers when they sold for a nickel back in South Dakota in the forties and at that time the consumer bought ice-cream cones for a nickel and cups of coffee for a nickel and Coke for a nickel, and he and she related those consumer items to each other as being worth about the same price. I remember a great debate in this town over whether the price of the *Free Press* should move from seven cents to a dime or seven cents to eight cents.

"How silly can newspaper publishers or owners be?"

Neuharth predicted that the circulation of both Detroit papers would be going up in years to come. Each had lost circulation in 1985, but Neuharth noted that *USA Today*'s entry into the market meant total readership had actually gone up, not down. "I think the total newspaper readership will continue to go up and I would expect that both the *News* and the *Free Press* will show circulation gains even if, or maybe *especially* if, they make it more convenient for the public to drop a single coin—like a quarter—into a vending machine rather than two dimes or a nickel and a dime."

The audience chuckled knowingly. So that was it: Neuharth was going to increase the *News*'s daily cover price to a quarter. The *Free Press* would follow, and soon both papers would be making money again. The competition, the journalists assumed, could then continue unabated without any merging of the papers. It was good news indeed.

While he had the floor, Neuharth took the opportunity to embarrass a *News* reporter. William Dunn, who was covering Neuharth's talk, rose to ask a question.

"What about Time and NBC?"

"The question is, 'What about Time and NBC?" Neuharth told the audience. He turned to Dunn. "What *about* Time and NBC?"

"Well," Dunn said, "it was reported that you were meeting with them, talking about a possible merger."

"Where was that reported?"

Dunn hesitated. "I believe the *Wall Street Journal.*"

"Are you sure?" Neuharth said. Dunn was turning red. "You aren't, are you? Well, it wasn't. No, it was not."

Dunn, a veteran reporter, had simply mixed up networks; Gannett's merger talks had been with CBS. But Neuharth couldn't let it go at that. Instead, while dozens of Dunn's peers watched uncomfortably, Neuharth let him have it. "What has been reported in the *Wall Street Journal* is that we've had some conversation with Time, Inc., and *CBS*. Totally different network. So let's be careful." Dunn sat down.*

Neuharth didn't show up in Detroit again until January, when he named four Gannett executives to a *News* "transition team." For the next month the team immersed itself in gathering intelligence on *News* operations, reporting directly to Neuharth each Monday at 8:30 A.M. The group was Maurice L. "Moe" Hickey, a veteran publisher who had riled Neuharth by declining to be publisher of *USA Today;* Louis A. "Chip" Weil III, a senior vice-president whose family had sold Gannett a batch of lucrative little papers in the 1970s; Nancy Woodhull, a senior *USA Today* editor; and accountant Thomas J. Farrell, business manager of *USA Today.*

Neuharth told his team little about his intentions for the *News.* But the executives got the strong impression he was there to compete. "He never said, 'Look, this is what you're going to do when we buy this thing,' " Tom Farrell later said. One day, though, Farrell recalled, Neuharth lectured his charges: "You have to keep in mind that this is going to be a very, very competitive situation. We're going to have to compete like we've never competed before."

*William Dunn later became a reporter at *USA Today.*

Farrell went away thinking, This is going to be our first big street battle. We're going to fight the long fight.

It would not be easy. The *News* needed a lot of work, and the market was like nothing the Gannett people had ever seen.

The *News* was run by a phalanx of middle-aged white men. Few women and fewer blacks played significant roles at the largest newspaper in Detroit, with a population that was 70 percent black. Gannett, by contrast, was the undisputed industry leader in the hiring and promotion of women and minorities. Neuharth, who had never forgotten his mother's struggles to provide for her boys in the twenties and thirties, personally saw to that. His company's next project would be the *Detroit News*.

The *News* was crawling with unionized workers. Nearly 80 percent of the *News*'s 2,250 employees belonged to one of eleven unions; by comparison, about 20 percent of Gannett's workers were unionized. One morning, Farrell was sitting in *News* controller Gary Anderson's office when workers suddenly left the area en masse. "What's going on?" Farrell asked. "Fire drill?"

"Coffee break," Anderson said. It was in the workers' contract.

Farrell had never met anyone quite like Elton Schade, the tough, cigar-chomping leader of Teamsters Local 372. With 1,350 drivers and circulation workers, the local was the two Detroit papers' single most powerful group of employees. Schade didn't hesitate to let Farrell know it. Unions loathed Gannett for taking tough negotiating stances at its small papers; Schade wanted to make it clear that Local 372 would not be bullied. "We've done things a certain way around here for a long time," he told Farrell. The union leader had a spooky cast eye that intimidated Farrell. The Gannett executive couldn't tell whether Schade was looking at him or not. "You're going to find," Schade told him, "that we do things in Detroit that are different than you do things in your other markets."

News publisher Bob Nelson ruled by fear and intimidation. Deputies who made mistakes, said the wrong thing at the wrong time, or mentioned Nelson's taboo—raising prices—risked a chewing out in one of the "electric chairs" facing Nelson's desk. "He reminds one of a Navy chief," a member of Gannett's transition team wrote in a memo. "Not a lot of original thinking is allowed to take place under his administration."

Bob Kurzawa frequently incurred Nelson's wrath. The former *Detroit Times* employee had risen to circulation manager since joining the *News* in 1960. Nelson regularly berated him for not boosting circulation higher, though Kurzawa never let the *News* numbers fall beneath those of the *Free Press*.

Once, Kurzawa made a thirty-thousand-dollar mistake in a year-end expense report. He was summoned to one of the "electric chairs."

"Are you a college graduate?" Nelson asked.

"Yes, I am," Kurzawa replied. He had gotten a bachelor's degree in mathematics attending night school at the University of Detroit.

"Hmmm," Nelson said. "Can you tell me how a college graduate could just *forget* thirty thousand dollars?" Kurzawa knew enough not to answer. Nelson dismissed him from the room.

The next day Nelson called Kurzawa in again. "You're a college graduate, aren't you?" he said.

Yes, Kurzawa answered again. Again Nelson wanted to know, "How the hell can a college graduate lose thirty thousand dollars?"

Nelson repeated the scene twice more before letting up. Kurzawa was a mess. He couldn't sleep for days. His palms sweated whenever Nelson summoned him. He expected to be fired.

Fear also set the tone for competition with the *Free Press.* The *News* led the market by nearly every measure of circulation and advertising share and revenue. But Nelson constantly told his charges that at any time Knight-Ridder could decide to bring its full financial weight to bear and simply crush the *News,* as it had the *Philadelphia Bulletin* in 1982. Nelson instilled less the will to win than the fear of losing. Fear begat insanity.

The *News*'s fifteen-cent cover price didn't come close to covering even the cost of newsprint and ink. Indeed, only twenty other dailies—less than 1 percent of the country's total—sold for as little. The *Free Press*'s daily twenty-cent cover price was lower than that of 95 percent of U.S. dailies, most of which sold for a quarter. Sunday pricing—both papers sold for seventy-five cents—was a bit more sane, though one of every five U.S. dailies had gone to a dollar or even a dollar and a quarter. Despite their relatively low prices, the Detroit papers were discounted even further in the effort to build circulation. In September of 1985, the *News* told the Audit Bureau of Circulations that it had discounted nearly 235,000 daily subscriptions in the previous half year, almost 102,000 more than the *Free Press.*

The *News*'s official advertising rates also were among the lowest in the country. But, to steal ads from the *Free Press, News* salespeople cut the rates further. Indeed, *News* ad sellers earned bonuses by increasing market share, not revenue. If you wanted a bigger bonus, you cut better deals for your customers.

The rate cutting was like a narcotic. The longer it went on, the more dangerous it became. Advertisers greedily whipsawed the papers for better and better deals. The *News* discounted its already low rates by 30 to 40 percent, gave away ads on Mondays, and slashed Saturday rates by more than 50 percent. The *Free Press* offered its own smorgasbord of bargains. Managers never could tell if salespeople were fibbing when they claimed to have lost a sale because the other paper was "giving ads away." The *News* blamed the *Free Press* for cutting rates, the *Free Press* blamed the *News*. But where the fault lay was irrelevant; both papers were losing money because they were cheating themselves out of precious advertising dollars, the source of 75 percent of their revenue, their means to profitability.

Nelson refused to raise prices for fear of losing market share to the *Free Press*. Whenever either paper raised newsstand prices or ad rates, it risked losing subscribers and advertisers. Nelson was convinced that, once share began to slip, the *News* would find itself on an irreversible fall into the graveyard for afternoon papers. Kurzawa and ad director Richard McClennen cajoled Nelson to raise prices selectively, arguing that the *News* could exploit its dominant position, especially on Sundays. Nelson wouldn't budge. "We weren't going to give the *Free Press* an inch," he recalled. Kurzawa and McClennen left Nelson's office with his bellowed profanities ringing in their ears.

The *News*'s competitive strategy was costly on the expense side of the ledger, too. The paper's all-day printing and distribution schedule required extra news staff and separate distribution networks for evening and morning. But if the *News* had not sold papers in the morning, it surely would have trailed far behind the *Free Press* by 1985. The *News*'s morning circulation kept it ahead—by a little. Even as Gannett's transition team scrutinized their new property, the *Free Press* was gaining.

Yet the *News* had other advantages: an 84,000-paper lead in Sunday circulation (838,000 to 755,000); nearly 62 percent of total advertising linage; and, perhaps most important, an enormous 72 percent of the Sunday classified ad linage. Classifieds were the linchpin of the *News*'s dominance. If you were looking for a job, recruiting new hires, shopping for a car, or selling a set of golf clubs, you *had* to advertise or shop in the *News,* where the market was twice the size of the *Free Press*'s. People bought the *News* at least as much for the thick sections of classifieds as for the news stories and conservative editorials.

Journalistically, the *News* was solid—perhaps too solid for Gannett tastes. "The impression is that the paper takes itself quite seriously," Robert Giles, editor of Gannett's Rochester papers, wrote in a memo in which he critiqued the *News* and pitched himself as the new editor of the paper. Stories were uniformly thorough—meaning too long, in Gannett's view—and the writing rarely sparkled. The paper was assembled in seemingly random order; readers might have to do some searching for features they regularly read. A feel for Detroit and environs was strangely lacking. The *News* seemed more interested in statewide affairs, reflecting editor Lionel Linder's belief that state government directly affected more *News* readers than did Detroit.

The local report suffered. The feature and business pages were lackluster, obituaries few. The daily television page didn't grab readers. Dull stories on taxes and the economy too greatly outnumbered stories on life-styles, entertainment, sports, and local businesses. Linder had added color and graphic elements to brighten the *News*'s appearance, but the execution was erratic at best. "Call in a *USA Today* fix-up crew in photo, engraving and the pressroom," Giles advised. Even many *News* editors privately agreed that the *Free Press* was more lively, better written, and better looking. On a big story, the *News* often would outreport its rival, but the *Free Press* would *look* as if it covered the story better because of its superior packaging, layout, and photos. Despite Linder's best efforts to spruce it up, most days the *News* lived up to its nickname of the Old Gray Lady.

When Al Neuharth was mulling how to improve his new newspaper, he sought advice from some *Free Press* veterans. On the weekend of January 11, 1986, he gathered half a dozen of them, along with Moe Hickey, at Pumpkin Center, his beach cabin in Cocoa Beach. There was Lee Guittar, a former *Free Press* president, now president of *USA Today;* Ron Martin, an ex-*Free Press* editor who was executive editor of *USA Today;* James Head, the president of King Features Syndicate who had once been a *Free Press* sports editor; Joe Urschel, another *USA Today* editor who had worked at the *Free Press;* and Derick Daniels, one of Neuharth's oldest newspaper pals, formerly executive editor of the *Free Press* and president of *Playboy* magazine. They chatted and munched candy in a conference room overlooking the Atlantic while Neuharth paced in a hooded gray sweatshirt. They didn't accomplish much—John Curley called it "an old buddies' party"—but Neuharth made sure his friends down the coast at Knight-Ridder knew his mind was on Detroit. He planted a story in Gannett's Cocoa Beach paper that included a photo of Neuharth, Head, and Hickey smiling absurdly at a three-day-old copy of the *News.* MEDIA LEADERS DISCUSS PLANS FOR *DETROIT NEWS,* the headline read.

On January 13, Neuharth surprised a *News* reporter by telling him he had no plan to increase the price of the *News* after all. "I kid a lot about charging what a paper's worth," Neuharth said. "There's a perception that the first thing we do is take off our hat and coat and raise the price. That generally isn't the way it works." Still, Gannett's pricing practices were the industry's most aggressive. Not one Gannett paper sold for less than a quarter daily, and many sold for thirty-five cents, *USA Today* for fifty.

Two weeks later Neuharth addressed the Economic Club of Detroit, a group of business, civic, and political leaders who gathered weekly to eat lunch and hear a speech. Behind the dais, a huge blue logo shrieked MOTOWN GOTOWN.

Neuharth castigated Detroit's media for portraying the city as crime-ridden and economically troubled, even though it was. "The fact is," he said, "that some local journalists join in the practice of the Journalism of Despair, which is the modus operandi of many in the media on the Eastern Seaboard." He said he wanted to balance that with "a new Journalism of Hope," which "should chronicle the good as well as the bad, the glad as well as the sad." The line was lifted from one of his speeches touting *USA Today.* The audience clapped and cheered.

A question-and-answer period followed. The first question, read aloud by *News* publisher Bob Nelson, asked if the Detroit papers would combine printing facilities.

Neuharth explained that the question referred to a joint operating agency, or JOA. "The answer to that question," he said, "is that there have been no discussions between Gannett, the owners of the *Detroit News* as of next month, and Knight-Ridder, the owners of the *Detroit Free Press,* on that subject at all, nor have we given any real thought to it."

Neuharth also was asked whether Gannett would raise the price of the *News.* Any increase, he said, would be made "only after a great deal of study and consultation."

Despite his many signals to the contrary, Neuharth was coming to the conclusion that raising the price of the *News* would be a mistake. Indeed, Neuharth was considering *cutting* prices, at least selectively. It would cost a few hundred thousand dollars, but it might cost the *Free Press* even more, either in dollars or in market share. Neuharth had a target in mind. The *Free Press* dominated the outstate market of readers and advertisers more than an hour's drive from metropolitan Detroit. The *Free Press* had staked a claim to those regions under Lee Hills in the 1950s and 1960s, and the *News* had never seriously countered. It wasn't a terribly valuable market—outstate circulation didn't attract much ad revenue because advertisers usually focused on the big Detroit market. But, as the last outpost of *Free Press* supremacy, outstate was an appealing—and vulnerable—target.

By mid-February Gannett was preparing to spend $12 million to double the printing capacity of the *News*'s Lansing printing plant and increase outstate sales of the *News* and *USA Today.* Moe Hickey, soon to be named publisher of the *News,* was readying to spend more than $1 million on new vending machines and promotion. Neuharth was thinking of reducing the price of the outstate *News,* which at the time sold for twenty cents, a nickel more than local editions.

At least for the moment, Gannett wasn't living up to its reputation for raising prices and boosting profits. Despite a memo by Larry Miller listing fourteen measures to bolster the *News*'s bottom line—including raising prices, cutting corporate overhead costs, eliminating the *News*'s Lansing and Washington bureaus, and improving marketing and promotion—Neuharth wasn't interested in making an immediate profit, or so he said. He talked with ENA's lame-duck bosses about putting the *News* on a five-year plan to ensure the paper a stronger market position vis-à-vis the *Free Press*.

"If we can do that," he told a private gathering of *News* and ENA officials in February, "we at Gannett are perfectly willing to take our lumps during some stages of that or the early stages of that. Nobody at Gannett has any [plans] of making a lot of money at the *Detroit News*. At the same time we would be dishonest if we didn't say that we believed the operation that you've developed here should return a respectable profit to its owner, ultimately. But we take the long route rather than the short route, and we will certainly take that here."

Neuharth was beginning to persuade a lot of people that he had no intention of backing off in Detroit. His assertiveness surprised some on Wall Street, where, from the day Gannett agreed to buy the ENA, stock analysts had been predicting that the *News* and the *Free Press* would move swiftly for federal approval of a JOA. At first, analysts didn't buy Neuharth's public saber rattling; certainly none of them thought Gannett would dare vie head-to-head with Knight-Ridder. Gannett always sought to avoid competition; Neuharth was accustomed to defending the practice of investing only in one-paper markets. Indeed, he told an interviewer in 1978 that Gannett "would not be interested in situations in Detroit, Cleveland, Chicago or Philadelphia." Now that he was in Detroit he avoided ruling out a JOA, but he talked enough about competing that, by early 1986, even some analysts started assessing Detroit without assuming a JOA. They were not pleased, of course, for continued competition probably meant continued losses. Their best hope was that Neuharth would raise prices at the *News* and lead both Detroit papers into a saner, more profitable era. John Morton, one of the industry's most oft-quoted analysts, had predicted that Gannett would raise prices almost immediately.

Gannett made its purchase of the ENA formal on February 18, 1986. Clark and Neuharth signed the closing papers in a brief ceremony at the Detroit law offices of Butzel Long. At 12:30 P.M. the two men joined more than eighty top *News*, ENA, and Gannett officials for a celebratory lunch. It was a last supper of sorts for some in attendance, because they soon would be losing their jobs. For now, though, they were glad to hear Neuharth assure them Gannett would fight the good fight. Neuharth, a sports nut who rooted for the New York

Yankees, compared the battle to a ball game. With Gannett's help, he vowed, "The *News* will win the playoffs and retire the trophy."

Peter Clark chimed in later that day at a party for staffers who gathered for champagne and cookies. "You ain't seen nothing yet," Clark said. "We will be stronger because of the resources that the Gannett Company will be adding—resources of money, personnel, talent, and energy. And it will be stronger specifically because of Al Neuharth's leadership."

The same day, Neuharth named himself chairman of the *News,* an extraordinary move, akin to the chairman of General Motors assuming sole responsibility for a single car division. He named Moe Hickey, fifty-one, publisher; Chip Weil, forty-four, president; Lionel Linder, fifty-four, editor; and Bob Nelson, sixty-one, special assistant to the chairman. A dozen members of the ENA corporate staff were quietly handed their walking papers, among them Clark's trusted financial deputy, Ed Frederickson. Soon top editors Linder and Ben Burns would be swept aside by a new wave of editors from Gannett's Rochester papers.

Before Neuharth left Detroit that February afternoon, he was interviewed by *News* reporter Richard Willing.

"Has the idea of a joint operating agreement been contemplated?" Willing asked.

"Not by me," Neuharth replied. "We will look at any and all options to preserve and enhance the *News*'s dominant position, so I won't rule out anything. But there is no reason for me to suggest that [a JOA] is a likely development."

There were plenty of reasons.

Even before Gannett made its bid for the ENA, Gannett accountants had been busy estimating the profits a JOA could generate. On August 9, 1985, accountant Larry Miller wrote his boss, Doug McCorkindale, "It appears that the only way this [ENA] investment could be self-supporting would be through substantial earnings gains at the *Detroit News.* Obviously, this would be very difficult without a JOA." On August 30, the day after Gannett agreed to buy the ENA, analyst John Kornreich of Neuberger and Berman asked McCorkindale why Neuharth was implying he would compete in Detroit. Don't worry, McCorkindale confided. "It's not hard to figure out what we're going to do."

All the talk of raising prices was a smoke screen. Aside from the possibility of losing market share, hiking prices incurred the risk of jeopardizing the legal argument for a JOA. To obtain the necessary federal approval of a JOA, the applicants would have to prove that either the *Free Press* or the *News* was in danger of failing. A price boost at the *News,* followed by the *Free Press,* might have made both papers profitable—and, thus, unable to satisfy the statutory test. Gannett was well aware of the risk. "Would we dare raise prices in the interim if that puts both entities into black?" accountant Miller scribbled to himself in August of 1985. A few days later McCorkindale wrote Neuharth: "Circulation pricing at the *News* is obvious, but we have to keep the JOA possibilities in focus."

In February, when Neuharth told *News* reporter Richard Willing that no JOA was under consideration—"not by me"—Gannett and Knight-Ridder had tentatively agreed on several important issues relating to a potential JOA.

The month before, when Neuharth told the Economic Club of Detroit that Gannett had not "given any real thought" to a JOA, his people were discussing it regularly with Knight-Ridder, and both companies had developed detailed bargaining positions. *Free Press* publisher David Lawrence, Jr., sitting on the dais with Neuharth, knew a JOA was being discussed and was aghast that Neuharth hadn't even tried to skirt the question. "If you tell me that big a lie, I've got no way to deal with it," Lawrence said later.

Even in November, when Neuharth told journalists gathered at the Detroit Press Club that there had been "no discussion, no consideration, no conversations" about a JOA, he himself had met at least twice and talked on the phone at least twice with Knight-Ridder executives about that very subject.

In fact, discussions had begun back in August. On August 6, three weeks before Gannett entered its formal bid for the ENA, Neuharth had placed a call to the Miami office of Alvah H. Chapman, Jr., the chairman of Knight-Ridder. Chapman was vacationing, so Neuharth spoke with James K. Batten, Knight-Ridder's president. Gannett, Neuharth explained, was mulling a bid for the ENA. He was curious as to whether Knight-Ridder would, at least in concept, consider a JOA between the *News* and the *Free Press.*

"Under the right circumstances," Batten said, "I am sure that would be something we could at least entertain."

That was all Neuharth needed to know.

6

JSK

Alvah Chapman couldn't have been happier. The skies were clear, the seas were calm, and his boat, a forty-six-foot Bertram with twin four-hundred-horsepower screws, was outracing the cruiser captained by his pal Armando Codina. It was August of 1985, and the Chapman and Codina families were enjoying their annual boating vacation to the Bahamas. "Captain Alvah," as Codina called Chapman, was surrounded by his wife, Betty, his two daughters, and four of his six grandchildren. He loved every minute of it.

The news from Jim Batten made things even better. Batten was Chapman's top lieutenant at Knight-Ridder, Inc., the company Chapman had run since 1976. When Chapman phoned him from an island dock, Batten related an intriguing August 6 phone call from Al Neuharth, who wanted to know if Knight-Ridder might be interested in a JOA in Detroit. Hearing Batten replay the conversation, Chapman nodded in agreement. He had pursued a JOA for years but could never come to terms with Peter Clark. With Clark out of the picture, talk of a JOA was sure to get more businesslike. Prolonging the Detroit battle would have little appeal for Neuharth, who already had a big money loser, *USA Today,* on his hands. A solution to the nagging Detroit problem might be near. But Chapman did not celebrate just yet. Stoic as ever, he returned to his vacation, saying nothing to family and friends. He made a mental note to call Neuharth as soon as he got back to Miami. It had been a good day. Just three years before he was scheduled to retire, it looked as though Alvah Chapman might finally have the chance to wipe away the one lingering blemish on his illustrious career.

When its second engine blew, the B-17 bomber, *Battlin' Betty,* dropped back out of the formation, naked in the German sky. Now the roving Messerschmitt fighters could finish it off.

Before they had the chance, the B-17 began to plummet, nose down, leveling slightly at intervals like a leaf, then falling again, trailing a black ribbon of smoke. Three circling German planes flew off to stalk other prey. A fourth fighter hung back to witness the crash.

At twelve hundred feet the last German fighter was shocked to discover the B-17 cruising under cloud cover. *It had not crashed.* As the German stared incredulously out the rear of his hatch, his eyes met those of the bomber pilot, Army Air Corps Captain Alvah Herman Chapman, Jr. One of Chapman's gunners blew the German to pieces. He was so close that chunks of his plane landed on Chapman's turret. With the aid of the clouds, Chapman and his crew guided their crippled plane to safety.

It was a miraculous escape. Even his fellow bomber pilots had figured Chapman was spinning to oblivion. But he had fooled them all, and saved himself and his nine crew members, by flying a risky "falling leaf" maneuver, which he had practiced for hours in the sky over Montana. Later, he would disavow any heroism in his deed, crediting instead his B-17: "one helluva airplane." That was Alvah Chapman. But he had also been prepared, and *that* was Alvah Chapman. He kept a cool head, and *that* was Alvah Chapman. Hero or not, he did what had to be done, and *that* was certainly Alvah Chapman.

He was just twenty-three and had yet to run a newspaper, but already he was shaping his simple but powerful management style: to see, without passion, what needed to be done and then, with tremendous passion, pursue it until it *was* done. Decades later, those who followed Chapman would marvel at his seeming ability to will things into being, however improbable or impossible they appeared. "Chap was cool, levelheaded, all business," recalled Chapman's navigator, retired Air Force Colonel C. M. Smith. "He'd fly straight and level, he wouldn't flinch, he'd just bore right in on the target. He was a born leader."

And a born newspaperman, third generation. Chapman's maternal grandfather, R. W. Page, had sold ads and kept the books for the Columbus, Georgia, *Ledger* before buying the paper with his brother-in-law in 1893. Page's son, Alvah Chapman, Sr., eventually took over and acquired a few other southern papers, including his main rival in Columbus, the *Enquirer,* and the Bradenton, Florida, *Herald.*

On Saturday nights in the late 1930s, teenaged Alvah junior was at the *Herald* switchboard, handling phones and reading page proofs. At 2:00 A.M. he went to work in the mail room. Two hours later he was in a truck, delivering to outlying routes. After Sunday school and church, Chapman was ready for bed. During the summer he collected bills and assembled type in the composing room. The freckle-faced boy with the pale blue eyes was learning to love the trade. "It was an opportunity to be in the center of things, an opportunity to make a difference," he would say later. Making a difference was important to the Chapmans, a close-knit family bound by a strong faith in God. Young Alvah would grow especially fond of the biblical proverb "For unto whomsoever much is given, of him shall be much required."

Much was expected in the way of discipline at The Citadel, the antebellum military college set along the Ashley River in Charleston, South Carolina. Freshman Alvah Chapman only reluctantly took to the oppressive maze of rules that seemed to govern everything a cadet did, from climbing stairs to folding clothes to using the latrine. For a "knob," as freshmen were called, humility became a survival technique. "You were a very low individual," Chapman ruefully recalled.

Each night, after taps, an upperclassman would rap on the door of each room and ask, "All right?" If all was as it should be, you answered, "All right." But if not, if for example your roommate was out of the room, you answered otherwise, and the upperclassman would investigate. Your roommate could get in trouble, but you did not lie. You did not cover for your roommate, and you did not expect him to cover for you. "In life at The Citadel, a man's word is his bond," said retired Army Lieutenant General George M. Seignious II, one of Chapman's classmates. "That's deeply ingrained."

By the time he was a senior, Chapman had so impressed The Citadel's faculty, officers, and cadets that he was chosen cadet regimental commander, the college's top rank. Chapman was an A student, intensely competitive but not boisterous, a leader of stern gazes and few words. His forte was discipline. The Citadel imposed a rigorous schedule of academic, athletic, military, and social activities. "Time was of the essence," Seignious said. "If a person didn't have the discipline, he would run out of time. Things would slip. Alvah just didn't let things slip."

Once Chapman had to discipline a fellow senior named Fritz Hollings. Hollings, a company commander, had covered for a roommate who missed a drill. He was stripped of his rank and forced to walk humiliating tours of the grounds for weeks. Years later, Senator Ernest F. Hollings, Democrat of South Carolina, praised Chapman for meting out deserved punishment: "There's a right and wrong in this world, and there's no fuzziness [about it] with Alvah Chapman."

In World War II Chapman flew thirty-seven bombing missions in the *Battlin' Betty,* nicknamed for his newlywed, Betty Bateman. There would have been more glamour in becoming a fighter pilot, but Chapman did not see himself as a lone wolf. He had studied business management at The Citadel, and as a bomber pilot he managed people. He soon became a squadron commander with responsibility for more than fifteen hundred men and their training, discipline, morale, and aircraft maintenance.

After the war Chapman returned to the *Columbus Ledger-Enquirer.* He wrote stories and sold ads, finding himself more comfortable with the business side of newspapering. In 1948 he became business manager. In 1955 the *Ledger-Enquirer* won a Pulitzer Prize for its reporting on vice in nearby Phenix City, Alabama, but by then, Chapman had been lured away by Nelson Poynter, the legendary Florida publisher. A feisty, independent man who favored bow ties, Poynter published the *St. Petersburg Times,* one of the finest dailies in the country. He believed owning a newspaper was "a sacred trust, a great privilege," as he put it in the fifteen-point manifesto, "Standards for Ownership of a Newspaper or Broadcast Enterprise," he wrote in 1947. To uphold that trust, he believed, a newspaper had to be financially strong. Chapman, he thought, could help the *Times* accomplish that as an executive vice-president and general manager.

First, though, Chapman had to take some tests. The tests, developed by a psychologist named Byron Harless, sought to determine whether Chapman had an aptitude for leadership. Poynter arranged for Harless and Chapman to meet, seemingly by accident, at the Tampa airport en route to a newspaper convention in New Orleans. He did not warn Chapman about the tests. "He didn't know a damn thing about what I was going to do with him," Harless recalled. In New Orleans Harless persuaded Chapman to cancel a dinner date and take his exams. Chapman was tired from traveling and had to give a speech the next day, but he sat down for six hours and completed the interviews and written tests. Harless was amazed at the young man's confidence and calm. Around five the next morning he called Poynter. "If I was running the *St. Petersburg Times,*" Harless said, "I would hire Alvah Chapman."

In 1957 Chapman went to Savannah, Georgia, as publisher, president, and minority owner of the *Morning News* and *Evening Press.* The papers were "unbelievably bad," Chapman recalled. For weeks on end the agenda of the Rotary Club's Monday morning meeting was the lead local news story. Local news, no matter how significant, never made the front page, which was reserved for world and national news. No staff reporters covered the state government in Atlanta, or the federal government in Washington, D.C. Advertising rates were based, incredibly, on how close an advertiser was to the printing plant. Classified ads, sports pages, news pages were sprinkled haphazardly throughout the paper, wherever they happened to fall during typesetting. The combined Sunday paper didn't come off the presses until 10:30 A.M.

Chapman revolutionized the *News* and *Press*. He added a food page, stock market reports, an outdoor writer, and bureaus in Atlanta and Washington. He hired new reporters and an executive editor, and the papers crusaded against illegal gambling and political corruption. He increased salaries. He reworked advertising rates to reflect actual costs and profit margins. He started running two presses instead of one. The Sunday paper came out earlier. Readership and advertising revenue increased. Profits more than doubled. He got to know his employees. "He could walk into the classified department to one of the ladies in the phone room and say, 'How are you, Sally?' " said Tom Coffey, then sports editor in Savannah.

Chapman also stepped on a few toes. The *News* and *Press* reported and editorialized on political corruption, slumlords, the poor local school system, and the need for an expressway. Friends of the banker who owned a controlling interest in the *News* and *Press* told him they didn't appreciate the aggressive coverage. The banker, Mills B. Lane, decided to sell. Among the potential buyers he approached was James Knight, one of the two brothers who published the *Miami Herald, Akron Beacon Journal, Charlotte Observer, Charlotte News,* and *Detroit Free Press.*

Knight was more interested in Alvah Chapman.

Chapman joined Knight Newspapers in August of 1960 as Jim Knight's assistant at the *Miami Herald*. By then Chapman was established in the South as one of the industry's rising stars, an articulate advocate of careful management and budgeting, a soft-spoken gentleman with an uncanny grasp of what it took to make money selling good newspapers. But Alvah Chapman was still just a whippersnapper. His renown paled beside that of the cranky, brilliant, irrepressible patriarch of his new company—John Shively "Jack" Knight.

Jack Knight never was eager to work for his father. When he returned from two undistinguished years as an infantryman in World War I, he bolted the family home in Akron, Ohio, for California, where he partied with the Hollywood crowd and squandered five thousand dollars he had won playing craps with his army pals in France. He finally agreed to join his father's newspaper, the *Akron Beacon Journal,* on two conditions.

"What's that?" asked Charles Landon Knight, known as C. L.

"If I don't like the work, I can get out," his son said. "If I'm no good, I'll be kicked out."

As it turned out, Jack Knight loved the work. And he was awfully good at it.

When his father died of cancer in 1933, thirty-eight-year-old Jack and his younger brother, James, inherited an *Akron Beacon Journal* that owed hundreds of thousands of dollars and paid employees in scrip, the Great Depression equivalent of IOUs. Akron was a wasteland of jobless workers, failed banks, and shuttered businesses. The Depression threw a lingering shadow over the newspaper business. A precipitous drop in advertising income plunged many papers into the red. From 1931 to 1936, more than 220 dailies closed their doors. Then came the recession of 1937. Ad revenues fell again, and meanwhile labor and production costs had risen; another 165 papers folded by the end of 1939. Startups did not offset failures. By 1945 the number of U.S. dailies would drop to a twentieth-century low of 1,744, representing a net loss of nearly 200 dailies since 1930.

Knight's *Akron Beacon Journal* was competing with the *Times-Press,* owned by the prosperous Scripps-Howard chain. The Knights were no match financially for Scripps-Howard. Still, Jack thought he could outmaneuver the *Times-Press,* which he figured would be hampered by the dictates and whims of its corporate parent. He hired more reporters, expanded local news coverage, and added comic strips, columnists, and other entertaining features. He believed superior quality sold newspapers. As his brother James later put it, "When we buy a newspaper, we spend money to improve the editorial product. That brings us more readers who read the paper more thoroughly, producing better results for advertisers. More revenues from added circulation and advertising produces better profit. And this we plow back into improving the editorial product still more."

"Get the truth," Jack Knight told his editors, "and print it."

When a strike in the rubber industry crippled Akron's economy in 1936, Knight increased space for news in the *Beacon Journal* even as advertising income ebbed to nearly nothing. Akron's mayor threatened violence against "radicals and Communists," prompting Knight to pen a bold front-page editorial, "No Room for Vigilantes," castigating the mayor and others who would resort to the bludgeon. The editorial was reprinted by the rival *Times-Press.* The strike hurt both Akron papers, but the *Beacon Journal* lured readers from the *Times-Press,* which had cut its newshole. In two years, the Knight brothers would absorb the *Times-Press,* leaving Akron the country's largest city with only one daily newspaper. "We are now solely responsible for printing and distributing information in this city," Knight told his editors. "And that, gentlemen, is sobering."

Knight ran things differently from his father, who had used the *Beacon Journal* to advance his pet political causes. When Jack once asked C. L. which candidate for sheriff the *Beacon Journal* would support in an upcoming election, his father blithely replied, "The one who gives us the county printing business." Repulsed, his son decided that any paper he published would be stubbornly independent of the railroads, breweries, utilities, political parties, and other interests that had manipulated publishers for decades. That meant, of course, that a newspaper had to stand on its own financial feet. Knight grew fond of quoting Dick Jones, an editor in Tulsa who said, "The penniless newspaper, like the penniless young lady, is more susceptible to immoral proposition than one well-heeled." Still, Knight worried that newspapers could so severely distance themselves that they would become as colorless and impersonal as a bank. "Far too many newspapers are languorous when they should be alert, cynical when they should be enthusiastic, cowardly when they should fight," he thundered in a speech at the University of Akron in 1936.

In 1937 the Knight brothers bought the *Miami Herald;* in 1940, the *Detroit Free Press;* four years later, the *Chicago Daily News.* Big-city competition did not scare Jack Knight. He would prevail in Miami and make enormous progress in Detroit, though he eventually would retreat from Chicago. He was a trim man in impeccable suits and gold cuff links, with thinning, slicked-back hair and a square, jutting jaw that fit his stubborn mien. The *Saturday Evening Post* profiled him in 1945. "The parallels between scientific crapshooting and newspaper ownership are not dwelt upon in colleges of journalism," the *Post* said. "But Knight, who never attended one anyway, has applied crapshooting principles to publishing with high success." Yet Knight thought craps had taught him caution in business. "Only a fool," he would say, "plays against the percentages."

He was a businessman born to newspapering, gifted with that intangible journalistic sixth sense, "a nose for news." Knight's biographer, Charles Whited, wrote: "Many publishers inherited newspapers and devoted their energies to business, and it made little difference to them whether the business involved newspapers or dry goods. Knight, on the other hand, devoted himself to news and editorials with aggressive energy." He threw himself into improving each new paper, prodding editors to add reporters, features, columns, and news space. Knight papers became trendsetters, embracing concise writing, human interest stories, and innovative design that made newspapers easier on the eyes. Knight hired smart people and didn't hesitate to mimic other publishers. "If I can borrow, adapt or steal a great idea, that's journalism at its peak," he said. And he was ready for traditionalists who carped about the changes: "A paper has got to be read before it informs anybody."

His editors got a good deal of leeway, but they could expect a steady flow of suggestions and critiques from his typewriter. He wanted tough, bare-knuckled journalism that carefully but unblinkingly exposed the failings and foibles of a community's institutions. "We fawn not upon the mighty," he once wrote. When a Miami politician asked, "What do we have to do at city hall to get right with you?" Knight replied, "Nothing, except be good public servants." Then he rapped out a note to his editor urging even more vigilant reporting on city hall.

The *Free Press* won the Knight group its first Pulitzer Prize in 1945, for stories exposing corruption in the state Legislature. Soon the *Free Press* won a second Pulitzer, the *Miami Herald* won one, and the *Chicago Daily News* snagged a pair. By the mid-1950s the Knight brothers' papers were netting $1 million a year in profits. They purchased the *Charlotte Observer* in North Carolina, then the competing *Charlotte News.* They were on a roll, making money, admired by journalists and businesspeople alike. Jack Knight was the star—the millionaire journalist, the journalist's publisher, courted by presidents, praised by his peers.

His dominance of the company was undergoing a subtle change, though. Brother James Knight, fifteen years Jack's junior, was asserting himself. While Jack got the attention, the accolades, and the quotes in the national magazines, Jim Knight tended quietly to what he called the "nuts and bolts" of the business—the printing, selling, and delivery of papers. He didn't say a lot—"shucks" was a favorite expression—and he was more at home in the pressroom than the newsroom. But he made decisions that were crucial to the future of Knight Newspapers.

In Miami in 1943, a newsprint shortage presented Jim Knight with a difficult choice between sharply reducing the *Herald*'s newshole or cutting advertising to almost nil. At the urging of *Herald* executive editor Lee Hills, Knight gutted advertising. The *Herald* nearly suffocated as the rival *News* gobbled up ad revenue. "It's probably a good thing for brother Jim," Jack Knight gloated to an associate. "Maybe he will get over some of that smug optimism that he enjoys so much." But readers hungry for war news flocked to the *Herald;* when newsprint was again plentiful, the *Herald* put the *News* behind it for good.

Jim Knight pushed for the expansion into North Carolina. Jack resisted buying the *Charlotte Observer,* which offered little of the prestige of operating in Chicago or Detroit. Jim, envying the potential of investing in a growing industrial pocket, insisted he could push the *Observer*'s gross profit to $1 million quickly and $1.5 million in five years. "I like this type of property better than any in Detroit," Jim Knight argued. "The earnings of these small units are terrific by comparison." Jack relented, but told Jim to run the paper. Charlotte would become one of the Knights' most profitable properties.

In the late 1950s the younger sibling again defied his brother by planning a sprawling new printing plant for the *Miami Herald.* He picked a breathtaking site on Biscayne Bay, hired a lawyer to acquire the land secretly, and prepared to make the biggest single purchase of printing presses in history. Jim Knight saw the chance to update the *Herald*'s printing technology, cut costs, add color production, and prepare for a south Florida population boom. Jack Knight saw $30 million being spent. "This is the monster that could kill us," he complained.

Jim was unfazed. "This is the *Miami Herald* plant we're going to need in 1980, maybe even before."

He was right, of course. The industry was entering a new, more difficult period. Television and radio were competing harder for advertising dollars. Printing and labor costs were spiraling upward. Newspapers being produced on ancient presses under decades-old work rules needed to modernize, but labor was asserting itself in strikes and wildcat stoppages. Although the industry was growing—from $2.4 billion in advertising and circulation revenues in 1950 to $4.1 billion in 1960—the players were becoming fewer and larger. By 1960, group operators published more than 550 dailies controlling almost half of the country's total daily circulation. Circulation was on a steady rise, but the number of dailies had leveled off at 1,763.

"It was obvious," Jim Knight said years later, "that the freedoms we enjoy, and which depend on citizens being accurately informed, could not be maintained if newspapers were forced out of business. It was either change or die."

Simply putting out a good paper was no longer enough to survive, let alone thrive. Editors and reporters could not be counted upon to lead the industry into the future. A new crop of newspaper empires was sprouting, a crop that would make the so-called chains of the past seem puny by comparison. They could not be managed by one man from a newsroom in Akron, no matter how brilliant or charismatic or scrupled he was. They required professional managers, schooled in the arts of finance and management, who could wrestle with unions, embrace the computer age, design billion-dollar financial structures, and navigate Wall Street. When Jim Knight went looking for a leader to shape his company for the coming decades, he found him in the publisher's chair in Savannah, Georgia. His name was Alvah Chapman.

Alvah Chapman didn't have to be around Knight Newspapers long to see he had a lot of work to do.

The Knight brothers put out fine papers and made a lot of money, but they were behind the times financially and managerially. They treated the company more like a loose confederation of fiefdoms than a budding empire needing a central genius to prepare it for the future. And there were fiefdoms within the fiefdoms. General managers, who tended to business matters, executive editors, who oversaw the news pages, and editors, who formulated the newspapers' opinions, operated in strict independence of each other, as prescribed by Jack Knight.

Corporate staff was nearly nonexistent, so there was no centralized planning or budgeting. The five newspapers reported financial results separately and differently, so the Knights had no clear idea of how the company as a whole was faring. Some $20 million lay dormant in a non-interest-bearing checking account. A top Knight deputy, C. Blake McDowell, explained that the Knights did not want to upset local bankers by moving the money. Chapman was incredulous. "It's *our* money," he insisted.

At the *Miami Herald,* Chapman found all sorts of little problems that threatened to become large ones. The *Herald*'s paper-and-pencil bookkeeping system was a disaster. Advertisers were regularly refused refunds when the *Herald* made an error in an ad. "A lot of customers were mad as hell at us," Chapman later said. The *Herald* was printing thousands of copies every day that were unaccounted for. When Chapman asked how unsold or returned copies were counted, a pressroom supervisor told him, "Oh, we just pick a number between one and ten."

As in Savannah, Chapman set about fixing things. Repairs made at the *Herald* were rapidly exported to other Knight papers. Chapman was fortunate to be named almost immediately to the Knights' new five-member executive committee, formed at the behest of Jack Knight, who felt his brother had gone behind his back to plan the new *Herald* printing plant. As secretary, "I kept the minutes, but more important, I set the agenda," Chapman recalled. "I could get them talking about things *I* wanted to talk about." In three short years Chapman was named to Knight Newspapers' board of directors. In 1967 he was promoted to executive vice-president of the corporation. By then he had doubled the *Miami Herald*'s revenues and tripled its profits. He would not run the parent company until 1976, but he was, from the start, just as vital a member of its inner circle as its titled leaders—the Knight brothers and their longtime confidant, Lee Hills.

Chapman installed modern budgeting and financial controls. A monthly "Headline Report" consolidated the newspapers' performance and offered month-to-month, year-to-year, and paper-to-paper comparisons. Periodic conferences gave managers and editors throughout the chain a chance to share ideas. A management-by-objective program provided incentive bonuses to, for example, salespeople who landed new advertisers and composing room managers who got pages out faster.

The company embraced computer technology, marrying it to writing and editing, billing and bookkeeping, record keeping and page makeup. Chapman recruited his friend Byron Harless—the same psychologist who had evaluated Chapman for the *St. Petersburg Times*—to professionalize hiring and training practices. The Knight brothers had hired people based on the glint in their eye and the feeling in their own guts. Harless designed psychological tests to analytically discern candidates to lead the company.

Meanwhile, Knight papers burnished their reputation for journalistic quality. In 1968 alone, the chain won an unprecedented three Pulitzers—one to Jack Knight for his column, "The Editor's Notebook"; one to the *Charlotte Observer* for editorial cartoons; and one to the *Detroit Free Press* for its coverage of a deadly race riot. Chapman tried not to disturb the Knights' policy of giving their newspapers great day-to-day autonomy. Until settling in Miami in the early 1970s, the parent didn't even have a central headquarters.

"The net of all this," Jack Knight told *Business Week* in 1970, "is that we don't have so many crises now. We're pretty orderly. But it isn't as much fun any longer." Knight was enjoying the business less and less. In 1966 he privately groused about his brother and Chapman obtaining a joint publishing contract—the equivalent of a JOA—between the *Miami Herald* and the rival *Miami News,* owned by the Cox family of Atlanta. Later he called his brother "a born monopolist," who should have left the *Miami News* to "turn slowly in the wind."

In 1969 he resisted taking the company public. Chapman pushed the idea, arguing that it would give the Knights capital with which to expand and stock that could be used to attract quality managers. Knight had no desire to answer to Wall Street analysts or commit his company to perpetual expansion. He finally gave in, but, addressing financial analysts in February of 1970, he sought to distance his papers from the cold will of the market. "We believe in profitability," Knight declared, "but we do not sacrifice either principle or quality on the altar of the countinghouse."

Knight had disparaging words for the purchase of two jointly owned dailies in Macon, Georgia. "When you've played in the major league," he said, "you don't have much interest in the minors." The same year, Knight voted not to buy the *Philadelphia Inquirer* and *Philadelphia Daily News* from Walter Annenberg. Knight thought the papers were woefully bad and would require a much larger investment than the $55 million purchase price. "I had ten reasons for not buying Philadelphia," Knight said later. "At our final meeting in Cleveland, I called Jim Knight outside and told him it was not too late to stop it. Jim brushed me off." Part of Jack Knight simply didn't want to let go. "Maybe," he admitted in a weak moment, "I just want to run everything." He was in his seventies and slowing down physically, but he still thought he knew as much or more than the younger men who were gradually taking control of Knight Newspapers.

He was increasingly uneasy with the idea of newspaper owners getting as big as companies that made steel, cars, or soap. "I think we have objectives other than simply trying to see how big we can become," he had reflected in a letter to his brother in 1967. "Sometimes the lure of bigness tends to make newspaper publishers forget their prime responsibilities."

His company didn't stop growing, though. In 1974 Knight Newspapers merged with Ridder Publications in what was then the biggest newspaper deal in history. Their stock swap created a new company, Knight-Ridder Newspapers, Inc., that published thirty-five dailies and eight weeklies from coast to coast. Knight-Ridder's total daily circulation of 3.8 million was the largest in America (though Gannett had more papers). The merger made eminently good business sense. The Ridder family owned nineteen small to midsized papers located in the West, the North and the Midwest, offering the Knights a hedge against the cyclical economies of Detroit, Miami, and Philadelphia. Few of the Ridder papers had direct competition. The Ridders—even more than, say, Gannett—were known more for making money than putting out good papers.

The Ridder empire had descended from Herman Ridder, a German immigrant who ran a small German-language newspaper, the *Staats-Zeitung*, in New York in the early 1900s. After his death, his sons, Bernard, Victor, and Joseph, took over and began to expand, buying the *New York Journal of Commerce*. By 1940 they owned papers in St. Paul and Duluth, Minnesota; Aberdeen, South Dakota; and Grand Forks, North Dakota, as well as an interest in the *Seattle Times.* As male heirs proliferated, the Ridders added radio and TV stations, and papers in California, Michigan, Kansas, Colorado, and Indiana. "We are Catholics," Victor Ridder explained. "We have many children and most of them turn out to be sons. We have to buy a newspaper for every son."

The practical, profit-minded Ridder clan made no bones about its priorities. "We'll buy any newspaper we can buy at the right price and bet money we can make a profit," Victor Ridder once said. "We are in this business as a business and if somebody offers us a good price for a newspaper, we'll sell it." The journalistic quality of a Ridder paper depended on who ran it. Some Ridder papers were good, some were marginal, some were terrible. Bernard Ridder, Jr., who became president of the parent company in 1969, liked to compare the various publishers to dukes ruling their own private duchies, oblivious of the rest of the kingdom.

It was Bernie Ridder who saw the wisdom in joining with the Knights. He had been frustrated in his attempts to get the company thinking as one, with common goals and a greater commitment to journalistic quality. Like the Knights, the Ridders had taken their company public in 1969. But some family members didn't believe or understand that going public brought new obligations. They preferred the status quo. Perceiving the company a rudderless ship, Wall Street avoided it.

The papers were making money, but Bernie Ridder thought they could have been faring better—*and* producing better papers. Many were bloated with aging employees, rooted in outdated business practices, and dangerously satisfied that they could forever ride the industry to prosperity. "Whether you were competent or not, whether you worked at it or not, if you were a Ridder, you got a job," recalled one family member. One top editor was said to have told a bright assistant he had little chance of advancement because, "What we need is a constant supply of mediocrity." P. Anthony "Tony" Ridder, the son of Bernie Ridder who would one day become president of Knight-Ridder, remembered, "No one really had control over what was going on, and Dad thought we needed to do something to increase professionalism."

The family also faced the dicey problem of deciding who of the next generation would run the company and get the coveted publishing posts. "It's inevitable in families," Bernie Ridder recalled. "You begin to get certain animosities and even jealousies, and even cliques within cliques." Merging with another company offered a solution. It would force objectivity on the Ridders by diluting the potency of family ties and emotional considerations in corporate decision making. The deal itself could spell out who would run the new company.

Bernie Ridder considered Gannett as a partner. He played golf now and then with Paul Miller and liked him. Miller had made it clear that he'd love to entertain a merger, and the two men once had even sat down with their financial advisers to discuss it. There was some overlap in the Gannett and Ridder chains, but not enough to scuttle a deal. Ridder was more concerned about Miller's ambitious number two man, Al Neuharth. He worried that Neuharth's ample ego would lead him to ease the Ridders out of any significant role in a new company.

Alvah Chapman and Lee Hills were easier to trust. Ridder admired the way the Knights produced such good newspapers while making a handsome profit. Serious negotiations followed a phone call from Chapman to Ridder in early 1974. A deal was announced in July. Lee Hills would be chairman, Bernie Ridder vice-chairman, Chapman president. Two Ridder family members—Joseph, the strong-willed publisher of the *San Jose Mercury News,* and Eric, publisher of the *Journal of Commerce*—opposed the merger. But in November the boards of both companies ratified it.

On December 2, the day Knight-Ridder officially was born, Hills, Ridder, and Chapman sent a letter to employees.

"We believe that editorial quality and economic profitability are inseparable. We believe in change, and our ability to plan and master it. Our primary task . . . is to forge a new company which maintains a singleness of purpose while retaining individuality and difference. It will not be easy."

Jack Knight did not oppose the merger, but he was not wildly enthused. Publicly he defended group ownership, believing his company had bettered every paper it bought. Privately, though, he groused that such mergers were yet another step away from the independence he so cherished. "If I were a younger man," he confided to an editor, "I'd lead a rebellion."

There would be no rebellion, of course. In 1976 Alvah Chapman became chief executive officer of Knight-Ridder Newspapers, Inc. The younger men were leading Jack Knight's company—and his beloved profession—into a new age that would severely test their ability to plan and master change.

By the summer of 1985, Jack Knight had been dead for four years and brother Jim was long retired. There were no other Knights to carry on the family tradition. None of Jim's four daughters was in the business. Two of Jack's three sons had died young; the third ran a Knight-Ridder newsprint subsidiary. The sole Knight who had shown promise of rising to the top of the company, Jack's grandson, Johnny III, had been murdered under scandalous circumstances in Philadelphia. But a good deal of Jack Knight—or JSK, as Knight-

Ridder's executives reverentially referred to him—lived on in the company he had built. Symbolically, jackets were still mandatory in the executive dining room, per JSK. But a more telling sign of his undying influence was the remarkable string of Pulitzer Prizes his papers won under Alvah Chapman.

From 1977 to 1985, Knight-Ridder papers won fourteen Pulitzers for reporting, writing, photography, and editorials. By comparison, the *New York Times* won eleven, the *Los Angeles Times* six, the *Washington Post* and the *Wall Street Journal* four each. Gannett papers won just two. In 1986, Knight-Ridder newspapers would win an unprecedented seven Pulitzers. The prizes weren't everything, but they didn't hurt a company's reputation; Knight-Ridder's was sterling, at least when it came to journalism. Chapman celebrated the prize winners by inviting them to the company's annual meeting for bows before the brass and the shareholders.

The CEO's baton, first at Knight Newspapers and then Knight-Ridder, had passed from Pulitzer-winning Jack Knight to businessman Jim Knight to Pulitzer-winning Lee Hills to Chapman, a businessman, not a journalist. "Knowing he was seen as a business-side operator, he wanted to make sure the journalism side was seen as strong," recalled Jim Batten, the newsman who was Chapman's heir apparent. "He didn't want to be thought of as someone who didn't appreciate the values of editorial excellence."

Knight-Ridder in 1985 was a $1.7 billion company, nearly three times the size it was when Chapman took over as CEO nine years before. Profits had nearly tripled to $133 million a year. The company had ventured into commercial and cable television, started the country's first videotext service, and acquired a couple of new dailies. Chapman's tenure had seen the launch of foreign news bureaus around the globe, an expansion of the Washington bureau, and the creation of a division that sold information on stock, bond, commodities, and money trading markets around the world.

Knight-Ridder was listed in the bestselling book *The One Hundred Best Companies to Work for in America,* cited for teamwork, a "family spirit," and a "human touch" in the managers among its twenty-two thousand employees. Recruits to the sixth-floor executive suites overlooking Biscayne Bay were amazed to find so little corporate backbiting. Executives boasted, with no self-consciousness, of Knight-Ridder "values," "integrity," and "morality." Knight-Ridder was a proud, self-assured company that let deeds do its talking—not unlike its proud, unassuming leader, Alvah Chapman.

Chapman wore conservative suits with drab striped ties and drove himself to work each morning after prayers with his wife, Betty, and a swim in the pool at his modest canal-front home. Just as when he flew the *Battlin' Betty* over war-torn Europe, he was a leader of few words. A steely glare or an appreciative nod was all Alvah Chapman needed to let someone know how he felt. He was well known and respected in his industry, but he did not seek attention for himself or his company. Even within Knight-Ridder he kept a low profile. The *Miami Herald* newsroom was one floor below his office, but on the rare occasion that he strolled through it, plenty of reporters and editors didn't recognize him.

Everything Chapman did was infused with purpose. Guests for fishing were welcomed with a typewritten list of assignments. He might catch a boatload of fish, but he was disappointed if they were the wrong kind or color. "When he took his boat to the Bahamas for the first time you would have thought he was taking the *Queen Mary* around the world," one Knight-Ridder executive said. He prepared for his first time snow skiing by jogging and reading two books on the sport. A game of golf with Chapman was never completely friendly. Tony Ridder once mistakenly hit the wrong ball, then looked to Chapman for sympathy. Chapman told him to take a penalty stroke. Another time, Bernie Ridder suggested they speed the game up by forgoing short "gimme" putts. Chapman wouldn't hear of it.

Nobody prepared like Chapman. "You never go to a meeting with Alvah without preparing," said John C. Fontaine, Knight-Ridder's top lawyer. "He will catch you up." The rigors of life at The Citadel had made Chapman a devotee of detailed lists, schedules, memoranda, and briefings. "He is the best-organized person most of us have ever met," Batten said. "He manages to get more done in a twelve-hour period than anybody I've ever known." When he wasn't running the country's second-largest newspaper company, Chapman made time to get buildings built, campaign against gambling, and fight the drug wars in Miami and Dade County. He likened his schedule to a box filled with croquet balls. "Most people would say it is full, but it isn't," he would say. "You can fit tennis balls in the cracks." And between the tennis balls, golf balls. And marbles between the golf balls, BBs between the marbles. He packed his daily schedule, using the slivers of time between meetings to, say, raise a few hundred thousand dollars for a bayfront project or jot an outline for an upcoming convention speech. Chapman did not leave things for tomorrow. When he left his office every evening, his desk was clean.

His immodest goal was to make Knight-Ridder the world's best newspaper company, by striving to serve equally well its five oft-conflicting constituencies: shareholders, readers, advertisers, employees, and the hometowns of each paper. To Chapman, the balancing act required caution and circumspection. Knight-Ridder was careful about borrowing and wasn't nearly as busy a shopper as, say, Gannett. Alvah Chapman had little of Al Neuharth's instinct for gambling and entrepreneurship. Gannett had ballooned into the country's largest newspaper company by buying and creating things, while Knight-Ridder, for the most part, quietly nurtured what it had. Chapman made no apologies. "If we were the biggest, fine, but that wasn't one of my goals," he would recall. He took more pride in the Pulitzers and in Knight-Ridder's selection as one of the country's best companies to work for.

The company's financial numbers were respectable, but hardly Gannett-sized. Knight-Ridder posted eight consecutive years of rising profits, healthy dividend growth, and a 15 percent margin of profit before taxes. But its return on equity and its growth in sales and profits consistently lagged behind the industry. And 1985 was shaping up as a problem year. Profits were headed lower than they had been in 1984. The profit margin would dip below 14 percent. And there was no recession to explain it away.

Four tumors were gnawing at Knight-Ridder's bottom line.

One was Viewtron, a futuristic service that supplied news, advertising, home banking and shopping via personal computer. Subscribers were scant; Viewtron was losing, on average, more than $7 million a year. Chapman would shut it down in the spring of 1986. Labor troubles were brewing in Philadelphia, the company's richest source of revenue. In September of 1985 the unions would walk off their jobs for forty-six days, costing Knight-Ridder more than $10 million. Meanwhile, profits were falling at the *Miami Herald,* which had lost touch with its increasingly Hispanic audience and was besieged by competition in Broward and Palm Beach counties to the north. Then there was the *Detroit Free Press.* The *Free Press* had lost $35 million since 1979 and was about to lose another $8.4 million in 1985. In fact, the paper represented a tremendous opportunity—if only it could overtake the rival *News* in daily circulation. But that might take years and, in the meantime, the struggle was terribly expensive.

"Detroit was a millstone around our neck," Chapman later recalled. "The analysts, wherever we went, wanted to talk about Detroit. We wanted to talk about other things." Editors at other Knight-Ridder papers grumped that the *Free Press* was bleeding their budgets. "You get tired of saying, 'If we didn't have Detroit, we'd be doing better,' " Knight-Ridder lawyer John Fontaine recalled.

Chapman was determined to fix Detroit before he retired in the spring of 1988. "It was a problem that had grown up on his watch and it had to be solved on his watch," recalled a close Chapman confidant. Winning the war, especially against a company with Gannett's financial muscle, would take longer than a couple of years. But a couple of years was plenty of time to get a JOA up and running and making lots of money.

Which is why Al Neuharth's August 6 phone message was so encouraging. When Chapman returned from his boating vacation, he returned the call. Soon the two men would meet face-to-face. And Alvah Chapman would have a chance to clear his desk before he walked away from his career.

7

Operation Tiger

David Lawrence, Jr., smelled a rat. The *Detroit Free Press* publisher was accustomed to Knight-Ridder requesting information, but never had he seen queries so voluminous and specific. Lawrence was sure something was up. He put in a call to Jim Batten in Miami. The Knight-Ridder president was an old friend who had once been an editor at the *Free Press* and, like Lawrence, had been executive editor of the *Charlotte Observer*.

"David, I can't talk right now," Batten said in his soft southern drawl. It was a Friday afternoon. "Call me at home tomorrow." On Saturday, Batten first instructed Lawrence that what he said had to be kept in strict confidence. Lawrence assured him it would. Knight-Ridder, Batten said, had begun talks with Gannett about forming a joint operating agency in Detroit. "We don't know where this is going to come out," Batten cautioned. "But a JOA is a possibility."

Lawrence's heart sank. The last thing he wanted was a JOA. Indeed, he had just written in his Sunday column, "Loose speculation about JOAs and such can contribute to a perilous sort of momentum toward something most of us would prefer to avoid." For seven years he had struggled to push the *Free Press* past the *News*. Now, just as victory seemed within reach, Knight-Ridder and Gannett would snatch it away by imposing a truce. Lawrence didn't play for ties. He was the kind of guy who dove for shots in office volleyball games. Once, hemmed in by a parking lot traffic jam, he instructed his senior managing editor, Neal Shine, who was driving, to purposely hit another car (Shine complied). Almost from the time he arrived in Detroit in 1978 there had been rumors that a JOA was in the works, but Lawrence had ignored them. After all, why would Knight-Ridder want a JOA when the *Free Press* could take the whole market? When, in December of 1984, Alvah Chapman told Lawrence he was being promoted from executive editor to publisher of the *Free Press,* Lawrence asked, "Do we have time to make a difference?" Chapman would recall saying he planned to "work like hell" to negotiate a JOA—but Lawrence hadn't heard that at all. He had heard that there *was* time to make a difference, to beat the *News* and claim victory. Now, Lawrence didn't quite feel betrayed to hear that JOA negotiations had begun, but it was a dismaying surprise, and he told Batten so.

Which didn't mean Lawrence would resist. He would do what he was told. Meanwhile, he could hope that Chapman and Al Neuharth would have trouble cutting a deal. With a little more time, maybe the *Free Press* finally could overtake the *News.* And Dave Lawrence could dispel the demons that had dogged him and the *Free Press* since his arrival in Detroit seven years earlier.

If there was a turning point in the fortunes of the *Detroit Free Press,* it was December 1, 1978, the day executive editor Kurt Luedtke left the paper and David Lawrence replaced him. Within two years, the *Free Press* would see its last dollar of profit. Detroit would confront the crippling double whammy of a national recession and a wave of cheap, high-quality Japanese imports precipitating an inexorable decline in the might of the Big Three auto manufacturers. The *Detroit News* would accelerate its assault on the *Free Press*'s turf—the morning market. It would be unfair to pin the blame solely on Lawrence. He was in the wrong place at the wrong time. Nonetheless, his arrival put a period to a splendid era, one defined by nearly thirty years of the *Free Press* director's baton passing from mentor to protégé, from Jack Knight to Lee Hills, Hills to Al Neuharth, Neuharth to Derick Daniels, Daniels to Kurt Luedtke, an era during which the *Free Press* became a supremely wonderful place for a reporter to report and a writer to write. Never again would journalists be so important at the *Free Press*—or, with few exceptions, at any American daily.

Jack Knight bought the *Free Press* for $3.2 million in 1940 from eighty-one-year-old Edward Douglas Stair, a crotchety millionaire who had amassed a fortune in theaters, real estate, banking, and Michigan newspapers. The stocky, snowy-headed Stair had run the *Free Press* with a banker's mien and a tyrant's will, intimidating editors, fending off unions, using news pages to stroke friends and buffet enemies. Franklin D. Roosevelt was among the many who, Stair decreed, were not to be treated favorably in the *Free Press.* Stair carped about night baseball because it lured people away from his theaters, and bad-weather forecasts because they discouraged shopping at his advertisers' stores.

His paper was Michigan's oldest daily, founded by John Pitts Sheldon in 1831 as the weekly *Democratic Free Press and Michigan Intelligencer,* a drab five-column sheet that pandered to the Democratic Party. Sheldon had published Michigan's first regular paper, the *Detroit Gazette,* and was once jailed briefly after writing a series of stories critical of the state Supreme Court. When he introduced the *Democratic Free Press and Michigan Intelligencer,* Detroit was just coming into its own as a major river port; the population quadrupled to nearly ten thousand by 1840.

The *Free Press* cast a skeptical eye on the few newspapers that claimed to be objective, explaining that, like a copperhead snake, "the neutral papers never show their colors before they apply their fangs." Subscribers in those days weren't looking for dialogue; they wanted their paper to parrot their political opinions. A paid subscription was tantamount to a party donation.

In 1835 the paper started publishing six days and was renamed the *Detroit Daily Free Press.* By 1900 the *Free Press* had a national reputation as an innovator. It had started Michigan's first Sunday newspaper, the country's first section strictly for women—called The Household—and the first overseas edition, printed in London. One editor, the tempestuous Wilbur Storey, boosted circulation with lurid stories of crime and scandal. "It's a newspaper's duty to print the news and raise hell," he said. A successor, William Quinby, reined in the sensationalism and injected new technology, including the typewriter, typesetting machine, telegraph, and web press. The *Free Press* offered a compendium of local and national news, satire and light humor, intellectual samplings such as poetry and book reviews, and useful features on child rearing, needlework, and women's rights.

It also was in financial trouble. Quinby departed in 1893 to be U.S. envoy to the Netherlands, leaving his two sons to mind the store. He returned in 1897 to find the *Free Press* mired in debt. James Scripps, owner of the *Detroit News,* nearly bought the paper in 1905, but a complication arose involving Ralph Booth, the brother of Scripps's son-in-law, George Booth. Quinby sold to a group of local businessmen led by Frank J. Hecker, who later brought in E. D. Stair, then owner of the daily *Detroit Journal*. By 1917 Stair controlled the *Free Press*.

When Jack Knight bought it in 1940, the once-liberal *Free Press* was as conservative as Stair, criticizing FDR, trade unions, and America's role in World War II. It had won its first Pulitzer Prize in 1932 for exhaustive coverage of an American Legion parade. But it lagged behind both the *News* and the *Detroit Times* in daily circulation. Knight expanded news coverage, added features, columns, and comics, and introduced a new, brighter typeface for headlines. He surprised local business and labor leaders by personally seeking their counsel and criticism. He also inserted the slogan "An Independent Paper" in the masthead on the editorial page. "Under the new ownership," Knight vowed in a page-1 statement, "the *Detroit Free Press* will be politically independent in its editorial policy. It will always be operated in behalf of the general public, uncontrolled by any group, faction or selfish interest and dedicated solely to the public service."

Early in Knight's tenure, an editor asked what to do with a story that would offend a major advertiser.

"You're the editor," Knight said.

"I'll run it," the editor happily replied.

Knight brought in executive editor Stuffy Walters to enforce his unconventional theories on concise writing, snazzy page layout, and human interest stories. Before leaving to edit the *Chicago Daily News*, Walters remade the Sunday *Free Press* into a colorful mix of how-to stories, personality profiles, and snappy pieces on social and cultural trends. "It's no sin to be interesting," Walters liked to say. Editorials remained conservative but were tempered with fairness. The *Free Press* even had an occasional friendly word for Roosevelt. Circulation rose by nearly 100,000. Profits exceeded $2 million a year. In September of 1946 the *Free Press* had a slim daily lead, with circulation of 417,336 to the *News*'s 412,605 and the *Times*'s 405,887.

By the time Lee Hills arrived in Detroit in 1951, the *News* had reclaimed a 12,000-paper lead. Knight had lured Hills from Scripps-Howard to be city editor of the *Miami Herald*. He had worked at newspapers since he swept floors and wrote school news for a tiny Utah weekly at the age of fourteen. Hills was a serious, immaculately dressed gentleman who, staffers joked, pissed ice water. He was a first-rate journalist: The *Miami Herald* under Hills had won a Pulitzer for exposing the involvement of organized crime in the local gambling trade. Hills himself would win one in Detroit for his coverage of the 1955 contract talks between the automakers and the UAW. As a manager, he had a gift for mastering the minutest detail; from his meticulous shorthand notes and memoranda emerged a brand-new *Detroit Free Press.*

Hills aimed to distance the *Free Press* from its afternoon rivals by honing its image as a morning product. Technically, the *Free Press* had long been a morning paper, but most of its first edition, delivered to homes in the morning, went to press at 7:00 P.M., lacking lots of late news and sports. Much of its circulation depended on fickle street sales. The morning market held great potential, but the *Free Press* hadn't had the production schedule or the product to exploit it. A *Times* editor called the *Free Press* "another afternoon paper with a morning hangover." Hills invested in new presses and composing room equipment so that the *Free Press* could print later and publish color photographs. Circulation workers hustled new subscribers via telephone, branching into the suburbs and outstate Michigan. Readers were polled on what they liked and didn't like. Hills reorganized the paper, giving sports its own section and introducing a "second front page" on page 3 to highlight local news and give the illusion of a more open paper. Regular features were set in the same place every day, prompting the slogan "Easy to read, easy to find." Editors stressed good writing and life-style features, especially those appealing to women and young people. Promotions touted "the friendly *Free Press.*" Hills wanted readers to think of the *Free Press* as a loyal, helpful friend, so that they would get emotionally hooked.

More and more, they did.

In September of 1959 the *Free Press* again passed the *News* in daily circulation—and then, for the first time ever, held the lead through the spring reporting period. It was a triumphant moment—but again it would not last. Within months the *News* would recapture the lead by buying the *Detroit Times.*

Jack Knight might have bid for the *Times,* but he did not trust the people at Hearst, the paper's owner. In 1956 he had discussed—secretly, he thought—buying Hearst's *Chicago American.* The *American* would have supplied the Sunday paper Knight's *Chicago Daily News* so desperately needed to survive that circulation war. A deal seemed imminent when the Hearst people suddenly announced they were selling the *American* to the *Chicago Tribune.* Knight felt double-crossed. "We did *not* want to leave Chicago," he said years later.

Instead of seeking the *Times,* Knight, Hills, and their young lieutenant, Al Neuharth, launched a daring counterattack: recruiting the *Times*'s circulation people and offering *Times* subscribers a facsimile of their old paper. It worked well enough, but still left the *Free Press* in a deep hole. In 1962, ten months after the *Free Press* had stopped printing its *Times*-like "Family Edition," the *News* led by 211,000 papers a day and claimed seventy cents of every dollar of advertising revenue.

In the next thirteen years, the *Free Press* would again overtake its rival in daily circulation, recapture gobs of advertising linage and revenue, and produce a snappy, irreverent, enterprising, unpredictable newspaper fueled by the counterculture passions of the Vietnam and Watergate years. People at "the *Freep*" reveled in their underdog role, peering down Lafayette Boulevard at their huge rival, "the *Snooze,*" with ridicule and contempt. The *News* was the Union army, lumbering along in its smug belief that brute force would prevail; the *Free Press* was Jeb Stuart's cavalry, countering with feint and ambush.

The period belonged to Derick Daniels and Kurt Luedtke. Daniels had been one of Neuharth's cronies at the *Herald*. Neuharth brought him to the *Free Press* as city editor in 1961 to replace John Driver, a much-loved newsroom chief who died of cancer. Daniels was the grandson of Josephus Daniels, the onetime secretary of the navy and patriarch of the North Carolina family that published the *Raleigh News and Observer*. Daniels, a dashing southerner with one brown eye and one blue, was at first regarded warily in the *Free Press* city room, where he was dubbed "Magnolia." He rose to executive editor and gradually made the *Free Press* better, sprucing up the design, hiring good people from faraway papers, and refocusing the staff on the needs and desires of the reader. He fervently believed newspapers were losing touch with their customers. To Daniels, reporters and editors were too caught up in keeping their distance and maintaining the illusion of objectivity. Daniels deplored the arrogance of newsroom types who imposed their own, outdated definitions of news on readers. "Today, newspapers and networks are big business," he wrote in 1970. "They cost money to operate, and make money when they do, and they are dangerously near forgetting why they're operating and whom they're operating for. While the communications industry has grown, it seems to me its willingness to pay attention to little voices has diminished. But the times are changing."

Daniels preached the need for what he called "kitchen news": stories that applied directly to the way Americans lived their lives, how they found jobs, chose their schools, cooked their meals, made ends meet. The modern reader, he wrote, was "hungry for information that will help him right now, to do something, or be something, or very simply, that will interest him." "Kitchen news" was not easy to prepare. Many newspeople preferred the familiar routine of covering dull but "important" governmental events. Daniels challenged journalists' traditional notions of news: "Our reader has the right to know what he wants to know and what he needs to know instead of what our outdated mythology dictates he ought to know."

The most tangible example of his ideas debuted on page 1 of the *Free Press* on January 14, 1966. "Action Line" offered the services of *Free Press* reporters and editors to help solve readers' everyday problems. Readers dialed 222-6464 with requests for help. They were looking for a builder who hadn't finished a job. They wanted a pothole repaired. They wondered what a housewife was worth, and whether Eliot Ness had committed suicide. "Action Line" tracked down the builder, got the pothole fixed, pegged the value of a housewife at $172.96 a week, and reported that Ness had had a fatal heart attack "just as he was about to make some real dough for the first time in his life."

"Action Line" gave a big chunk of the front page to readers, who loved it. So many calls came the first day "Action Line" ran that Michigan Bell had to shut the line down. *Free Press* circulation soared by 10,000 in a week, 27,000 in six months, 90,000 in a year. At the *News*, editors sneered at "Action Line" as pandering, but two years later introduced their own version, "Contact 10." Daniels had stolen an idea from the *Houston Chronicle* and refined it into a smart-alecky showcase that played to the public's growing disillusionment with authority and bureaucracy. It was a splendid way to reach middle-class readers in the turbulent 1960s.

Kurt Luedtke wrote the column for its first six months. Then just twenty-six, he had come from the *Miami Herald* branded an impatient young man brimming with talent—and himself. He had left the *Herald* after giving the managing editor a foolish ultimatum: Fire the city editor or let me go. In Detroit, the brash Luedtke quickly made his plans clear. "He wanted to be king of the *Free Press* and he didn't want to wait until he was forty-five," said Neal Shine, then chief assistant city editor of the *Free Press.*

Luedtke got his big break on a hot Sunday afternoon in the summer of 1967. As an assistant city editor, he came in to run the city desk when a disturbance in an inner-city neighborhood festered into a full-fledged race riot. Luedtke sank his teeth into Detroit's biggest story of the decade and never let go. The riot raged for eight days. Forty-three people died. A twenty-block-by-twenty-block ghetto was looted and burned. Army paratroopers and national guardsmen descended on Detroit with tanks and jeeps. At the *Free Press,* working with Neal Shine and the bulk of the city desk staff, Luedtke planned the coverage, deployed reporters, edited stories, and wrote a few himself.

Spot coverage at the *Free Press* and the *News* was detailed and exhaustive. But the *Free Press* distinguished itself with a five-week-long investigation laying bare how each of the forty-three dead met his or her end. The report was remarkable because it was researched by three white journalists—Barbara Stanton, Gene Goltz, and William Serrin—who ventured into riot-scarred areas populated largely by angry blacks who were not inclined to be forthright with the established media. Unlike their latter-day counterparts, Stanton, Goltz, and Serrin could not search databases or demand police documents under the Freedom of Information Act. Computers were a novelty and officialdom wielded great control over journalists' access to its secrets. Legwork and street smarts were the reporters' primary tools; Goltz, an old-timer who once had his nose broken by a Texas police chief he had sent to jail, occasionally used a cheap bottle of wine to loosen up a source.

Their thorough and gripping report did much to rebut the popular notion among whites—and reinforced by some of the *News*'s coverage—that blacks were killed because they broke the law. In an introduction written by Luedtke, the *Free Press* concluded: "A majority of the riot victims need not have died. Their deaths could have been—and should have been—prevented." The coverage won a Pulitzer Prize, the paper's greatest single journalistic triumph over the *News*.

They were heady days. The *Free Press* had nearly quadrupled its yearly profits in the 1960s, pushing the profit margin from 5 percent to 12 percent. In 1969 the *Free Press* added more subscribers than any daily in the country.

The editorial page underwent a transformation. Long as conservative as the *News*, the *Free Press* under editorial page editor Mark Ethridge, Jr., son of the legendary Louisville editor, veered left with Ethridge's passionate criticism of U.S. involvement in Vietnam. In 1969 the *Free Press* backed Richard Austin's losing bid to become Detroit's first black mayor. Under Joe Stroud in the mid-1970s, editorials vigorously supported civil rights, urban renewal, and other liberal causes. Stroud would endorse Jimmy Carter for president, marking the first time the *Free Press* had backed a Democrat since Grover Cleveland.

Luedtke reigned in the newsroom, which he ran as Derick Daniels's protégé even before being named executive editor at the age of thirty-three in 1973. He was a slight, intense, chain-smoking man given to profane outbursts and dazzling displays of writing skill. "I've seen him take copy in which there hid a great story and Kurt would run it through his typewriter and it would get legs and walk around," said Jim Batten, who worked for Luedtke on the city desk. Luedtke called himself a "commercial" editor, for his passion was to sell newspapers. "You don't know," he once told Batten, "how it kills me personally when we're not selling newspapers the way we ought to."

He believed good writing sold papers. He wanted the *Free Press* to take readers where they would never go in the stodgy *News.* "We hoped to create a sense of deprivation in the reader," he recalled. "Do not ever let 'em be able to predict what's going to show up in their morning *Free Press.*" There were run-of-the-mill news stories and there were "*Free Press* stories." Luedtke usually defined the latter, often as he stood next to a reporter's desk, dragging on a cigarette, rocking back on his heels as the reporter pitched an idea. "A good story was something that a lot of people wanted to read," he recalled, admitting, "It might not be real high on true import or deep sociological meaning."

The investigation of the riot deaths was a "*Free Press* story." So was a snarky feature on the wives of several wealthy businessmen opening rival chocolate shops. Or the in-depth look at the reasons for the Kent State shootings. Or the feature on the pretty young woman hitching a ride on the Lodge Freeway. Or the funny piece on the *Free Press* reporter trapped in the mayor's washroom. "If more than two of us thought it was interesting," one of Luedtke's protégés recalled, "we'd go out and [do the] interview." They were the kinds of stories Detroiters talked about over their morning coffee. They were also the kinds of stories people at the *News* talked about, but didn't get into the paper.

There were *Free Press* ways of doing things, too. Like sending a reporter to London when rumors of Paul McCartney's death were rampant. Like having a reporter from the women's section travel the Mideast writing on the aftermath of the Six-Day War. Like getting an exclusive interview with Arthur Bremer's parents by paying for their flight from Wisconsin to Baltimore, where their son was in jail for shooting George Wallace. Like stealing stories that ran in the *News*'s lightly circulated suburban sections, doing them over, and slapping them on page 1 of the *Free Press.*

The *Free Press* had two-thirds the *News*'s staff and a much smaller newshole, so it didn't even try to be a paper of record. Outnumbered staffers prided themselves on finding ways to outdo the *News.* "We were the scrappy little underdog," said Christina Bradford, then a *Free Press* city editor. "If we couldn't be bigger than the *News,* then by God we were going to be better." (A decade later, Bradford would leave Gannett's Rochester papers to become managing editor of the *News.*)

"The only thing we had to sell was entertainment," Luedtke recalled. Writers were his stars. Grunts at most papers, general-assignment reporters at the *Free Press* were the highest form of life. They got the adulation, the juiciest assignments, the best trips. Luedtke stroked them regularly over drinks at the Money Tree and the Detroit Press Club. He hired from all over the country, looking for ambitious young people who wanted to use the *Free Press* as a stepping-stone to better things. If they were a little more rebellious or idealistic than the button-down types that appealed to deans of journalism schools, so much the better—as long as they could write the socks off a story.

A remarkable array of talented reporters and editors plied their trade at the *Free Press* under the auspices of Derick Daniels and Kurt Luedtke. Jim Batten, of course, would one day be president of Knight-Ridder. Gene Roberts would go on to win a batch of Pulitzers as executive editor of the *Philadelphia Inquirer.* Van Gordon Sauter would become president of CBS News. Ellen Goodman would become a nationally syndicated columnist. Ron Martin would be editor of *USA Today* and the *Atlanta Journal and Constitution.* Daniels himself would be president of *Playboy* magazine. Scads of reporters would go on to successful careers at the *New York Times,* the *Washington Post* and the *Los Angeles Times.*

At the *Free Press,* journalism truly mattered. Writing great stories mattered. Knight-Ridder was a faraway company barely mentioned in the newsroom. The grimy task of running the *Free Press*'s business was for bean counters, ad hustlers, and other money changers. The really important work of putting out a paper people wanted to read was done in the *Free Press*'s one-block-long third-floor newsroom, by a bawdy collection of eccentrics, intellectuals, and pseudohippies who drank and partied and slept together, from Sauter, "the Bear," holding court in the easy chair he kept next to his metal desk; to Jim Schutze and Bill Michelmore, renting rabbit costumes to trick-or-treat for beer in Detroit's downtrodden Cass Corridor; to the delicate Barbara Stanton, the writer's writer, who would wear her sunglasses while she wrote to hide her intense emotions.

Their grail was to pass the *News* and stay ahead, once and for all. They *knew* their paper was better, but they craved the numbers to prove it. "We came up with some crazy ideas," recalled *Free Press* reporter Jack Kresnak. "Like, everybody buy three papers on the way home. We figured once we topped 'em, they'd be eating our dust." They almost made it. In the third quarter of 1975 the *Free Press* passed the *News* in daily circulation for the first time in fifteen years. Its average daily circulation of 622,916 gave it an unofficial lead of 8,100 papers a day. Staffers popped champagne corks and pinned on makeshift "We did it!" buttons. They believed it had everything to do with what they'd done for the paper.

But, as before, the triumph was short-lived. By the following March the *News* had recaptured a 5,000-paper lead. Then the *News* began to sell morning papers printed at its new plant in suburban Sterling Heights. The *Free Press* slipped further behind. Luedtke and his charges still believed they would prevail, but some momentum had been lost. Even Luedtke admitted, "The *Detroit News* scares the hell out of me."

Exactly why isn't clear, but as the 1970s wore on, the *Free Press* seemed to lose its edge. Perhaps it was because Luedtke lost interest. Perhaps it was because Luedtke's abrasive personality wore thin. Many staffers grew weary of his tantrums and the coddling of his latest newsroom favorites. If you weren't on Luedtke's A list, life could be miserable. "Kurt made as many enemies as friends," said Gary Blonston, one of Luedtke's A writers. "He's brilliant, no question about that," said another of his reporters. "But he rules by crisis." Yet another put it this way: "He managed by yelling at people and kicking ass." Even Luedtke knew he wasn't a sensitive boss. Once he saw himself in a videotape of a *Free Press* editors meeting, lounging back in his chair, smoking, looking defiant, making wisecracks. You little asshole, he thought. How does anybody work for you?

For the first time in years, *Free Press* people defected to the *News*. First fashion writer Marji Kunz, then reporter George Cantor, film critic Susan Stark, handicapper Al Coffman, cartoonist Larry Wright, and, finally, star sports columnist Joe Falls. "It was pretty clear there was something wrong with Kurt's relations with people," recalled Joe Stroud, editor of the editorial page. "It was sort of a test of wills whenever you were dealing with Kurt." In fact, Luedtke was bored. At thirty-nine, when many a talented reporter had just begun the transition to editor, Luedtke figured he had the best job in newspapering he would ever have. He couldn't see himself spending another twenty years in it.

A few tears were shed when, in October of 1978, Luedtke told the *Free Press* staff he was leaving. To those he left behind, he wasn't the nicest guy in Detroit, but he was one hell of a newspaperman, maybe the best in the city. As Neal Shine recalled, "People who gladly would have punched Kurt in the mouth recognized that this was going to be a significant change in our lives."

David Lawrence, Jr., was about to make certain of that.

With the departure of Kurt Luedtke, David Lawrence became by default the brightest, youngest rising star in Knight-Ridder. At twenty-five he had been an editor at the *Washington Post.* At twenty-eight he shared in a Pulitzer Prize for directing a project on migrant farm workers at the *Palm Beach Post.* At twenty-nine he became managing editor of Knight-Ridder's *Philadelphia Daily News.* At thirty-three he was executive editor of the *Charlotte Observer.* Now, at thirty-six, he took up his company's greatest challenge—winning the Great Detroit Newspaper War.

The quest was perfectly suited to Lawrence, a compulsive workaholic who refused to accept being number two at anything. He took his newspapering cues from his beloved father, an upstate New York farmer who switched to journalism and became the respected capital bureau chief for the *Orlando Sentinel*. Growing up as one of nine children, Lawrence junior recalled, "You were expected to make something of yourself. And there weren't really any excuses."

He made it plain from his first day that, under David Lawrence, the *Free Press* would be the best at *everything*—amassing readers, selling advertising, making money, breaking stories, writing features, correcting mistakes, stroking angry customers. "I never was interested in playing for a JOA or playing for a tie," Lawrence recalled. Winning would take time, though Lawrence didn't behave as if he had much. In his first two months on the job, he spoke one-on-one with each of the *Free Press*'s 225 editorial employees, many of whom had never had more than a brief chat with an executive editor. To get a feel for Detroit, he rode with police on night patrols, attended different churches every Sunday, and visited readers who had written with suggestions or criticisms. Luedtke had avoided community involvement, but Lawrence embraced it, arranging lunches with local power brokers and offering himself to arts and charity organizations.

He charged around the newsroom in stocking feet, shirttails flying, papers crumpled in one hand, a pen in his teeth. Lawrence never went off duty. He toted page proofs and tear sheets with him on fishing trips, to an art auction, to Detroit Tiger games, to an editor's wedding. "Dave was the kind of guy who would call you up at night and say, 'There's a comma out of place on page 11B,' " one of his editors recalled. While other editors passed delivery complaints on to the circulation department, Lawrence personally attended to every one he received. "It was a fetish with him," Joe Stroud said. If Lawrence was having dinner with someone who didn't take the *Free Press,* he would likely as not have them signed up to a trial subscription by dessert. He often drove with a car phone in one hand and some reading spread on the steering wheel; Alvah Chapman finally ordered him to hire a driver so he wouldn't kill himself or somebody else. And then he would order his driver to run an occasional red light.

His wife, Bobbie, a light sleeper, might wake him in the dead of night with a news tidbit she heard on the radio, and Lawrence would be on the phone to the city desk. Editors arrived each morning to tear sheets scribbled over with Lawrence's blue marking pen. The staff finally gave him a set of rubber stamps bearing his pet phrases: "How can this happen?" and "BASIC!" He surprised reporters with complimentary notes they dubbed "Dave Raves," and personally responded to every reader who wrote him, dictating hundreds of personal letters to his secretaries.

His immediate goal was to make the *Free Press* more complete. Under Luedtke, the paper had experienced tremendous highs, but its scattershot approach did not suit Lawrence. He didn't want to gamble on readers buying the *Free Press* to supplement the *News;* fewer and fewer people were reading even one paper a day, let alone two. "Completeness" became his mantra. Lawrence's *Free Press* would offer *everything* readers needed. Some staffers recoiled at the prospect of the *Free Press* becoming as starchy and predictable as the *News,* but Lawrence insisted the paper would change without sacrificing its quirky feel.

He hired more staff and expanded the newshole. He named a national editor and opened bureaus in Atlanta, Toronto, Vienna, and Zimbabwe. Feature sections were repackaged, columnists added, suburban coverage bolstered, business news expanded and showcased. It was classic Jack Knight strategy: Give readers a better product and more will buy it.

Lawrence also tried to instill a more professional management style, seeking staff input, answering staffers' questions promptly and often in writing, holding periodic meetings to discuss methods and ethics, toning down the favoritism that had marred the Luedtke regime. "Dave was almost a textbook public administrator," recalled Stroud. Lawrence installed systems designed to institutionalize fairness for pay hikes and promotions.

He made it his personal mission to court and coddle readers. His signed Sunday column invited them into the *Free Press* newsroom to see and hear how reporters and editors concocted story ideas, followed leads, crafted headlines, chose photographs, and decided which news went where and why. It apologized for mistakes, second-guessed and sometimes defended reporters, questioned editors' judgment, profiled janitors, and gave perturbed readers a forum in which to speak, the publisher standing faithfully by their side. The *Free Press* already printed more letters to the editor than the *News,* but Lawrence believed readers deserved a more prominent place to air their gripes. If that occasionally exposed the paper's faults and foibles, Lawrence thought, so be it. "Readers want to know we're human, imperfect and not very different from them," he told the *Wall Street Journal* in 1983. His column often ended with a plea for readers to write him: "What do you think?"

The column was not universally loved in the *Free Press* newsroom, where some felt it pompous and self-serving, not to mention a bit cuddly for hard-nosed newspeople. "Huggy Bear journalism," some called it. A few worried that it undermined their ability to do their jobs. To those critics it was, at times, as distasteful as a coach singling out a player for public criticism. "It was a joke, of course," said reporter Kresnak, who otherwise respected Lawrence. "You dreaded being in it." At the *News,* Lawrence was viewed as an opportunist making points with readers at the expense of his staff. *News* managing editor James Vesely said the *Free Press* was "friendly" in "the same sense a guy's friendly who's selling you a vacuum cleaner."

For all the improvements Lawrence tried to make, something still seemed amiss. To many veteran staffers, putting out the *Free Press* wasn't as much fun as it used to be. Lawrence seemed more manager than editor, and the *Free Press* "became more like any other operation, a matter of numbers and budgets and so on," one top editor said. As reporter Blonston recalled, "Everybody [had] a college education and made too much money." The newsroom took on an almost corporate feel, as if, with enough memos, plans, and meetings, you could somehow impose order on the disorderly nature of covering the news. Editors became more important than writers. Marketing and reader surveys replaced the delicious intuition that governed Luedtke's *Free Press.* Things were fairer and more predictable, but Lawrence couldn't always rally his troops as Luedtke had. You wouldn't see Lawrence holding court over Cuban manhattans at the Money Tree bar, or posing as a Coast Guard officer to inveigle an interview with the survivor of a shipwreck, as Luedtke once had.

The *Free Press* began losing money. The paper had been handsomely profitable for twenty-five years—save 1968, the year of the nine-month-long labor strike. In 1980, Lawrence's second full year on the job, the *Free Press* lost $4.6 million. The loss grew to $7.8 million in 1981 and hovered in the $7 million to $8 million range through 1985. Counting Michigan's single-business tax and the fees the *Free Press* paid to Knight-Ridder for accounting and other services, the *Free Press* from 1979 through 1985 lost nearly $66 million.

Lawrence's efforts to improve the *Free Press* were expensive. The ratio of labor and employee benefit costs to the *Free Press*'s total revenues rose from 42 percent in 1978 to 51 percent in 1985, representing an increase of nearly $40 million. Newsprint costs also soared as national prices jumped from $300 a ton in 1976 to $535 a ton in 1985. Revenues couldn't keep up, in part because *Free Press* president Don Becker started discounting ad rates to try to boost the *Free Press*'s market share. Total revenues, which had grown by 13 percent a year in 1976, 1977, and 1978, grew by only 8 percent in 1979 and 1981 and declined in 1980 and 1982. Even when revenues were higher than expected, costs often raged out of control. In November 1983 Chapman complained of "incredible inattention to management, when our costs exceed budget by $504,000 in a month when revenue exceeded budget by $274,000. There is no reason to have a budget unless Don Becker and the other *Detroit Free Press* department heads pay some attention to it."

The *Free Press* ad department floundered in confusion, running through five ad directors between 1979 and 1985. Pressmen struggled with the modern equipment in the *Free Press*'s new, $47 million plant on the Detroit River. Planning for the plant had been poor; production problems grew so severe that Byron Harless commuted for months from Miami to ease tensions between unionized pressmen and their nonunion bosses. Daily delivery was a quagmire of mistakes. Hal Bay, president of the *Free Press*'s ad agency, asked to withdraw from bidding on the account because so many people in his own shop couldn't get the paper delivered on time. "If it weren't so sad, it would be almost funny," an embarrassed Bay told Jim Batten.

Michigan's economy, battered by a national recession, was no help. In the late 1970s and early 1980s, nervous Americans weren't buying cars the way they had a few years before—or at least not American cars. U.S. auto sales and production hit twenty-year lows. Michigan unemployment soared to 17 percent, as auto, steel, forging, and heavy equipment plants closed, forcing tens of thousands of workers out of jobs. Many left Michigan to hunt work in the Southwest. Sales of Texas newspapers with their bulging help-wanted sections boomed in Detroit. Ford reported billions of dollars in losses, while the federal government reluctantly rescued Chrysler from bankruptcy.

People didn't stop buying newspapers. On the contrary, the unemployed had time to read and needed help-wanted ads; circulation at both Detroit papers dipped slightly in 1980 and then rose for the next several years. The recession's negative impact was more insidious. Advertisers couldn't afford to spend as much when consumers weren't buying as many cars, dishwashers, and dining room sets. Dozens of supermarkets and a welter of big retailers simply closed for lack of business. J. L. Hudson, Detroit's biggest and oldest retailer, padlocked its downtown location, leaving the city without a single major department store. With fewer rivals, surviving retailers had less need to advertise.

The city and state governments verged on bankruptcy. The Reagan administration shut off the flow of federal funds that Jimmy Carter had funneled to his good friend, Detroit mayor Coleman A. Young. Suicides and welfare claims soared. Shops along Woodward Avenue, once the glittering main thoroughfare of the Motor City, were gutted, burned, boarded up, or cowering behind ugly iron grates. Downtown became a ghost town that workers fled for suburbia as soon as their jobs were done each day. The rest of the city had pockets of bustle and civility, but much of it was a bleak landscape of abandoned buildings and once-proud neighborhoods suffocating in poverty and crime.

Elsewhere, big-city dailies were strangling in the recession's grip. In 1981 and 1982, newspapers in New York, Washington, Philadelphia, Buffalo, and Cleveland stopped publishing. Corporate parents shut many of the weaker papers in cities where they owned two dailies, or simply merged the papers. Afternoon papers, besieged by changing life-styles and daytime traffic jams that complicated delivery, bore the brunt of the closings.

America's big dailies were being swept under by a wave of societal changes for which they had few and feeble responses. The cities they had served and thrived with for decades were riddled with poverty, crime, joblessness, and population loss. Suburban sprawl stretched their newsgathering resources thin and fueled the growth of suburban dailies and weeklies. Television gobbled up more and more national advertising dollars while local "shopper" papers and direct mail nibbled at local advertising. People were less trusting of all the media, viewing them as "rude and accusatory, cynical and almost unpatriotic," *Time* magazine wrote in 1983.

Thousands of small retailers had gone out of business in the 1970s, crushed or swallowed by national chains that trained a stingier eye on ad spending. As the stores consolidated, fewer people made the decisions on where and how much to advertise, and they based their choices increasingly on the cold demographic data churned out by computers. Increasingly, they were reluctant to buy space in more than one big daily in the same market. Better, they figured, to target the slice of the market that bought the bulk of their products—and forget the rest. So, as newspaper expert Leo Bogart has noted, a paper like the *Philadelphia Bulletin* could suffocate on a deficit of $21 million in a market where advertisers spent $1.8 billion in 1981.

Still, newspaper companies weren't exactly struggling; their own industry's steady consolidation helped the corporate goliaths endure the bad times. Profit margins were double the average for all U.S. corporations; in 1982, in the depths of recession, profits at the big publicly held companies rose by an average of 8 percent. But the deaths of the *Philadelphia Bulletin*, the *Washington Star*, the *Cleveland Press*, and other dailies were grim reminders that the business wasn't as easy as it once was. Newspapers had weathered downturns before, but this one hurt more because it inflicted permanent damage on the smokestack industries that were the economic lifeblood of heartland metropolises like Detroit, Cleveland, and Pittsburgh.

In Miami, Knight-Ridder executives scrounged for ways to heal the festering Detroit sore. Alvah Chapman and Bernie Ridder flew to Atlanta to try to peddle the *Free Press* to Cox Enterprises. Cox said no thanks. The Newhouse chain also took a pass at buying the paper. A JOA in Detroit was beginning to look attractive. "There's no reason to believe that the Detroit-area economy will rebound sharply anytime soon," Jim Batten wrote Chapman in October of 1981. "Unless we're prepared to slug it out for five to ten more years, gradually wearing down the *News,* our most attractive possibility is to shoot for an acceptable [JOA] arrangement in the next two, three or four years."

Chapman already had discussed a JOA at least twice with Peter Clark. The first time, in January of 1981, they met in Chapman's Palace Hotel suite in New York. Chapman told Clark the dire economy offered an unusual opportunity for a JOA. The Newspaper Preservation Act of 1970 required that at least one paper be "failing" to qualify for an agency. Chapman's lawyers had advised him that both the *News* and the *Free Press* already were "failing," but a few more years of losses would make their application "ironclad." Clark said it would be "difficult" to agree to a JOA that interfered with the *News*'s independence. In further discussions over the next year, Clark repeatedly let it be known that the *News* didn't need a JOA. In any case, Clark said, no JOA would be acceptable to the owners of the *News* unless they controlled the arrangement. Moreover, they insisted, the *News* would publish the sole Sunday paper and be permitted to retain enough morning circulation to remain Michigan's largest daily. "The *News* is the mother lode," Clark told Chapman. "If we have to subsidize it for ten years with other parts of the company, we will do so."

Chapman dispatched Knight-Ridder executive Richard Capen, Jr., to talk with Bob Nelson. They did not get along. Nelson was even more stubborn than Clark, insisting that the "dominant" *News* control any JOA. Chapman thought their demands outrageous. The *News* surely was losing more money than the *Free Press—twice* as much, according to Chapman's advisers. Clark insisted otherwise, but he would not show Chapman actual figures. Chapman began to wonder if his people were guessing wrong. His top financial executive, Robert Singleton, reassured him: "Using [Clark's] logic and adjusting it for some of my own lends even more credence to our estimate."

The *News* people dug in deeper when the trade magazine *Editor and Publisher* quoted an unnamed Knight-Ridder official saying "it is just a matter of time" before the *Free Press* would prevail. An enraged Nelson fired off a reply: "If the Knight-Ridder big shots in Miami really believe that money and time alone will solve their Detroit problems, they are stupid beyond measure and arrogant beyond belief. And rich, they will remind me."

The war in Detroit was heating up for everyone to see. BITTER SHOW-

DOWN IN MOTOWN, blared a headline in *Time* magazine. RIVAL PAPERS IN DETROIT BAR NO HOLDS IN FIGHT THAT ONLY ONE MAY SURVIVE, said the *New York Times*. WILL THE NEWS SURVIVE? asked *Monthly Detroit* magazine.

When the *Free Press* started giving away papers at McDonald's, the *News* matched the deal at Burger Chef. The *News* printed a major investigation of judicial corruption; the *Free Press* suggested it was racially motivated. The *Free Press* ran a baseball trivia contest; the *News* published the answers in advance. The *Free Press* won a Pulitzer in 1981 for photographs taken in a Michigan prison; the *News* won one in 1982 for its investigation of the strange death of a navy recruit—a story the *Free Press* initially had broken. The *Free Press* retaliated by hiring one of the *News*'s two Pulitzer-winning reporters; someone from the *News* sent Lawrence a cactus with a note reading, "Thanks for taking more of our dead wood."

"It used to be more like a cricket match with a lot of 'good show' and 'well played,' " Neal Shine, the *Free Press*'s senior managing editor, lamented to the *New York Times* in 1982. "Lately it has gotten more serious. I think people know the stakes are a lot higher now." In case that fact slipped their minds, in Lawrence's office stood a display of delivery boxes from defunct papers, bearing the inscription LEST WE FORGET.

By 1984 any hope of armistice had dissolved. "Detroit is KRN's number-one problem," Knight-Ridder vice-president Frank Hawkins, Jr., wrote to the company's top managers in January. Hawkins was a former wire service reporter whose job was to stay in touch with Wall Street analysts, who frequently asked when and how Knight-Ridder would fix the *Free Press*. "The continuing losses in Detroit are a major factor in holding down our [stock price] and damaging our performance record vis-à-vis the other companies in our industry. Absent Detroit, KRN's record is easily one of the best in the industry."

It was time for a bold stroke. The people at Knight-Ridder and the *Free Press* called it Operation Tiger.

The blueprint for Operation Tiger was drafted in a series of secret, all-day sessions at the Boca West resort in Boca Raton, Florida, and the Sonesta Beach Hotel on Key Biscayne in February and March of 1984. The upbeat sessions were led by Jim Batten and attended by nine other Knight-Ridder executives and the *Free Press*'s field generals, executive editor Dave Lawrence, publisher Don Becker, and editor Joe Stroud. Also in attendance were Sam McKeel and Eugene Roberts, Jr., publisher and executive editor, respectively of the *Philadelphia Inquirer*.

McKeel and Roberts were invited because they had won a newspaper war on a scale approaching that of the Detroit battle. During the 1970s the *Inquirer*'s mortal enemy had been the *Philadelphia Bulletin,* owned by the McLean family, who were friendly with Peter Clark and Bob Nelson of the *Detroit News.* Like the *Free Press,* the *Inquirer* was a morning paper that trailed its afternoon rival in daily circulation. "Nearly everybody reads the *Bulletin,*" went the jingle. Also like the *Free Press,* the *Inquirer* journalistically was a nimble, lively, choose-your-spots competitor, while the *Bulletin,* like the *Detroit News,* was a lackluster paper of record. The *Inquirer* had advantages the *Free Press* lacked, such as the dominant share of Sunday classified advertising and the indirect aid of Knight-Ridder's *Philadelphia Daily News,* an afternoon tabloid that appealed to blue-collar readers who might otherwise have bought the *Bulletin.*

The Knights had hired Gene Roberts away from the *New York Times.* He had learned the trade as a reporter and city editor under Lee Hills and Derick Daniels at the *Free Press.* At the *Inquirer,* the Frog, as his staff affectionately called him, hired some eighty reporters, expanded the newshole, opened foreign bureaus, and pushed investigative reporting. He keyed his reporters to knock-'em-dead coverage on the biggest stories, like the 1979 nuclear mishap at Three Mile Island, for which Roberts deployed nearly his entire staff. Beginning in 1975, the *Inquirer* won Pulitzer Prizes for six consecutive years.

Meanwhile McKeel, together with Roberts's other business-side counterparts, went after the *Bulletin*'s money. They stole the popular *Doonesbury* cartoon from the *Bulletin* and added a batch of other strips. They increased spending on promotion, targeted suburbs for circulation and advertising growth, and countered *Bulletin* attempts to steal Sunday classified share with cut-rate deals. In the mid- to late 1970s, the competitive strikes were part of a carefully plotted strategy called the Win Plan.

By 1980, *Bulletin* publisher William McLean III, grandson of the paper's founder, was seeking a JOA. A deal was at hand when McLean abruptly backed off. He had a buyer for the *Bulletin*—Charter Media Company, a partnership of oil and magazine magnate Raymond Mason and newspaper publisher Karl Eller, who had sold his company, Combined Communications Corporation, to Gannett for $370 million. Charter didn't want to spend the millions necessary to keep the *Bulletin* strong while the JOA application was pending. Instead, it laid off workers, froze wages, and remade the *Bulletin* into an eye-catching spread of color photographs, elaborate graphics, and investigative projects. But it was too late to stanch the bleeding. The *Bulletin*'s belated launch of a morning edition in 1978 failed to stop the *Inquirer* from vaulting into the daily circulation lead in 1980. With the daily lead went the advertisers, and the *Bulletin* lost a total of $35 million in 1980 and 1981. When Charter again sought a JOA, Knight-Ridder declined. The *Bulletin* was too crippled financially to make a JOA worthwhile.

On January 29, 1982, the *Bulletin* closed.

Two years later, Knight-Ridder hoped to export the Philadelphia Win Plan to Detroit. The Operation Tiger sessions were called to develop a plan that would make the *Free Press* dominant by every measure of circulation, advertising, and editorial content. The final objective was two-pronged: gradually become profitable by gaining dominance of the Detroit market or, failing that, exert enough pressure on the *News* to force its owners back to the JOA bargaining table. Detroit, Jim Batten told the Knight-Ridder board, was "a prize worth fighting for."

The Tiger plan, named for Detroit's heavy-hitting pro baseball club, called for all sorts of costly editorial improvements, including more staff, more newshole, more color, more news of affluent suburbs, enhanced coverage of sports and business, new specialized sections, and an expanded TV guide. Production would be revamped to produce more papers printed after midnight. Preliminary planning would begin for a multimillion-dollar expansion of the riverfront printing plant.

Circulation workers would attack *News* strongholds in the city and blue-collar Macomb County while in addition targeting affluent areas where the *Free Press* traditionally fared better than the *News*. An advertising push would focus on boosting the *Free Press*'s share of the all-important classifieds. Circulation and advertising prices would be gradually pushed up. Promotion on radio, TV, and billboards would be increased, as would research of reader desires. Ultimately, the planners hoped, *Free Press* daily circulation would rise to 670,000 by the fall of 1986—which in theory would give it a slim lead over the *News*. Meanwhile, they projected, the paper's share of Detroit's advertising linage would rise to 50.9 percent by the end of 1987.

Lawrence, Becker, and Stroud authored a "mission statement" brimming with confidence: "To the *Detroit News,* the strategy, as it unfolds, will be like watching wave upon wave of assault troops pour across the line and against every point in the perimeter of its base camp." Batten told the Knight-Ridder board: "It has been a long war. We are proposing to strike now with force, to convince the *Detroit News* management that this is not simply one final lunge but the stepped-up offensive of a durable competitor." Addressing Wall Street analysts in October of 1984, Chapman said, "You might ask why we're adding these improvements now. The answer is, in our judgment, the timing is right and we can afford it. We clearly believe the momentum is in our favor."

Knight-Ridder and *Free Press* people did not expect immediate results.

The first phase of Tiger would cost nearly $27 million, and losses exceeding that were budgeted for 1984–86. The original Tiger plan didn't target a date for profitability. Chapman himself cautioned the Knight-Ridder board that "we should not enter this program unless we are willing to stay with it for a long enough time to fairly assess the results." The primary goal was to overtake the *News* in daily circulation. All else—the Sunday lead, ad linage, revenue, profits—would follow.

A year later, Knight-Ridder was comfortable enough to give a reworked "Tiger II" added firepower: $22.3 million worth of new printing presses for the riverfront plant. The board—save two of its sixteen members—bought Lawrence's argument that the added presses were crucial to gaining "total dominance" in Detroit. Lawrence argued that Tiger had been such a success that the *Free Press*'s printing plant could not handle new business and, more important, *potential* new business. Press capacity was a chronic impediment to circulation growth; the *Free Press* was printed on fewer presses than almost any daily in the country. New presses would enable the paper to print more copies with late sports scores, blunting the key advantage of the *News*'s morning edition. In a memo to the board, William A. Ott, Knight-Ridder's senior vice-president of operations, called the expansion "crucial to our winning dominance in one of the nation's top half-dozen markets." If the *Free Press* had been a baseball team, the plant expansion would have been the clutch relief pitcher acquired in August to take the team to the pennant.

The new equipment wouldn't be up and running until 1987, but again, Knight-Ridder was willing to wait. The executives were certain the *News* was losing a lot more money than the *Free Press.* And by now there were ominous signs that the Evening News Association might actually lose the paper in a scrape with restive shareholders. Indeed, a couple of investors considering a bid for the ENA—a Hollywood producer by the name of Jerry Perenchio and a Nashville meat-packer and TV station operator named George Gillett—had been asking whether Knight-Ridder might like to combine in a JOA if they could snag the ENA.

In January of 1985 Dave Lawrence became publisher of the *Free Press.* The move was a departure from Jack Knight's decree that business and editorial managers be equal partners, for Lawrence now oversaw both sides of the *Free Press.* Chapman had long disagreed with Knight's beliefs on this count, arguing that a single person had to be held accountable for a newspaper's performance. Knight-Ridder promptly gave Lawrence as deputies two generals from the Philadelphia war, Jerome Tilis and Robert Hall.

Knight-Ridder had its share of Tiger doubters. Board member Clark

Clifford, the eminent Washington lawyer and lobbyist, voted against buying the new presses. Bernie Ridder abstained because he felt the investment wasn't worth it. Amused at the bravado of Lawrence, Tilis, and Hall, Ridder promised to buy them all Cadillacs after they had the dominant share of classified advertising, something he was sure he would never see. "You're going to tell me you won in Philadelphia and now you're going to win in Detroit," Ridder lectured them. "Don't forget in Philadelphia you were fighting the Italians. In Detroit, you're fighting the Germans."

Indeed, Tilis and Hall quickly discovered that Bob Nelson was not Charter Media. When the *Free Press* cut a rate for this or that customer, the *News* promptly matched or beat it. Yet Nelson avoided across-the-board discounts, aiming his counterpunches to frustrate *Free Press* efforts to boost share in such moneyed areas as Oakland County and the Grosse Pointes. Bulldog Bob Nelson was determined not to get beat by "those clowns from Philadelphia," as he referred to them. He even had a couple of ex-*Bulletin* bosses, Richard McClennen and Frank Ferriolo, directing ad sales. They wanted Tilis's and Hall's blood. "We'll go out and fight fire where we've got to fight fire," Nelson exhorted his troops.

None of which fazed Dave Lawrence and Company. Though the *Free Press* many months ran hundreds of thousands of dollars behind budget, it was making progress in several circulation and advertising niches. Most important, it was steadily chipping away at the *News*'s daily circulation lead. And the centerpiece of the Tiger plan—the riverfront plant expansion—wasn't even in place yet. When the *Free Press* broke ground for the project in 1985, Chapman said, "This investment reaffirms our confidence in our prospects in the Detroit market and in our newspaper and its management and employees."

As the takeover noose tightened around the Evening News Association, the mood in the *Free Press* newsroom turned jubilant. The war seemed to be nearing an end. Staffers whooped and exchanged high fives. "There was this almost arrogant feeling of victory at the *Free Press,*" recalled *Free Press* reporter David Everett. William Mitchell, then an assistant managing editor of the *Free Press,* remembered, "The psyche of the place was, [the *News*] was going to be bought by Jack Kent Cooke or those other bozos, Lear and Perenchio." Even the emergence of Gannett didn't dampen the mood much. Lawrence and his bosses in Miami figured Al Neuharth would raise prices, as he had at most Gannett papers. The *Free Press* could then hike its own prices, start making money again, and pass the *News* anyway, since it was a better paper sold when most people wanted it, in the morning. Certainly businessman Neuharth wouldn't perpetuate Nelson's masochistic practices. And certainly Gannett couldn't hope to compete journalistically with Knight-Ridder. Sure, Neuharth would gussy up the paper with color and other graphic gimmicks. Beyond that, though, what could he bring that was new and vital to big-city, competitive newspapering? He hadn't played Detroit hardball in more than twenty years.

By early 1986 the *Free Press* had narrowed the *News*'s daily circulation lead to a few thousand copies. The first critical step toward winning the war—overtaking the *News* in daily circulation—was at hand. Dave Lawrence could taste it. He knew a JOA might be in the works, but he was thinking victory. Preparing a major Knight-Ridder presentation, he wrote, "Take a look past your current impressions of Detroit and look at the *Free Press*. You'll find the makings of a winner."

Alvah Chapman had other ideas.

Two weeks after Al Neuharth's overture to Jim Batten on August 6, 1985, Chapman returned the call to confirm Knight-Ridder's interest in a JOA.

Chapman and Neuharth met face-to-face in the Gannett suite, 38-H, at the Waldorf Towers in New York on September 25. Chapman brought Batten and financial executive Bob Singleton. Neuharth was accompanied by Gannett president John Curley and vice-chairman Doug McCorkindale. They chatted mostly, getting reacquainted, touching on little of substance. Chapman told Neuharth he wanted as close to a fifty-fifty deal as possible. The Knight-Ridder chief had been coached extensively by Singleton and Knight-Ridder's top lawyer, Jack Fontaine. Fontaine had urged him in a memo, "We must make it clear that while we would prefer an agency on a fair and reasonable basis, we don't *have* to have one. We believe long-term the tides are in our favor, and if necessary, we'll stay the course. If Gannett can carry *USA Today*, we can carry Detroit."

Neuharth and his deputies listened, then Neuharth smiled charmingly and said, "As you know, Alvah, we're the new guys in town. We don't know quite as much about the market as you. We appreciate the details you've offered, but I hope you won't mistake our silence for acquiescence or agreement." Curley, stifling a smile, was reminded of two heavyweight boxers circling each other in the ring.

A half-hour cab ride away on Wall Street, wishful rumors were circulating that a JOA was in the works. "For Knight-Ridder, the entrance of Gannett into the Detroit newspaper war zone is an unmitigated windfall," analyst John Kornreich wrote. He envisioned JOA profits of $93 million within five years.

By the time Chapman, Neuharth, and their lieutenants met February 4 at the Eden Roc Hotel, Yacht and Cabana Club in Miami Beach, they were close to agreement on several important issues. Neuharth agreed early that Gannett and Knight-Ridder would share the profits of a JOA close to evenly, setting aside Peter Clark's demands for as much as 70 percent of the take. Neuharth also jettisoned Clark's insistence that the *News* retain some home-delivered morning circulation, agreeing with Chapman that having both the *Free Press* and the *News* delivered mornings would be inefficient. However, Neuharth held fast to Clark's rejection of a JOA controlled by Knight-Ridder. On this point, Neuharth was inflexible, which was no surprise to Chapman. This would be the biggest JOA in history, and Neuharth's ego would not tolerate it being seen as anything but Gannett's.

The issue was so important to Neuharth that he refused to call the talks serious so long as control remained unresolved in his favor—hence his fibs when asked publicly about JOA prospects. Still, his lawyers and accountants were busily exchanging financial data and bargaining positions with Knight-Ridder. Even before Gannett closed its purchase of the *News* on February 18, the JOA talks were further along than they ever had proceeded when Peter Clark headed the *News*.

Some of Neuharth's closest advisers were surprised at how swiftly the negotiations were progressing. Neuharth obviously wanted this deal badly. "Just get it done," he kept telling his associates. Doug McCorkindale, the shrewd ex–Wall Street lawyer, was Gannett's top dealmaker; he was hardly a circumspect type, but he felt uneasy proceeding at such a pace. Move too fast and you risked not making the best possible deal. Certainly one of McCorkindale's criteria never was to "just get it done." But Neuharth was in no mood to wait. He made that abundantly clear on March 5, two days before he and Chapman had scheduled another meeting in Washington. On Gannett's sixteenth day in the Great Detroit Newspaper War, Neuharth fired a shot across Knight-Ridder's bow: He cut the price of the *Detroit News*.

8

Sabbath

Dave Lawrence couldn't believe his ears. *Detroit News* reporter Walter B. Smith was telling him Al Neuharth had announced that, effective March 31, 1986, the *Detroit News* would reduce the newsstand price of its outstate editions by a nickel, to fifteen cents. The white-haired Smith was one of the *News*'s oldest and best business reporters. He didn't enjoy being lectured by his sources, but he dutifully noted the homily Lawrence bestowed on him on March 5, 1986. "Why would you lower your price if you believe your readers are getting a good value at the price you are charging?" Lawrence ranted into the phone. Smith had no answer. "Readers are smart," Lawrence said. "They're willing to pay for value."

Cutting the price truly seemed absurd, even to such a battle-scarred veteran as Lawrence. Both Detroit papers had held off on needed price increases before, and of course their rampant discounting had been costing them millions of dollars every year. But never in Lawrence's memory had either publicly *reduced* prices. He told his staff that the *Free Press* intended to stand pat. "We place value in what we do," he declared.

Again, Alvah Chapman had other ideas. When he heard about Neuharth's price cut, he ordered it matched. It would cost the *Free Press* $1 million or so, but money wasn't the issue. "We needed to let Gannett know if they wanted to fight a war, it was going to be a long one," Chapman recalled. Tony Ridder, who had just left Knight-Ridder's San Jose paper to become president of the company's Newspaper Division, called Lawrence to tell him the *Free Press would* follow the *News*'s price cut. Lawrence was beside himself; Knight-Ridder almost never overruled its local executives. The publisher argued briefly, but Ridder told him the decision was final. Lawrence appealed to Chapman, to no avail. The edict from Miami portended an unsettling new reality for Lawrence: he was but a small player in a game of psychological warfare he knew little about. It was disturbing enough to have Miami calling the shots; worse, though, was the specter of Al Neuharth manipulating the *Free Press* from afar.

By the end of the day, Lawrence announced that the *Free Press* would match the *News*'s price reduction. "We are simply doing what the *News* has done—no more, no less," he insisted. "We will meet our competitor on every front."

The front on March 7 was suite 1000 in the fashionable Capital Hilton in Washington, D.C. Neuharth, John Curley, and Doug McCorkindale faced off against Chapman, Jim Batten, and Byron Harless. Before the meeting Neuharth told Curley and McCorkindale, "We're through farting around. They have to understand that the issue is control and there's no backing down on that."

The meeting dragged on for five hours. Neuharth grew impatient. Chapman made another speech detailing the *Free Press*'s advantages: It dominated the morning market. It attracted more upscale readers. People who read both papers favored the *Free Press*. It had greatly narrowed the daily circulation gap. It looked sharper and was stronger journalistically. It had a strong, young management team. Neuharth had heard all of this before. When Chapman finished, he blew up.

It wasn't a full-blown tantrum, but Neuharth left no doubt that he was fed up with talk. "Life's too short for me to go over all this stuff again," he fumed. "Let me make it clear: There is some room for negotiation on the profit split. There is *no room* for negotiation on the question of governance in Detroit. None. We're going to have control. Period."

Harless looked at Neuharth and said, "It seems to me it gets down to basically one thing, and that's control."

"You got it," Neuharth shot back. Furthermore, he declared, these talks were finished until Knight-Ridder decided Gannett would control any JOA in Detroit.

Why was control so important?

For several reasons, some of which—but not all—had to do with running a business well. If asked, Neuharth would say he believed equal partnerships led to indecision, and indecision, in turn, to trouble. With one company firmly in control of the JOA, there would be no indecision. In Detroit, that company had to be Gannett. Neuharth believed Gannett, which was in seven JOAs, was more savvy about running the peculiar operations than Knight-Ridder, which was involved in JOAs in Miami and Seattle. Also, Gannett had ceded control in other JOAs, with disastrous results.

Since his impoverished childhood, Neuharth had steadfastly avoided trusting his fate to others. Even in the doomed *SoDak Sports* venture he had made sure he controlled 51 percent of the enterprise's ultimately worthless stock. "If he doesn't control it, he's not interested," said Charles Overby, Neuharth's longtime right-hand man. "He doesn't have the patience to sit around and try to come to consensus. He wants to get it done."

Control also would indicate which paper had won the Detroit battle, a reality to which both companies were highly sensitive. In interviews, Neuharth would insist it didn't matter to Gannett, since the company had not been in Detroit long enough to get credit or blame for the war's outcome. But Neuharth didn't want to look as if he had caved in to Knight-Ridder and Chapman. He was sure he could outfox Chapman at the bargaining table. "He thought Chapman was a Sunday school teacher," said one of Neuharth's closest colleagues. To Neuharth, Chapman was "a prissy person who didn't have guts, who didn't have the drive" of Al Neuharth. In his 1989 autobiography, Neuharth would call Chapman "a careful, cautious member of the church consistory. Delay and pray is his style. If in doubt, he won't reach for a deal."

Chapman acted the gentleman. He was occasionally amused by Neuharth and his indulgences, but Chapman rarely said anything about his rival. Even when others joked about Neuharth's flamboyant style, Chapman kept a poker face. Still, the rivalry was palpable. The JOA talks were not just a simple negotiation, but the natural extension of a bitter and protracted war. Neuharth hadn't been involved in that war in many years, but he and Chapman had deep roots in it nonetheless. "They were competitors," said a top Gannett executive who was intimately involved in the negotiations. "You knew it in the industry. That's normal between two [company] heads, but this was even more so because they had both been in the same organization at the same time. You could see it. It was a little bit of one-upsmanship as you went through the negotiations."

Chapman was at least as sensitive as Neuharth to the perception of who prevailed in Detroit. He did not want to discourage *Free Press* people, who deeply believed they were on the verge of winning. But the *News*'s circulation and advertising advantages wouldn't permit the *Free Press* to claim unconditional victory, at least not yet. "We hoped to move eventually to an agreement [in which] neither side would be seen as having lost the battle of Detroit, for the sake of our people at the *Free Press,* for the sake of the *Free Press,* for the sake of Knight-Ridder," Jim Batten recalled. Said Bernie Ridder: "The idea was to say we fought to a draw. That was very important to Alvah."

To qualify for the antitrust exemption that made a JOA attractive, one of the papers had to prove it was in probable danger of financial failure. But it wasn't easy to discern which Detroit paper was more likely to expire. Chapman and Neuharth considered having both papers file as "failing," but their lawyers dissuaded them, arguing that such an unprecedented approach would be risky. Because the *Free Press* had lost more money and trailed the *News* by most measures of circulation and advertising, Chapman and Neuharth agreed that the *Free Press* would be the "failing newspaper" for the sake of the JOA application.

Chapman accepted this with characteristic stoicism. "I regarded it as one of the difficult things we had to do to get from A to B," he recalled. Being tagged a failure would no doubt hurt the *Free Press* people, but the sting would be forgotten once the JOA went into place. With the morning market to itself, the *Free Press* would swiftly become Michigan's largest daily. And if the *News* could not stave off the circulation cancer that afflicted so many other afternoon dailies, the *Free Press* might one day have all of Detroit to itself.

The short term promised pain, though. If Chapman surrendered control of the JOA, Neuharth would have two whips with which to lash the proud people of the *Free Press.* Control of the JOA and the "failing" label each could be portrayed as evidence that the *News* had won the newspaper war; and if, by chance, someone inferred that Gannett and Al Neuharth had engineered the victory, Neuharth wouldn't mind one bit.

Worse, the "failing" tag stood to actually harm the *Free Press.* If government approval of the JOA didn't come quickly, the *Free Press* risked scaring away advertisers and top-notch employees. If the JOA was denied after a lengthy legal fight, the *Free Press* might be so crippled that it would have to close—and Gannett would have vanquished Knight-Ridder. Neuharth secretly referred to this scenario as the "big win." "Winning," he would write in his autobiography, "is the most important thing in life. Everything pales in comparison to the feeling of winning."

If Neuharth's March 7 tantrum at the Capital Hilton was more than theatrics, though, the JOA was in jeopardy. The outstate price cut signaled it was a mistake to think Neuharth would raise prices—even though his accountants were churning out memos showing how higher prices and an end to subscription discounts could push the *News* into the black. Chapman had no more stomach for these suicidal games. He had to find a way to give Neuharth the control he wanted without fully ceding Detroit to Gannett.

In the Gannett camp, Neuharth had focused on control to the exclusion of nearly all other issues. His top advisers, including Curley, McCorkindale, and lawyer Bill Keating, urged him to drive a harder bargain on several fronts. Neuharth ignored them.

Keating had assembled the Gannett-run JOA between Cincinnati's *Enquirer* and *Post*, and was intimately familiar with Gannett's other agencies. He was convinced that Neuharth should try to negotiate a so-called host-tenant structure. In a host-tenant JOA, one newspaper dominated absolutely. It hired the business-side workers and ran all the business operations while the other paper existed solely as a newsroom. Because the union contracts and business practices of the dominant paper prevailed, there was no need to reconcile differing union contracts, develop new work practices, or choose between conflicting systems, all difficult and costly processes. The host-tenant arrangement avoided cultural clashes over policy issues such as pricing, promotion, and labor negotiations. It was cleaner, simpler, and more profitable. Given the egos involved, it may have been difficult to negotiate. Neuharth did not pursue it.

In memos and meetings, Neuharth's advisers urged him to seek a profit split more closely reflecting the *News*'s 60-plus percent share of advertising linage and revenue. Neuharth wasn't interested. They argued that the *News*'s huge Sunday circulation lead entitled it to produce the entire Sunday paper in a JOA. Knight-Ridder was arguing for jointly produced weekend products. "Joint news publications don't work because of staff jealousies and coordination problems, which obviously affect the product," McCorkindale had written to Neuharth in January. But Neuharth agreed to the joint weekend papers. "He wouldn't take advice," complained a top Gannett executive. "He was told not to do the deal we did. He *had* to do a goddamn deal. He was in a hurry to get something done.

"It was an ego trip. He was so anxious to beat up on Alvah and gain control that some of the pieces of the picture were missing. Some of us felt the *News* was in a much stronger position than others. We weren't [in Detroit] long enough to really know all the pluses and minuses."

Another Gannett executive involved in the negotiations said Neuharth pursued three items with great vigor: First was control. Second, he wanted a slightly larger than 50 percent share of the profits in the first few years of the JOA's hundred-year duration. Third, he wanted the *News*'s name to appear first in the masthead on the jointly produced Saturday and Sunday papers, as in the *Detroit News and Free Press.* "Anything else was not significant because [those three points] would make it look like he had prevailed in the negotiations—he *Neuharth,* not Gannett, he *Neuharth,*" the executive said. "It was personal for him."

Shortly after the disappointing March 7 meeting, Chapman and his wife, Betty, visited Israel with a group of influential Miami citizens. The annual pilgrimage was intended to strengthen ties between the city's Christian and Jewish leadership. Singing hymns, holding hands, weeping together, the businessmen and their wives forged strong emotional bonds as they visited memorials of the Holocaust and sites sacred to the life of Christ.

On the Mount of the Beatitudes overlooking the Sea of Galilee, Chapman was asked to recite Christ's Sermon on the Mount. In his reedy Georgia accent, he read from his own Bible: "Blessed are the poor in spirit, for theirs is the kingdom of heaven . . ."

For a few blessed days Chapman forgot about Detroit.

Returning to Miami, he focused again on the JOA. He thought he had a way to break the impasse over control of the agency. He jotted a list of items—he called them "shareholder concerns"—that he believed had to be exempt from Gannett control in a JOA. He phoned Neuharth. Gannett's board of directors was scheduled to meet in Miami Beach March 24 and 25. Chapman invited Neuharth to his home on March 23, a Sunday.

Neuharth played hard to get. "I always like getting together with you, Alvah, but it's going to be a busy weekend."

Chapman persisted. "I just think that if you and I sat down, alone, privately, with no one else in the room, we might be able to move this thing along."

Neuharth remained coy.

"While I love being with you and I love being with the Knight-Ridder people, there's no point in us meeting unless you are prepared to settle the issue of control."

"Well," Chapman said, "I think under certain conditions, if we can agree on a lot of other things that are important to us, we can get over that hurdle."

Neuharth was glad to hear it.

* * *

The midday sun peeked through the shuttered windows in Chapman's den. Neuharth sat on a sofa, sipping an iced cola. Chapman settled into an easy chair to Neuharth's left. A Bible rested on a table within Chapman's reach. The men exchanged small talk and wished each other a happy birthday. Chapman had turned sixty-five on Friday, Neuharth sixty-two on Saturday.

The cramped room in Chapman's suburban Miami home seemed too modest for a man who had earned more than eight hundred thousand dollars the previous year. Besides the sofa and easy chair, there was barely room for a desk, a swivel chair, and two end tables. One wall was stacked to the ceiling with books on American history, business, newspapering, and Christianity. The pecan paneling was crowded with photographs of Chapman's father, his father-in-law, Nelson Poynter, Byron Harless, Bernie Ridder, and buddy Don Shula, head coach of the Miami Dolphins. Amid replicas of his war medals, an oil painting depicted a young, uniformed Alvah Chapman at The Citadel. An assortment of plaques recognized his devotion to civic affairs in south Florida. Behind his desk hung a photograph of Jack Knight. "To Alvah and Betty Chapman," read the inscription, "whose support and encouragement have meant so much to me during trying and difficult days."

On this Palm Sunday, Neuharth had spent a relaxing morning reading newspapers and jogging near the Alexander Hotel in Miami Beach. Chapman had attended services at the Coral Gables First United Methodist Church. A touch of flu had left him with a slight fever. To Neuharth, he seemed a little tense. "Maybe I was," Chapman would recall. "There was a lot at stake."

Chapman started the meeting. He told Neuharth that, though he might be willing to cede control, Knight-Ridder intended to take an active role in the JOA. "If you have in mind a genuine partnership and I can be convinced of that," Chapman said, "then I believe I can get over the issue of control."

"That's what we had in mind from the beginning," Neuharth said matter-of-factly. "But, again, there can't be a partnership without someone in control." Neuharth argued that Gannett was more "objective" in assessing Detroit, because it had not been embroiled in the war for the past twenty-five years. The newcomer bore no ill will or hard feelings that could distort its perspective. He did not mention his own Detroit past, his days battling the *News*, his departure from Knight-Ridder, his unspoken rivalry with Chapman.

"The *News* is in the dominant position," Neuharth intoned, "and we're sure as hell not going to piss that away by agreeing to be equal partners. You've seen how we compete. We'll cut prices or we'll increase the newshole, we'll put the pressure on, we'll use all the resources necessary to dominate the market. And without a JOA, you and I both know there's going to be one newspaper in this market."*

Chapman wasn't sure which paper that might be. He didn't think Neuharth arrogant enough to think Gannett could force Knight-Ridder out of Detroit. He figured Knight-Ridder could last as long as Gannett, if it came to that. Of course, it would be costly, assuming the *News* didn't raise its prices. The JOA offered a much safer route to profitability.

Chapman proposed a compromise. Gannett could control the JOA if it agreed that certain actions could be taken only with the agreement of *both* partners. Quite simply, there were areas in which Chapman didn't feel Gannett should have a right to dictate to Knight-Ridder. For example, Chapman said, "Let's assume you get your control. If you want to build a $100 million plant, are you just going to send us a bill for our $50 million?"

"Oh, no," Neuharth said.

Chapman handed him a list of the so-called shareholder concerns he had developed on his return from Israel. It specified nine matters in which Gannett and Knight-Ridder would have equal say. For example, both partners would have to agree on large capital contributions—say, to build a new printing plant. Both parties would have to agree to sell a large item such as some printing presses or a chunk of valuable real estate. Both parties would have to agree to change the JOA contract or take on a large amount of debt. On other management issues, Gannett would govern the JOA by virtue of holding three seats on the agency's management committee to Knight-Ridder's two.

Neuharth wasn't about to commit to specific language, but he liked the concept. That satisfied Chapman. With the caveats he had designed, control of the JOA no longer seemed so important. As a practical matter, the merger wouldn't work well anyway if Gannett used its three-to-two edge to bully Knight-Ridder. Besides, the *Free Press* would have the stronger morning market, and once the *Free Press* became the dominant paper, the economic leverage would be Knight-Ridder's.

There was another issue of concern to Chapman. He insisted that an "independent" chief executive, as Chapman termed it, be hired to manage the JOA's day-to-day affairs and answer to the five-member management committee. He proposed Charles Brumback, a top Tribune Company executive who had impressed Chapman as publisher of the *Orlando Sentinel*. Neuharth de-

*Neuharth's version; Chapman does not recall Neuharth using this language.

murred. He already had a chief executive picked out: William J. Keating, the Gannett general counsel and former congressman who had assembled Gannett's successful JOA in Cincinnati. Gannett had acquired Keating when it bought the *Cincinnati Enquirer* in 1979. He was an able politician who Neuharth figured could calm potential opponents of the JOA and smooth the way for federal approval. Chapman agreed to meet him.

A white limo whisked Neuharth from Chapman's home around 3:00 P.M. He and Chapman had a deal. Neuharth had his precious control and Chapman had the protections he desired. There would be much haggling over details in the days to come, but the stiffest barrier to a JOA in Detroit finally had been swept aside.

Dave Lawrence was scheduled to fly to Boca Raton on Monday, March 31. On Tuesday, April Fool's Day, he, Jerry Tilis, and Bob Hall were to make a major presentation to Knight-Ridder executives on the promising future of the *Free Press.*

Tony Ridder called to ask Lawrence to stop first in Miami.

At Knight-Ridder headquarters, Lawrence sat down to lunch in a private, sixth-floor dining room with Ridder, Alvah Chapman, Jim Batten, Byron Harless, and Larry Jinks, the company's senior vice-president of news and operations.

Lawrence sat in stunned silence as Chapman told him the Detroit newspaper war was ended. Knight-Ridder was about to sign a joint operating agreement with Gannett. "The only moment I could remember more painful," Lawrence recalled, "was the death of my own father." The next day, Lawrence dutifully made the optimistic *Free Press* presentation as planned, artfully dodging a question about the possibility of a JOA. "I spend all my time thinking about the problems I've already got and the least time thinking about what might happen," he told his audience. Tilis had never seen his friend looking so down. Lawrence was always upbeat, full of energy. Today he looked ashen, as if he had lost one of his best friends. "Something wrong, Dave?" Tilis asked.

Lawrence's reply was curt: "Let's agree right now that you won't ask me any more questions."

Shrimp cocktail and champagne were on the buffet in Al Neuharth's suite at Detroit's Hotel Pontchartrain on the evening of Sunday, April 13. Neuharth had gathered about twenty *Detroit News* editors and executives to tell them about the JOA that would be announced to the world Monday morning.

The contract had been signed two days earlier by Doug McCorkindale and Bob Singleton in the Washington offices of Hughes Hubbard and Reed, Knight-Ridder's legal counsel. Lawyers for Hughes Hubbard and Gannett's outside counsel, Nixon, Hargrave, Devans and Doyle, had toiled around the clock for more than a week to put the final touches on the seventy-nine-page contract and accompanying partnership and licensing agreements. Chapman and Neuharth wanted the deal wrapped up by the weekend so they could announce it early Monday morning, when the stock markets opened.

Things were going according to plan when Neuharth convened his soiree at the Pontchartrain. "He was absolutely dancing on his tiptoes," said a *News* executive who attended the gathering. Neuharth quickly laid out the terms of the deal: The *News* and the *Free Press* would combine all of their printing and business operations, such as circulation, advertising, accounting, marketing, and promotion, into a newly created entity called the Detroit Newspaper Agency, or DNA. Bill Keating, whom Neuharth called "the most knowledgeable person on JOAs in the country," would run it, answering to a management committee of three Gannett designees—Neuharth, McCorkindale, and John Curley—and two from Knight-Ridder—Chapman and Batten. Profits would be split evenly for the last ninety-five years of the hundred-year agreement. For the first five years Gannett would get a slightly larger share, starting with 55 percent in the first year and gradually sliding back to 50 percent.

The newsrooms would remain separate and independent. On weekdays, the *Free Press* would publish in the morning, the *News* in the afternoon. On weekends, the papers would jointly publish the *Detroit News and Free Press*. On Saturdays, the *Free Press* staff would produce world, national, state, local, and sports news while the *News* staff produced softer stuff on entertainment and life-styles. Those roles would be reversed on Sundays. Both days, there would be two editorial pages, one for the *News*, one for the *Free Press*.

What the deal meant, Neuharth gleefully concluded, was that the *News* had won the war. The *Free Press*, not the *News*, would file the application for government approval as the "failing newspaper." The *News* would control the JOA. "This deal," Neuharth told his assembled charges, "was made possible for two reasons. One, the *Detroit News* established and maintained the number one position with the leadership of Bob Nelson and others. And that number one position, as we inherited it, put us in a good negotiating position. The second fact is that Gannett brought—you interpret this as you will—additional muscle, if not charm, to the table."

He winked as he said "charm."

Nelson gloated, telling everyone, "We beat their ass." But the mood in the room wasn't quite jubilant. The others dutifully applauded their chief's little speech, but it was hard to feel triumphant about surrendering the key to their victory, the morning circulation they had worked for a decade to develop. Even Neuharth noticed it. "I'm sure not everybody in the room went home dancing up and down," he recalled.

Meanwhile, across the Detroit River in Canada, Alvah Chapman was addressing a somber group of *Free Press* executives dining in a private room at the Windsor Hilton. Neal Shine, who had been at the *Free Press* since the early 1950s, didn't want to believe what he was hearing. Christ, he thought, we've been fighting this fight for twenty-six years and now it's a scoreless tie? *Free Press* executive editor Kent Bernhard, an old-style newsman who reveled in the daily skirmishes with the *News*—"The sun comes up and the guns go off," he liked to say—seethed, though he held his tongue. Editor Joe Stroud struggled with the idea that the *Free Press* had failed. "I thought we were winning," he later recalled. "We had been *told* we were winning, even by our own financial people." Jerry Tilis, veteran of the Philadelphia war, was disappointed that he wouldn't "win another Super Bowl ring" but glad he might be able to leave Detroit, a city his wife loathed.

One member of the group had been through many more battles than the rest. *Free Press* circulation director Myron Didyk had received one of those chilling middle-of-the-night telegrams when Hearst sold the *Detroit Times* in November of 1960. He had fought the *News* in the streets for twenty-six years. And he had just helped the *Free Press* put up its best first-quarter circulation numbers in history. But now, as Alvah Chapman told him the war was ending, Myron Didyk's eyes filled with tears.

Neuharth and Chapman made the deal public in a 10:00 A.M. news conference at Detroit's Omni International Hotel. Wall Street got the good news via the Dow Jones news wire.

Amid the click and whir of cameras, Dave Lawrence introduced the two gentlemen to a roomful of reporters, many of them from the *Free Press* and the *News*. By now the *Free Press* publisher had put behind himself much of the shock and dismay at learning the newspaper war was ending. He had asked to do the introduction today, considering it part of his personal therapy. "This is," he told the assembled reporters, "a momentous day in the history of journalism in Detroit and Michigan."

Up stepped Chapman and Neuharth, the rivals-turned-partners who had set aside their warring papers' differences for the sake of a profitable peace. Both were smiling broadly. Chapman was in his customary dark blue suit and conservative red tie. Neuharth wore a light gray double-breasted suit, a black silk tie with silver and white stripes, and a billowing black-and-silver pocket puff. Tacked on his right lapel was a brass "News #1" pin.

For the next half hour they sought to persuade their skeptical audience that the JOA was not about revenues or profits or divvying up a lucrative market, but about preserving newspapers. Chapman said the deal meant Detroit would have "two strong and independent editorial voices for at least the next century." Neuharth said that after "extensive study and very thoughtful consideration," he had concluded that Detroit could not support competing dailies. "The demise of either newspaper in this market would be tragic, not just for its employees . . . but for readers, for advertisers, and for the general public."

But neither man would say which paper would have died if Gannett and Knight-Ridder hadn't agreed on a JOA. *News* reporter David Markiewicz pressed Chapman on the point. "Would the *Free Press* in fact have failed?" Markiewicz asked. "And if it would have, how long [from now]?"

Chapman skirted the question, explaining instead that the "failing newspaper" designation meant merely that the *Free Press* had been losing money for a long time.

Markiewicz wasn't satisfied. "Would the *Free Press* have folded if this hadn't come about?"

Chapman wasn't smiling anymore.

The question was important because it suggested another that was on everyone's mind: If the attorney general did not sanction the JOA, would Knight-Ridder then close the *Free Press*?

In fact, Chapman had not in recent months seriously considered closing the paper. Knight-Ridder directors had briefly discussed the option in the spring of 1985, Chapman warning them that the conversation was never to leave the room for fear of discouraging *Free Press* people. But closing the *Free Press* never was prominent among the detailed alternatives considered during the Tiger deliberations. More recently, Chapman had thought the largest hurdle to a JOA was negotiating the agreement. He wasn't expecting much trouble getting it approved, and had not given serious thought to the consequences of a denial.

He deflected Markiewicz's question a second time: "I will not choose to comment whether the *Free Press* would have folded and how soon. The *Free Press* has been losing money for a number of years and Knight-Ridder has no obligation to continue to support a losing newspaper indefinitely."

A statement released jointly by Knight-Ridder and Gannett said the Detroit papers had battled to a "virtual draw." Chapman had insisted on including the phrase, which he coined, and Neuharth did not resist. The phrase did not please the lawyers, who figured anyone opposing the JOA could use it against the publishers. "When a number of us saw that press release, we about had a heart attack," one Gannett lawyer recalled. After all, if the war had ended in a tie, who could say whether the *Free Press* truly was the "failing newspaper"?

Neuharth, of course, had no plan to close the *News,* JOA or not. If the merger was approved, Gannett would get half the take in a hundred-year monopoly. If it was denied, Neuharth was willing to bet that the "failing" tag by then would have so damaged the *Free Press* that it would expire anyway.

Either way, Neuharth would win.

The companies planned to file a formal application for JOA approval in a few weeks. Because it was such a "simple, straightaway proposition," Chapman said, a swift sanction was expected. "You'd be safe to say about a year."

Strangely, neither Chapman nor Neuharth could remember how their negotiations began.

"I don't remember when the JOA was first mentioned," Neuharth said in reply to a reporter's question.

"Could it have been before you bought the *Detroit News?*" the reporter asked.

"Oh, no," Neuharth said.

Another sore subject was JOA profit projections. When a reporter inquired about them, Chapman glanced at Neuharth and chuckled. Neuharth just smiled. "You still have the mike," he demurred. Chapman offered a nonanswer. "As public companies, once the agency is approved and implemented, our financial progress will be reported," he said. The companies expected the JOA to make profits from the start. How much, Chapman wasn't saying. It simply wouldn't do to talk about the tens of millions of dollars in profits the companies expected, not when Knight-Ridder was about to plead poverty to the government.

News publisher Bob Nelson watched from the back of the room, smoking and gloating. "This is all bullshit," Nelson confided to passing *News* employees. "We kicked their asses." Dave Lawrence found himself surrounded by reporters asking if the *Free Press* had lost the war. "Absolutely not," Lawrence insisted. "The truth of the matter is I believe the *Free Press* will be the dominant morning newspaper" under the JOA. He had a lot of company in that belief, including his Knight-Ridder bosses, Wall Street analysts, and even a few

News editors. Chapman had circulated a memo to Neuharth predicting that the JOA would drop the *News*'s daily circulation from 656,000 to 520,000. Nelson himself had given Neuharth a memo showing how, by surrendering its morning share, the *News* almost immediately would become number two.

Neuharth insisted otherwise at the press conference. "The *Detroit News,* at great expense and with some difficulty, has converted some of its former afternoon readers to morning in recent years," he said. "We think those loyalties to the *Detroit News* are pretty strong, and that the conversion will take place back to the afternoon. It is our expectation that the relative circulations are likely to remain about the same."

Neuharth ended the press conference with a wave of his hand, telling the reporters, "You all have deadlines to meet."

The announcement of the JOA delighted Wall Street. "A super deal," said analyst R. Joseph Fuchs of Kidder, Peabody. "Very good news," said Victoria Butcher of Eberstadt Fleming. "An excellent deal for both the companies," said Bruce Thorp of Lynch, Jones and Ryan. The companies' stock prices, which had been rising on rumors that a JOA was imminent, rose again on news of the deal, Gannett's by a quarter, Knight-Ridder's by half a buck.

Several analysts projected the companies splitting annual pretax profits in the range of $100 million within five years of a JOA start-up. Gannett and Knight-Ridder didn't publicly dispute the guesses; some of their own projections were more cautious, though hardly pessimistic. Preliminary Knight-Ridder estimates saw a JOA earning about $50 million in its first year, rising to near $100 million by year ten. One Gannett scenario projected a small loss in the first year, quickly becoming an operating profit of $50 million by the third year; another foresaw a $51 million first-year profit rising to $107 million in the fourth year.

Expectations were high. In private chats with analysts, Doug McCorkindale played them down, while publicly Neuharth played them up. Addressing analysts in San Francisco, he took issue with an April 15 report by John Reidy of Drexel Burnham Lambert. Reidy had projected 1991 JOA revenues of $700 million and an operating profit of $112 million, for a margin of 16 percent.

"What he forgot," Neuharth bragged, "is that the governance of the Detroit Newspaper Agency is in the hands of the Gannett Company by a three-to-two margin, and 16 percent operating margins are simply not acceptable at the Gannett Company. So, while we appreciate the specifics and the interest, John, I suggest that as you get into the late eighties and early nineties, while we don't project earnings for you, we don't want to see you embarrassed by being off as much as 100 percent, and we suggest you might want to revise your numbers upward."

The mood wasn't quite so sanguine along Lafayette Boulevard, where sadness and uncertainty hung like a cloud. Chapman and Neuharth had admitted some "redundant" workers would lose their jobs in a JOA, though they couldn't say yet how many. *Free Press* workers donned buttons reading, I'M NOT REDUNDANT.

Beyond the immediate concern for their jobs, workers at both papers grieved the passing of an era. "A black day for Detroit journalism," lamented one *News* reporter. Barbara Stanton, the Luedtke holdover who had shared in the *Free Press*'s 1968 Pulitzer, summed it up neatly on the front page of her paper: "In Denver and Dallas and a few other towns there are competing newspapers, and they think they are slugging it out for dominance in their markets. What do they know?" Some veterans of the war simply refused to accept its end. Circulation workers at the *Free Press* had T-shirts printed with the slogan WE'RE STILL FIGHTING. Anticipating the angst, Neuharth and Chapman vowed that, though business rivalry would end, journalistic competition would continue unabated. But the rank and file had trouble seeing how the JOA would better their lives.

Maybe Dave Lawrence did too. On the day of the announcement he repeatedly told his staffers to stay the course, keep putting out a good paper, trust the people at Knight-Ridder. All day he swallowed his own hurt, focusing on the future, trying to forget that a publisher's role in a JOA would probably be skimpy. That night, when he and two other *Free Press* officials were walking to the parking lot, a long black car pulled out from an underground ramp. Lawrence suddenly leapt forward and lay prone on the pavement in the car's path.

Then he just as quickly scrambled to his feet, laughing. Veteran *Free Press* reporter Jeanne May was watching from a few steps behind. She didn't know whether to laugh or cry.

The days following the announcement of the JOA were sumptuous icing for Alvah Chapman. On April 17, Knight-Ridder papers were awarded a remarkable seven Pulitzer Prizes (the *Free Press* was not among the winners). A few days later, Chapman was elected president and chairman of the American Newspaper Publishers Association, the industry's leading trade group.

On May 20, Neuharth surprised shareholders at Gannett's annual meeting in Washington by announcing he was stepping down as chief executive in favor of John Curley. He appeared to choke up a bit as he told his audience, "I am not going away. I love this company and the business and profession we are in. I plan to continue as your very active chairman until my contract expires in March of 1989, when I will be sixty-five."

The announcement culminated a spring of milestones for the onetime poor kid from South Dakota. The day before, Neuharth had announced that Gannett would purchase Louisville's prestigious *Courier-Journal,* calling it the final jewel in his "triple crown" of newspaper purchases, including the *Detroit News* and the *Des Moines Register.* So, Neuharth's last year as CEO was distinguished by $1.3 billion in acquisitions and the apparent resolution of the Detroit newspaper war. The deal in Detroit seemed especially fitting, for it brought Neuharth's career full circle. If he had left loose ends when he reluctantly left the *Free Press* in 1963, now they finally were tied up—in a neat hundred-year package that promised to make Gannett many billions of dollars. Perhaps that was why he had been so eager to get the deal done.

But even as the Gannett and Knight-Ridder lawyers prepared a JOA application for Attorney General Edwin Meese, rough edges were appearing. Although Neuharth had been a gentleman at the April 14 press conference, privately he was touting Gannett's control of the JOA to anyone who would listen. Over lunch with *News* executives on April 14, he bragged that his earlier price cut had "scared the shit" out of Knight-Ridder. Word of Neuharth's boasting found its way to the *Free Press,* where Dave Lawrence at first tried to downplay it as typical Neuharthian bluster.

Shortly after the JOA was announced, the *News* hosted a party to mark the paper's victory in the war. "Let's celebrate!" read posters tacked up around the building. "Free beer, pretzels and chips in the *News* cafeteria." Hearing of it, Lawrence was repulsed. "It was cynical," he later recalled. "People being told they were winners were among those who would lose jobs. Someday they would wake up and they would have had a free beer and free soft drink and ended up losing their job."

A front-page *News* story published Sunday, April 20, quoted an unnamed *News* executive—it was Bob Nelson—crowing about the power Gannett would wield over the JOA. Neuharth had coached him well. "First of all," the anonymous Nelson was quoted as saying, "when do you come out on the street? When do you put the papers in the rack? When do you take the other guy's papers out of the rack? How do you promote it? How do you use the Sunday paper to build five-day readership? The DNA [Detroit Newspaper Agency] is going to have to make all of those decisions and, when that control lies with Gannett, sort of common sense says they're going to favor the *News.*"

The gloating disturbed Lawrence enough that he asked the *Free Press* staff to prepare a story clarifying what control of the JOA meant. Lawrence didn't understand it to mean the *Free Press* would stand by while Gannett toyed with its loyal morning readership.

He also didn't appreciate Neuharth advancing the idea that the *News* had won the war. Hadn't Neuharth agreed that the papers had fought to a "virtual draw"? Hadn't Neuharth come seeking the JOA in the first place? "It angers me," Lawrence wrote his staff in *The Friendly Fast Facts,* an in-house newsletter, "when anybody tries to use this situation, which is tough for everybody, to their own advantage."

Lawrence got so fed up with Neuharth's chest thumping that he dashed off a note to Alvah Chapman and Jim Batten. "Minimally, please be angry," he pleaded. "This is not building trust." Lawrence's bosses told him to calm down; Neuharth was just being Neuharth. Besides, the JOA would render moot all claims to victory. Chapman and Batten were supremely confident the merger would be sanctioned. FAST APPROVAL PREDICTED FOR NEWSPAPER DEAL, read a front-page headline in the April 20 *Free Press.*

But everyone wasn't climbing aboard the publishers' bandwagon. From the day the JOA was announced, voices began to rise up in opposition, feebly at first, getting louder by the day. "I've never seen a JOA where people didn't get hurt," said Elton Schade, the leader of Teamsters Local 372, the newspapers' biggest union. "I see nothing positive in it," declared Donald Kummer, administrative chief of Newspaper Guild Local 22, the papers' second-largest union. "We won't stand still for this," vowed Louis Mleczko, the *News* reporter who was president of Guild Local 22. "How can you call a newspaper that has a circulation of 630,000 daily and is neck-and-neck with its competitor a 'failing' newspaper?" asked Lee Dirks, a onetime *Free Press* executive turned newspaper broker.

Alvah Chapman and Al Neuharth might not have believed it, but the newspaper war was a long way from ended—longer than either of them could have known.

Part Three

Unseemly Haste

9

Welfare for the Rich

It took the lawyers less than a month to transform the *Detroit Free Press* from a paper with the "makings of a winner" to one in "probable danger of financial failure." The *Free Press*'s losses were the centerpiece of the voluminous application for a joint operating agency the newspapers filed with the Justice Department on May 9, 1986. Strictly on operations, the *Free Press* had lost nearly $44 million during the 1980s. Adding the Michigan single-business tax and fees paid to Knight-Ridder for corporate services, the losses came to $64 million, a bit more than $10 million a year. The *Detroit News* wasn't doing much better. Although the *News* made a razor-thin profit in 1985, it had lost nearly $21 million on operations in the 1980s, $46 million if you counted the state tax and corporate fees. Furthermore, both papers expected to lose millions more in 1986.

The publishers complemented their seventy-two-page brief with several cardboard boxes of memos, reports, and other documents purporting to support the case for the JOA. In the next two months, Knight-Ridder and Gannett would supply the government with some two hundred thousand pages filling more than sixty cartons. The companies hoped the information would be sufficient to obviate any need for a costly and time-consuming public hearing on the matter.

Two lawyers for the companies already had pleaded the case to the

Justice Department's Antitrust Division, which had first crack at analyzing the application and advising the attorney general what to do about it. Representing Knight-Ridder was gravel-voiced Calvin Collier, a former chairman of the Federal Trade Commission, whose friend Charles "Rick" Rule was the top deputy in the Antitrust Division and point man on the JOA application. At Collier's side was Lawrence Aldrich, who had joined Gannett after six years in the Antitrust Division, where he had tried the unsuccessful case to halt a JOA between the *Seattle Times* and the *Seattle Post-Intelligencer* in the early 1980s.

Collier and Aldrich made an informal presentation to Antitrust Division staffers on April 14, the day the JOA was announced. While Neuharth and Chapman chatted up the press in Detroit, the lawyers offered rough charts and graphs augmenting the companies' three central arguments for the JOA: (1) the *Free Press*'s losses were severe and irreversible; (2) the shrinking Detroit market could no longer support two major dailies; and (3) the *Free Press* could not overcome the *News*'s leads in a plethora of circulation and advertising categories.

The latter point focused on the *News*'s dominance of the "primary market area," the three-county region composing metropolitan Detroit. The area was crucial because it supplied the *News* and the *Free Press* with 75 percent of their advertising revenue, which in turn accounted for 75 percent of the newspapers' total revenue. The *News*'s lead in daily circulation in the tricounty area was more than 105,000; in Sunday circulation, a considerable 242,000. Consequently, the *News* collected more advertising dollars—$180 million in 1985 to the *Free Press*'s $112 million. The *Free Press* had more circulation than the *News* in Michigan's more far-flung, outstate areas, but advertisers were keener on reaching Detroit and its suburbs.

The argument aimed to puncture the notion that the *Free Press* was close on the heels of the *News,* as evidenced by the narrow, 5,000-paper gap between the papers in overall daily circulation. The primary market area, the companies contended, was the true test of the *News*'s dominance. That key advantage, the argument went, effectively blocked the *Free Press* from increasing circulation and advertising rates enough to stem its burgeoning losses. Unless the *News* hiked prices first, the *Free Press* did so only at the risk of losing price-sensitive subscribers, which would translate into diminished ad revenue—and bigger losses.

The *Free Press,* the companies argued, had survived solely due to the largess of Knight-Ridder, which was not obliged to bear the *Free Press*'s losses indefinitely. As the application put it, ". . . the only alternatives in Detroit are a JOA or the eventual loss of a vigorous editorial voice." It did not specify which voice might be lost. Knight-Ridder and Gannett further argued that the JOA should be approved quickly, for delay would lead to further deterioration of the *Free Press* and the potential of greater job losses than the JOA otherwise would require. Prompt approval, the companies said, "is in the best interests of both newspapers, their employees, and the communities they serve."

The arguments were sound, Collier and Aldrich thought, but neither lawyer was optimistic that the Antitrust Division would accept them. They both knew people in the division whose free-market beliefs did not incline them to favor an industry with special treatment. Indeed, the division had a deep mistrust of the law that permitted JOAs. Which should have been no surprise, given the peculiar circumstances surrounding the passage of the law and the controversies that arose as newspapers succumbed to the temptation of a legislated monopoly.

Richard Milhous Nixon was no friend of the press. The secretive Nixon White House had kept the media at bay with every legal means available, making history by obtaining a court-ordered halt to publication of stories on the Pentagon Papers. Vice President Spiro Agnew conducted a systematic public assault on the press, brandishing the phrase "nattering nabobs of negativism." Yet in 1970 Nixon did the newspaper industry a large favor by signing into law the Newspaper Preservation Act.

Enactment of the law culminated three years of intense lobbying that engendered bitter debate about the growing might of the press. "The Newspaper Preservation Act was not considered or passed on its merits, which were hardly considered, but rather as a result of a skillful lobbying campaign among legislators who did not need much convincing," researcher Ralph H. Johnson concluded in a 1975 dissertation. Indeed, the legislation of the Newspaper Preservation Act had the unseemly feel of the back-room dealing and political arm-twisting that newspapers regularly abhorred on their high-minded editorial pages.

The Failing Newspaper Bill, as it was originally titled, was designed to circumvent court rulings in the case of *Citizen Publishing Co.* v. *the United States.* Voting 7–1, the Supreme Court had affirmed a lower court decision ruling illegal a JOA between the *Tuscon Daily Citizen* and the *Arizona Daily Star* that had been in existence since 1940. The case might never have arisen had the Small family, owners of the *Citizen,* not exercised an option to buy out their partners at the *Star.* In 1964, President Johnson's Justice Department was seeking just such a case to test the applicability of the antitrust laws to JOAs.

Though price-fixing, profit-pooling, and other monopolistic practices had been common in newspapering since the first JOA in 1933 in Albuquerque, the Sherman and Clayton acts had been only infrequently invoked against newspapers, and rarely to attack such impediments to competition as a JOA might pose. No one was sure why newspapers had avoided the enforcement endured by other industries. Some thought it due to the limited resources available to the Antitrust Division. Some theorized that the First Amendment made the industry immune to antitrust laws, despite at least one Supreme Court decision holding otherwise. Others wondered whether the government was chary of taking on people who bought ink by the barrel.

After the Small family's plan to buy their competitor was revealed, Representative Morris Udall, Democrat of Arizona, complained to Attorney General Nicholas Katzenbach that a Republican owner was taking over the last major Democratic newspaper in the state. On January 4, 1965, the Antitrust Division filed a complaint charging Citizen Publishing with profit-pooling, price-fixing, seeking to dominate the newspaper business in Tucson, and restraining competition. Three years later, U.S. District Judge James A. Walsh found the Tucson papers guilty as charged. They appealed to the Supreme Court. On March 10, 1969, the court ruled for the first time that a JOA violated the antitrust laws. Justice William O. Douglas, writing for the majority, quoted from a previous decision involving the Associated Press: "Freedom to publish is guaranteed by the Constitution, but freedom to combine to keep others from publishing is not."

Panic shot through the newspaper industry, for the ruling endangered not only the Tucson JOA but twenty-one similar agencies in Miami, San Francisco, St. Louis, Pittsburgh, Nashville, Albuquerque, Tulsa, Shreveport, and other cities. Advertisers in Tucson and San Francisco promptly filed lawsuits seeking to break up the local JOAs and end monopolistic ad pricing. Congress set to work on a pair of new bills designed to blunt the ruling's effect by retroactively legalizing all JOAs and providing a framework for the creation of future JOAs. Different versions of the law had died in the previous Congress, but the determined sponsors, most of whom hailed from states that were home to JOAs, would not be denied. Their proposals were recast in the Ninety-first Congress as the Newspaper Preservation Act. In its final form, the law provided that newspapers would be entitled to an exemption from the antitrust laws in cities where one paper could prove it was in "probable danger of failure." The standard was a less stringent variation on the traditional "failing company" defense that exempted companies facing "grave probability of a business failure." The law stated public policy to be in favor of "maintaining a newspaper press editorially and reportorially independent and competitive in all parts of the United States."

Publishers argued that the bill would preserve dual editorial voices in cities, and that many papers would die lacking the shelter of a JOA. Due to closing and mergers, the two-newspaper town was headed for extinction. In 1923, 502 cities enjoyed head-to-head daily competition; by 1945 that was down to 117 cities and by 1971, just 37. "Without the economic capacity for anyone to go to press, there certainly can be no free press," declared Representative Spark Matsunaga, a Hawaii Democrat who supported the bill. Matsunaga argued that the central issue before Congress was "a free press versus the sanctity of our antitrust laws."

Strangely, though, virtually no testimony was offered as to how many newspapers would be preserved by the bill or would go out of business if the bill did not pass. The bill included no mechanism for requiring publishers to rescue papers through JOAs. In fact, publishers resisted the inclusion of language requiring the maintenance of separate editorial voices on grounds it would violate the First Amendment.

The law legalized existing JOAs and authorized the attorney general to decide where future JOAs were warranted, despite efforts by Michigan senator Philip A. Hart and others to vest that power with the courts. Critics, including academics, unions, suburban publishers, and lawyers from the Justice Department's Antitrust Division, attacked the law as special-interest legislation that favored not only a specific industry but an industry niche. Suburban dailies and weeklies feared being driven from business by powerful joint operators. Moreover, opponents argued, the law would most greatly benefit chain owners, who were partners in many existing JOAs and could use their financial might to coerce smaller rivals into agencies. Stephen Barnett, a law professor at the University of California at Berkeley, told a House antitrust subcommittee that the bill's new title was a misnomer. "What the publishers really want is not relief from financial hardship, not preservation of the second newspaper, and not an economic situation in which the paper can make a decent profit. All these advantages are available under the present law. What the publishers want is protection from competition and the right to pile up monopoly profits."

Representative Clark MacGregor of Minnesota and fellow Democrat Abner Mikva of Illinois argued that the industry's refusal to make public financial data on the existing JOAs was reason enough to scuttle the law. The secret financials showed "more black figures than red ones," Mikva charged. Others claimed the legislation would speed the growing concentration of newspapers in the hands of large corporations. At least three influential dailies—the

New York Times, the *Wall Street Journal,* and the *Washington Post*—opposed the law editorially. "If the precedent holds, you won't have to be going into bankruptcy," syndicated columnist Nicholas von Hoffman wrote. "You'll only have to poor-mouth and make it seem that you are."

Indeed, publishers downplayed their fortunes while lobbying for the JOA law, prompting *Forbes* magazine to call newspapering the "liveliest corpse" in U.S. industry. Senator Hart called the bill "a poverty program for the rich." In one session at which congressmen were analyzing newspaper finances, Senator Everett M. Dirksen of Illinois was heard to remark, "My God, those people make a lot of money." But even Dirksen became a supporter as the bill gained momentum in both chambers of Congress. Editors and publishers descended on Washington to squeeze hands and twist arms. Lobbyists were hired by the newspapers' powerful trade organization, the American Newspaper Publishers Association, at the urging of Scripps-Howard, Hearst, and other chains that participated in JOAs. "The lobbying which went on for this bill may well have set new records," said Senator Thomas J. McIntyre, a New Hampshire Democrat who opposed the measure. Perhaps none of the advocacy, though, was as important—and as unseemly—as that endeavored by Richard Berlin, president and chief executive of the Hearst Corporation, whose *San Francisco Examiner* was a partner in a JOA.

Berlin targeted the man whose signature would make the Newspaper Preservation Act law: President Richard M. Nixon. Berlin had reason to be concerned about Nixon's views. The Justice Department, led by Assistant Attorney General for Antitrust Richard W. McLaren, staunchly opposed the bill. No one in the administration had spoken in support of it—that is, until Berlin wrote a pair of not-too-subtle letters.

As reported by media critic and former *Washington Post* editor Ben H. Bagdikian in his book *The Media Monopoly,* Berlin wrote slightly different letters to Nixon and McLaren. The letter to Nixon was properly solicitous. "I am taking the liberty of addressing myself to a matter of common interest to both you and me," Berlin wrote. "Many other important publishers and friends of your administration . . . are similarly situated. All of us look to you for assistance." He mentioned the Cox, Worrell, Newhouse, Scripps-Howard, and Knight newspaper chains. The companies owned but a handful of papers actually affected by the JOA law, but Berlin spoke with the might of their dozens of other newspapers, their broadcast stations, and their magazines, all of which helped to shape public opinion of the president.

Berlin was more direct in his letter to McLaren. "Those of us who strongly supported the present administration in the last election are the ones most seriously concerned and endangered by failure to adopt the Newspaper Preservation Act. . . ." He mentioned that Nixon had received nearly unanimous support from newspapers favoring the law. "It therefore seems to me that those newspapers should, at the very least, receive a most friendly consideration." Nixon received a copy of the letter.

The threat was palpable, but it did not affect McLaren, who continued to testify against the JOA bill. He argued that the antitrust laws permitted several ways in which competitors could work together—by printing jointly, for example—to rescue a financially troubled voice. Allowing any business to fix prices or share profits "would flout the basic principles of the free enterprise system," he said. "If any company . . . can be saved only by eliminating all competition between it and its competitors, we doubt that any good case can be made for the preservation of so lifeless an enterprise."

Three months later, though, a Commerce Department official told the House antitrust subcommittee that the Nixon White House supported the bill. The panel members were incredulous. Chairman Emanuel Celler, noting that the Bureau of the Budget had approved both positions, said the bureau "apparently lights a candle for Christ and a candle for the devil and takes no chances." McLaren subsequently reiterated the Justice Department's opposition, while admitting the Commerce Department spoke for the administration. It was, to say the least, an embarrassment.

Nixon offered no explanation. Years later, transcripts of taped White House conversations revealed that Nixon thought McLaren a "good little antitrust lawyer" who had been dominated by "all these bright little bastards that worked for the antitrust department for years and years and years and hate business with a passion." Could Nixon's animus have prompted the administration's two-faced view of the Newspaper Preservation Act? Or did Berlin's petitions win the day?*

The Senate passed the bill by 64–13, the House by 292–87. Nixon signed the bill into law, without comment, on July 24, 1970. In 1972, American newspapers gave Nixon the highest percentage of political endorsements of any presidential candidate in the modern era. Remarkably, every Hearst, Cox, and Scripps-Howard paper endorsed Nixon. Two years later, threatened with impeachment, Richard Nixon resigned. His fall was precipitated by the Watergate scandal, the best reporting of which was done by the *Washington Post*—coincidentally, one of the few large dailies to oppose the Newspaper Preservation Act.

*Nixon declined to be interviewed for this book.

Gannett did not actively lobby for the law but philosophically supported it. Jack Knight, who believed passionately that newspapers should not seek favors from the government, would have nothing to do with the publishers' lobbying campaign. Some speculated that he would have preferred an end to JOAs so that he could be rid of his own JOA partner, the *Miami News*. But Knight did not lobby against the Newspaper Preservation Act. As Alvah Chapman recalled, " 'Indifferent' is a good word" for how Knight felt. "He said, the hell with it, we don't need to go to Congress for anything."

Controversy dogged the law for the next fifteen years. The first new JOA was approved by Attorney General William Saxbe in 1974 between the *Anchorage Daily News* and the *Anchorage Times*. It ended in divorce five years later after the *News* sued the *Times*, alleging a conspiracy to create a monopoly. Yet the *News*, which had filed the JOA application as the "failing newspaper," eventually passed its rival in daily and Sunday circulation after a new owner, the McClatchy chain, spent heavily on a new printing plant, a Sunday paper, and expanded news coverage. Soon McClatchy was bragging that the *News* was "the best 40,000-circulation daily in the country." In 1992 the *Times* would close. In Anchorage at least, the "failing" paper was not predestined to fail.

In 1977 Scripps-Howard applied for a JOA between its *Cincinnati Post*, which claimed to be "failing," and the *Cincinnati Enquirer*. The Scripps-Howard board vowed to close the *Post* if the JOA was denied—although the company refused to consider selling the paper. The *Post* had lost about $10 million in the past five years, but opponents of the JOA, including the Newspaper Guild, argued that the *Post* lost money deliberately—by not following its rival's price hikes or aggressively cutting costs—in the hopes of qualifying for a JOA. Attorney General Benjamin Civiletti approved the agreement, which took effect in December of 1979.

The *Times* and the *News-Free Press* of Chattanooga, Tennessee, were next to seek a JOA. They sought emergency approval, claiming the *Times* could last only a few more weeks. When the Justice Department's Antitrust Division recommended that immediate help be denied, the papers assembled the JOA anyway. The Antitrust Division initially urged denial of the arrangement, but softened on consideration of arguments made by Cahill, Gordon and Reindel, the Washington law firm of the *New York Times*, which was controlled by the same Ochs family as the *Chattanooga Times*. When Attorney General Civiletti sanctioned the JOA in September 1980, rumors circulated that President Jimmy Carter's appointee had merely capitulated to the nation's most powerful newspaper in an election year.

In Seattle, where the *Times* and the *Post-Intelligencer* sought a JOA, the Antitrust Division recommended that it be denied. The "failing" *Post-Intelligencer* had lost $14 million in the past twelve years, but the Hearst Corporation refused to consider selling it, though several parties, including Australian media baron Rupert Murdoch, had expressed interest in buying the morning paper. (Knight-Ridder owned a 49.5 percent interest in the *Times.*) An administrative law judge and Attorney General William French Smith thought the JOA was justified, and eventually they were upheld by the Ninth Circuit Court of Appeals. The Supreme Court declined to hear an appeal by a group of newspaper employees, advertisers, and suburban publishers who opposed the JOA, which went into place in 1983.

Two JOAs that were grandfathered by the Newspaper Preservation Act also came under scrutiny. In 1983, the Newhouse chain said it would close the *St. Louis Globe-Democrat,* which was the morning paper in a JOA with the *St. Louis Post-Dispatch,* owned by the Pulitzer family. The *Globe-Democrat* was losing more money than the *Post-Dispatch* was making, so the partners were splitting losses. Though one paper was to close, the partners intended to share the profits of a one-paper JOA. Critics of the Newspaper Preservation Act blanched: This was preserving editorial voices? The Antitrust Division forced a sale of the *Globe-Democrat,* but the young buyer, Jeffrey Gluck, had neither the resources nor the experience to survive against Pulitzer and Newhouse. The *Globe-Democrat* went out of business for good in 1986.

Scripps-Howard closed the *Columbus Citizen-Journal,* a morning daily, after the owners of the *Columbus Dispatch* declined to renew their twenty-six-year-old JOA. The *Citizen-Journal* had the advantageous morning market and a growing circulation, but it trailed the *Dispatch* by about 80,000 subscribers a day and lacked its own printing plant. After the *Citizen-Journal* closed at the end of 1985, the *Dispatch* angered suburban publishers by creating its own chain of free weeklies and buying up other small papers.

Despite the three years it took to pass it and the more than five thousand pages of *Congressional Record* its debate consumed, the Newspaper Preservation Act was hardly a model of thoughtful and well-crafted legislation. By 1986 the scholarly literature on the law was rife with criticism. It had survived two challenges to its constitutionality, but legal scholars, newspaper executives, judges, and journalists still had not divined precisely what constituted a "failing newspaper." The proliferation of suburban papers, magazines, cable networks, and radio and television stations had effectively rendered the stated purpose of the law—preserving editorial voices—obsolete. (One study suggested that readers *didn't care* whether they had competing newspapers.) Even executives in the corporate suites of Gannett and

Knight-Ridder would concede—though only in private—that the law had outlived its usefulness.

It was true that JOAs sustained, at least temporarily, a handful of editorial voices that otherwise might have been stilled. And, as one study concluded, papers in JOAs tended to be slightly better journalistically than those in strict monopolies. But the law had numerous shortcomings. Newspaper closings in Washington, Philadelphia, Buffalo, Cleveland, and other cities showed that it didn't necessarily save editorial voices. The St. Louis and Columbus cases implied that publishers weren't as interested in diversity of voices as in monopoly—which the law helped them procure. Chattanooga suggested that politics could taint the quasi-judicial process under which JOAs were granted. Seattle was evidence that a "failing" paper might be valuable enough that its owner wouldn't sell it. Cincinnati demonstrated that losing money had its own reward. Anchorage showed that "failing" papers aren't necessarily failing.

The cases confounded judges, angered executives, lined the pockets of lawyers, and, at times, defied common sense. Detroit would put them all to shame.

The Detroit JOA would easily be the biggest ever. The *News* alone had more daily circulation than both papers in either Seattle or Cincinnati. Even under the probusiness Reagan administration there would be political pressure to give the Detroit deal more than a passing glance. By some measures the *News* and the *Free Press* were close competitors—especially in daily circulation, the standard measure by which the industry ranked newspapers. The papers' low prices also raised the question of whether a simple price increase could erase the deficits. And it was arguable that the *News,* not the *Free Press,* was the "failing" paper. Just before filing the JOA application, Alvah Chapman told a reporter covering Knight-Ridder's annual shareholder meeting, "The *News* qualifies. The *News* could file on the same basis that papers in other markets qualify." Indeed, Chapman and Al Neuharth had let their lawyers decide which Detroit paper was "failing."

At the Antitrust Division, neither of the two men who would oversee the Detroit papers' petition was inclined to look kindly on JOAs. The chief of the division was Assistant Attorney General Douglas H. Ginsburg, a cool, forty-year-old intellectual who had taught at Harvard for ten years. His top deputy and soon-to-be successor was Rick Rule, thirty-one, protégé of former Antitrust Division chief William Baxter, who had forced the sale of the *St. Louis Globe-Democrat* when the Newhouse chain hoped to close it quietly and enjoy

JOA profits in peace. Ginsburg and Rule were alumni of the University of Chicago Law School, birthplace of the so-called Chicago school of economics and law. The Chicago school of thought held that the market itself, unobstructed by government or other intervention, was best able to determine how the economy ought to work. As the theory went, only when a severe threat to the market's efficiency loomed was government or judicial intervention appropriate. It was a key underpinning of the Reagan administration's free-market policies.

Indeed, the administration moved aggressively to excise regulatory and other barriers from what Reaganites perceived to be the "free market." That included rethinking the antitrust laws or, at the least, the way they were enforced. Under chiefs Baxter, J. Paul McGrath, and Ginsburg, the Antitrust Division adopted a more benign view toward large corporate mergers and sought ways to discourage antitrust suits by individuals, while focusing enforcement attention on illegal price-fixing and bid-rigging. It was a controversial position. Critics charged the Reaganites with lax antitrust enforcement designed to curry favor with big business. The new thinking certainly found friends on Wall Street, where lawyers and investment bankers were reaping enormous fees for engineering the megamergers of the early to mid-1980s.

On the surface, the Reagan White House certainly seemed the place to get a rubber stamp for a JOA. In a memo to Chapman and Jim Batten in the fall of 1985, Knight-Ridder senior vice-president Bob Singleton wrote, "[T]he political climate is right for a JOA. During the next three years, it is essential that we get this accomplished if there ever is to be a JOA in Detroit. We qualify now and during the next two years we will continue to qualify. . . ." After all, the JOA was just another merger—and a partial one at that, since the newsrooms of the *Free Press* and the *News* would remain separate. Why would an administration that let Gulf Oil and Chevron exchange vows in a $13.2 billion marriage stand in the way of a newspaper combination worth a mere $400 million a year?

Ironically, the answer was the Newspaper Preservation Act. Ginsburg and Rule didn't much like the law, precisely because it interfered with the workings of a free market. To them, the Newspaper Preservation Act was crass special-interest legislation, an aberration rooted in politics that amounted to little more than a subsidy. Worse, the law appeared to create an incentive to *lose* money. Not that newspapers *wanted* to lose money, but they could *afford* to as part of a grander strategy—to gain market share, for instance—if they could fall back on a JOA. The notion was disturbingly detectable in the Detroit application. "It was absolutely clear that there were tons of red ink being spilled on those two newspapers' books," Rule recalled. "But it looked awfully voluntary. It looked like it was a conscious, rational decision, because they were investing in this billion-dollar pot of gold." From the beginning Rule worried that sanctioning the Detroit JOA could trigger a chain reaction: "If we allow this one to go, is there any way you could ever stop a JOA? Do we basically create the incentive for every two-newspaper town in the United States to either become a one-newspaper town or go into a JOA?"

Gannett lawyer Larry Aldrich was all too familiar with this kind of thinking. In his years working at the Antitrust Division, he had come to feel its mistrust of the JOA law was as visceral as it was intellectual. It was born in the division's embarrassment at the congressional hearings on the law, and nurtured in the Seattle case, where the division's recommendation for denial was ignored by Attorney General William French Smith. Aldrich had led the division's assault on the Seattle JOA, but he now questioned even his own intellectual honesty because he never had persuaded himself that Seattle could have supported two dailies without a JOA. He expected the division to try to derail the Detroit case.

The division, however, would not have the last word. Its charge was to prepare a factual report that would recommend the attorney general's next step: approve or deny the JOA, or order a public hearing. If a hearing was called, the division would participate and make another recommendation to an administrative law judge. The judge would make his own recommendation to the attorney general, who could then decide the JOA application as he wished.

The Antitrust Division lawyer assigned to the case was Seymour Dussman, a nineteen-year department veteran who volunteered for the task. Dussman, raised on Detroit's southwest side, also had attended the University of Chicago Law School. He found the Newspaper Preservation Act a puzzle. "It doesn't take long to read it," he later commented. "It takes a lot longer to figure out what the hell it means." He had never tried a newspaper case; now he had a bit more than two months to decipher the law, pore over the newspaper documents, and interview executives, advertisers, community leaders, and anyone else who could shed light on the Detroit papers. With the help of a few division staffers, he would draft a report that would be edited by Rule, signed by Ginsburg, and submitted to Attorney General Edwin Meese III.

Ed Meese was a favorite of newspaperpeople, not so much for his politics or administrative ability as his unfailing penchant for making news. Meese always seemed to be in trouble. He was linked to the Wedtech kickback scandal. He was said to have received payments for his political support of a pipeline that was never built. He was calling the American Civil Liberties Union a "criminals' lobby." He was being investigated for allegedly rewarding friends with government jobs.

It wasn't easy to predict how Meese might feel about the JOA. The lifelong lawyer and politician had never handled a case involving newspapers, and his legal interests ran more to criminal than civil matters. He had lobbied for capital punishment and a hobby was monitoring police calls on a home radio. As a conservative Republican, he might have been expected to accommodate big companies like Gannett and Knight-Ridder. Then again, he might have been just conservative enough to frown on a special-interest deal like a JOA. Knight-Ridder and Gannett hoped the former was the case, but they really hadn't a clue as to what Meese thought. And, of course, Meese wasn't saying.

Time was of the essence to Knight-Ridder and Gannett. The faster the *Free Press* and the *News* ended their rivalry, the faster the parent companies could get down to making some money. In public, however, executives were less likely to talk about profits than to drop a veiled threat: more jobs would be lost if the JOA was delayed and the newspapers' financial position was allowed to deteriorate. Bill Keating, who would run the JOA's combined business operations, insisted that no more than a thousand jobs would be lost in the merger, but he never missed a chance to warn that matters would be worse if approval was delayed.

Privately, the lawyers were saying Meese was likely to order a public hearing—the last thing Knight-Ridder and Gannett wanted to hear. The Seattle and Cincinnati cases had gone to hearings and both took more than two years to be approved. In Detroit, two years could mean $40 million or more in losses—not to mention a small fortune in attorneys' fees. The companies did what they could to avoid a hearing. Their voluminous application attempted to replicate the types of information ultimately required in Seattle and Cincinnati. "Delay in this proceeding threatens Detroit's future as a city with two vigorous newspapers," the application declared. Keating, a former congressman, gladhanded Michigan civic leaders and retailers, soothing them with assurances that, while the newspapers were likely to boost ad rates under a JOA, they would do so cautiously.

To some, the publishers' efforts to avoid a hearing were hypocritical. Detroit mayor Coleman Young noted, with a trace of exaggeration, that hardly a day passed when a Detroit paper wasn't badgering the city for something under the state's Freedom of Information Act. "Now why the hell are they trying to push this damn thing through without a hearing?" Young demanded. Even

News publisher Moe Hickey thought it foolhardy to try to dodge a hearing. "I don't give a shit how many documents you show [the public]," he told one of his reporters, "they want to hear you talk about it."

The issue supplied a focus to a nascent JOA opposition movement that was otherwise disorganized. Kurt Luedtke emerged as the best-credentialed critic of the JOA. The former *Free Press* executive editor had become a successful Hollywood screenwriter, earning an Oscar nomination for his first script, *Absence of Malice,* a seamy story—based in truth, Luedtke insisted—about a reporter who had slept with a source. Still enamored of his old paper, he was livid when he heard the *Free Press* had declared itself "failing." "This should be given a very careful look," Luedtke told a *Free Press* reporter, "because I believe it's indefensible."

State Senator John Kelly of Michigan, who thought the JOA a shameless grab for monopoly, introduced legislation to allow the state attorney general to block the merger. Most citizens, Kelly claimed, were against the JOA. "By God," he declared, "you don't mess with your morning *Free Press,* your church or your baseball team."

On a Sunday in June, an essay on the *Free Press*'s op-ed page criticized the JOA in detail. The authors were Luedtke and Hillel Levin, executive editor of *Metropolitan Detroit* magazine. Levin previously had written that the JOA "smacks of the big-business collusion that the *Free Press* derides, and yet remains the sort of government-sponsored perversion of the free-market economy that the *News* opinion writers so often condemn. Talk about your shiftless welfare cheats." In their *Free Press* essay, Levin and Luedtke argued that the *Free Press* was gaining on the *News* in several key circulation areas and would improve its position when its printing plant expansion was complete. "The paper is not operating at all like a company on the verge of bankruptcy," they wrote. "There have been few significant attempts at price increases or budget cutting." At a minimum, they argued, the JOA plan should be reviewed at a public hearing.

The newspapers weren't concerned with Kelly, Levin, or others attacking the JOA, but Luedtke was worrisome. His knowledge of newspapering and the *Free Press* threatened to legitimize the swelling arguments against the JOA. Luedtke was a veteran of the war and a *Free Press* loyalist who had worshiped Jack Knight and the lean, resourceful *Free Press* that never failed to turn a profit. Luedtke's involvement also implied criticism of David Lawrence's stewardship of the paper. Lawrence had worked hard to slip the shadow of his fabled predecessor. Now it hung ominously over his paper again.

Luedtke's anti-JOA fervor only went so far. He thought it arrogant of the newspapers to oppose a hearing, but he wasn't prepared to actually fight the JOA in court. One day he visited his old haunt, the Money Tree, and sat around the bar exhorting *Free Press* staffers to mobilize against the JOA. They looked at him bemusedly, as if to say, "We thought you left." Luedtke and Levin made a halfhearted attempt to organize an anti-JOA coalition, calling on local politicians and some of the bigger retailers. Few were eager to take on the newspapers and their parent companies. "It was like a joke," Luedtke recalled. "I remember thinking, The newspapers are taking us seriously, and we don't have plan fucking one."

John Kelly's anti-JOA bill crashed on takeoff. At a hearing at the Detroit Press Club, Kelly faced a daunting roomful of dark-suited Gannett, Knight-Ridder, *News* and *Free Press* lawyers who imbued the proceeding with a stony silence. The newspapers' executives declined to participate, and the one person who testified for the papers, Detroit attorney James Robinson, argued that the state could not override a federal statute. Michigan's attorney general already was saying the same thing. Kelly's fellow senators declined even to adopt a resolution recommending a hearing. A bit of lobbying by David Lawrence, who had spoken privately with the state's legislative leaders, had paid off. Meanwhile, Keating persuaded the Michigan Merchants Council, a trade group representing Sears, Kmart, Hudson's, Kroger, and other big retailers, to take no position on the JOA.

Even so, Luedtke and Levin cobbled together a group of influential Michiganders who wrote Meese a letter requesting a public hearing. The group included former Governor William Milliken, UAW president emeritus Douglas Fraser, state AFL-CIO president Sam Fishman, wealthy suburban publisher Philip Power, and Mayor Young. Two Michigan congressmen, Democrats John Dingell and William Ford, also wrote letters urging a hearing. A local auto dealer paid $25,308 for an ad in the *Wall Street Journal* that blared in big, black letters, LESS FOR MORE. THAT'S WHAT YOU CAN EXPECT IF THE JOA GOES THROUGH.

By opposing a hearing from the start, Knight-Ridder and Gannett had handed their critics one small, easily understandable tidbit to rally around. The JOA was a peculiar, hard-to-fathom device, but it was not difficult to fathom the newspapers' hurry to get one. By the summer, Meese had before him a pile of letters urging a hard look at the JOA. Doubts had been raised by congressmen, business leaders, retailers, suburban publishers, and lots of average citizens, the kind of people the *Free Press* and the *News* would have liked to have had on their side. Still, few, if any, had the will or the wherewithal to fight the JOA.

But there were other, much heavier guns trained on the JOA. The Teamsters, the Newspaper Guild, the Graphic Communications International

Union, and the Communications Workers of America, representing more than thirty-five hundred workers at the *Free Press* and the *News,* had the most at stake, the money to launch an all-out assault, and the deep emotional reserves to sustain one. This was, after all, Detroit, a union town through and through, from the smoky beer-and-a-shot joints nestled by the car assembly plants and downriver foundries, to the brick fortress of the UAW's Solidarity House on the Detroit River. What better place was there for proud laborers to take a stand against America's two largest newspaper companies?

10

Fighting Words

Bruce Miller figured he was wasting his time when he saw John Jaske, a glum-looking Gannett labor lawyer, waiting in Bill Keating's makeshift office in the Hotel Pontchartrain. There would be no deal today. Miller was an attorney for Detroit Newspaper Guild Local 22, the union that represented more than nine hundred editorial, business office, and janitorial employees of the *Detroit Free Press* and the *Detroit News*. He had asked to meet with Keating in the hope that they could reach some understanding that would persuade Guild Local 22 not to formally oppose the JOA.

They sat in an unremarkable suite of beige walls, shell-colored carpeting, and a curtained view of the Detroit River fourteen floors below. This was Bill Keating's temporary home and office. He tended to business in one room, slept in another, and made himself an occasional hot dog or peanut-butter sandwich in a cramped kitchenette. On weekends he commuted to his hometown of Cincinnati, where his wife, Nancy, and most of their seven children and fifteen grandchildren remained. He and his wife planned to move to Detroit so that he could manage the Detroit Newspaper Agency for at least the first few years of the JOA before they retired back to Cincinnati. For now, though, Keating's task was to help get the JOA approved. Part of the job was meeting with union chiefs and their attorneys.

Miller stated his business: Local 22's Representative Assembly would be meeting that night, June 10, 1986, to decide whether to request a public hearing on the JOA. The union was concerned that it stood to lose about half of its membership under a JOA—and, thus, half its annual dues income and, in theory, half the leverage it would bring to future contract negotiations. Miller wondered if something could be worked out to avert the membership loss in return for the union supporting the JOA. Surely Gannett and Knight-Ridder would be pleased to have the Guild sit on the sidelines through any legal battle.

Jaske explained, in level, final-sounding tones, that the understanding Miller hoped to reach was illegal. The law prevented the Detroit Newspaper Agency from protecting Guild members. Miller had expected this. He told Jaske he knew the law, but he also knew of ways to comply while solving the Guild's problem. "The issue," Miller later recalled saying, "is whether both sides want something to happen. If your position is that it's illegal, then you're telling me we have nothing to talk about."

Miller was throwing down a gauntlet of sorts, but Bill Keating's expression remained blank. Keating was a regular guy, the consummate midwestern achiever. The son of a wealthy dairy executive, he had been an all-American high school swimmer, a municipal judge, and a popular city councilman in his hometown of Cincinnati. He eagerly accepted the challenge of learning the newspaper business at the relatively late age of forty-six, when multimillionaire investor Carl Lindner asked him to return from Congress to run the *Enquirer*. After Gannett bought the *Enquirer* as part of its 1979 merger with Combined Communications Corporation, Keating rose swiftly in Gannett's corporate ranks, taking charge of the company's vast Newspaper Division in 1984 and becoming general counsel and executive vice-president a year later.

Al Neuharth chose Keating to manage the Detroit JOA less for his newspaper skills than his political acumen. The conservative Keating was well connected in GOP circles; he had defended President Nixon through the Watergate scandal and was a close friend of President Gerald Ford. More important, with a wink, a smile, a well-placed compliment, a hand gently placed on a shoulder, Keating knew how to put people at ease. He was the right kind of person to calm advertisers and employees fretting over the JOA.

Keating had another side too. When it was time to do business, particularly business with Detroit's many aggressive newspaper unions, his easygoing affability could quickly disappear. His blue eyes lost their playful sparkle and his smile became a tight frown. Now, with lawyer Jaske at his side, Keating showed his frown to the Guild's Miller. A JOA in Detroit, Keating declared, was inevitable. As Miller recalled it, Keating added that the Guild could do nothing to stop the JOA. Miller was surprised to hear that. Keating had lived through the lengthy Cincinnati JOA proceedings, in which the Guild played a major role in delaying the merger between the *Enquirer* and the *Post.*

Miller warned Keating that he could be wrong. For instance, the Guild might argue—to the attorney general or, perhaps, a federal judge—that the *Free Press*'s losses actually were investments in the future. Keating's expression then, it seemed to Miller, changed ever so slightly. But, as Miller recalls, Keating merely repeated, "There's nothing the Guild can do to hurt us." Keating's recollection differs. He remembered saying that the JOA was inevitable, but insisted that he did not say specifically that the Guild could do nothing to stop it. Rather, he said, he simply told Miller that he saw no way for the DNA to solve the Guild's problem within the law.

Whatever Keating said, however he said it, Miller did not take it well. His suburban Detroit law firm of Miller, Cohen, Martens and Ice had built a national reputation for battling big companies on behalf of steelworkers, coal miners, pipe fitters, electricians, and other blue-collar laborers. Miller, a tough-talking native of Brooklyn, wasn't about to be intimidated by Keating. "Well, Mr. Keating," Miller recalled saying, a tone of irritation creeping into his voice, "if I were you, I would check your references. I'm not here to blow my own horn, but check us out." The brief meeting was over. That evening, Local 22's Representative Assembly voted 17–0 to file papers urging Attorney General Edwin Meese to order a public hearing on the JOA.

Bill Keating was hardly alone in thinking the Newspaper Guild could not threaten a big daily newspaper. The Guild had never been the most powerful or militant newspaper union. In 1986 it seemed less likely to fight than ever before.

The union was born in 1933, when poorly paid reporters nationwide rallied to the call of columnist Heywood Broun of the *New York World-Telegram.* Printers and other newspaper workers had organized years before, but journalists had balked, fearing that organization would somehow taint the ethical purity or diminish the romance of their profession. The Great Depression helped change their minds. By 1938 the Guild had been involved in twenty strikes and won contracts with seventy-five newspapers and the United Press wire service.

Forty-eight years later, the Guild counted thirty-three thousand members at some 150 news organizations in the United States, Canada, and Puerto Rico, including the *New York Times,* the *Washington Post, Time* and *Newsweek* magazines, and the Associated Press. Pay had climbed from as little as a dollar a day in the 1920s to an average top salary in 1986 of $585 a week, or $30,420 a year. Reporters and editors at a handful of the biggest dailies could make upwards of $2,000 a week. Still, journalism remained a relatively underpaid white-collar profession, especially for those just starting out, who could expect annual salaries well below $20,000. In Detroit, Guild Local 22's contracts called for top minimum salaries of $647.84 a week at the *Free Press* and $644.34 at the *News*.

National Guild membership increased in the 1980s, but employment in the newspaper industry was growing more than twice as fast. Although the Guild had wooed other types of newspaper workers, nearly half its membership still worked as reporters, editors, photographers, or white-collar clerks. All could be replaced easily, depriving the union of the ability to pose a viable strike threat. Indeed, walkouts weren't nearly the bane to newspapers they once had been, for managers were being trained to operate the computers, presses, composing devices, and other high-tech equipment used to put out a paper. Automation decimated the leverage most newspaper unions once enjoyed.

The Guild resorted to tactics such as byline strikes and antidiscrimination lawsuits, but these lacked the financial or public relations impact of a strike. The union also tried to bolster its clout by merging with the typographers' union, but the effort failed. In the 1980s a few Guild locals were forced to simply watch while other newspaper unions negotiated contract terms that were in turn forced on the Guild.

It was a dark decade for all unions. President Reagan had effectively declared war on organized labor by breaking the strike of the air traffic controllers early in his first term. Businesses became increasingly inventive and courageous in their efforts to bend unions that had wrested healthy wage hikes and other concessions in the 1960s and 1970s. Union representation of wage-and-salary workers dropped from nearly 25 percent in the mid-1970s to 17.5 percent in 1986, continuing a decades-long trend. Many of the nation's biggest unions—including auto, steel, and mine workers—were forced to retreat from previous gains in wages, benefits, and working conditions.

Even as the newspaper industry flourished, the Guild suffered setbacks or achieved only modest gains in bitter contract fights in Washington, New York, Milwaukee, Philadelphia, and Detroit. It spent heavily on the unsuccessful bid to waylay the Cincinnati JOA, then watched the fight over the Seattle JOA from the sidelines. The union continued to organize new papers, but gains were partly offset by the loss of members at newspapers that closed.

Fifty years after the birth of the Guild, journalists still struggled with the notion of belonging to a union. In the 1980s they considered themselves bona fide professionals, not unlike lawyers and doctors. They aspired to be the social, cultural, and financial equals of their bosses, and they weren't certain how a union could help them achieve that. As Guild historian Daniel J. Leab said in 1989, "The problem today is the same problem that made it so hard to organize the Guild in the first place. Journalists are unable to come together because of ideological hangups; they think they're management when they're not."

Detroit Newspaper Guild Local 22 was formed by *Detroit Times* staffers in 1934. Despotic *Free Press* owner E. D. Stair blocked efforts to organize until 1940, when one of Jack Knight's first acts as new owner was to sign a contract with the union. For decades, *News* workers remained loyal to the paternalistic Evening News Association, which kept all of its workers on partial pay throughout the nine-month strike of 1967–68. But *News* workers flocked to the Guild nest in 1974 following the "Monday morning massacre" in which forty-eight editorial staff were fired by editor Martin Hayden and managing editor Paul Poorman.

In 1986, Local 22 was as solid as any Guild unit in the country. It had reelected its president, *News* reporter Louis Mleczko, four straight times since 1977, and Donald Kummer was a trusted administrative officer. Still, some members grumbled that Local 22 had little clout when it came to confronting the publishers. The Guild could present a solid front, but Teamsters Local 372, led by the inscrutable Elton Schade, could always cut the Guild off at the knees. The Guild would hold out for so much money, the Teamsters would make their own deal, and the Guild's leverage would disappear. The reason was simple enough: the papers didn't really need the Guild's members. If the Guild walked out, the *Free Press* and the *News* could hire out-of-work journalists or fill the papers with wire copy. A strike by the Teamsters, hundreds of drivers who actually got the papers to readers each day, would shut down both buildings on the spot.

Yet Local 22 was hardly a shrinking violet. Its spiritual leader was Mleczko, the son of a UAW member, who had come to the *News* in 1971 from the *Akron Beacon Journal*, where he was arrested while covering the Kent State shootings. (He had forgotten his press credentials and arrived at the scene in a Volkswagen Beetle festooned with a peace sticker.) Angered by the treatment older reporters suffered in the "Monday morning massacre," Mleczko played a leading role in bringing Local 22 to the *News*.

Mleczko (pronounced Muh-LETCH-koh) was a compact, balding man whose pugnacious reporting uncovered construction flaws in the heavily used Zilwaukee Bridge near Michigan's thumb and found cost overages in Mayor

Coleman Young's prized People Mover project in downtown Detroit. He wore muddied construction boots with his khaki slacks and kept a yellow safety helmet on his desk. As president of Local 22, Mleczko wore his inveterate mistrust of authority on his sleeve. In his eyes, few of the publishers' deeds weren't motivated by greed or the desire to intimidate. Even within the Guild he attacked officialdom, lambasting the union's international leaders for mismanagement and fiscal irresponsibility.

Friend and partner Don Kummer had joined the *News* as a press operator out of high school in 1951. He soon got involved in the Pressmen's Union Local 13 and was elected president of the local in 1973. He shined by trading job cuts for lifetime job guarantees and improved pensions, but was voted out of office after an ill-fated strike at the suburban *Oakland Press*. Both the Pressmen and Guild Local 22 lost their *Press* shops when scab workers replaced the striking union members. Kummer took the fall, but he blamed Teamsters Local 372, which had crossed the picket lines, enabling the *Press* to publish without missing a day.

Mleczko lured Kummer to the Guild. While Mleczko fulminated, the taciturn, chain-smoking Kummer plotted strategy and managed the Guild's daily affairs. Reporters could count on him for a sarcastic quip now and then, but he largely endeavored a calming role, reminding Mleczko that the Guild was not a platform for ideological crusades but a tool for bettering workers' lives. Soon after the JOA was announced, Kummer took Mleczko aside. Mleczko had been publicly attacking the JOA every chance he got. "Look, Lou," Kummer pleaded, "if we can work out a satisfactory agreement, we have to be quiet on this, because we have to look out for the membership."

One afternoon shortly after the JOA was announced, Kummer and Pressmen's Local 13 president Tom Brennan met with Keating, Jaske, and *Free Press* negotiator Tim Kelleher at the Pontchartrain. Kummer might as well have waited outside. Throughout the brief session, Keating addressed Brennan as if Kummer weren't present.

Walking back to their adjacent Book Building offices, Brennan asked his old friend, "Did you get the same impression I did?"

"Sure did," Kummer said. "They were basically ignoring the Guild." Kummer didn't get it. In twenty-seven years as a union official, he had been shouted down, given the runaround, laughed at, and lied to. He wasn't often ignored.

A complex underlying problem threatened to paralyze negotiations from the start: Among Local 22's nine-hundred-odd members were more than three hundred who worked in the *Free Press* business offices as ad sellers, circulation clerks, data processors, and marketing service staff. Under a JOA, they would become employees of the DNA. The Guild's other members—primarily journalists—would remain employees of the *Free Press* and the *News,* whose newsrooms would be separate from the DNA. Keating made it clear the DNA would not recognize the Guild's office workers as members of a union. The Guild could try to organize the workers once the JOA took effect, but the DNA would not stand idly by. Further, the DNA wouldn't need all the workers after merging the two papers' business staffs; some would be asked to leave. The Guild had a "successor clause" in its contract with the *Free Press* requiring a new owner of the paper to honor the contract in full; but the DNA, which would not own the newspaper, had no intention of fulfilling that provision. As Keating saw it, the Guild's only members in the JOA would be in the newsrooms, so there was no reason for him to talk to Kummer.

Complicating matters was Teamsters Local 372, which represented a passel of similar office workers at the *News.* Those workers also would join the DNA, unrecognized as union members, probably in some of the same departments as the *Free Press* business workers. All of which created the disconcerting prospect of the DNA, the Guild, and the Teamsters pulling in a three-way tug-of-war for several hundred workers. The unions wanted to bargain to retain their own members, but the DNA begged off, invoking a law barring a company from getting involved in union competitions for workers. The DNA could have worked around the law via negotiations—as it later would with the Teamsters—but Gannett and Knight-Ridder wanted as little union participation in the DNA as possible. For one thing, the status quo sought by the unions would be costly; the DNA was not going to permit the unwieldy prospect of different unions representing similar types of workers. "We were not going to sell out our employees," a DNA executive later insisted. "It would be *their* choice" whether to join a union. Further, Keating was determined not to have his JOA hiring constrained by union contracts; he wanted to hire the *best* workers, who might not necessarily be the most senior. Meanwhile, the Guild and the Teamsters were each maneuvering to represent *all* of the disputed workers, even those who did not already belong to their respective unions. Thus, the DNA, shielded by the law, had effectively set its two biggest unions on a collision course.

But if Keating didn't want to address the overlap problem, how could Kummer keep those Guild members? He needed leverage, and the best available was to somehow bottle up the JOA. He and other union leaders consulted Thomas Kauper, a University of Michigan law professor who had headed the Justice Department's Antitrust Division in the mid-1970s. Kauper stressed that no JOA ever had been rejected. Kummer wasn't sure what to do. A challenge would be expensive and time-consuming. If it failed, it could divide Local 22. But hundreds of Guild jobs were at stake. Kummer and Mleczko had to act. Mleczko was set on opposing the JOA. "This whole deal stinks," he told Kummer. "You and I both know that neither newspaper is failing. At least we're going to go down swinging. If they're going to destroy us as a union, they're going to do it publicly."

Kummer preferred the bargaining table to the courtroom. Guild attorney Miller offered to meet with Keating and appeal for negotiations on the overlap issue. When Kummer heard Miller's report of the brief encounter with Keating, he felt his dander rising. *There's nothing the Guild can do to hurt us.* The words Bill Keating allegedly had said rang in Kummer's ear like a dare. Whether Keating actually uttered them or not, Kummer couldn't get them out of his head.

"It wouldn't be like Keating to say, 'Go get fucked,' " Kummer later recalled, "but that's what it amounted to.

"From then on, it was a fight."

Elton Schade was not spoiling for a fight, but he would fight if he had to, as the Detroit publishers knew only too well from bitter experience.

One minute after midnight on November 16, 1967, members of Teamsters Local 372 had walked off their jobs at the *Detroit News,* precipitating one of the longest, costliest, most divisive strikes in newspaper history. When the strike ended in August, Detroiters had gone nine months without newspaper coverage of some of the most important stories of a turbulent decade. During those months the key forum for a healing dialogue in the wake of the '67 race riot disappeared. Workers struggled to get by without weekly paychecks. The unions lost members and their once healthy strike funds were badly depleted. Detroit businesses were deprived of a crucial advertising vehicle. The newspapers lost tens of thousands of subscribers and millions of dollars, while the competitive balance between them shifted dramatically; suddenly, the *Free Press* was within reach of the once invincible *News.*

Behind it all was a dour, calculating twenty-six-year-old who aspired to be the next Jimmy Hoffa. His name was Elton Schade. On the night of November 15, 1967, Schade roused a roomful of his Teamster brothers to take to the picket lines, even though the *News* had made the wage-hike proposal he had demanded only two days before. There was fire in his eyes and fear in his rhetoric; a Teamster had been shot to death in a recent holdup at a *News* delivery substation. Schade and his union brothers were unhappy with the

News's plan for enhanced protection. When they walked out, they surprised their own international officials and angered other union leaders who thought Schade was going too far too fast.

In the 1960s, newspaper strikes were as common as the change of seasons in big northern cities like New York and Chicago. Just a few months before the Detroit strike, a protracted walkout in New York helped to kill the *World-Journal-Tribune*. As the *News* opined after the lengthy Detroit blackout, "labor contracts have produced mere interludes between strikes in an industry with limited mechanism to predict a coming shutdown and no machinery to restore peace when multiple unions walk out and then vie with one another as to which will return with the richest settlement." The *News* and the *Free Press* endured more than a hundred labor-induced stoppages between 1955 and 1967, including a 134-day halt in 1964.

Across the country, newspaper bargaining was an impossibly tangled mess of political and practical conflicts. Because of the diversity of jobs required to put out a newspaper, big dailies found themselves bargaining every few years with a mind-boggling smorgasbord of unions. In Detroit, the Big Three automakers sat down at the bargaining table with the UAW, while the *Free Press* and the *News* squared off with fourteen union locals to negotiate twenty-three different contracts. The unions whipsawed the papers for a better deal, while the papers played antagonistic unions against one another. On the surface, the most polarizing issues were usually wages and benefits, but other, less tangible matters were nearly as divisive: How many persons does it take to operate a press? When should automation be allowed to replace workers? Should unions or the newspapers control supervisors of unionized employees? When is overtime pay justified?

After the 1967–68 strike, the publishers and union leaders vowed to find better ways to communicate. But two decades later, labor relations in Detroit were as strained as ever. The Teamsters struck the *Free Press* in 1980 on the eve of the Republican National Convention in Detroit, sabotaging months of expensive newsroom preparations. The publishers retaliated, however feebly, by printing an unprecedented joint edition. In 1983 negotiations for a new contract took more than a year. Many of the same problems that had bedeviled negotiations in the 1960s persisted. The newspapers, bargaining jointly, dealt with eleven locals affiliated with half a dozen different international unions. The unions were split into rival camps, one led by the Teamsters, the other by the Guild and the Pressmen. After the demise of the Evening News Association, both groups were immediately wary of Gannett, which had a reputation for preferring to do without unions.

To make matters worse, the union groups' respective leaders, Schade and the Guild's Don Kummer, despised each other. Kummer felt Schade had betrayed him on several occasions, in particular during the ill-fated *Oakland Press* strike. Schade held a grudge for some uncomplimentary things Kummer allegedly had said after contract talks in 1980. Each considered the other a double-dealer, though Schade had the better reputation, at least with the publishers, for keeping his word. "You get a room full of union leaders, you get a room full of egos," explained Tom Brennan, president of Pressmen's Local 13. The biggest belonged to Schade and Kummer, who seemed constantly vying for supremacy among the motley collection of Detroit newspaper union bosses. Each wanted to be the spokesman for all the unions, and each resented it when the other was quoted more prominently in news stories about negotiations. They avoided face-to-face confrontations, but the tension at meetings involving both men was palpable. No one seriously thought they could call a truce long enough to join forces against the JOA.

Elton Schade rarely hesitated to go his own way, as long as it served Local 372 of the International Brotherhood of Teamsters. He had grown up on Detroit's east side, peddled the *News,* and later became a "jumper," the person who hops on and off a newspaper delivery truck unloading bundles. At eighteen he joined the Teamsters, and in five years was elected recording secretary of Local 372. In 1966 he was elected to secretary-treasurer, the local's most powerful position. Rival union chiefs cringed as Schade stood before them, pie-faced and humorless, his cast eye disorienting, an oversized cigar clenched in one hand, declaring, "Local 372 will do what it has to do." That might mean it would cut its own deal, the other locals be damned, or it would cross another union's picket line. Schade believed deeply in the labor movement, but he was no more loyal to the Guild or the Pressmen than he was to the *News* or the *Free Press.* His sole, obsessive loyalty was to the Teamsters and Local 372. He worked seven days a week and took no vacations. Except for an occasional Detroit Red Wings hockey game, his social life was virtually nil. He lived with his elderly parents and spent most evenings with Teamster pals at Carl's Chop House, a venerated steak joint not far from the Teamster complex in the shadow of Tiger Stadium. When his parents moved to North Carolina, he took an apartment by himself but spent little time there. "He was a very lonely man and he always wanted people around him," recalled his longtime secretary, Gretchen Schumann. Those people almost invariably were Teamsters, for Schade wasn't comfortable around outsiders. He took pains to keep a distance, refusing to let any non-Teamster from the *News* or the *Free Press* buy him lunch or a drink. There were occasional girlfriends, but nothing serious. Schade was wedded to his work.

When the JOA was announced in April of 1986, the unions were in the middle of a three-year contract set to expire in June of 1987. Shortly after the JOA was announced, Keating told the union chiefs the DNA hoped to negotiate "phantom contracts" that would take effect when the JOA did. He met throughout the summer and fall of 1986 with the leaders of the biggest unions—Schade, his Teamsters brother Joel Wilson of Mailers Local 2040, Tom Brennan of Pressmen's Local 13, and Dave Gray of Typographers Local 18. Guild Local 22 was, for the most part, excluded. Keating and the other leaders got to know each other, though little progress toward contracts was made. To Schade and the other unionists, Keating seemed straightforward and willing to listen. They did not appreciate his occasional reminders that the JOA was a certainty that obliged labor's support, but they figured he was parroting a company line. When push came to shove, they figured, Keating couldn't possibly want a strike to further complicate the enormous chore of combining the business operations of the *Free Press* and the *News*.

That worked to Schade's advantage, because no one could hurt the publishers more than the Teamsters. The first and most important task of a JOA would be to deliver papers on time to readers who would already be anxious about the JOA's higher prices and the newfangled, jointly produced weekend editions. Yet the DNA could not hope to replicate the complex machinery of drivers, jumpers, district managers, and other Teamsters that moved papers from the printing plants to coin boxes and people's doorsteps every day. Knight-Ridder and Gannett could conscript nonunion journalists from their other papers to write and edit stories, but they could not hire someone who could quickly learn to navigate a coin-box-and-convenience-store route through Lincoln Park.

Schade had his own problems. One was an overlap dilemma similar to the one faced by the Guild. The Teamsters represented *News* office workers who could be out of a job or out of the union in a JOA. The DNA also was arguing that district managers, who supervised route drivers and some carriers, legally did not belong in a union. Schade hoped to resolve the problems in negotiations, but if he failed, he stood to lose more than 400 members, a third of Local 372's membership of 1,350.

Meanwhile, Teamsters at the *News* were clamoring not for negotiation but opposition to the JOA. They didn't want to share their heftier pension fund with *Free Press* Teamsters. They didn't like the publishers' plan to dovetail the papers' Teamster seniority lists, which meant some *News* Teamsters would lose seniority to *Free Press* Teamsters. Seniority was crucial because it conferred rights to choose which area of metropolitan Detroit a driver or district manager would work in, which in turn determined how much money he or she would make. *News* Teamsters believed they had won the newspaper war and therefore should surrender nothing in a JOA. If the seniority lists weren't to be placed end to end, *News* Teamsters had no use for a JOA.

Schade heard them, but he wasn't sure, in the summer of 1986, what to do. If he played it cool and dickered with the DNA, Schade risked alienating more than eight hundred *News* Teamsters. If he postured militant, negotiations could get difficult; ultimately, he could lose a big chunk of his membership. In the next Local 372 election, that could cost him his job—to Schade, his very life.

Part of the problem was predicting whether the JOA would be approved. If, as Keating insisted, it was a certainty, why waste time and money opposing it? It was tempting to let the Guild carry the ball while Schade quietly cut a deal for the Teamsters—but Keating wasn't dealing. Keating seemed to think the unions should support the JOA strictly on principle. It was a nonposition, as Schade saw it, a stick without a carrot.

And it wasn't a very big stick. No one, not Alvah Chapman, not Jim Batten, not Dave Lawrence, would say the *Free Press* would be closed if the attorney general denied the JOA. The *Free Press*'s claim to be a "failing newspaper" implied that it might succumb without a JOA, but whenever Knight-Ridder executives were asked to confirm that, they equivocated. Which made Schade and the other union bosses all the more skeptical of the publishers' intentions: Was "failing newspaper" a truly descriptive term, or was it merely the semantic key to unlock a legalized monopoly?

Schade was apprehensive, but not impatient. He had learned much from the strike of 1967–68, when rival union chiefs and even his Teamster brothers vilified him for getting carried away by emotion. Nineteen years later, while the Lou Mleczkos of the world were railing against the JOA, Elton Schade kept his passions in check. He met with Keating and bided his time, awaiting a sign. It came in July, from an unexpected source: the Reagan administration.

11

Bean Counters

Doug Ginsburg didn't disappoint the lawyers who thought the Justice Department's Antitrust Division would dislike the Detroit JOA. The report by the assistant attorney general for antitrust was released the night of Wednesday, July 23. Cal Collier and a flock of other Knight-Ridder lawyers waited at the Pennsylvania Avenue offices of Hughes Hubbard and Reed, not far from the main Justice Department building at Tenth and Constitution Avenue. Around eleven o'clock, someone from Justice called to say the report was ready. A junior associate was dispatched to pick it up. When he returned, the lawyers quickly scanned the eighty-three-page report for Ginsburg's conclusion, which they found on page 2:

> Based on the information currently available and the Antitrust Division's investigation, I have concluded that the applicants have not yet sustained their burden of proof of showing that the *Detroit Free Press* is a "failing newspaper" within the meaning of the Act and that approval of the application would effectuate the policy and purpose of the Act. On the other hand, one cannot conclude that this burden is incapable of being met. Therefore, I recommend that a hearing be held for the purpose of developing evidence with respect to the issues set forth in my report and summarized below.

In minutes, Collier was on the phone to Jack Fontaine at Knight-Ridder headquarters in Miami. Fontaine, a partner at Hughes Hubbard as well as Knight-Ridder's chief in-house counsel, listened briefly and turned to Alvah Chapman. Chapman was disappointed, but Fontaine assured him the report was no surprise and didn't necessarily bode poorly for the JOA's chances before Ed Meese. Meese didn't have to follow Ginsburg's recommendation, Fontaine said, and, even if he did, a hearing wasn't likely to hurt the case. At Gannett headquarters, lawyer Larry Aldrich gave his bosses a similar spiel, stressing that approval might take a bit longer than hoped, but it was hardly in jeopardy.

Ginsburg himself hadn't done much work on the report, but he concurred with those who did the bulk, mainly Rick Rule and Seymour Dussman and a handful of other staff lawyers and economists. Dussman and his crew had been busy. They spent days digging through the boxes of documents submitted in support of the JOA application. They read the one hundred letters sent to Meese concerning the JOA (ten urging immediate approval of the JOA, twenty-seven requesting a hearing, fifty arguing for denial). Dussman and staff attorney Gregory Hovendon traveled to Dussman's hometown to tour the *Detroit Free Press* and its riverfront printing plant and to talk with local advertisers, suburban publishers, politicians, and union officials. In Detroit and Washington they interviewed Alvah Chapman, Al Neuharth, Dave Lawrence, Peter Clark, and other people in business suits whose names and faces weren't easy to keep straight. Neuharth surprised Dussman by asking which paper his parents had subscribed to when Dussman was a boy. It was the *News*.

The *News* troubled Ginsburg nearly as much as the *Free Press*. In his report he wondered why Gannett had been so eager to get a JOA if the *Free Press* was in fact "failing." And why would Gannett share fully half the profits with a partner it supposedly was dominating? "It is not unreasonable to infer," the report said, "that Gannett felt that if it increased prices in order to improve the profitability of the *News*, the *Free Press* would then have pricing flexibility of its own. The consequence—reduced losses or even profits for the *Free Press*—could well eliminate the possibility of its entering a JOA in the future." In other words, Gannett couldn't afford to raise prices because that might jeopardize a JOA. And, while a price increase might nudge both papers into the black, profits wouldn't approach the bounty of a JOA. Ginsburg said the companies "demonstrated an almost unseemly haste in considering the possibility of a JOA even before Gannett had successfully bid for the Evening News Association."

He was not unimpressed with the *Free Press*'s losses, but he questioned whether the paper's prospects were as bleak as Knight-Ridder's lawyers painted them. Detroit had suffered a recession, but a recovery was under way. He noted *Free Press* gains in daily circulation and ad linage and revenue. Operation Tiger had seen mixed results, but a key component, the riverfront plant expansion, was not yet in place. *Free Press* personnel costs had risen faster than at the *News*. Losses had not prompted serious consideration of closing the *Free Press*—to the contrary, Knight-Ridder had increased spending in Detroit and postponed making profits. Indeed, Ginsburg suggested that the *Free Press*'s losses might be more aptly viewed as investments in the future, evidence of Knight-Ridder's willingness to trade short-term pain for a long-term bonanza. He was raising what would be the case's pivotal question:

> When a newspaper owner consciously and deliberately decides to sacrifice short-term profits in a quest for greater long-term profits, indeed potential monopoly profits, should a JOA be available as a "second-best" alternative? This issue is especially important here because the *Free Press* has not lost the battle; rather, it and the *News*, according to the statement of the chairmen of the parent companies, have "fought to a virtual draw."

There were those words again.

Open season on Ginsburg's report began the morning after it was released. Analyst Bruce Thorp dismissed the report as "typical lawyer talk." Other analysts played it down, but the stock prices of Gannett and Knight-Ridder dropped $2.00 and $2.25 a share, respectively. Neuharth griped that Ginsburg's opinion was tainted by politics. "We made a factual case, but we didn't jump up and down and get on a soapbox and wave the flag like those who were opposed to it," he told the *Washington Post.* Keating said Ginsburg "is dealing with a lot of maybes. You can't go on forever with these kinds of losses." Kurt Luedtke was happily surprised, telling the *News* he hadn't expected Ginsburg to deliver so sharp a rebuke.

In the fall, Douglas Ginsburg would be nominated to the U.S. Circuit Court of Appeals for the District of Columbia, one of the most distinguished appellate panels in the land. A year later, in the wake of the Robert Bork fiasco, President Reagan would nominate Ginsburg to replace Justice Lewis Powell on the Supreme Court. The nominee would withdraw after admitting he used marijuana in the 1960s and 1970s. In the newsrooms of the *Free Press* and the *News,* the cynical would snicker that Ginsburg must have been indulging again when he wrote that damning opinion on the JOA.

* * *

The newspaper lawyers flayed the Ginsburg report in a brief to Meese on August 25. The assistant attorney general, they said, ignored the enormity of the *Free Press*'s losses. Circulation and advertising trends favorable to the *Free Press* were isolated and, anyway, they had not overcome the *News*'s sizable market share advantages or prevented huge and growing losses. Ginsburg raised hypothetical questions about the future of the *Free Press*—might it become profitable if the *News* raised prices?—that could not be answered at a public hearing or anywhere else. He had not challenged the validity of the losses, they said, nor had he made a case that management of the paper was unreasonable.

The *Free Press,* they argued, was a victim of the unique economic characteristics of the newspaper industry. History proved, with rare exception, that second-place newspapers in large cities ultimately succumbed. The publishers relied heavily on analysis by Dr. James Rosse, a Stanford University professor and one of the preeminent experts on newspaper economics. Rosse held that economies of scale helped larger newspapers make more money than their smaller rivals at relatively the same prices. Simply, that was because most of the cost of producing a day's ration of papers is contained in producing the day's very first copy. Duplicating that paper thousands or hundreds of thousands of times adds relatively little to the overall cost, as the theory goes. So, the bigger a newspaper's circulation, the more it spreads its costs, the wider its margin of profit per paper. With a larger profit margin, the paper can better afford to hold down prices than a smaller rival, which has smaller economies of scale and hence a smaller margin. If, for competitive reasons, the larger paper decides to price so low that it is losing money, it loses less. Add to that the strains of increased competition, from television, suburban papers, and direct mail for a limited pool of advertising dollars, and the smaller paper simply cannot—and, in most cases, did not—catch up.

The publishers also accused Ginsburg of failing to consider the *Free Press* as a stand-alone entity, as required by the Newspaper Preservation Act. Minus Knight-Ridder's financial lifeline, the *Free Press,* they wrote in their reply, "would long ago have followed into history the *Washington Star,* the *Baltimore News-American,* the *Philadelphia Bulletin,* the *Cleveland Press,* the *Buffalo Courier-Express,* and numerous other newspapers that once competed successfully but are now only memories." Ginsburg's assertion that the publishers had displayed "unseemly haste" in seeking a JOA demonstrated his "underlying hostility" toward the Newspaper Preservation Act. In other words, they told

Meese, they never had a chance with Ginsburg, because he plainly did not like the law.

The companies continued to insist a hearing wasn't needed, but now they hedged their bets. If the attorney general was to order a hearing, they argued, he should set an "expeditious schedule." The newspapers were losing a combined $450,000 a week—the equivalent of $23 million a year. "Under these circumstances," the lawyers argued, "all speed is necessary and appropriate."

Yet, unwittingly or not, they were themselves delaying a decision. By law, Meese could not rule until the end of a thirty-day period for public comment on the Ginsburg report. The Justice Department twice extended the deadline because it needed more time to consider Knight-Ridder and Gannett's plea that seventy thousand pages of their documents be kept confidential. The companies finally aborted the request in October, agreeing to release all but about fifteen hundred pages. Reporters digging through the new paper were puzzled to find that much of it duplicated material released previously.

On September 25, one year to the day after Neuharth and Chapman first met to discuss a JOA, Guild Local 22 voted unanimously to oppose the JOA at a public hearing or, if Meese approved the merger without a hearing, in federal court. "The newspapers will not get a JOA as fast as they want one," Don Kummer vowed. Yet only 40 of the local's 950 members found time to come to the Detroit Press Club for the vote. The future of Detroit newspapering was being decided, and no one showed up.

The Guild vote displeased Elton Schade; he didn't like being upstaged by Kummer, and he had hoped to have more control over the unions' response to the publishers. Privately, he was girding Teamsters Local 372 for battle. The Ginsburg report suggested that the JOA wasn't the sure thing Keating insisted it was; certainly there was leverage to be gained by opposing the merger, at least for now. On October 8, Local 372's executive board voted to mount its own legal challenge to the JOA.

A week later Alvah Chapman showed up in Detroit with some interesting news for *Free Press* executives: the JOA might be in place by the middle of 1987, perhaps even sooner. Chapman said he was encouraged by what was happening at the Justice Department, though he could not be specific, and spoke of "a strong possibility" that action could come very soon. What Chapman could not, or would not, say was that the publishers had been given a valuable bit of intelligence concerning the attorney general's thinking about the JOA. It had come from Jerald F. terHorst, a former *News* Washington correspondent who had worked briefly as President Ford's press secretary before resigning in protest when Ford pardoned Nixon for the Watergate scandal. In 1986 terHorst was the chief of Ford Motor Company's Washington public relations staff. At a social function one night that fall he had found himself chatting with Attorney General Edwin Meese.

TerHorst had met Meese a couple of times covering presidential campaigns, but he did not know the attorney general well. As terHorst recalls it, when Meese heard that the Ford flack once had worked for the *News,* the attorney general grimaced and said, "I've got that JOA thing on my calendar and I've got to make a decision." In terHorst's view, Meese wasn't eager to make what he characterized as a close call. TerHorst recalls the attorney general asking what public sentiment toward the JOA was like in Detroit. It was a strange and probably improper question, since Meese was supposed to base his decision on whether the *Free Press* was a "failing paper." Besides, the case record was crammed with letters from Michigan citizens, most of which urged Meese at the very least to call a public hearing. TerHorst said he didn't know much more than what he read in the newspapers, but he offered to make a call or two if Meese was interested. Meese was. "I'd kind of like to approve it if I could, but I'm not sure I can do it just like that," Meese said, snapping his fingers for emphasis. "If you can sound it out, get the lay of the land, I'd appreciate it."*

TerHorst called Bill Keating, who was to run the JOA. After listening to terHorst's story of what Meese had said, Keating told terHorst the publishers were hoping for a swift approval of the JOA so that they could put it together before either paper deteriorated further. Keating called terHorst a week or so later to stress that a public hearing probably wouldn't do much good, since it was unlikely to alter the entrenched positions of either the newspapers or the unions. That concluded terHorst's inquiry into public sentiment in Michigan. He dutifully relayed what he had learned to one of Meese's aides.

Encouraged by terHorst's hopeful news, Keating and the executives at Knight-Ridder and Gannett geared up JOA implementation planning, preparing to begin interviewing workers at both papers for jobs in the new Detroit Newspaper Agency. Every day it seemed, rumors circulated that Meese was prepared to approve the JOA at any moment. Of course Keating and his bosses did not share what they knew with the employees. Instead they filed additional

*Meese does not recall this conversation and says he seriously doubts it ever occurred. "We were scrupulously careful not to discuss what my decision would be," he says.

briefs with Meese noting that the *Free Press* had lost $12.4 million and the *News* $10.6 million during the first nine months of 1986, arguing yet again that a hearing would be "costly and unnecessary."

Dave Lawrence tried to ease the tension on his staff by giving them as much information on the JOA as possible—though the terHorst leak was never mentioned. Lawrence met with dozens of employees, set up a telephone hot line for quick answers to JOA questions, and posted queries and answers weekly on office bulletin boards. Often he replied to questions himself, as in an October 1 edition of *The Friendly Fast Facts:*

> QUESTION: A rumor in the composing room last night was that a decision has already been made that if the JOA doesn't go through, Knight-Ridder will close the paper. Is that so?
>
> ANSWER: Nothing I know confirms that. In fact, I have been assured by the highest officers of Knight-Ridder that no decision has been made.

Just before Thanksgiving, Lawrence and Keating flew to Washington for a visit to Capitol Hill. A few days later Michigan's senior congressmen, Democrat John Dingell and Republican William Broomfield, cosigned a letter to Meese asking the attorney general to decide the JOA by December 8.

Their timing could have been better. The very day they sent the letter, Meese and President Reagan were at a news conference answering questions about the administration's use of profits from the sale of arms to Iran to aid the contra revolutionaries in Nicaragua. It would erupt into the worst scandal of the Reagan years, and Meese would be squarely in the middle of it.

On December 8, Assistant Attorney General John R. Bolton replied to Dingell and Broomfield with a two-page letter assuring them the department was proceeding as quickly as it could. On January 26, Meese made a speech at the Detroit College of Law. He politely declined to answer questions on the JOA but assured reporters a decision was forthcoming within a week to ten days. First Boston Corporation analyst Kevin Gruneich, who happened to be in Detroit at the time, called his Wall Street office and ordered Knight-Ridder and Gannett placed on the "buy" list, touching off a minor rally in the companies' stock prices. It finally seemed the time to cash in on Detroit.

Every day there were rumors. Keating couldn't meet with anyone from the *News* or the *Free Press* without newsroom gossips whispering that a decision was imminent, the JOA would be approved, and Keating was ready to throw the switch on the merger. *Free Press* staffers put $104 into a betting pool on the day and hour Meese would make the call. The attorney general didn't help matters. On February 3 and again on February 20 he again publicly promised a decision in a week to ten days. An anonymous *Free Press* poet vented frustration on a bulletin board:

Edwin Meese said, Let me see
I'll make my decision 'bout quarter past three
But at that time, he said, Wait some more
And I'll spill the beans at ten to four
At ten to four, we got no jive
And at four thirty-six, he said, See ya at five
At five nineteen—still no clue
A reporter spread a rumor 'bout six oh two
By six thirty-nine, there was still no fate
They said, Come back tomorrow 'bout twenty past eight
But all the reporters knew better this time
They ain't showing up 'til half past nine!

By then, Meese's top deputy, William Bradford Reynolds, was urging the attorney general to call a hearing. In a February 13 memo Reynolds outlined several unresolved issues, including what he called "the ultimate issue: whether the *Free Press* more likely than not will be unable to return to profitability without a JOA. I believe that we need a hearing to answer [the issues] confidently."

At about quarter past two on February 25, Meese released a two-page order for a public hearing on the Detroit JOA. At a news conference in Washington, Associate Deputy Attorney General John C. Harrison admitted that Iran-contra had delayed the decision slightly. "It would have been possible to make a decision on the merits" of the JOA, Harrison told reporters, "but the attorney general was not confident that that would have been the right decision, because he was not confident that he knew enough about what was going on." So Meese was erring on the side of caution. Keating and his bosses at Knight-Ridder and Gannett assumed Iran-contra had cost them a quick approval of the JOA. Meese would later insist that Iran-contra had had nothing to do with it.

For all of the bold predictions of the executives and the lawyers, the JOA was going to a hearing. Chapman dismissed it as delaying the inevitable, but now, it seemed to many of the *Free Press*'s twenty-two hundred employees, approval was not by any means certain. Doug Ginsburg may have been mistaken, but he wasn't crazy or stupid. Perhaps the Knight-Ridder lawyers were mistaken. "I fear what Knight-Ridder would do with the *Free Press*," veteran *Free Press* reporter Jack Kresnak said. "If [the JOA] is not granted, what's Knight-Ridder going to say, 'We didn't mean it'? I'm afraid they'd close the *Free Press* down." But the company avoided that question yet again. Asked about Knight-Ridder's intentions, company spokesman Frank Hawkins enigmatically told a *News* reporter: "The *Free Press* has been part of our life-style since 1940."

Wall Street prepared for another year of losses, expecting as much as $17 million at the *Free Press* alone. The prices of Gannett and Knight-Ridder stocks took a tumble. The impatient publishers prayed for a speedy conclusion to the hearing and a swift—and favorable—decision from Meese. But Kevin Gruneich, the young First Boston analyst, had it exactly right: "Anybody who thinks this thing is going to be over in months," he confided to a *News* reporter, "is kidding themselves."

"On the record, please."

It was 10:00 A.M. on a muggy Monday, August 3, 1987. More than a year had passed since Douglas Ginsburg had issued his troublesome report. Courtroom 237 in the federal courthouse in downtown Detroit was packed. Elton Schade was there with his sidekick, Tom Minielly of Teamsters Local 372. So were union chiefs Don Kummer of Guild Local 22, Joel Wilson of the Mailers, Tom Brennan of the Pressmen, and Dave Gray of the Typographers. Reporters from the *Free Press*, the *News*, the Associated Press, and a bevy of radio and television stations mingled in the aisles. *Free Press* reporter Stephen Jones joked, "Detroit media held hostage—day one."

In the back of the modest, high-ceilinged room sat Peter Clark, looking tan and healthy, chatting with a friend. A couple of rows in front of him were the *Free Press*'s Dave Lawrence and Bob Hall, sitting with Chip Weil and Moe Hickey of the *News*. They looked fairly placid for four men who had been squabbling for much of the summer over how the JOA would work if it ever was approved. At the front of the room, beyond a thigh-high wooden railing, a throng of lawyers in dark suits scurried to their places. There were about a dozen representing the Detroit papers and their parent companies, three for the Antitrust Division of the Justice Department, another eight or so for Mayor Coleman Young and six union locals, who were there to oppose the JOA. Calling the room to order was Morton Needelman, a retired administrative law judge who had come from Washington to conduct the hearing on the JOA.

Mort Needelman was a fifty-six-year-old Brooklyn native and graduate of Harvard Law School who had spent thirty years toiling in a variety of posts at the Federal Trade Commission. The cases he had handled in thirteen years as an FTC administrative law judge involved, among others, the auto, candy, moving, lumber, and broadcast industries, but never newspapers. He was tall and lanky, like Ichabod Crane in a business suit. His smallish face, with its doleful, hooded eyes, beaked nose, and cropped black mustache, was faintly reminiscent of Groucho Marx, though Needelman rarely made a joke and hardly ever smiled, at least in the courtroom. Lawyers encountering Needelman in the courthouse elevators learned they would get nothing by way of chitchat but a clipped "Good morning."

Needelman had a reputation as a bright, hardworking judge who ran a no-nonsense courtroom, but the lawyers for Knight-Ridder and Gannett were wary. As a field investigator and director of the FTC's Bureau of Consumer Protection, Needelman had antagonized many a large corporation. In Washington legal circles, some felt Needelman was inclined to lean ever so slightly in favor of the so-called underdog—that is, whoever opposed a corporation. "What we assumed from the outset," recalled Philip Lacovara, Knight-Ridder's lead attorney, "was that Judge Needelman would start out thinking that nothing in our value system is as sacred as the antitrust laws and, therefore, anyone seeking to get such an exemption must be up to no good, they must be trying to do something that is fundamentally un-American."

The publishers had a fleeting opportunity to have the judge removed. In April of 1987 a group called the Federal Administrative Law Judges Conference (FALJC) complained to the Justice Department that Needelman's appointment was improper. An active judge, the group argued, should have been appointed instead of a retiree. Lawyers for Knight-Ridder and Gannett wondered if the appointment might be grounds for appeal of the ultimate JOA decision. That would be a help if the JOA was denied, a problem if it was approved. Dethroning the judge would take time; meanwhile, the JOA would be in limbo. Though the lawyers didn't expect Needelman to look kindly on their case, there was no guarantee a replacement would be friendlier. A failed removal bid might simply irritate the judge, like swatting at a wasp. Finally, the lawyers decided to take their chances on Needelman. It was a decision they would regret.

If the judge was hostile to the JOA, he didn't show it. He was clearly impatient, acerbic, skeptical, but his philosophical bent was inscrutable. At a prehearing conference in April he said he intended to pursue the "very vigorous testing" of the application he thought the attorney general desired. At a July conference he described the newspapers' case as "formidable." He granted virtually all of the opponents' requests for newspaper documents over the objections of the publishers' attorneys, but warned the opponents not to focus their case on "snippets" of mismanagement. Questioning the Antitrust Division's approach to the case, he said, "What I thought the attorney general had in mind was alternatives to a JOA, not this sort of second-guessing. It's not an alternative to a JOA to have a perfect staff, because no one has a perfect staff." Yet he challenged the newspapers' suggestion that Detroit followed the pattern of smaller cities that were unable to support competing dailies. "Why didn't Congress just say that every city that has two newspapers could have a JOA?" Needelman asked rhetorically. "You can't prove the death of a newspaper in Detroit by the death of a newspaper in Anchorage, Alaska, can you?" He seemed to relish arguing with lawyers of all stripes.

Needelman would begin each of the sixteen days of the hearing with a businesslike, "On the record, please." Today, he asked the lawyers to introduce themselves, then turned to the tables on his left, where attorneys for Knight-Ridder, Gannett, the *Free Press*, and the *News* sat, two rows deep.

"Opening statements for the newspapers?"

"Thank you, Your Honor."

Standing before Judge Needelman at a lectern in the middle of the courtroom, his hands clasped gently at his back, stood a dark, barrel-chested man wearing delicate, rimless spectacles. Knight-Ridder's lead attorney was Philip A. Lacovara, partner in charge of Hughes Hubbard and Reed's Washington office and one of the most distinguished members of the District of Columbia Bar. The onetime newsboy, *magna cum laude* Georgetown, *summa cum laude* Columbia Law, had, at the age of thirty, argued the Nixon tapes case before the Supreme Court—and prevailed, precipitating the first and only presidential resignation in history. When President Ford pardoned his predecessor, young Phil Lacovara protested by resigning from Leon Jaworski's Watergate prosecution team.

He had grown up on Long Island, the son of a bank lawyer, and made his reputation in Washington, where he served as assistant to then-Solicitor General Thurgood Marshall and later as a deputy solicitor general. At thirty-one he had opened Hughes Hubbard's Washington office. Now, at forty-four, he reigned as the firm's Washington litigator par excellence. His presence attracted complex cases, including many that found their way to the high court. His clients included Ford Motor Company, Northwest Airlines, Pfizer, and Texas Air. When Laurence Tribe, the Harvard law professor and renowned expert on constitutional law, needed an attorney to investigate the tapping of his phone, he called on Lacovara.

He had been working on the JOA since Meese ordered the hearing. Prior to that, Calvin Collier had been Knight-Ridder's lead counsel, but Collier was less litigator than strategist and number cruncher. At the prehearing conference in April, Lacovara had argued for a tightly regulated hearing schedule and a June 1 start. When he pointed out that the hearing in the Seattle JOA had proceeded on such an expedited basis, Needelman trumped his ace by saying he had spoken with the judge in the Seattle case, Daniel Hanscom, and Hanscom had said it was a difficult experience.

"I'm only suggesting it is possible," Lacovara pleaded, "and that case shows you can have—"

"Do you want to give me an affidavit from Dan Hanscom that that is possible?" Needelman interrupted.

"I don't think he'd deny it," Lacovara said. "The case was fully and fairly tried. That is all I was getting at."

"All right," the judge shot back, "but you haven't tried to get that affidavit from him?"

"I wouldn't try to get such an affidavit from a presiding officer."

"Right. Don't."

Lacovara had more success persuading Needelman to allow Knight-Ridder and Gannett to submit their witnesses' initial testimony in writing, a procedure common to administrative cases but unusual in other litigation. Witnesses submitted detailed written statements, which then were tested in live cross-examination. Hughes Hubbard used the approach often in cases involving government agencies; it was simpler and saved time. Gannett's lawyers had their doubts; they wondered if a judge might, subconsciously or not, discount written testimony in favor of more dramatic live cross-examination. But they did not press the point; Neuharth had instructed that, since the *Free Press* had filed as the "failing newspaper," the case was Knight-Ridder's to win or lose.

Anyway, neither the Knight-Ridder nor the Gannett lawyers thought cross-examination could disturb the testimony offered by their well-paid witnesses, including two accountants, an industry analyst, an economist, and a handful of executives, among them Neuharth and Alvah Chapman. They had seen nothing in the months prior to the start of the hearing to suggest the Antitrust Division, the unions, or Mayor Young would raise any sort of novel challenges to their essential argument, which Lacovara, without the aid of notes, succinctly summarized for Judge Needelman.

"We are here this morning to begin a hearing on the question of whether the *Detroit Free Press* is in probable danger of financial failure. That question, I think, is illuminated by what you will hear from the first two witnesses this morning, Mr. Thibault and Mr. Kahn. The plain, simple, and irrefutable fact in this case is that the *Free Press* has, for a considerable period of time, since the beginning of this decade, been incurring real, substantial, and continuing losses. If it were not for the subsidies of its parent, Knight-Ridder, the *Free Press* would not be publishing this morning. It is publishing this morning because the *Free Press* has received $178 million in cash advances."

Lacovara could not have looked more confident. He stood almost perfectly still and relaxed, gesturing sparingly, occasionally resting his hands on the lectern. "What's more remarkable, Your Honor, about the testimony that you'll be hearing from the witnesses being presented by the Antitrust Division and the intervenors is that they do not really take issue with the fundamental and undeniable reality of long, continuing, real, and substantial losses. . . . In all of their testimony, with all of the abstruse theories that they have advanced, they have not been able to come up with the magical solution for how to turn this newspaper from the financial travail in which it finds itself into a profitable newspaper."

That was true, but beside the point, as Seymour Dussman, the Antitrust Division's lead attorney, pointed out early in his opening remarks. "It is the applicants," the moonfaced lawyer admonished, "who have the burden of proof in this proceeding."

Technically, the role of Dussman and his two colleagues, Gregory Hovendon and Mary Beth McGee, was to ferret out information the attorney general would need to make a sound decision. According to the statute, and as Dussman saw it, the Antitrust Division was to be fact finder rather than antagonist. If asked, Dussman would readily assert that the division had not determined how Meese ought to rule on the JOA.

However, no one on the newspaper side believed that, as had become clear at the prehearing conference in April. At one point, Needelman had called all the lawyers to the bench to ask if the case could be settled without a hearing. Gannett lawyer John Stuart Smith of Nixon, Hargrave, Devans and Doyle had said the publishers would be glad to settle if the Antitrust Division would host the meeting at which the *Free Press* and the *News* would jointly raise circulation and advertising prices—which, of course, would have been a gross violation of the antitrust laws. It was a snide suggestion, intended to imply that the Antitrust Division, for all its criticism of the JOA, could offer no better solution. Dussman had found it mildly amusing. No thanks, he'd said.

Now Dussman was telling Needelman that losses alone did not automatically qualify the *Free Press* for a JOA. "If losses were sufficient to qualify," Dussman argued, "there would be no need to explore most of the issues set forth in the attorney general's order. . . . If the history of losses were sufficient to demonstrate that a paper is failing, then the *News* presumably would be failing. Instead, the applicants and their witnesses say that it is the *News* that is the paper with insurmountable competitive advantages, vis-à-vis the *Free Press*. . . . A question which we believe has not yet been answered is why the largest newspaper company in the country would agree to forgo hundreds of millions of dollars in profits if it truly believed that its only metropolitan daily newspaper competitor in Detroit was failing."

In other words, the *News* would not have been publishing that morning if not for the subsidies of Gannett. It was a more critical question than even Dussman could have imagined.

Duane F. Ice was scowling. The big redheaded lawyer for Guild Local 22 never could hide his contempt for the newspapers' case. He was one of two lead lawyers for the six newspaper unions and Mayor Young. Assistant Attorney General William Bradford Reynolds had approved the unions as "intervenors" in the JOA hearing because they stood to lose jobs, the mayor because he represented the wider public. Reynolds turned away several others who had asked to participate, including a college professor who once wrote for the *Free Press*, a group of conservatives called Citizens for Newspaper Competition, state Senator John Kelly, and W. Edward Wendover, publisher of a small suburban tabloid.

Ice was a forty-year-old labor lawyer who grew up in rural Michigan and clerked at Bruce Miller's firm while attending Wayne State Law. He joined the firm as an attorney in 1974 and in four years was a partner. He worked hard, was fastidiously well organized, and kept after witnesses like a bulldog. Ice relished the David-and-Goliath clashes a labor lawyer frequently confronted. In the biggest case of his life, he had coordinated the legal efforts of hundreds of copper miners striking Phelps Dodge Corporation in Arizona in the early 1980s. On one occasion he exhorted a large group of the miners, "I believe that the company seriously underestimated you people. For some reason, they thought you were a soft touch." He might have said the same to Detroit's newspaper unions.

His cocounsel was Eugene Driker, ten years Ice's senior and an antitrust specialist and partner in the Detroit firm of Barris, Sott, Denn and Driker. Driker was a native of Detroit who also had graduated from Wayne State Law.

His firm's clients were predominantly corporate. In Driker's most celebrated case, he had defended a Michigan utility, Consumers Power Company, in a multimillion-dollar lawsuit filed by Dow Chemical involving Consumers' failure to complete a nuclear power plant. The case was settled after two years at trial, in no small part due to Driker's meticulous dissection of the true intentions of Dow Chemical's executives. When Teamsters Local 372 approached him to handle the JOA case in the spring of 1987, Driker was intrigued, as he had been since bumping into Dave Lawrence at a social gathering the previous fall. The *Free Press* publisher had told Driker how strong was the newspapers' case, and Driker had asked to see a copy of their arguments. On a cursory reading they seemed solid, but Driker figured there had to be another side. A look at the Ginsburg opinion, which Lawrence obligingly passed along, had confirmed his suspicion.

Representing the union would not be a lucrative assignment. Elton Schade, sensing Driker's personal interest, made it clear that Local 372 couldn't afford much. Driker figured the case would generate a fair amount of public interest and be over reasonably quickly. And it appealed to his competitive instinct, which was sharp. No opponent had ever won a JOA case, and the odds were slim that he and the Guild's counsel were going to beat the publishers' formidable coterie of Washington lawyers. That cinched it for Driker. He told Schade that, rather than charge by the hour, he would do it for a flat fee of $175,000. "We gave it away," he later said.

Driker and Ice met at the prehearing conference in April. Their clients had been squabbling publicly over which union would represent noneditorial workers under the JOA. At the same time, the unions' leaders, Schade and Don Kummer, were futilely trying to overcome their personal animosity to forge an alliance to oppose the JOA. Judge Needelman forced them together by ordering that the unions speak with "one voice" at the hearing. That was fine with Driker and Ice, who had no time for bickering. They had just four months to cull through tens of thousands of documents, prepare exhibits, interview the newspapers' witnesses, find their own witnesses, and develop a strategy for attacking the publishers' case, now more than a year in preparation. They had the Ginsburg opinion for a guide, and neither of their clients was totally new to the case, having prepared briefs urging Meese to call a hearing. But, compared with the lawyers for Gannett and Knight-Ridder, Driker and Ice were rank novices when it came to understanding part-run circulation, rate card discounting, cost-per-thousand, and the myriad other nuances of newspapering.

Although six unions were sanctioned as intervenors, the Teamsters and the Guild—meaning Driker, Ice, and a few junior associates—carried the bulk of the legal load, with a little help from Mayor Young's attorneys. Andrew Zack of Driker's firm and Hanan Kolko of Ice's firm flew to Washington to see the documents filed there. At the cramped, windowless public reading room at the Justice Department they saw boxes stacked four high along the walls and decided they couldn't possibly get the job done there. When Needelman charitably ordered the cache sent to Detroit, the truck hauling the boxes broke down en route, delaying delivery by three precious days.

Ice flew to Washington hoping for guidance from Dussman, but the Antitrust Division lawyer offered little but a vague index to the documents. Driker and Ice had a more fruitful meeting with Kurt Luedtke. The former *Free Press* executive editor expounded on the *Free Press,* the *News,* Knight-Ridder, and Al Neuharth for most of a sunny afternoon while the lawyers sipped iced tea on the back porch of Luedtke's suburban Detroit home. Someone joked that they should have checked the bushes for bugging devices.

Driker and Ice sought expert help from academics, editors, and others steeped in the business, but they were either too busy, too expensive, or too timid. "Everybody suggested that I talk to somebody else," Driker recalled. "It was clear to me that nobody wanted to take on Gannett and Knight-Ridder." Some undoubtedly believed the case for the JOA was solid.

It didn't matter much to Driker, though, because he was sure the companies' documents would be the key to the case. The Consumers Power–Dow Chemical trial had convinced him that a few handwritten notes scribbled on a cocktail napkin could be worth more than a thousand pages of testimony sculpted by a lawyer. Day after day Driker's deputies, Zack and Morley Witus, plowed through the mountain of documents with Ice's young associates, Kolko and Russell Linden, and two of the mayor's attorneys, George Koklanaris and Cynthia Yott. They began by separating documents into some three dozen categories, then broke them down into stacks tailored to the newspapers' witnesses. Slowly, the scattered pieces of the puzzle began to come together. Now and then, Zack or Witus would scurry down the hall to Driker's office clutching a newly discovered document: "Look at this, Gene! Look at this!"

Driker had been less confident than Ice that the JOA could be stopped. By the time the hearing began August 3, Driker thought their chances were better than even. The newspapers' case struck him as very good—perhaps *too* good. The written testimony was polished to a high gloss, replete with nifty charts and graphs. The experts were the most prominent available. Their conclusions left no room for disagreement. Driker thought of it as a panzer division deployed to steamroll the opposition—perhaps he and Ice could string a wire across the road.

Their own witnesses were less than promising. The best they could offer was a couple of obscure financial consultants with no background whatsoever in the newspaper business. So Driker and Ice focused on the publishers' witnesses. Their initial testimony, delivered to Needelman in neatly packaged, white three-ring binders, was concise and simple: the accountants and other experts testified that the *Free Press*'s losses were real; the executives testified that management of the *Free Press* had been reasonable. That was the gist of it.

A more complex picture emerged from the documents Zack, Kolko, Linden, and Witus had rummaged through. For all of their searching, the young lawyers could not find any documents that spoke of the *Free Press* as a paper doomed to fail. There were no letters or memoranda that sharply questioned or criticized the performance of Dave Lawrence and his deputies. On the contrary, executives in Miami and Detroit seemed, overall, encouraged. They weren't happy about the *Free Press*'s losses, but they weren't planning on profits anyway for quite a few years. Only after the JOA application was filed had people started writing about bleak prospects at the *Free Press*. Until then, there were no documents in which anyone seriously contemplated closing the *Free Press*. Over and over, the bosses in Detroit and Miami wrote of gaining "dominance," of investing in the future, of winning the war—and, here and there, of the possibility of getting a JOA.

"We emphasize most strongly the contemporaneous records," Ice told Judge Needelman. He was in the middle of his opening statement. Driker was working distractedly at the intervenors' table, poring over notes he would use to cross-examine the first of the publishers' witnesses. "What were these executives doing and saying?" Ice said. "It's clear they did not want to report to each other the *Free Press* is failing, we have got to lose it, the losses are not reversible. There is no contemporaneous record remotely resembling that. On the contrary, their own statements and records reflect confidence, reflect the thinking the *Free Press* would win, that it would remain viable. Even Gannett conceded the viability of the *Free Press* when it granted a fifty-fifty JOA unlike any other JOA in both its terms and its duration.

"The *Free Press* cannot prove and has not proved that its losses are irreversible. First of all, there is no record that they tried. What the record shows is that, since 1980, the goal has been JOA and downwards. At no time since 1980 has the short-term, direct, and immediate goal been to get profitable either this fiscal year, the next, or even the one after that." Ice was delivering notice that he and Driker would use the publishers' own words and deeds against them. That did not alarm the lawyers for Gannett and Knight-Ridder, who could not imagine more than the slimmest chance that they would be rebuffed.

The newspapers' first witness was accountant Robert H. Thibault. He was a tall, broad-shouldered man whose chin jutted defiantly whenever a question displeased him. Thibault gave the strong impression of being somehow irritated at having to answer the queries of strangers. He certainly would rather have been in the mountains of North Carolina, where his family was vacationing.

Thibault was the partner in charge of the audit staff at the Miami office of the national accounting firm of Ernst and Whinney, Knight-Ridder's auditor. Knight-Ridder paid Ernst and Whinney eight hundred thousand dollars a year to handle its books, and had paid a hundred thousand dollars for the preparation of Thibault's written testimony, consisting largely of an audit purporting to show that the *Free Press* would be insolvent if not for $178 million advanced by its parent. The audit also offered what is known in the accounting trade as a "going-concern opinion," concluding that the *Free Press* "may be unable to continue in existence."

What dramatic tension had built during the lawyers' opening statements quickly gave way to the tedium of Thibault's matter-of-fact assertions concerning paid-in capital and intercompany charges. Gregory Hovendon of the Antitrust Division completed his cross-examination without leaving a scratch.

After the lunch recess, Gene Driker stepped up to where Thibault sat at Needelman's left elbow. "Good afternoon, Mr. Thibault," he said. He began by establishing what Thibault was not: neither a financial analyst, an economist, an investment banker, nor an appraiser—not someone who could necessarily render a conclusive business judgment about the future of the *Free Press.* As he grilled Thibault, Driker paced between his lectern and the witness stand, firing question after question without seeming to ponder what the witness had just testified. He was a bantam rooster of a man, with a few silver hairs pasted across his balding pate. A pair of half-glasses dangled from a cord around his neck. He did not ask questions so much as suggest answers. "I take it you are aware, Mr. Thibault, that there are many corporations, including some of the giants of American industry, that have had going-concern qualifications in the last five years and are very much alive today. Isn't that so?"

Driker was not terribly familiar with the arcane realm of public accounting, and he did not expect to tear large holes in Thibault's highly technical testimony. But he hoped to leave Needelman with a sense that all was not as tidy and simple as Knight-Ridder and Gannett would have had the judge believe.

Driker produced a memo Thibault had written five months earlier saying Ernst and Whinney would prepare an audit questioning the *Free Press*'s ability to survive.

Peering through the half-glasses perched on the end of his nose, Driker read: " 'This conclusion is based on the following facts and circumstances.' "

He looked up at Thibault.

"Then you list the three facts and circumstances, do you not?"

"Yes," Thibault replied.

"The third is, 'In the filing with Justice, KRI has asserted that DFP is a "failing" newspaper.' "

"Yes."

Driker hoped it was clear that Knight-Ridder had claimed the *Free Press* was failing based, at least in part, on its accountant's dire assessment—while the accountant had based his evaluation, at least in part, on the assertion that the paper was failing.

Driker kept Thibault on the stand for four hours. He asked why Knight-Ridder would first classify a $71 million advance to the *Free Press* as a loan, then reclassify it as a long-term investment, then, when the JOA was in the works, call it a loan yet again, thereby making the *Free Press*'s financials look worse. He wondered why Knight-Ridder didn't put some value on the *Free Press*'s hefty losses as a means of reducing the corporation's income tax.

Thibault had reasonably good answers for most of the questions, yet he was clearly exasperated with the diminutive, circling, relentlessly curious Driker. By the end of the day Thibault was acting as if the attorney had him on the run. His jaw clenched. His face burned red. He fidgeted in his chair. His cluster of attorneys, watching from a few feet away, wondered how Driker had gotten to him so.

Thibault seemed more relaxed the next morning, when Lacovara questioned him on redirect. The attorney's simple questions sought to dispel whatever doubts had been created by Driker's lengthy inquiry. Thibault gladly confirmed that none of the accounting vagaries attached to the *Free Press*'s bookkeeping had any material effect on the newspaper's immense losses.

On recross, Driker focused on April 14, 1986, the day the JOA was announced. Prior to that day, he asked Thibault, "did any of the responsible executives of the *Free Press* ever tell you that they believed that the *Free Press* was no longer a viable financial entity?"

"Not that I recall," Thibault replied.

"Did anyone from Knight-Ridder tell you, prior to April 14, 1986, that they viewed these infusions of funds . . . as money that was going down a rathole that they'd never see again?"

"They didn't characterize it that way, no."

Driker bored in on the one impression he wanted most to leave with Needelman: that an accountant had no business predicting the future of the *Free Press.* Thibault had repeatedly asserted that the *Free Press* would, without Knight-Ridder's largess, have a difficult time borrowing enough money to survive. Driker chose this small point to help make his larger one.

"If you were managing the *Free Press,* if you were the owner of the *Free Press,* Mr. Thibault—let's pretend that you take off your auditor's hat and put on a management hat—and your auditor walked in and he said, 'You know what? You people are going down the tubes tomorrow. You're going to fail tomorrow,' because, as Mr. Lacovara said yesterday, without the help of Knight-Ridder, the *Free Press* couldn't have published yesterday morning. Let's assume you're running this stand-alone enterprise and your auditor walks in and says, 'It's all over. Turn out the lights.' And you ask why, and your auditor says, 'Well, it's because you need more money and there's no ability to get it.' And you say, 'Well, how do you know there's no ability to get it?' And the auditor says, 'Well, based upon my experience, I don't think you can get it.' Now, if you were the owner of the *Free Press,* Mr. Thibault, wouldn't you try?"

"Yes," Thibault said, "and I might ask a second opinion, too."

"You mean of another auditor?"

"Of another auditor or someone else skilled in obtaining financing."

"But the best way to find out about whether you can raise debt or equity is to try it, isn't that so?"

"Yes."

"And you sure wouldn't turn out the lights before you did try it, would you?"

"No."

Walking the two blocks back to his office, Driker thought, We're going to have fun with this case.

Stewart J. Kahn, the publishers' next witness, wasn't nearly as uptight as Thibault. The accountant for Arthur Andersen and Company actually liked Driker, who had quizzed Kahn in preparation for the hearing. In the courthouse corridors, Kahn and Driker had ribbed each other about the pennant race between Kahn's favorite baseball team, the New York Yankees, and Driker's Detroit Tigers.

Driker had fun with Kahn on the witness stand as well. Kahn's firm had prepared, at a cost of nine hundred thousand dollars, a two-inch-thick stack of financial analyses that, like Thibault's testimony, concluded that the *Free Press* would be defunct without the help of Knight-Ridder. What had caught the skeptical eye of the JOA opponents was a predictive analysis called the "A-score."

The A-score had been developed by Arthur Andersen with the help of Dr. Edward I. Altman, a professor of finance at New York University and the father of the Z-score, a statistical model for predicting bankruptcy. The A-score was calculated by multiplying five financial ratios—for instance, current assets to current liabilities—by a coefficient. The result was a number, usually between a positive 2.6 and a negative 1.0, that purported to forecast whether a company was in imminent danger of going bankrupt. The lower the score, the higher the chance of financial distress.

Not surprisingly, the model predicted doom for the *Free Press.* For 1985, the *Free Press*'s A-score was a negative 3.837, translating into a 99 percent chance of severe financial trouble. That was the year the *News* was in the throes of a takeover and *Free Press* bosses Bob Hall and Dave Lawrence figured their foe was finally ready to succumb. The *Free Press*'s score had been calculated from the Ernst and Whinney audit and did not take into account Knight-Ridder's competitive strategies for the *Free Press.* Arthur Andersen had prepared a limited A-score analysis for the *News,* but that had been "discarded," Kahn testified.

Late that Wednesday afternoon Driker zeroed in on the A-score. "If you are a businessman," he asked Kahn, "and Arthur Andersen's engagement partner tells you you have got a low A-score, you don't simply shut the lights and send out pink slips and go home and close the door to your business, do you?"

"Some people might," Kahn said, "but probably most of them would not."

"Most of them might probably find a way to improve their business conditions so they get back up among the enviable people who have plus A-scores, isn't that so?"

"Yes, Mr. Driker."

Driker produced a list of fourteen companies that had received exceptionally low Z-score ratings in 1975. Lacovara objected, because Kahn's testimony had focused on the A-score, not its precursor, the Z-score. Needelman, visibly annoyed, reminded Lacovara that Kahn's written testimony alluded several times to the Z-score.

Driker asked Kahn if he had tracked the fourteen members of "murderers' row," as Driker called it, to see whether they had survived for the past twelve years. He had not.

"I'm sure you will be surprised to know I did," Driker said.

"I'm not at all surprised," Kahn said ruefully.

For the next half hour Driker proceeded through the companies on the list—Mohawk Data Sciences, Electronic Associates, Todd Shipyards, Puerto Rican Cement Company, ICN Pharmaceuticals, Memorex Corporation, and so on—to show that all but one, despite their dismal Z-scores, had avoided bankruptcy. Several were still struggling financially. Some had sold off substantial parts of their businesses. A few were sold or merged into other companies. But all, save one, had defied the prognosis of the Z-score. Arthur Andersen itself recently had given at least two of the companies clean bills of financial health. Lacovara again objected; Needelman again silenced him. "You had no reservations when you tried to impress upon the administrative law judge and, through me, the attorney general the usefulness of this device," Needelman lectured. "Mr. Driker has every right to ridicule it."

To Driker, it didn't matter whether the Z-score or A-score was on trial. The point was, the equations failed to account for the real world. *Of course* these abstract models predicted the *Free Press*'s demise—as they would have for the *News*. The *Free Press* had suffered enormous losses—as had the *News*. All Driker meant to suggest was that there were *reasons* for the losses, reasons that led back to corporate boardrooms in Miami and suburban Washington. No statistical model could fathom those reasons and no audit could lay them bare. The losses were not paper losses, but neither did they come close to telling the whole story.

Kahn tried to resuscitate the A-score during Lacovara's redirect, but it was no use. It was as if Driker had gotten a witness to admit he had lied; no amount of demonstrating that the witness later told the truth could restore his credibility. At Lacovara's able prompts, Kahn obligingly reiterated his opinion that the *Free Press* was in danger of failing. It was, Kahn said, in worse shape than any of the other four newspapers that had applied for JOAs.

Driker could not let that stand. "Of the four JOA corporations included in your inquiry, that is, the four newspapers previously granted JOAs, how many of those four companies intentionally incurred operating losses as part of a deliberate strategy?"

"I don't know," Kahn said.

Kahn had testified that only an event that would "materially affect the operations of the *Free Press,* such as the closing of the *News,*" could save the *Free Press.* Driker asked if such an event might be the *News* raising its circulation price, which in turn might prompt the *Free Press* to do the same.

"Well, you know," Kahn equivocated, "there are so many factors to consider," such as how many people would stop buying both papers, whether circulation would decline, how advertisers might react. "I mean, if somebody with a magic wand waved it and said, 'Here is $35 million more of revenue and nothing bad is going to happen to you,' that would be a major event."

"Would you agree," Driker asked, "that probably the people most qualified to make those kinds of predictions and analysis would be the top management of Gannett and the top management of the *Free Press,* or Knight-Ridder? Do you understand my question? You said you're just a—"

"Bean."

"Bean counter," Driker said, "a garden-variety accountant. I'm suggesting to you that the people to really make the intelligent decision about what would happen . . . would be people like Mr. Chapman or Mr. Neuharth or the top executives of these two very sophisticated newspaper chains."

"I would think so," Kahn said.

"Thank you," Driker said. "I have no further questions."

It was 6:45 P.M. "Thank you very much, Mr. Kahn," Needelman said. "You're as much a bean counter as Mr. Driker is a potted plant."

Free Press general manager Bob Hall, the last of the accountants to take the stand, was a bus driver's son who grew up in Philadelphia, had delivered the *Inquirer* and the *Bulletin,* graduated from Drexel University, married a Philadelphia woman, and spent his entire career in the City of Brotherly Love, first as a CPA at Ernst and Ernst, then as an executive at the *Inquirer* just before it launched the "Win Plan" assault that vanquished the *Bulletin.* Unlike many of his peers, Hall was not an executive who hopped from newspaper to newspaper in the corporate chain, collecting promotions while training one eye on a job at headquarters. Yet when Jerry Tilis, a former *Inquirer* colleague, asked Hall to come to Detroit in early 1985, Hall was intrigued enough to say yes. Detroit offered the chance to relive the exhilaration of bare-knuckled, head-to-head competition. Knight-Ridder seemed as committed to overtaking the *News* as it had been to defeating the *Bulletin.* Hall was impressed with Operation Tiger and heartened to see Knight-Ridder willing to spend $22 million on the expansion of the *Free Press* printing plant so crucial to Tiger's ultimate success.

But Hall, like Tilis and Dave Lawrence, was kept in the dark about the JOA until the deal was virtually done. Until then, he exhibited no pessimism or doubt about the *Free Press*'s future. On the contrary, Hall, with Tilis and Lawrence, had touted the *Free Press*'s competitive strengths at Knight-Ridder meetings in Boca Raton just days before the JOA was announced. But once Knight-Ridder proclaimed the *Free Press* as "failing," Hall's thinking quickly fell into step. In his written hearing testimony he said he was "convinced" there was no way for the paper to reverse its losses, "especially now that the resources of Gannett Co. stand behind the *News.*" Unlike the *Inquirer,* Hall said, "the *Free Press* simply has insufficient strengths on which to build in competition with a paper as formidable as the *News.*"

But, as he admitted under questioning by Dussman, Hall had not completely changed his mind until the JOA was announced and he saw documents showing that Knight-Ridder and the *Free Press* had woefully overestimated the size of the *News*'s losses and underestimated the *News*'s ability to get advertisers to accept rates slightly higher than those charged by the *Free Press.* Gannett's willingness to plumb its deep pockets, Hall said, reinforced his growing belief that the *Free Press* could not prevail.

Throughout two days of testimony, Seymour Dussman and Duane Ice relentlessly probed what Hall had thought *before* the JOA was announced. Hadn't the *Free Press* expected to lose money? Hadn't Knight-Ridder endorsed that expectation by approving annual *Free Press* budgets? Hadn't Operation Tiger been cheated out of a fair chance to succeed? Hall replied with a string of bluff confessions to *Free Press* failings and shortcomings: It couldn't raise prices on its own. It had failed to fulfill many Tiger projections. It hadn't grown circulation enough to need the printing plant expansion. It was losing more money than anyone had predicted. The only genuine advantage Hall would admit to was the paper itself—the stories, photographs, and editorials—and that wasn't enough to stanch the losses.

Lacovara took it a step further. "Do you have a judgment," the attorney asked his client, "about what the condition of the *Free Press* would be today if it had been operating as a stand-alone company in the last five years?"

"I believe the *Free Press* would probably be closed," Hall said.

"Do you have an expectation of what would happen to the *Free Press* if a joint operating agency does not go into effect?"

"Knight-Ridder would have a very tough decision, and I think they would close it."

Someone finally had said it.

But Hall was not the person who would make that decision, as Seymour Dussman, on recross examination, sought to make clear.

"Have you discussed that matter with Mr. Chapman or Mr. Batten or any other official of Knight-Ridder?" the lawyer for the Antitrust Division asked.

"No, sir, I have not," Hall replied.

"So you have not made any such statement to them—is that correct?"

"That is correct, yes, sir."

"Have you made any such statement in any forum where it might have come to the attention of Mr. Chapman or Mr. Batten or any other Knight-Ridder official prior to this courtroom this afternoon?"

"I do not believe so, no, sir."

"You of course, then, have no indication or no idea of what Mr. Chapman's views and the Knight-Ridder board of directors' views would be on the advisability of continuing to operate the *Detroit Free Press* were this JOA to be denied?"

"Absolutely not, no."

Soon enough, though, everyone in Needelman's courtroom would know exactly what Alvah Chapman thought.

12

Bolt Out of the Blue

Al Neuharth was having a delightful summer. Still two years from retirement, the flamboyant Gannett chairman had gone off on a retiree's junket he called BusCapade. Neuharth billed the jaunt as a way to get closer to average Americans. It also was a way for Americans to get closer to Gannett or, more specifically, *USA Today*. BusCapade was classic Neuharth, mixing equal parts journalism and hucksterism.

For months he traveled the country in a $350,000 Blue Bird Wanderlodge, outfitted with cellular phones, a microwave oven, a liquor cabinet, and a driver named Joel Driver, visiting every state, chatting with citizens, dropping in on governors, and writing happy accounts of his impressions for *USA Today*. As was often the case with Neuharth, appearances differed a bit from reality. He occasionally eschewed the motor home for Gannett's luxurious Gulfstream IV jet. An entourage of reporters did legwork and fed him quotes for his "Plain Talk" columns. Staff from Gannett papers were dragooned into toiling for BusCapade. When it rolled into Michigan, *Detroit News* automotive reporter Edward Miller was told to set up a Neuharth interview with Roger B. Smith, chairman of General Motors. Interviews with the boss of the world's largest company usually were arranged weeks in advance, but Neuharth had a tight deadline—that day. Miller dutifully called a GM public relations person, who was surprised at the request, since Neuharth and Smith had dined the night before at the swank Oakland Hills Country Club in suburban Detroit. Another meeting was arranged, and Neuharth's "Plain Talk" column on Michigan included an innocuous quote from Smith on his work with Detroit Renaissance, a local redevelopment group.

BusCapade was in South Dakota when Neuharth received a telegram saying *USA Today* had turned its first monthly profit. "Staff betting you'll forgive us for ruining your prediction that we'd have to wait until end of year," the missive read. It was more proof that Neuharth's ego was bigger than Mt. Rushmore; though the telegram was signed by Gannett president and CEO John Curley, Neuharth had written it and had Curley send it to him so he could show it off to his South Dakota pals. (Neuharth gleefully revealed this in his autobiography.) As for *USA Today,* despite its brief flirtation with profitability, the newspaper would continue to post financial losses for years to come.

The *Detroit News* also continued to lose money, but that didn't worry Neuharth in the least. So far, his Detroit strategy appeared to be working beautifully. The *News* was moving aggressively—if expensively—to improve its market position, while the *Free Press* was suffering, financially and psychologically.

Though total daily circulation in Detroit had climbed to an all-time high, the *Free Press* now trailed the *News* by nearly 40,000 papers a day, the widest gap since the early 1970s. "Morale is at an all-time low," Knight-Ridder executive Donald Nizen declared in a memo in November of 1986. "Myron Didyk says circulation personnel on the *Free Press* are worried about their job security, not circulation figures." *Free Press* president Jerry Tilis recalled, "When winning is removed from the picture, you have no idea what it does to your people." It was like telling a football team late in a close contest that it would have to concede defeat. "You can't be a leader of troops in the field *and* be the guy saying, 'We're gonna die, let's sue for peace.' If the people in the field start thinking about suing for peace, you're in trouble."

Five hundred *Free Press* employees attended stress seminars sponsored by the paper. Some bolted for other papers: seventeen journalists, including a few of the *Free Press*'s best reporters, during the first half of 1987. Several moved down Lafayette Boulevard to the *News,* where ex-*Free Press* editor Christina Bradford was dangling hefty pay raises. Moves to the *News* hadn't been common since the twilight of Luedtke's tenure. Executive editor Kent Bernhard quit in disgust. Managing editor Scott Bosley took a Knight-Ridder job in Washington.

Tilis, Bob Hall, and Dave Lawrence scrambled to keep *Free Press* losses from breaking the $20 million-a-year barrier. Holes in the staff were left unfilled. Promotion budgets were trimmed. The "failing newspaper" tag wore heavily. "You bleed a lot more once you stand up and say you're failing," Tilis recalled. *News* ad salespeople told customers the *News* was going to control the JOA, so it would behoove them to deal exclusively with the *News.* An official at the Ontario Ministry of Tourism told a *Free Press* salesperson, "Well, we'll be working with the folks at the *News* after the JOA, won't we?"

The *Free Press* shied away from raising ad rates, in part because of the signal it might send about JOA pricing. Yet some customers accused the paper of deliberately lowballing rates to increase its losses and buttress its application. First Boston analyst Kevin Gruneich observed that the *Free Press* couldn't stop discounting, lest opponents of the JOA argue it wasn't necessary in the first place. A much-needed expansion of the *Free Press*'s mail room was shelved. *Free Press* executives Pete Pitz and Robert Burns had advised in a memo that "the announcement of a construction project by the 'failing' paper will be at the least misunderstood by many. It could, regrettably and wrongly, contribute to delay for JOA."

At the *News,* publisher Moe Hickey and president Chip Weil went for blood. Publicly, they parroted the company line in support of the JOA. Privately, they sneered at their *Free Press* counterparts and pulled for denial of the merger. They expected the *News* would be so far ahead by the time Meese scuttled the merger that Knight-Ridder would have to pull up stakes. Hickey loved letting the *Free Press* know who was boss. At JOA planning meetings he reminded Hall and other *Free Press* executives that any unresolved issues could go to a vote of the Detroit Newspaper Agency board—which, of course, Gannett controlled. The executives had to agree on a wide range of business and editorial matters, from when the papers would be printed each day to how the joint weekend editions would be structured. Negotiating the look of the weekend nameplate, Weil offered a prototype with the *Free Press* logo in minuscule type beneath a huge *News* logo, and another with the *Free Press* logo inside the paper—"to pull their chains a little bit," Weil later said. Hall, who exchanged angry words with Hickey on more than one occasion, complained to Knight-Ridder of "turf protection" and "a still-present attitude of 'winner' and 'loser' " among *News* officials. Bill Keating acted as referee, trying to ease tensions by insisting that the partners-to-be reach consensus on all issues and refusing to invoke Gannett's 3–2 vote.

Meanwhile, Hickey was buying circulation. He spent millions on *News* television and radio ads, subscription discounts, reader contests, new carriers, and hundreds of red newsboxes that sprouted on street corners all over outstate Michigan, northernmost Ohio, and across the Detroit River in Windsor, Ontario. Much of the far-flung circulation was useless to major advertisers who wanted to reach metropolitan Detroiters, and a good many subscribers halted delivery when a contest or a discount ended. Bob Nelson wrote a memo warning that the new circulation would be difficult to maintain, but he was ignored. The new subscriptions lasted long enough to count in the six-month circulation average and put the *Free Press* farther behind. Circulation workers were reaping big cash rewards and trips to the Bahamas, Las Vegas, and Hawaii. The pricier prizes made it worthwhile for workers to buy extra papers themselves. Those counted as new circulation, even if they were immediately tossed into the trash. But when *News* circulation gains were announced, Hickey shamelessly boasted of "new management, new ideas, new results."

Weil maintained the *News*'s ad market share by keeping rates low and cutting deals that delighted advertisers. Saturday ads sold at fire-sale prices; Weil called them "Saturday specials." "In some cases we were losing money, but we were driving the *Free Press* crazy," he later boasted. In one memo to Lawrence, *Free Press* president Jerry Tilis fumed, "I don't know what's happening at the *News,* but apparently the JOA filing period might be characterized as a period of total irresponsibility."

News executive editor Bob Giles spent freely to improve the paper, adding space for news, expanding the staff, enticing veterans into early retirement, aggressively recruiting and promoting minorities and women. Changes to the paper itself were vast, ranging from a halt to the use of courtesy titles such as *Miss* and *Mrs.* to a recasting of the front page. George Rorick, designer of *USA Today*'s weather page, dressed the Old Gray Lady in the eye-catching garb of many another Gannett paper. Even skeptics who expected much less from Gannett conceded that the *News* had become a cleaner, brighter, more thoughtfully organized newspaper. Its daily report took on a harder, more locally focused edge. The *News* looked less and less like Lionel Linder's reflective afternoon paper, more and more like a nimble, quick-to-react morning paper—indeed, more like the *Free Press.* Tom Bray's editorial page did not veer from its archconservative bent, but the rest of the paper was remarkably different and, many people thought, better.

All of it cost money. After posting a marginal profit in 1985, the *News* lost $13 million in 1986 and posted a $5 million loss in the first quarter of 1987, just $20,000 less than the *Free Press.* Neuharth didn't bat an eye. At Knight-Ridder, of course, *Free Press* losses were viewed as a deadly virus. At Gannett, where *USA Today* had lost hundreds of millions, *News* losses were seen as a sort of miracle elixir, the key to the future. In fact, they were an unavoidable part of what Neuharth termed the "win-win" plan: win by getting the JOA or win by forcing the *Free Press* to surrender. The pending JOA abetted the strategy. The *Free Press* couldn't exactly match the *News* dollar for dollar in improvements, then plead poverty to Ed Meese. While the legal proceedings and the "failing" label took a toll on *Free Press* morale, *News* people exulted in their rising numbers. Moe Hickey and Chip Weil weren't the only ones pulling for a denial of the JOA.

On Monday, August 10, a limousine deposited Al Neuharth at the front steps of the federal courthouse in Detroit. A flock of TV cameras recorded the arrival, while Alvah Chapman, whose testimony was to follow Neuharth's, slipped by almost unnoticed after walking over from the Hotel Pontchartrain. Neuharth took a seat at the front of the courtroom gallery with Bill Keating. Chapman sat across the aisle with his top lawyer, Jack Fontaine, and his chief public relations person, Frank Hawkins. They listened while Peter Clark, former president of the Evening News Association, testified that he had willingly accepted losses in the hope of either outlasting the *Free Press* or obtaining a JOA.

Neuharth took the stand late that afternoon. Under questioning by Justice's Greg Hovendon, Neuharth refused to characterize the *News*'s 1986 deficit of $13 million as a loss, preferring to call it an "investment" designed "to maintain or enhance our dominance in circulation and advertising." "Dominance" was a word he repeated often during his testimony. He seemed to be quite fond of it.

It puzzled Hovendon, though. Hadn't Gannett and Knight-Ridder declared that the newspapers had fought to a "virtual draw"? Neuharth dismissed that as a sop to Chapman. "I was wearing this '*Detroit News* No. 1' pin at that press conference, as I'm wearing it today, and as all or most employees of the *Detroit News* wear it," Neuharth declared. "That would seem to me to be concrete evidence of which newspaper was number one, and had been long before we acquired it." Chapman's face reddened. He didn't enjoy listening to this, but if he wanted a JOA, he knew he would have to endure a few Neuharthian commercials.

Neuharth's testimony was a lesson in Orwellian discourse. Losses became investments. A tie became a victory. Neuharth had not lied when he repeatedly denied there had been JOA negotiations because those were only "informal discussions." The *Free Press* could not survive without its "life-support system," Knight-Ridder, but that wasn't necessarily true of the *News*, even though the paper had lost tens of millions of dollars in the 1980s.

Before Hovendon finished, Neuharth made a little speech. He had told the court he believed that, absent a JOA, the *Free Press* would have gone out of business, leaving the *News* a monopoly. Then why agree to a JOA? Hovendon wondered. Why not wait for the whole pot of gold?

"I think you have to understand," Neuharth said, "and, I hope, *believe* the history and traditions of Gannett's, if you will, philosophy, policy, and style."

Gannett, Neuharth pointed out, could have allowed rivals in Honolulu, Nashville, and Shreveport to die but had benevolently allowed them to survive in JOAs. Gannett's competitors in Honolulu and Nashville might have disagreed, but, alas, they were not in the courtroom today. (In 1991, after Neuharth had retired, Gannett would decline to renew the Shreveport JOA, forcing the closing of the ninety-six-year-old *Shreveport Journal.*) Neuharth conveniently failed to mention Little Rock, where Gannett's newly acquired *Arkansas Gazette* was trying to run the rival *Arkansas Democrat* out of town, with nary a thought of obtaining a paper-saving JOA.

Yes, profits would be greater if Gannett had Detroit to itself, Neuharth said, but profits weren't always as important as preserving two newspapers. "This is not a new revelation," he insisted, knowing full well that many in the courtroom, especially the reporters, didn't believe a word of it. What *was* a revelation was his avowed desire to rescue the *Free Press* from what he saw as certain death at the hands of Gannett.

"I worked for three years at the *Detroit Free Press,*" Neuharth said. "I gained tremendous respect for the product, the job it was doing in this market, for its people. I worked ten years for the parent company, Knight-Ridder, and it would not have given me any satisfaction to engage in practices here that would have resulted in the demise of the *Free Press.* My objective was to help it survive." Even Judge Needelman found Neuharth's testimony puzzling. Later he would remark that he didn't quite understand this "newspaperman's code" of feeling attached to a competitor.

The next day, Gene Driker arrived at the courthouse two hours before his cross-examination of Neuharth was to begin. Keating spied him poring over exhibits in one of the conference chambers adjoining the courtroom.

"What are you doing here so early?" Keating asked.

Driker smiled. "I want to be on my game for the big man."

Now Driker stood at the attorney's lectern with his arms folded across his chest, looking directly at Neuharth. He asked if Neuharth thought the *News* was being adequately managed when Gannett bought the Evening News Association. Neuharth thought it was "very well managed," despite its considerable losses.

"Yet," Driker said, "you found it appropriate to bring in quite a bit of new management talent from other Gannett properties to Detroit."

"Yes, sir."

"That management," Driker said, "has succeeded in increasing the operating losses of the *Detroit News.* Is that correct?"

"That management has managed to exceed in many areas," Neuharth said. He wore the wry hint of a grin. "The one that you mentioned is one of them." In fact, Neuharth admitted, the *News* could not hope to be profitable and maintain its daily circulation lead, at least not in the short run. Neuharth had no idea how long it would take to overwhelm the "failing" *Free Press.* Meanwhile, the *News* would lose money, largely because it kept its prices so low.

Driker was most curious about why Gannett, known for its aggressive pricing, had not raised prices at the *News.* Hadn't Gannett done so twice at *USA Today,* and hadn't circulation continued to grow? Yes and yes, Neuharth replied. (*USA Today*'s losses were primarily due to its inability to attract sufficient advertising revenues.) Didn't memoranda prepared by Doug McCorkindale and Larry Miller prior to Gannett's purchase of the ENA contemplate price hikes at the *News?* Yes, but they were preliminary thoughts, not to be taken seriously, Neuharth said.

Driker reminded Neuharth that when Gannett agreed to buy the ENA, Neuharth had told a news conference about Gannett's formula for improving the profits of its papers: put more news in the paper, sell harder for readers and advertisers, raise the prices for circulation and advertising. Was Gannett on that path with the *News?* Driker asked.

Neuharth said it had taken only the first two steps.

"You do intend to take [the next] steps at the appropriate time, do you not?" Driker asked.

"Perhaps," Neuharth said. "But I certainly couldn't define the appropriate time."

It was a convenient reply.

Driker showed Neuharth a transcript of the chat Neuharth had had with *News* and *Free Press* employees at the Detroit Press Club in November of 1985, when he said both papers might show circulation gains if they made it more convenient for the public "to drop a single coin, like a quarter, into a vending machine rather than two dimes or a nickel and a dime."

"I may have said, 'like a quarter,' " Neuharth said. "However, the fact is that at that time in November of 1985 we were seriously considering whether that single coin should be a dime or a quarter." That was news. However, there wasn't a shred of contemporaneous evidence in the record to support it. Needelman and Ed Meese would just have to take Neuharth's word.

Gannett didn't raise prices, Driker suggested, because it was afraid the *Free Press* would promptly follow—as it would have, Bob Hall had testified—and become profitable, thus jeopardizing the JOA. Driker showed Neuharth memos from McCorkindale and Miller alluding to precisely that point.

Neuharth didn't remember them clearly. "In point of fact," Driker said, "you considered from the first moment you thought that a JOA was possible in Detroit, right up to the time you filed the application, what impact on the JOA application a circulation price increase at the *News* would have, isn't that so?"

"No."

"You never thought about that?"

Neuharth backpedaled. As reporters who had interviewed him knew, one of Neuharth's standard practices was to qualify and requalify his very own words until what he actually said and what he said he intended often were at odds. He may not have been a liar, but he was a dissembler of the first rank.

"That's not true," Neuharth said. "I didn't say I never thought about it. But that was not a primary consideration."

A moment later, Neuharth admitted he "may have considered" how a price hike would affect a JOA's chances, but, he insisted, that had not influenced his business decisions concerning the *News*. Whatever he did, he said again and again, was to assure that the *News* was the "clear winner" by every measure of circulation, advertising, and journalistic excellence.

All the while, of course, as he had so passionately testified earlier, he was trying to assure the survival of the *Free Press*.

Inside Driker's lectern was a stack of transparencies. He pulled one out and placed it on an overhead projector to Neuharth's left. The screen showed a page of handwritten notes. In the upper right-hand corner was scribbled, "AHN on DET., 4/20/86." The notes were of a meeting of the *Detroit News* board of directors, convened by Neuharth in Detroit six days after the JOA was announced. They had been jotted down by Madelyn P. Jennings, Gannett's senior vice-president for personnel and a member of the *News*'s board, which was chaired by Neuharth.

Neuharth had never seen the notes. Handwritten memos were not permitted to reach his desk. Driker was glad to hear that. Neuharth was more likely to have trouble disavowing something he was unfamiliar with. Of course Driker had seen the notes many times during the course of his preparation. In fact, though, not until early that morning, as he huddled in the conference chamber outside the courtroom, had he truly comprehended their significance. Jennings couldn't possibly have known what a wrench her innocent memorandum would throw into the JOA machine.

On the first of three pages Jennings had written, "Entirely new deal (but ain't a sure thing)." Driker suggested that it meant that Neuharth had wanted to impress upon his deputies the need to keep one eye on JOA approval while managing the *News.* Neuharth disagreed. He said he simply hadn't wanted them letting up on the *Free Press* while the JOA was pending. The notes went on: "Review everything DN is doing or planned + review all approaches + strategy (dir. compet.). Subtle chg. w/ objective: DN *even stronger* going in to JOA than now or *much* if JOA not approved."

An outline of strategic steps followed. One was: "Cont. circ. push. . . . No price incr now." Another was: "Ad—increase share of field. No thought to more realistic rate card pricing *now.*" So Neuharth had ordered that no prices be increased while the JOA was pending. He told Driker that he did not consider that a change in strategy, despite what Jennings had written. It was merely the way to protect the *News*'s dominant position while awaiting a JOA outcome. Driker wanted Neuharth to admit that he had ordered prices held down because to raise them would have risked the *Free Press* following the price hikes and becoming profitable—thus dooming the JOA. Neuharth didn't take the bait, but neither did he succeed in discrediting the insidious suggestion of Jennings's notes. They would not be forgotten.

It was getting late. Driker had grown weary of Neuharth's chest thumping about the *News*'s dominance. To Driker, the financial data plainly showed that Gannett needed the monopoly profits of a JOA to justify the $717 million purchase of the ENA—unless the company was willing to increase the price of the *News.* Besides, Driker pointed out, the *News* would quickly become the junior paper once the JOA took effect.

Driker removed his glasses. He looked impatient.

"The fact is, Mr. Neuharth, that it is Gannett that needs this JOA in this market to justify its investment in the *Detroit News,* isn't that so?"

"No, sir."

"It is Gannett that needs the JOA to earn the kinds of profits that you expect from your newspapers, isn't that so?"

"No, sir."

Driker had hardly expected Neuharth to answer in the affirmative, but his questions were not designed so much to elicit replies as to drive home his point about Neuharth's cynical strategy. Judge Needelman listened carefully.

When Driker finished, Needelman turned to Gannett's lead attorney, John Stuart Smith, for redirect. "Your Honor," Smith said, "applicants have no questions." Smith later told reporters that redirect wasn't necessary because Neuharth's testimony had done nothing to hurt the publishers' case. Driker chuckled when told this; he had assumed Neuharth's exit reflected the executive's desire to get out of that courtroom as fast as he could.

Outside the courthouse, Driker could barely contain himself. "The last thing they were interested in was making the *News* profitable, because the *Free Press* would also become profitable," he insisted to a group of reporters. He was almost shouting. "It wouldn't allow a JOA." Driker felt wonderful. The cameras were whirring, the reporters were scribbling, and Neuharth was long gone in his limousine. Brick by brick, Driker told the reporters, the opponents were building a case against the JOA.

It wasn't until later that Driker remembered the detail that had so buoyed his mood that afternoon. He was questioning Neuharth when, like any good lawyer, he glanced at the witness's hands for any sign of nervousness or doubt.

As Gene Driker saw it, Neuharth was gripping the witness stand like the edge of a cliff. His knuckles were white.

Until the summer of 1987, Alvah Chapman had not given much thought to closing the *Detroit Free Press.* He had figured all along that the biggest and perhaps only hurdle to the JOA was cutting an acceptable deal with Gannett. When the Antitrust Division asked in writing whether the *Free Press* might be closed if the JOA was denied, Knight-Ridder's lawyers called it "an unattractive option" that had not been seriously discussed. Indeed, until the hearing, the only newspaper executive willing to speculate publicly on the consequences of a JOA denial was Neuharth, who told a group of Wall Street analysts in March of 1987 that the *Free Press* certainly would have to be closed without a JOA. "Our *Detroit News,*" he conveniently added, "would have the whole market." Jim Batten, asked by a *Free Press* reporter to comment on Neuharth's assertion, testily replied, "Whatever Neuharth is saying, he is saying on his own hook." Batten and Chapman regularly dodged the question of the *Free Press*'s ultimate fate, in part because they did not wish to alarm the newspaper's staff or unnerve advertisers, but also because they truly had not settled on an answer.

Chapman himself had raised the question when Phil Lacovara, Jack Fontaine, Gerald Goldman, and the other Knight-Ridder lawyers were preparing his written direct testimony for the hearing. The executive wanted to make crystal clear to the employees of the *Free Press* and, especially, the unions and Mayor Young that the publishers' pursuit of the JOA was not just a game that would have no real consequence. But the lawyers argued that broaching the subject of closing the *Free Press* could put the publishers in the difficult position of having to somehow *prove* it would happen. Since the law required no such proof, the publishers were better off leaving it alone, the lawyers said. If the question was asked at the hearing, Chapman could respond then. The executive reluctantly agreed. But at their regular meeting in June, he told Knight-Ridder's directors what he planned to testify, if asked: that he would recommend closing the *Free Press* in the event the JOA was denied.

By the time Chapman took the witness stand late on Tuesday, August 11, he was certain the question had to be answered. Dussman, Driker, Ice, and their corps of aggressive young assistants had raised serious questions about the publishers' case. Although Knight-Ridder's lawyers still insisted that they would prevail, they allowed as how their opponents' skillful presentation of certain isolated documents might distract Judge Needelman from the facts that entitled the *Free Press* to a JOA. Lacovara and Cal Collier agreed that it certainly could not hurt the case if Chapman spelled out what it would mean if the judge were somehow confused by their opponents. Besides, if the opponents asked, Chapman had no choice but to answer.

The question didn't come up during Chapman's first brief stint on the witness stand Tuesday afternoon. That evening, in Lawrence's fifth-floor office at the *Free Press,* Chapman informed the publisher of what he intended to testify. Lawrence took the news with grim resolve, telling his boss it was the absolutely correct thing to do. They both slept well that night.

The next morning, under questioning by Dussman, Chapman testified that Knight-Ridder had grown increasingly interested in a JOA as the *Free Press* lost money for a third straight year in 1981. "It was a goal," Chapman admitted. "It became a higher-priority goal in later years, but it was a goal at that time, yes, sir." Profits also were a goal, but they were elusive, because the *News* kept prices so low. *Free Press* executives had considered a couple of circulation price increases that would have made the *Free Press* profitable, at least for a short while, but Chapman said price hikes probably would have doomed the paper because it would have lost huge amounts of circulation. Had Gannett raised the *News*'s prices, the *Free Press* would have had more pricing flexibility, he said.

Dussman was especially intrigued by a letter Chapman had sent Neuharth on January 20, 1986. The six-page, single-spaced missive outlined the many advantages the *Free Press* had over the *News,* including the morning position, a modern printing plant, upscale demographics, and improving circulation and advertising trends. The *Free Press* described in that letter certainly did not sound like a failing enterprise. Chapman tried to shrug it off as little more than a negotiating stance.

Dussman wasn't buying that. He asked, with a touch of sarcasm, if Chapman had thought he could put something past Neuharth by playing games with circulation and advertising numbers.

"I don't consider the presentation of those figures as playing games," Chapman insisted.

"Well," Dussman smartly retorted, "that's exactly my point, Mr. Chapman. You *weren't* playing games."

Dussman had quizzed Chapman for six hours without asking the ultimate question. Duane Ice had no plan to ask it. Nor did Lacovara. One of the cardinal rules of cross-examination is never to ask a question to which you do not know the answer. Dussman knew the rule well. Technically, though, it did not apply to him. By law, he was a fact finder, not an adversary.

It was midafternoon. Dussman had one last question.

"Mr. Chapman, it is true, isn't it, that Knight-Ridder has made no decision yet as to whether or not to continue publication of the *Detroit Free Press* if the joint operating arrangement is not approved, is that correct?"

"I would like to respond to that," Chapman said. "And I will respond to it, but it is going to take a minute or so."

For the next six minutes the only sound in the courtroom, except for Chapman's level voice, was the faint scribbling of reporters trying to get every word he said on paper. Dussman stood patiently at the lectern, waiting for the executive to finish. Chapman held his back straight and his head high; despite the bleak finality of what he felt he had to say, his face was its usual hard, inscrutable mask. Chapman was too tough to let himself show it, but it pained him deeply to say that he would personally seek the closing of a newspaper. The Knights had never closed one of their own papers. Chapman had no desire to be the CEO who violated that tradition, especially with a paper that Jack Knight had purchased and personally nurtured. Like the disciplined soldier who refuses to contemplate defeat, Chapman never had allowed himself to seriously doubt that the JOA would be approved. But his courtroom oration was an admission, if not of defeat, then certainly of doubt, a doubt that left him no alternative but to threaten Jack Knight's 156-year-old paper with death.

Most of what he said was not new. The *Free Press* could not raise its advertising rates because advertisers already were paying more per thousand subscribers than when they advertised in the *News*. The *Free Press* could not raise circulation prices; the last such move, a twenty-five-cent hike on Sundays, had precipitated a Sunday circulation decline that still hadn't ended thirty-one months later. Nor could the *Free Press* cut payroll or newsprint costs; it already had to give readers and advertisers as much as the *News* with less revenue.

"Absent a JOA," Chapman said, "with no prospects to overcome the revenue deficiency, no prospects to move this newspaper into the black, the *Free Press* would be in a very, very difficult situation. And Knight-Ridder would have to take very serious action. It would not be my unilateral decision to close the *Free Press* if the JOA were turned down and no possible appeal were available. But it would be the decision of the Knight-Ridder board of directors to do that. However, as much as it would pain me to do that, if this JOA were to be turned down, it would be my recommendation that we do that."

Reporters covering the hearing rushed out to call their newsrooms. Driker and Ice were first dumbfounded, then a little angry that Chapman would threaten the court, and, finally, buoyed by what they viewed as an act of desperation. To them it was obvious that Knight-Ridder and Gannett felt their case was in trouble. Chapman had had lots of opportunities to say this before, but he never had taken them—until the opponents of the JOA mounted their attack at the hearing. His soliloquy obviously was scripted, they thought. Ice and Driker didn't think Chapman was lying, but they did not believe he would have made this declaration before the hearing. Was Chapman really so arrogant as to try to make Judge Needelman—or, by extension, Ed Meese—responsible for closing the *Free Press?* Ice and Driker wondered. Perhaps, they thought, this implied challenge would backfire. Perhaps Needelman would be offended by an eleventh-hour threat. Maybe Meese would be too.

Ice set out to cast doubt on Chapman's declaration. He asked when the executive had reached his decision.

"I'm not sure when I decided that," Chapman replied.

Subtle sparks raced between the two adversaries. Chapman didn't like the lawyer. Ice wore his repugnance for the JOA in an ever-present scowl, looking like someone who could not rid himself of a sour taste in his mouth.

"Can you tell us what year?" Ice asked.

"I can't."

"Can you tell us if you made that decision before or after the application for the JOA was filed?"

"I would assume," Chapman said, "that I made it sometime after it was filed and sometime before I made it public."

Had he consulted his top deputies? No. Had he asked for pertinent studies or analyses? No. Had he prepared any memoranda for the board of directors? "I don't think I'll have to write that memorandum," Chapman said. He seemed offended that Ice would challenge what he had said.

Still, Chapman would not rule out selling the *Free Press* in the event the JOA was denied, though he said he doubted a "reputable" buyer would come forward. Anyway, he said, the *Free Press* was not for sale, at least for now.

Banner headlines in both Detroit papers heralded Chapman's declaration. Curiously, the news was not received with great dismay at the *Free Press.*

Like Driker and Ice, many employees remained skeptical of Knight-Ridder's plans. In the days following Chapman's testimony, Lawrence polled hundreds of *Free Press* workers on their reaction. About half returned slips of paper saying they didn't believe the *Free Press* ever would close. Lawrence was amazed. His people refused to let go of the notion that, if the JOA was denied, the *Free Press* and the *News* would simply return to unfettered, head-to-head competition. Which shouldn't have been so surprising, since Lawrence and Chapman had for more than a year given them no reason to believe otherwise. There was no escaping the idea that Chapman's testimony was a desperate attempt to rescue a foundering case for the JOA.

The people at the *News* certainly saw it as that. A few found dark humor in the juxtaposition of Chapman's dire assertion with Neuharth's boasts that the *News* could not lose. *News* reporter Edward Miller quipped to a fellow staffer: "Looks like *JOA* stands for 'The joke's on Alvah.' "

Four days after Chapman delivered his prospective death sentence, a Northwest Airlines jet carrying 155 passengers and crew lifted off Runway 3-Center at Detroit Metropolitan Airport. The jet struggled to stay aloft, careening left off the runway, barely forty feet above the ground. The pilots had neglected to set the wing flaps properly. Still, the jet might have stayed up in the humid Sunday evening air had its left wing not clipped a forty-eight-foot-tall light pole in a rental car parking lot. Flight 255 slammed into the ground in a ball of billowing orange and crimson flame, skidding along Middle Belt Road under the overpass at Interstate 94. The crash instantly killed 154 people on the plane and 2 who had the misfortune to be driving past. Miraculously, four-year-old Cecelia Cichan survived.

It was the second-worst disaster in U.S. aviation history—and the biggest local story the *News* and the *Free Press* had covered since the 1967 riot. Within minutes of the crash, reporters from both papers were on the scene, picking through the charred wreckage, interviewing tearful witnesses, tracking down airport and government officials to find out how and why the catastrophe had occurred. The story dominated the papers for the next two weeks. Nearly one hundred pages of stories, photos, and graphics ran the first week alone. Dozens of reporters were deployed in Detroit, Washington, Chicago, Phoenix, and Minneapolis to try to piece together the complex details of a gripping tragedy.

For many of them it would be the most intense, exhausting, and exuberant few days of their careers. "This was the Big Story, the one you waited for, prepared for," *News* assistant city editor Nolan Finley wrote. News staffs at both papers were driven by the fear of being beaten by their competitor. Each night, as deadlines neared, editors and reporters prayed they had not missed even the tiniest detail the other paper might have, let alone the really big hit—the clue that would reveal the true cause of the crash. By evening, they were more anxious to see their rival's early papers than their own. When the *Free Press*'s next-day first edition arrived at the *News* around 8:45 every evening, editors quickly scanned it for material the *News* had overlooked. The *News*'s later deadlines allowed time to "chase" a story, as the editors put it, into the early edition. If the *Free Press* hadn't broken anything major, the *News* editors savored a delicious moment of relief before launching into the nightly round of criticism and scorn for the *Free Press*'s report, however similar it might have been to the *News*'s. They hadn't produced a paper yet, but they were congratulating each other: "We kicked their ass!" It was a tension-easing ritual that would be repeated down the street, despite the smug claims of many *Free Press* staffers that they never bothered to read the *News*.

When the crash coverage finally died down at the end of August, both papers would lay claim to the bragging rights for having done the better job. But it would be impossible to say whether one had outdone the other. Both had covered every possible detail, from the failure of the wing flaps to the frequency that the number 255 was played in the state lottery. They also repeated each other's mistakes, like misspelling the name of the tiny survivor. Most readers didn't have the time or inclination to compare, but whichever paper they read, they got a lot for fifteen or twenty cents.

It was a remarkable season for news. Pope John Paul II visited Detroit. Henry Ford II died. Chrysler bought American Motors. A wave of drug-related shootings of children beset the city. The Tigers raced for a pennant. There was a commuter plane crash that killed nine, a fatal tornado, a warehouse blaze that felled three firemen, an all-night siege at a suburban motel in which three police officers were fatally wounded. Each time, waves of *Free Press* and *News* reporters set upon the stories, determined to deliver the best to their readers.

At the time, it seemed to matter. Daily circulations at both papers were climbing to record highs. The journalists could tell themselves they were having an actual effect on the business competition. It was as if, with one tremendous surge of vigor and imagination, the journalists could make everyone forget the JOA. It was a stirring thought, but an empty one. As the reporters sifted through the rubble and carnage of Flight 255, impeccably attired lawyers were finishing their work in Judge Needelman's courtroom. What the journalists did was of little concern to them.

* * *

Hanan Kolko, one of Duane Ice's young associates, was entertaining reporters in the corridor outside the courtroom. After Chapman, the hearing had become tedious and anticlimactic, and Kolko was trying to lighten things with an impromptu impression of *Free Press* publisher David Lawrence on the witness stand.

" 'Mr. Lawrence, can you tell us if it is Wednesday?' " Kolko said, aping Ice. Then, mimicking Lawrence's slight southern accent, Kolko gave the reply: " 'Well, let me put that in context. I'm on this side of the international date line . . .' " Jacquelynn Boyle, a *Free Press* reporter, shook her head in disgust. Lawrence "is such an embarrassment," she said. Like many of her *Free Press* colleagues, Boyle often referred to Lawrence as "Skippy," a nickname he detested. No one was quite sure how he had gotten it or why it had stuck; maybe because the childish nickname mocked the ultraserious, patronizing tone Lawrence was wont to lapse into. He seemed to have a knack for taking himself more seriously than others did.

When he took the witness stand at the JOA hearing, Needelman had asked him his name and profession.

"David Lawrence, Jr., newspaperman," Lawrence had announced. A groan was in order, but this was a courtroom. Needelman just scowled.

"By whom are you employed?" the judge demanded.

"The *Detroit Free Press.*"

"You are the publisher, right?"

"Yes, sir."

Lawrence was equally exasperating under cross-examination, lecturing lawyers Ice and Gregory Hovendon on the fundamentals of newspapering—"It ain't the same as toaster ovens"—and going on about readers' "love" of the *Free Press,* the legacy of Jack Knight and Lee Hills, and the "soul" of the *Free Press.* Lawrence's legendary memory failed him at times, though it seemed sharper when his lawyer, Phil Lacovara, was asking the questions. Driker passed a note to the Knight-Ridder lawyers: "You sandpapered him up so much he looks like the Manchurian candidate."

Lawrence was called by the Antitrust Division because Knight-Ridder had not offered him as a witness. The Knight-Ridder lawyers thought it would be difficult for someone so emotionally wrapped up in the competition to testify. Their concern was well founded, as it turned out. Under cross-examination, Lawrence could not bring himself to say the *Free Press* was a failing newspaper.

Ice had counted on that.

"I take it you have concluded that the *Free Press* is a failing newspaper," the lawyer taunted Lawrence. "Is that correct?"

"I don't know specifically," the publisher replied. Few people could equivocate like Dave Lawrence. "I do not have any intimacy of understanding of the term 'failing.' I am comfortable with the integrity of what is proposed."

In a string of rambling replies, Lawrence strained, without much success, to recast the optimistic things he had said and written about the *Free Press*'s prospects before the JOA application was filed. He allowed that it made him feel "a little foolish" to be faced with them again. He called the *Free Press*'s decision in early 1985 to raise the Sunday cover price to seventy-five cents an "unmitigated disaster," then recanted after admitting that the increase, while costing about thirty-eight thousand Sunday customers, had improved the bottom line. "I wish, in retrospect, that my mother had never taught me the word 'unmitigated,' " he ruefully admitted.

Back at the *Free Press,* Lawrence read the as-yet unpublished story his reporters, Boyle and Stephen Jones, had written about his testimony. The lead sentence said Lawrence had "backed off" his "unmitigated disaster" statement. Lawrence let his editors know he didn't like that phrasing, and they asked Boyle, who had written the lead, to change it. Furious, she refused. "Since when do we let subjects of our stories rewrite them?" she ranted. An editor made the change. The next day Lawrence apologized to Boyle and Jones for the way he had handled the matter, but said he had no qualms about the change itself.

John Morton was even less effective as a witness. The tweedy, pipe-smoking former newspaperman was the most oft-quoted financial analyst in the industry, operating his own research firm as an arm of the New York brokerage of Lynch, Jones and Ryan. For years he had been publishing reports saying the *Free Press* was the more likely to win the newspaper war. He changed his mind only after the JOA was announced—and Gannett subsequently hired him to testify on its behalf. Just two months before the JOA was announced, Morton had testified in an antitrust case in Arkansas that the *News* was at greater risk. Driker and the Antitrust Division's Mary Beth McGee trapped the analyst in a cage of past assertions from which he could not escape. By the time Morton stepped down, his own attorneys wished they had never hired him.

James Rosse, the Stanford University economist whose theory of economies of scale was a linchpin of the publishers' case, came under sharp scrutiny by Needelman himself. The judge had asked a few questions here and there of other witnesses, but he interrogated Rosse for more than an hour. Though Needelman pointedly cautioned the lawyers against inferring anything from his questions, it was clear he had doubts about Rosse's opinions.

The witnesses for the unions and the Antitrust Division weren't any more impressive. J. Chester Johnson, a municipal finance expert hired to paint a positive picture of the Detroit economy, admitted that some of his reference materials appeared to be "in error." Marilyn J. Simon, an Antitrust Division economist, conceded there was no unilateral means by which the *Free Press* could become profitable. The lawyers for Gannett and Knight-Ridder had more trouble disturbing economist Kenneth Baseman's analysis that the JOA's fifty-fifty profit split (for the last ninety-five years of the contract) represented a recognition by Gannett that Knight-Ridder would have continued to compete for at least seven years without a JOA.

Of the hundreds of thousands of words spoken during the hearing's sixteen days, those that rang truest were spoken on the final afternoon by Bob Nelson, the former *News* publisher who now assisted Neuharth much of the time from a condominium on Florida's Gulf Coast. The gist of his testimony was that the *News* had had to keep its prices low to keep the *Free Press* from overtaking it. Indeed, he said that following the *Free Press*'s Sunday price hike in 1985 was "one of the dumbest things I ever did."

When the lawyers finished with him, Needelman asked Nelson, "Do you share Mr. Neuharth's attachment to preserving the well-being of the *Detroit Free Press*?"

"Well," Nelson said, "I guess I feel sorry, Your Honor, for the people that may lose their jobs. But my general remorse for the *Free Press* probably passes after ten or fifteen seconds."

Needelman flew home to Washington to begin sifting through the record of the hearing. He had stayed in Detroit for the entire hearing, spending weekends reviewing testimony and taking strolls along the Detroit River. He had grown fond of the city, the friendly people, the restaurants in Greektown, the homemade soup at Nick's deli across the street from the courthouse. He found himself rooting for the Tigers. It saddened him to see hollowed-out buildings and the downtown abandoned so early in the evening. The heart of Detroit did not seem to have much of a heartbeat.

One morning when he was buying a *New York Times,* the face of the man behind the newsstand counter had lit up with recognition. "I know who you are," the man exclaimed. "You're the coach of the Detroit Red Wings!" Needelman, who bore a passing resemblance to hockey coach Jacques Demers, smiled. But he did not correct the man. The judge treasured anonymity—and its complement, inscrutability. Before adjourning the hearing, he called the publishers' attorneys to the bench. "Inform the newspapers not to call me from this point on," he commanded. "I realize you don't have control over newspapermen. Tell your clients not to call me—at all." The lawyers felt Needelman had conducted a fair and expeditious hearing—and that it was nearly impossible to predict what he would tell the attorney general.

The parties filed briefs with the judge on September 23. The Antitrust Division, surprising no one, argued for denial of the JOA. A final round of briefs was filed October 14.

The case boiled down to this:

The *Free Press,* at the behest of Knight-Ridder, had sustained enormous losses as part of a conscious, two-pronged strategy to either dominate the Detroit market or force the *News* into a JOA. The jury was still out on the vehicle for this strategy, Operation Tiger, which had had only limited success, perhaps because it was never fully implemented. Executives at Knight-Ridder and the *Free Press* had been confident they would prevail, and continued to be even after Gannett had emerged on the scene. The *News,* under the aegis of the Evening News Association and then Gannett, essentially was holding the *Free Press* hostage in its number two position by keeping prices low. The *News* also had suffered huge losses. In fact, neither paper could survive without its corporate parent—though both parents had, until April of 1986, willingly accepted the consequences of their struggle for dominance. The future of the *News* and the *Free Press* depended on their owners' willingness to sustain the struggle. Neuharth, under oath, had vowed to continue it. Chapman had said he would not.

The opponents had offered no prescription for the *Free Press,* acting alone, to cure its financial ills. They had not disturbed the notion that the *Free Press*'s losses were real and continuing. But they had raised serious questions about the meaning of those losses—questions that weighed heavily on Needelman.

As a young FTC attorney, Needelman had tried an antitrust case against a renowned lawyer. Dazzled by the famous man's skills, the presiding judge had written an opinion that everyone on the case, even the big-name lawyer, recognized as a fairy tale. The young Needelman had concluded that a judge could not trust advocates to tell him the truth; he had to make his own diligent search, while keeping in mind the imbalance in legal skill and resources that could arise when large corporations were pitted against foes of lesser wherewithal. As Judge Needelman put it, he had to be wary of getting his pocket picked.

To Needelman, the truth most often could be found not in the carefully crafted statements of lawyers, but in the memoranda, notes, letters, and other documents that had been written, in unaffected candor, *before* a case came to trial. Needelman felt his job was to listen carefully for how testimony matched up against what witnesses had written and said *before* they knew they would face a specific legal test. In fact, the judge's intellectual approach, which he never discussed in court, was not much different from that of the opponents of the JOA.

The law set no deadline for Needelman to complete his work, but he promised himself he would finish by the end of the year. He worked in a spacious office at the main Justice Department building at Tenth and Constitution. Lined up along one wall were five tables laden with volumes of hearing transcript and exhibits, written direct testimony, legislative history, and legal briefs. Working long days and weekends, Needelman first prepared a lengthy list of "findings of fact." He took pride in this step; appellate courts in the past had said kind things about his facts while disagreeing with the conclusions he derived from them.

The judge then began writing his discussion, which would conclude with his recommendation to the attorney general. Assuming he proceeded as in the past, Needelman must have drafted two discussions—one recommending approval of the JOA, one denial. He then would have analyzed and edited until he felt one version more consistently reflected his findings of fact. That one would wind up on the desk of the attorney general.

Needelman finished on December 29. He hated to release such an important opinion during a holiday, but he didn't feel he could withhold it for the sake of convenience. The next day a clerk in the Justice Department's Management Division notified the attorneys that the judge's recommendation was ready.

The 129-page opinion came down hard on the publishers. Needelman found that the *News* was not clearly dominant and that the *Free Press* was not in the classic downward spiral of circulation and advertising that historically characterized "failing" papers. Indeed, Needelman noted, the papers themselves had asserted that they had fought to a "virtual draw." Their negotiation of a JOA, he found, reflected a "distaste" for competition. "The objectives of dominance and future profitability were pursued by both papers (and their parents) in the belief that failure too had its reward in the form of JOA approval," Needelman wrote.

The judge found no convincing proof that Detroit was unable to support two profitable papers. In fact, he said, Knight-Ridder and Gannett viewed the city as a "choice plum" that could yield profits if the newspapers raised prices. It was no surprise that Detroit had trouble sustaining two profitable papers "when both are practically being given away," Needelman wrote.

Neuharth's insistence that he would not raise prices "requires acceptance of the odd notion that a rational and self-interested firm will persist in unprofitable behavior."

Needelman dismissed Chapman's vow to recommend closing the *Free Press* in the event the JOA was denied. "The record . . . contains no convincing evidence that he seriously considered closing the *Free Press* prior to his witness-stand bolt out of the blue and, accordingly, I have assigned little weight to this threat," the judge wrote. Needelman did not mean to suggest that Chapman had lied, merely that the Knight-Ridder chief's statement was not supported in the record.

Above his signature on the final page of his opinion Needelman wrote, "The administrative law judge recommends that the attorney general issue the following order:

> Upon consideration of all of the facts and applicable law, it is hereby ordered that the application by *Detroit Free Press,* Incorporated and the *Detroit News,* Inc., for approval of a joint operating arrangement pursuant to the Newspaper Preservation Act, 15 U.S.C. S 1801 *et seq.*, be, and the same is, hereby denied."

Part Four

Hearts and Minds

13

Drastic Measures

It was a grim New Year 1988 for Alvah Chapman. For days he did not sleep well, and he spent the holiday weekend poring over Needelman's damning opinion. He was furious with his lawyers, who had promised so much and delivered so little. Even now they were telling him Needelman had made many errors and Attorney General Edwin Meese would find ample reason to overrule the judge. "That's when we made the decision we were not going to let the lawyers run the damn thing anymore," Chapman later recalled.

He sat down with Jim Batten, Bob Singleton, and Tony Ridder and prepared an exhaustive, point-by-point analysis of Needelman's bomb. Then he called all of his top Knight-Ridder deputies and *Free Press* executives to a strategy session in Miami on Monday, January 4. Seven hours of brainstorming yielded no good answers. The lawyers tried to reassure, but none of the executives, not even the usually indefatigable Chapman, could dredge up much optimism that Meese would overrule his administrative law judge *and* his Antitrust Division. It looked like it might be over.

At night, Chapman lay awake, thinking and praying. Where had he gone wrong? It was true that he had involved himself less directly in the effort to secure approval of the JOA than he normally would have in a project of such importance. Chapman had entrusted that task to his attorneys, believing he would be more useful overseeing preparations for the actual merger of the newspapers. After all, he was a businessman, not a lawyer. Besides, the case for the JOA seemed so clear, the *Free Press*'s huge losses so convincing, that he couldn't imagine how the lawyers could stumble. Obviously, that was a mistake. Less obvious was another important truth: Chapman's decision to leave to others the pursuit of his ultimate goal was totally out of character. When Alvah Chapman wanted something important done, he rarely deferred to anyone else. Personal leadership and hands-on commitment were the hallmark of his private work in Miami, where he had been the single most determined, persistent, and effective catalyst behind nearly every significant commercial development in the city's downtown renaissance of the 1970s and 1980s.

When he embarked on a project close to his heart, he made a practice of first jotting down names of all the people and institutions with a stake in it. Then he would personally contact each one, seeking a firm commitment, frequently of dollars, long before the project was public knowledge. In the wake of the 1980 race riot in Miami, Chapman and another local business leader raised $8.5 million in a few weeks, largely by going directly to the chiefs of the area's biggest companies and asking for sums as large as a half million dollars. With the JOA, though, Chapman didn't follow his own tried-and-true practice. He never even made his customary list of constituents with a stake in the project. He and Al Neuharth phoned the mayor and the governor and a few of the local corporate chiefs, but those were courtesy calls, perfunctory at best. Chapman left the courting of the politicians and the large advertisers—what little courting there was—to Bill Keating. Many groups with vital interests in the JOA—small advertisers, suburban publishers, the unions, the citizens of Michigan—were simply told what was going to happen. Chapman never reached out to them, never sought to get them to buy into the JOA, as he might have sought their sanction of, say, the construction of a shopping mall on the Detroit riverfront.

It was arrogant and it was naive. Chapman was a willful man who, once he believed his objective was correct, refused to entertain the possibility that it could be wrong. Those who did not agree were mistaken, in Chapman's view, and they would eventually come around or clear out of his way. He also had an innate trust in the American legal system. If there was a law, such as the Newspaper Preservation Act, and a citizen or a corporation complied with the law, the system ultimately would support that person or company. Which was why Needelman's opinion threw Chapman for such a loop. He could not fathom that justice, properly applied, could deny Knight-Ridder the benefits of the Newspaper Preservation Act. As he saw it, Knight-Ridder was a victim of a historical hostility to the law that Needelman, the onetime antitrust cop, shared with the Justice Department's Antitrust Division. The proof was that Needelman had refused to believe the simplest piece of evidence before him: that the *Free Press* would be closed if the JOA was not approved. That Needelman would dismiss the assertion as a "witness-stand bolt out of the blue" infuriated Chapman. Since his days at The Citadel, where truth equaled honor, Alvah Chapman had prided himself on being a man of his word. Needelman was the first person he could recall who had ever publicly doubted him.

But the perceived slight was unimportant. Of graver import was that everyone who had a stake in the Detroit newspapers might now doubt that Chapman would do what he had said he would do. That would be tragic, Chapman thought, for he was not bluffing. More than two thousand jobs would vanish and the people of Michigan would lose a friend that had been with them for more than 150 years, longer than the *Detroit News,* longer than the Detroit Tigers, longer than General Motors or Ford or Chrysler. Knight-Ridder could try to sell the paper, of course, but it was unlikely that anyone with the wherewithal to duel Gannett would take such a dare. The Wall Street analysts, who certainly believed Chapman's threat, already had pronounced that no publicly held company would buy the *Free Press,* which virtually assured that none would, since the analysts would devalue the company for doing so. If the JOA was denied, the *Free Press* was, in all likelihood, doomed. In retrospect, Chapman almost wished he had made that clear from the start, when he and Neuharth announced the JOA in April of 1986. But his lawyers had told him that was unnecessary.

Now, though, the fate of the *Free Press,* at least in Chapman's eyes, was certain without a JOA. The executive's mission was to convince anyone and everyone who cared.

One of those first few nights of January 1988, Chapman lay awake while his wife, Betty, slept at his side. Frustrated with his insomnia, he asked God for help, silently repeating a verse from the Gospel of Matthew: "Come unto me, all ye that labor and are heavy laden, and I will give you rest." As he prayed in the dark, it dawned on Chapman that this was not a time for rest, this was a time to get to work. God had spoken to him. Chapman immediately left the bed, pulled on a robe and slippers, and hurried downstairs to his office. He took out a yellow legal pad and began to make a list of all the key people in Michigan whose support he believed he would need to persuade Attorney General Edwin Meese to approve the JOA. It was a list he should have made long before.

* * *

Alvah Chapman unveiled his plan to rescue the JOA in a meeting with Al Neuharth and other Gannett executives and lawyers at Hughes Hubbard and Reed's Washington offices on January 7, 1988. Knight-Ridder and the *Free Press,* Chapman said, would ask dozens of key Michigan citizens—corporate leaders, clergy, politicians, government officials—to write letters urging Attorney General Meese to approve the JOA, lest the *Free Press* be shut down. To convince the Michigan citizenry of that dire possibility, Knight-Ridder's board of directors would convene a special meeting to confirm what Chapman had threatened on the witness stand. Further, Knight-Ridder would try to negotiate a settlement with the newspaper unions to result in the unions renouncing their opposition to the JOA. *Free Press* publisher David Lawrence already was working on Mayor Coleman Young to reverse his stance.

Neuharth and his deputies listened with interest. Gannett president and CEO John Curley made a suggestion. "If you're going to talk about Detroit," he said, "maybe that's the place to hold the [Knight-Ridder board] meeting." Chapman said he'd consider it. Neuharth said Gannett would support Chapman's strategy, without actively participating. "It's your ball game, the burden of proof is on you, and we think you should decide how to go about it," he told Chapman. Neuharth wanted to avoid the controversy he was certain a public relations campaign would stir. "I didn't want to get into a pissing match," he later recalled. "I thought that this company and the *Detroit News* were somewhat above that because of the position they were in." Nonetheless, he reassured Chapman that Gannett remained fully committed to the JOA. "We thought in the beginning a JOA was in the best interest of all parties," Neuharth told him. "We think that now."

At the *Detroit News,* however, Neuharth's underlings were anticipating the fall of the *Free Press.* Before Judge Needelman's opinion came out, executive editor Bob Giles had bumped into a reporter who asked, in jest, what Giles wanted for Christmas. Two things, Giles said: the Cleveland Browns in the NFL playoffs and a denial of the JOA. The Browns made the playoffs, then lost to the Denver Broncos, 38–33, in the AFC title game. After Needelman did what he could to grant the second wish, Giles circulated a memo seeking suggestions on how to exploit "the clear advantage we have coming off the Needelman recommendation."

Business reporter Kathleen Kerwin was assigned to interview industry experts about how the *Free Press* could be run profitably; one was Moe Hickey, who had left the *News* to run the *Denver Post* for owner William Dean Singleton. "You've got to raise prices and pare down expenses," advised Hickey, who had eagerly chopped prices and lost millions while at the *News.* An analytical story accompanying Kerwin's piece was headlined, GANNETT HOLDS ALL THE CARDS, MOST AGREE. *News* publisher Chip Weil sent a letter exhorting employees to increase the *News*'s circulation and advertising leads in the wake of the Needelman decision.

Lionel Linder, the ENA holdover who had retained his title of editor with little of the responsibility, confided to a *News* reporter that Bob Giles and Chip Weil "think they see they're going to win the whole pot of gold." But, Linder added, without a trace of irony, "They don't trust Meese. He might not go along with Needelman."

David Lawrence didn't know whom or what to trust. Like Alvah Chapman, Lawrence no longer felt confident that legalities alone would carry the day. To sway Meese there had to be something extra, something new, something more tangible than ad linage analyses and abstract theories about economies of scale.

Lawrence had his own middle-of-the-night epiphany. Around 4:00 A.M. on January 8 he left his bed, made coffee, and padded down to the computer in his basement study. "I am worried," he typed. "The *Free Press* could die." It would be his column, which appeared every Sunday on the page opposite the editorials. For more than 950 words, Lawrence went on about the "unthinkable" calamity that would confront his newspaper if the JOA was denied. He did not discuss the possibility that the *Free Press* could be sold. He did not explain why Knight-Ridder had waited more than a year to spell out the peril threatening the *Free Press*. He did not mention the enormous profits the JOA was expected to generate once it was in place and the *Free Press* and the *News* raised prices.

Instead, he wrote of an elderly woman who had sent him a check for fifteen dollars to ease the *Free Press*'s financial burden. She apologized for not sending more, but, "I am handicapped for 43 years with multiple sclerosis, and that puts me into a disadvantageous situation," she wrote. Another woman, Lawrence wrote, sent him a letter urging him to raise prices: "The *Free Press* enriches my brain. So feel free to deplete my purse."

"People care so much," Lawrence wrote. "But the checks won't do it. We lost $18 million last year. There is nothing we could do on our own, the judge conceded, that could ensure profitability." It was the only bit of Judge Needelman's findings Lawrence saw fit to cite in his desperate missive. "A JOA provides no perfect world," he conceded. "But it provides the only real future for readers and the people who produce your *Free Press*. . . . Isn't the JOA—

whose purpose is to preserve voices and, thus, entirely separate, and fully competitive, news and editorial departments of the two newspapers—the better way to go? It is, moreover, the one way to protect most of the jobs." Lawrence wanted it understood, however, that his own job wasn't at issue. "Please do not see this as self-serving," he begged. "None of this is to save my job. I am trying to save your newspaper." Whatever happened to the *Free Press,* Lawrence's landing would be soft. Knight-Ridder already was talking about bringing him south to be publisher of the *Miami Herald.* Lawrence ended most columns with a plea for readers to write him. In this column he asked, "What does the *Free Press* mean to you and what would you miss the most? It would mean a lot to me to know. Please write to me. . . ."

The column was cleared with Knight-Ridder lawyer Cal Collier and faxed to Chapman, who was delighted with it. In Detroit, editor Joe Stroud and new *Free Press* executive editor Heath J Meriwether, who had come from the *Miami Herald* to replace Kent Bernhard, wondered if the column should run on the front page. Decades earlier, front-page editorials had been common in big dailies. Lawrence could remember his father running them in the *Sarasota News.* But the *Free Press* hadn't run one for as long as anyone could remember. Not during the 1967 race riot, nor the Vietnam War, nor even when Chrysler in the late 1970s was on the verge of bankruptcy and more than a hundred thousand jobs were on the line. Then again, had Chrysler owned a newspaper, it might well have published a front-page column pleading for help.

Lawrence wanted his column on the front page, but the decision was Meriwether's. He didn't hesitate. "This was a survival issue," he recalled. "If there was an appropriate time for the publisher to go to page one, this was the time." Alan Lenhoff, assistant to *Free Press* general manager Robert Hall, also was urging front-page play. "One of my fears throughout this whole process," Lenhoff later told a *Free Press* reporter, "has been that the paper would shut down and someone at a cocktail party a month later would say, 'Why didn't you *really* tell me you were in trouble?' I thought we ought to tell people. There are no rewards for failing in a genteel manner."

So Dave Lawrence's column, headlined, MATTER OF LIFE OR DEATH FOR YOUR *FREE PRESS,* ran down the length of the left side of the front page of the *Free Press* on Sunday, January 10. In case readers missed that, *Free Press* columnist Hugh McDiarmid's similar piece ran the length of the left side of page 3A, the first thing readers saw when they opened the paper. McDiarmid predicted that, "sometime later this year, you'll wake up to a *Free Press* with a big, black headline saying: 'Goodby [*sic*] Detroit.' Save it. It will be the last one. It will also be tragic."

Reaction to Lawrence's column was impassioned and sharply divided. In one week, more than a thousand *Free Press* readers responded with letters bemoaning the possibility that their paper might soon disappear. Their notes bespoke a remarkable attachment to the paper they turned to each morning over coffee or juice. They talked about it as if it were a live, breathing human being, not an inanimate bundle of newsprint and ink.

"Our *Free Press* is a warm and caring friend," wrote two brothers from the rural community of South Lyon. "I consider everyone on the *Free Press* to be a friend of mine," wrote a man from the affluent suburb of Bloomfield Hills. "Like a good friend," wrote a woman from Westland, a blue-collar suburb, "my *Free Press* has been there—to challenge, make me laugh, make me think." They wrote of the comforting "wake-up thud" of the *Free Press* against their front doors and the "empty feeling" that ensued when it came late. They declared their love of the comics, the sports page, the columnists, the crossword puzzles, and ridiculed the *News* as "cold, wizened, wrinkled, undesirable." A nun promised prayers. A woman told how she had recently buried her father with a copy of his beloved *Free Press*. Lawrence was overwhelmed. In twenty-five years of professional newspapering, he had never seen such an outpouring of affection for a newspaper. He read every letter and kept his secretary busy typing personal replies.

But not everyone was enamored of Dave Lawrence's column.

Jeanne Towar, the outspoken publisher of the *Daily Tribune* in suburban Royal Oak, exploded in a news story run in the *Free Press*. She was a devout *Free Press* reader who didn't know how to start the day without the paper, she said, but Lawrence's plea wasn't about saving the paper. "This is all about making $100 million a year," she said. "If Mr. Lawrence would make some of the hard choices the rest of us have made, he wouldn't have to write the damn self-serving piece he wrote on the front of the paper. And yes, I do think it's self-serving. The fact that he said it *isn't* says something."

The day after Lawrence's column ran, Michigan governor James Blanchard, who had been publicly neutral on the JOA, told three *News* reporters in an interview that he believed Detroit could support two newspapers without a JOA and it was "hogwash" to think otherwise. With characteristic glibness, Blanchard said the *Free Press* needed to improve its quality—"get some reporters, some features, and some columnists"—to survive. "I think they have a quality problem. I really do. There isn't a lot of news in there, and then they're losing a lot of it. The *Detroit News* is hiring everybody that worked at the *Free Press*. You got the publisher begging on the front page for letters on Sunday . . . and they're charging less than the cost of paper to print it."

Before they were even published, Lawrence heard about the governor's comments in a phone call that evening from *News* reporter Charlie Cain. Late that night Lawrence called Blanchard at home. The publisher seemed quite upset, Blanchard later recalled. Lawrence couldn't believe the governor would make such nasty remarks about the *Free Press* at such a stressful time—and to its competitor, no less. Blanchard was equally surprised, or at least acted as though he were. He hadn't expected the *News* to take his remarks so seriously, he told Lawrence. He certainly didn't expect the *News* to print what he'd said, which he considered the kind of off-the-cuff chitchat that reporters knew to keep out of the paper. While he had found problems with a few *Free Press* editorials of late, Blanchard admired Dave Lawrence for his extensive work on community affairs and had no wish to embarrass the publisher so. Now that seemed unavoidable, though, for the *News* was running a story the next day. Lawrence asked Blanchard for the courtesy of a follow-up interview with the *Free Press* if Blanchard felt the *News* had misconstrued his words. The next day the *News* ran a front-page story—with no small measure of glee, Lawrence thought—and a partial transcript of a tape of Blanchard's remarks, which included several digs at the *Free Press* and the governor's questioning of the need for a JOA.

On the front page of the following day's *Free Press,* Blanchard was suddenly a fan of the *Free Press* and the JOA. His criticism of the *Free Press,* he said, was colored by recent *Free Press* editorials that had dismayed him. His disparaging comments were nothing more than "jokes at lunch." In fact, Blanchard said, it would be a tragedy if the *Free Press* had to close, and now he wasn't so certain both papers would survive without a JOA.

In newsroom slang, it was a "skinback"—the awkward act of correcting or modifying something one had previously written or said. Politicians regularly skinned back, of course, but rarely in such stark juxtaposition. It was embarrassing for Blanchard, confusing to readers, and a bit silly for the papers, who appeared to be engaged in a childish exchange of "Did!" and "Didn't!" Lawrence denied having tried to influence the governor, despite his late-night phone call, and Blanchard dismissed the notion that he could be unduly influenced.

Lawrence's Sunday column pleading for support infuriated the heads of the newspaper unions. Their lawyers, Duane Ice and Gene Driker, detected a sinister motive. It seemed obvious to them that the publisher wanted readers to write to Attorney General Edwin Meese, which possibly would violate so-called *ex parte* rules barring contact with the decision maker. In fact, Lawrence's column hadn't even hinted at writing Meese—although some readers took precisely that meaning. Indeed, a friend of Lawrence, Diane Edgecomb, the boosterish leader of Detroit's Central Business District Association, orchestrated a letter-writing campaign aimed at the attorney general.

The unions responded with their own letter to Lawrence calling his column a "corporate propaganda advertisement mouthing the Knight-Ridder line." "For three weeks last August . . . all parties had the opportunity to present the facts in this application thru [*sic*] documentation or direct testimony," the two-page letter read. "To now solicit opinions outside that legal forum to directly influence the attorney general is not only unethical but illegal. To unleash a campaign of corporate terrorism on the employees of the *Free Press* and the citizens of this state, fueled by Knight-Ridder's refusal to operate without the guarantee of monopoly profits, is unconscionable."

Lawrence, undaunted, defended his column as "in the greatest traditions of American journalism going back 200 years." The sniping irritated him. Was he supposed to simply stand by and watch the *Free Press* perish? Lawrence felt he had a moral obligation to tell the readers exactly what would happen if the JOA was not approved. If some chose to view that as a threat, so be it. Lawrence was more concerned that no one think it a bluff. Needelman may not have believed Alvah Chapman, but Dave Lawrence certainly did. Chapman was plenty tough enough to pull the plug on the *Free Press*. As for selling it, Knight-Ridder would have to get a handsome price—$100 million at least—to justify not simply padlocking the place and hauling the printing presses to Philadelphia, where they were badly needed.

The union chiefs' letter also accused Lawrence of violating journalistic ethics. "[Y]ou give *new meaning* to the old adage in the newspaper industry that 'freedom of the press belongs to those who own one,' " the letter said. "The timing, subject and placement of Sunday's column violates every known journalistic standard." Some of Lawrence's own reporters felt the publisher had crossed the line between informing readers and using the paper to further its self-interest. Arguably, Lawrence had bent, if not broken, the *Free Press*'s ethical guideline instructing staffers to "avoid using their *Free Press* positions to obtain personal or financial benefit for themselves, family, or friends." John Saunders, a *Free Press* business reporter who was about to leave the paper for the *Toronto Globe and Mail,* echoed the feelings of many when he said, "The way things are going, this paper will die of shame before they have a chance to close it."

Lawrence didn't lose any sleep. He felt the *Free Press* had covered the JOA fairly and accurately and had let the critics—including Saunders, whose damning quote was published in the *Free Press*—have their say. Lawrence's column was *his* say, and he wasn't about to apologize for it.

Had he abused his privilege as publisher to shill for his bosses? Or simply exercised common sense in making an important statement as forcefully as possible? It was tempting to imagine Lawrence as torn by inner conflict over those questions. But Lawrence wasn't torn at all. If ever he had agonized, it was in the spring of 1986, when he first learned a JOA would cut short his quest to win the Great Detroit Newspaper War. He made a decision then to stand by Knight-Ridder and the JOA. For Lawrence, there was no turning back. His commitment was absolute.

At the hearing before Judge Needelman, Lawrence had testified that he believed part of his job was to set "a tone of morality and integrity" for the *Free Press*. Now, while he tolerated those who castigated him, he told himself—and anyone who asked—that his and the *Free Press*'s integrity was intact. He was doing what he had to do to save the JOA and the *Free Press*—with no regrets. Extreme situations sometimes required extreme measures. If Lawrence had pushed the envelope of journalistic ethics, he would push it even further before this mission was complete. Purity was not a luxury he and Knight-Ridder could afford right now.

So Lawrence had no qualms whatsoever about his phone call to Gerald Greenwald, chairman of Chrysler Motors Corporation, Chrysler's carmaking subsidiary. Lawrence wanted a favor. At Alvah Chapman's urging, Knight-Ridder had tried to procure the services of Timmons and Company, one of Washington's top lobbying firms. William E. Timmons, a onetime White House aide to Presidents Nixon and Ford, had some of the best Republican connections in town. The *Washington Post* called him "one of Meese's favored advisers." His partner, Tom C. Korologos, had helped Ed Meese win Senate confirmation as attorney general. But Timmons's firm had a policy of concentrating on a dozen or so regular clients who paid annual retainers, and it wasn't seeking new business.

Chrysler, however, had Timmons on retainer. Lawrence called Greenwald, whom he knew from a variety of community activities, to ask if Knight-Ridder could borrow Timmons for a bit. Greenwald passed the request on to Timmons, who agreed to help. (Korologos also recalled a telephone call from Chrysler chieftain Lee A. Iacocca, who told him, "Make it happen.") Lawrence offered to pay for the lobbying services, but that was impractical because Timmons didn't charge by the hour. So Chrysler, via its annual retainer, picked up the tab.

As it turned out, Timmons and Korologos did little for Knight-Ridder. But Lawrence had pushed the ethical envelope a bit further. He had asked a favor of a company that was in the news columns of the *Free Press* almost daily. He'd offered no quid pro quo—and Greenwald did not infer one—but there was the clear appearance of a conflict of interest, the kind of unseemly appearance for which the *Free Press* and scores of other newspapers regularly criticized public officials like Ed Meese.

And there was more to come.

The tall, hoary-headed man who stood at the head of the conference table was impeccably dressed, in his customary pin-striped, double-breasted suit with a high shirt collar and French cuffs, smiling broadly at the men arrayed before him, his chiseled face still dazzlingly handsome at eighty-one. Clark M. Clifford was also one of the most influential men in Washington. He had convened this January 14, 1988, meeting of Knight-Ridder's lawyers and executives and a few select guests to explore how they could persuade Attorney General Edwin Meese to ignore the recommendation of Judge Morton Needelman and grant the *Detroit Free Press* a JOA.

Clark Clifford had only recently been consulted. Alvah Chapman himself had flown to Washington to visit the lawyer in the hushed, paneled confines of Clifford's twelfth-floor office, where Clifford, if he peeked through the permanently drawn blinds, had a view of the White House, the Washington Monument, and the Capitol. Chapman had told the older man that Knight-Ridder dearly needed his help with the greatest crisis it had ever faced. Chapman wanted a fresh perspective on the case for the JOA, a new way of approaching it that would snatch the *Free Press* from death's jaws.

Clifford had been on Knight-Ridder's board of directors since the 1974 merger of the Knight and Ridder chains. He was an old friend of Walter Ridder, who ran the chain's Washington news bureau and had invited Clifford to join the Ridder board. After the merger, Clifford was the only outside director asked to stay on. He was regarded as Knight-Ridder's Washington hand, the link to an inscrutable and sometimes distasteful realm from which Chapman and his lieutenants preferred to keep a distance. Jack Knight, of course, had reveled in the swirl of political Washington, hobnobbing with Nixon, Eisenhower, and Johnson, delighting in the rancorous debates of the day. Chapman left such matters to his reporters and editorial writers, confining his own political interests primarily to greater Miami and Florida. When a window on Washington was needed, he could always turn to Clark Clifford. Clifford's firm, Clifford and Warnke, was not Knight-Ridder's primary counsel, however; Hughes Hubbard and Reed was. But Hughes Hubbard's lawyers had disappointed Alvah Chapman. Although he had no intention of dismissing them, he intended to get them some help.

Clifford's credentials were the envy of every lobbyist, politician, and policymaker in Washington. He had been a confidant to Presidents Truman, Kennedy, Johnson, and Carter. He was the ghost writer of the Truman Doctrine. He had confronted the chieftains of the steel industry when Jack Kennedy thought they were gouging the public. As secretary of defense, he had nudged LBJ toward ending the Vietnam War. Clifford and Warnke had represented Standard Oil, RCA, Phillips Petroleum, TWA, and dozens of other corporations and foreign nations. The archetypal superlawyer, Clifford was rumored to have been the first attorney in America to earn a million dollars a year.

Before Chapman approached Clifford, he had talked it over with Jack Fontaine, Knight-Ridder's general counsel. It was a ticklish matter for Fontaine, because he also was a partner at Hughes Hubbard and spent a lot of time at the firm's New York office. He knew that Phil Lacovara and the firm's other Washington lawyers would not look kindly on a new firm intruding on their case. But Fontaine agreed with Chapman. "We as a company, and our lawyers," Fontaine later recalled, "had not appreciated that the [JOA] issue was much broader than a legal issue, that the context was not only legal but political, in a small-*p* sense, that you had to win the hearts and minds of the people. We also thought we needed a very visible, eloquent advocate who would deliver the legal message in a more evangelical style than we did at the hearing."

Clifford had been hearing about the JOA at board meetings for two years, though he had not gotten involved in the lawyering. Lacovara seemed to have things under control; his reports to the board were invariably optimistic. Clifford was surprised and dismayed to hear that the administrative law judge had recommended that the JOA be denied. He was not surprised, however, when Chapman asked for his help. By now, the JOA was not a creature of businesspeople and journalists in Detroit, but of politicians and bureaucrats in Washington. Clifford agreed to drop everything and devote himself to the JOA. He spent hours reading the transcript of the hearing and Judge Needelman's opinion, which powerfully impressed him. Though he disagreed with the judge's conclusion, Clifford thought Needelman had so crisply and forcefully explained himself that it would be foolhardy, lacking some new argument or evidence, to expect Meese to differ.

Needelman's view struck Clifford as hypertechnical; the judge had focused narrowly on the letter of the law and ignored the spirit. Yet the spirit of the law was crucial because, as was obvious to Clifford, the case had broad public policy implications for the future of two-newspaper cities. In Clifford's view, the judge—and everyone opposed to the JOA, for that matter—assumed that the choice in Detroit was between a JOA and a continuation of combat between the *Free Press* and the *News*. That was not the choice at all. The choice was between a JOA and a one-newspaper city. "That's where we've gotten off the track," Clifford told Chapman.

Now Knight-Ridder had to act boldly, Clifford told Chapman, or the JOA—and, hence, the *Free Press*—would be lost. "I concluded," Clifford recalled, "that we needed to change the direction of the case." He and Chapman devised the twin tactics of having the Knight-Ridder board confirm that the *Free Press* would be closed, and negotiating with opponents to get them to withdraw from the case. Clifford also combined Chapman's idea—seeking the support of community leaders—and Dave Lawrence's plea—for letters from readers—into a plan to seek signed letters from key political, civic, religious, and business leaders and submit them to Attorney General Meese. The purpose of the January 14 meeting in Clifford and Warnke's main conference room was to discuss how to pursue the three-pronged strategy *within the law.*

Chapman sat at the conference table with Jim Batten, Jack Fontaine, Dave Lawrence, and Phil Lacovara. Next to Clifford was his splendidly coiffed protégé, Robert Altman. Lobbyists Bill Timmons and Tom Korologos were there, along with Theodore H. Mecke, Jr., a retired vice-president of public affairs for Ford Motor Company, whom the *Free Press* had hired to help plan the courting of Detroit's corporate and civic elite. They listened as Clifford deferred to Chapman, who set the tone with the curious statement that Knight-Ridder wanted to save the *Free Press,* though not at the expense of the company's reputation.

Phil Lacovara also was concerned about reputations—his own and that of his law firm. Lacovara was just as determined as Clifford to save the *Free Press,* but he was not comfortable with the plans his client and its newly hired counsel were contemplating. Now he told them so. The Needelman opinion, he said, was a setback, but hardly the final word. Meese was not bound by the recommendation and could dispute the facts of the case, Needelman's interpretation, or both. The judge had made many findings consistent with Knight-Ridder's view, including one—that the *Free Press* could not return to profitability through any action of its own—which by itself provided a strong basis for approving the JOA. Needelman did not agree with Knight-Ridder, Lacovara said, because he obviously didn't like the Newspaper Preservation Act. Meese surely would be able to see that. As a cabinet member and overseer of public policy, Meese also would find it more difficult to dismiss the risk that the *Free Press* would close. Forced to choose between the views of Needelman and those of Knight-Ridder, Lacovara argued, Meese would side with the latter.

Lacovara conceded that it might help to get the unions and Mayor Young to rescind their opposition. Meese might also be subtly influenced by outsiders such as business and political leaders, so long as they represented a broad political spectrum, lacking any partisan taint. Supplying him with the outsiders' declarations of support would be permissible if they were fashioned as submissions by *amici curiae*—"friends of the court," who regularly participated in administrative cases. The rules for submissions were somewhat vague in this case. They said the attorney general should base his decision on "the hearing record, the examiner's recommendation, and any exceptions and responses filed"; but they were silent on whether those exceptions and responses could include comments offered by outsiders.

There were risks to Clifford and Chapman's political strategy, Lacovara said—risks that he and his colleagues felt outweighed the potential benefits. The political appeal could backfire if Meese and his top deputy, William Bradford Reynolds, perceived an obvious attempt to manipulate; if they thought they would be viewed as capitulating to corporate interests, they might well opt for the safer course of adopting Needelman's stance. The letter-writing campaign might provide opponents with a basis for judicial appeal. There also were questions of appropriateness, which Lacovara had discussed with his partners, Cal Collier and Gerald Goldman. Though the mechanics of the campaign were technically permissible, Lacovara told his audience, neither he nor Hughes Hubbard and Reed was inclined to pursue such a strategy. "We continued to believe [that] on the merits Meese would decide in our favor," Lacovara later said. "This was not a time for drastic measures."

Clifford politely begged to differ. The stakes were too great and the risks of losing the *Free Press* too high to continue to pursue a course that thus far had failed. He respected his esteemed colleague's concerns, but this was no time to be punctilious. "We're going to lose," Clifford later recalled saying, "if we don't do something new."

Phil Lacovara could not win this argument. It wasn't because Clark Clifford was more eloquent than Lacovara, though perhaps he was. It wasn't because Clark Clifford could mesmerize a room, as he had today, with his mellifluous oratory and the subtle gestures—the spidery fingers pressed thoughtfully to his temples—that implied a level of sagacity the younger Lacovara could not approach. Lacovara could not prevail because Alvah Chapman had lost his innocence—and arrogance—about Washington. Chapman had trusted Washington, and Needelman had burned him. So he'd decided the JOA was not about the law. It was about politics.

Which meant Lacovara wasn't the right man for the job, and he knew it. He didn't say so to the people in Clifford's conference room, but to him, there were two ways to be a Washington lawyer: "the lawyerlike way and the influence-peddling way," as he later put it. "I was happy to concentrate in my career on the lawyerlike ways of getting things done," he recalled, "and trusting the fate of my clients to the outcome of that process, even though sometimes they lost." That was, in a way, why he had resigned as counsel to the Watergate special prosecutor the day after President Ford pardoned Nixon.

Lacovara did not quit the JOA, though from that day on his role was diminished. He made it clear to Alvah Chapman and Jack Fontaine that he and his colleagues would continue preparing briefs and crafting arguments, but they would not participate in lobbying or favor seeking. Lacovara felt he could not resign from the case outright because he had concluded that Knight-Ridder's political strategy was within the law. Withdrawing would be irresponsible inasmuch as it drew attention to whether Knight-Ridder's new strategy was appropriate or not.

Personally, though, Lacovara had had it with the JOA. He had been superseded by a highly visible lawyer who was handling *his* case in a way he would not have handled it. No matter the outcome, Lacovara stood to look bad. If Meese denied the JOA, he would be blamed. If Meese approved it, Clifford would get credit for a miraculous rescue. No one would ever know whether Lacovara could have prevailed on the merits.

Serendipity provided an escape. Sometime in January, Lacovara received a call from Benjamin Heineman, Jr., a friend who had become general counsel at General Electric. Heineman wondered if Lacovara could recommend an attorney to oversee GE's worldwide litigation. "Depending on what you've got in mind and how it's structured, I might be interested," Lacovara told Heineman. In fact, Lacovara wasn't as happy as he could have been at Hughes Hubbard. His superiors had found his performance at drumming up new business wanting; indeed, Lacovara himself found hustling for clients distasteful. With a case as important as the JOA on his hands, Lacovara normally wouldn't have considered leaving Hughes Hubbard. But the case was no longer his. By summer, he would be gone.

14

The Falling Leaf

The Knight-Ridder board of directors came to Detroit on a dreary winter Thursday to rubber-stamp Alvah Chapman's promise to close the *Free Press* in the absence of a JOA. Chapman hadn't any doubt the board would do his bidding. His board was as typically American as Wonder bread—white, male, and stacked in favor of management. Five of the eighteen members were company officials: Chapman, Jim Batten, Tony Ridder, Bob Singleton, and Richard Capen, publisher of the *Miami Herald*. Another five, though not managers, were bona fide insiders: three Ridders, Chapman's pal Byron Harless, and seventy-eight-year-old Jim Knight. Two others, Peyton Anderson and Ben Morris, had joined the board after Knight-Ridder bought their newspaper companies. One member was female—Barbara Hauptfuhrer, who served on half a dozen other boards—and one was black—Jesse Hill, Jr., president of the Atlanta Life Insurance Company. Rounding it out were Chapman's close ally, Clark Clifford, and top executives of Xerox, Raytheon, and Goldman, Sachs.

Of the thirteen who gathered in person around a long, rectangular table in the Family Dining Room at the Detroit Club on January 21, none was inclined to buck Chapman. Many had lived with the *Free Press* since the mid-1970s, and while they appreciated its special place in the lore of the Knight legacy, they were weary of the suicidal war with the *Detroit News*. Only Jack Knight might have argued for sustaining the fight, but he was long gone.

Indeed, it was conceivable that even the fiery former publisher of the *Free Press* would have let the paper die, just as he had walked away from the *Chicago Daily News* when he saw he could not prevail. Knight probably could not have stomached the campaign being waged by Chapman, Clifford, Dave Lawrence, and their lobbyists and flacks. More than a few *Free Press* journalists were shaking their heads and wondering aloud if Knight was turning in his grave.

Since the verdict of the Knight-Ridder directors was a *fait accompli*—indeed, one director, Raytheon chairman Thomas Phillips, called in his vote *before* the meeting—it had been easy to script the three pivotal days Chapman would spend in Detroit. Lawrence, capitalizing on the countless hours he had spent working for community causes, arranged for more than 150 of Detroit's business, political, and social elite to grace a private cocktail reception that would follow the Knight-Ridder board meeting. He set up meetings for Chapman with multimillionaire investor Max Fisher, a Republican who had raised more than a million dollars for George Bush in the Michigan presidential primary; Governor James Blanchard; and a passel of influential Michigan labor chiefs, among them Bobby Holmes of the Teamsters and former UAW president Douglas Fraser.

Meanwhile Jim Batten, former reporter, had helped set the stage by playing press secretary. With Jack Fontaine in tow, he had visited the *Wall Street Journal, U.S. News and World Report,* the *Washington Post,* and the *Washington Times,* where former *Detroit News* editorial writer Tony Snow was editing the archconservative editorial page. (Snow recalled telling Batten, "Let me do you a favor; we *won't* write about the JOA.") Batten phoned friends at the *Los Angeles Times* and the *New York Times.* He wanted these influential papers' editorial support, but he also expressed his fervent hope that they would cover the Knight-Ridder board meeting in Detroit. It was important, in Batten's view, that the whole country know what would happen to the *Free Press* if the JOA was denied. Clips from the publications he contacted also regularly found their way to Ed Meese.

The Knight-Ridder board meeting began at 1:30 P.M. Jim Knight and Walter Ridder did not attend. Barbara Hauptfuhrer and Peyton Anderson participated via conference call. Chapman and Fontaine began by updating the board on Needelman's recommendation and the next steps in the legal process. Tony Ridder and Gene Falk, then a top business executive for Knight-Ridder's Philadelphia papers, discussed plans for a new printing plant in Philadelphia, including how the *Free Press*'s presses could be used there.

Around 2:30, nonboard members were asked to leave. A somber hush fell over the room. Bob Singleton offered a detailed analysis of what a shutdown of the *Free Press* would cost Knight-Ridder—a net loss of $20 million to $25 million after the presses were moved, the property was sold, and the employees had received severance. Chapman told the board he didn't think the *Free Press* could be sold, citing the unlikelihood that anyone would offer a price high enough to offset the benefit of moving the presses to Philadelphia. Clark Clifford dominated the board's discussion, passionately stressing his view that Knight-Ridder had to make unequivocally clear what could be lost to the readers, the advertisers, the employees, and the unions—the "stakeholders," as Clifford called them. Ed Meese was a stakeholder, too, Clifford argued, for he would not want to be remembered as the man who could have saved the *Free Press* but did not. Only the Knight-Ridder board could present Meese with such a stark choice.

Chapman and Fontaine had assembled a contingency plan—"Plan B," they dubbed it—in a pair of unlabeled, black three-ring binders. Plan B sketched a thirty-day schedule in which Knight-Ridder would hire a newspaper broker to offer the *Free Press* for sale. If no buyer emerged, the paper would then be closed. Among the materials in Plan B were an appraisal of the *Free Press*'s valuable Detroit riverfront property and a draft press release announcing that the *Free Press* would halt publication. Chapman had not shown it to anyone in Detroit, but he kept it in sight on his desk in Miami as a constant reminder of the *Free Press*'s grave situation. "It kept me very, very humble," he recalled.

The meeting adjourned at 4:15. Chapman headed to the *Free Press* building to face the press. Reporters from *Time, Newsweek,* the *New York Times,* the *Washington Post,* the *Los Angeles Times,* the *Wall Street Journal,* the local television and radio stations, and, of course, the *Free Press* and the *News* packed room 100, a big, high-ceilinged chamber off the main lobby on Lafayette Boulevard. Sitting amid the working press were Clark Clifford, Bernie Ridder, and other Knight-Ridder directors. Anxious *Free Press* staffers lined the walls, which were wrapped in murals depicting loggers, fur traders, and Native Americans in early Michigan. A painting of Benjamin Franklin, *Printer,* smiled benignly on the throng, a feather pen in his right hand.

Chapman stood at a lectern on a slight podium in a corner of the room. He was not tall, but today he seemed to tower over the journalists who waited anxiously for a chance to cast doubt upon his resolve. The camera flashes captured the face of a man who had put everything but this moment behind him, whose flat blue eyes and grim, thin-lipped frown said that he had finally acknowledged the possibility of defeat, but now his indomitable will would take over and force the specter of failure to its knees.

"My optimism for approval of a successful JOA is much higher than it was on the thirtieth of December," Chapman declared. He held in his hand a single typewritten page he had carried from the Knight-Ridder board meeting—the resolution that the directors had unanimously voted to adopt. It read:

> RESOLVED, that after careful and deliberate review of all relevant consideration, the Board of Directors of Knight-Ridder, Inc., hereby reaches the following conclusions and takes the following action:
>
> 1. There is no feasible business strategy by which the *Detroit Free Press* can be operated profitably absent a joint operating arrangement with the *Detroit News*.
>
> 2. Approval of a joint operating arrangement with the *Detroit News* is in the best interests of (a) the readers, advertisers and employees of the *Detroit Free Press,* (b) the many constituencies in Detroit and the State of Michigan who depend on and benefit from the existence of two independent editorial voices, and (c) the shareholders of Knight-Ridder, Inc.
>
> 3. Approval of the application for a joint operating arrangement between the *Free Press* and the *Detroit News* must be pursued with full vigor.
>
> 4. If the application for a joint operating arrangement between the *Detroit Free Press* and the *Detroit News* is not approved, it would not be in the best interests of the shareholders of Knight-Ridder for the Company to continue to subsidize losses of the *Detroit Free Press* and, accordingly, in such event the Company will no longer support the operations of the *Free Press.*
>
> 5. In the unfortunate event that the Detroit joint operating arrangement is not approved, the relocation of the presses and other production equipment of the *Detroit Free Press* to the proposed new Philadelphia satellite plant would permit that plant to be equipped with modern presses at the least cost possible and would be in the interests of the shareholders of Knight-Ridder.
>
> 6. The appropriate officers of the Company are directed to take all necessary steps without delay, in the event the application for a joint operating arrangement is not approved, to shut down the operations of the *Free Press* and to relocate its assets to other operations of the Company and to sell or otherwise dispose of any assets not so relocated.

Closing the *Free Press,* the Knight-Ridder board said in a prepared statement, would be "the most anguishing event" in Knight-Ridder's history—but there would be no hesitation to carry it out. Chapman remarked that the *Free Press* printing presses "would fit very nicely" in the new Philadelphia plant. Wasn't that arm-twisting? a reporter asked. Chapman's eyes flashed with contempt. "The action taken by the board today is to help people *understand* the position," he retorted. "I don't consider it arm-twisting. Teachers don't teach school by arm-twisting. They do it by educating."

If the journalists thought Chapman might waffle, they were disappointed. Needelman's opinion, he said, was "legally flawed." The opponents of the JOA were "misguided." There was "no likelihood" that the *Free Press* could be sold if the JOA was not granted. "We don't see that there's a formula for anyone to successfully run the *Free Press,*" he said. A decision by Mayor Coleman Young and the unions to end their opposition to the JOA would be "a very positive development," which Chapman hoped to make happen soon. In fact, he said, the *Free Press* was "entitled" to the unions' support. Chapman wasn't worried that *Free Press* editors were journalistically constrained because the paper had sought favors of people who showed up daily in its news columns. "If there's a job to do," Chapman said, "they'll do it."

The questions came, one after another. Chapman never flinched. He gave his answers in the cool, clipped, supremely confident tones he must have used commanding his bomber squadron over war-torn Germany. He could have been in his leather bomber jacket again, eluding Nazi fighter planes with the ruse of the "falling leaf" maneuver. Except now the *Free Press* was the falling leaf, spinning toward seemingly inevitable doom. Alvah Chapman could only hope he would find a cloud bank of refuge before he crashed and burned.

Chapman, Batten, and Clifford returned to the Detroit Club, where a who's who of Detroit's business and social elite had assembled at the behest of Dave Lawrence and Ted Mecke. Among the nearly two hundred guests were General Motors chairman Roger Smith, state Supreme Court Justice Dennis Archer, Detroit Edison Company chairman Walter J. McCarthy, Jr., Lieutenant Governor Martha Griffiths, state Senate Majority Leader (and governor-to-be) John Engler, Wayne State University president David Adamany, National Bank of Detroit chairman Charles T. Fisher III, *Detroit News* publisher Chip Weil, and former *News* publisher Martin Hayden, an old friend of Clifford. Some already had written to Lawrence in support of the JOA, and Knight-Ridder's lawyers were preparing to include their letters in the upcoming submission to Attorney General Edwin Meese.

As he informed the group of Knight-Ridder's verdict, Chapman couldn't help but be encouraged by the solemn silence that enveloped the room. The message finally was sinking in: the choice was a JOA or no *Free Press*. Clark Clifford took over. His audience seemed in awe of the elder statesman, who had perched at the elbow of presidents and witnessed firsthand the unfolding of history. Clifford invoked Winston Churchill, whom he had gotten to know in 1946 on a train to Fulton, Missouri, where Churchill told the world that Eastern Europe was riven by an "iron curtain." Borrowing from Churchill's wartime exhortations of his countrymen, Clifford ended with the plea: "Never give up, never give up, never give up." The implication was inescapable: the fate of the *Free Press* was out of Knight-Ridder's hands; it was up to the people of Michigan.

Richard Kughn, a millionaire real estate developer, emerged from the reception to tell a *Free Press* reporter, "It must happen—period. We need two different points of view, and we aren't going to get it without the JOA." Of the attendees quoted in the next day's papers, only one admitted to being skeptical of Knight-Ridder's threat. The Reverend William Cunningham of Focus: HOPE, one of Detroit's most visible charitable organizations, told a *Free Press* reporter, "When a bum comes up to me and asks for a dollar or he'll commit suicide, I don't believe that. I may give him the dollar, but I don't believe he'll commit suicide."

Chapman's next appointment was with the heads of the newspaper unions. Elton Schade, Don Kummer, and the other labor leaders waited at the Hyatt Regency Hotel in neighboring Dearborn, within sight of the Ford Motor Company headquarters. With Bob Hall, Bill Keating, and *Free Press* vice-president for labor relations Timothy Kelleher at his side, Chapman asked the unions to negotiate an end to their opposition to the JOA. Slowly he read the grim resolution Knight-Ridder's board had adopted that afternoon. "If I worked for a company," he told them, "the last thing I'd want to do is work for a company that's losing money." But the union chiefs weren't the friendly audience Chapman had faced at the Detroit Club. Their opposition to the JOA was their bargaining leverage. What was in it for them to help Knight-Ridder? Why should they come to the aid of a company that had essentially ignored them for two years?

Chapman wasn't saying just yet. But he left them with a story he liked to tell about an African villager who had felled an elephant deep in the jungle. He returned to his village seeking help to lug the giant back to the town. As his neighbors helped haul the beast, the villager exulted over "my elephant." But, the hunter told his helpers, if they succeeded in getting the creature to the village, the beast would be "our elephant," and everyone would share in its meat, its hide, and its ivory. "This," Chapman said, referring to the *Free Press*, "is *our* elephant. Prior to the hearing, it was Knight-Ridder's elephant. You don't have the option now of opposing us philosophically." In other words, Chapman was saying, the unions had made their point. Now it was time to save the paper.

The next morning the unions agreed to negotiate.

Chapman's campaign was going beautifully. In the days to follow, the boards of Detroit Renaissance and the Greater Detroit Chamber of Commerce, comprising many of Detroit's wealthiest and most powerful citizens, listened to Chapman's personal plea and voted to back the JOA. Senators Donald Riegle and Carl Levin volunteered their help. Letters continued to pour in, only a handful of them critical of Knight-Ridder's campaign. The sixteen hundred letters the *Free Press* ultimately would receive represented but a tiny fraction of the paper's daily circulation, but it was an extraordinary volume for any single subject.

A special meeting of the Economic Club of Detroit was arranged by Ted Mecke, a past president of the club. On January 27—two years to the day after Al Neuharth misled the same group about discussions of a JOA—Alvah Chapman asked them to believe the *Free Press* would be gone without a JOA. He had the audience of 650 in the palm of his hand before he even spoke. The Reverend David Eberhard, a Detroit city councilman, opened the luncheon with the invocation: "Dear Lord, bless the *Detroit Free Press* and the *News*. Grant them jobs, opportunities, and approval." When Chapman recited the address of Attorney General Edwin Meese, his listeners chuckled and scribbled it on napkins and business cards.

The same day in Washington, D.C., Clark Clifford and Jim Batten took their case to Michigan's congressional delegation. A meeting had been arranged by Clifford, Governor Blanchard, and Congressman John Dingell, chairman of the powerful House Energy and Commerce Committee.

Dingell's role was a bit ironic; he had voted *against* the Newspaper Preservation Act in 1970, reflecting his belief that the antitrust laws should be weakened only under pressure of the direst need. Publicly, he had been neutral on the Detroit JOA until he was persuaded the *Free Press* would close without it. When Batten called the day of the Knight-Ridder board meeting, Dingell was glad to offer his help. The congressman angrily dismissed the suggestion that he was bowing to people who regularly covered Congress and periodically endorsed candidates for political office. Dingell hadn't been seriously challenged for reelection in years. He didn't need the blessings of the Detroit papers, and in fact was criticized by both as often as not. "I have regularly told the *News* and the *Free Press* to go to hell and so have many of my colleagues," Dingell told *News* Washington correspondent Michael Clements.

Sixteen of Michigan's eighteen congressmen gathered in room 2218 of the Rayburn House Office Building. Governor Blanchard, who just two weeks earlier had said the *Free Press* could survive without a JOA, introduced Clifford, Batten, and Neal Shine. Clifford made another stirring speech about the choice between a JOA and the demise of the *Free Press.* The politicians were as spellbound as Clifford's Detroit Club audience. Most of them knew almost nothing about the Newspaper Preservation Act. Most were Democrats like Clifford; given a choice, they might have preferred that the conservative *Detroit News* be under the gun.

Neal Shine listened uncomfortably. The *Free Press*'s senior managing editor didn't like going hat in hand to people his paper was supposed to cover without fear or favor. He had to make a short speech, but he wished he were somewhere else. Batten, who once had worked for Shine at the *Free Press,* had asked his old boss to attend. "I'd rather be covering night police," Shine grumbled to *News* reporter Clements.

Born and raised on Detroit's east side, Shine had joined the paper in 1950 as a part-time copyboy at $3.55 a day. He had held virtually every position in the newsroom, from beat reporter to managing editor. Along the way, the ruddy-faced Irishman had become the *Free Press*'s unofficial father confessor, who could buck up a struggling young reporter with a few words of good humor and encouragement, or take a wayward veteran to the woodshed and know that he or she would still be a friend when the unpleasantness passed. In and around Detroit, Shine was the *Free Press*'s best-known emissary, at least as familiar as Dave Lawrence. *Free Press* reporter Barbara Stanton once wrote of him: "He is widely revered for having a heart soft as an Irish rain, a ready wit, and an unflagging affection for his city, his newspaper, and his colleagues—not to mention numerous assorted waifs, wastrels, and worthy causes, uncovered and aided in his four decades as a newsman." Now Neal Shine was forced to think of the *Free Press* as a cause. It was torture.

After the meeting with the Michigan delegation, Shine spoke with *News* reporter Clements. Clements wanted to know how this quintessential journalist, the kind of newsman who didn't know the home-delivery price of his paper and didn't care, felt about asking favors of politicians. The brief interview was doubly painful because Shine had to do it with someone from the *News.* Shine hated the *News.* "There are some things I would not do to save the *Free Press,*" Shine told Clements. "We have not come close to any of those yet. I would not come before a member of the delegation or any other delegation and ask them for a favor, because I would not be interested in any sort of quid pro quo resulting from it."

No? Wasn't that what he had just done?

"They asked us to come and explain what was going on," Shine protested. "Knight-Ridder asked me if I would come along and I said sure. . . . When one of the congressmen said, 'What can we do?', Clark Clifford said, 'That's entirely up to you. Do whatever you feel you should do or can do or want to do.' "

But Clifford didn't have to ask, did he? Clements said.

"No," Shine admitted, "it's implied."

Shine obviously was wrestling with his conscience. "Clark Clifford doesn't work on the *Free Press* city desk, doesn't have any say in our endorsements or editorial policy," he argued. But then, as if to confess, he said, "I do. I was there and I loaned myself to that kind of a process." He could not help but feel he had crossed some invisible line, and it hurt. But it hurt more to imagine the end of the newspaper that had served his beloved city, given him voice, and fed his family for thirty-eight years.

Clifford's suggestion that the congressmen do "whatever you feel you should do" was hardly innocent. Several already had agreed to sign a letter to Attorney General Meese, who had been criticized as a charlatan by some of the very Democrats who now would beseech him to save the *Free Press* (indeed, Clifford himself once called Meese's close friend and boss, President Reagan, an "amiable dunce"). The letter had been drafted by Knight-Ridder's attorneys and circulated on Capitol Hill the day before the meeting with the delegation.

Some of the legislators did not appreciate it. "Frankly, it smacks of intimidation to have them come and, in essence, lean on us," complained Jeff Eller, a staffer for Democratic Representative Bob Carr. "I'm not so sure anybody will sign that letter." He was underestimating Carr's colleagues. Only Carr, Democrats John Conyers and Bill Ford, and Republican Paul Henry declined to sign. (Representative George Crockett initially signed but shortly after withdrew his endorsement.) Conyers accused Knight-Ridder and Gannett of being interested primarily in "megaprofits." "The only rationale that I can attach to this kind of a ploy is that their legal case is weak," Conyers told the *News*.

Knight-Ridder and Gannett filed a 129-page brief with the Justice Department on January 29. For the first time, the legal papers bore the imprimatur of Clark M. Clifford and Robert A. Altman of Clifford and Warnke.

Phil Lacovara and his colleagues at Hughes Hubbard and Reed had prepared the bulk of the legal argument. In a nutshell, they argued that Judge

Needelman himself had made the findings necessary to conclude that the *Free Press* was "failing"—chiefly, that it had lost enormous amounts of money and had no way to return to profitability—but he had misunderstood the Newspaper Preservation Act and mistakenly applied legal standards such as the supposed need to be in a "downward spiral." The brief closed by succinctly addressing the seven questions the attorney general had posed in ordering a hearing nearly a year before.

The argument was sandwiched between two sections that essentially were the province of the Clifford camp. Appended to the brief were thirty-seven letters signed by Michigan business and political luminaries, including President Gerald Ford, General Motors chairman Roger B. Smith, Ford chairman Donald E. Petersen, local retailers Stanley J. Winkelman and Joseph L. Hudson, Jr., Dow Chemical president Frank Popoff, Detroit Edison chairman Walter J. McCarthy, Jr., Stroh Brewery chairman Peter W. Stroh, president of the NAACP's Detroit branch Arthur L. Johnson, and Jewish Community Council executive director Alvin L. Kushner. The selection included none of the heartfelt missives sent by less well connected *Free Press* subscribers, who, presumably, carried little clout with Ed Meese.

Governor James Blanchard's letter was typical. In part, it said:

> The loss of the *Free Press* would be a tragedy for the paper's employees, suppliers, and carriers; a tragedy for the millions of Detroit and Michigan readers who rely on the *Free Press* each morning; and a tragedy for the marketplace of diverse ideas and free speech so vital to our nation.
>
> More than 2,200 *Free Press* jobs would be eliminated and additional supplier jobs put in jeopardy if the paper were forced to close it [*sic*] doors. The City of Detroit would lose a major taxpayer and a conscientious corporate citizen.

Clark Clifford himself had crafted the *pièce de résistance*: a six-page preamble that placed responsibility for the future of the *Free Press* squarely in the lap of Meese. In it, Clifford informed Meese of the Knight-Ridder board resolution, which was appended. "The Board acted with deepest regret, without rancor, and not with the purpose of threatening the community or anyone else," Clifford assured Meese. "The Board merely concluded that the time had come to face the stark reality of a hopeless situation." Clifford found eight occasions within the twenty-three spare paragraphs to mention the possibility of the *Free Press* shutting down or Detroit becoming a "one-newspaper city" (never mind the *Oakland Press, Macomb Daily,* or dozens of other community papers scattered throughout the metropolitan area).

The preamble concluded:

> We have attempted to clarify this basic issue as well as we can for the Attorney General.
>
> The issue becomes very clear under the changed circumstances that have taken place. Approval of the JOA ensures two newspapers for the Detroit area. Denial of the JOA means that the *Detroit News* will be the only remaining paper.
>
> Applicants are confident that the Attorney General will recognize that the denial of the JOA would lead to the unfortunate paradox that the Government had the opportunity under the law to continue Detroit as a two-newspaper city—but chose not to do so.

So it was Ed Meese, a career politician whose scant business experience was running part of an aerospace company for a year, who would shut down the *Detroit Free Press.* With Clark Clifford's insidiously brilliant preamble, Knight-Ridder washed its hands of the newspaper's fate.

Time magazine called it "a risky game of chicken." The *Quill,* a magazine published by the Society of Professional Journalists, printed an essay by Ron Dorfman accusing Knight-Ridder of waging terrorism and blackmail. A cartoon in *Crain's Detroit Business* portrayed Chapman as a gangster with his gun to Lawrence's head, saying, "Give me half of da JOA profits, or da kid is dead!" Andrew Zack, the young lawyer who had helped Gene Driker dismantle the case for the JOA, watched in astonishment as the campaign unfolded on the front pages of the *Free Press* and the *News.* "It's impressive what the media can do," he commented sarcastically to a *News* reporter. "If we ever needed a demonstration of the power of the media in America, boy, we got it."

The publishers truly were flexing their muscles. Knight-Ridder led the charge, courting an attorney general, bending its own journalistic rules, trampling on Jack Knight's grave. Gannett, though conveniently silent, was a partner nonetheless, having agreed to share costs of the campaign. It wasn't as obviously cynical and unseemly as the industry's crusade for the Newspaper Preservation Act in the late 1960s, but it carried, at the very least, the appearance of impropriety, the scent of political manipulation, the taint of greed.

Though not by the reckoning of Alvah Chapman and Dave Lawrence. They would tell anyone who asked that they were simply trying to save the *Free*

Press. All that mattered was whether their campaign worked—and it was working well. Their snowball had swallowed up citizens and corporate heads, politicians and pillars of the community. Next were the unions. They had their price. For one, though, the price would be greater than for the rest.

15

Divided They Fall

David Everett had an errand to run for a few of his fellow members of Newspaper Guild Local 22. The *Free Press* reporter was supposed to submit a resolution to be voted on at the local's annual membership meeting scheduled for February 11, 1988. Everett knew there was a deadline for submitting such things, but he had forgotten what it was. Anyway, he didn't think Don Kummer, the local's administrative officer, would let a technicality scuttle a vote on a matter of such grave importance: a resolution to renounce Local 22's opposition to the JOA.

Everett had prepared the resolution at the request of *Free Press* reporters Jane Daugherty and Patricia Chargot. Daugherty, an accomplished feature writer who had come from the *Miami Herald* in 1985, and Chargot, a reporter who had joined the *Free Press* during Kurt Luedtke's reign, believed the Guild's opposition to the JOA had gone far enough. Both deplored the thought of the *Free Press* and the *News* being joined at the pocketbook, but they were convinced that Alvah Chapman and the Knight-Ridder directors weren't bluffing. They refused to stand idle while their beloved paper perished and hundreds of fellow employees—not to mention Daugherty and Chargot—lost their livelihoods. If the Guild could help avert the tragedy, they believed, at the very least the union could and should discuss the matter with its members.

Don Kummer was well aware of their thinking, and he resented it. For one thing, the Guild's bargaining position would be severely undercut if its membership unilaterally voted to support the JOA. Opposition was the sole trump card Local 22 could play to get the publishers to protect members whose jobs would be imperiled if and when the *Free Press* and the *News* merged their business operations. Because the newsrooms would remain separate, the JOA posed no threat to the jobs of journalists, such as Daugherty and Chargot. Which was why, Kummer assumed, most journalists had been indifferent about the Guild's militant stance. After all, fewer than 50 of Local 22's 950 members had found time for the September 1986 meeting at which the union voted to oppose the merger. Kummer saw Daugherty, Chargot, and Everett as Johnny-come-latelies who were out to save their necks now that Chapman had put them on a chopping block with his vow to close the *Free Press*. Kummer didn't believe Chapman, at least not yet. And he suspected that Dave Lawrence was behind this eleventh-hour bid to split the Guild, though he had little but rumor to support his belief.

Still, Kummer had a duty to consider the members' resolution—*if* it was presented in accordance with Local 22's bylaws. When Everett walked into Kummer's thirty-third-floor office in the Book Building on Friday, February 5, he was a day or so late. The agenda for the meeting had been printed and part of it had been mailed. When the reporter handed over the typewritten resolution, Kummer promptly told him it could not be added to the February 11 meeting agenda. Everett asked Kummer to think about it.

The last thing Don Kummer needed was an insurrection in his own union. Even as Jane Daugherty and friends were fomenting discord in Local 22, the fragile six-union coalition that had battled the JOA for two years was beginning to crumble. On February 1, *Free Press* negotiators had offered a severance package that would take effect if the JOA was turned down and the newspaper closed. The $12 million program was to give employees as much as a year's pay, two months of health benefits, and help finding new jobs. Separately, the publishers had improved a previously crafted plan under which employees would be paid to leave voluntarily if a JOA was achieved. The unions considered the offers modest, but the publishers, for the moment at least, were standing firm.

The day after the offers were made, Kummer and other local union chiefs—Elton Schade of the Teamsters, Joel Wilson of the Mailers, Tom Brennan of the Pressmen, Dave Gray of the Typographers, and Jerry Deneau of the Photoengravers—had met in Washington with international officials of their respective unions. After huddling for two and a half hours at the K Street headquarters of the Communications Workers of America, the labor bosses released a stinging joint statement calling Knight-Ridder's public relations campaign "an act of bad faith." Kummer, emerging from the meeting, told reporters, "At least we've agreed to stay together."

Joel Wilson didn't see it that way. In 1986 the stout union boss had been a strong advocate of the decision by mailers across the country to defect from the International Typographers Union and affiliate with the Teamsters—a move that had endeared Wilson to Teamsters Local 372 chief Elton Schade. Wilson was one of Schade's few confidants; rarely did Wilson make a significant decision regarding Mailers Local 2040 without consulting Schade.

Wilson's 340 members stuffed papers with preprinted ad inserts and did other menial tasks. Increasingly, automation threatened their jobs. There had been a day when mailers stacked, bundled, tied, and even mailed the papers. As fast as they worked—"You could barely see their hands moving," Neal Shine once told a researcher—machines were faster. Local 2040's immediate future wasn't so dire, though. Bill Keating, chief executive of the Detroit Newspaper Agency, had told Wilson his union wasn't likely to lose full-time jobs under a JOA, partly because it had a lot of part-timers, partly because the weekend insert load was likely to be heavy. As well, both newspapers' mail rooms were antiquated, and it would be a while before the DNA could afford to upgrade.

Wilson's primary concern, then, was with the fate of his members should the JOA be denied. He harbored no doubt that Knight-Ridder would close the *Free Press.* The local's Detroit attorney, Sam McKnight, believed Meese would view his decision as largely political and, therefore, almost certainly would grant the JOA. So, aside from showing loyalty to the other unions, Wilson had little incentive to hold out for a better deal he didn't know he would get. He certainly wasn't about to tarry for the sake of Don Kummer, whom he didn't like much anyway. When Wilson left the meeting in Washington, he went his own way. Although several attendees said the international chiefs had made it plain that the unions should stay united, Wilson insisted he had heard instructions to try to settle. Back in Detroit, that's what he set out to do.

On February 7, Mailers Local 2040 voted to support the JOA. Wilson, grinning broadly beneath tinted glasses, told reporters he had never been prouder of his members. The publishers had guaranteed their jobs while offering a buyout of eight weeks to one year of pay in return for voluntary departures. First rights to the slots vacated would go to any members of Schade's local who lost jobs because of the JOA. Naturally, Schade had given his blessing before the agreement went to a vote.

Keating was glad to get the Mailers out of the way, but he and his negotiators—Bob Hall and Tim Kelleher for the *Free Press*, John Jaske for Gannett and the *News*—had a lot of work to do. They wanted to get all six unions and Mayor Young to renounce their opposition to the JOA by February 16, the deadline for opponents to submit final arguments.

Strictly as a legal proposition, the strategy was of dubious value. The same arguments that had persuaded Judge Needelman to reach his conclusion would survive whether the opponents continued their challenge or not. As a practical matter, though, the publishers hoped the withdrawals would send a strong signal to Ed Meese that the nature of the case had changed. Meese also wouldn't have to worry that his decision would be appealed in federal court, since all the potential challengers would have been swept away (the Antitrust Division was barred from appealing the attorney general's decision). Which was why it was crucial to get rid of at least one of the two unions with the will and wherewithal to pursue the case further—the Guild and the Teamsters.

The publishers would have loved both out of the way, but that appeared an unlikely prospect. Kummer and Schade were still fighting over whose union would represent office and circulation workers under the JOA. Each constantly bothered Keating with accusatory questions about what the other was secretly extracting from the publishers. Keating kept telling them—and any reporter who asked—that the Detroit Newspaper Agency would not interfere in the unions' dispute. "We do have to run a shop, we do have to make a profit, we do have to get a return on our investment," Keating told a *News* reporter. "Short of that, there won't be any deal." Sometimes, Keating thought, it seemed Kummer was more concerned about the Teamsters and Schade more worried about the Guild than they were about their own unions.

Whether he knew it or not, Kummer had good reason to worry. Of the two unions, the publishers preferred to accommodate the Teamsters. Local 372 had the most members. Schade, the publishers thought, was easier to deal with than Kummer. They also believed the Teamsters had the better attorney in Gene Driker. And Schade was not facing the nasty internal rift festering around Kummer. The publishers were well aware that the Guild faced the prospect of being done in by its own members.

The Guild's membership meeting was set for Thursday, February 11. On Tuesday, Schade and officials of the Typographers, Pressmen, and Photoengravers reported progress at the bargaining table. Not so Kummer. On Wednesday, a Guild negotiating session with the publishers lasted just seven minutes. A fuming Kummer told reporters, "They either don't give a damn whether the union drops their opposition, or they're waiting for the palace coup."

Jane Daugherty's quest for a vote on the Guild's JOA opposition was attracting more sympathizers, primarily from within the *Free Press.* She held her ground despite personal attacks from fellow journalists at the *Free Press* and the *News,* some she had considered friends, who accused her of cozying up to management. Coincidentally or not, Dave Lawrence was meeting regularly with small groups of *Free Press* staffers to answer questions and reinforce Knight-Ridder's commitment to closing the paper. While Kummer publicly accused the publisher of meddling in union matters—"He's the most active unpaid member we have"—Lawrence denied having urged anyone to join Daugherty's movement. (Daugherty denies ever speaking with Lawrence about her effort.)

As the Guild meeting neared, the "contras," as Daugherty's band of dissidents had come to be known, vowed to press for a vote, Local 22's bylaws be damned. "Thursday night," Kummer told Local 22 president Lou Mleczko, "is going to decide the future of this local."

But first, Mayor Coleman Young had something to say.

To say Coleman Young didn't like the *Free Press* or the *News* would be a gross understatement. The mayor loathed the papers, which had caused him more grief than he cared to remember. They criticized his policies. They made fun of his projects. They investigated his friends and allies. They badgered his lieutenants with requests for information. They portrayed him in editorial cartoons as a grinning, arrogant buffoon. Their politics didn't seem to matter; the liberal *Free Press* was as likely to skewer Democrat Young as was the conservative *News.* But what undoubtedly rankled the mayor most about Detroit's powerful dailies was that they represented the Establishment. Coleman Young had been fighting the Establishment for most of his sixty-nine years.

In the late 1930s and 1940s, Young was a zealous labor activist who once swung a lead pipe to defend himself against one of Ford Motor Company's antiunion thugs. He organized Detroit garbage haulers and hospital workers, and became the first black named to a powerful Detroit council that organized union chapters across the country. Young's radicalism came under harsh scrutiny in the anti-Communist fervor of the 1950s. He was questioned by the House Un-American Activities Committee and hounded by the FBI. Broke, jobless, forsaken even by some of his union allies, Young dropped out of political life, a victim of the Establishment.

He reappeared in the late 1950s with the passing of the McCarthy era. By 1973 he was a Michigan state senator eyeing a run for mayor of Detroit. He rode to victory on a campaign that focused on a controversial police program viewed by blacks as a racist vehicle of police brutality. In place of white Establishment oppression, Coleman Young, Detroit's first black mayor, offered hope and optimism for a shattered city that would include all of its people in a brilliant rebirth.

The renaissance never truly took hold. For every ray of hope that gleamed off a new riverfront skyscraper, there were darkening clouds of crime, unemployment, and poverty in the city's decaying neighborhoods. Yet somehow the popularity of Coleman Young—fiery orator, infectious charmer, crusader for his people—grew unabated. Pundits anointed him "mayor for life."

Like many an entrenched ruler, Young grew distant and isolated from his subjects. He had long been a solitary man; stung by the disappointments of his youth, he trusted almost no one. He certainly did not trust Detroit's media, which to him were part of the Establishment that had tormented him and his fellow blacks all his life. Though they were his primary conduits to the people of Detroit, he choked off the flow of information from city hall, forcing reporters to seek him out as the last and sometimes only authority on what was happening behind the castle walls.

City officials regularly stonewalled the simplest requests for information. One *News* reporter seeking to buy a city map was told he would have to file a written request under the Freedom of Information Act. Interviews with Young and other mayoral aides took weeks and months to schedule. City officials avoided speaking to the press without Young's permission. On at least two occasions, Young loyalists went to jail rather than honor court orders to release information on city business. When bad news about Detroit proliferated, the mayor called a news conference and blamed it on the media. He frustrated TV and radio reporters with his unfailingly profane language. At press conferences he occasionally called on *Detroit News* city hall reporter Bruce Alpert as "the motherfucker from the *News.*"

It was no surprise when Young came out against the JOA shortly after it was announced in April of 1986. His rationale seemed immaterial; no one expected Coleman Young to grant any request by the newspapers without some resistance. But Young had his reasons. He figured the JOA would give the papers even more power than they already had. And, in Young's view, the power would be concentrated in the hands of Gannett, which dominated the JOA's ruling board. That was not good because, of the two dailies, Gannett's *News* was the more hostile to Young's administration. At a dinner he hosted in May of 1986, Young told some seventy Michigan journalists the JOA would make Detroit effectively a "one-newspaper town." "I appreciate the honest intentions of the editorial staffs of the *News* and *Free Press* to continue to exert their independence," he said. "But I do not believe you can have honest competition when you're controlled by one party."

Young's bark was sharper than his bite, though. The attorney he assigned to the JOA, Edward Bell, was dying of cancer. Bell let Gene Driker and Duane Ice do most of the work on the JOA hearing, while the city declined to share in paying Driker's and Ice's fees. "The mayor was only in it for publicity reasons," the Guild's Don Kummer recalled.

Dave Lawrence sensed all along that the mayor's challenge was more symbolic than substantive. The *Free Press* publisher also felt Young misperceived the JOA; Lawrence certainly didn't intend to cede control of the *Free Press* to Gannett. He met with Young on a few occasions to make his case, but the mayor would not be swayed—at least until February of 1988.

Lawrence had had a brief exchange with Young about the JOA at a community dinner in November. Seeing the publisher strolling past his table, the mayor had joked, "I'm against the JOA because I want Dave Lawrence to stay in town." Lawrence had recently been of help to Young, raising more than $6 million for a new chimpanzee exhibit at the Detroit Zoo. He saw the mayor's gibe as a chance to reopen their JOA discussions. "You need to know," he confided to Young, "this is real serious and it's no game." On December 8 the two talked for more than two hours over lunch at the London Chop House. Lawrence raised the possibility of the mayor changing his position, but Young, Lawrence recalled, said, "I can't tell you how difficult it would be for me to do that. You'd be lucky if you got me neutral."

Publicly, Young did not alter his stance. Two days after Lawrence's controversial front-page column on the JOA appeared, the mayor told a press conference the JOA "would be the end of the free press, the freedom of the press that we talk about so loudly." Later that day Young met with Lawrence and promised to keep quiet. That wasn't enough for Lawrence. "Mr. Mayor," he pleaded, "this is such a serious situation that standing mute won't help us at all." Young *had* to publicly withdraw as a JOA opponent.

On January 18 Lawrence took Alvah Chapman to Manoogian Mansion, the mayor's stately riverfront residence. Chapman had met Young at the 1979 and 1985 groundbreakings for the *Free Press* riverfront plant. Today's gathering wasn't so festive. Chapman and Lawrence were ushered to a second-story office, where the mayor received them in a robe and slippers. He had obviously slept late, as was his custom. They talked for about an hour. Again Young said he would have trouble changing his position.

"But I'll think about it," he said.

Young gradually was coming to believe that Chapman wasn't bluffing.

Months before, when there was no gun to the head of the *Free Press,* it was easier to hold out against the JOA as a matter of principle. But when Chapman told him the Knight-Ridder board would vote to shutter the paper, practical matters such as jobs and tax revenues suddenly loomed larger. Whether Knight-Ridder's position was blackmail—and Young thought it was—was immaterial. It was a hardball ploy that a hardball politician could appreciate.

Three days later, as the Knight-Ridder board met in Detroit, Young gave the first signal he might back off. At a U.S. Conference of Mayors meeting in Washington, he told reporters he was giving "serious consideration" to withdrawing. When the Detroit Renaissance board voted to support the JOA on January 27, Young didn't quibble. But he also vowed not to break with the newspaper unions until they had extracted "maximum concessions" from the publishers. "You shouldn't walk out on the one who came with you to the dance," he told reporters. But six days later he tempered his stance, saying he would withdraw when convinced the publishers were being "reasonable" in bargaining.

By now it was clear that Young was prepared to withdraw. The question was when. The publishers felt he had to pull out before February 16, when the last briefs were due to Attorney General Meese. But they also thought an earlier withdrawal by labor's longtime ally could put subtle pressure on the newspaper unions to settle. It certainly wouldn't hurt if Young pulled out before the crucial February 11 Guild meeting.

On February 5 Young told a group of two hundred Baptist ministers that he intended to seek a fifth term. His plans surprised no one, though the election was more than a year away. On February 9 the *Free Press* responded with an editorial that essentially endorsed Young months before the campaign would begin. The headline read, TOP JOB: SO FAR, THE BEST CANDIDATE TO SUCCEED MAYOR YOUNG IS MAYOR YOUNG. "Mayor Young's unofficial decision to seek a fifth term next year—if he doesn't change his mind—is both good and troubling news," the editorial read. "It's good news because it suggests his continued concern for his city, and because there simply is no one else on the political horizon who could be expected to do a better job than, or as good a job as, the incumbent." The "troubling" part concerned the "paucity" of potential replacements for Young. The editorial ended with a cheerful toast: "[H]ere's to the longest-serving mayor in Detroit history—and to his continued vigor and good health."

The next day, a Wednesday, Lawrence was on the phone to Young, pleading for the mayor's JOA support. The Teamsters and other unions were reporting progress in bargaining. Only the Guild was at an impasse, with the pivotal Thursday meeting looming. On Wednesday evening, Lawrence phoned Young three times. Finally the mayor told him, "I think things are at a stage that I can come out of the rain now."

Young announced his intention to withdraw at a news conference Thursday. "I took a position in opposition to the JOA based on my assumption that we could have a choice between two independent newspapers and a JOA," he said. "I've been convinced that the *Free Press* will close, and that eventuality reduces the choices to JOA or one newspaper." He said he was concerned about the potential loss of jobs and tax revenues, which would be greater if the *Free Press* closed than under a JOA. As for the unions, "I was happy to note that the Mailers settled just the other day," he said, "and I know that both the Guild and the Teamsters are in stepped-up sessions with the *Free Press.*" Young had to have been lying or misinformed, for it was no secret that the Guild was getting nowhere at the bargaining table.

Young insisted his decision had nothing to do with the kind *Free Press* editorial published two days before. Lawrence grew indignant when a *News* reporter suggested a connection. "The most precious asset this newspaper has is its integrity," he snapped. "We've been in business a hundred and fifty-six years being honest every day, not being honest when it suits some particular interest." Young and Lawrence also denied that the announcement of the mayor's withdrawal was timed to pressure Guild members scheduled to meet Thursday night. The issue became moot when a swirling blizzard forced a last-minute postponement of the meeting.

"The paper's got the mayor," Kummer cracked to a *News* reporter, "but we've got God."

The next day, Jane Daugherty's dissidents filed a lawsuit seeking to force a membership vote on the Guild's opposition to the JOA.

The union was coming apart.

Daugherty's forces, a loose-knit collection of mostly *Free Press* journalists, were lined up against the Guild leadership, many fellow *Free Press* staffers, and virtually all the three hundred Guild members at the *News*. Daugherty and her cohorts, reporters David Everett, Patricia Chargot, Rob Musial, Patricia Montemurri, and others, tried to work something out with Don Kummer and Lou Mleczko, but the Guild leaders would not budge. Daugherty was astonished that the Guild would block a vote on such a crucial issue. "Unions are nothing if not democratic, or so we thought," she recalled. "I don't think it occurred to anybody that Guild members would be disenfranchised. It's not reasonable for people who see their careers as advancing democracy to say you can't vote in your union." Look, she told Kummer, you don't want to have this fight in public. The dissidents didn't have the votes to win. Just let us walk in and lose, Daugherty pleaded.

For their part, Kummer and Mleczko were appalled that Daugherty and her colleagues would try to strip the union of its leverage at so delicate a point in negotiations. Their last-minute bid was nothing short of mutiny. Didn't they understand the jobs of some 450 Guild members—400 of them at the *Free Press*—were at risk in a JOA? Why had they remained quiet for more than a year while the Guild squared off against Knight-Ridder and Gannett? "This was a nightmare," Kummer recalled.

To a point, the union leadership sympathized with the dissidents. "I didn't blame them for their fear, I blamed Lawrence," recalled Kate DeSmet, secretary of Local 22 and the *News*'s religion writer. "The problem was, Daugherty and her group focused the fear on the Guild instead of focusing on their owners and editors, who were fanning the flames of hysteria. It's like your boss denies you a raise and you go home and beat up your wife."

In fact, the dissidents were torn about their last-ditch maneuvers. They abhorred the thought of a discredited politician such as Meese deciding their future. Some resented Knight-Ridder for having put the *Free Press* in such an untenable position. And more than a few had to admit they hadn't been attentive to the issue early on. "I participated in the Guild like most journalists around the country, in a half-assed way," Daugherty recalled. Still, the thought of the *Free Press* publishing a final edition headlined, GOODBYE, DETROIT! was too much to bear.

Whether you stood with or against the Guild depended almost entirely on whether you believed Knight-Ridder. Daugherty and her allies obviously did. Mleczko, Kummer, and other Guild leaders were either unable or unwilling to see why. It was a curious position for those people, many of whom were journalists trained to consider all sides of an issue. They felt the dissidents were naive to accept Knight-Ridder's word in the wake of Judge Needelman's assault on the JOA. Yet the dissidents thought the Guild leaders equally naive to expect professional journalists not to challenge them. To some it seemed Kummer and Mleczko were demanding blind allegiance. "That was too much to ask," Everett recalled.

The mood was ugly when more than four hundred members of Guild Local 22 filed into Detroit's Cobo Hall for their annual membership meeting on Monday, February 15—one day before final submissions were due to Attorney General Edwin Meese. Earlier that day, Wayne County Circuit Judge John R.

Kirwan had declined to order the Guild to allow a vote on its JOA stance. Nevertheless, Daugherty's dissidents intended to make themselves heard. Kummer opened the meeting by outlining the Guild's final proposal to the publishers: job reductions through attrition, improved severance and retirement plans, and provisions that would give the Guild a fair shot at representing merged departments that would include employees represented by competing unions, such as the Teamsters. The publishers had rejected the proposals and given the Guild until 1:00 P.M. Tuesday to accept their final offer. Kummer asked the members to vote on a resolution supporting the local's bargaining committee—in effect, a vote to continue opposing the JOA.

The members debated for nearly two hours, cursing, shouting, and calling each other names. The contras chanted, "Keep the *Freep,* keep the *Freep,*" while Mleczko frantically pleaded for order. Dissidents who tried to address the meeting were greeted with hoots and groans. "Thanks for fucking us over," one told DeSmet after the meeting ended. At one point, *News* reporter Chris Singer asked if the Guild would survive the JOA. Mleczko made a little speech, telling of Guild attorney Bruce Miller's tense meeting with Bill Keating shortly after the JOA was announced.

"We were not opposed to the JOA on philosophical grounds, but we wanted job protection," Mleczko said. "Miller gave me permission to give you Keating's answer: he said, 'Nothing the Guild can do to the agreement can hurt us and it is inconsequential to this agency.' With that he showed Miller to the door. From that time to the present, they've refused to bargain in good faith and have held this union in contempt.

"They terribly underestimated our resolve."

The vote was anticlimactic. By a show of hands, Local 22's members polled 349–84 to support their bargaining committee—and continue fighting the JOA.

By 5:00 P.M. Tuesday, February 16, all of the unions had renounced their opposition to the JOA and urged Attorney General Edwin Meese, in writing, to approve the merger.

Except, of course, Guild Local 22.

After the Mailers succumbed February 7, the Pressmen, Photoengravers, Typographers, and Teamsters bargained until the last possible moments. None of the agreements reached by the unions and the Detroit Newspaper Agency involved wages and work rules; those negotiations would come later. Instead, the five unions accepted severance and early retirement packages along with a smattering of deals tailored to each local.

While Guild members quarreled at Cobo Hall, Pressmen's Local 13N of the Graphic Communications International Union had its own heated debate. The Pressmen eventually voted 115–86 to accept severance benefits and a promise that they would not lose jobs at the outset of the JOA. President Tom Brennan reluctantly endorsed the settlement. "The bad thing about it," he complained to reporters, "is that the whole union movement is going to hell in this country when we're faced with situations like this one, where it's really a no-win situation."

The Typographers and the Photoengravers fell next. Members of Typographers Local 18 were assured lifetime job guarantees they had negotiated in 1975. Photoengravers Local 289 had some job overlaps with the Pressmen and the Typographers. Despite what the publishers repeatedly said about the Detroit Newspaper Agency staying out of jurisdictional disputes, the DNA helped work out a three-way deal that assured the Photoengravers of survival under the JOA.

The DNA cut a sweet deal for Elton Schade and Teamsters Local 372. It was just what the Guild's Kummer had feared. The publishers agreed to count one hundred circulation office workers at the *News* as part of a single bargaining unit with the field circulation crew. Because the field workers already were Teamsters, the office workers were all but certain to vote to become Teamsters too. It meant Guild circulation office workers at the *Free Press* were likely to lose their jobs—even though Bill Keating felt they were better qualified than their counterparts at the *News*. When it came to buying off the unions, the publishers' oft-stated policy of hiring the best people apparently did not apply.

The DNA also enhanced the union's pension plan and agreed to extend to 1993 the expiration deadline on the Teamsters' "unit clarification letter." The letter, negotiated by Schade years before, promised that the publishers would not ask the National Labor Relations Board to remove circulation district managers from the union as managerial employees. It effectively kept more than four hundred Teamsters in the union who otherwise would have been ousted. The letter was set to expire in 1992; Schade wanted it extended for the rest of his life. He got one year.

No such deals were available to Guild Local 22. The DNA refused to assure the union that even one of its 450 office and maintenance workers would have a job, let alone be a member of the Guild. The publishers clearly did not want to include the Guild in their new business operation. "We knew the Guild would be angry," one of the newspapers' top executives recalled. "It struck me that their size within the business unit was small enough not to be significant." In fact, the Guild had more members in the newspapers' business operations than the Typographers, the Photoengravers, or the Pressmen. But the publishers apparently saw an opportunity to place at risk half the membership of their second-biggest union—and they took it. "I really felt sorry for Donny (Kummer)," Mailer president Joel Wilson recalled. "They were out to kill him."

In his Book Building office, Kummer fumed. Just a few days before, Bill Keating had told Kummer that, while he did not concur with the Guild's determined stand, he admired it. Then he'd turned around and cut a deal with Schade. Kummer felt betrayed—by the publishers and, once again, by the wily Elton Schade.

In Washington late Tuesday afternoon, Guild attorney Hanan Kolko waited for orders to file the unions' final JOA briefs. Around 4:00 P.M., Duane Ice called to tell him Teamsters Local 372 would not take part, even though Teamsters attorneys Andrew Zack and Morley Witus had spent much of the weekend helping Kolko and Ice finish the briefs. Guild Local 22 was on its own.

It was a bittersweet day for Gene Driker, who had led the Teamsters' legal assault on the JOA. The feisty attorney could tell himself he had done his job well; his advocacy had provided his client with leverage that helped it negotiate an agreement. But part of him, a part close to his heart, yearned to try this case to the end. Driker wanted to test in the courtroom Knight-Ridder's public relations campaign, which struck him as the height of arrogance and cynicism, a deplorable attempt to subvert the legal process. When the publishers had filed the Knight-Ridder board resolution and their letters of support on January 29, Driker had angrily suggested that the JOA hearing be reopened so that he could cross-examine Knight-Ridder directors. That, too, was a rough day for Driker; he had just put his father in a nursing home and, in a few days, he would die. When the Teamsters withdrew, Driker could not resist a parting shot. "The newspapers," he told a *News* reporter, "are daydreaming if they think that just because the unions have gotten out of this thing it is a free ride home." He dashed off a letter to Seymour Dussman at the Justice Department's Antitrust Division: "You . . . are to be greatly congratulated for pursuing a course that I certainly believe is the right one in this case, and for sticking with it."

For Guild Local 22, things just got uglier.

On February 19 Jim Fitzgerald, the *Free Press*'s grandfatherly presence on the back page, attacked Guild president Lou Mleczko in a column headlined, I DON'T LIKE TO BE TOLD THAT I'M BEING TERRORIZED. Fitzgerald was one of six *Free Press* columnists who recently had received bonuses for staying at the paper while the JOA was pending. Bob Talbert, Hugh McDiarmid, Nickie McWhirter, Susan Watson, Mike Duffy, and Fitzgerald received immediate lump-sum payments of 25 percent of their salary and the promise of a like amount to be paid at the time of the JOA decision. (Star sports columnist Mitch Albom declined the bonus.) A select group of *Free Press* executives and editors also got bonuses, including editor Joe Stroud, whose first draw was in the neighborhood of thirty-five thousand dollars. The bonuses rankled some Guild members who thought the columnists were being induced to shill for the JOA. Dave Lawrence and executive editor Heath Meriwether defended them as necessary to keep key employees from leaving.

Fitzgerald had bemoaned the prospect of the *Free Press* closing long before he got any bonus. Even before the JOA hearing, he had complained that his Guild union dues were being spent on an effort he did not support. His February 19 column castigated Mleczko for remarks the Guild leader had made to *Metro Times,* a local weekly. Mleczko had accused Knight-Ridder of committing a "terroristic" act and said he had "never seen . . . a company beat up on its employees as badly as the *Free Press* has."

Mleczko was "full of crap," Fitzgerald wrote. Further:

> I think it's past time for Guild leaders to wake up and smell the stench of their stubbornness. They are now the only official Detroit opposition to the JOA. I'm far from persuaded that Edwin Meese will pay any attention to whatever the Guild or other unions tell him. But the life of this newspaper is on the line; time has run out, and to me the Guild's position is outrageous.

Fitzgerald did not mention his bonus.

The column infuriated Kate DeSmet, the *News*'s religion writer and Guild Local 22 secretary. She mailed a reply to Fitzgerald that said, in part:

> . . . you use newspaper space to campaign again for the company. You take cheap shots at one of the finest reporters and union presidents this town has ever seen. As for Lou Mleczko's union leadership, how the hell would you know a thing about him or what union leadership should do? In eight years of attending monthly Representative Assembly meetings and general membership meetings, I've seen you at how many? One? Last Monday?
>
> . . . William Sloane Coffin Jr. put it brilliantly—there is no smaller package in the world than a person wrapped up in themselves. And that is how you and the most strident of the JOA

> supporters appear—spoiled bratty yuppie-types who care for nothing but yourselves, your bonuses, and your rear ends.

Fitzgerald showed DeSmet's letter to Daugherty, who wrote to DeSmet. Her slightly more civil missive assailed DeSmet for unfairly labeling dissident Guild members, some of whose personal activities—buying food for the homeless, caring for elderly parents—disqualified them for "yuppie-dom." "Let me also suggest," Daugherty wrote, "that you read a little more William Sloane Coffin Jr., maybe dip into Eugene Debs and Heywood Broun a bit more before you decide to stick labels on people who simply believe that their union dues are as good as yours and should entitle them to a right to a vote that may decide the fate of their newspaper and their jobs."

The contras got their vote at a Guild meeting February 29 at the Fort Street Presbyterian Church. Again they were defeated, this time 303–111. Again the debate degenerated into a shouting match. At one point, contra Rob Musial yelled to be recognized while Mleczko refused to yield, declaring, "The chair will control the microphone." It was a painful moment for Musial, who had helped organize the Guild's *News* unit in 1974. "We were looked at as traitors," he recalled. "It was very weird times."

The publishers invited the Guild back to the bargaining table. "We'll give you back your union," one executive chided Kummer. But the talks stalled again as the Guild demanded to represent all advertising sales staff under the JOA, as it did at the *Free Press.* Knight-Ridder, which hoped to erase any chance of a court appeal of a favorable JOA ruling, was willing to negotiate the issue, but Gannett was not. In a fit of pique, *Free Press* general manager Bob Hall told *News* reporter David Sedgwick, "This is an issue that could kill the *Free Press,* and Gannett is saying no."

On March 10 Assistant Attorney General Harry H. Flickinger had a dozen cartons of JOA materials delivered to the office of Attorney General Edwin Meese. The boxes contained seventeen volumes of transcript, twenty-nine binders and eleven accordion folders of exhibits, Judge Morton Needelman's opinion, and the last round of briefs filed by Knight-Ridder and Gannett, the Antitrust Division, and Guild Local 22. In an accompanying memo to Meese adviser Brad Reynolds, Flickinger noted, "Neither the Newspaper Preservation Act nor Department regulations set an outer time limit in which the Attorney General must render his decision."

Nearly two years had passed since Alvah Chapman and Al Neuharth had had their fateful chat in Chapman's den. Now the deal they'd cut on that balmy Sunday was finally in the hands of the man who would decide whether they could consummate it.

16

Pulling Punches

Ed Meese wore a wide grin. All around him were scores of Detroiters sporting bright yellow buttons bearing the slogan KEEP THE FREEP. It was April 25, 1988, and the attorney general had come to tell the Economic Club of Detroit about the Reagan administration's war on drugs. Before the lunch, *Free Press* staffers Jane Daugherty and Patricia Chargot had scurried about Cobo Hall placing buttons on tables. "I don't think this is tampering," Daugherty insisted. "This is free speech. If I thought it was tampering, I wouldn't do it." Meese declined to talk about the JOA, except to say a decision would come "in the next very few months." But he was clearly amused by the buttons.

He hadn't had much reason to smile of late. A special prosecutor was preparing a report outlining a litany of instances of questionable conduct by Meese. Two of the attorney general's top deputies recently had resigned after criticizing Meese to President Reagan. He was enmeshed in scandals involving an Iraqi oil pipeline, the Wedtech kickback scheme, and the Justice Department's investigation of the Iran-contra intrigue. Some of Reagan's top advisers were urging the president to jettison his old friend. MEESE IS A PIG! posters were plastered all over Washington. Even the *Detroit News,* a staunch Reagan ally, had called for the attorney general's exit in an editorial published the day before he addressed the Economic Club. But Meese clung to his job, insisting it would be wrong to surrender in "a lynch-mob atmosphere."

His travails were of great concern to Knight-Ridder and Gannett, though not because he was a notable newsmaker. As calls for Meese's resignation grew louder, the publishers began to worry that he might step down before rendering his decision on the JOA. The national media were saying the Justice Department was in disarray; things weren't getting done because Meese was too distracted by his own legal dilemmas to focus on the country's. Even as Meese insisted that was not the case, the media speculated that he would be gone by summer.

No one was certain what would happen if Meese left office with the JOA in abeyance. Could an acting attorney general make the call? Would a new decision maker need yet more time to reach a conclusion? What if the decision spilled over into the next administration? What might George Bush or Michael Dukakis's attorney general think of the JOA? God forbid, might the process have to start all over again?

Knight-Ridder had a more immediate worry: that Meese might not even consider its public relations campaign. Assistant Attorney General Harry Flickinger was sending form letters to people who had written Meese directly about the JOA. "Because the Attorney General will be the decision-maker in this matter, the regulations governing the case require that he act only on the basis of the record in the case," Flickinger wrote. "The rules do not permit the department to place your document into the record of that hearing and it accordingly may not be otherwise considered by the Attorney General." However, Flickinger's letter did not address letters appended to briefs filed by the parties to the case. In a note to Flickinger, Clark Clifford argued that those letters should indeed be considered. As if to flaunt Flickinger's directive, Clifford sent a copy of his note to Meese himself.

Unbeknownst to the publishers, Meese's staff was taking steps to shield the attorney general from outsiders seeking to sway him. Brad Reynolds, Meese's top adviser, gave Flickinger a memo saying that "letters *actually appended* to official record documents should not be removed or separated. Necessary precautions will be taken during the Attorney General's record review to insure that such extra-record materials receive no consideration and have no influence on the Attorney General's decision."

When Meese was scheduled to chat with lobbyist Tom Korologos about gun control, Steve Matthews, the attorney general's executive assistant, reminded his boss in a memo that Korologos was working for Knight-Ridder and "it would be advisable . . . either to take careful notes or to have someone else present in order to verify later that the Detroit joint operating agreement was not discussed." When Flickinger told Meese's chief of staff, Mark Levin, that scores of letters had arrived at the department, Levin said, "Great—keep 'em." The staff warded off attempts to contact Meese by routing them away from the attorney general's office to Justice's Management Division. That was how they dealt with a "Dear Ed" letter from Detroit multimillionaire and GOP supporter Max Fisher suggesting a meeting with the attorney general. "AG cannot read this communication, let alone hold a meeting," read a memo attached to Fisher's letter.

"We were aware [of the letters] but we made a conscious decision that that was extraevidentiary," recalled Frank Atkinson, Meese's deputy chief of staff at the time. "We were also aware of reasons that it was suspect, as any fact would be that is produced during the pendency of litigation and might be designed to affect the litigation. When you have developments occurring within the context of a pending administrative proceeding, you recognize that it might be more tailored to influence the litigation than as an actual reflection of what the thinking is on the part of the parties."

The staff could not always shield Meese. On June 7, at a private gathering of congressional Republicans, Meese was handed a letter by Representative Carl Pursell of Michigan. "Michigan needs a decision," the letter read. "Many professional employees are in limbo and are leaving to accept other positions. I personally believe Michigan needs two major newspapers (JOA) to promote competing ideas." According to Pursell, Meese allowed that some people might perceive a delay in his deliberations. Meese did not, however. "I will do everything I can to make this decision soon," he told Pursell.

On July 5 Meese told the assembled Washington press that he would be "vindicated" by a forthcoming report by special prosecutor James McKay; with his innocence settled, he would step down as attorney general by early August. (In fact, while McKay would not seek Meese's indictment, the prosecutor's report would conclude that the attorney general probably broke three laws.) Meese did not say whether he would rule on the JOA before leaving. His spokesman, Patrick Korten, said the JOA was not a "major consideration," prompting *Free Press* columnist Jim Fitzgerald to bitterly observe, "What the hell, there's no hurry. Maybe such a low-priority matter as the JOA will be left for the next attorney general to decide, if he's not too busy ducking the cops."

At the *News* and the *Free Press*, the rumor mill was working overtime. People speculated that Meese would approve the JOA because Republicans couldn't afford to upset big publishers in an election year. Others guessed Meese would deny the deal to silence a liberal voice that frequently criticized the Reagan administration. It was taking this long, some said, because Meese couldn't find a politically acceptable way to deny it. No, argued others, it was dragging on because Meese couldn't find a way to refute Judge Needelman's arguments.

For some reason people started thinking Meese would disclose his decision on a Friday; at the *Free Press,* "Thank God It's Friday" became "Oh God, It's Friday." City editor Chip Visci sent the newsroom staff a message via computer: WHEN THE HELL IS ED MEESE GONNA GET OFF HIS BUTT!!!??? In fact, Meese wasn't taking much longer than attorneys general had in the Seattle and Cincinnati cases. At the Justice Department, official spokesman Mark Sheehan got so fed up with addressing silly rumors that he threatened a *Free Press* editor, only half in jest, that he would go public with the weirdest inquiries.

Free Press reporter William Mitchell spent part of a day tracking down a *Free Press* security guard who had casually speculated that the ruling was imminent. After all, Rufus Sharp parked Bill Keating's car. "I couldn't imagine that Bill Keating was going to confide in Rufus Sharp," Mitchell later confessed. "But I figured stranger things have happened; why should I draw the line there?"

The *Free Press* was taking no chances.

Bill Day drew editorial cartoons for the *Free Press.* His job—to look hard at the events of the day and decide what he thought of them—was one of the most visible at the newspaper and one of the simplest. Doing his job, though, became painfully complicated when it concerned Attorney General Edwin Meese—and led to a sad and embarrassing moment for the *Free Press.*

Day had been at the *Memphis Commercial Appeal* when the competing *Press-Scimitar* closed, and the *Philadelphia Bulletin* when it published its farewell edition. "Everybody said it didn't have to happen," Day recalled. "That is little consolation when you're getting your last paycheck." He did not doubt that Knight-Ridder would close the *Free Press* if it didn't get a JOA. But, for Day, the thought that Ed Meese would determine whether he would relive the horror of burying a newspaper was repugnant. Day was a passionate liberal whose stark, darkly humorous sketches were despised by many a Michigan conservative; he believed Meese was a disgrace to his office and his country. Telling the truth, Day believed, required that he comment on the attorney general.

So he did. Early in 1988 he sketched a cartoon of an enormous sewer pipe running through the White House. The pipe was marked in large letters with the words "Iraqi pipeline scandal," and a voice from inside was saying, "Look . . . If Ed Meese says this is storm sewer piping, then I believe him!" Editor Joe H. Stroud rejected the cartoon. As chief of the *Free Press* editorial page, that was his prerogative; Stroud routinely asked Day to make changes to cartoons and occasionally turned them down outright.

Joe Stroud was no ideological fan of Ed Meese. Stroud had come to the *Free Press* during the 1967–68 strike to be associate editor of the editorial page.

As a young reporter in his home state of Arkansas and an editorial writer and editor in Winston-Salem, North Carolina, he had grown intensely interested in the civil rights movement and how it would unfold in America's big cities. Detroit, still recovering from the '67 riot, was fertile ground for a liberal thinker like Stroud. With editor Mark Ethridge, Jr., Stroud helped move the once-conservative *Free Press* far left of the *News.* He took over the editorial page in 1973.

Nor did Stroud harbor illusions about Meese's character. In 1984 his page had urged the Reagan administration to withdraw Meese's nomination. "Mr. Meese, it seems, is not as scrupulous as he might be about avoiding the appearance of impropriety," the *Free Press* opined in March of 1984. Later, the paper called Meese "woefully unqualified" to be attorney general. Even after an independent counsel had cleared Meese of wrongdoing in several questionable circumstances, the *Free Press* said he was "a long, long way from being the best possible nominee."

The *Free Press* published at least eight editorials on Meese while the JOA was before the attorney general. All either took issue with his policies or urged the Reagan administration to clear up questions about the attorney general's ethics. The *Free Press* never called for his resignation. Its language sometimes seemed tortured, as in, "With the resignation of two of the Justice Department's ranking officers and four of their aides, President Reagan's support of Attorney General Edwin Meese III becomes increasingly difficult." However, the *Free Press* was known for editorials that, in an apparent effort to be fair, equivocated. A reader in 1986 had sent a sarcastic letter to the editor saying the *Free Press* editorial staff deserved the "Dare to Be Wishy-Washy Award" for frequently using the words "but," "yet," "however," "tendency," "gesture," "implied," "signal," "good start," "perhaps," and "maybe."

With Meese, Stroud felt he couldn't win. If the *Free Press* defended Meese, critics would accuse it of apple-polishing; if it criticized Meese, some would say it was trying to bully him. Still, those concerns hadn't troubled him much until Judge Needelman rendered his opinion and it suddenly appeared that the JOA, and therefore the *Free Press,* was doomed.

In five of the eight Meese editorials, the *Free Press* disclosed its potential conflict of interest by noting that the JOA was pending before the attorney general. No such disclaimers, however, appeared in the two Meese editorials run before Needelman issued his opinion. "It probably never occurred to me in that earlier period," Stroud later explained. "I think what intervened in part was [Lawrence's] very visible campaign . . . so it became a much more political issue."

The *Free Press* published five Bill Day cartoons critical of Meese *before*

Needelman released his opinion. But when Day offered his pipeline cartoon shortly after the judge's recommendation became public, Stroud showed the cartoon to *Free Press* publisher Dave Lawrence. Lawrence thought it needed a disclaimer. That seemed impractical within the cartoon itself, but the possibility of running a disclaimer in print next to the cartoon either didn't come up or was quickly dismissed.

Stroud told Day the cartoon simply would not run. Stroud said he didn't feel the graphic form allowed for explanation of the *Free Press*'s conflict of interest. In an editorial on Meese, the writer easily could mention that the attorney general was deciding a matter of importance to the paper. Such a disclaimer was not practical in a cartoon, Stroud said. Day's initial reaction was anger. "We felt like we had to handle [Meese] with kid gloves," Day later complained. "I didn't agree with that." He didn't think the *Free Press* should be pulling punches with what he called "one of the sleaziest attorneys general in history." Perhaps naively, Day thought the JOA would be decided on its merits, regardless of what the *Free Press* editorialized.

Day kept drawing, though, offering the *Free Press* two more cartoons. One showed a group of "forgetful" elephants, gathered at the national GOP convention, who couldn't remember who Ed Meese was. Another depicted Meese as a Baltimore Oriole, alluding to a major-league baseball team in the process of losing its first twenty-one games of the season. Both cartoons were rejected. When associate editor Jacqueline Thomas showed the Oriole sketch to Lawrence, the publisher told her that running it would be akin to the scene in the film *Public Enemy* when Jimmy Cagney jams a grapefruit in Mae Clarke's face.

Day drew a fourth cartoon that he didn't bother offering to his bosses. It showed the White House at night. "Ron, what does your horoscope say?" asked Nancy Reagan. "Nan," the president replied, "I don't believe that bunk anymore." In the sky, a constellation blazed with the words FIRE MEESE. Although that cartoon and the others did not run in the *Free Press,* they found their way into other papers because Day, in keeping with a long-standing agreement with Stroud, passed them on to a syndicate.

Day wasn't the only cartoonist whose opinions were being censored. *Miami Herald* editor James Hampton had ordered cartoonist Jim Morin not to draw cartoons about Meese—for the *Herald* or any other paper. Although other Knight-Ridder papers freely commented and cartooned on Meese, Hampton felt the *Herald,* as the company's flagship, might be viewed as reflecting the corporate mind. "You can couch it in all the fancy words you want to and rationalize it all you want to, but what it comes down to is the fact that tens of millions of dollars and 2,200 jobs are riding on Meese's decision," Hampton told *Herald* reporter Celia Dugger. "That affects this newspaper as well as Knight-Ridder. That's a conflict of interest."

Thomas Bray, editorial page editor of the *Detroit News,* didn't see it that way. Cartoonists Draper Hill and Larry Wright drew several cartoons lampooning Meese. Bray's taboo was cartoons on the JOA. When Wright offered one of someone threatening to toss a *Free Press* newsbox off a tall building, Bray turned it away. He also rejected a Hill parody of a *Free Press* TV commercial that showed Meese and wife gazing at a sunrise over the caption "Awake to the morning—You love your morning *Free Press.*" Bray later explained, "We felt there wasn't much to be said or to be gained by talking about" the JOA.

None of the *News*'s editorials on Meese made reference to the JOA. "I think we and [the *Free Press*] can address issues and not allow our personal interests to interfere with our judgment," Bray recalled. "You can't put the whole world on hold because a decision is pending." *News* editorials stopped short of defending Meese while criticizing congressional "scandal-mongering" and the "unconstitutional" use of a special prosecutor. The editorial urging Meese to resign was tempered with praise for his judicial selections. "Mr. Meese deserves to be considered innocent until proven guilty," the *News* opined, "but he also owes it to the country and the president to step aside if his personal legal problems begin to overshadow his official duties."

On July 19, two weeks after Meese said he would resign, the *Washington Post* published a story headlined, NEWSPAPER TREATS MEESE GINGERLY. Media reporter Eleanor Randolph's story said *Free Press* editorializing had been "comparatively gentle." More damaging was the revelation that the *Free Press* and the *Miami Herald* had kept cartoons on Meese out of the papers. Editors Stroud and Hampton insisted they had acted on their own, not under orders from Knight-Ridder. In the *Herald*'s case, that wasn't entirely true, because Hampton had conferred with *Herald* publisher Richard Capen, Jr., who was a Knight-Ridder director and member of the executive committee. Cartoonist Bill Day told Randolph, "The danger in censorship is how it corrupts those who practice it."

The day the *Post* story appeared, Stroud was in Atlanta at the Democratic National Convention. Reporters started calling from the *News* and other Michigan papers, and it struck Stroud that most of them had a vested interest in the JOA, one way or the other. Yet they seemed to have little sympathy for his position. Their questions frustrated him; he thought he had done his best *not* to succumb to the temptation to avoid commenting on Meese. Perhaps he had made the wrong decision, he thought, but it was not a dishonorable one. Now he would be embarrassed before hundreds of thousands of Michigan readers. He explained himself as best he could, and Lawrence backed him up. But it hurt to have the *Free Press*'s and his integrity so publicly called into question. Later, Stroud would wish he had allowed the cartoons to run with an appended disclaimer, however awkward it may have appeared.

The day after the *Post* story ran, the *Free Press* dutifully published its own version, along with Day's four cartoons, on the front page. The wire services and *USA Today* picked up the story and it circulated around the country. It had to have been especially embarrassing for Stroud, who at the time was president of the National Conference of Editorial Writers. *Free Press* staffers were red-faced; down the street, *News* employees snickered and sneered. *Free Press* columnist Jim Fitzgerald took his paper to task in print. *Crain's Detroit Business,* a well-read weekly that had opposed the JOA, opined that the "cartoon fiasco reveals that the second, independent editorial voice in the city isn't independent of the financial needs of its $2-billion-a-year parent company."

Readers wrote nasty letters, which the *Free Press* gamely published. "So the *Free Press*'s 'holier than thou' ethics aren't so holy," wrote W. Edward Wendover, publisher of a weekly newspaper in suburban Detroit. "If you keep up that disregard for your public trust, there won't be any value to the Morning Friendly for Knight-Ridder to sell." Another reader empathized. "It's so easy for another publication or another media outlet to take potshots at you while you're walking a tightrope," wrote Mort Baldock. "Please know you have supporters and believers out here." Bill Day himself wrote a column that focused on censorship. "Actually," he wrote, "cartoons at many other American newspapers have long been the victim of 'that word.' Just ask Garry Trudeau of 'Doonesbury' fame. The irony is that whenever censorship happens, it always seems to create more controversy than if the censored cartoon had been used in the first place. That certainly is what happened in my case."

By far the sharpest public criticism came from *Washington Post* business columnist Jerry Knight. Knight, no relation to Jack Knight, wrote that Knight-Ridder had "taken the prize for perfidy by ordering editorial cartoonists at two papers to lay off Attorney General Edwin Meese." He scored the company for seeking the aid of politicians "who have much to gain from being on the good side of a powerful newspaper chain." He called it "a sad story, unworthy of a great newspaper chain, an embarrassment to the fine journalists who work for Knight-Ridder, such an embarrassment to the profession that few people in the news business want to write about it." The episode reminded the world "that news is just another business, one no closer to perfection than peddling aluminum siding or making $300 hammers for the Pentagon."

Dave Lawrence fired back in a letter to the *Post* editor. "There is—and

I feel this both personally and professionally—too often a smugness in our business, a self-righteousness about others' morals," he wrote. "I have never known that so clearly as in these past two years. The one thing we at the *Free Press* have tried our damnedest to hold on to (in addition to the newspaper itself) is our integrity."

Lawrence had been defending the *Free Press*'s honor ever since he wrote the front-page column saying the paper might die. Then came the courting of politicians and other public figures the *Free Press* covered. And the hiring of lobbyists. The editorial praising Coleman Young. The bonuses to the *Free Press* columnists. Now the censored cartoons. Each time, Lawrence insisted the *Free Press*'s integrity was its most precious possession. Each time, he was less convincing than the last. That wasn't necessarily Lawrence's fault. It probably owed more to one of the rules of the game that newspapers play every day: sometimes there is nothing more damning than a denial.

Amid the lawyerly trappings of the Justice Department offices at Tenth Street and Constitution Avenue in Washington, a trio of bright young attorneys descended upon the record of the Detroit papers' application for a JOA. In spring of 1988, Frank Atkinson, William Levin, and Michael Socarras brought a fresh perspective to the case. None of them was familiar with it, and none ever had handled a case involving the Newspaper Preservation Act.

Atkinson, thirty, was a graduate of the University of Virginia Law School who had worked closely with Meese counselor Brad Reynolds in Reynolds's early days as chief of the Justice Department's Civil Rights Division. He had been Meese's deputy chief of staff since January of 1988. Levin, thirty-one, had joined the Justice Department to work on the ill-fated nomination of Robert Bork to the Supreme Court. The Yale Law School alumnus stayed on as a special assistant in the Office of Legal Counsel. He had a keen business sense, having earned an MBA at Yale and worked on Wall Street as a financial analyst. Socarras, twenty-six, had met Levin while both were law clerks for federal Appellate Judge James L. Buckley, brother of famous conservative William F. Buckley. Socarras, a Cuban émigré, had degrees from the London School of Business and Yale Law School. Reynolds hired him as a special assistant in December of 1987.

The job of the three lawyers was to cull through the record, weigh the evidence, and prepare memoranda for Reynolds analyzing whether various aspects of the Detroit application satisfied the requirements and intent of the law. Reynolds then would distill the briefs and pass them along to Meese.

Ultimately, Meese, with a good bit of help from Reynolds, would decide whether the newspapers were entitled to a JOA. If Meese was the judge, then Atkinson, Levin, and Socarras were his law clerks.

Their task was daunting. For one thing, the record was enormous. Sorting through, organizing, and absorbing a dozen cartons' worth of material would take weeks. By the time most matters reached Meese's office, they had been pared to several succinct arguments. But the JOA had arrived as a sprawling, argumentative mess. Before Meese's advisers could focus on the handful of key issues that would shape the ultimate decision, they had to wade through hundreds of pages to figure out what the issues were.

The job didn't get any easier after that. Applying the Newspaper Preservation Act in Detroit was difficult if only because there was no fitting historical guide. What few precedents there were—Seattle, Cincinnati, perhaps Tucson—looked nothing like Detroit. "The paradigm case reflected in legislative history is one where there's a dominating newspaper and a newspaper that is either in or on the verge of the downward spiral," Atkinson later explained. "This really wasn't that case. This was a case where the parties found themselves in the position they found themselves in by virtue of head-to-head competition from fairly evenly matched positions."

That by no means disqualified Detroit. The Newspaper Preservation Act essentially required two things: that one paper be in "probable danger of financial failure," and that the JOA "effectuate the policy and purpose" of the law, which was to keep newspapers alive. "It was clear that we were dealing with a situation where there was special importance attached to the second prong of the analysis," Atkinson recalled.

In other words, Atkinson, Levin, and Socarras had to decide whether, as a practical matter, the *Free Press* was likely to continue operating if no JOA was available. Was it likely, in fact, to cease to exist? Indeed, would it exist today were it not for the largess of Knight-Ridder? The latter question was crucial because the law required that the *Free Press*'s condition be assessed "regardless of its ownership or affiliations." And yet the probable mortality of the *Free Press* could not be the sole deciding factor; otherwise, couldn't any two newspapers get a JOA simply by declaring that one would be closed?

The law itself did not help the lawyers much. "It was not an easy statute to understand," Levin recalled. "It was not a well-drafted statute." The attorneys struggled to discern precisely what the law meant by "probable danger of failing," and how that applied in a case where *both* papers were in financial distress. Congress obviously had not foreseen such a case, where there was no crumbling market, no downward spiral, no greatly menacing competition from suburban papers. Yet, it struck the young lawyers, if the *Free Press* could not compete itself out of its problems, then wasn't Detroit precisely the kind of case for which the Newspaper Preservation Act was designed?

Indeed, the Detroit case underscored the inherent difficulty in designing laws to fulfill one public policy—in this case, editorial diversity—that conflicts with another held to be equally valuable—that of the antitrust laws. "The facts in this case made it very difficult to reach any conclusion," Levin recalled. "There was no easy answer as to whether [the newspapers] were entitled to the benefits of a JOA." In Levin's opinion, even the parties to the case failed to construe the law properly. "There was no single submission," he recalled, "that accurately applied the facts to the law."

As they had in their clerking days, Levin and Socarras, who shared an office at the Justice Department, had long, intense conversations about the case. Probably sometime in June, Levin gave Atkinson a lengthy memorandum, which Atkinson reworked and then passed on to Brad Reynolds.* Around this time Meese got involved. Reynolds and Meese talked the case over at lunch and through at least one transoceanic plane ride. On at least one occasion, Meese had Levin, Socarras, and Atkinson in to answer questions.

Reynolds, the cranky southerner who was closest to Meese, was not enamored of the JOA law. He didn't see why the media deserved special treatment. "It seems to me that the media outlets in this country can either survive or not survive as legitimate businesses under the rules that everybody else has to play," he later said. "If you're going to get in there and play with the big boys, then you've got to take your lumps. If you fail, you fail." But Reynolds didn't think it was his place to second-guess Congress. He felt he had to work within the bounds of the Newspaper Preservation Act, however wrong-headed it seemed.

By mid- to late July, Meese, Reynolds, and their three advisers had reached a tentative decision. It was, as each of them later described it, a close call. According to Reynolds, at least one of them disagreed "right up to the end." Neither Reynolds nor the others would say who. At the heart of the dissent was the issue that had haunted the case from the very beginning: whether the *Free Press* could survive without a JOA.

*The author made exhaustive attempts to retrieve this memo or others like it via the Freedom of Information Act. No such memos could be located. Justice Department officials said they could have been destroyed, misplaced, misfiled, or removed from the department.

To answer that central question, Reynolds recalled, Meese and his advisers chose to assess the *Free Press*'s financial condition not as it stood in May of 1986, when Knight-Ridder and Gannett applied for the JOA, but as of the spring of 1988. "That was when we froze the lens," Reynolds recalled. By 1988, of course, the *Free Press*'s losses had escalated, its market positions had deteriorated, and the Knight-Ridder board had voted to close the paper. Indeed, the *Free Press* scrutinized by Meese, Reynolds, and their young counselors was quite different from the one Judge Morton Needelman had analyzed. The *Free Press* of 1988 certainly was less likely to survive than the *Free Press* of 1986. If it wasn't a "failing paper" then, perhaps it was now.

If Meese wanted to approve the JOA—as he supposedly told Jerry terHorst in that idle conversation in the fall of 1986—he would have to overrule his own Antitrust Division and Judge Needelman. If he denied the JOA, the publishers were sure to appeal in federal court. Meese himself felt he should take a broader perspective than those who had assessed the application before him. "One of the things the ultimate decision maker has to do," Meese recalled, "is stand back and look at the thing in its entirety . . . and not get so bogged down in all the factual aspects that he can't see the whole picture."

On July 20, Justice Department spokesman Patrick Korten told reporters for the *Free Press* and the *News* that Meese would rule on the JOA before he left office in mid-August. By then, Reynolds was already working on a first draft of Meese's opinion and order.

17

Wishful Thinking

Later the same day, Frank Hawkins, Knight-Ridder's official spokesman, was chatting on the phone with a Washington reporter for the *Detroit News.* Hawkins was a onetime Associated Press correspondent who had covered, in his globe-trotting career, the 1973 Middle East war and the terrorist hostage taking at the 1972 Olympics in Munich. As Knight-Ridder's primary contact for the media and Wall Street analysts, he spent a good deal of his time answering questions. Today, though, Hawkins was asking the questions. He liked reporters and wasn't afraid to admit that sometimes they knew more than he did. He wanted to know what the *Detroit News* reporter had heard about the JOA decision.*

The reporter hadn't heard much, but he enjoyed bantering with Hawkins, who, unlike some corporate flacks, had a good sense of humor. The rumor, the reporter told Hawkins, was that Meese would rule on the JOA the following week.

"What's he gonna do?" Hawkins asked.

"I have no idea," the reporter said.

"What do you *think* he's gonna do?"

*The reporter was the author.

"I think," the reporter guessed, "if you don't get the Guild out, he's gonna deny it."

It was rank speculation, of course, but in these tense days for Knight-Ridder, it was plausible enough for Hawkins to hurry down the hall of Knight-Ridder's sixth-floor executive offices in Miami to tell P. Anthony Ridder.

Bernie Ridder's tall, slim, stylishly dressed son was Knight-Ridder's rising star. As publisher of the *San Jose Mercury News,* Tony Ridder had used the Silicon Valley boom to create the ideal modern newspaper, one that made dazzling profits while winning Pulitzer Prizes. He had made his reputation as a ruthless cost cutter, but at San Jose at least, the cutting hadn't come at the expense of the product. On the contrary, Ridder had increased editorial spending while persuading his unions to accept money-saving automation in the mail room and printing facilities.

In 1986, Ridder had moved to Miami as president of Knight-Ridder's Newspaper Division, entrusted with transplanting the San Jose success to the chain's thirty-odd other papers. He was an impatient forty-seven-year-old who thrived on getting things done quickly, whether he was solving a delivery problem, running the New York City Marathon, zipping through the Atlantic Ocean in his Cigarette powerboat, or wolfing a hamburger for lunch. "I enjoy speed," he once told *Business Week* magazine.

He hadn't been deeply involved in the JOA. Lately, though, he had been offering his services in the effort to get Guild Local 22 to withdraw as an opponent. Ridder knew Charles Dale, the Guild's beefy, white-haired international president, from contract negotiations on the West Coast. The men liked and respected each other. Ridder thought their relationship might help to thaw the frosty relations between Local 22 and Knight-Ridder.

The Guild and the publishers hadn't negotiated since March. In the meantime, Knight-Ridder had taken a few public swipes at the union. Alvah Chapman had chastised it at the company's annual meeting, and Hawkins always had a caustic comment ready for the media, as in, "The Guild's kamikaze-like attitude in all this continues to baffle me." Knight-Ridder still wanted the Guild out of the way, figuring that, even if it didn't influence Meese, at least there would be no one to file a court challenge if the JOA was approved.

Ridder had called Dale, who agreed to meet. They chatted briefly in Dale's Washington office on July 15. On July 19, Dale and Don Kummer had dinner with Ridder and *Free Press* general manager Bob Hall at a Georgetown steakhouse. Kummer told Ridder and Hall he wanted his members protected in the merger of the papers' business functions. Hall said he wanted the Guild's support, but he could not promise the union wouldn't lose members if and when the combination took place. The four agreed to meet again on Tuesday, July 26. But on July 20 Hawkins told Ridder of the gossip from the *News*'s Washington reporter. Ridder immediately got on the phone to Dale and requested an earlier meeting.

At 3:00 P.M. Friday, July 22, Ridder, Hall, Dale, and Kummer met at the Guild's Georgetown headquarters. They had agreed to talk without the usual retinue of second-tier negotiators—and without John Jaske, Gannett's icy lead bargainer. Kummer, who blamed Jaske for the publishers' unbending positions, was delighted. Hall was glad a potential Gannett veto wouldn't be hovering over the talks. Gannett wasn't even consulted; Bill Keating was informed only shortly before the Friday meeting.

Characteristically, Ridder had planned to wrap up quickly; he had dinner guests waiting at his vacation home in North Carolina. Around 7:00 P.M. he phoned his wife to say he wouldn't be making it. Kummer was prepared to go all night. "We didn't know if we were going to come out Friday night or Saturday night or Sunday morning," he told a *Free Press* reporter, "but we knew this was it."

The negotiations went slowly. At 11:00 P.M. the four men broke for supper at Mamma Regina, an Italian restaurant in nearby Silver Spring, Maryland. Ridder and Hall ate at a different table from Kummer and Dale. They had been meeting together and caucusing separately for eight hours, with little movement on either side. Kummer was in a tough spot. It was becoming clear that Knight-Ridder, even without Gannett at its side, wasn't going to budge on its refusal to let the Guild represent members who would become employees of the Detroit Newspaper Agency. But Ridder and Hall were offering other carrots Kummer could not ignore. If he rejected them now, he might never see them again. If Meese approved the JOA, the Guild would lose most of its leverage, unless it waged a successful court fight—a risky and expensive proposition. Kummer had to decide when the publishers truly had made their best offer.

Around 2:00 A.M. Dale and Kummer caucused yet again.

"You want to give up on this thing?" Dale asked. "It looks like nothing's going to happen."

"If it's going to break down," Kummer said, "let them call it off. It's their show."

In another room, Ridder's lanky frame was stretched out on a sofa, in a deep sleep. Dale nudged him awake. Tony, he said, let's talk some more.

"Chuck," Ridder protested, "I can't understand a thing you're saying. I'm still asleep."

They talked some more. Setting jurisdiction aside, Kummer pressed for a guarantee that no Guild members would be laid off. Ridder and Hall had been willing to guarantee there'd be no more than one hundred layoffs, but now they came down to seventy-five. They also promised none of the Guild's janitorial workers at the *News* would be laid off. The DNA or the *Free Press* newsroom would simply have to find jobs for Guild business and janitorial workers who might otherwise have been eliminated. "I guess Dave Lawrence will have a lot of extra help in editorial," Ridder joked. Ridder and Hall also offered a half-million-dollar fund for retraining of displaced workers. And, *Free Press* Guild members who were at least fifty-five years old would get pension benefits equivalent to what they would receive at sixty-five. The package would cost at least $3 million.

Throughout the night, Ridder kept Bill Keating informed via telephone, while Keating stayed in touch with Doug McCorkindale at Gannett. Keating didn't like this at all. He feared Knight-Ridder would hand away job cuts that were crucial to the JOA's financial success. It was frustrating enough that the papers had for months ignored his pleas not to fill vacancies. Now he was being dictated—over the phone in the middle of the night, no less—terms that would further hamper his ability to streamline the JOA operations. Keating also knew that, the minute a Guild deal was signed, Elton Schade would be all over him to find out if the Guild had gotten anything the Teamsters didn't get. Ridder sympathized, but he thought Keating was overreacting a bit. "The kinds of issues Bill was having a problem with, when weighed against getting the Guild out, were not important," Ridder recalled.

Dawn was fast approaching. Kummer and Dale wearily considered whether to accept Knight-Ridder's offer. Dale recalled an old union saying: When you reach the point where you're swallowing the cow, don't choke on the tail.

Kummer and Dale did not choke. Around 5:00 A.M. Ridder called Alvah Chapman to tell him there was a tentative deal. All that remained was for the Guild's executive board to ratify it.

That was far from certain.

Kummer caught the first flight to Detroit. Back at his Grosse Pointe Park home, he immediately called Lou Mleczko, who happened to live down the street. Mleczko stopped mowing his lawn and tromped down to Kummer's house. Kummer was sitting at his kitchen table, smoking his umpteenth cigarette of the last twelve hours. His heavy-lidded eyes looked droopier than usual, partly from exhaustion, partly from what he had to tell his old and dear friend Mleczko.

Kummer quickly outlined the deal he had struck with Ridder and Hall. Mleczko did not look happy. He thought it was a strong package overall, but it appeared Kummer hadn't gotten the one crucial thing Local 22 had sought from the start.

"Where's the jurisdictional issue, Don?" Mleczko asked.

Kummer just shook his head. Mleczko thought he saw tears in his eyes. "I couldn't get the jurisdiction," he said.

"Well," Mleczko said, "I've got to think this through."

Mleczko returned home, crestfallen. For nine years he and Don Kummer had worked side by side, partners and friends. Mleczko always had marveled at how compatible they were, how they never seemed to disagree, how they always were able to work through what minor differences of opinion they had.

The difference they faced now wasn't minor at all. Mleczko simply could not live with the deal Kummer had made. As much as he deplored the idea of merging the papers, as much as he despised Gannett and Knight-Ridder for bringing an end to the newspaper war, Mleczko had resigned himself to swallowing the bitter pill of a JOA—but if, and only if, each and every member of Guild Local 22 had a future assured with one of the newspapers or the Detroit Newspaper Agency. Kummer's deal did not satisfy that condition.

So Mleczko had to fight it.

Local 22's bargaining committees were hastily convened Sunday night. It soon became apparent that Kummer and Mleczko were on opposite sides. Kummer detailed the proposed settlement with Knight-Ridder and Mleczko lobbied his colleagues to vote against it. "People were looking at each other saying, 'What the hell is going on here?' " Mleczko recalled.

The committees did not have the last word, though, because the membership had authorized the thirty-five-member executive board (also known as the Representative Assembly) to decide whether the Guild would continue to oppose the JOA. Committee members could have made a recommendation to the board, but after meeting for two and a half hours they were too polarized to vote.

The executive board met the next morning at 7:30 in a conference room adjoining Kummer's office on the thirty-third floor of the Book Building in downtown Detroit. More than thirty people stood along the walls or sat around long folding tables bunched at the center of the room. Kummer passed out copies of the settlement, already signed by Bob Hall.

Knight-Ridder wanted a decision by noon.

Mary Birkett, a *Free Press* circulation trainer, started the discussion.

"We have obligations to the people we represent," she said. "But we also have to recognize the long-range effects of this. The JOA is bad for unions and it signals what companies can get away with. I recommend we reject this proposal." Her sentiment went to the heart of what Kummer had feared all along—that philosophical distaste for the JOA would obscure the reality of the collective bargaining process. Emotion was useful so long as it did not blind people to facts. The facts were, in Kummer's eyes, that the Guild had to get on the JOA bandwagon now or risk being forever isolated.

Luther Jackson spoke next. A business reporter and the *Free Press*'s unit chairperson, Jackson had steadfastly opposed the JOA, even through the contentious Guild rift in February. Now he was softening. "I oppose JOAs too," he said. "But as unit chair, I have to think of the people impacted by this."

"I don't think it matters if we drop our opposition," argued Deborah Kaplan, a *Free Press* reporter. "What they're doing is trying to get us out of a position of strength by making us drop our legal fight if Meese approves the JOA."

Dave Jobse, a *News* maintenance man, agreed. "With this tentative agreement, and an approved JOA, we in the *News*'s maintenance unit would no longer be represented by the Guild. We have sent in our Guild dues every month to fight the JOA. Ours is the oldest unit. And now you want to strip us of our affiliation. We are totally opposed to this tentative agreement."

Someone asked Guild attorney Duane Ice if the union's withdrawal would mean anything. "I expect if the Guild changes its position, that would be a significant factor for Meese," Ice said. "Then there's no one else left to challenge his opinion. If we don't get out and he approves the JOA, we can still go forth and block it. Knight-Ridder will close the paper if the JOA is not approved, though. Gannett has not tried to make the JOA happen."

Mleczko's blue eyes flashed. He reminded the group that Local 22 would be surrendering the rights to represent more than 300 members. "We're offering them a hundred-year monopoly," he said. "We live with that beast forever." He admitted there was a risk to his position: if the JOA was rejected, the *Free Press* could close and the Guild would lose 650 members. But he did not believe the *Free Press* would close; it might be sold, but it was too valuable to shut down.

"If we stay as intervenors and the JOA is rejected, can we get an injunction to stop closure of the *Freep*?" Kaplan asked.

"We don't have a chance," Ice said. "You can't stop the *Freep* from closing."

Kummer looked sad and exhausted.

"This is the first time I've ever had a difference of opinion with Lou in ten years," he said. "I don't think this local got involved because we could set new standards for the world. What we did get involved in was a process to expose [the JOA] for what it was. I think we're stuck with one monopoly in Detroit. It's either Gannett or the agency. We got in this for the best deal for our people. I don't think there are any more deals. We've got nothing to be ashamed of. We helped people. We got more than we had in February and March."

Luther Jackson offered his support. "By fighting this," he said, "we've kept jobs going for two years. But I've also got to represent people at the *Freep* who are going to want answers."

He moved that the board accept the settlement.

Local 22 secretary Kate DeSmet took a roll-call vote. It was 13–13 when it came to Mleczko, who voted to reject. DeSmet's "no" made it 15–13, with one abstention.

Every head in the room turned as Kummer abruptly stood up and announced, "I do not feel I can go back to the general membership of this union and sell them what you've just handed me.

"It's been fun, folks."

And he walked out. Don Kummer had resigned.

The crowded room exploded with angry shouts and accusations. Some of the people were crying. Some were calling for another vote. Some were heading for the door, feeling alone and confused and weary of the fight. What was happening to their union, once so strong and unified in the face of the publishers' attempts to dominate them? Had they finally been beaten? Would the JOA tear Local 22 in two?

Mleczko had won. He could have gaveled the meeting to a close and walked away victorious.

Instead, he called a five-minute recess.

He found Kummer sitting at his desk, smoking a cigarette, staring out the window. Kummer himself was surprised at what had just happened. He had always said he would step down if ever the union forced him to sell something he felt he could not honestly sell. That day had come. But Kummer hadn't thought of quitting until he saw the vote come around to Mleczko and realized that his hard-earned deal would die.

Mleczko was angry. He wanted to yell, "Kummer, get your ass back in there and face the music!" But he kept his temper and, instead, made a halfhearted joke. "Well, chief," he said, "this is another fine mess you've gotten us into."

Kummer said nothing. Perhaps it was in that instant that Mleczko knew the Guild's fight was over. He had left home that morning vowing to hold his ground. "I don't care if I'm the only no vote on this," he had told his wife, Lorraine. "I'm not changing my stand." But he had not foreseen the bitterness and anger that would divide his union brothers and sisters. He had not imagined that his friend Kummer would quit.

Now Mleczko told himself that it simply could not go on like this, with members suing each other, calling each other names, threatening a vote to decertify the local. If they walked out of the Book Building that morning with the 15–13 vote as the last word on the JOA, the scars might never heal.

Mleczko asked Kummer to come back to the meeting. He would call for a second vote, he said, and he would recommend acceptance of the settlement. Kummer stood up from his desk.

The chaos in the conference room had subsided. Mleczko called the meeting back to order. "If we leave with a split vote, we'll have a split union, and possibly the end of the union," he said.

Someone suggested calling a vote of the entire membership. But it was too late; Knight-Ridder wanted a decision now.

"There's a time to fight," Ice said, "and a time to deal."

Mleczko had made his choice. He was not alone. Others in the room had voted their conscience, assuming the settlement would be approved anyway. They were prepared to change their votes. "As president," Mleczko said, "I was making hard comments against this. It is also clear, if we had a general membership meeting now, I think they'd approve this. Because of that feeling, I will change my vote and recommend we accept it and vote it unanimously."

There was a show of hands—15–9 in favor of settling.

Mleczko called his wife. She had supported his stance from the beginning. Indeed, it was Lorraine Mleczko who first had exhorted her husband to fight the JOA on the day Alvah Chapman and Al Neuharth announced it. "You can't let this happen," she had told him. "What are you going to tell your grandchildren?" Now she listened as he told her that the fight was over, that *he* was finally responsible for ending it. She could feel his hurt, his frustration, his lingering doubt that he had done the right thing. He was inconsolable. But at least he was distracted; he had to circulate at the *News* and tell his fellow Guild members what had happened that morning at the Book Building.

Lorraine Mleczko wasn't so fortunate. She hung up the phone, went down to the basement, sat on the floor next to the cat litter box, and wept.

* * *

On Sunday, August 7, Al Neuharth called about a dozen high-level editors and executives of Gannett and the *News* to a secret meeting at the Hyatt Regency in Dearborn, a fifteen-minute drive from downtown Detroit. Among the dozen or so participants were John Curley, Doug McCorkindale, and John Quinn from Gannett, *News* publisher Chip Weil, and editors Bob Giles and Christina Bradford.

The first order of business was a bet. Neuharth loved making wagers; at baseball games, he liked to gamble on what the next pitch would be. Today, he asked his charges to wager twenty dollars apiece on how Attorney General Edwin Meese would rule on the JOA. Without exception, they bet that Meese would deny the merger.

It wasn't so much wager as wishful thinking.

By now, no one in the room really wanted a JOA, least of all Bob Giles, the *News*'s executive editor. Giles, a taciturn fifty-five-year-old who favored broadly striped shirts and suspenders, felt the *News* deserved to win the Great Detroit Newspaper War outright. In the latest six-month circulation period, the *News* had widened its daily lead to 40,448, its biggest advantage since 1974. In Giles's opinion, the *Free Press* just wasn't getting the job done. For months he had been asking for a *News* story detailing how the *Free Press* could be run at a profit. The assigned reporters weren't able to come up with a story that satisfied him.

Giles had great respect for Knight-Ridder, but he also had a little something to prove. He had worked for Knight Newspapers as a reporter and editor at the *Akron Beacon Journal* for seventeen years. He fondly remembered riding with Jack Knight and Richard Nixon from the Cleveland airport in 1959; forbidden to take notes, Giles had memorized what Nixon said so he could write a story when he returned to the newsroom. As managing editor, Giles had directed the *Beacon Journal*'s Pulitzer-winning coverage of the Kent State shootings. He became executive editor in 1972, but resigned three and a half years later after an intramural skirmish with former *Free Press* editor Mark Ethridge, Jr. It left a bad taste in Giles's mouth. "They left me to twist in the wind," he later remarked. After leaving Akron, he taught for a year at the University of Kansas before Gannett hired him to edit the two Rochester, New York, papers.

Giles was a fiercely competitive man; when the *News* broke an especially good story, he might have a copy of the paper hand-delivered to the home of the *Free Press*'s Neal Shine with a note attached—"Thought you'd like to see this." No small part of what had lured him to Detroit was the chance to beat Knight-Ridder. "I thought this was an opportunity to let Knight-Ridder know I was still around," he recalled.

But Giles's pale blue eyes didn't usually indicate fires burning within. Shy by nature, he rarely put his emotions on display. One *News* reporter half-jokingly labeled Giles's management style as "productive reticence," the craft of getting things done without saying anything. Occasionally, though, Giles indulged his pride, as when one of his reporters interviewed him in November of 1986. Giles was riding high then. The *News* was steadily increasing its lead while the *Free Press* labored under its "failing newspaper" tag. The reporter asked how the *News* planned to retain its rank after surrendering the morning market in the JOA.

"We intend to stay on top," Giles insisted. "We don't intend to give the *Free Press* an opportunity to overcome the *News*. There's more to this than the bottom line. There is a tremendous amount of pride in having the *News* remain number one. You have the commitment of Al Neuharth. That's a very important ingredient in this. He knows how to use control of the JOA to make good things happen with the *Detroit News*. I want to be number one. If we are number two, I won't feel that I've succeeded, no matter how much profit the JOA makes." Giles smiled conspiratorially. "I don't think the people at the *Free Press* understand what Gannett control means. This is going to be the place to come. I don't expect this to be a happy marriage. The interests of the *News* and the *Free Press* within the [Detroit Newspaper Agency] will be in a state of constant tension. That's why Gannett control is so important."

Two years later, Giles no longer was so cocky. Neuharth had long ago disengaged himself from Detroit. First he'd gone off on BusCapade and now the irrepressible Gannett chairman was circling the globe on JetCapade. (The trip prompted a joke that Neuharth arranged meetings with Fidel Castro and other world leaders not so he could meet them, but so they could meet him.) Neuharth's "commitment" to the *News* had fallen victim to his notoriously short attention span.

By May of 1988 Giles was frantically concerned that the *News* was doomed to number two status under a JOA. With a decision imminent, *News* circulation people had produced estimates showing the *News* wasn't likely to stay on top for long after the JOA was in place. Giles had pleaded with Chip Weil to do something to preserve the *News*'s position, to no avail. Weil figured that was a matter for Gannett. So Giles went over Weil's head in a memo to Neuharth, Curley, McCorkindale, and John Quinn, Gannett's vice-president for news. The memo projected the *News* losing 83,000 subscribers at the JOA's launch, and another 65,000 within ninety days. The *Free Press* would immediately take the circulation lead, increasing it to 98,000 within a year. The shift would have serious consequences, Giles's memo argued:

a. The strategy initiated in 1986 by the *Detroit News* Board to be the dominant Detroit newspaper, with or without a JOA, would have failed. And so would our strategy of building statewide circulation, as well as the more recent commitment to push for morning readership.

b. The *News*'s role and influence as a statewide newspaper would be diminished. The *Free Press* would be left as the only true statewide paper in Michigan.

c. Whatever advantage was anticipated in translating the *News*' dominant position on Sunday into daily readership would be lessened.

d. One of the planning objectives of DNA, as I understand it, was to maintain circulation parity because two papers of relatively equal size would influence advertisers to buy in combination. If the DNA begins with the afternoon newspaper as number two by 100,000, it may not be possible to meet the DNA goal of parity. The trend toward morning readership would then be more likely to follow the normal pattern in Detroit. The result would be a gradual deterioration of the readership of the *News*. Over time—say 10 years and beyond—there could be an impact on advertising, as well as circulation revenue. As the gap between morning and evening circulation widens, combination buys become less attractive to advertisers.

e. If the *Free Press* goes from failing paper to number one, the reaction in the press, among market analysts and readers would not be in the best interest of Gannett.

The perception would be that Knight-Ridder outmaneuvered Gannett, even though Gannett controls the JOA.

The idea that Detroit was a "win-win" for Gannett would seem less so.

None of the *Detroit News* people who carried the fight to the *Free Press* or will be expected to do so after the [JOA] are prepared for this turn of events.

Giles wanted Gannett to negotiate for an even earlier press start than the 6:15 A.M. to which Knight-Ridder had reluctantly agreed. Curley told Giles he appreciated the editor's sentiments, but there wasn't much he could do. The JOA contract said the *News* was an afternoon paper; not many afternoon dailies went to press at 6:15 A.M. Curley thought Knight-

Ridder had gone to great lengths to accommodate Gannett. A deal was a deal, after all.

So no one could have been happier than Bob Giles to hear the topic of Al Neuharth's clandestine meeting at the Hyatt Regency on August 7. Neuharth wanted to talk about how the *News* would exploit its newfound advantages when Meese denied the JOA and Knight-Ridder closed the *Free Press.* "It will be a whole new ball game," Neuharth told his troops. He wanted them to think hard about how the *News* would "out-*Free Press* the *Free Press.*"

For Neuharth, it was a nostalgic return to 1960, when he and Lee Hills were plotting the *Free Press*'s countermoves to the *News*'s purchase of the *Detroit Times.* Hills's genius was in offering *Times* readers a paper that looked and felt like a familiar old friend, like the *Times* itself. Neuharth wanted to know how the *News* could publish a morning edition that would cater to the habitual expectations and desires of *Free Press* devotees. Except on the editorial page, the *News* wasn't radically different from the *Free Press* anymore. But the "Morning Friendly" still had certain characteristic attributes and quirks that earned the loyalty of hundreds of thousands of readers.

Should Gannett buy the *Free Press*'s name? Would it need the *Free Press*'s printing presses? And the subscription lists? Which of the *Free Press*'s editors and reporters ought to be hired? How many of the *Free Press*'s features and columns should run in the morning *News?* How quickly could the *News* move to lock up the metropolitan Detroit market for a daily newspaper?

It was a preliminary exercise, but an exciting one. Neuharth hadn't been this worked up over Detroit in months. As for Giles and the others, "I think their saliva was running," Neuharth later recalled. Thoughts of the *News* suffering a humiliating plunge to number two gave way to thoughts of the *News* emerging as the undisputed victor of the newspaper war. Neuharth adjourned the meeting with instructions for everyone to do some serious brainstorming. When the Meese denial came down, the *News* would be ready to leap into action.

In Washington, reporters were told on the morning of Monday, August 8, that Meese would be releasing his JOA decision that afternoon. It would be his last official act as attorney general.

Around 4:00 P.M. about twenty reporters hovered outside a small office in the Justice Department building at Tenth and Constitution. On a table inside rested a thick stack of copies of Meese's decision. The *Free Press* had sent reporter Patricia Montemurri, one of Jane Daugherty's contras, to help Washington correspondent Patricia Edmonds cover the story. When the reporters were beckoned into the room, Montemurri shouldered her way past the others and literally ran to the stack of opinions. Snatching one up, she flipped immediately to Meese's conclusion.

A wave of utter relief washed over her face.

Meese had approved the JOA.

His decision was but fifteen pages long. Like Judge Morton Needelman, Meese had found that neither Detroit newspaper was in the so-called "downward spiral." Like Needelman, he had concluded that the *Free Press* did not face "external market forces," such as rising costs, that would portend failure. Like Needelman, Meese saw no market declines in circulation or advertising such that the *Free Press* was doomed to perish. In fact, Meese had accepted Needelman's findings of fact without exception. But he had interpreted them differently, and reached a different conclusion.

The linchpin to Meese's view was the Ninth Circuit Court of Appeals' decision in the Seattle JOA. The court had found that "the probable danger standard is, by the plain meaning of the words, primarily an economic standard: Is the newspaper suffering losses which more than likely cannot be reversed?" Not surprisingly, Meese had applied just such a "common-sense construction" to his decision, a view that was consistent with how the Reagan administration often interpreted American laws. Meese was impressed by the *Free Press*'s record of losses. "Indeed," he wrote, "were it not for a major infusion of millions of dollars by its parent, there is every reason to assume that the *Free Press* would have failed long ago." Knight-Ridder might be equipped to forestall the *Free Press*'s demise, Meese felt, but that did not diminish the probability that the paper would fail.

Knight-Ridder's high-stakes gamble that the *Free Press* could overtake the *News* had been offset by the *News*'s pursuing a similar, win-at-all-costs strategy. "Both have been frustrated," Meese concluded. That the companies then looked to a JOA as an option was evidence merely of "prudent management judgment," Meese found. "Certainly, newspapers cannot be faulted for considering and acting upon an alternative that Congress has created."

The attorney general dismissed Needelman's suggestion that both papers could become profitable by raising prices. "Gannett has made clear that it has no intention of embarking on such a course, either unilaterally or in conjunction with Knight-Ridder. While [Needelman] questioned the testimony of Gannett officials to this effect, it hardly reflects unsound business judgment to retain awhile longer the *News*' current depressed pricing practices with so many indications that the *Free Press* and Knight-Ridder have abandoned all hope of market domination."

Knight-Ridder's public relations campaign had had no influence,

Meese said. "Since those maneuvers occurred after the close of the record, they have not been included in any consideration of the instant application," he wrote in a footnote. However, he said, he could not wholly disregard Alvah Chapman's vow to recommend that the *Free Press* be closed. It would not be illogical for Knight-Ridder to do just that, Meese found.

In short, Meese was convinced the *Free Press* would go out of business if the JOA was not approved. "To stand by and watch the paper's demise would poorly serve the Act's policy disfavoring a newspaper monopoly in the City of Detroit," he wrote.

When news of the decision reached the *Free Press,* a great cheer went up in the newsroom. Reporters and editors whooped and high-fived, hugged and kissed, laughed and cried. "If I had to think of the worst days and the happiest days of my years at the *Free Press,*" Neal Shine said, "they all would be rolled into today." Cartoonist Bill Day rushed into Dave Lawrence's office shouting, "I didn't do it! I didn't do it!" The publisher shook his hand and cracked, "Not for lack of trying."

Someone broke out champagne. Jane Daugherty uncorked a twelve-year-old bottle of Haitian rum she had been saving for a celebration. Lawrence strode into a hastily called meeting of *Free Press* managers to thunderous applause. It took him a moment to collect his emotions. "I think we have seen the end of a very long process," he said. "I will never have a moment like this in my life." Later he told a *News* reporter, "I can't imagine a better day."

Not everyone was merrymaking, though. In other quarters of the *Free Press,* business-side workers soberly wondered whether they would have jobs when the JOA was formally assembled ten days later. Five hundred of them at the *Free Press* and the *News* were to lose their jobs, either through layoffs, early retirement, or voluntary severance. "I guess I'll retire," *Free Press* printer Don Floer told a reporter. "They don't want a sixty-year-old man anymore."

The mood was just as restrained at the *News.* There, too, business-side workers contemplated futures without employment. Newsroom staffers, many of whom had opposed the JOA to the end, braced for sweeping schedule changes that would come with the elimination of the *News*'s morning home delivery. Bob Giles and Chip Weil, obviously disappointed, had no comment for the public. "This is not a perfect world," Weil told the newsroom staff. "Some things I like, some things I don't like."

There was no talk of the *News* becoming the number two paper, but Giles knew what his reporters and editors were thinking. "Gannett," he reassured them, "intends to exercise the advantage of that majority [on the Detroit Newspaper Agency board] to the benefit of the *Detroit News.*" Al Neuharth insisted in an interview that the *News* would simply convert morning readers to afternoon delivery. "What most of you are hung up on," he snapped, "is this morning business, which I think is an unrealistic [concern]. Most of the *News*'s A.M. readers are former P.M. readers. Maybe it's as easy to switch them back to afternoon from morning as it was to switch them to the morning."

When Alvah Chapman heard about Meese's decision, he was boating in the Bahamas, just as he had been that day in August of 1985 when Neuharth first talked to Jim Batten about the prospect of a JOA. Again Chapman and family were vacationing with pal Armando Codina. Codina's cruiser, *What A Country*, was equipped with a telex. Late Monday afternoon, Chapman clambered aboard his friend's boat to watch for JOA news. Shortly after 4:00 P.M. a message slowly unfurled. First came the sender, "Knight-Ridder, Inc.," then the company address, and then, finally, "J . . . O . . . A . . . A . . . P . . . P . . . R . . . O . . . V . . . E . . . D."

Chapman was elated. He rushed to shore at Treasure Cay to call Miami. "Eight," he excitedly told Batten, "has always been my lucky number." It was 8/8/88. Chapman had his JOA. The Detroit problem was all but solved. All that remained was to whip the operation into shape and start making some money.

Finally, Alvah Chapman could retire in peace.

Or so he thought.

Part Five

The Downward Spiral

18

To Kill the *Free Press*

No one had opposed the JOA longer than John Francis Kelly—and no one had been so thoroughly ignored. The diminutive state senator with the charming smile and piercing blue eyes had registered his displeasure with the newspapers' plan within days after it was announced in the spring of 1986. His attempt to pass a state law blocking the merger went nowhere. His public hearing at the Detroit Press Club was a bust. His bid to participate in the hearing before Judge Needelman was denied. Two letters to Ed Meese got him a perfunctory form letter in response. He got Dave Lawrence to answer his letters and have breakfast with him once or twice, but, predictably, failed to persuade the *Free Press* publisher the JOA was wrong for Detroit.

The thirty-six-year-old lawyer, born and bred on Detroit's east side, had been in Michigan's Legislature ten years since whipping an incumbent on a platform of neighborhood revitalization. Fellow lawmakers saw him as a smart, well-intentioned maverick who loved a spotlight, frequently spoke before he thought, and had surprisingly little clout for a three-term legislator. Kelly's bluntness and unpredictability saved him from obscurity. He was the definitive loose cannon. He once publicly berated the speaker of Michigan's House—a fellow Democrat—as an "ignorant, uninformed, half-baked hillbilly." In a close-fought tax fight in 1985, Kelly openly snubbed Democrat Governor James Blanchard to side with the Republicans. Another time he told a television reporter that crime was so bad where he lived that he watched TV with a shotgun and his wife slept with a revolver handy—exaggerations he later recanted. When a voter castigated him for getting a ticket for careless driving, Kelly sent a telegram suggesting that the voter "suck eggs." "John's my friend," said one Michigan politician who knew him well. "But he's flaky."

Yet Kelly kept getting elected. That was partly because, for all his bluster and hyperbole, he was eminently likable. And he worked hard to keep his constituents happy. His district straddled the Detroit city line, taking in one of the city's poorest areas and a slice of the well-to-do enclave of Grosse Pointe Park. Working from their cramped Mack Avenue office, he and his staff tended assiduously to constituent requests and complaints. Kelly always could be counted on to organize a community parade or raise money for a worthy cause. He was bright, too; he had a master's degree from the University of Michigan and was working toward a Ph.D. in political science at Georgetown University.

In early 1988, while other Michigan politicians fell in step with Knight-Ridder's JOA campaign, Kelly went on the attack. In a scathing letter to Attorney General Edwin Meese, he wrote, "The fear of closing the *Free Press* has been fueled by a vicious, aggressive campaign . . . to chill those who were in opposition and to intimidate political and community leaders into legitimizing the unholy JOA alliance." He argued that the JOA wouldn't preserve diversity because the papers would draw "nourishment . . . from a common source." Stories and editorials would "amount to little more than ventriloquism by the Detroit Newspaper Agency."

Kelly believed the JOA would ultimately lead to one paper, a daily *Detroit News and Free Press.* That would create problems for a marginally influential politician like John Kelly, who had learned over the years that he often could get publicity only by playing one paper's newsroom off of the other. If the *News* knew the *Free Press* was working on it, the *News* might pursue a story it otherwise would have ignored.

Kelly also disliked bullies; thanks to his intemperate tongue and Irish temper, he had tangled with a few in his day. To him, Knight-Ridder and Gannett had been bullying their employees, their unions, the people of Michigan, and even Meese. When the Knight-Ridder board voted to close the *Free Press,* Kelly imagined gun-toting terrorists trotting out hostages before television cameras. "I vowed to myself that they couldn't get away with this," he later said. He didn't figure to beat America's two largest newspaper companies, but he was fiercely determined to get their attention. In the wake of Meese's approval of the merger, John Kelly took one last, desperate shot at stopping it.

On August 8, 1988, Kelly had just ten days to wage his private war on the JOA. By law, that period was set aside for court challenges before the publishers actually combined their business operations. No challenges were expected in Detroit, because none of the official JOA opponents remained, except for the Antitrust Division, which was barred from suing the attorney general.

Using a log he had kept of everyone who had called or written him about the JOA, Kelly set about assembling a new group of opponents. He and his staff started making calls. By Sunday, August 14, about forty people had said they would stand with Kelly, many of them employees of the newspapers. At the same time, Kelly was scrounging for legal help. Though a lawyer himself, he didn't have the experience to mount an effective challenge. Nor did he have the money to hire a first-rate antitrust attorney.

For the moment he settled for Matt Beer, a friend studying at Detroit College of Law. Beer was a thirty-five-year-old ex-reporter who had worked at the *News*, *Detroit Monthly* magazine, and the *National Enquirer*, the latter for just four weeks. His father was a retired judge and semifamous bigamist who for thirty years secretly had kept two families. The younger Beer had gained his own notoriety writing "Yours Truly," a puckish gossip column that regularly skewered Detroit celebrities. Just before he left the *News* for *Detroit Monthly* in 1986, Beer raised a stink with a showcase story about a bar where men amused themselves by using water-filled tommy guns to wet the panties of female dancers. Executive editor Bob Giles wrote a public apology after scores of readers sent angry letters. After "Rambo Wet Panty Night," few *News* editors missed Matt Beer.

Beer shared Kelly's mistrust of the JOA, as well as an almost visceral dislike of Dave Lawrence. To Beer, a lifelong *Free Press* reader, Lawrence had ruined the paper with his commitment to "completeness," which Beer thought had dulled the sharp journalistic edge Derick Daniels and Kurt Luedtke had honed. Beer also thought Lawrence's outrageous JOA campaign was unbecoming a respectable journalist, even to one who, like Beer, had spent much of his time in the profession dealing in rumor and innuendo.

On the weekend of Saturday, August 13, Beer plunged into research of the Newspaper Preservation Act while John Kelly went off to Army Reserve drills in western Michigan. From there Kelly put in a call to Stephen Barnett, a law professor at the University of California at Berkeley. Barnett had made a cottage industry of writing, always critically, about the Newspaper Preservation Act; Kelly had noticed his name in *Free Press* and *News* stories. Barnett wasn't interested in joining the JOA fight, but he urged Kelly to approach Public Citizen, a nonprofit organization founded by Ralph Nader. The Washington outfit regularly tangled with big business and big government in the name of protecting the average American consumer. It had lawyers for hire at attractively low rates—free, in fact. Barnett had heard Public Citizen might be interested in the Detroit JOA.

In fact, Barnett recently had spoken with someone else trying to fashion a new anti-JOA force—Guild Local 22 president Lou Mleczko. Although Mleczko's dramatic about-face had removed the Guild from the fight, Mleczko personally could not give it up. Publicly he adhered to the Guild's neutral stance; privately he toiled to defeat the JOA. For Mleczko, it had become a holy crusade. He called on Nader, whom he knew from the early 1970s, when Mleczko was the *News*'s hell-raising consumer reporter and Nader's nascent Public Citizen was giving corporate America fits with exposés of unsafe cars and other products. In 1988 Nader wasn't as visible, but his nonprofit advocacy group had its pesky fingers in nearly every issue affecting Americans' lives, from pesticides to prescription drugs. Nader listened to Mleczko's plea and referred him to a lawyer named William Schultz.

Bill Schultz worked for the Public Citizen Litigation Group, the legal arm of Public Citizen. He was a youthful-looking man of forty who had litigated many a case concerning the safety of food and drugs. As an undergrad at Yale, Schultz had admired Nader from afar as someone who fought injustice but did so within the system. While clerking for a federal judge in Washington in 1975, he heard of the Public Citizen Litigation Group and called for an interview. The group could offer no more than eleven thousand dollars a year in salary, but its docket was crammed with fascinating cases. Schultz took the job. By 1988 he probably could have gone to one of Washington's prestigious private firms and made three or four times the fifty-five thousand a year he was making. He never gave it much thought. Schultz had traded wealth for interesting cases and the option of wearing blue jeans to work.

When Mleczko called, the lawyer was interested in the JOA, but he explained that, for Public Citizen to get involved, the case had to encompass some broad legal or public policy issue. Mleczko promised to send materials he hoped Schultz would find persuasive.

When Schultz sat down with the inch-thick stack of paper Mleczko express-mailed him, he was instantly enthralled. The newspaper war was fascinating. Judge Needelman's analysis was penetrating and, Schultz thought, correct. Inexplicably, Meese had disagreed in what Schultz thought was a remarkably thin and poorly reasoned opinion. How in the world, the lawyer wondered, could Meese have accepted *all* of Needelman's factual findings and come to the opposite conclusion? Schultz thought the case was likely to focus on how much deference the courts should give an agency decision maker such as Meese, a legal conundrum that regularly confronted Schultz and his Public Citizen colleagues in the D.C. Circuit Court of Appeals.

On the afternoon of Sunday, August 14, Schultz was working in his drab seventh-floor office at Public Citizen's Washington headquarters when another stranger called, this one going by the name of John Kelly. Schultz told him he was interested in the JOA but needed to do more research before committing to working against it. In his heart, though, Schultz already was on the case. Later that day he called his friend and fellow Public Citizen lawyer David Vladeck, who was visiting his mother's summer cottage in upstate New York. "I've got a great case for you to work on," Schultz said. "Do you have time?" Vladeck knew Schultz well enough to know that if Schultz said it was a good case, it was a good case.

On Monday, Schultz and Vladeck told Mleczko, Kelly, and Beer they would charge no fees, but Public Citizen would gladly accept donations. They had a lot of work to do.

First order of business was getting a temporary restraining order, to halt the actual merger of the JOA while the opponents appealed Meese's decision in federal court. To get a TRO, Schultz and Vladeck would have to show that someone would be "irreparably injured" by the merger, meaning the lawsuit needed Michigan plaintiffs, real people who could testify that the JOA would harm them. Mleczko mentioned one W. Edward Wendover, a suburban publisher who had said some unkind things about the JOA. There would have to be affidavits, signed by whatever plaintiffs could be found. There would have to be a legal brief. And it all would have to be ready, Schultz figured, by Tuesday morning.

They had twenty-four hours.

In the Sunday paper, the *News* had run an item saying Public Citizen was mulling a challenge of the JOA. "It's too early to tell what we'll do," Bill Schultz was quoted as saying. Appropriately, the item topped the gossip column, formerly written by Matt Beer, "Yours Truly."

The news didn't faze Bill Keating. The chief executive of the Detroit Newspaper Agency was a lawyer as well and, in his mind, no attorney worth his wing tips could believe a challenge had any chance of succeeding. Indeed, no new opponent could even be *allowed* to sue. In Keating's mind, every constituency that could be affected by the JOA—the public, advertisers, employees, shareholders—already had been represented in one fashion or another by the companies, the unions, and Mayor Young. Besides, Keating told himself, Meese was right.

Keating let the Knight-Ridder and Gannett lawyers worry about it. He was busy enough preparing for the merger of the circulation, advertising, production, and promotional operations of the *Free Press* and the *News*. When midnight struck to end Wednesday, August 17, Knight-Ridder and Gannett would sign papers that would officially launch a joint operating agency in Detroit for one hundred years. And the *Free Press* and the *News* could start making money for the first time in nearly a decade.

For Keating and his lieutenants at the newspapers, the week since Meese's decision had been a dizzying whirl of eighteen-hour workdays. The birth of the Detroit Newspaper Agency was a monumentally complex task, and ten days of labor wasn't nearly enough time to accomplish it perfectly. Keating's goal was to have the new organization in place, get unions signed to new contracts, and have people ready to get newspapers where they had to go when they were supposed to be there.

The day after Meese released his decision, Al Neuharth and Alvah Chapman came to Detroit to announce who would help Keating run the DNA. When Neuharth saw Chapman, he pumped his old rival's hand and said, "You're the first guy I know who's happy about having a fishing vacation interrupted." They named as Keating's two top deputies *News* publisher Chip Weil, to manage marketing and advertising, and *Free Press* general manager Bob Hall, to oversee circulation. *News* veterans were pegged to fill four of the six vice-president slots, including the crucial posts in circulation and advertising. Already, it seemed, Gannett was exploiting its 3–2 control of the DNA management committee.

Jubilation mixed with wariness at a joint press conference to announce the appointments. When Dave Lawrence was asked how the *Free Press* news pages might improve under the JOA, he shot back, "We're not about to tell the *Detroit News* what we're going to do." Weil, looking flustered, blurted, "We're going to tell the same thing. We're not going to tell the *Free Press* what we're going to do." Everyone chuckled uneasily.

Labor negotiations began immediately. The unions were hungry for more money; they hadn't had a contractual raise in more than two years, and they wanted retroactive pay. The publishers were more interested in discussing how to get more workers off the payroll. Still more buyouts and early-retirement plans were put on the table. Keating talked optimistically about having agreements before the launch, though he knew the Teamsters' Elton Schade would probably negotiate until the last possible moments. Keating had to have the Teamsters if the JOA launch was to succeed, because his biggest headache would be getting papers delivered on time. The first day of the JOA, hundreds of drivers would suddenly be faced with unfamiliar routes. Newspaper carriers, who answered to Teamster district managers, would grapple with new schedules and routes, due mostly to the joint editions on Saturdays and Sundays. Printing schedules would change, especially for the *News*, jeopardizing timely delivery.

It wasn't the only logistical challenge facing Keating and the Detroit Newspaper Agency. Circulation staffers were moving from the *News* building to the *Free Press,* while advertising staff shifted in the opposite direction. Additional phone lines were needed to answer customer queries. Dozens of managers had to be trained. New DNA stationery was needed. Salary and benefit schedules were being reworked. A television commercial had to be shot, launching a million-dollar ad campaign. Deeds, warranties, contracts, and other legal papers were being readied for transfer from the newspapers and their parent companies to the DNA. Ad rate cards had to be redone—but couldn't be until the JOA was in place, because antitrust laws barred the papers from sharing rate data until then. The DNA didn't wait for the actual launch to announce new newsstand prices: The *Free Press* and the *News* would go up a nickel each daily, to twenty-five and twenty cents, while the joint Saturday edition would be twenty-five cents and the joint Sunday paper a dollar. New prices meant thousands of coin boxes had to be adjusted.

For all the planning that had been done over the past two and a half years, no one was certain how the launch would proceed. "What struck me," one *Free Press* executive later said, "was all the questions being asked that nobody had answers to." There had been dozens of meetings, reams of plans and schedules produced, but much of it was intangible—"blue-sky planning," as one *News* executive put it. The planners had no dry delivery runs or actual rate cards to go on. Even studies of JOAs in other cities were of limited use, because none were as big as the Detroit merger. Remarkably, there had been little serious thought given to how two groups of longtime rivals would be taught to work productively together, let alone get along. There were plans to have "DNA" coffee cups made up, but otherwise the publishers seemed to assume that workers would warm naturally to their new employer since for the first time in years they would actually be succeeding in the marketplace.

For now, though, hundreds of workers had to be told whether they would have a job, whom they would work for, what their duties would be, and how much they would be paid. If there was any thought of waiting until the JOA was in place to make such wrenching changes in people's lives, it was dismissed. Keating wanted to start the JOA completely fresh, without lingering reminders of the past. Besides, keeping unneeded people would be costly. No one, least of all Keating, gave much thought to the possibility that the JOA would be halted before it came together. No one believed—or wanted to believe—it could happen.

Someone brought it up in a managers' meeting run by Keating that Sunday. Most of them had seen the item in "Yours Truly." One of them asked whether it was wise to plan on implementing the JOA while the prospect of a court challenge loomed. The questioner alluded to Seattle, where a group of citizens successfully had halted the JOA with a federal court action. Keating, recalled one executive who was present, set his hands firmly on the table and stared straight ahead, as if the person who had asked the question weren't there. He wore a determined frown and his eyes were flat behind thick bifocals. "Nothing's going to stop us," he declared.

While Kelly, Mleczko, and Schultz conferred, the layoffs began. *News* and *Free Press* employees were called into one-on-one meetings where they learned what kind of future they had, if any, with the Detroit Newspaper Agency. Outside, ambulances waited for potential victims of shock or heart attacks. The payroll had to be trimmed by five hundred. A few hundred had previously been pared through attrition or early retirement. As it would turn out, fewer than fifty would be asked to leave involuntarily. Many others, however, were forced to choose between a job they did not want and unemployment, with severance pay. And the DNA wanted their answers almost immediately.

The meetings were brutally efficient. There was little time for consolation or explanation. Workers waited in line to go into an office where a manager from the *News* or the *Free Press* waited behind a desk. Fifteen minutes later they emerged with their lives rearranged. Joe Grech was one of the newsbearers. "It was a day I'll never forget," recalled the *Free Press*'s assistant retail advertising manager. "If they could have shot the messenger, I would have been shot a lot of times that day."

For some, there was good news—a job they would enjoy, a higher salary, a promotion. For others, there was just relief at knowing they would continue to get a weekly paycheck. Some had to accept jobs for which they felt overqualified. Some had to swallow their pride to work for their counterpart at the other paper. It wasn't easy to be told you weren't considered as good as the person you had competed against for years.

Even the lucky ones suffered watching close friends and coworkers struggle with the notion of being unwanted. "It was like a concentration camp where you watch your friends executed," said Anne Kilgore, an advertising layout clerk. For the unlucky, there was no job, just instructions to clean out their desks. As generous as the severance package was, it could not fully cushion the blow of being abruptly cut off from a way of life. The Great Detroit Newspaper War was over. Before these sad days, that had been merely an idea; now it was reality, hard and unbending. This was life in the real world of newspapering, outside the fantastic realm where newspapers lost thirty-five thousand dollars a day and kept publishing.

They had fought the good fight for so many years, and now, in fifteen minutes, it was over. Some reacted with anger, some with tears, some with the brave stoicism of soldiers who knew they had outlived their usefulness. A few, the older employees ready to retire and the youngest ones eager to try something new, welcomed the end.

At least the uncertainty finally was behind them. For twenty-eight months the JOA had been holding up their lives. Especially at the *Free Press,* people had put off buying homes and cars, getting married, refurbishing their houses, committing to anything that required the certain knowledge that they would be employed. At least now they knew what tomorrow, if not the more distant future, would hold. At least now they could get on with their lives—unless, of course, John Kelly and his friends at Public Citizen succeeded in their quixotic quest.

Four stories over the quaint burg of Plymouth, Michigan, William Edward Wendover paced the plank-board deck outside his loft apartment, a long-necked bottle of Rolling Rock beer in one hand and a portable phone pressed to his ear with the other. He was listening to a Washington lawyer named Schultz, who was trying to talk Wendover into joining a group planning to try to stop the JOA. Wendover was a tall, gangly man in faded blue jeans, balding on top, with longish locks on the sides and a bushy walnut beard. At forty, he still looked like the hippie he had been at twenty-one, except that now he was a businessman, father, and respected citizen of Plymouth, a small suburb twenty miles west of Detroit. His business—and passion—was newspapers.

Ed Wendover published the Plymouth-Canton *Community Crier,* a tabloid weekly with a circulation of about 20,000. In its cramped, disheveled offices, the *Crier* bravely chronicled the doings of the twin communities of Plymouth and Canton Township, from high school soccer to fiftieth wedding anniversaries to the machinations of the local zoning board. When the post office couldn't pass a safety inspection, the *Crier* ignored local officials' pleas for silence and reported it. A *Crier* reporter went undercover to find out if a new massage parlor in town was selling sex, and came back with a story that the going price for fellatio was fifty dollars. When the mayor buried his family dog in the public cemetery at taxpayer expense, Wendover published a story even after the mayor, a good friend, begged him not to. For a while the *Crier* published a regular column critiquing local school lunches—until the schools started withholding menus.

Wendover himself never shied from slapping hometown officials and politicians, people he regularly bumped into, in editorials and his regular column, "With Malice Toward None." As the title suggested, it was nothing personal; the gregarious Wendover was known to share an occasional pitcher of beer with the very people who were skewered regularly in the pages of the *Crier*. He was a sixties-style hell-raiser who was content to protest within the system. As a young man, Wendover had sent his draft board letters critical of the Vietnam War printed on ungainly cement blocks and sheets of plywood, knowing the agency had to save all correspondence, no matter the form. Now and then he would call the board, collect, from wherever he happened to be, like, for example, a pay phone in an underground cave in Kentucky. "Of course they would refuse the calls, but it bugged the shit out of them," Wendover boasted. Summoned for a physical exam prior to induction in the military, he showed up in a tiger costume, playing "Alice's Restaurant" on a kazoo. When the sergeant demanded why he was wearing the outfit, Wendover innocently replied, "What?" "You're out of here," the sergeant growled back, ruling Wendover undesirable.

Knight-Ridder experienced Wendover's brand of citizen activism at the annual shareholders meeting in April of 1987. He showed up in a dark blue suit and dress shoes without socks. While directors, executives, and shareholders mingled at the premeeting coffee, Wendover passed out fliers urging them to STOP THE JOA!!! The flier made a pocketbook appeal, suggesting that Knight-Ridder might be better off trying to win in Detroit rather than settling for half the profits. "Perhaps the short-term, safe buck has risen above long-term profit and social responsibility on management's priority list," the flier said. Wendover probably would have been asked to leave had he not owned ten shares of Knight-Ridder stock.

Wendover's investment in Knight-Ridder was the least of his concerns with the JOA. Though he ran a small business, he considered himself above all a journalist, and he instinctively disliked the idea of newspapers joining forces, however limited the merger. As a businessman, Wendover thought it unfair that two companies would be granted, in effect, an exclusive franchise of the Detroit market—for *one hundred years,* no less. If one paper truly could not survive, then its demise might allow other voices to replace it—perhaps not in quite the same form, but as viable, evolving substitutes nonetheless, he thought. Actually, though, Wendover believed Detroit could support both dailies. The *Free Press*'s claim to be "failing," he felt, was belied by its gains on the *News* in the 1970s and early 1980s. If either paper was in trouble, Wendover thought, it was the *News.* Still, he agreed with Judge Needelman's assessment that both papers could be modestly profitable if they simply raised prices a bit.

Like John Kelly, Wendover had expressed his reservations with the JOA early on, in a May 1986 letter to Alvah Chapman. Chapman's two-sentence response suggested Wendover review the JOA application, where, Chapman wrote, "I believe you will find the answers to all of your questions." The condescending reply did not sit well with Wendover, who thought he deserved more respect from a fellow newspaperman. He sought the government's permission to participate in the JOA hearing but, like Kelly, was denied. Occasionally the *Free Press* or the *News* quoted him as one of several local "critics" of the JOA, but Wendover knew the observations of an outsider meant little. All he really could do was watch and stew.

Until Bill Schultz called. Schultz offered a chance to finally *do* something. At first Wendover balked. What were the chances, after all, that this juggernaut could be stopped? Not good, Schultz told him—but the odds would be better if Wendover signed up as a plaintiff. After all, he was a competing publisher who could demonstrate that he would be hurt by the JOA. Wendover wasn't certain of that, though. One could argue that the JOA would *help* small publishers, because when the Detroit papers raised their prices, everyone could follow. On the other hand, the *Free Press* and the *News* could use their market power to soak up the area's finite pool of advertising dollars, thus depriving smaller competitors of revenue they needed to survive.

Wendover was more concerned that he couldn't afford a public legal fight. He worried that it would spur a backlash among the conservative people of Plymouth and Canton. They subscribed to the *Free Press* and the *News,* and they might wonder why Wendover would take action that could deprive them of one of their papers. Neither did he have a lot of time to spend on this quixotic challenge. Like most small-town publishers, Wendover did just about everything at the *Crier,* from writing stories to laying out pages to taking the occasional classified ad over the phone. The *Crier* was hardly coasting. Wendover's company earned 5 to 10 percent a year on about a million dollars in revenue, but most if not all of the profit came from outside printing jobs rather than the newspaper.

Wendover also had friends in the newspapering community who

might not appreciate his getting involved. Indeed, he was on the Michigan Press Association board of directors, which had not taken an official stance on the JOA. He didn't know anything about filing lawsuits in federal court. He didn't know John Kelly. Bill Schultz was just a voice on the phone.

Wendover paced his deck on that warm autumn evening, listening to Schultz, wanting to be convinced. He hung up without giving Schultz an answer and called his mother. She told her son that his late father, a man Wendover had admired, would have done what his son was considering doing. Wendover's father had been an engineer, not a journalist, but that wasn't the point. The point was whether it was the right thing to do.

It was right for Ed Wendover. He called Schultz back to tell him he was in—so long as Schultz had no problem with Wendover keeping Chip Weil and Dave Lawrence informed of the group's intentions. He felt he owed his publishing colleagues at least that professional courtesy.

On Tuesday, August 16, a group calling itself Michigan Citizens for an Independent Press filed suit in the U.S. District Court in Washington, D.C., to overturn the approval of the Detroit JOA. The defendant was Attorney General Richard Thornburgh, the former Pennsylvania governor who had replaced Meese. The plaintiffs were John Kelly, Matt Beer, Ed Wendover, two minor advertisers, a former *News* employee and neighborhood newspaper publisher, and a part-time *Free Press* printer who stood to lose his job. That morning, Wendover called Weil and Lawrence. Weil told him he had expected a challenge. Lawrence was unavailable, so Wendover left a message. When Lawrence returned the call, the first thing he said was, "You're going to kill the fucking paper." Wendover was offended—after all, it would be Knight-Ridder's decision to close the *Free Press*, not his—but all he said was he was sorry Lawrence felt the way he did.

The case was assigned to U.S. District Judge George Revercomb, who was on vacation. Judge Joyce Hens Green, standing in for Revercomb, scheduled a hearing for 10:00 A.M. Wednesday, August 17—just fourteen hours before the JOA was to take effect. Public Citizen lawyers Bill Schultz and Dave Vladeck were the only representatives of Michigan Citizens for an Independent Press in Judge Green's courtroom that morning. Kelly, Beer, and Wendover, the president, secretary, and vice-president of the group, waited anxiously in Detroit. They probably could have afforded five-hundred-dollar flights to Washington, but they didn't want to spend the money for what they figured was a long shot.

Sitting at Judge Green's left, the short, compact Schultz and tall, gangly Vladeck were the Mutt and Jeff of the courtroom. And they were psyched up. They had been running on adrenaline for three days, preparing. They were up against two of Washington's best-known lawyers, Clark Clifford and Philip Lacovara. Yet they felt good about their chances. And they knew that, win or lose, they would have a decision in a few hours.

Schultz and Vladeck had to persuade Judge Green of two things: that their clients would suffer "irreparable injury" if the JOA was assembled, and that they had a fair chance of ultimately winning their appeal. In a twenty-three-page brief, they noted that the publishers already had announced their intention to hike prices. Also, once the JOA went together, hundreds of employees would lose jobs and readers would have to settle for joint weekend editions instead of separate products. Even if Knight-Ridder was serious about closing the *Free Press,* which the lawyers doubted, it surely wouldn't snuff the paper before its legal options were exhausted.

Just before the hearing began, Lacovara approached Schultz and handed him a sheaf of papers. Scanning it quickly, Schultz saw it was an order by a Detroit judge barring David Kersh, one of Schultz's seven plaintiffs, from suing federal officials. Kersh, it turned out, was a litigious fellow who had worn out his welcome in Detroit's courts. It was news to Schultz. Oh, shit, he thought. It was not the best way to start. Schultz thought it classy of Lacovara to show him the document, but it also was a reminder of the formidable resources arrayed against the Public Citizen lawyers. Lacovara's legal team had unearthed the obscure document in less than a day.

Judge Green was a fifty-nine-year-old Carter appointee known as a champion of individual rights and affirmative action. In the past twelve hours she had read the Michigan Citizens brief and two from Knight-Ridder. Now she wanted a smooth proceeding because she had to leave soon for a funeral. Green summoned Schultz first to argue what she called "a most interesting matter."

Schultz's nineteen-minute argument focused on the apparent conflict between Meese's decision and his acceptance of Judge Needelman's findings of fact. Schultz also alluded to the critical assessments of the JOA by the Antitrust Division and former Assistant Attorney General Douglas Ginsburg, who now was a judge in the D.C. Circuit Court of Appeals. "The point is," Schultz said, "everybody but the attorney general who reviewed the evidence found that the parties had not made their case that there was a likelihood or that it was probable that, absent approval of the JOA, the [*Free Press*] would fail."

From the phalanx of dark-suited lawyers on the other side of the courtroom, Phil Lacovara stood to speak for the *Free Press.* The barrel-chested attorney was at General Electric now, shuttling between Connecticut and Washington to fulfill his duties as president of the D.C. Bar. Since his departure from Hughes Hubbard and Reed, two other Washington partners, Cal Collier and Peter Kreindler, had left to take corporate jobs, and eleven other lawyers were preparing to defect to another Washington firm. Lacovara hadn't had much to do with the JOA of late, but Jack Fontaine, Knight-Ridder's top lawyer, had asked him to argue today. Though Clark Clifford was now the chief JOA legal strategist, he hadn't argued a case in court in years. Lacovara still knew the JOA matter better than anyone, and he was familiar to the judges of the D.C. District Court. Besides, the lawyers for Knight-Ridder and Gannett expected to win easily.

Lacovara began with a plea for mercy.

"The two-year delay has been a very wrenching experience," he said, "not just a financially troubled period for these two papers, during which they've lost perhaps another forty-five or fifty million dollars. This has been an extremely troubling experience for the people of Detroit, not just the employees of the paper, and the people in the entire Michigan community." Those people, Lacovara said, wanted Green "to remove the uncertainty under which these employees as well as the papers have been suffering."

One by one, Lacovara questioned the opponents' claims that the JOA would hurt them. He pointed out that one plaintiff, a furniture store operator, had not signed his affidavit and was quoted in that day's *News* as denying involvement in the appeal. Another, Kersh, who published an entertainment passbook, apparently ran ads only at Christmas. The part-time printer in danger of losing his job belonged to a union that now supported the JOA. A five-cent increase in the price of the papers, Lacovara argued, wasn't big enough to hurt anyone. Besides, Judge Needelman himself had said the papers could become profitable only by raising prices.

Judge Green asked a few questions. None hinted strongly which way she was leaning. Schultz and Vladeck were more encouraged that she asked how future court proceedings might be scheduled. She warned the lawyers not to call her office, lest they interrupt the preparation of her decision. "Have your runners ready," she said. "It is going to be, undoubtedly, the very last part of the afternoon or into the evening before this will be out."

She called a recess at 11:12 A.M.

Bob Giles and Chip Weil strode side by side through the newsroom of the *Detroit News*, wearing the broad grins of Cheshire cats. They were smiling because, less than five hours before the JOA was to begin, Judge Joyce Hens Green had called a halt.

At 7:15 P.M. Green issued a temporary restraining order barring the newspapers from merging their business operations until September 17; meanwhile, Judge George Revercomb would take it up at a hearing scheduled for September 8. Green's tough, twenty-two-page opinion said it appeared that Meese's approval of the JOA had been "arbitrary and capricious," unsupported by the evidence, and contrary to law. The publishers might prove otherwise when the court took a more thorough look, she said, but for now, "it will be very difficult to reassemble this egg once it has been scrambled."

The news spread quickly, first through the *News* and *Free Press* buildings, then through the local pubs where scores of employees were attending farewell parties. Workers who had cleaned out their desks that afternoon suddenly faced returning to work in the morning. Some cheered, some groaned, some threw up their hands in bewilderment. "I made the hardest decision of my life when I retired," said Jack Millard, a *News* classified advertising manager. "Now they're telling me it doesn't matter." Philip LaPorte, a *Free Press* ad manager, had laid off eight fellow workers that day. "This has been the worst day of my life," he moaned, "and now they do this." John Walls, an operating engineer who had kept his job, directed his anger at Kelly. "I think John Kelly ought to be on the end of my size 9s," he said. "They've been messing with people for two and a half years and now they're going to mess with them some more? People have been crying when they walk out of this building. Now they're going to cry again."

Ed Wendover wasn't crying. Within minutes of the ruling he was getting calls from people wanting to join the nascent Michigan Citizens for an Independent Press. Matt Beer, who had been studying, returned home to a jangling telephone. It was John Kelly.

"It's over," Kelly announced.

Beer felt a tinge of disappointment. "Well," he said, "at least we tried—"

"No, no, no," Kelly interrupted. "The *JOA* is over." Beer flicked on his television. The first thing he saw was Dave Lawrence's anguished face. Beer couldn't help but laugh. He laughed at the absurdity of what was happening, at the impossible thing he and a bunch of ragtag strangers had accomplished against the two largest newspaper companies in America. Most of the "Michigan Citizens" had never even met. Their campaign had been conducted almost entirely by telephone and fax machine.

Amazingly, the *Free Press* and the *News* had no contingency plan for a court-ordered halt. Both papers had to scramble to sell advertising and prepare news material for separate weekend papers. Union contract negotiations abruptly ended. Readers flooded the *Free Press* and the *News* with calls to ask what the papers would cost and when they would be delivered. Some just canceled subscriptions in frustration. "I've taken more stops than I can count over the past few days," one customer service clerk told reporters.

The *Free Press* went into shock. The demon of uncertainty, seemingly banished by Ed Meese, was back. "It was a terrible moment," Lawrence later said, "one of the very worst I ever lived through." He and Bob Hall decided not to call workers back until morning. "After what all these employees have gone through," Hall told reporters, "a phone call at home tonight would not be the best thing." Alvah Chapman, who had resumed his Bahamian boating vacation, was returning from some night fishing when Jim Batten radioed with the news. "It was a body blow," Chapman later said. The lawyers had let him down again.

There was little such anguish at the *News.* When Chip Weil heard about Judge Green's ruling, he thought, I've got a new lease on life. He immediately called *News* security. "You've got to keep all the *Free Press* people out of this building," Weil happily ordered, "because this thing's been turned down." Bob Giles was equally delighted. Now the *News* might have a chance to win the war outright after all. He was mildly amused when his own paper mistakenly quoted him, instead of Lou Mleczko, as saying he was "getting some measure of satisfaction out of this." The quote was only technically inaccurate. Weil ordered employees back to work immediately. "We're back in business," he told the staff. "Let's go out and kill the *Free Press.*"

Weil didn't mean it literally, but when Bob Hall saw the quote Thursday in the *News,* he wondered. "*Kill* the *Free Press,* Chip?" he asked at a meeting that morning. "Hey," Weil replied, "this is a competitive world and we are now great competitors." Later, Dave Lawrence made a point of telling Weil, "I would never knowingly hurt a competitor." Weil just shrugged. "I guess we're from different schools."

The *Free Press* and the *News* had been just four hours and forty-six minutes from becoming partners for a hundred years. Now their rivalry was beginning to look more bitter than ever.

19

Jerking Around

"What you did to me and my colleagues this week was cruel," *Free Press* reporter Renee Murawski wrote to John Kelly. "After 28 months of not knowing whether I'd have a job the next week, of not knowing whether I could take an apartment with a year's lease, of not knowing whether any friendship I formed would only come to an end because I'd have to move, I thought my pain and uncertainty were over. You have ensured that they will continue."

Murawski was one of scores of *Free Press* employees and readers who wrote or called to lambaste Kelly in the days following Judge Joyce Hens Green's halt to the JOA. Sixty-two *Free Press* staffers signed a letter urging the state senator to reconsider: "Whether we agree with the JOA or not is, at this point, immaterial. What is important is what this is doing to our lives and the lives of our families." Another wrote, "I must admit it appears that you are only trying to get publicity . . . and in the process you are putting the jobs of many employees on the line." One wondered sarcastically if Kelly was on Gannett's payroll. Yet another asked simply, "How can you sleep at night?"

Matt Beer and Ed Wendover also got their share of angry and profane messages. Beer heard from a few former colleagues and competitors who didn't like him much anyway. Wendover chuckled at the nasty phone calls until his young daughter, Jessica, inadvertently answered one. One night, Vaughn Derderian, a friend of Wendover who ran the Anchor Bar, the watering hole for many *News* and *Free Press* workers, cautioned Wendover against making a planned visit. "An evil wind is blowing through," Derderian warned.

Most critics focused their anger on Kelly, the opposition group's most visible spokesman. They questioned his sanity and his motives. Among the less vulgar terms, they called him heartless, vain, cavalier, mistaken, and misguided. "The beauty of language is, you can express the intensity," Kelly later said. "They expressed it." Kelly did not back down, though; if anything, the attacks firmed his resolve. He wrote combative letters printed in the *Free Press* and the *News* asserting, "I am not a Johnny-come-lately." He threatened shareholder lawsuits, a repeal of the Newspaper Preservation Act, and a public commission to regulate newspaper pricing. "I don't know how to say it without sounding self-promoting," he later said, "but I don't like being pushed around by anybody. It's like a bar fight—either you're going to kick his ass or he is going to kick yours."

Kelly also was getting more publicity than he ever got battling tax hikes or trading insults with fellow legislators. His face and his voice were all over Detroit television and radio, and the *Free Press* ran a big photo of him smiling behind copies of the two Detroit papers. If he minded, it didn't show. "You put a microphone or camera in front of John and his eyes light up," Wendover recalled. A Michigan politician who knew Kelly well later said, "He was having the time of his life." Kelly himself told *News* reporter N. Scott Vance the court challenge was fun.

Besides, Kelly was getting calls and letters from supporters, too. By early September, Michigan Citizens for an Independent Press counted five hundred members. "I don't know you," a *News* employee wrote Kelly, "but I'm so proud and happy there are people like you willing to fight the big guys and their contempt of justice." Dozens of *News* staffers signed petitions in support of Kelly's cause. Some two hundred readers sent preprinted coupons expressing support; the slips had been circulated by *News* carriers who stood to lose weekend routes under the JOA. Another sympathetic writer invoked the Book of Ephesians: "For we wrestle not against flesh and blood, but against principalities, against powers, against the rulers of the darkness of the world, against spiritual wickedness in high places."

Kelly even had sympathizers at the *Free Press*. One was Bill McGraw, one of Detroit's most respected all-purpose reporters. Among McGraw's myriad assignments in eleven years at the *Free Press* were city hall, the federal courts, the Detroit Tigers, and the Detroit Red Wings. He was a friend of Kelly and Matt Beer, and had opposed the JOA from the start. Shortly after Judge Hens Green blocked the merger, McGraw wrote a two-page letter, which he posted on *Free Press* bulletin boards. The letter eventually was signed by twenty-six *Free Press* journalists and published on the editorial pages of both Detroit papers:

> It was not Guild leaders who terminated, bought out and retired hundreds of loyal *Free Press* employees August 17—even though the temporarily approved JOA was endangered by the threat of an appeal. It was not the Guild that called them back to work the next day and told them to keep working until they have to be terminated, bought out or retired again.
>
> It was not John Kelly who launched a pro-JOA public relations campaign last winter that has embarrassed the *Free Press* in journalistic circles across the nation.
>
> It was not Matt Beer who threatened to close the paper if the corporation did not get its way, the kind of corporate behavior that the *Free Press* used to condemn.
>
> It was not Ralph Nader who has refused to give *Free Press* employees a raise for the two years that the JOA has dragged on. . . .
>
> . . . [W]e hope that our colleagues will not allow Knight-Ridder to pit worker against worker while it pursues a policy whose true beneficiaries are not employees, readers or advertisers, but only the coffers of Knight-Ridder and Gannett, the two biggest media conglomerates in America.

The companies had a touch more sensitivity than McGraw's letter allowed. Both were permitting employees who had been involuntarily laid off to leave immediately with their allotted severance pay, if they wished. Still, the letter must have been painful for the bosses at Knight-Ridder and the *Free Press* to read, because so much of it was true.

Kelly and his cohorts got more substantive help from a stranger nine hundred miles away in Little Rock, Arkansas. His name was Walter E. Hussman, Jr., and his newspaper, the *Arkansas Democrat,* was in a bloody war with the *Arkansas Gazette,* owned by Gannett. Hussman called Public Citizen lawyer Dave Vladeck one day in late August to ask how he could aid the cause of Michigan Citizens for an Independent Press. At first Vladeck didn't understand the purpose of Hussman's call, but as the publisher related the story of the competition in Arkansas, the lawyer began to think Little Rock and Detroit weren't far apart, after all.

Hussman, a feisty, wisecracking Arkansan, had worked wonders with the *Democrat* since his family bought it for $3.5 million in 1974. In the late 1970s, the paper was all but dead when Hussman went hat in hand to the rival *Gazette* looking for a JOA. The *Gazette*'s owners at the time, the Patterson family, declined, figuring Hussman's paper wasn't worth the trouble. After all, the Pattersons' *Gazette* had about 80 percent of the market's ad revenue, more than twice the *Democrat*'s daily circulation of 55,000, and a healthy circulation lead on Sundays.

But Hussman, a kindred spirit of the *News*'s Bulldog Bob Nelson, would not surrender. "It was a matter of pride," he later told the *New York Times*. "I couldn't deal with the prospect of losing." He switched the *Democrat* to morning publication, slashed prices, started printing color, expanded news staff and space, and began offering free classifieds. He offered cut-rate deals to his four biggest advertisers. It was crazy and it was costly—the *Democrat* lost nearly $20 million after taxes between 1974 and 1984—but it worked. Hussman's *Democrat* made steady gains on the *Gazette,* which countered with an antitrust suit charging Hussman with predatory pricing. The *Gazette* lost the case in 1986 and promptly sold out to Gannett for $51 million.

Gannett thundered into Little Rock vowing to spend the money necessary to win the war. Al Neuharth had no interest in a JOA or the diversity it supposedly would preserve; Gannett fully intended to vanquish this opponent and collect the spoils. Gannett's *Gazette* immediately matched *Democrat* price discounts and offered free classifieds. Gannett paid for more staff, a bigger newshole, new bureaus, and new presses and mail room equipment. The paper changed dramatically. The *Gazette* had long been Little Rock's version of the *Detroit News,* an unfussy paper of record that had won two Pulitzers for coverage of the Little Rock school desegregation crisis of 1957. Gannett applied its tried-and-true formula, adding color and new sections, shortening stories, putting softer features on page 1, and lessening the emphasis on hard news. Some Arkansans wondered if the *Gazette* would alienate traditional readers while seeking a wider, younger audience.

By the summer of 1988, Gannett's *Gazette* led Hussman's *Democrat* by 37,000 copies on weekdays and nearly 15,000 on Sundays. Both papers were losing millions of dollars a year. Gannett drew on the profits of its other papers, billboard operations, and TV and radio stations; as Peter Clark had with the Evening News Association, Hussman siphoned profits from his company's handful of other little dailies and cable TV properties.

Gannett turned up the heat on August 14—the Sunday following Attorney General Edwin Meese's approval of the Detroit JOA. A front-page item by *Gazette* publisher William T. Malone told readers the paid-in-advance home-delivery price of the paper would be cut by an astonishing 57 percent—to eighty-five cents a week, or about twelve cents a day. Malone said the cut was to make the *Gazette* "more competitive in this most competitive newspaper state and to give our readers some good news as inflation seems to be creeping upward again." It may have been the first time in history that a publisher *reduced* prices because of inflation.

Hussman saw it as a naked ploy to take the Detroit strategy southward. It appeared that Gannett, believing the Detroit matter settled, now planned to focus on eliminating competition in Little Rock. As it had in Detroit, that meant slashing prices to increase its rival's losses until the rival either succumbed or acquiesced to a Gannett-run JOA. Except that, in Little Rock, Gannett had no interest in a JOA, and neither did Hussman. The fight would be to the death.

Against such a formidable foe, Hussman had to use everything at his disposal to survive. Which is why he called Dave Vladeck. So long as the *News* and *Free Press* remained enemies, Gannett had fewer dollars and management hours to devote to the battle at Little Rock. Hussman also was concerned that Meese's approval of the JOA effectively sanctioned the bleed-your-rival tactics Gannett was using in Little Rock and that Hussman felt were predatory and, perhaps, illegal. If stopping Gannett meant fighting a piece of the Little Rock battle in a Washington courtroom, that was fine with Walter Hussman. "It was a way of shooting back," he recalled.

Vladeck was intrigued. The involvement of the *Arkansas Democrat* would suggest to the court—and, more important, higher courts—that the JOA had implications beyond Detroit. He suggested that Hussman file a friend-of-the-court brief.

The *Democrat*'s nine-page *amicus* brief argued that Meese's opinion, if upheld by the courts, would "provide a blueprint for eliminating competition in all remaining two-newspaper towns, including Little Rock." Further, "A dominant newspaper owned by a chain with a deep pocket can always force its rival into unprofitability." Congress, the *Democrat* said, "did not intend the Newspaper Preservation Act to reward this type of conduct."

Gannett's scornful, seven-page reply countered that Hussman's only consistent position seemed to be that aggressive pricing was acceptable so long as he was the only one engaging in it. The *Gazette*'s 57 percent circulation price cut, for example, had simply brought Gannett's paper in line with Hussman's *Democrat*. Hussman himself had plumbed the "deep pocket" of his other properties to force the Patterson family, which had owned only the *Gazette*, out of Little Rock, Gannett said. If Hussman truly felt Gannett was pricing illegally, he could file a predatory-pricing lawsuit, to which Gannett would be "eager" to respond. However, Gannett maintained, Hussman's complaints were irrelevant to the Detroit case.

Judge George Revercomb disagreed, allowing the *Arkansas Democrat* to participate in the JOA case. For Walter Hussman, it was but a small step toward the much larger victory he would eventually win over Gannett in Little Rock.

The voice on the other end of Bill Schultz's line was a sonorous baritone. "Hello, Mr. Schultz," it said. "My name is Clark Clifford. I'm a lawyer here in town."

Clifford said he was phoning as a courtesy. He had once practiced in St. Louis, he said, where it was customary for opposing counsel to make such a call before a case began.

In a few days, Clifford and Schultz would confront each other before U.S. District Judge George Revercomb. Now, though, Schultz couldn't help but smile. He hadn't even been born when Clifford was practicing in St. Louis. And it was almost comical to think of Clifford as just another "lawyer in town." If any other high-powered Washington attorney had introduced himself that way, Schultz would have considered it false modesty. But with this elegant old man, counsel to four presidents, there was something charming about it. The men had a friendly chat, Clifford asking a lot of innocuous questions about court procedure. Of course the crafty old lawyer had his own associates to answer such questions; he obviously was trying to feel out his opponent.

Clifford now was officially Knight-Ridder's lead JOA lawyer. After the loss before Judge Hens Green, Phil Lacovara and Jack Fontaine had agreed it would be best if Lacovara removed himself altogether. "We had been thinking about it," Fontaine recalled. "The outcome of the [temporary restraining order] certainly pushed us over the edge."

Shortly before 9:00 A.M. on September 8, Clifford alighted from a limousine in front of the U.S. District Court on Constitution Avenue, smiling for TV cameras whirring in the cool sunlight, looking deeper in a gray double-breasted suit and charcoal fedora. In the courtroom he moved among the other lawyers and executives, shaking hands and introducing himself to people he hadn't met. "Hi, Clark," said Gannett lawyer Larry Aldrich. "Hello, Mr. Aldrich," Clifford deferred. He sat at the head of the long table to Judge Revercomb's right, with his partner Robert Altman, Gerald Goldman of Hughes

Hubbard and Reed, and the Justice Department's Thomas Millet. Sitting around them was a coterie of Knight-Ridder and Gannett executives and lawyers, including Alvah Chapman, Jim Batten, Doug McCorkindale, and Bill Keating. The entourage spilled over to the other side of the aisle, where Bill Schultz and Dave Vladeck sat lonesomely preparing their notes. Their clients did not attend. The presiding judge, George Revercomb, was a Reagan appointee known among D.C. lawyers to be scholarly, courteous, and fair.

The day before, Revercomb had denied Michigan Citizens' request that Edwin Meese be ordered to answer questions about outside attempts to influence him. Meese submitted an affidavit saying he had not been influenced by letters or other efforts to sway his decision. That was good enough for Revercomb, whose ruling essentially put to rest the question of Meese's decision being affected by Knight-Ridder's public relations campaign. It was a minor setback for Michigan Citizens; Schultz and Vladeck hoped to do better at today's hearing.

They had to show that Meese's decision was "arbitrary and capricious"—a heavy burden. It would not suffice for Schultz and Vladeck merely to demonstrate that Judge Needelman's conclusion was preferable to Meese's. The crux was whether Meese had reached a reasonable conclusion, given the facts placed before him. As the publishers repeatedly reminded the court, the attorney general was not bound by law to follow the advice of his administrative law judge or his Antitrust Division. On the contrary, Congress had designated the attorney general as decision maker, and as such he had broad discretion to interpret both the facts and the law. Only if his decision was unreasonable—"arbitrary and capricious," in legal lingo—could the court overturn it.

Schultz told Revercomb that Meese, in his written decision, had an obligation to explain his reasoning as well, especially since he had chosen to accept Needelman's fact findings as accurate but had reached a different conclusion. "What he has to do when he does that is cite evidence in the record that he is relying on and explain how he came to a different conclusion," Schultz said. "Again, he didn't do that." The argument did not go particularly well. Schultz barely had begun when Revercomb started interrupting with questions. Still, Schultz did not sit down thinking he would lose the case. A curious judge wasn't necessarily a hostile judge.

Clark Clifford was next. It was a moment of some drama, because Clifford had not argued a case in court in years. When reporters asked, he smiled and said he couldn't remember the last time he had. "It used to be my life," he told them.

Now the gaunt attorney stood before Revercomb without any notes in hand. On the podium rested a single sheet of paper listing three or four handwritten points. "Good morning, Your Honor," Clifford began. "A rather careful examination of the record indicates that there has been presented to you and placed upon your desk approximately 1,059 pages of material in this case. It occurred to us that possibly that was getting very close to unusual punishment for Your Honor. I would hope to be of some assistance in moving through this plethora of paper. . . ."

Clifford went on for thirty-five minutes, essentially making a speech. He was magnificent. His posture was straight, his voice perfectly modulated, his hands those of a conductor leading a symphony. The judge interrupted just four times, twice merely to make observations with which Clifford happily agreed. Clifford reviewed the law. He recounted the financial straits of the *Free Press*. He reminded Revercomb that Meese had rejected Needelman's conclusion that a paper had to be in a "downward spiral" to be considered failing (though this was only implicit in Meese's brief opinion). He read from Alvah Chapman's hearing testimony about closing the *Free Press*.

It was a simple, elegant argument that a seventh-grader could have understood. "We didn't want to say so publicly, but the fact is, we've lost" the newspaper war, Clifford intoned. "We come now to say we've lost. We are not going on anymore. It's like having a bleeding artery in your foot. We can't stand the losses any longer." When Clifford finished, Chapman and the other Knight-Ridder executives and lawyers quietly exulted. A few felt like applauding. Schultz and Vladeck groused that Revercomb hadn't asked more questions. "It was a bad sign," Vladeck later admitted. "I was disheartened."

He had reason to be. Six days later Revercomb released an eighteen-page decision concluding that Meese was "not unreasonable" to have approved the JOA. Michigan Citizens said it would appeal and asked the Court of Appeals for the D.C. Circuit to again block the merger while the opponents sought to quash it altogether. "This is just the middle innings," Vladeck said. "The ball game isn't over yet."

Knight-Ridder hoped it was. An emergency meeting of Knight-Ridder and Gannett executives and lawyers was called for Thursday, September 15. The *Free Press*'s parent was ready to put the JOA in place as soon as the court allowed.

Unfortunately for Knight-Ridder, Gannett was not.

Until September 15, 1988, Alvah Chapman hadn't harbored the slightest doubt that Gannett would enthusiastically launch the JOA when the time came. He was aware of the saber rattling by Chip Weil and Bob Giles, and the speculation on Wall Street that Gannett would prefer not to have a JOA, but he didn't believe for a minute that Al Neuharth or John Curley would try to back out of the deal. Indeed, when Revercomb released his decision, Neuharth and Curley had issued a statement saying they were "gratified."

Besides, in Chapman's mind, a clause on pages 4 and 5 of the JOA contract made it plain when the merger was to be consummated: the tenth day after either the attorney general gave the nod or after "the removal or elimination of such injunction, restraining order, or other court process" blocking the JOA. In other words, when any legal barriers were lifted. That point was rapidly approaching. The D.C. Circuit Court of Appeals had entered an emergency stay blocking the merger while it considered whether to keep the JOA on hold while Michigan Citizens pursued its appeal. The court was expected to rule any day now on the lengthier stay. Meanwhile, the publishers had to decide when and how they would implement the JOA if, as Knight-Ridder anticipated, the court declined to hold it up any longer.

The lawyers and executives met at Hughes Hubbard and Reed's Washington offices. Al Neuharth, Jim Batten, and Bill Keating couldn't make it, but Chapman, Clark Clifford, John Curley, and Doug McCorkindale were there. Clifford made yet another senatorial oration, urging the publishers to launch the JOA as soon as possible after the stay was lifted. Judge Revercomb's ringing affirmation of Meese was the last word, Clifford said. Curley, an unpretentious veteran of the Associated Press, marveled at Clifford's theatrics, the eyes closed tight, the fingers pressed to the temples. His plea was certainly dramatic, Curley thought, but almost purely emotional. "We were just supposed to defer to Clark," Curley later said. "It was typical Clifford, where he was speaking without doing his research."

The executives looked next to John Stuart Smith. The partner at Nixon, Hargrave, Devans and Doyle, Gannett's outside counsel, was an average-looking man whose most distinguishing attribute was his ever-present fedora. John Smith also was one of the country's most knowledgeable attorneys on the subject of the Newspaper Preservation Act. He and Larry Aldrich had worked side by side with Knight-Ridder's attorneys since the JOA application was filed. They found it occasionally frustrating because they had a good deal more background in such matters than most of Knight-Ridder's lawyers—yet the Gannett attorneys were under orders to defer on most matters of strategy because the onus was on Knight-Ridder to prove the *Free Press* was "failing." That had not been a serious problem because the two camps got along well and hadn't encountered any sharp disagreements.

Now they had one. And Gannett wasn't about to defer.

Chapman and his Knight-Ridder colleagues listened in stunned silence as Smith explained why Gannett was ill-advised to launch the JOA while Michigan Citizens waged its appeal. Smith argued that a JOA, in and of itself, violated the antitrust laws; otherwise there would be no need for the Newspaper Preservation Act. If the Detroit JOA started up only to be nullified later by an appellate court, Knight-Ridder and Gannett would be, for the period during which the JOA operated, in violation of the antitrust laws—and, therefore, liable for costly damages if the Justice Department or an outside party such as a suburban publisher brought an antitrust action. The crucial question was, what were the odds of a court dismantling the JOA once it was in place? Clifford had argued that they were slim. No court, he said, would strike down the JOA after it had been approved by the attorney general and affirmed by a federal court. The complexity of undoing the merger and the harm it could cause the companies, papers, and employees would be discouragement enough.

The argument was plausible, though Clifford had cited no cases to support it. Smith asked Gary Valby, one of his partners at Nixon, Hargrave, to speak. Clifford smiled; this one-two punch obviously had been scripted. In fact, Valby and his staff had found more than twenty cases that, directly or indirectly, contradicted Clifford. In each case, a court had overturned a prior decision and voided some form of business combination that was already in place. The cases weren't precisely analogous—none were JOAs—but they illustrated Smith's point: that Knight-Ridder and Gannett couldn't expect a court to bless the JOA just because it was consummated. Valby started relating his cases one by one. When he had finished with two or three, the annoyed Knight-Ridder lawyers asked that he simply give them the citations.

Chapman said nothing, but he kept clearing his sinuses—a sign that he was uneasy. To him, Gannett's arguments amounted to a lot of legal hair-splitting that ignored the hard reality of the *Free Press* losing forty-five thousand dollars a day. Still, there was no point making an issue of it yet. Curley and McCorkindale hadn't said they definitely wouldn't implement the JOA. It was mostly lawyers making the disagreeable noises, and the lawyers had been wrong so many times by now that Chapman was tuning them out. The meeting concluded with an agreement to put off a decision on implementing the JOA until after the D.C. Circuit Court ruled on the stay. If the stay was granted, the question would be moot. In the meantime, Gannett would leave it to Knight-Ridder to file papers asking the court to remove the stay.

Two days later, Knight-Ridder got a clearer picture of Gannett's intentions. Chapman happened to be in Detroit, attending a reunion of his 401st

Bombardment Group. He woke to a story in the *Detroit News* headlined, 2 PAPERS AT ODDS OVER JOA. It quoted an anonymous Gannett source saying that Gannett would not implement the JOA even if the stay *was* lifted. "We've got to be satisfied that it's a done deal in every respect," the source said. "We are just not going to jerk our workers around and jerk our readers around again." Chapman was livid. Only Neuharth would play this kind of game. He got Curley on the phone. As Chapman recalls it, Curley reassured him that Gannett had reached no such decision. "That's just Al talking," Chapman remembers Curley saying. Curley remembered differently: "We had no intention of going forward until it passed its last hurdle," and Chapman was aware of that, he recalled.

Other evidence suggests Knight-Ridder was caught unaware. Dave Lawrence was quoted in the *Washington Post* as saying that Knight-Ridder intended to launch the JOA "at the first moment that we have the legal wherewithal." Tony Ridder told the *Free Press* that Knight-Ridder "would probably start the JOA" if the stay was lifted. It may have been wishful thinking, but Knight-Ridder was determined to get the JOA started as soon as possible.

Knight-Ridder gave the D.C. Circuit Court of Appeals a bound, 106-page volume of exhibits to go with a 26-page brief arguing that the stay ought to be lifted. Among the exhibits was a 6-page affidavit by one Thomas D. Francek. Francek was a psychologist and mental health therapist who counseled *Free Press* and *News* employees suffering from substance abuse and stress.

Francek's testimony noted a "steady monthly escalation of stress and trauma" among newspaper employees, particularly at the *Free Press*. Counseling had increased to as much as 50 hours a week through early August of 1988, then exploded to more than 150 hours while the papers prepared for the abortive JOA launch. Workers were on a "traumatic roller coaster," Francek wrote. To cope, some were turning increasingly to drugs and alcohol. Domestic violence was on the rise. "In at least one case, a child was thrown into a wall in an incident which in my professional opinion was directly related to abuse of substances, which in turn was related to job stress," he wrote. In an interview with *Free Press* reporter William Mitchell, Francek said, "I've got reports of people using cocaine and marijuana with total disregard for their jobs now, because they've been told they won't have a job." He didn't name names, but his quote narrowed the pool of candidates to the forty or so who had been told they would be laid off.

Employees at the *Free Press* and the *News* were appalled. To them, the Francek affidavit was cynical in the extreme. One *Free Press* staffer, in an in-house newsletter, called it "the most shameless, ill-conceived, and unethical misuse of employee counseling I have ever seen." Employee sessions with Francek and his associates were supposed to be strictly confidential. But here was a public document, reported in both newspapers, testifying to employee drug and alcohol abuse, raising the ugly specter of a child being dashed against a wall! Workers felt violated and exploited. And to what purpose? The ostensible point of the affidavit was that the sooner the JOA was in place, the sooner the employees' mental health would improve. But a more insidious message seemed to be that the court was somehow responsible for the employees' troubles, which, to the workers, was preposterous. No one was more responsible than the people at Knight-Ridder and Gannett who had pursued the JOA in the first place.

Popular columnist Pete Waldmeir, who had written about hundreds of crooks, con men, and other lowlifes in his forty years with the *News,* wrote a column calling the Francek affidavit "an all-time low for sleaze." "This shrink apparently talks to workers in confidence and then tells management what he hears," Waldmeir fulminated. He singled out Dave Lawrence, referring to him by the nickname Lawrence detested. "Skippy's a guy who has steadfastly asserted he has nothing but the highest personal regard for his workers," Waldmeir wrote. "And then he uses specific examples of their personal lives for corporate advantage."

Later, Knight-Ridder and *Free Press* officials could not remember whose idea it was to use Francek, although Lawrence admitted he'd had something to do with it. In the *Free Press*'s in-house newsletter, he insisted the affidavit was submitted not to advance the cause of the JOA, "but to support the request that the case not be unduly delayed." It was a distinction without a difference. He gratuitously quoted Francek as saying he regretted using the example of the child being abused—as if Francek, not Knight-Ridder's two-hundred-dollar-an-hour lawyers, had total control over what the affidavit contained. Lawrence assured employees that no one in management had seen counseling reports. Francek "helps people," Lawrence wrote. "We would not do anything to compromise that."

At the *News,* Chip Weil fired Francek. Guild Local 22 called on Lawrence to do the same, but Lawrence refused, calling Weil's action "totally unfair" to Francek, "who has worked hard for this newspaper and cared about the people here."

Whatever its intent, the Francek affidavit did not sway the court. On September 20 a three-judge panel ordered the JOA postponed indefinitely and set oral arguments for October 28.

The next day a *Free Press* story confirmed it was indeed Al Neuharth who had said Gannett would not move immediately to launch the JOA. Neuharth told reporter Bill Mitchell that Gannett was no less interested in a JOA, but, "We don't want any more of that jerking around" of readers and employees. "Our contract . . . is very firm," he said. "Both parties will see this through until we have a done deal or we don't have a done deal." The contract actually said nothing about a "done deal"; it said the JOA should be launched when legal barriers were lifted. For now that issue was moot, but Neuharth made it clear that Gannett would ultimately decide when and how the JOA would begin, if ever.

"I don't want to make a big deal out of this, but the point is that the JOA is structured so that we have three votes and they [Knight-Ridder] have two," he said. "But nobody is mad at anybody. Nobody has any sharp hang-ups. When you have five people involved in a decision and you have a three-to-two vote, you have some differences about how you get there."

And, to Alvah Chapman's dismay, there were more to come.

While the companies bickered, Clark Clifford took a feeble stab at settling the case out of court. One afternoon that fall, he invited Bill Schultz and Dave Vladeck to his Connecticut Avenue office. Once the Public Citizen lawyers had settled into a rich maroon leather sofa, Clifford launched into another speech. Judge Revercomb's strong opinion, he said, would be nearly impossible to overturn. Meanwhile, the *Free Press* was losing forty-five thousand dollars a day. People were laboring under the great burden of uncertainty this unnecessary process had placed upon them. Wasn't it time to call it a day? What would it take to persuade Michigan Citizens to give up its challenge?

The problem was, Clifford had nothing to trade. Michigan Citizens wasn't seeking anything, like money, that could be negotiated. Clifford spoke vaguely of altering the JOA contract to accommodate the group's concerns, but Schultz and Vladeck were unimpressed. They left Clifford's office puzzling over his purpose in inviting them. Had he thought he could intimidate them into dropping the case? Had he suspected they were having doubts about where the case ultimately might lead?

Schultz and Vladeck were in fact concerned that the *Free Press* could be closed. They had no desire for Ralph Nader's seminal organization to be seen as sending a newspaper to its grave. If they succeeded in stopping the JOA and—for no other reason than spite—Knight-Ridder shut the *Free Press,* Detroit would wind up with the monopoly Michigan Citizens was trying to avoid.

Schultz and Vladeck had to ask themselves if they were on a kamikaze mission: Was there any realistic chance the *Free Press* could survive without a JOA? To satisfy their concerns, they did some amateur exploring in the business world. They contacted a potential buyer of the *Free Press,* and spoke with an investment firm about the possibility of an employee buyout of the paper, but the talk never got serious. The lawyers had a more fruitful exchange with the father-in-law of a friend who once had worked with them at Public Citizen. The father-in-law was an investor in Omaha, Nebraska, by the name of Warren Buffett.

Buffett was a legend in American investing. From ten thousand dollars he'd made delivering newspapers as a boy, he had amassed a personal fortune estimated at $1.6 billion. While Wall Street profited from junk bonds and hostile takeovers, Buffett sat in Nebraska, making money largely by picking stocks and running businesses that produced goods and services. His company, Berkshire Hathaway, traditionally invested in blue-chip concerns with good names and solid franchises, among them the Washington Post Company, Capital Cities/ABC, and Geico, the big auto insurer. The handful of largely unknown companies owned by Berkshire Hathaway made candy, furniture, vacuum cleaners, uniforms, industrial compressors, and newspapers.

To Buffett, the onetime newsboy, newspapering was the most interesting of his ventures. In 1977 he had purchased the *Buffalo News* for $32.5 million after several other companies had passed, believing an evening daily not worth the trouble. When Buffett bought it, the *Buffalo News* dominated the competing *Buffalo Courier-Express* in weekday circulation and advertising, but it had no Sunday paper, a serious disadvantage. Buffett started a Sunday edition and offered introductory discounts to attract subscribers. The *News* steadily built its Sunday base, suffocating the *Courier-Express,* which relied heavily on Sunday ad revenues. Both papers were losing money when in 1982 Cowles Media Company of Minneapolis decided to close the *Courier-Express.* Even as Gannett was launching *USA Today,* Buffalo joined a procession of cities, including Washington, Philadelphia, and Cleveland, witnessing the funerals of daily newspapers.

Over the 1980s, the *Buffalo News* became a highly profitable newspaper that also earned respect for its journalism. So Buffett seemed qualified to make a few observations on the Detroit situation. At Schultz and Vladeck's request, Buffett's son-in-law, Allen Greenberg, arranged for the three to speak via conference call one evening that fall.

Buffett had a working knowledge of the Detroit market. He followed the media business closely as an investment opportunity, and his partner, Charles Munger, had owned stock in the Evening News Association (and sold it shortly before Gannett made its huge offer in 1985). In 1985, Buffett had taken a cursory look at Detroit when Salomon Brothers asked if he wanted to purchase the ENA. He had observed then, as he now told Schultz and Vladeck, that it was almost impossible to predict which Detroit paper would prevail. Though the *Free Press* trailed the *News* in several categories, Buffett said, the deficits weren't so large as to be irreversible. Schultz and Vladeck heard that to mean someone might want to buy the *Free Press* if the JOA was denied and Knight-Ridder didn't want to operate it anymore.

Buffett didn't have all the facts. But Schultz and Vladeck hung up feeling more comfortable with their mission. As Schultz later said, the conversation "said to us, there had to be a market, there had to be someone who would buy that paper." Only Knight-Ridder could know what it would do. Schultz and Vladeck could only guess, and their guesswork told them they were doing the right thing. So they pressed on.

The news from Miami sent a chill through the *Detroit News.*

On Friday, October 14, Cox Enterprises announced it would close the *Miami News* at the end of the year if it could not find a buyer for the paper. Cox, a nineteen-daily chain controlled by a pair of billionaire Atlanta doyennes, said it was "highly improbable" a buyer could be located. Any newspaperman or -woman would have been saddened to hear that another daily was on the brink, but the death sentence pronounced on the *Miami News* had special meaning for the people of the *Detroit News,* because the *Miami News* was in a JOA with Knight-Ridder's *Miami Herald.* Just as the *Detroit News* would be in *its* JOA, the *Miami News* was the junior paper with a shrinking afternoon audience. The JOA that was supposed to protect the *Miami News* appeared to have failed in Miami. It wasn't scheduled to expire until 1996. Why would the *Miami News* be closing now if it still had ten years to live in the shelter of a JOA?

The answer: Cox and Knight-Ridder wanted more money.

Since it began in 1966, the Miami JOA gradually had become a problem for Knight-Ridder. Under the contract with Cox, Knight-Ridder printed, delivered, promoted, and sold ads for the *Miami News.* In return for roughly 15 percent of the JOA's profits, which were generated chiefly by the *Miami Herald,* Cox provided a newspaper every day but Sunday. As the *Miami News*'s circulation dwindled, pressure on the JOA's profitability increased; by 1988, Knight-Ridder was losing $9 million a year on the *News* alone. But the *Herald*'s profits more than made up for the shortfall, so both Knight-Ridder and Cox reaped a profit on the JOA, and Miami readers enjoyed the assumed benefits of news and editorial diversity. The *Miami News* staff still produced a scrappy, respected paper that had won five Pulitzers in its ninety-two years.

Still, the paper was not pulling its financial weight, a fact that figured prominently in a lengthy set of negotiations between Cox and Knight-Ridder over whether to extend the JOA contract beyond 1996. Knight-Ridder, weary of the *Miami News*'s losses, had been trying since the late 1970s to persuade Cox to alter the agreement; Alvah Chapman's offer to sell Cox the *Free Press* was one of the inducements, though a dubious one. Cox grew more interested in talking about the JOA as the 1990s neared. Without an extension of the agency, the *Miami News* was destined to go out of business, and Cox would no longer be permitted to sponge off of the *Herald*.

In 1986 Cox bought a sizable chunk of Knight-Ridder stock, the kind of move that in the predatory 1980s was often prelude to a takeover bid. Cox denied any interest in a takeover—as did most of Wall Street's raiders in the early stages of one—and pressed for more negotiations over the JOA. In January of 1987 the companies signed an agreement granting Cox an option to extend the JOA until the year 2021, with two important changes: Cox would get a smaller share of the JOA's profits, and Cox would absorb the operating losses of the *Miami News*.

Because Cox had no intention of funding those losses, the amended JOA pact doomed the *Miami News*. But for the next thirty-three years Cox would continue to take money out of Miami—about 10 percent of the *Herald*'s profit, or an estimated $165 million. In an incredible something-for-nothing deal, Cox was, in effect, getting paid *not* to publish a newspaper. It didn't seem to be exactly what the drafters of the Newspaper Preservation Act had intended. But then, as with most JOAs, this was not about preserving editorial voices. This was about money.

Cox exercised its option in October of 1988 and almost immediately announced its intention to close the paper. Predictably, Cox and *Miami News* executives defended the deal as reflecting the hard realities of newspapering. David Easterly, president of Cox's Newspaper Division, said there were "economic circumstances so severe that editorial considerations come in second, and I guess $9 million losses are those kinds of circumstances." Cox chairman James C. Kennedy said the paper had only ten thousand subscribers who didn't also subscribe to the *Herald*—therefore, "no one is listening" and "there is no alternative voice." Asked if the JOA was a failure, Kennedy said, "The paper was dead twenty-two years ago. We prolonged it for twenty-two years."

Their pious assertions were so disingenuous as to approach outright lies. Cox, with annual revenues of $1.8 billion a year, was *not* losing $9 million a year in Miami; in fact, its annual share of the JOA's profits had ranged from $5 million to $8 million for the past several years. It had taken $93 million out of Miami since 1966. True, the *Miami News* was taking in $9 million a year less than Knight-Ridder was spending to produce it, and the overall JOA profit was reduced by that amount. But that was precisely the kind of situation in which a JOA was supposed to protect a troubled paper. The Cox executives implied that their paper might have been saved if it were earning its own profit within the JOA—but if both Miami papers had been profitable on their own, they wouldn't have needed a JOA.

Kennedy's smug claim that Cox benevolently had saved the paper from certain death twenty-two years before was technically accurate, but misleading. Cox had not saved the paper; the Newspaper Preservation Act had. And now the company was perverting the law to its own financial benefit. Cox didn't have to extend the JOA. The company could have continued operating the *Miami News*—and earning a tidy multimillion-dollar profit—until 1996. Instead it chose to foreshorten the life of the paper—and the alternative voice it offered—so that Cox could prolong its ride on the *Miami Herald* gravy train. As Easterly explained to *Herald* reporter Joel Achenbach, "If you're a business person, you've got to make a decision to extend the income stream."

Easterly's telling quote illuminates what was—and is—patently wrong with the Newspaper Preservation Act. The underlying principle of the law is that our notion of what is fair in business, as embodied in the antitrust laws, can be set aside in special instances to preserve editorial diversity, which Congress deemed vital as a matter of public policy. The law says nothing about setting aside the antitrust laws so that wealthy corporations can extend their income streams, but the lack of clarity in the act leaves it open to cynical and pernicious interpretations. "Editorial diversity" has almost nothing to do with decisions to close a paper or keep it alive. Journalists don't make those decisions; "businesspersons" do. "Editorial diversity" isn't their concern; the "income stream" is. In effect, Congress left interpretation of the Newspaper Preservation Act to people who can't have as their primary concern preserving newspapers, as Cox's decision to kill the *Miami News* so poignantly demonstrated. The death of the *Miami News* was a travesty on the law—but the law invited such travesties on itself.

The Miami situation struck fear into the people of the *Detroit News* because they suddenly could envision the same thing happening to them. In their worst nightmares, the *News* would waste away in the afternoon market and gradually become a financial drag on the JOA. Gannett and Knight-Ridder would decide the *News* was no longer needed. Gannett's executives would call the paper's demise a tragic reminder of how difficult it is to survive in the modern newspaper business, even as they looked forward to many decades of sharing in the profits of a one-paper JOA.

There were no serious buyers for the *Miami News.* Cox and Knight-Ridder had virtually assured that. According to their agreement, a buyer would not participate in the JOA, and Knight-Ridder would continue printing the *Miami News* for only one more year. After that, the new owner would have to find its own source of printing. The Justice Department opened an investigation of the amended JOA, but nothing came of it. The *Miami News* published its final edition, and the journalists scattered to new jobs, new papers, new lives, while the businesspersons at Cox headquarters prepared to stay busy counting the Miami money for another thirty-three years.

"Mr. Clifford?"

Clark Clifford stepped to the lawyers' podium in the U.S. Court of Appeals for the District of Columbia Circuit and smiled broadly at the three judges peering down at him.

"May it please the court . . . ," he began.

It was October 28, a pivotal day for the *Detroit Free Press.* On this chilly gray morning, Clark Clifford and his fellow Knight-Ridder lawyers were full of hope that they could finally end the long wait for the JOA. Ed Wendover and Senator John Kelly, the leaders of Michigan Citizens for an Independent Press, had declared before the oral argument in the D.C. Circuit that the group might give up its challenge if the court rendered a unanimous decision affirming Ed Meese's approval of the JOA.

The publishers had not drawn the friendliest panel, though. Presiding today was Spottswood W. Robinson III, a seventy-two-year-old appointed by President Johnson, whose penchant for writing lengthy, detailed opinions had earned him the nickname "Mr. Footnote." To his right sat Ruth Bader Ginsburg, fifty-five, a law professor and Carter appointee known as one of the brightest members of the court (and no relation to Douglas Ginsburg, the former assistant attorney general who also was a D.C. Circuit judge). Because of their liberal views, neither Ginsburg nor Robinson was expected to look kindly on the decision by ex-Attorney General Meese.

Sitting to Robinson's left was the *Free Press*'s best hope, Judge Laurence H. Silberman. Silberman, fifty-two, was one of seven Reagan appointees who were transforming the ideological bent of the D.C. Circuit, which, next to the Supreme Court, is perhaps the most influential court in the United States.

The day had passed when social-minded groups such as Public Citizen could expect a sympathetic hearing in the D.C. Circuit. Led by the now-departed Robert Bork, the court's conservative wing repeatedly had disappointed liberals and made it more difficult for anyone to sue the government. Most of the lawyers in the courtroom today believed Silberman, a bald, bespectacled man of sharp intellect and acerbic wit, was most likely to defend Meese's decision. But it was no sure thing, for Silberman occasionally went off on his own. "Silberman's independence is on display sometimes during oral argument," *American Lawyer* wrote. "He is not afraid to think aloud and test out his own legal theories."

Earlier that October morning, Silberman's thinking aloud had made things difficult for Bill Schultz. Nearly every time Schultz started to make a point, Silberman had jumped in with a question. The judge did not buy the argument that Meese had erred in accepting testimony that the *News* would not raise prices. Indeed, Silberman detected a flaw in Michigan Citizens' crucial arguments on pricing. Sardonically, he had asked, "Is this case a situation where everybody agrees that the proper thing to do is for us to call the *Detroit News* and the *Detroit Free Press* into the back room and say, 'Please raise your prices and we will give you immunity to do it,' and you make the agreement right there? That is almost the smell of the briefs." At one point he had said the *Free Press* was "clearly going to lose" the competition. If he owned the paper and was denied a JOA, he said, "I would go out of business. I can't imagine any reason to stay in business." Schultz and Vladeck hadn't expected to get Silberman's vote, but they worried that he was using the bench as a bully pulpit. Silberman, Vladeck later complained, "was not only dead set against us, he was dead set in his intention to try to sway the votes of his colleagues."

Clifford now rose before the panel in his trademark double-breasted suit, looking every bit as calm and confident as he had in the district court. He spoke without notes. His argument focused on Meese's conclusion that the *Free Press* would close if the JOA was not approved. "If at some point you want me to read that one sentence," Clifford said, gently pressing the point, "I would read it, because he states it so clearly."

He was breezing along when Judge Ginsburg asked a question about how narrowly the court should view the JOA as an exception to the antitrust laws. It was the kind of technical question to which lawyers who argued regularly in the D.C. Circuit were accustomed. It alluded to a canon of law holding that exceptions to the antitrust laws were to be narrowly construed; in other words, when a case was close, the decision would lean toward the antitrust law rather than the exception. The Ninth Circuit, in the case of the

Seattle JOA, had reaffirmed the canon. But in the Detroit case, the American Newspaper Publishers Association, a trade group, had argued in a friend-of-the-court brief that the Newspaper Preservation Act should not be so narrowly construed.

Ginsburg asked Clifford to reconcile the conflict.

"I accept the premise that an exception to the antitrust laws must be narrowly construed," Clifford said, and started to discuss how the notion applied to the Newspaper Preservation Act.

Silberman stopped him. "Excuse me, counsel. It seems to me the question that Judge Ginsburg asked you is a very important one. Do you concede that it is our obligation to insure that this statute be interpreted as a narrow exception to the antitrust laws?"

"I don't accept the general principle—"

"Well, now wait a minute," Silberman interrupted, "the question is, do you concede that it is our role to insure that the attorney general's opinion or decision is a narrow interpretation of an exception to the antitrust laws?"

Clifford had to be careful. This canon, in and of itself, did not help his case. "I'm not sure that there is any adequate answer to that," the lawyer said, "because I think that it is so general. I say to you that I accept the principle that exceptions to antitrust laws should be narrowly construed. But then when you take into consideration, Your Honor, what the aim was of the Congress, they said in the preliminary language of the act, the purpose of this act is an effort to see if we cannot perpetuate two newspapers in the various cities of our country."

"What significance," Silberman asked, "does *Chevron* . . . have with respect to the question that Judge Ginsburg and I asked you?" Silberman was referring to a 1984 Supreme Court case, *Chevron U.S.A.* v. *Natural Resources Defense Council,* which dealt with a ruling by the Environmental Protection Agency concerning the Clean Air Act. On appeal, the D.C. Circuit had overturned the EPA in an opinion written by Judge Ruth Ginsburg—which then was overturned by the Supreme Court. In his majority opinion, Justice John Paul Stevens wrote that the EPA's decision, while debatable, was nonetheless reasonable. Because Congress had empowered the EPA to decide—just as Congress had empowered the attorney general to apply the Newspaper Preservation Act—the agency's view was entitled to great deference, the high court found. In other words, unless an agency's call was flat-out wrong, a court could not substitute its own thinking. Because government decisions frequently were on trial in the D.C. Circuit, *Chevron* came up almost daily.

In theory, *Chevron* bolstered Knight-Ridder's case, for it instructed the appellate court not to set aside Meese's decision simply because he *could have* reached a different one. The Justice Department's brief defending Meese's decision discussed *Chevron*'s relevance for three pages. Knight-Ridder's brief listed nineteen cases as authorities; *Chevron* was one of four marked with an asterisk as principal authorities. Schultz and Vladeck, worried that *Chevron* could hobble their argument, had downplayed the case in their brief. They cringed when Silberman asked about it. They saw the question floating down to Clifford like a fat, hanging curveball waiting to be whacked out of the park.

But Clifford missed it completely.

"I know that you are familiar with" *Chevron,* Clifford began. Then he hesitated. For a fleeting instant his voice seemed to lose its familiar ring of certainty and purpose. "We have been familiar with it," he said.

Lawyers on both sides of the courtroom listened in astonishment. What kind of answer was this? Was Clifford equivocating about a case that obviously helped him?

"I am not in position to say that I feel that it has any important impact upon this particular instance."

The lawyers sitting around and behind Clifford, those who knew what *Chevron* meant, sat in stunned, embarrassed silence. If they had not been in a courtroom, they might have gasped. A single thought flashed sickeningly through their minds: *Clifford does not know the case.* It didn't seem possible, but no lawyer who understood *Chevron*—say, Phil Lacovara—could have given Clifford's reply. Those who saw how Clifford had fumbled this opportunity wondered if he truly thought *Chevron* unimportant, if he had read his own brief, if his associates had prepared him, if he had simply forgotten the case, if his years had gotten the better of him. Clifford later said he had read *Chevron,* and thought it indeed helped Knight-Ridder's case, though not in a decisive way. Better, he thought, to emphasize that Meese had adopted the Ninth Circuit's thinking in affirming the Seattle JOA—that a paper should be judged deserving of a JOA if, in all probability, it could not survive without one. The Ninth Circuit's standard consumed *Chevron* in this case, Clifford thought, though he did not make that argument in response to Silberman.

Clifford was fortunate to have Douglas Letter to bail him out. Letter, a youthful man of thirty-five with a clean-shaven face and close-cropped hair, was the Justice Department's lead appellate litigator on the Detroit case. He had successfully defended Attorney General William French Smith's approval of the Seattle JOA, and in his ten years with the department had argued scores of cases in every appellate circuit in the country. Letter found the Detroit case fascinating. Even after Seattle, he was struck by the raw viciousness of the rivalry between the *Free Press* and the *News.* The case also posed intriguing legal and political questions, not least of which was how the court would treat an opinion by a man who was being sullied on MEESE IS A PIG posters all over Washington. Letter himself was ambivalent about Meese's decision. Under *Chevron,* it was eminently defensible—but Letter thought he could just as easily have defended a denial of the JOA.

When he heard Clifford's answer, Letter knew he would have to correct it. His own brief had used *Chevron* to defend Meese's decision. Shortly after he stood to argue, Silberman said, "I hope, Mr. Letter, you realize that there was a sixty-four-dollar question that Judge Ginsburg and I put to Mr. Clifford, the answer to which I think, if his answer was correct, would probably lose the case."

"Your Honor," Letter replied, "I think it is a sixty-four-*million*-dollar question."

Silberman smiled. "It may be."

Later, in part because of the way Clifford handled the *Chevron* question, Knight-Ridder would replace him with yet another litigator.

As they filed out of the courthouse at 11:45 A.M., lawyers for both sides were subdued. No one was predicting victory, except, of course, John Kelly, who told reporters, "I think we clearly won." The Knight-Ridder lawyers had come hoping for a clean sweep, but now that seemed an unlikely prospect. Silberman looked like a vote for the JOA. Ginsburg seemed doubtful. Robinson, who had not asked a single question, was impossible to read.

20

The Big Win

Ed Wendover almost dropped his coffee. He was eating breakfast in Grand Rapids, Michigan, where the Michigan Press Association, of which he was a director, was hosting its annual meeting. What startled Wendover so was the cutline beneath a big color photograph of John Kelly on the front page of that Saturday morning's *Detroit News.* It quoted Kelly as saying, "I'd love to argue [the JOA] before the Supreme Court."

What the hell is he thinking? Wendover thought. He didn't mind when Kelly ran off his mouth at the publishers, but this outburst was an affront to Bill Schultz and Dave Vladeck, who had worked so hard to get Michigan Citizens this far. Kelly did most of his arguing in the raucous chamber of the Michigan Senate, where grandstanding and glad-handing were the accepted methods of debate. They wouldn't do before the highest court in the land. Wendover made up his mind that, if Michigan Citizens took its case to the Supreme Court, Kelly would watch from the gallery.

It was January 28, 1989. The day before, the U.S. Court of Appeals for the D.C. Circuit had handed down a 2–1 decision affirming Meese, with Judges Silberman and Robinson voting in the majority. The two-pronged majority opinion, written by Silberman, relied heavily on the *Chevron* precedent, saying that if the attorney general's interpretation was reasonable, "it is entitled to deference under *Chevron.*" Meese was rational to conclude that the *News* would not let up on the *Free Press*—by raising prices, for example—if a JOA was unavailable, the judges found. "Debatable, the Attorney General's appraisal may well be, but [it was] hardly unreasonable," the opinion read.

In her dissent, Judge Ruth Ginsburg argued that Meese hadn't cogently explained how the *Free Press* met the standard of being in "probable danger of financial failure." Rather, she found, "market dominance is now beyond the grasp of the *News* as well as the *Free Press.*" Meese's reliance on testimony by Al Neuharth and Alvah Chapman permitted the publishers "artificially to generate and maintain the conditions that will yield them a passing JOA," resulting in a "self-serving, competition-quieting arrangement," Ginsburg wrote. That was well beyond Congress's intention of saving weak papers from stronger competitors in markets that could not support two newspapers. *Chevron,* while allowing Meese some leeway, did not permit him such an expansive reading of the Newspaper Preservation Act, Ginsburg wrote. She advocated sending the JOA back to the attorney general for reconsideration.

The court ordered the stay blocking the JOA dissolved in seven days, meaning Knight-Ridder and Gannett could implement the merger anytime after. When Wendover had heard the news Friday afternoon, he'd gone looking for *Free Press* general manager Bob Hall, who also had come to the Michigan Press Association meeting. Hall was already driving back to Detroit. Wendover reached him on his car phone and exhorted him not to launch the JOA until Michigan Citizens decided what, if anything, its next step would be. Hall was noncommittal, but Wendover hoped the publishers wouldn't force his group to rush to seek yet another stay. "I think we ought to be able to handle this in a gentlemanly way," he said.

He was, of course, mistaken. On Sunday, January 29, the companies convened an emergency strategy meeting at Hughes Hubbard and Reed's Washington offices. Over sandwiches and chocolate chip cookies, Neuharth, Chapman, Jim Batten, John Curley, and Doug McCorkindale took less than an hour to agree the JOA should start on February 6. They had no intention of waiting for Kelly and Wendover; indeed, they wanted to give their opponents as little time to act as possible. Curiously, there was little of the legal debate that marked the September meeting, when Gannett had hinted it wasn't eager to launch. Neuharth didn't say a thing about "jerking readers around," even though Michigan Citizens was saying it might try to block the JOA once more. At 6:00 P.M. the publishers issued a terse press release saying they would launch the JOA unless the courts entered another stay, which they considered unlikely. "We seem to be on the homestretch," Dave Lawrence told *News* reporter Keith Naughton. "I feel some calm and quiet optimism about this coming to pass."

While the press release was being faxed to reporters in Washington,

Detroit, and Miami, Wendover, Kelly, and Matt Beer were wandering around downtown Detroit in a cold drizzle looking for a place to talk. They had met at Reedy's saloon near Tiger Stadium, but, like nearly everything downtown on a winter Sunday, it was closed. They settled on Musial's, a homey blue-collar pub hard by the Lodge Freeway. The place was nearly empty. The three leaders of Michigan Citizens sat by a pool table in the back of the bar, where one wall was covered with black-and-white photographs of the Three Stooges.

Wendover was fuming. By now he had heard about the publishers' plans and told reporters he considered them "coldhearted." He vented his anger at Kelly before the first pitcher of beer arrived. "There's no way in hell you're going to argue our case before the Supreme Court."

"I was misquoted, Ed," Kelly insisted. Beer backed him up. Kelly said he had merely meant to emphasize that Michigan Citizens could proceed with the challenge if Bill Schultz and Dave Vladeck deemed the mission too futile to continue. That didn't mollify Wendover, who stormed out of the bar to find a copy of the Saturday *News* bearing the six-inch-by-four-inch photo of Kelly with the offending quote. This was Sunday, though, so there were none in coin boxes. He finally found a leftover in the lobby of the *News* building. A security guard ordered him not to take it, but Wendover slapped a quarter down and rushed out. Back at Musial's, he resumed his griping. He said he was fed up with Kelly telling the press what the group would or wouldn't do before Wendover had had a chance to consult with him. Wendover made it clear he could get his own lawyer, who could make the First Amendment arguments that Wendover had been urging on Schultz and Vladeck. (The lawyers didn't believe the First Amendment was relevant to the case.) "You can do whatever you want, Ed," Kelly said, but Michigan Citizens was going to take the case to the Supreme Court, if necessary. Kelly had polled more than a hundred group members in the past forty-eight hours and they were overwhelmingly in favor. Besides, Kelly said, he was tired of Wendover informing Chip Weil and Dave Lawrence of Michigan Citizens' doings. They were the enemy, after all.

The two men really were bickering over who was the true leader of Michigan Citizens for an Independent Press. Kelly felt entitled because he had researched legal issues, rounded up charter members, and lent his name when everyone said the cause was futile. Wendover saw himself as the group's conscience, representing the journalists who made up much of Michigan Citizens. "It was pretty crazy," Beer later said. "People had to do some yelling at each other." The Musial's regulars had never seen such a shouting match between men who weren't even drunk. "It was hot," Wendover later said. "We were a group of people who couldn't agree on the time of day."

Wendover calmed down after Kelly agreed to be more careful about what he told the media. Beer ordered more beer. They got Schultz on the pay phone. The lawyer was willing to proceed with the case, though he didn't sound as enthusiastic as before. He didn't care about Kelly saying he would argue; by now Schultz had learned not to take the senator literally. But the lawyer felt obliged to tell his clients their best shots at winning were behind them. They could request an infrequently granted rehearing by the three-judge circuit panel; seek *en banc* review by the entire circuit court, even rarer; or go directly to the Supreme Court, where their chances of being heard were extremely slim. Their decision, Schultz cautioned, could not be made lightly; they had to weigh the very real possibility that they ultimately would lose. Would they like the Newspaper Preservation Act to get a public seal of approval from the Supreme Court? Schultz wanted to press on, but his clients were such an impulsive bunch that he felt a dose of hard legal reality was needed to assure a sober and reasoned choice. Public Citizen would have many more cases before the D.C. Circuit and the Supreme Court; it couldn't afford to bring actions that were less than serious.

Schultz held the line while Wendover, Kelly, and Beer talked it over. They had been joined by Lou and Lorraine Mleczko, who urged them to keep up the fight. Luckily, no one else wanted to use the pay phone. Around 9:00 P.M., Wendover, whose credit card was paying for the call, told Schultz that Michigan Citizens wasn't ready to give up. He, Kelly, and Beer signed a twenty-eight-word resolution authorizing Schultz and Vladeck to appeal the case as quickly as possible to whichever court they deemed appropriate.

Schultz announced a plan the next afternoon at Public Citizen's Washington offices. While reporters filed into a cramped reading room for the news conference, Vladeck had to be reminded to don a tie and shoes. Schultz said Michigan Citizens would ask the D.C. Circuit Court to review the case *en banc*, but he would not commit to seeking Supreme Court review if the *en banc* bid failed. "We haven't decided that yet," he said.

First they had to get another stay. The publishers had resumed contract negotiations with the unions and begun preparations for the launch of the JOA. "So we'll be the whipping boy again," a bitter Wendover told a *News* reporter. Kelly, unfazed, said the newspapers "have decided on a collision course and we say, 'Okay, we'll play chicken with you.' "

On Wednesday, February 1, Michigan Citizens filed a short request for the entire D.C. Circuit Court to halt the JOA temporarily. Few expected it to succeed. Even Guild Local 22 leader Don Kummer was telling members to assume the JOA would begin the following Monday. Still, at the *Free Press*, staffers tried not to get their hopes up, for fear of having them dashed again.

At the *News,* staffers dreaded a JOA start-up. "The mood around here is like a mausoleum," reporter Bonnie DeSimone wrote in a computer-generated message to a fellow reporter. "New sked posted with tons of p.m. and weekend shifts; loss of part of our weekend paper; prospect of strike vote (most folks including me think it'll be another freep-news bloodbath in the union mtg) & general feeling that bad guys won. i'm mostly pissed about them trying to ram this thru again after they said they'd wait out the appeals process. i keep thinking of the line in 'animal house': 'you fucked up. you trusted us.' " Many in the newsroom shared her sense of betrayal and apprehension.

At 5:15 P.M. Thursday, a clerk from the D.C. Circuit Court called a reporter at the *News.* "The stay has been approved," she said. The vote was 9–0, with Judges Douglas Ginsburg and Kenneth Starr not participating (Ginsburg because of his prior involvement; Starr because he had been nominated to replace Charles Fried as solicitor general). The reporter told an editor, who immediately typed the message into his computer and, with the touch of a button, transmitted it to every terminal in the *News* newsroom. As the messages flashed at the top of the computer screens, a cheer swept through the second floor, where most of the reporters and editors worked. A few *News* staffers uncorked a bottle of champagne and sang, "Stay, just a little bit longer . . ." Kelly gloated over the surprise victory, small though it was. "The mighty Soviet army has been defeated again by the *mujaheddin,*" he joked. Schultz was elated. Even Judges Silberman and Robinson had voted for the stay. The lawyer celebrated with a cold beer in his office.

The jubilation did not last. On February 24 the D.C. Circuit Court voted 5–4 not to review the case *en banc.* Michigan Citizens had needed six votes; again Spottswood Robinson had deprived them of a win. But Schultz took comfort in Chief Judge Patricia Wald's dissent, which seemed to signal the Supreme Court that the case begged for further review. Two days later, Michigan Citizens said it would ask the high court to extend the stay indefinitely—but even without an extension, the group would press an appeal. "We want no ambiguity," Kelly said. "We're firing this volley and we're waiting for tactical response from the newspapers." For the moment, though, the newspapers had none. "Each company is checking with their own attorneys," was all Bill Keating would say. Alvah Chapman suggested the executives not meet until after the high court had considered whether to extend the stay.

Michigan Citizens filed its request for a stay on Thursday, March 2. The next day, a story in the *News*'s business section hinted strongly that Gannett would not agree to launch the JOA even if the Supreme Court denied the stay. Ed Wendover read the story that morning in his bathroom, surrounded by paraphernalia he had collected spoofing Presidents Nixon and Reagan. His daughter, Jessica, got concerned when she heard her dad whooping and yelling. "Dad, are you okay?" she asked. "I'm great!" Wendover shouted back. "We don't need a stay anymore!" If the court didn't provide one, Wendover assumed, Gannett would.

That afternoon, Chief Justice William Rehnquist declined to extend the stay. Schultz and Vladeck immediately appealed to Justice William Brennan, Jr., who extended the stay until the full court could discuss it at a scheduled March 17 conference. On the morning of Monday, March 20, the court rendered a three-sentence verdict: No stay. Justices Harry Blackmun and John Paul Stevens dissented, though an actual vote count was not disclosed. Michigan Citizens vowed again to ask the Supreme Court to review the case. "We lost one battle in the war," Schultz told a *Free Press* reporter. But Supreme Court watchers did not believe the court would choose to hear the case. Harold Spaeth, a Michigan State University professor who monitored the court closely, told the *News,* "Even though the fat lady has not begun to sing, most assuredly she's clearing her throat."

Gannett and Knight-Ridder scheduled a meeting for the next afternoon to determine their next step. After nearly three years, there no longer were any barriers to their newspaper merger in Detroit. Except, perhaps, for the people who had launched the JOA quest: Al Neuharth and Gannett.

Two black Cadillac limousines waited at the brass canopy entrance to 815 Connecticut Avenue, home of Clifford and Warnke. At 1:17 P.M. Alvah Chapman, Jim Batten, and Bob Hall strode from the building, with lawyers Clark Clifford, Jack Fontaine, and Gerald Goldman in tow. The limos ferried them to the Roosevelt Bridge and across the Potomac River to Rosslyn, the corner of Arlington, Virginia, where the gleaming twin silos of *USA Today* and Gannett Company, Inc., loomed over Wilson Boulevard.

The Knight-Ridder entourage left their limos in a parking garage in the Gannett tower and took a series of elevators to the thirtieth floor. They emerged into a glittering receiving area of brass and onyx marble, the air tinged with soft golden light. Behind the receptionist, a spiral staircase ascended to the offices of Al Neuharth and John Curley. Chapman and the others were ushered down a corridor into the White Room. The walls, the polished floor, the upholstered chairs, and the long, egg-shaped table dominating the trapezoidal chamber were a dazzling white. A wall of ceiling-high windows offered a bracing view of Washington across the Potomac.

Neuharth sat at one end of the table. He would preside over today's crucial meeting, one of his last as leader of Gannett. The next evening, hundreds of invited guests would ascend the same tower to attend a lavish dinner commemorating Neuharth's twenty-six years with the company and marking his impending retirement. There would be crown roast of veal, Château Latour 1979, irreverent video testimonials from the likes of Walter Cronkite, Donald Trump, George Steinbrenner, and Oprah Winfrey, a glossy thirty-two-page booklet on Neuharth's career, and gifts, including a waterproof metal detector, which McCorkindale would suggest Neuharth use "the next time he wants to walk on water." Neuharth, set to retire on an annual pension of four hundred thousand dollars, would talk of how Gannett came to "outsmart our enemies . . . and outcharm our friends."

It was nearly three years to the day since Neuharth and Chapman had agreed to the JOA on a Sunday afternoon in Miami. In the last few weeks it had begun to look as if the deal might come apart. Gannett was sending disturbing signals. A story that appeared March 3 atop the business page of the *Detroit News* outlined the risks Gannett faced in launching the JOA before all legal challenges were exhausted. If the Supreme Court were to order the merger undone after it had been assembled, the *News*'s future would be in jeopardy. Once the egg was scrambled, the *Free Press* would become the daily circulation leader because the *News* would no longer have morning home delivery. The *News*'s dominance of classified advertising would disappear because the papers would combine advertising—including Sunday ads, in which the *News*'s claim to more than 70 percent of the classifieds was its most decisive advantage. If the court then ordered the JOA dismantled and the papers to start competing again, the *News* would find itself woefully outflanked, almost certain to perish. As one unnamed *News* official was quoted, "There is all risk for Gannett and none for Knight-Ridder." Further doubt was cast on Gannett's intentions in a front-page *News* story March 16 in which John Curley hinted that Gannett would not start the JOA until the Supreme Court either declined to hear the case or ruled in the publishers' favor. The stories had not gone unnoticed at Knight-Ridder. Queried publicly, Chapman and Batten dismissed them as speculative, but the executives could not hide their dismay as they seated themselves in the White Room on that Tuesday afternoon. Chapman looked particularly grim. He was overdue for retirement but had put it off, vowing not to leave until either the JOA was in place or the *Free Press* was closed. Now he finally had been granted permission to close the grueling final chapter in his career. At last he could save the *Free Press*.

But Al Neuharth was standing in his way.

Chapman was determined to convince the Gannett executives and lawyers that launching the JOA was the right thing to do. He had ordered Jack Fontaine to bring the merger closing documents. He wore the same willful face he had shown the roomful of reporters at the *Free Press* on the day the Knight-Ridder board rendered its bleak verdict on the paper's future. And, again, he relied heavily on Clark Clifford to argue his case, to sway the people in the White Room as he had swayed the politicians and businesspeople of Michigan, to use his impassioned eloquence to make the Gannett people see that Knight-Ridder was correct.

Neuharth called the meeting to order and asked Clifford to speak. The old man stood with his back to the windows, the aerial tableau of Washington spread behind him.

"The Supreme Court has said, 'You are free to close the JOA,' " he said. " 'We are washing our hands of this case. We are not interested in this case. We will not hear this case.' " With a 7–2 vote against the stay, Clifford argued, the court had supplied a clear signal that it would not grant a review of the case, also known as *certiorari*. Only four votes were needed for *certiorari*, but obviously no more than two justices were interested. Once the JOA was launched, Clifford said, the court would be even less inclined to hear the case. "There is no chance this court will grant *certiorari*," Clifford intoned, repeating it several times, as if he could hypnotize the Gannett people.

Neuharth was pacing in a corner of the room. He looked to John Stuart Smith, Gannett's lead counsel. "Well, John," he said, "how do you feel about that?"

Smith already had heard the gist of Clifford's argument in phone conversations with Knight-Ridder's lawyers. He was prepared to tear it apart. "I really am in full agreement with the sentiments Mr. Clifford expressed," Smith said, "and I wish the court had said those things. I wish Mr. Clifford had been a justice of the court. But the court did not say that it would not grant a petition for *certiorari*, and it did not say it would not reverse the lower court's decision."

The vote against the stay wasn't necessarily 7–2, Smith said. All that was certain was that Justices Stevens and Blackmun favored the stay; the other votes were not disclosed. Occasionally, individual justices did not record their votes on stays. Justice Brennan, who had temporarily halted the JOA so that the full court could consider a stay, was likely to have favored a longer halt, Smith argued. Justice Thurgood Marshall, the court's liberal champion of civil rights, also may have been inclined to vote for a stay. The point was, no one could be sure. The vote may well have been 7–2, Smith said, but it also might have been 5–4. Four votes were enough to grant *certiorari*.

Clifford interrupted. "But the full court *never,* after having denied a stay, has granted a petition for *certiorari.*"

"We looked into that matter," Smith calmly replied, "and we found some cases where the court had denied applications for stays and subsequently granted *cert.*"

"Well," Clifford said, "the Supreme Court has been around for two hundred years, and if you go back far enough, you can find anything."

"That is true, of course," Smith conceded. "But because we are only interested in this court, we have only inspected the decisions of the Reagan court."

Weeks before, Smith had assigned a group of junior lawyers at his firm, Nixon, Hargrave, Devans and Doyle, to research all cases since 1980 in which the Supreme Court had considered a stay. It was painstaking work, because the court did not keep good records of such matters. The team, led by Corinne Yu, had sifted through hundreds of cases, finding six in which the court had granted *certiorari* after denying a stay. In four of those, Smith said, the court ultimately reversed the lower court's decision—playing out what would have been Gannett's worst nightmare.

Chapman and Batten sat stewing. One of them asked if Smith would please discuss one of the cases.

He was happy to oblige. He chose *Palmore* v. *Sidoti,* a case argued in 1984. After divorcing from her husband, Linda Sidoti Palmore was awarded custody of their three-year-old daughter. Anthony J. Sidoti sought to alter the arrangement on the grounds that his ex-wife was living with a black man, whom she later married. A Florida court, finding that living in a racially mixed household might hurt the child, granted the ex-husband's request and was upheld on appeal. Linda Palmore petitioned the Supreme Court for *certiorari* and requested a stay that would have kept her child from being moved to the home of her ex-husband while the case was argued. The court denied the stay but granted *certiorari,* and ultimately ruled in favor of the ex-wife, reversing the lower courts. "In some circles," Smith told the Knight-Ridder and Gannett executives, "a decision to take a child away from its parent is not as significant as a decision to permit two businesses to merge. But in other circles, it's more important. And I believe that is a concern that would be shared by some people on the court."

So the court wasn't necessarily shy about denying a stay and then taking a case. But would it overturn the JOA? The Nixon, Hargrave research team had explored that question too. Smith had a theory that a decision maker's vote on the JOA could be predicted by his or her attitude on antitrust matters. If he was proenforcement, like Judge Mort Needelman, he would be against the

JOA; if he was probusiness, like Ed Meese, he would be for it. All of the prior decision makers in the Detroit JOA—with the exception of Circuit Judge Spottswood Robinson—had followed the pattern. Smith's aides had analyzed all of the Reagan court's decisions in antitrust cases. It was hardly scientific, but Smith wasn't looking for a precise prediction, just an indication of how the court might lean. Although his gut told him the court would look kindly on the JOA, "When the stakes are this high, I never trust my instincts," he later said.

The result was a chart showing how each of the justices had voted in some thirty antitrust cases.* Justice Stevens, for example, had favored the plaintiff—the party alleging an antitrust violation—in twenty-two of thirty-four votes. Chief Justice Rehnquist, on the other hand, had voted for the defendant in twenty-five of thirty-three votes. Assuming that justices who most often voted for the plaintiff would vote against the publishers, Justices Stevens and Thurgood Marshall were most likely to vote against the JOA; Rehnquist, Anthony Kennedy, and Sandra Day O'Connor were most likely to vote for it. Too close to call were Justices William Brennan, Harry Blackmun, Byron White, and Antonin Scalia. White, for example, had voted seventeen times for the plaintiff and thirteen for the defendant. But, strictly on Smith's seat-of-the-pants numbers, the JOA would lose 5–4, with Stevens, Marshall, Brennan, Scalia, and White in the majority.

Smith wasn't saying the publishers were likely to lose. Rather, he was arguing that, despite Clifford's impassioned claims to the contrary, the facts showed that the court's denial of the stay did *not* ensure that the court would deny *certiorari* and did *not* ensure that the court would affirm the JOA. "Talk about nailing it," Gannett lawyer Larry Aldrich later bragged. "I don't think it was a fair fight, because John had done his homework and Clifford had not."

The Knight-Ridder people did not agree. Later, Knight-Ridder attorney Jack Fontaine called Smith's argument "the most inane, jumbled, unprincipled presentation I've ever seen." The uncharacteristic outburst by the taciturn Fontaine said a lot about the frustration his camp felt in the White Room that afternoon. Their contract with Gannett was straightforward. It said the JOA would start after "the removal or elimination of [any] such injunction, restraining order, or other court process" blocking it. It did not say the launch could be stopped if one of the parties thought there might be further litigation. The

*For Justice Anthony Kennedy, a relatively recent addition to the court, the Nixon, Hargrave lawyers used antitrust cases he had heard on the Ninth Circuit Court of Appeals.

Knight-Ridder people believed Neuharth and his cronies were using legal technicalities to avoid their overriding obligation. As Chapman recalled, "There was a clear indication on my part and Clark Clifford's that they were doing an immoral, illegal thing."

But Gannett was holding up the JOA for two simple reasons that had little to do with morals: the company stood to lose a great deal if the Supreme Court dismantled the JOA *after* it was in place, and it stood to gain a great deal if the Supreme Court struck down the JOA *before* it was in place. Gannett was trying to avoid the most dire consequences of Neuharth's deal with Chapman while exploiting the legal proceedings to gain a monopoly.

Neuharth's deal virtually guaranteed that the *News* would wither away under a JOA, because he had blithely dealt away the paper's competitive advantages. Strictly as a business proposition that wouldn't matter much, because Gannett would still get its half of the JOA profits anyway. Cash made by the *Free Press* would spend as easily as cash made by both papers. But if the Supreme Court ordered the JOA disassembled, Gannett not only was likely to lose the *News,* it would lose its guaranteed hundred-year income stream. It would be obvious that Alvah Chapman had gotten the better of Al Neuharth. Gannett stood to fare much better if the JOA never happened. If the Supreme Court rejected the JOA and the *Free Press* closed, Gannett would rule Detroit and Neuharth could retire knowing he had brought Knight-Ridder, the mighty bastion of the journalistic establishment, to its knees. In his words, Neuharth would achieve "the big win."

Publicly, Neuharth insisted Gannett was not as interested in money as in preserving two editorial voices in Detroit, but that was hard to believe given what was happening high in the Gannett tower on March 21, 1989. In fact, Gannett wasn't at all enthused about a JOA anymore, but there was no legal way out of it. So the lawyers were holding it up until the Supreme Court legally could hand Neuharth his "big win." "People were feeling real good about it: Wouldn't it be great if we won the whole thing?" McCorkindale later said. Did that figure in Gannett's blocking the launch? "I'm sure it did," he said.

However, McCorkindale, Neuharth, and Curley didn't discuss that reason with their Knight-Ridder counterparts. Instead they emphasized the danger a premature launch posed to the *News.* The Knight-Ridder people understood the concern, but they didn't see how it was relevant. "If that's the position they wanted to take, they should have taken it back when they negotiated the agreement," Fontaine later said. He kept telling the Gannett people this was "a lousy way to start a hundred-year partnership." It was hard not to wonder whether Gannett ever was truly commited to a JOA.

Knight-Ridder was not innocent, though. At one point, Smith took Fontaine aside and offered a possible solution: If the JOA went together and the Supreme Court struck it down, Gannett would have the right to buy all of the publishers' hard assets in Detroit, including the printing presses. Gannett would print the *Free Press* under contract to Knight-Ridder—but the *News* would get first claim on press times, meaning the *News* would become the morning paper. Fontaine quickly dismissed the offer. Later, he recalled thinking: "*(a)* it would look awful; *(b)* it would be illegal. I sensed that the proposal was something they knew we would not, could not, accept."

More curious was the offer Knight-Ridder didn't make. Chapman never sought to reassure Gannett that Knight-Ridder would close the *Free Press* if the JOA was assembled and the Supreme Court later undid it. For more than a year he had been telling anyone who asked that the *Free Press* would die without a JOA. But the meeting at Gannett revealed an asterisk on his promise: He had no intention of closing the paper if the JOA started up and the Supreme Court ended it. By then the *Free Press* would, as if by magic, be the dominant force in Detroit, and the *News* would be "failing." Knight-Ridder would gladly rescind its promise rather than walk away from its newfound gold mine. If the *News* perished, that would be Gannett's problem.

So there was no shortage of cynicism in the Gannett tower on the first day of spring in 1989. The meeting that day wasn't about morals or partnerships or saving editorial voices. It was about money. And it was about winning.

It dragged on for five hours. The lawyers met, the executives caucused, Chapman and Batten pleaded, and, finally, John Curley said no, Gannett would not go ahead. John Smith suggested asking Michigan Citizens to agree to file their petition for *certiorari* quickly in return for a promise not to launch the JOA. The lawyers were concerned that Michigan Citizens might file the petition too late to be considered before the court recessed at the end of June, which would mean the case might not even be heard until 1990. Smith phoned Bill Schultz, who gladly accepted the deal.

The meeting broke up shortly after 6:00 P.M. There had been no shouting or table pounding, but Chapman and his entourage "were damned unhappy and [Gannett] knew it," Fontaine recalled. "Alvah was very angry. [But] Alvah does not shout or rant or curse. He just spoke very forcefully. All the warmth went out of the room, if you will." When two reporters ambushed Chapman as he approached his limo in the parking garage, he insisted, "We're gonna go together." That wasn't quite so. Upstairs, a weary Jim Batten told reporters, "Both companies remain firmly committed to the pursuit of the JOA and implementation at the earliest possible moment." Gannett did not believe that moment had come. Asked why, Batten snapped, "You need to talk to your friends at Gannett."

The Knight-Ridder group returned to Clifford and Warnke for a debriefing. Talk of filing a lawsuit was quickly dismissed. Gannett couldn't be forced to launch the JOA; besides, as Fontaine later said, "How the hell could you operate the newspapers for ninety-nine years if you couldn't get through this part?" They had been delayed by Ed Meese, Mort Needelman, Joyce Hens Green, the D.C. Circuit Court, and, now, their supposed partners. But they would wait again as they had waited before. If they had to wait for a year, it would cost them at least another $20 million. That was a small price to pay for billions.

Chip Weil wasn't sure how to act or what to say. The jocular, smooth-talking *News* publisher rarely was at a loss for words, but tonight he had unexpectedly found himself in an elevator with Supreme Court Justice Byron White. Weil wasn't cowed by greatness—after all, he had worked for Al Neuharth for nearly twenty years—but he didn't think he ought to be chatting up Supreme Court justices while the JOA was before the high court. White introduced himself and his wife, and when the elevator doors opened at the twelfth floor and Weil offered to get the justice a cocktail, White said he would join the publisher at the bar.

It was Sunday, April 2, and White was in the Presidential Suite at the Capital Hilton in Washington, D.C., where the *Detroit News* was hosting a private buffet supper. The soiree marked the end of the Gridiron Club weekend. Each year the Gridiron Club, a group of sixty Washington newspaper journalists, staged a white-tie dinner for a horde of celebrities from the worlds of business, politics, sports, and entertainment. The primary purpose of the dinner was to roast official Washington in a variety show produced and performed by the journalists. Saturday's main event was followed by a reprise on Sunday afternoon for friends and family of Gridiron members and other lesser mortals who had not been invited the night before. Traditionally, the *News* hosted a cocktail reception for the performers and guests on Saturday night, and on Sunday a more modest get-together for a few top editors and the staff of its Washington news bureau.

This year, Justice White was the guest of veteran *News* correspondent and Gridiron member Richard A. Ryan. Ryan had volunteered to invite White when the justice's name came up at a Gridiron Club meeting in January. The *News* reporter thought it would be interesting to meet the justice, a football

All-American at the University of Colorado who had played halfback for the Detroit Lions in the 1940s. It never entered Ryan's mind that White might soon be helping to determine the fate of the Detroit papers.

On Sunday night, White and Weil were standing by themselves at a bar in a corner of the hotel suite when White, making polite conversation, asked, "So how's your new business venture going in Detroit?"

Weil's face turned crimson. "It's not going, Mr. Justice," he said.

"Why not?" White asked.

"Because it's before your court."

The conversation ended. White did not speak to Weil again that evening. Later, a *News* reporter asked the justice an innocuous question about the possibility that the JOA case would be granted *certiorari;* White immediately changed the subject.

The justice must have felt uncomfortable. It is hard to believe he would have ventured into a room full of *News* reporters and editors had he known the paper was party to a case before his court, but evidently he did not know. Although the court had considered Michigan Citizens' request for a stay, the group had not yet filed its petition for *certiorari,* which would have formally put the case before the court. White apparently assumed the JOA had been assembled after the court denied the stay.

Michigan Citizens filed its petition for *certiorari* April 5. Lawyers Bill Schultz and Dave Vladeck placed two questions before the court. The first involved the *Chevron* case that Clark Clifford had slipped up on in the D.C. Circuit. Michigan Citizens asked whether *Chevron* required courts to defer to an agency's decision even if the decision conflicted with the rule that antitrust exemptions should be granted sparingly. The second asked whether a JOA could be granted solely on the basis of two newspapers showing that they had lost money and one—the *News,* in this case—asserting that it would not raise prices.

Schultz and Vladeck's chances of getting *certiorari* were slim. The court deigned to review only 150 to 175 of the 5,000 cases submitted each term. It usually did not grant *certiorari* when the solicitor general urged it not to, as with the JOA case. Generally, the court accepted two kinds of cases: those that involved broad constitutional issues, and those that had produced conflicting rulings in different circuit courts. Neither criterion applied to the JOA case. Still, that did not bar the Supreme Court from taking it up; the court could review anything if at least four justices found it interesting as a matter of public policy. Though they weren't optimistic, Schultz and Vladeck thought the JOA might be that special kind of case.

Lawyers for Knight-Ridder and the solicitor general filed twenty-three- and seventeen-page briefs urging the court not to take the case. Gannett offered a sentence: "The *Detroit News* Inc. and its parent, Gannett Co. Inc., remain fully committed to the joint operating arrangement in Detroit, and urge this Court to deny the petition for *certiorari* as expeditiously as possible." A clerk told Gannett attorney John Smith the brief was the shortest ever submitted to the court. (Later, Smith proudly displayed a miniature copy of the one-page brief on an end table in his Washington office.) Smith believed silence was Gannett's most eloquent argument for the JOA. By implying that it wasn't as keen about a JOA as Knight-Ridder, Smith believed, Gannett would discourage justices from thinking the papers were equally in need of one. Knight-Ridder's lawyers, now more suspicious of Gannett's motives than ever, did not fully agree with Smith's strategy, but they could not force Gannett to file something more substantial.

The Supreme Court took up Michigan Citizens' petition for *certiorari* at a private conference on Friday, April 28. Their decision was to be announced the following Monday. Knight-Ridder executives talked of starting the JOA one week later. Gannett executives said nothing.

At 10:00 A.M. on Monday, May 1, any thoughts of start-up dissolved amid a loud roomful of reporters scanning eleven pages' worth of orders released by the Supreme Court. The court had denied eighty-nine petitions for *certiorari* and granted five. Among those granted was *Michigan Citizens, et al.*, v. *Thornburgh, Atty. Gen. of U.S.*

The JOA was going to the highest court in the land. No one but the justices and their clerks knew at the time, but Justice Byron White had not participated in the decision to grant *certiorari*. His reasons for withdrawing remain unknown.

At the *Free Press,* workers stoically braced for another year of uncertainty. The Knight-Ridder lawyers had been wrong so many times now that the *Free Press* staff's greatest fear was of the lawyers predicting victory yet again. "If there's a color darker than black, that's what we would call today," said Rosemary Doherty, a *Free Press* ad saleswoman.

At the *News,* staffers celebrated with cheers and handshakes. Someone adorned a bust of *News* founder James Scripps with a scrap of paper scribbled with "Hooray!" The *News*'s front page bore a six-inch-by-five-inch color photo of John Kelly standing in front of the *News* building, holding his arms as if he were bearing the newspaper on his shoulders. A *News* story for the first time alluded to Gannett executives talking of the "big win."

Later that week, when *News* reporter Keith Naughton showed up at

Knight-Ridder's Miami headquarters to cover a JOA strategy session, Jim Batten angrily rebuffed him. "I don't have any idea what we're going to do and I'm not going to talk to you about it," the normally affable executive snapped. The *News*'s celebration following the Supreme Court's decision, he said, "was very unprofessional behavior." The next day in Detroit, Batten indulged his temper again, thanking *Free Press* staffers for withstanding "petty harassment from those outside this building who are not fit to hold your coat—egocentric politicians, odd publicity seekers, and competitors who do high fives at what they regard as a harbinger of the *Free Press*'s demise. You have exhibited great heart and class."

But the most difficult test of the *Free Press*'s heart was yet to come.

21

A Matter of Survival

Something changed in Elton Schade on the day the Supreme Court announced it would take up the case of the Detroit JOA. Even though his union had long ago withdrawn as a formal opponent of the JOA, the secretary-treasurer of Teamsters Local 372 had remained personally opposed. Schade was able to afford that philosophical luxury because he had long believed the JOA ultimately would be approved. He also viewed Knight-Ridder's vow to close the *Free Press* as little more than a bargaining ploy. But when he heard that the Supreme Court had agreed to review Michigan Citizens' challenge, his certainty about the outcome of the JOA vanished.

On that day, Schade was attending a Teamsters convention in Fort Lauderdale with Joel Wilson, president of Detroit Mailers Local 2040. All that evening Schade kept going to Wilson's hotel room to worry aloud about the future of the *Free Press*. "They're going to close the *Free Press,*" he kept telling Wilson. "The Supreme Court has agreed to hear the appeal, and I am absolutely convinced the Supreme Court is going to kill the JOA." Wilson tried to reassure his friend, but Schade was inconsolable. He would pace Wilson's room for a while, ranting about the dire consequences facing the *Free Press* and the hundreds of Teamsters who worked there, then go back to his own room only to return to Wilson to rant some more. When Schade chatted over the phone with his secretary that day, she remarked that he sounded morose. "I think this is the first time I really believe the *Free Press* is going to close," he said.

Schade feared, in a way, for his life. As he saw it, if the JOA was struck down and the *Free Press* closed, his union brothers and sisters would blame him. Even though the Teamsters no longer officially opposed the JOA, the union's lawyers had helped assemble the formidable case Bill Schultz was using to try to stop the merger. Schade faced an election in the fall. Though he was regularly reelected by wide margins, he had convinced himself that the JOA would be his downfall this time. He could even foresee himself losing if the JOA *did* survive the Supreme Court, because hundreds of Teamsters would have to change jobs as the publishers combined *News* and *Free Press* seniority lists.

The thought of losing was unbearable for Schade, because the Teamsters was all he knew. "That was the only thing that was important to him," recalled his sister, Julie Eberspacher, whom Schade visited each year for two days at Christmas. "He gave everything he could to those men. He didn't have much to share with his family." Besides leading Local 372, Schade was secretary-treasurer of Joint Council 43, which governed twenty-one Teamster locals in Michigan. He was active in myriad other union activities, and hoped one day to ascend to national office. That hope had dimmed in the past year. Schade's national aspirations were linked to the fortunes of his friend and mentor, Detroit labor leader Bobby Holmes. The year before, Holmes had backed a run for national office by Weldon Mathis, who sought to succeed Jackie Presser as international president. When Mathis lost, Schade lost his best chance to become head of the Teamsters' new national Newspaper Division. He had hoped his handling of the JOA would make him a top candidate, but someone else got the job.

Schade was content to remain at Local 372, but the last three years had made him increasingly restive. First the Evening News Association got into the takeover mess. Then Gannett, with its open disdain for unions, rumbled into town. Then the publishers began their pursuit of the JOA. And now that was bogged down in a court system over which Schade had no control. So much had changed so quickly. So much change still was to come. Schade hated change. He clung to order and routine, as suggested by his unvarying daily drill: mornings in the office or at meetings, lunch and a steam with right-hand man Tom Minielly, a Canadian Club and water and dinner at Carl's Chop House, home to his apartment by eleven. Each day he recorded his weight in an appointment book he kept solely for that purpose, though his weight never varied by more than a few pounds. On Saturdays he would come to his office alone and open the safe where he kept several thousand dollars of his own. The cash was stowed in a batch of envelopes marked with the amount each contained and the date Schade last counted it. He would remove the money, count it, re-mark the envelopes, and return them to the safe. The ritual appeared to serve no purpose other than to reassure Schade that the money was as he had left it.

Everything that had happened in the last three years now threatened to disrupt Schade's obsessively ordered existence. If he lost the election, he would lose all of his official Teamster positions and the routines he attached to them. The union probably would find him another office job, but he would have none of the power he wielded as head of Local 372. He couldn't stand before hundreds of cheering members and boast that he had negotiated a contract that met their needs. He couldn't stride into the lobby of the *News* and announce to the receptionist, "Please tell Mr. Nelson that Elton Schade is waiting." His life would never be the same. He was paranoid, of course, to think he would lose the election, and paranoid to expect the JOA to be rejected simply because the Supreme Court had taken the case. But Schade, in some secret corner of his mind, perhaps on those lonely Saturdays in his office, had convinced himself he was doomed. "He just saw everything he worked for going down the drain," Joel Wilson recalled. Schade kept his feeling well hidden, though; to the members of Local 372, he was their unflappable leader.

Shortly after the Supreme Court granted *certiorari,* the publishers succumbed to union pressure to negotiate an interim contract. The eleven unions split into two camps, one led by the Teamsters, the other by the Guild and the Pressmen. The Guild talked openly of setting a strike deadline, while Schade took a more cautious stance, saving the threat of a strike for the launch of the JOA. Schade sought a $30-a-week raise while the Guild-led group pushed for $45, then $40. On May 31 the seven unions led by Schade and the Teamsters settled for $22. The Guild group vowed to fight for more, but the game was over. Once again, Schade had dictated the terms of the Guild's agreement.

But Schade himself was coming apart, and his friends were beginning to notice. He seemed especially out of sorts one Monday in the middle of June. All that morning he was in and out of the offices of Tom Minielly and Joel Wilson. "He came to my office at least a dozen times and just sat there and looked at me," Wilson later recalled. Schade was worried the publishers weren't going to pay the portion of the $22-a-week raise that was retroactive to May 1, even though they had agreed to it at the bargaining table. Schade called Keating, who was puzzled by Schade's concern, but nevertheless made a few phone calls. He called Schade back to assure him the retroactive pay would be in paychecks that Thursday.

An annual dinner for retiring *Free Press* Teamsters was scheduled for the afternoon. Schade told Minielly he wasn't going. Minielly couldn't believe it. Schade loved attending those dinners. "Al, you're going," Minielly told his old friend. "You have a lot of friends there, they expect you there, you need a little time to see your friends, have a little drink." Schade acquiesced, but he didn't seem to have his usual good time. He asked Minielly to make his speech for him, and when Minielly refused, Schade offered a clipped testimonial devoid of the union leader's usual passion. Afterward, Schade and Minielly returned to the office before Minielly headed home for the evening.

No one knows for sure what happened to Elton Schade that night. Minielly later tried to retrace his friend's steps. Schade, he said, went to Carl's, but did not eat. He left around 10:00 P.M. and returned to the office, where he took off his watch and rings—one a gift from Jimmy Hoffa—and locked them in a drawer. Schade then went to the Teamster steam room he and Minielly frequented at the lunch hour. Minielly later found a folded towel Schade evidently had used as a pillow. Schade apparently lay there alone among the girlie posters tacked to the wall. He might well have been thinking that he was about to die.

Sometime after 2:00 A.M., Schade was standing in an alley behind a pair of cinder-block storage sheds near his office building on Trumbull Avenue. His 1987 Lincoln Continental was parked out front, where the security cameras in the Teamster parking lot could not spy it. According to Detroit police accounts, Schade fired three times from a handgun. The first shot missed, the bullet scuffing the wall of the building behind him. The second shot grazed his head. A Wayne County medical examiner later said Schade may have been building the courage to kill himself. If so, he succeeded with the third shot, firing into the right side of his head, the bullet tearing into his brain. Schade slumped against a garbage bin and collapsed to the ground, his blood spreading across asphalt gravel and broken bits of glass. He was pronounced dead at Detroit Receiving Hospital.

Police called it a suicide. A witness told police she thought she had seen things that indicated Schade was murdered. Becky Bradley was sitting on the porch of her nearby home when she saw Schade walking in the alley. He had both hands above his head, she said, and he did not have a gun. He kept his hands near his head while Bradley saw a flash and heard a shot. A second shot dropped him to his knees, and a third shot pitched him forward to the ground, Bradley said. But she did not see an assailant. When the paramedics came, Bradley thought she saw one of them take a pistol from the back of Schade's belt. She also thought she saw a ring on one of Schade's fingers. Police tried to confirm Bradley's version, without success.

No one can say for certain why Elton Schade died. There is no doubt that he had been depressed and apprehensive. He may well have felt that way because he feared for his job. Or he may have believed his life was in danger for some unknown reason. His close friends say Schade had a personal problem that he took to his grave. They would not discuss it. "It was a small thing," said one of them, "but with him it was immense."

If Schade did commit suicide, his friends and associates feel it almost certainly had something to do with his inability to accept the changes that had enveloped him and his dear Teamsters Local 372. But Schade was not alone in his unwillingness to part with the past. Virtually no one touched by the long and anguished end of the Great Detroit Newspaper War wanted to relinquish what was close and familiar and certain. They wanted their lives to go on as they had. Alas, the price—tens of millions of dollars in losses—had grown too great. For Elton Schade, the price may have been his life.

At the *Free Press,* they waited. And they bid farewell.

Neal Shine retired June 30. The *Free Press*'s beloved senior managing editor had been at the paper thirty-nine years. At 6:00 A.M. on his last day, a group of *Free Press* staff led by senior reporter Brian Flanigan trundled the contents of Shine's office—desk, computer, telephone, coffee machine, book of Irish verse—from their home on the third floor to the sidewalk in front of the *Free Press* building. When Shine arrived at 9:20, two hundred people stood around the makeshift work area and applauded. A police sergeant issued Shine a ticket for blocking pedestrians. "We figured you started out on the street," Flanigan explained, "and you should end up on the street."

A month later, Dave Lawrence announced he would leave to become publisher of the *Miami Herald.* Bob Hall would replace him as publisher of the *Free Press.* Lawrence fought back tears as he told the staff of his decision to accept Knight-Ridder's long-standing offer. "In my life," he said, "there can never be another newspaper like this one." Few were surprised; his departure had been rumored for months. Even while he stumped for the JOA, Lawrence had taken Spanish lessons and studied Latin American culture to prepare for his next post.

Some couldn't help but see him as a captain fleeing a sinking ship. Lawrence had promised more than once to stay at the *Free Press* until the JOA was decided one way or the other. He broke his vow because he felt he could do nothing more to help the *Free Press,* and his move to the *Herald* had been on hold for two years. "It is unhealthy for both institutions and for the people of both institutions to know leadership will be changing . . . and not consummate that change," Lawrence told the staff. He often had told his crew he did not plan to stay on beyond the JOA itself. Lawrence had too much pride to become a publisher in name only, who would oversee the *Free Press* newsroom but have little or no control over the paper's crucial business functions. Nor did he desire to work for the Detroit Newspaper Agency, where he would have to toil with his former rivals. "Too much of me had been spent doing things the other way," he later said. Before he left, an anonymous staffer left Lawrence a dozen white roses in a black vase. A note read: "Chief, you fought one hell of a fight."

The Supreme Court set October 30 for oral arguments. Mindful of Clark Clifford's performance at the D.C. Circuit Court, Knight-Ridder hired yet another law firm to argue its case before the high court. Clifford helped select Mayer, Brown and Platt, the Chicago-based Supreme Court specialists. The case would be argued by Stephen M. Shapiro, a former deputy solicitor general who had won fifteen of the eighteen cases he had tried before the court. Gannett was not consulted. And when Clifford, Shapiro, and Alvah Chapman met with the solicitors general who would be defending Ed Meese's opinion, Gannett's lawyers were purposely left out. After the bitter disappointment in the Gannett tower, "We weren't feeling very friendly," Jack Fontaine later said.

Michigan Citizens for an Independent Press and the *Arkansas Democrat* filed briefs urging the Supreme Court to reject the JOA. Instead of the *Chevron* question emphasized in its petition for *certiorari*, Michigan Citizens focused on how approval of the JOA would subvert the intent of the Newspaper Preservation Act. Under Meese's interpretation, Bill Schultz and Dave Vladeck argued, competing papers "would have an incentive to engage in price wars with the goal of achieving dominance and monopoly profits or, alternatively, approval of a lucrative JOA." In other words, the Detroit JOA would offer an improper road map to other papers desiring a JOA. Schultz told a *News* reporter, "Maybe the Newspaper Preservation Act should be renamed the Newspaper Profitability Act."

Knight-Ridder and Gannett responded in separate briefs August 11. Both argued that price wars would rage whether JOAs were available or not, simply because pricing often dictated which of two competing papers would survive. Knight-Ridder's fifty-page argument called the *Free Press* a "shell" that would have perished long before if not for its parent's financial aid. Gannett in its thirty-eight-page brief distanced itself from the J0A, saying it was "contractually obligated," while noting that the *News* "finds itself in what [Al Neuharth] has characterized as a 'win-win' position." *Amicus* briefs supporting the JOA came from the unions, three Detroit business organizations, Governor Blanchard, the American Newspaper Publishers Association, and an ad hoc group of *Free Press* reporters and editors led by Jane Daugherty, erstwhile leader of the "contra" faction that had tried to get Guild Local 22 to renounce its opposition to the JOA.

The Daugherty brief was an unusual, twenty-one-page mélange of arcane legalism and journalistic passion prepared by nine *Free Press* reporters and editors and their Detroit lawyer, Barbara Harvey. Accompanying it was a bulky, portfolio-sized binder of recent showcase *Free Press* stories, including an investigation of Detroit banks' lending practices and a poignant exploration of the twenty-year aftermath of the 1967 race riot. Forty-two people signed the brief. Most were *Free Press* journalists, but there were also a few big-name editors, including Gene Roberts, the *Free Press* alumnus who had won a flock of Pulitzers at the *Philadelphia Inquirer,* and the *Oakland Tribune*'s Robert Maynard, the first black editor of a mainstream U.S. metropolitan daily. They agreed "most reluctantly" that the *Free Press* needed a JOA. "*Amici* would prefer that what has been called the 'last great American newspaper war' would go on forever in Detroit," the brief said. "Without the help of the Newspaper Preservation Act, it cannot."

The heart of the brief was an eloquent, ten-page statement written in large measure by Barbara Stanton, the veteran *Free Press* reporter who had shared in the paper's Pulitzer Prize for coverage of the 1967 riot. She wrote, "In an era when the one-newspaper town has become the norm, when Americans get most of their information from a local monopoly newspaper or television's bite-size bits of news, Detroit still enjoys two serious, spirited, greatly dissimilar newspapers." By drawing pointed distinctions between the *Free Press* and the *News,* Stanton, Daugherty, and their colleagues hoped to persuade the Supreme Court of the value of having different editorial voices in the same city. The argument seemed convincing on the surface, but much of its unscientific analysis was rooted in the past. For example, on race relations, an area of coverage Daugherty et al. chose to emphasize, the *News* of 1989 was hardly the paper it had been in 1968, when it published a daily totting of muggings that described suspects by race. Nor did the *News* of 1989 shy from investigative work, another area Daugherty and friends stressed. The two papers' editorial pages still clashed almost daily, but otherwise it was hard to argue that the *Free Press* and the *News* weren't looking and acting more like each other all the time, just as newspapers across America had come to look and act more like each other since the advent of *USA Today.*

At its core, the brief sought to convince the court that the *Free Press* mattered. Indeed, the journalists who signed the brief were asserting, in a way, that *they* mattered. They wanted the court to know—or perhaps they were trying to convince themselves—that the stories they wrote and the photographs they shot counted for something, that what they did for a living ultimately would play a role in deciding the fate of the *Detroit Free Press.* In fact, though, the hardest lesson of the three long years of waiting for the JOA was that the journalists did not matter. At least not much. The journalists at the *Free Press* hadn't had a thing to do with the decisions to launch Operation Tiger and lowball ad rates and expand the printing plant and suck up a few years of multimillion-dollar losses to get a JOA. Their precious scoops and photographic coups played no role in the attempt to persuade Ed Meese and the courts to approve the merger. That very spring of 1989, the *Free Press* had won a Pulitzer Prize for Manny Crisostomo's intimate photographs of life at a Detroit high school. But it quickly became old news as attention turned to the Supreme Court's decision to take up the JOA. If the *Free Press* did survive and ultimately overtook the *News,* it would not be because the journalists at the *Free Press* had put out a better paper, but because of a deal cut by a couple of business executives in a distant city. Indeed, the Great Detroit Newspaper War now was being waged in Washington by a lot of lawyers who didn't even read the *Free Press* or the *News.*

The journalists at the *News* were no less irrelevant than their counterparts at the *Free Press;* they just weren't as aware of their impotence because they weren't toiling under a spreading shadow of imminent death. The *Free Press* people had lost their chance to win the war outright, had lost their leaders, and now stood to lose their paper. For three years they had been hearing that they worked for a "failing" enterprise while their enemies at "the *Snooze*" bought their way to bigger circulation and advertising leads. Perhaps because they knew no other way, they kept on fighting, like some misguided battalion of soldiers who have not heard that the war is over.

On Friday, October 13, less than three weeks before the Supreme Court was to hear oral arguments on the JOA, more than forty *Free Press* reporters, photographers, and editors gathered in room 100, the high-ceilinged chamber where Alvah Chapman had solemnly told them their paper had to have a JOA or it would die. Today, though, they weren't thinking about the JOA. Instead, they listened to a pep talk from city editor Ron Dzwonkowski and senior reporter Brian Flanigan. Then they fanned out across the city with their cameras and notebooks to take a twenty-four-hour snapshot of life in Detroit's drug culture. It was an ambitious project—and maybe, they knew, their last chance to show the world what a bold, idealistic, and irreverent paper the *Detroit Free Press* could be.

For the next day, they followed an addict who sold a boombox for eight dollars to spend on crack cocaine. They photographed a crack-dependent infant fighting for life on a respirator. They saw dealers making scores at a heavily traveled intersection. They listened to a former addict belt out a gospel song at a rehabilitation center. They watched a four-year-old boy "assume the position" as police raided his mother's apartment for illegal drugs. They visited drug dens, a police interrogation, a hospital emergency room, a telephone help line, the scene of a shooting, a courtroom, a morgue, and the ritzy suburban homes of the leaders of a cocaine ring.*

Back at the *Free Press,* newsroom staff took reporters' calls, processed film, and planned the layout of the twelve-page special section—"24 Hours: The Drug Menace"—to be published that Sunday. It was an enormous effort, involving more than ninety *Free Press* journalists, many working around the clock. The one at the center of it all, hunched over a computer keyboard in the third-floor city room, shaping the welter of disparate images and quotes into a compelling, hour-by-hour narrative, was a squat, muscular forty-three-year-old in a graying goatee and a Harley-Davidson T-shirt.

His name was Brian Flanigan, and he was a reporter's reporter, one of the best in Detroit. Neal Shine liked to say that Flanigan was not born of a mother, but chiseled out of a glacier where he had been preserved since Ben Hecht created him as a mythical 1920s Chicago newspaperman. For most of his ten years at the *Free Press* his beat was crime, and nobody covered it like Brian Patrick Aloysius Michael Dennis "Beep" Flanigan. Year after year, Flanigan charmed his hordes of well-placed sources, beat the *News* to juicy stories, and wrote in a simple, hard-edged style that subtly bespoke his compassion for the downtrodden and disadvantaged. Flanigan seemed to know everybody in Detroit—certainly every cop—and to the few people he hadn't met, he delighted in introducing himself as "the best-looking Irishman you'll ever know."

*A minor controversy arose concerning the reporting of this project. After the story was published, a photographer admitted paying a crack addict twenty dollars for a Sony Walkman. The addict used the money to buy drugs. The photographer and a reporter did not immediately tell their bosses of the purchase. They were suspended briefly without pay, and the *Free Press* did not nominate the project for any journalism awards.

He was a Detroit native, the oldest of eleven children, who served two terms in Vietnam as a marine and came home to live with a group of radical writers and activists in the Cass Corridor, one of Detroit's toughest neighborhoods. He worked passionately for civil rights and other liberal causes, wrote free-verse poetry, and struggled with heroin, cocaine, and alcohol abuse. In 1974 he joined the staff of the *Michigan Chronicle,* Detroit's black-owned weekly, covering crime, courts, sports, the jazz scene, and anything else he fancied. The day he befriended Jack Kresnak, the *Free Press*'s young police reporter, they were sitting in a park adjoining police headquarters and the Wayne County Jail. "Wanna smoke a joint?" Flanigan offered. They did.

From the time he started as a journalist, Flanigan talked about working for the *Free Press.* Kresnak helped him get hired there in 1979. Flanigan soon became the dominant figure in the newsroom, an intense, comic, obnoxious dervish of energy and passion who routinely used language that wouldn't be tolerated in hell. Staffers arriving at the *Free Press* city room could count on Flanigan greeting them with a gruff, "Good morning, shithead," a sure sign that Flanigan liked them. "Shut up and stay with me, kid," he would tell young journalists, "and I'll take you to the top." He swaggered around the room in Hawaiian shirts and cowboy boots, always up, always excited about the story he was working on that undoubtedly would infuriate "the pukes down the street."

He loved beating the *News.* He loved the pressure of writing on deadline, which he called "jam and jelly time." He cared deeply about the *Free Press* and everything that went into it. "He was as passionate about four un-bylined paragraphs buried deep in the A-section as he was about stories that stretched beneath his name across the top of Page One," Shine once wrote. Though he won his share, Flanigan disdained journalism awards, of which he would say, "Don't pull on my dick, it's long enough." He loved his *Free Press* comrades, from the janitors to the librarians to the people who sold ads and took customer complaints. Many had the honor of being nicknamed by Flanigan. Shine was "Gramps." Kresnak, Flanigan's longtime partner, was "the Raw Dog." Flanigan's wife, science writer Nancy Ross, was "Doc." Flanigan also is believed to have tagged Dave Lawrence with the "Skippy" moniker the publisher so detested.

In Flanigan's mind, there was nothing he and his *Free Press* family couldn't do. One day he came to Shine with one of his cockiest grins. "Gramps," he said, "this is maybe the best I've ever been." He was working on a story of an infant, abandoned to the elements, who had been saved by a stray dog. "Daugherty and I are going out to find the mutt," Flanigan vowed.

A few hours later he returned muttering profanely about the impossibility of finding one dog in a city of strays. Shine shook his head. "The difference between you and me, Brian," Shine said, "is that I would have come back with a dog."

"*A* dog?" Flanigan defiantly shot back. "Or *the* dog?"

He drove his editors crazy. Few reporters worked harder or faster, but if an editor disagreed with Flanigan's angle on a story, or tried to make a Flanigan story something Flanigan didn't think it was, Flanigan could be counted on to storm around the newsroom threatening to throw people out windows.

He drove the *News* crazy. *News* reporter Ric Bohy once staked out a suburban home where a fugitive criminal supposedly was hiding. He was planning on a scoop until a *Free Press* reporter rolled up beside him. Bohy later found out that a neighbor had called local police with the license plate of the car he was in. When a cop traced the car to the *News,* the cop called Flanigan to let him know a story might be brewing. "That's how the guy was wired," Bohy said. "The cops called *him.*"

The *News* had tried to hire Flanigan several times. *News* managing editor Christina Bradford, a *Free Press* alumna who had worked for Kurt Luedtke, had aggressively recruited him. Flanigan couldn't keep this to himself, of course. Every now and then he would stomp into Shine's office with some minor complaint and declare, "Fuck it. I'm calling Christy." Fed up, Shine finally told him, "Brian, don't come to my office anymore unless it's to tell me you're going to the *News.*" He figured Flanigan would not be able to bring himself to defect.

A few days later Flanigan burst in on a meeting Shine was having with Larry Jinks, Knight-Ridder's senior vice-president for news. "Fuck it," Flanigan said, "I'm staying. If the goddamn place goes down, I'm going with it." And he stomped back out.

"What was that all about?" Jinks asked.

"I think," Shine replied, "that was Brian's way of telling me he's not going to the *News.*"

Flanigan didn't like the idea of a JOA and initially opposed it. But eventually he resigned himself, believing the JOA was the only way to keep the *Free Press* alive. His name appeared on Jane Daugherty's *amicus* brief.

He was at his frenetic best the Friday night and Saturday of the *Free Press*'s twenty-four-hour drug culture watch. "He just pumped everybody up," executive editor Heath Meriwether later said. "He wouldn't let you get tired. He wouldn't let you get down." The project was all Flanigan had talked about for weeks. It meant a lot to him, partly because he knew firsthand the damage drugs could do, partly because he relished the challenge of spinning dozens of different threads into the colorful fabric of a story. Flanigan hadn't planned to go to work Friday until 2:00 P.M., but he woke at 5:00 A.M. and fiddled at home until he couldn't take the waiting anymore. He got to the *Free Press* before noon.

All that night and the next day, Flanigan periodically called Nancy, his wife, to relate vignettes and details. Earlier that week she had had a biopsy, which had Flanigan worried. Nancy was his greatest passion. They had met when she came to the *Free Press* in 1982 as a summer intern. Flanigan had asked her out the first time by shouting across the newsroom, "Hey, Toots, had dinner yet?" He took her to a barbecue in the backyard of a law office in the Cass Corridor and, from then on, they were inseparable. They married on the roof of the *Free Press* building in the fall of 1984. Flanigan reluctantly donned a tuxedo; when the priest asked if he took Nancy as his wife, he replied, "Why else would I be dressed this way?" Nancy worried about Flanigan, too, as he worked his two-day shift on the drug project. He had been suffering chest pains and was scheduled for stress tests the following week. Friday night he lay down for a few moments, but was too worked up to sleep.

The story he wrote opened with the image of a twenty-six-year-old addict drinking wine and beer to prepare for a night of hunting crack. "Tim's on the launching pad," Flanigan began. More than eighty column inches later, the tale ended with an image of Tim, twenty-four hours older, polishing off a forty-ounce bottle of Pabst beer. In between came vivid pictures of handcuffed young men, frustrated cops, frightened mothers, gun-toting teenagers, and a man injecting heroin into his groin. Flanigan finished twenty minutes before deadline. His colleagues gave him a standing ovation. He was glowing when he called Nancy Saturday evening to say he was coming home. A couple of other people got on the phone to tell her what a terrific job he had done, maybe his greatest performance ever.

But the sight of Flanigan at the door of their home gave Nancy a start; he was gray all over and deep circles rimmed his eyes. The buoyant energy she had felt on the phone seemed to have left him. Flanigan wanted to celebrate, though. He changed clothes and they went out for dinner. He seemed better then, talking excitedly about the project.

He woke early Sunday and went out for a *Free Press.* He and Nancy planned to spend a quiet day at home. Sometime after noon he complained of feeling suddenly exhausted. Something was wrong, he said. He felt horrible. He was having chest pains and they were moving into his arm. No, he told Nancy at first, don't call the doctor, I'll be okay. The pain worsened. He thought he was having a heart attack. Nancy called an ambulance. Flanigan lay down on their bed. Hurry up, he said, I don't know if I can make it. Before he passed out, he told Nancy he loved her. She performed CPR until the paramedics took him away.

Shine heard about the heart attack when he arrived home from the annual *Free Press* marathon. He rushed to the emergency room at St. John's Hospital, where he found editor Joe Distelheim and a handful of other *Free Press* people. Distelheim just shook his head. Flanigan was dead. Shine began to cry. Kresnak was there; he had burned up a clutch driving over. Heath Meriwether was in grass-stained sweatpants; he and the *Free Press*'s touch football team had just beaten the *News*. Reporter Patricia Chargot was there, unbelieving and angry. "God is fucking with our minds," she said.

The *Free Press* staff paid tribute in a lengthy front-page story that called Flanigan "one of the best damn reporters ever to work the streets of Detroit." Shine wrote, "I suppose there might be journalists somewhere who care more about what they do than Brian Flanigan cared about his work. I never happened to meet one. And never expect to." Cops praised Flanigan as a man of honor; a priest called him "the perfect Detroit journalist"; *Free Press* security guards and custodians called Nancy to offer sympathy. Even readers who did not know Flanigan were touched. "Never in my life have I read such a moving account of a man's life and his heartbeat," one wrote to the *Free Press*. "Just as Brian Flanigan put his whole heart into his job, so did the *Free Press* staff put their whole hearts into writing their final farewell to a cherished friend."

For a few days, the *Free Press* newsroom was eerily quiet. Flanigan's desk became a shrine. Someone laid a piece of black velvet at his computer terminal, and friends left flowers, poems, and messages. People just couldn't believe he wasn't there. In the days following his death, some would glance at his desk and weep silently for what had been so cruelly stolen away.

As much as they loved Flanigan, perhaps his *Free Press* colleagues were mourning more than just his sudden passing. Perhaps they were grieving, too, for three years of uncertainty and turmoil, for the unrelenting threat to their lives and livelihoods, for the inexorable passing of an era they had loved. A *Free Press* editorial described Flanigan as the epitome of the *Free Press* and Detroit: "tough and gritty, street smart and iconoclastic, motivated by a core of principled compassion." Now he was gone—and maybe their paper would soon be gone too. How much more would they have to endure? How much more *could* they endure? "It was like Brian's death," his wife recalled, "was the last blow."

Flanigan would have understood. He too had lived with the pain of watching his paper edge closer to the brink, and he undoubtedly would have wished he hadn't made matters worse. At his memorial service, attended by five hundred family members and friends, a part of one of his poems was read. Flanigan's simple lines, written years before, could not have spoken more eloquently to the ordeal his friends were suffering through now:

it was never a matter of choice
only a matter of survival

22

Five Hundred Miles Away

A warm October sun bathed the marble steps ascending to the majestic portico that welcomes the public into the United States Supreme Court. On one step stood Bill Keating, making small talk with Michigan state senator John Kelly. Just introduced, the chief executive of the Detroit Newspaper Agency and the chief opponent of the JOA chatted until a news photographer approached. Keating suddenly looked uncomfortable. "No photos," he insisted, waving the photographer away. Kelly, always happy to get his mug in the paper, thought the executive was kidding around. But Keating walked away.

It was Monday, October 30, and the Supreme Court was about to hear oral arguments in the attempt by Michigan Citizens for an Independent Press to block the Detroit JOA. The case was scheduled second on the afternoon docket. By 1:00 P.M., when the first case began, the courtroom had nearly filled with executives, lawyers, and others who had come from Detroit and Miami to watch. Many were seeing the room for the first time, and they marveled at its imposing grandeur, the two dozen Sienna marble columns, the forty-four-foot-high ceiling, and the nine leather swivel chairs waiting behind the high mahogany bench.

John Kelly wore a new suit. "I want to put my best foot forward and look as credible as the corporate captains sitting on the other side," he explained. Ed Wendover had rented a motor home so he could bring his daughter, Jessica, and a group of friends from Plymouth. He also flew his mother up from Florida because, he said, "It's not every day your family gets a case heard in a big court." Wendover was in awe. Waiting in line to enter the courtroom, he fidgeted and sweated. "Dad," his daughter whispered, "it'll be all right." Wendover kept thinking of the high school teacher who had taught him that in America, anyone could take a case all the way to the Supreme Court. It was the kind of thing you heard but never really believed. Until it happened.

Jane Daugherty, leader of the *Free Press* "contras," brought her eight-year-old, Ryan, who told his mother the justices looked small sitting behind the bench. Lou and Lorraine Mleczko drove out with their fourteen-year-old daughter, Carrie. Just before they left, Mleczko had gotten into a verbal joust with Frank Hawkins, Knight-Ridder's wiseacre spokesman. Hawkins, aware that Mleczko had helped organize Michigan Citizens, described the Guild chief to a *News* reporter as having "the face of baby Jesus, the brain of a terrorist, and the tongue of Satan." Mleczko, amused, noted to the same reporter that he was an atheist.

Alvah Chapman, who finally had stepped down as chairman of Knight-Ridder, flew up on the company jet with Jim Batten, Tony Ridder, and Dave Lawrence, now publisher of the *Miami Herald.* John Curley and Doug McCorkindale came over from Gannett. *Free Press* publisher Bob Hall and his wife, Ronna, flew down from Detroit, but fog grounded the *News*'s Bob Giles. Al Neuharth, busy promoting his newly published autobiography, *Confessions of an SOB,* also was a no-show, though no one seemed to miss him.

Sitting to the justices' right were Bill Schultz, Dave Vladeck, and Public Citizen's head lawyer, Alan Morrison, representing Michigan Citizens. A few of their Public Citizen colleagues were in the gallery, along with Schultz's wife, *Washington Post* reporter Sari Horwitz, and his sister and father. Franklin Schultz, himself an attorney, had been a classmate of Justice Byron White at Yale Law School, and they had stayed in touch over the years. When Bill Schultz had argued his first case before the high court, White had passed a scribbled note to the young lawyer's father in the gallery. "Frank," it read. "Chips and blocks and things like that. Congratulations." But the younger Schultz lost the case, with White and every other justice voting against him.

The publishers brought their usual legion of lawyers. There were more than a dozen, from each of the parent companies and the four law firms on the case—Nixon, Hargrave, Devans and Doyle, for Gannett; and Hughes, Hubbard and Reed, Clifford and Warnke, and Mayer, Brown and Platt, all for Knight-Ridder. Representing Acting Solicitor General Lawrence G. Wallace were

Thomas W. Merrill and Michael Lazerwitz of his office, and Douglas Letter, the Justice Department lawyer who had bailed out Clark Clifford in the D.C. Circuit Court.

Knight-Ridder's hiring of star Supreme Court advocate Stephen M. Shapiro of Mayer, Brown and Platt came at least partly to naught. Shapiro had helped prepare Knight-Ridder's brief, but he would not be allowed to argue today. Instead, Deputy Solicitor General Tom Merrill would defend the decision of former Attorney General Edwin Meese. The court had declined to let both Knight-Ridder and the solicitor general argue. Traditionally, the Supreme Court gave each of the two sides in a case half an hour to present its arguments. Occasionally the court allowed parties on the same side to split the half hour, but the Rehnquist court increasingly had frowned on the practice. In the JOA case, the court denied two requests for so-called divided argument.

Either Shapiro or Merrill could argue, but not both. The lawyers for Knight-Ridder and the solicitor general chose the latter, not because Merrill was the better lawyer, but because the court seemed to expect the government to defend its own decisions. Still, Knight-Ridder was concerned the solicitor general might not put enough emphasis on the real-world consequences of a denial of the JOA—that is, the closing of the *Free Press.* Clark Clifford, tapping his contacts in the solicitor general's office, had asked that Merrill be assigned to argue because Merrill had agreed to consult with Knight-Ridder on his presentation. The government lawyer met several times with Clifford and at least once with Alvah Chapman. When the day for oral argument arrived, the Knight-Ridder people were confident that Merrill understood their perspective, though they still wished they could have had Shapiro face the justices.

The first case ended at 1:34 P.M. Just before Chief Justice William Rehnquist called the JOA case to order, Justice Byron White stood up from the chair directly to Rehnquist's left and disappeared behind the maroon velvet curtain that hung behind the bench. Only eighteen days before, the court had disclosed that White had withdrawn from the case, citing unspecified "personal reasons." Newspaper reports speculated that White had recused himself because of a longtime acquaintance with Clark Clifford. (Clifford later insisted he did not have a close relationship with the justice.) White did not say. It is possible the recusal stemmed from White's awkward conversation with *News* publisher Chip Weil in the Capital Hilton seven months earlier. White officially was out of the case as of May 1, the day the court granted *certiorari.* There was no mention of his not participating in the March 20 decision to deny a stay of the JOA. Assuming White *did* participate in the stay decision, something must have happened between then and May 1 to make him think he should withdraw—and, as several court observers since have agreed, it could well have been the chat with Weil. Only Justice White knows the true reason.*

Simple arithmetic dictated that White's absence would hurt the JOA opponents: to win, Michigan Citizens now needed five of eight votes instead of five of nine. Gannett's informal analysis had White leaning slightly toward plaintiffs in antitrust cases, theoretically making him a vote against the JOA. In effect, White's recusal was a vote *for* the JOA. Indeed, it raised the possibility of an unusual 4–4 vote—which would allow Knight-Ridder and Gannett to consummate the merger. The publishers' lawyers played down this possibility, not wishing to acknowledge the case could be so close. But Schultz and Vladeck fretted, for they expected a narrow margin, and a tie would mean they once again had fallen a single vote short of victory.

The courtroom quieted as the lawyers from the previous case collected their briefcases and filed out. All attention focused on Bill Schultz, who now rose to the lectern set before the eight black-robed justices and the solitary empty chair.

"Mr. Schultz," Rehnquist said, "you may proceed."

"Mr. Chief Justice, and may it please the court . . ."

Schultz had spent the morning in the Supreme Court library, rereading cases and going over his six-page outline. He was ready, but nervous nonetheless, because an attorney could never be totally prepared for a Supreme Court argument. The justices were unpredictable. They could ask whatever they wished. They might not even listen to an attorney's carefully plotted argument; they might interrupt until his or her allotted time suddenly was gone. Oral argument at the high court was a severe test of a litigator, an intellectual duel with some of the sharpest minds in the country—minds that more than likely were already made up. Among Washington lawyers, the theory was that you could not win a case at oral argument; you could only lose. By the time you faced the justices, so the theory went, they already had decided the case on their reading of the briefs. But a lawyer couldn't know if the court was with him or against. He couldn't know if a justice holding a crucial vote had not settled on how he or she would cast it. So he had to argue well.

*The author wrote White seeking an answer. "I can be of no help to you," the justice replied in a one-sentence letter.

Schultz had hoped to go over some of the key facts before the justices started asking questions. He began by arguing that the Detroit papers were competitive equals, as they admitted by asserting they had fought to a "virtual draw." In every other JOA, Schultz said, "there was one paper that was dominant and profitable, and a second paper that was junior, losing money and had been losing both circulation and advertising."

Justice Antonin Scalia, sitting at the far end of the bench to Schultz's left, stopped the attorney. "Well," the dark-eyed jurist said, "the only difference here . . . is that [the *Free Press*] wasn't losing circulation, but it *was* losing money year after year, was it not?"

"The *Free Press* was losing money," Schultz said, "but the *News* here was also losing almost as much, whereas in the other situations, the paper not designated failing was profitable."

"So you consider that a stable situation? In which both newspapers are losing money every year?"

"Well, I didn't say—"

"That is stability?" Scalia insisted.

Justice Anthony Kennedy seemed equally skeptical. "If we're intending to ensure some competition *before* a JOA agreement," he said, "it's hard for me to understand how you criticize the fact that the Knight-Ridder operation fought the other newspaper to a draw. I think that's exactly what you want to encourage. . . . I mean, what's wrong with each newspaper fighting hard?"

Schultz then offered his "road map" argument, essentially that sanction of the Detroit JOA would supply other newspapers with an easy-to-follow guide to monopoly: refuse to raise prices, promise to close one paper without a JOA, and collect.

Again, Scalia seemed unimpressed.

"All they have to do is lose money for five years and gamble on the fact that, having lost that many million, some attorney general will approve the JOA?"

"Well—"

"Would you invest in that paper?" the justice asked. "You know, that seems to be a pretty risky gamble."

Schultz argued that, while the newspapers' losses were real, they were a direct consequence of the publishers' desire for a JOA. "We agree that this conduct may be rational," the attorney said, "if at the end of the road you can be assured or even have a good chance of getting a joint operating arrangement." But, Schultz argued, the decision to grant a JOA had to rest on more than the publishers' self-serving claims. Indeed, he said, the crucial question before

Attorney General Meese was whether Gannett would raise its prices if the JOA was denied.

Justice John Paul Stevens zeroed in on that question almost immediately after Deputy Solicitor General Thomas Merrill stood to address the court. Merrill had been in the solicitor general's office for two years, having practiced at the Chicago firm of Sidley and Austin and taught at Northwestern University and the University of Chicago. He did not regard the JOA case as a plum assignment. He and his colleagues in the solicitor general's office could not fathom why the court was interested, which made preparing all the more difficult. "You couldn't really tell what the legal issue was," Merrill later said. At the time, he wondered if the court simply wished to get to the bottom of a case that, as Merrill later observed, had an "odor of irregularity," what with Meese's rebuff of his administrative law judge, the divided circuit court, and the strong dissent on the plea for *en banc* review.

Merrill wore the traditional morning coat donned by government lawyers addressing the high court. He began by pointing out that, despite Michigan Citizens' suggestions to the contrary, the decision of the attorney general—not the beliefs of the administrative law judge or the Antitrust Division—was all that counted.

Justice John Paul Stevens cut him off.

"Mr. Merrill, it is true, though, that the attorney general *did* accept all the factual findings of the ALJ, did he not?"

The inference wasn't fair, Merrill replied. Meese never *adopted* Judge Needelman's findings, he merely *accepted* them as accurate. Stevens pressed on. He was setting a trap.

The justice wanted to know what Merrill thought of Al Neuharth's testimony that the *News* would not raise its prices so long as it competed with the *Free Press*. "Do you think we should accept that testimony as true, that the chief executive of a large newspaper, which has been losing money for years, millions and millions of dollars, would continue to lose money until he is successful in driving his competitor out of the market? That's the substance of what he testified to."

Merrill was beginning to see where Stevens was headed. He attempted a diversion. "I don't—I do not think that the court either needs to accept or not accept that testimony as true."

"And if that testimony is the truth," Stevens continued, "and if [Neuharth's] program were carried out after a JOA were turned down, would that be lawful or unlawful conduct in the opinion of the United States?" The justice was alluding to predatory pricing—the illegal practice of pricing below cost in order to force competitors out of a market.

"The claim has been made here that somehow it would constitute predatory pricing," Merrill said. "let me—let me address that directly."

"I'd like an answer to the question," Stevens said.

"Hm?"

"I'd like an answer to the question."

"I will try to answer the question."

"Yeah."

"There is absolutely no evidence in this record about predatory pricing," Merrill declared. "Predatory pricing, I take it, would mean—"

Stevens interrupted. He sounded impatient. "The testimony I've just described is strong evidence of an intent to engage in predatory pricing for the purpose of acquiring a monopoly."

Merrill gamely tried to deflect the unanticipated attack. Neuharth's testimony alone, he said, couldn't prove the existence of predatory pricing. It would be unfair to raise an issue that neither Judge Needelman nor the Antitrust Division had raised, he said. Of course, the justices could raise whatever issue they wished. But Stevens had made his point anyway: Not only might it be irrational for Gannett to persist in its kamikaze pricing strategy, it might well be illegal. And, more germane to the case at hand, if the strategy was in fact illegal, it would be sufficient grounds upon which to deny the JOA—a point that Merrill himself accepted.

Justice Scalia had one more problem. Meese and Judge Needelman had agreed Detroit could support two newspapers. "And it seems to me, once you make that finding, why would you ever want to grant a joint operating agreement?" Scalia asked. "Here you go in and say, this city can have two completely independent newspapers, but since it can't have two independent newspapers, we'll grant a joint operating agreement. I don't understand that."

"Sad to say, Justice Scalia," Merrill said, "but there are a lot of cities in this country that could support two newspapers, but that do not *have* two newspapers." Pricing low to retain market share doomed many a paper, he said. "In that sort of situation, the competitive reality is that the papers will not price at levels which are sufficient for the two of them to last."

Schultz picked up on the point in his rebuttal. Meese, he said, "found that Detroit can support two profitable newspapers if prices are at market—so that focuses the whole case on the issue of price and nothing else."

It ended at 2:34 P.M.

Alvah Chapman and the other Knight-Ridder executives hurried away, trying to avoid the reporters. They weren't thinking they had lost, nor were they counting on a win. After their long string of disappointments, they couldn't help but wonder if one more awaited. They thought back on the questions.

Justices Sandra Day O'Connor, Harry Blackmun, Thurgood Marshall, and William Brennan hadn't asked one. Rehnquist and Kennedy seemed friendly to the JOA. Scalia was inscrutable. Stevens, the old antitrust curmudgeon, was definitely hostile. There had to have been four votes to grant *certiorari*. Was there one more that would doom the *Free Press*?

While the executives scurried to their cars and limousines, Bill Schultz stood on the steps outside the Supreme Court, grinning and accepting hugs and kisses and congratulations from his friends and family. You were great, you were marvelous, you were terrific, they told him again and again. Even Clark Clifford had gone out of his way to compliment Schultz in the courtroom. Reporters crowded around him. He refused to predict victory, but said, "We think we have a good shot at winning."

Ed Wendover, in a suit with suspenders and a wide, 1960s-vintage American flag tie, beamed and smoked a big cigar. He admitted that, early in Schultz's argument, he had figured his cause was in trouble. By the end, though, he said, "I wanted to buy Justice Stevens a beer." Only John Kelly, of all people, restrained himself. The man who had predicted an 8–0 win before the argument now declined to make a forecast. "You never know what they are really thinking," he told reporters. "If Justice Stevens writes the opinion, I think we're in pretty good shape."

That night they celebrated at Bill Schultz and Sari Horwitz's home in northwest Washington. People crowded into the little house to eat pasta and drink wine and congratulate Schultz and Dave Vladeck for taking on the biggest newspaper companies in America. They chattered excitedly of Justices John Paul Stevens and Antonin Scalia, of how someone finally had grasped what Wendover and Kelly and Mleczko—and Gene Driker and Duane Ice and Don Kummer and Elton Schade—had seen all along, of how their quixotic, maligned mission had been validated by the highest court in the land.

And how maybe, just maybe, they would win.

Almost.

On the second Monday after the oral arguments, the court issued a one-page order that brought the forty-three-month JOA ordeal to a close: "The judgment of the court of appeals for the District of Columbia is affirmed by an equally divided court." It meant the court, minus Justice Byron White, had deadlocked, 4–4. It meant Knight-Ridder and Gannett could proceed with the JOA.

The decision was heartbreaking for the members of Michigan Citizens for an Independent Press, not only because they had lost, but also because the court was silent. Tie votes did not require a written opinion, and none was provided.* The opponents never would know what the court thought of their arguments or the Newspaper Preservation Act. Still, the closeness of the vote suggested their positions weren't as outrageous as the publishers had portrayed them. "If we had won and the *Free Press* had closed, that would have been a political black eye for us," Dave Vladeck rationalized. "So we're going to piss and moan about getting no decision, but this in some ways is better."

Indeed, if Michigan Citizens initially set out to emasculate the Newspaper Preservation Act, the group succeeded admirably, in effect winning its case even before the court's decision. Other newspaper owners would think hard before seeking a JOA, especially if they thought they could otherwise overcome a weaker rival. Competition was costly and fraught with risks, but at least direct combatants weren't at the uncertain mercy of the legal system. "The fact that we did get this far," Matt Beer said, "is a message to anybody who wants to pursue a JOA, that they will do so at their peril."

The opponents could have asked the Supreme Court to rehear the case and try to break the tie. Even if they had then lost 5–3, at least they would have gotten a written opinion. But the court almost never granted rehearings; Schultz wasn't inclined to seek one. In a noon conference call on November 15, Kelly, Wendover, and Beer decided to give up. "To me," Wendover told a *News* reporter, "this is as sad a day as when the *Detroit Times* closed in November of 1960."

Only Kelly pushed hard for a rehearing. Even after Michigan Citizens announced it would halt its campaign, he mailed a tortured letter to Byron White, asking the justice to rethink his decision to withdraw. "You alone," Kelly wrote, "appear to have created an irreversible manifest injustice by allowing one of our most sacred principles—freedom of the press—to be attacked by your omission. . . . The people have a right to know the reasoning behind this unexplained outcome." But the people did not have a right to know. Justice White sent a one-sentence reply saying Kelly's thoughts were "duly noted."

Free Press people responded to the court's decision with predictable joy and relief. At the *News,* where many had hoped the JOA would be shot down, there was posturing. John Curley, Neuharth's successor, sent a telegram

*Rehnquist, O'Connor, Kennedy, and Scalia voted to uphold Meese's approval of the JOA. The vote was disclosed in the late Justice Thurgood Marshall's papers, made public in early 1993.

that Bob Giles eagerly shared with his staff. "Please convey to your colleagues at the *News* my congratulations on winning the newspaper war in Detroit," Curley wrote. "While the competitive structure changes under a JOA, it doesn't mean there is any less competition. In fact, the *News* has momentum on its side and I expect it to continue to be the best newspaper in Michigan and again be the Best of Gannett."

The telegram did not mention that the *News* would swiftly become Detroit's junior newspaper. A story detailing how the *News* would lose its circulation lead was kept out of the paper. A front-page tag line identifying the *News* as "Michigan's largest newspaper" was quietly changed to "Michigan's No. 1 newspaper." Matt Beer, the onetime *News* columnist, observed, "We'll just have to wait and see whether the *Detroit News* will stay a competitive newspaper, and see whether the corporation will let it wither on the vine like what happened in Miami."

The JOA implementation machine cranked up a third time. Nonunion workers again were called into brief meetings with their bosses to be told whether or not they would have a job. The unions and the publishers returned to the bargaining table. Some noneconomic issues remained to be settled, but the biggest obstacles were wages and benefits. The unions wanted raises totaling $160 a week, spread over three years, plus a signing bonus equal to five weeks of wages; the publishers, represented by the Detroit Newspaper Agency, offered $35 a week over two and a half years, plus a two-week bonus. With the unions demanding a fair share of the JOA profits, the publishers started talking of how difficult it would be to make money in the merger's first year. The pleas of poverty failed to impress the unionists. "If these [publishers] are going to make $100 million to $150 million every year, they're going to have to offer us something decent," one angry Teamster driver said. "People are really fed up." Still, though a strike seemed likely for a while, the unions eventually caved in, settling for an $80-a-week raise and a two-week bonus.

Once again, Teamsters set the agenda. Although the Pressmen angered the other unions by settling first, Teamsters Local 372 and Mailers Local 2040 held out for more. A strike deadline loomed when the unions were handed a bit of last-minute leverage. Kmart Corporation, the country's second-largest retailer, with headquarters in suburban Detroit, threatened to pull $1 million worth of Christmas advertising if a settlement wasn't reached. After a night of frantic bargaining, the unions agreed to new contracts fifteen minutes before Kmart's 7:00 A.M. deadline—but extracted only $10 a week more than they previously had been offered. That morning, lead Gannett bargainer John Jaske was in Keating's office, bragging. "We really got them, Bill," he said.

Members of other unions complained bitterly that the Teamsters and their Mailer brothers had settled for too little. "The implication—if not the outright promise—that we've heard since the joint operating agreement process began was that at the end of this road we'd find a big rock-candy mountain," one *Free Press* worker groused. "Instead, we got a hazardous waste dump." The Mailers had been eager to settle because they were concerned Kmart would pull all of its future holiday circulars—costing them inserting jobs. As in the past, the Guild and other unions had to take what the Teamster locals got. The only difference was, they didn't have Elton Schade to blame.

The joint operating agency between the *Detroit Free Press* and the *Detroit News* became official at 12:01 A.M. Monday, November 27. Bill Keating, Bob Hall, and Bob Giles signed the documents that formally merged the newspapers' business operations into the Detroit Newspaper Agency. Onetime rivals began working side by side at the DNA. *Free Press* advertising staffers moved down West Lafayette Boulevard to offices in the *News* building, trading places with *News* circulation workers shuttling to quarters at the *Free Press.* Advertisers got higher rates; discounting was to become a thing of the past. Readers started paying more for the papers—at newsstands, twenty-five cents on weekdays and a dollar on Sundays.

The news and editorial departments of the papers remained separate and, technically, independent of the DNA. They would continue to compete for news on weekdays. On Saturdays and Sundays they would produce joint editions of the *Detroit News and Free Press.* "We're joined at the wallet," *Free Press* reporter Joe Swickard said, "but not at the heart."

The Great Detroit Newspaper War was over.

Sounds of laughter and clinking glasses drifted up past the crystal chandelier to the vaulted oaken ceiling in the Anderson Room, where Jack Fontaine stood before half a dozen tables full of dark-suited men, reciting a poem he had composed for Clark Clifford. It was January 31, 1990. At the behest of Alvah Chapman, Knight-Ridder was hosting a dinner in honor of Clifford at the Metropolitan Club, one of Washington's oldest and most exclusive social fraternities.

The purpose of the affair was to pay homage to Clifford for his role in getting the JOA approved. On the sixth floor of Knight-Ridder headquarters in Miami, Clark Clifford was a hero, the silver-haired sage who had come to the company's rescue in Detroit. Fontaine, Chapman, Jim Batten, Bernie Ridder, Bob Singleton, and Dave Lawrence flew up from Florida especially for the dinner. Bob Hall came in from Detroit, and there were lawyers from Hughes Hubbard and Reed; Mayer, Brown and Platt; and, of course, Clifford and Warnke. Even Thomas Merrill and Michael Lazerwitz of the solicitor general's office and Douglas Letter of the Justice Department came, after agonizing briefly over the propriety of accepting gratuities from a private corporation.

No one from Gannett or the *Detroit News* was invited.

The menu featured poached filet of sole with Chassagne-Montrachet 1983 and a roast tenderloin of beef with Château Beychevelle 1979. Guests received commemorative glass paperweights. A program bore a photograph of a smiling Clifford, dapper in a checkered suit, and a replica of the Supreme Court's one-page, 4–4 decision. Chapman, Batten, Lawrence, and Supreme Court lawyer Stephen Shapiro each rose to praise the old man beaming in their midst. Clifford himself finally addressed the group, thanking each of the lawyers in the room by name, then mesmerizing his audience with tales of his early life in St. Louis. It was an evening he would never forget.

A bit of levity was supplied by Fontaine, whose poem was a tortured parody of Ernest Lawrence Thayer's "Casey at the Bat." "C.C. at the Bar" traced the JOA story from the time Clifford entered the case. It ended:

Oh somewhere in this favored land the sun is shining bright
The band is playing somewhere and somewhere hearts are light
And somewhere men are laughing and somewhere children shout,
But there is no joy in Naderville—Bill Schultz is finally *out!*
Oh yes—in paradise next to Windsor, the sun is *shining bright*
And sixth-floor hearts, once heavy, are warm again, and light
But there's gloom at the second paper, *sly smiles are now a pout*
There is no joy on the other team—Billy Schultz is finally *out!*

The audience exploded in laughter and applause as Fontaine presented the appreciative Clifford with a copy of the verse. And the men, feeling warm and relaxed from the rich food and drink, settled back with brandy and cigars to savor this splendid evening and congratulate each other on their hard work and persistence, their shrewdness and vision, on all they had accomplished and overcome to finally gain what they had pursued for nearly four years of their lives. There wasn't a great deal of talk about the JOA itself, now two months old. Five hundred miles away from the Metropolitan Club, things were not going so grandly.

* * *

In Detroit, the JOA was a disaster aborning.

Readers were angry and confused. Advertisers were furious. Workers at the Detroit Newspaper Agency and in the *News* and *Free Press* newsrooms were demoralized and embarrassed. They had known the launch of the JOA would not go perfectly; merging two huge, vastly different organizations couldn't come off without a hitch. But they hadn't expected it to go this badly, to *look* so terrible to their customers and to their peers at newspapers across the country. In the first public assessment of the JOA, the *Wall Street Journal* published a highly critical story that began, "Here in the Motor City, the nation's two largest and most powerful newspaper chains appear to be accomplishing the impossible: Having a monopoly, and blowing it anyway."

It seemed everything that *could* go wrong *did* go wrong. Deliveries were late or missed. Some subscribers got two weekend papers, some none at all. Drivers got lost on new routes. Newsracks all over the city were empty for days at a time. Entire news sections were missing from the paper. Whole pages were blank. Ads were lost. Preprinted ad circulars, TV guides, and comics sections were left out. Classified ads were scattered haphazardly throughout the papers. Crossword puzzles and lottery-number listings shuffled randomly about the papers from day to day. The jointly produced weekend sections baffled readers with mixed typefaces, dual indexes, and occasionally duplicative news stories. Subscribers trying to reach the Detroit Newspaper Agency got busy signals for hours on end; the DNA was getting as many as nine thousand calls a day. Dozens of callers did succeed in reaching a flabbergasted Detroit bank vice-president—because the *News* had printed an incorrect telephone number.

Through it all, Bill Keating insisted the JOA was going as well as could be expected. "I don't think anybody will ever realize what a good job these guys did in getting out the papers," he told a *News* reporter shortly after the launch. "Anybody who expected our first day we would be operating like we were in business for five years had their heads in the sand. The people did an absolutely outstanding job."

Maybe the customers had *their* heads in the sand, because they did not agree with Keating. One reader dubbed the JOA "junk on arrival," another "joke on America." In particular, they were offended that the publishers would raise prices before the new contraption was running smoothly. "They should take care of the problems first and think about the money later," one reader told *Free Press* reporter Lori Mathews. Said another: "Maybe they're thinking we need them more than they need us." James Lipson, one of the DNA's top ad sellers, complained to a *News* reporter, "I can't go anywhere without my friends, my family, everyone who knows me, bitching about the JOA." Angry letters poured in. "Businesses that consider their own convenience over that of their customers invariably fail, as, doubtless, will your contrivances," one reader wrote. Another wrote that he felt "embarrassed to admit that I was completely suckered into supporting the JOA through its many stages of controversy." Wrote another reader: "The new name of greed is JOA."

Greed was only one of the reasons for the JOA debacle. There also were bad luck, lousy timing, legal hindrances, impatience, shortsightedness, and good old-fashioned hubris.

Customers might have been more sympathetic had the DNA not raised prices so quickly. Ad rates rose by as much as 300 percent. The increases fell heaviest on small, local retailers who had long enjoyed steep discounts. Normally a publisher would have tried to accommodate those accounts by offering "zoned" advertising—cheaper ads published only in editions circulated in specific geographic areas. But the JOA began without zoning because it posed difficult production challenges. The timing of the rate hikes couldn't have been worse; many advertisers already had planned their holiday ad budgets. Now they had to swallow the higher prices along with repeated mistakes in the publication of their ads. "How many times did I hear from advertisers, 'You screwed us in our most critical season,'?" one DNA executive ruefully asked. Gradually, many advertisers cut spending or stopped advertising altogether. A few big customers, including Sears and grocer Farmer Jack, withdrew ads, costing the DNA millions of dollars in revenue. Most would eventually return to the papers, but for many, their presence would be diminished. Bad feelings would linger for years.

The publishers defended the rates as competitive with those in other major markets when measured on a so-called CPM basis—the cost of an ad per thousand subscribers.* Many advertisers, particularly smaller, local ones, didn't care about the comparisons one way or the other. For years they had feasted on a steady diet of discounts, and they couldn't be weaned overnight. Out of arrogance or ignorance, the publishers seemed to think their customers should simply accept the price hikes in gratitude for the years of deals they had

*For example, a full-page Sunday retail ad in the *News* and the *Free Press* had a CPM of $20.95—lower than in the *Los Angeles Times* and *San Francisco Chronicle,* but higher than in newspapers in New York, Chicago, Washington, and Philadelphia. Similarly, the CPM of daily retail ads in the Detroit papers was higher than in New York, Chicago, and Washington.

enjoyed—as if the newspapers' kamikaze rate cutting were charitable. Not surprisingly, the customers saw things differently. They weren't about to automatically boost their ad budgets because the newspapers finally had decided to enter the modern era. "We were supposed to look at it more from the customer's point of view than we used to, and we didn't," a Knight-Ridder executive admitted.

Circulation snafus had much to do with a "mass bid," in which hundreds of Teamsters chose the districts where they would deliver papers. Virtually all wound up with new routes and new carriers in unfamiliar areas. Late papers, missed deliveries, and empty newsracks were predictable. Yet the Teamsters' contract called for another mass bid several months into the JOA; without any certainty of keeping their current routes, Teamsters had little incentive to properly develop them. "I don't know why we negotiated it," John Curley later grumbled.

A major circulation problem was duplicate deliveries of the weekend papers. According to Keating, most of the complaints the DNA took in the JOA's early going were from customers wanting to cancel one of the two identical papers they were getting on weekends. The problem arose largely because the DNA had no clear idea where or who its customers were—because it had no circulation database. Amazingly, the information gatherers had a paucity of information on the people who mattered to them most, their customers. Two decades into the computer age, the *Free Press* had a primitive computer system and the *News* was just developing one. Why were they behind the times? Partly because the Teamsters who controlled the widely scattered delivery operation—in metro Detroit, more than 350 districts were supervised by 640 district managers—weren't eager to part with such valuable information. Also, with much of their money going for discounts and promotions, neither paper had had the wherewithal to invest in a database. As the JOA approached, there was talk of having a common database created by a neutral third party, to allay antitrust concerns. But the idea was dismissed, in part because each paper feared the other would tap into the source and gain an advantage. They didn't trust each other.

A sharp "us versus them" mentality pervaded from the start. *News* and *Free Press* rivals couldn't easily break their competitive habits. One Gannett executive called it "brutal, undeclared civil war." A well-placed Knight-Ridder official said, "Virtually everyone underestimated the human dimension. You simply did not have a coherent, smoothly functioning merged organization." *News* people criticized ex–*Free Press* executive Bob Hall, now the DNA's circulation chief, for not promoting their paper. *Free Press* veterans chafed under the autocratic management of ex-*News* executive Dick McClennen, now head of DNA advertising. They hid information from each other. They bickered over doing things "the *Free Press* way" or "the *News* way." They worked hard to solve their own paper's problems, while giving short shrift to those of the other paper. In short, coworkers continued to act like competitors. Coffee cups embossed with the DNA logo did little to remedy the sniping and backbiting.

Cynicism pervaded the news-gathering staffs, especially at the *News*. "The reality that newspapers are, basically, a business, comes home more and more, as decisions appear to be made solely for business and production reasons, the reader be damned," a *News* assistant city editor wrote in response to an informal survey. In the same survey, 60 percent of the *News* and *Free Press* reporters, editors, and photographers polled said they felt their papers had become worse journalistically since the JOA started. Both, they felt, were hurt by the lack of competition on Saturdays and Sundays. Many thought the *Free Press* was struggling to adapt to its unfamiliar role as market leader. Instead of asserting itself as Michigan's newsiest, agenda-setting paper, the *Free Press* repeatedly let the *News* beat it on big local stories. At the same time, many felt the *News* was lowering its standards by hyping crime and entertainment stories with splashy front-page displays and loud headlines, apparently in a bid to increase street sales in the absence of morning home delivery. The *News*'s daily circulation plummeted anyway. And the *Free Press,* now sole provider of the home-delivered morning paper, picked up little of the *News*'s lost circulation. DNA executives couldn't explain it. Tens of thousands of readers were simply abandoning the papers.

Competitors leapt to exploit the papers' woes. Suburban papers launched Sunday editions and expanded their daily offerings, while radio and TV stations flogged the JOA in commercials. "For the cost of one quarter-page ad in the Detroit papers," boasted one radio station, "you can advertise for a whole month on WLTI." Auto dealers, miffed at JOA ad rates, began publishing their own free weekly, distributing it via direct mail.

Wall Street's expectations of huge JOA profits evaporated as it became clear the publishers had not cut costs or increased income enough to make the operation even marginally profitable. The DNA had hired too many people, partly because Bill Keating had tried to placate *News* and *Free Press* executives who had lobbied to have their own deputies placed. In a few cases, he hired two people to do similar jobs, defeating one of the JOA's main purposes. The publishers also had not won sufficient job reductions from the unions, and they were stuck with most of the costly work rules and featherbedding that had bedeviled them in the past. Just to get the JOA going, Knight-Ridder and

Gannett had had to concede more than they had hoped. For this they could thank Judge Morton Needelman, who in calling for denial of the JOA had handed the unions tremendous leverage. The publishers might have avoided the dilemma had they made a serious effort in 1986 to gain labor's support. But, thinking the JOA would be approved easily, they had held the workers at arm's length. Now they were paying for it.

Nothing haunted the launch more than the nearly four years of legal squabbling that repeatedly had delayed it. It had confused readers and advertisers. It had deepened bad feelings between the papers, particularly as Gannett and the *News* appeared to back away from the deal. It had put the papers further behind financially, making it harder for them to recoup their losses and more tempting to raise prices to imprudent levels. Through the many false starts and legal surprises, inertia had set in. "It destroyed planning," Bob Hall later said. "Part of the planning is having people charged up to work on the plan. And that comes from knowing when you're going to launch it." Antitrust concerns also had hampered planning. Keating had believed that the *Free Press* and the *News* couldn't actually merge circulation lists or plug their individual rate cards into a new pricing system until the JOA was formally in place, else they risked an antitrust violation. Consequently, much of the planning in those crucial areas was hypothetical. It was, as one DNA executive saw it, like General Motors and Ford trying to jointly produce a car without allowing their engineers and production people to actually see the blueprints or assembly line. "Do you think that son-of-a-bitch would run?" the executive asked.

Bill Keating got the bulk of the blame for the botched start-up, not all of it deserved. Besides overseeing the vast and myriad details of an unprecedented merger, Keating constantly was arbitrating disputes, some important and some not, between the many conflicting JOA factions—Knight-Ridder and Gannett, the *Free Press* and the *News*, management and labor, one union and another. He would not wield the hammer of "control" that Al Neuharth had negotiated in Gannett's 3–2 advantage on the DNA management committee. Instead, viewing the JOA as a partnership, Keating strove for consensus. It wore him out.

Perhaps his greatest failure was in never moving to Detroit. For four years he lived out of a hotel room and, briefly, an apartment, commuting to Cincinnati most weekends. He never got close to the community he needed to know intimately. Even to many of his own employees he seemed aloof and unengaged. His sparsely furnished office in the *News* building always had the look of temporary quarters, lacking pictures on the walls or other mementos to suggest he intended to stay. Keating and his wife had shopped for a house but grew wary of buying as the outcome of the JOA became less certain. Meanwhile, Keating relied on Dave Lawrence and Chip Weil to connect with the community. By the time the JOA went into place, both were gone. Shortly before Lawrence departed for Miami, Weil had left the *News* to become publisher of *Time* magazine's U.S. edition. Weil had relished competing, but he dreaded the thought of working with *Free Press* people. "I didn't want to run a newspaper factory," he later said. (In 1991 he would leave *Time* for the jointly owned *Arizona Republic* and *Phoenix Gazette.*)

Keating left Detroit in March of 1990. John Zanotti, publisher of the *Cincinnati Enquirer,* had unexpectedly left the paper, and John Curley granted Keating's request that he be sent home to replace Zanotti. After four years, Keating was burned out on the JOA. He had had enough of coddling enormous egos, standing off union bosses, battling with stubborn editors, and reading how badly the JOA had turned out. He also had been dragged into a national scandal involving his brother, Charles H. Keating, Jr., accused of using an Arizona savings and loan to bilk the government out of billions of dollars. Bill Keating had nothing to do with it, but the blot on his family's name bothered him a lot. Once, when *News* reporter Jon Pepper asked him about it in an interview, Keating angrily ejected Pepper from his office. It was the first time anyone in Detroit could remember Keating losing his temper. When he got the chance to escape to the comfort of his old digs in Cincinnati, Keating jumped at it.

He wasn't the only one going home. The same day his departure was announced, Knight-Ridder said Bob Hall would return to Philadelphia to run the *Inquirer* and the *Daily News.* To replace him at the *Free Press,* Knight-Ridder coaxed Neal Shine out of retirement. The *Free Press* staff seemed dispirited and unfocused; Jim Batten hoped Shine could remind them of the joy and reward in putting out a daily newspaper. Lee Hills, who had commanded the *Free Press* so ably in the 1960s, called the old Irishman to urge him to return. Shine happily acquiesced. At the official announcement in room 100, ebullient *Free Press* staffers doused Shine's Donegal tweed jacket with champagne and bestowed him with kisses, hugs, and two standing ovations. "I love every one of you," Shine told them. "If there's a crisis of morale, I'll do whatever I can to fix it. I know it's not going to be enough for me to go out and tell funny stories and give them my best lines." He was right about that. Something of the *Free Press*'s spunk had dissipated in the agonizing wait for the JOA. The paper would be recovering for a long time.

But at least it could boast of being Michigan's biggest daily. Circulation reports released April 17, 1990, confirmed that the *Free Press*'s daily total had eclipsed the *News*'s by an insurmountable 114,000 papers, 639,767 to 526,147. There was, however, little celebrating at the *Free Press,* where the people recognized that their ascent wasn't so much the result of street fighting as of boardroom negotiations. Still, in just four months the *News* had lost nearly 165,000 customers, and the numbers continued to fall. Bob Giles blamed it on the loss of morning home delivery, late press starts, and JOA launch problems. Nervous *News* staffers wondered aloud how long the paper could survive. Giles assured them there was no reason to despair. Once the start-up wrinkles had been smoothed over, he promised, the *News*'s numbers would rise again. Privately, he began telling deputies that Gannett and Knight-Ridder would have to restore morning home delivery to the *News;* in fact, he said, the *News* might even get sole responsibility for the Sunday paper and its 1.2 million in circulation, which would, in turn, help the *News* lure more daily readers. But Giles was mistaken.

At Knight-Ridder and Gannett, the executives watched in frustration and disgust as their gold mine produced nothing but rubble. A recession that hit all newspapers hard hurt the Detroit operation badly. Advertising kept falling. Costs came down only slowly. The *News*'s circulation continued to drop; the *Free Press*'s numbers fell too, though not as fast. No one was thinking about $100 million a year profits now.

Whenever they were asked publicly, the newspapers' executives insisted their hobbled beast would one day get up and walk. "It can't miss," DNA ad chief Dick McClennen told a *News* reporter in the summer of 1990. "The JOA is a muddled mess, but it's going to be a success. History will prove me right." But more than two years passed, and still Gannett and Knight-Ridder were losing money and readers in Detroit.* By the end of 1992, the companies had lost more than $100 million since announcing the JOA in the spring of 1986—not counting more than $10 million they spent on lawyers and forgettable consultants. To recoup their losses, they probably would have to wait until the next century.

Meanwhile, they had manipulated and demoralized their employees. They had confused and angered their customers. They had bent their own ethical rules to achieve their financial ends. They had tarnished the good name of Detroit journalism.

*The companies declined to discuss specific income figures. Knight-Ridder spokesman Frank Hawkins said his company had a "nice bottom-line profit in 1992," but admitted that it did not account for Knight-Ridder's share of $25 million in buyouts negotiated with the unions.

Were Gannett and Knight-Ridder totally to blame? No. The unions, led by the Teamsters and the Guild, had stubbornly resisted surrendering any of what they felt was their due, no matter the harm their actions threatened to the papers. Petulant advertisers had refused to accept the realities of a new day. Ed Meese and his Justice Department had dawdled; perhaps the merger would have proceeded smoothly had it not been fraught with doubt and pent-up hostility that built up over the long wait. Michigan Citizens, motivation aside, had prolonged the delay.

Still, at the end of the war, Gannett and Knight-Ridder had to accept most of the responsibility for the debacle it became. They were, after all, America's largest newspaper publishers, by many accounts the companies that would lead the industry into the twenty-first century. No one had forced them to seek the JOA. No one had forced them to persist even after their pursuit seemed doomed. They did what they did, they said, for the sake of having two voices in Detroit. By the time they had succeeded, their two voices were the *Free Press,* a paper whose soul had been eviscerated, and the *News,* which now looked to be Detroit's true "failing newspaper." As their battle faded into memory, the *Free Press* and the *News* found themselves waiting again for the money finally to come and sustain them. For all the blood they had spilled, in a way—a sad and senseless way—nothing had changed.

23

Conclusion: Waking Rip van Winkle

Nearly every one of the half-dozen times I interviewed Al Neuharth for this book, he remarked on the poor performance of the JOA, and how it never would have turned out so badly had he been in charge. "I would have been there with my sleeves rolled up," he told me. He frequently criticized Gannett—to me and to other reporters—for not having exercised the "control" of the Detroit Newspaper Agency he had so brilliantly negotiated with Alvah Chapman. He went so far as to insist that the *Detroit News* should have remained Michigan's largest daily paper, even after departing the home-delivery market, per his deal with Chapman. Gannett's control, Neuharth said, should have enabled the *News* to retain the top spot, through manipulation of the press times, pricing, and delivery runs. "It's very simple," he told me. "You have to have the smarts and the balls to do it." Never one for details, he declined to be more specific. When I pressed him, he grew impatient, showing a glimpse of his legendary temper. "I don't have to fucking explain that to you," he snapped.

Neuharth was engaging in revisionist history. True, he was not in charge when the JOA finally took effect in late 1989; but he was still chairman of Gannett when the companies made their first, abortive attempt at implementing the merger in 1988. I was in Detroit for those frenetic days, covering the story, and I don't recall seeing Neuharth with his sleeves rolled up. He was only in Detroit for a day. He also had personally signed off on all the decisions affecting the future of the *News,* including press times, pricing, and delivery. Later he tried to explain—feebly, in my opinion—that he was no longer "acting like a CEO," since he had relinquished the title to John Curley; in other words, Neuharth was saying, it was Curley's fault.

So far, "control" hasn't been much of an advantage for the *News.* Gannett's 3–2 majority on the DNA board has been diminished greatly by the contractual exceptions requiring Knight-Ridder's acquiescence to nearly any significant change in the JOA—for example, one allowing morning delivery of the *News.* Those exceptions, of course, were proposed by Chapman and accepted by Neuharth on that Sunday afternoon in Chapman's den in 1986. Today, one could argue that possession of the morning market, the daily circulation lead, and an equal share of the revenues give Knight-Ridder the economic leverage to control the JOA. If ever a sharp dispute arose, Knight-Ridder would appear to have less to lose in a divorce than Gannett.

Today, at the *Detroit News,* Al Neuharth is a pariah. The people who work for the *News*—and former *News* employees on the DNA payroll—recall Neuharth's boasts about the *News* remaining Michigan's top newspaper, and they feel betrayed. They see the *News* circulation continue to fall, and they feel foolish for ever believing he was serious about competing. No one at the *News* would be surprised to hear that Neuharth's last letter to me was addressed to the "Detroit Press." "He sold us down the fucking river," *News* executive city editor Mark Hass told me in the summer of 1990. "He just wanted to get this over with, make the big announcement, and be a big hero on Wall Street. He didn't know how good a paper he had here." At that time, the *News*'s circulation had fallen by less than 200,000; by now, it has dropped by 300,000—about the circulation of the *Houston Post* or the *San Jose Mercury News.* Bob Giles keeps telling me, as he has nearly every time I've seen him in the past two years, that the numbers have leveled off. In fact, though, no one really knows when the paper will hit bottom. I saw John Curley on the subway in Washington one day, sitting with a battered briefcase in his lap. We talked about the JOA, and I asked when he thought the *News*'s circulation would bottom out. He just shrugged.

There are many reasons for the decline. Most important, the *News* lost the morning home-delivery market. The paper has aggressively sought single-copy street sales, but, as of early 1992, the Detroit Newspaper Agency still was having mixed success getting copies of the paper in coin boxes before 9:00 A.M. The *News* also rid itself of a lot of "water," the costly circulation, sold at discount and in far-flung areas, that newspapers tolerate in head-to-head competition. Undoubtedly, the *News* lost customers during the troubled JOA launch. And prices are higher than before the JOA.

Naturally, you have to wonder whether the product—the paper itself—has alienated readers. That is difficult to determine, and I, being one of the people who put out the *News,* don't feel qualified to judge. The paper certainly isn't so bad as to have driven away tens of thousands of readers; on balance, the *News* is a pretty good paper delivered at the wrong time of the day. Still, at times it strikes me that my paper is behaving more and more like one on the brink, like a cancer patient willing to try anything to stave off the inevitable. Since the JOA began, the *News* has undergone several redesigns and introduced a bevy of new features aimed at luring new readers, including a young black columnist, a section for teenagers, an expanded weekly auto package, and a columnist writing from a gay perspective. As good as some of the additions seem to be, the profusion of changes has made it harder—for me, at least—to detect a central sense of purpose to the paper—a graspable identity, if you will.

A journalist's perspective on journalism often cannot be trusted, but I read the *News* every day, and I sense that its approach to covering the news has been changing almost constantly. One day the *News* is the crime journal, replete with tabloid-style headlines and gory detail. The next day it's a serious afternoon paper, analyzing yesterday's news. The next day it's touting the Teenage Mutant Ninja Turtles at the top of page 1. There's something to be said for unpredictability—it worked for the *Free Press* in the 1970s—but there's something as well to be said for the sense of familiarity between a reader and his or her newspaper that breeds loyalty. I used to have some sense of what the *Detroit News* stood for. No more. Maybe I am being unfair or shortsighted; after all, the *News* is, like so many other papers, struggling to redefine itself in a new era. Perhaps one day I will look back on its seemingly erratic sense of mission and see the kind of daring and imagination that other papers would do well to emulate. For now, though, I am not so sure, and many of my *News* colleagues have told me they feel equally ill at ease. "A lot of people share [a feeling] of disconnectedness," one *News* staffer wrote me. "No one really seems to understand where this paper is heading intellectually (or, for that matter, financially)."

Which leads to a question dozens of people have asked since I began working on this book: How long can the *News* survive? The simple answer is that it can survive as long as Gannett wants. But that's too simple. Publishing the *News* could become less attractive to Gannett if the paper's circulation continues to fall. As the circulation drops, advertisers will become less willing to buy dual advertising in both the *News* and the *Free Press.* If advertising in the *News* then declines, circulation is almost certain to follow—and the *News* will enter the deadly "downward spiral." The JOA then would be carrying a "failing paper," much as Knight-Ridder carried the *Free Press* and Gannett has been carrying *USA Today*. It can't go on forever.

Critics of the JOA like to argue that Gannett could stop publishing the *News* and continue to collect its share of the JOA pot. Technically, that is a mistaken notion; as currently written, the companies' agreement requires both partners to produce news and editorial material to participate in the JOA. Of course, the contract could easily be changed. If the *News*'s performance continues to decline, the paper eventually will become a drag on the entire operation, affecting Knight-Ridder's profit as well as Gannett's. It will become increasingly tempting—and, perhaps, financially prudent—to either close the *News* altogether or merge the papers into a daily version of the *Detroit News and Free Press* now produced on weekends. Both papers could have an editorial page in the merged paper, and Gannett and Knight-Ridder could further cut editorial, production, and delivery costs.

Such a change in the structure of the JOA probably would require the approval of the Justice Department, but that wouldn't be difficult to obtain, especially if Gannett and Knight-Ridder threatened to close the *News* if the amendment was not allowed (an irony Alvah Chapman surely could appreciate). One might ask if such a change would not be a de facto violation of the Newspaper Preservation Act. The answer is no, because the Newspaper Preservation Act is a law without teeth. As Seymour Dussman, the Justice Department lawyer who advocated denying the Detroit JOA, told Ed Wendover in a letter in March of 1990, the law "contains no enforcement provisions or penalties." The Justice Department "cannot police or enforce the contractual terms of JOAs." The department could sue Knight-Ridder and Gannett under the federal antitrust laws, but it would be difficult to argue that competition has been stifled where there has been no competition, at least between the two papers, since 1989.

Will the *News* survive? Ask a Gannett, *News*, or DNA executive and he or she will tell you it will. "It's a no-brainer," the DNA's latest chief executive, Frank Vega, told me. (Vega replaced veteran Gannett executive Joseph Ungaro, who had replaced Bill Keating.) Bob Giles says people who question the future of the *News* don't understand Gannett's commitment to the paper. John Curley told me, "I really don't see [the demise of the *News*] as a likelihood. It's one for the guys in the saloons to kick around." In early 1993 rumors again swirled that the *News* would have morning home delivery restored. *News* editors whispered hopefully about executive changes at the Detroit Newspaper Agency; a few managers with Knight-Ridder or *Free Press* backgrounds had been shunted aside in favor of Gannett veterans. Dominance of the DNA, it was theorized, would enable Gannett to force Knight-Ridder to allow the *News* back into the morning market. And maybe it will. Such a power play would hardly reflect the "partnership" of which Al Neuharth and Alvah Chapman spoke so fondly in 1986. But maybe it's what Neuharth had in mind when he sought control of the JOA.

The *News* is hardly Gannett's top priority. Primacy of place lies with *USA Today,* which continues to lose money ten years after its ballyhooed birth. By 1992 the "Nation's Newspaper" had lost more than $1 billion, according to unofficial estimates. But Gannett will carry *USA Today* longer than it will the *News,* if only because the national paper finally has provided Gannett visibility and a degree of journalistic prestige the company hitherto lacked. *USA Today* also may have greater earning potential than the *News,* assuming it finally convinces Madison Avenue of its advertising viability.

The JOA and *USA Today* aren't the only problems Neuharth has bequeathed to Curley. *USA Today on TV,* the television show modeled on the newspaper modeled on television, was a bust. Gannett suffered a humiliating defeat in Little Rock, where Neuharth had decided a JOA was unnecessary. Gannett's *Arkansas Gazette* frittered away its circulation and advertising advantages, and the take-no-prisoners plan to crush Walter Hussman's *Arkansas Democrat* bogged down in a swamp of losses exceeding $20 million a year. In 1991 Gannett sold the *Gazette* to Hussman, who promptly closed the paper. The recession battered Gannett profits in 1990 and 1991. For the first time in twenty-two years, the company reported a quarterly earnings decline—a fact Neuharth liked to mention to interviewers seeking his opinion of Curley's stewardship. Gannett also survived a brief takeover scare when the Gannett Foundation, an independent philanthropic organization created by Frank Gannett, offered to sell its 10 percent block of the company's stock. Ultimately Gannett bought the stake for $670 million, but the sale could have put the company into play. It was engineered by the chairman of the Gannett Foundation—none other than Neuharth.

Neuharth did not fall far from the company that had helped make him rich and famous. He moved to an office at the Gannett Foundation, directly across the street from the Gannett tower, and renamed the organization the Freedom Forum. His new quarters look strikingly similar to his old ones, with the big marble desk, a bank of televisions overhead, an ancient typewriter at the ready, a lovely view of the Washington Monument. Even as John Curley has done away with the limousines, hotel suites, and other profligate leftovers from the Neuharth era, Neuharth has drawn criticism for his lavish spending at the foundation. Naturally, he doesn't mind the attention. As he was with Gannett, Neuharth is determined to make the Freedom Forum the most visible entity in its field. Meanwhile, his former employer pays him $399,992 a year—to shrink to $299,992 after 1994—per his retirement plan. He gives speeches, travels almost constantly, and writes a weekly column for *USA Today*. And he never misses a chance to tweak his former colleagues. While the industry lobbied Congress in 1992 to stop the regional Bell operating companies—the so-called Baby Bells—from entering the information services business, Neuharth accused publishers of trying to limit press freedoms. "Can you imagine," he asked, "the gall of any newspaper owners or publishers screaming 'monopoly' at anyone else?"

It could be argued that Al Neuharth saved the *Detroit News*. Had Gannett not bid for the Evening News Association, the *News* might have been sold to people who would have settled for less in a JOA or, worse, closed the paper immediately. On the other hand, Gannett did not buy the ENA solely or even primarily for the *News*, and the company has profited handsomely from other ENA assets, especially the CBS affiliate in Washington.

Neuharth might have won the Great Detroit Newspaper War outright, had he been willing to fight on the battlefield of the market. Instead he tried to use the Newspaper Preservation Act to hold the *Free Press* at bay while his troops advanced. His scheme to claim the "big win" fell short, and now the *News*, which outfought the *Free Press* by nearly every measure, is at risk. Viewed strictly as a business transaction, Neuharth's JOA probably was a fair compromise. Throw journalism into the equation and you have to conclude that Neuharth blew the biggest deal of his career. What Knight-Ridder had lost in the streets, Alvah Chapman won back at the bargaining table with Neuharth. Neuharth might have had his "big win," but, apparently, he didn't have the "smarts" or the "balls" to go for it without the help of lawyers and bureaucrats. With nothing of his own to lose, he gambled with the future of a newspaper and the trust of the people who worked for it. Maybe those people—myself included—will find a way to rescue the paper from Neuharth's JOA. So far, though, it appears we are the losers of his cynical bet.

Like Neuharth, Alvah Chapman hasn't let retirement slow him down. He chairs the board of trustees at Florida International University, stays active at his church, plays some golf, and does a lot of fishing. He continues to chair Knight-Ridder's executive committee and keeps a modest office at company headquarters. In the summer of 1992 he accepted Florida governor Lawton

Chiles's invitation to chair a commission on the homeless, and then, after Hurricane Andrew ripped through south Florida, acceded to President Bush's request that he head a task force to rebuild the devastated area. "I'd love to have my old job back," Chapman has joked to Jim Batten. "It would be easier."

Chapman was as frustrated as anyone with the JOA's troubles, but at least he could rest assured that the *Free Press* had a secure future. For that reason, he made no apologies for his handling of Knight-Ridder's public campaign for the JOA, the threat to close the *Free Press,* the lobbying of public officials, the censored editorial cartoons; indeed, he was—and is—proud of what he did. "The dishonorable thing," he told me, "would have been to fold the *Free Press* and send those twenty-two hundred people out without jobs." Chapman is hardly a pariah at the *Free Press.* Some question his motives—after all, he was only saving the paper from his own self-serving threat, they say—but even his critics are glad the *Free Press* has a future. Chapman's lieutenants within Knight-Ridder and the *Free Press* beamed with pride whenever I asked about Chapman's one-to-one negotiation with Neuharth. "Alvah whipped his butt," one executive after another told me. Almost no one at Gannett or the *News* disagreed. Even Neuharth's closest deputies and pals thought Chapman had prevailed.*

Which makes it all the more ironic that the *Free Press* has struggled since the JOA began. Only in 1992 did the paper begin to reassert itself. Even diehard *Freep*sters admit that the *News* has consistently bettered the *Free Press* on major breaking stories. Meanwhile, the *Free Press* has failed to pick up any of the circulation lost by the *News.* As of the spring of 1993, the *Free Press* had lost 52,000 in circulation since the JOA's onset. "After three-and-a-half years of living under the guillotine, we became less free-wheeling than we had been," Neal Shine told the *Washington Post.* "A lot of the zest was neutralized." The *Free Press* didn't seem comfortable in the leadership role thrust upon it by the JOA—as if, with the tangible objective of overtaking the *News* forever removed, the *Free Press* couldn't find a source of motivation to replace it. "I think there is a psychological turning of the corner when you finally get this thing out of the way," Heath Meriwether told University of Michigan researcher Barbara K. Petersen. "We've got to look for the future. We're either going to build ourselves into a great newspaper, or not."

*One exception was Charles Overby, Neuharth's longtime assistant and president of the Freedom Forum, who said Neuharth had negotiated "the business deal of the century."

The *Free Press* staff needed time to recover from the JOA ordeal. Because the alternative was so grim, many expected the JOA to make everything right from the start. The myriad pitfalls of the new arrangement made some wonder if they had suffered for nothing. Some felt a sense of uncleanliness, as if they had violated some unwritten journalistic code by hoping the JOA would save their jobs. "There was this sort of anticorporate feeling about the whole thing," one *Free Press* staffer told Petersen. "Here you've got the corporation getting its JOA. It's got to make its profits, and Lawrence is gone on to his next life in Miami, and we're all still here, and we got this shitty $30-a-week raise, and well, whoop-dee-doo. Then they bring in this business guy, Bob Hall—whom we don't know—to be publisher, and Heath's not around, and Neal retired, and Flanigan died, and just some people who had really been part of the woodwork and soul of the place were no longer around, and people were kind of saying, 'What's it all about?' "

As the 1990s began, the same sort of question was being asked by newspaper executives and editors across America. They were questioning the role of the daily newspaper, reconsidering the ways they did business, rethinking their product and how to make it more compelling and urgent to people who allowed less and less time for reading newspapers. The most vocal and passionate of them was Jim Batten, Alvah Chapman's successor as chairman and chief executive of Knight-Ridder. Batten, the onetime *Free Press* editor, stumped for "customer obsession" in an industry that had gotten lazy about such fundamentals as delivering papers on time and attending to readers' everyday needs. "Newspaper plants are populated by people who think they were born on third base," Batten told *Business Month* magazine. "They've always been successful, and they assume they always will be successful. If the world weren't changing, they could get away with that attitude. But the world is changing."

The changing world, it appeared, required fundamental changes in the thinking of newspaper businesspeople and, especially, journalists. Industry leaders took up Neuharth's longtime call for an end to "editor-knows-best" newspapering and a return to genuine concern for what readers themselves wanted in their daily paper. Marketing specialists and pollsters were commissioned to plumb customers for their thoughts and suggestions. Many papers, mimicking *USA Today*, worked harder to get readers actively involved in the paper itself, with call-in surveys, guest columns, and other interactive features. A veritable struggle for the soul of newspapers was engaged as publishers, editors, marketers, graphics specialists, reporters, and readers debated the merits of information versus entertainment, hard news versus soft, simplicity versus sophistication, form versus function. For the first time, newspaper companies started putting money into research and development. Several chains undertook ambitious efforts to rethink their missions, most visibly at Knight-Ridder and Gannett. Knight-Ridder used a radical remake of its Boca Raton, Florida, paper to study how to appeal to baby boomers between the ages of twenty-five and forty-three. Gannett's "News 2000" project required editors at all of the company's papers to measure their progress in satisfying reader wants and needs.

Nothing motivated the companies as much as the recession. Advertising fell stubbornly; for the first time since the Great Depression, the industry in 1990 and 1991 suffered back-to-back declines in ad revenue. Profits throughout the industry declined. The industry counted a net loss of eighteen dailies in 1991, including the *Arkansas Gazette* and the *Dallas Times Herald.* In a speech in early 1992, Batten observed "an edge of fear in the air. Our complacency has melted into apprehension about newspapers' future." A few astute observers, led by analyst Kenneth T. Berents of the investment firm of Alex. Brown and Sons, talked of newspapers undergoing a structural upheaval—a "secular slide," as Berents termed it—that was masked by the recession's effects. Newspapers would never again be the dominant medium, journalistically or financially, they had been in the past, Berents warned. New competitors, swiftly advancing technology, and sociological changes unforeseen even in the 1980s were forcing newspapers to rethink the way they interacted with the public. Readers and advertisers could no longer be, as Jim Batten put it, "a factor . . . to be managed, controlled, kept in line, distrusted, put up with."

If only those lessons had been learned before Gannett and Knight-Ridder birthed the Detroit JOA. For indeed, the JOA epitomized the complacent way of thinking that had crept into the newspaper business as it savored its success of the 1970s and 1980s: jack up the prices, tell customers the way things are going to be, and wait for the money to roll in. As newspapers and newspaper companies try to change their old, bad habits, the Detroit papers are trying to change theirs. It will be years before we know if either truly has succeeded. Meanwhile, it is at once ironic and appropriate that Gannett and Knight-Ridder are the companies struggling to cure the ills of the Detroit JOA. For they are, indisputably, the leaders of the industry as it looks anxiously toward the twenty-first century. They embrace the widest geographical sweep, they are the strongest financially, they have spearheaded the most ambitious efforts to redefine newspapers in the early 1990s. The problems and challenges

Gannett and Knight-Ridder face at their papers across the country are magnified ten times in Detroit. If they can solve Detroit, it would seem, they can solve anything.

Crises followed David Lawrence, Jr., to Florida and his new post as publisher of the *Miami Herald.* For months he feuded publicly with Jorge Mas Canosa, leader of a powerful Cuban organization who felt the *Herald* was too soft on Cuban dictator Fidel Castro. There were threats on Lawrence's life and Mas Canosa plastered city buses with placards reading, "I don't believe the *Miami Herald.*" Mas Canosa backed off shortly before Hurricane Andrew tore into Florida. As the *Herald* struggled to get the paper out in the disaster's aftermath, Lawrence took to the top of a station wagon to fling papers on customers' lawns. The *Herald*'s coverage of the hurricane won the 1993 Pulitzer for public service. Lawrence kept abreast of what was happening in Detroit, but as always, he focused on what he called "the intensity of today." Time and again he told me, "I try my hardest not to dwell on the past." Yet behind his desk he hung a framed sketch of himself testifying at the JOA hearing. He would never forget his eleven years at the *Detroit Free Press.* He would never experience that kind of exhilaration and pain again.

When I last visited Clark Clifford, a carpenter was working in the receiving lobby of his Connecticut Avenue office. The scrawny young man in blue jeans, a baseball cap, and a long, green-hued ponytail had just finished walling off a passageway that for years had led to the well-appointed warrens of the many fine attorneys who once toiled for Clifford. The corridor was no longer needed because the lawyers had departed, leaving their mentor to his presumed shame and disgrace.

Advocating for the JOA was Clifford's last good moment in the public eye. In 1991, he and his partner, Robert A. Altman, were implicated in the scandal enveloping the Bank of Credit and Commerce International. They protested their innocence, but in 1992 federal prosecutors accused them of lying to regulators, taking bribes, and falsifying records to help BCCI illegally acquire U.S. banks. By then, Clifford and Warnke had broken up. The brass letters on the door to the firm were changed to LAW OFFICES OF ROBERT A. ALTMAN. At eighty-six years old, frail and weary and burdened of a failing heart, Clark Clifford faced the terrible ordeal of clearing his name before he died.

Clifford's able adversary, Bill Schultz, took a job on the staff of Congressman Henry Waxman of California. Schultz's partner, Dave Vladeck, continues to litigate for Public Citizen. Whenever I interviewed them for this book, they always seemed amazed, and a little gratified, to hear that the JOA was so troubled. Matt Beer passed the bar exam and set up his own practice in suburban Detroit. John Kelly was reelected as state senator in 1990, but lost in the Democratic congressional primary in 1992. Both times, the *Free Press* endorsed his opponents, describing Kelly as "mercurial and frequently quixotic." Ed Wendover has continued his personal war against the Newspaper Preservation Act, starting a national organization to lobby Congress to repeal the law—as Congress should. He likes to say the only good thing to come of the JOA was his relationship with a pretty blond named Sally Repeck. They met at a fund-raiser for Michigan Citizens for an Independent Press, fell in love, and were married in March of 1992 in the front window of the Penniman Delicatessen in downtown Plymouth.

Judge Morton Needelman went back to retirement in Washington. Phil Lacovara left General Electric to become general counsel and managing partner of Morgan Stanley, the Wall Street investment firm, which he left in early 1993 to pursue other, unspecified opportunities. Gene Driker and Duane Ice kept reading the *News* and the *Free Press,* wishing they could have been the ones to try their case before the Supreme Court. Don Kummer and Lou Mleczko oversee a smaller and, perhaps, closer Guild Local 22, determined to heal the divisive wounds inflicted by the JOA. During contract negotiations in 1992, the Guild's *News* unit faced off Gannett's bid to eliminate contractual pay raises in favor of raises based solely on merit. As the possibility of a strike loomed, *Free Press* Guild members, who did not face a similar threat from Knight-Ridder, phoned their *News* brothers and sisters to say they would stand by them to the end. Gannett finally gave up.

Bulldog Bob Nelson and his wife built a gorgeous contemporary home overlooking Boca Ciega Bay near St. Petersburg. Docked in front is Nelson's cruiser, *Newsboy.* Nelson just shakes his head and laughs whenever asked about Neuharth and the *News.* "He didn't know what he had," Nelson says. On the other side of the country, Peter Clark and his wife retired to an equally beautiful home in the desert near Palm Springs. They live what Clark has called "a blessed life" of traveling, reading, scuba diving, and enjoying their children and grandchildren. Because he remains on Gannett's board of directors, Clark feels it ungentlemanly to comment on the outcome of the newspaper war he fought for twenty-five years. But he cannot fully hide his feelings. When I spoke of what had become of the *News* under the JOA, his face told me how much it hurt him.

* * *

My friends ask me whether the JOA was a good thing. You would think that, after seven years of living the story, three and a half years covering it, and three years writing a book about it, I would have a simple answer. But there is none.

It is good, I suppose, that the *Free Press* didn't close. It is good that all those hardworking people didn't lose their jobs and put their families at financial risk. A few are friends; I would not like to see them suffer.

But such a view is shortsighted if the *News* does not survive.

The people who run Gannett and Knight-Ridder might like me to say it is good that Detroit has "diversity of editorial voices." By now it should be plain that I don't believe the JOA—or the newspaper industry in general, for that matter—is terribly concerned with the preservation of editorial diversity. Even if it were, I'm not sure the *News* and the *Free Press* are all that different from each other anymore. They are adequate, not dissimilar papers going about essentially the same difficult, perhaps impossible, task of trying to be everything to nearly everybody. Both aggressively seek the same affluent segments of the Detroit market; neither can afford to be too different from the other, without risking alienation of those crucial audiences. In other words, surviving means working *against* diversity, not for it. Since the JOA began, both papers have dropped longtime subscribers who are too expensive to maintain because they live too far away or in isolated areas. Forget "diversity"; those readers no longer hear even *one* of the Detroit dailies' voices.

At the risk of sounding heretical, I'll grant that it's *nice* to have two papers in Detroit, just as it was *nice* to have the Be-Mo potato chip factory in Kalamazoo, Michigan, when I worked there. I loved Be-Mo potato chips, but the company was too small to compete with Frito-Lay and other big food producers. So it closed. No one rushed in with government subsidies or special favors to rescue it. I and lots of other Kalamazooans were disappointed, but we started buying other brands.

I can hear the journalists screaming already: "Newspapers are more vital to democracy than potato chip factories!" Of course, diverse sources of information are more important in a democracy than diverse sources of potato chips. But who says newspapers—or, as the Newspaper Preservation Act assumes, big-city daily newspapers—ought to be the primary source?

In the 1990s there is no shortage of sources of information and opinion. This is the age of cable television, talk radio, fax machines, CNN, direct mail, audiotext, videotext, desktop publishing, computer bulletin boards, and a modern heyday in small community papers. Indeed, the notion of "two-newspaper" cities seems outmoded when you consider that urban and suburban sprawl has strengthened some smaller papers while diminishing the reach of many large papers—a natural rearrangement of the market that, while surely not healthy for the big-city dailies, isn't necessarily bad for the community at large.

With technology advancing at such a rapid pace, with Japan, Europe, and the United States vying for technological superiority, there is no telling what new channels of communication will open in the next decade. As Thomas Curley, younger brother of John and president and publisher of *USA Today,* has written: "Artificial barriers to markets, such as geography, will intensify. . . . New media will be launched as entrepreneurs and those with messages to communicate grasp the possibilities of electronic communications systems." Newspaper companies are beginning to invest in the very technologies that, on their own, pose legitimate competitive threats. As Al Neuharth is fond of saying, more people around the globe want more information than ever before—and there are more ways than ever of getting it to them.

All of which suggests that two-newspaper towns have become rare for a good reason: they aren't needed anymore. Does that mean people are necessarily getting less or less-diverse information? Of course not. It just means big-city dailies aren't supplying the bulk of it. The people most concerned about that are newspaper people, for obvious reasons.

Consider the industry's sanctimonious campaign to block the regional Bell operating companies from getting into information services. Newspaper publishers—including Gannett, Knight-Ridder, and most other chain operators—have a valid complaint that the Baby Bells could monopolize the news business because they control phone lines. But newspaper publishers accusing another industry of monopolization borders on the comical. Further, the publishers could have secured a foothold in information services years ago, when the Baby Bells were legally precluded, but the publishers were too busy buying TV stations, boosting their dividends, and sending executives on multimillion-dollar global junkets like Neuharth's JetCapade. Now, fearing the Baby Bells will siphon off the mother lode of classified advertising revenue, they would like Congress to save them from their shortsightedness. Meanwhile, a few smart publishers have quietly begun talking with phone companies about joint ventures from which both could benefit. Eventually the publishers and the Baby Bells will find ways to work together, and we'll stop hearing about the big, bad phone companies and their monopolistic ways.

My point is that publishers aren't as concerned about preserving voices as getting a piece of the action. That's what JOAs are about, including Detroit's. They might not admit it publicly, but the executives at Gannett and

Knight-Ridder know we no longer need "two-newspaper towns"; that is, cities with two large dailies. They are *nice* to have, but not necessary (coincidentally, the same thing Al Neuharth always has said about journalism prizes). That's why Gannett, Knight-Ridder, and other publishers have happily combined papers in towns where they owned both, figuring they could cut costs and increase profits by operating with a single staff and production schedule.

Critics of the Detroit JOA like to insist that Detroit still could have two independent, competing papers. I disagree. Given the nature of newspaper economics, the problematic Detroit economy, the recent national recession, and the fiscal objectives of Knight-Ridder and Gannett, one of the Detroit papers almost certainly would be gone by now had there been no JOA. Having said that, I propose that that wouldn't necessarily have been bad; indeed, Detroit might have been better off.

My hometown is a deeply troubled city that cries out for one excellent, financially strong newspaper instead of the two adequate, financially weak papers it has today. Had there been no prospect of a JOA, maybe by now Detroit would have that one excellent paper. I don't see why that paper could not—out of a sense of public duty—offer a diverse range of opinions and perspectives. Lots of other newspapers do it, *USA Today* foremost among them. (Indeed, the Detroit papers themselves do it every Saturday and Sunday in their hybrid editions.) The notion that a newspaper must necessarily be "liberal" or "conservative" is as outdated as the idea that individual Americans can easily be placed in such a box. As George Bush learned in 1992, they cannot.*

It would have been interesting to see how other media—even one of the suburban Detroit dailies—would have sought to fill the void left by the failed paper, whichever it might have been. I'm not suggesting that an *Ann Arbor News* or an *Oakland Press* would have replaced the *Free Press* or the *News*, but undoubtedly the vacuum would have been filled, probably in bits and pieces, by an assortment of other voices. Publishers of large dailies are fond of citing statistics showing that major cities have lost newspapers, when in fact many cities have benefited from the expansion of smaller papers in surrounding

*Many newspapers in 1992 did not endorse a presidential candidate—some 559 representing nearly twenty-three million in circulation, according to *Editor and Publisher* magazine. Shortly before the election, Richard Harwood wrote in the *Washington Post* that newspapers "to a considerable extent have depoliticized themselves. As often as not they are spectators rather than participants in our political wars."

communities. A good example is Los Angeles, where the *Orange County Register* has become one of the most successful and progressive dailies in the country. In Detroit, the incentive to claim audience and ad revenues left behind by the failed paper would have been tremendous. That would have been the natural order of the market.

Instead, the JOA foisted an unnatural order on the Detroit media market, and everyone suffered. The prospect of getting a JOA prolonged the insanity of the newspaper war. The artificially depressed price structure hurt television, radio, and suburban publishers as well as the *Free Press* and the *News*. Consumers and advertisers benefited for a while, but now they are paying for the free lunch. Meanwhile, both Detroit dailies fell woefully behind the industry in modernizing their business operations, leaving them ill-prepared to compete in the 1990s.

Only in 1992 did Gannett and Knight-Ridder persuade the Teamsters to agree to a streamlining of the antiquated circulation operation. Only in 1992 did they get the Pressmen to reduce "manning" minimums that had the Detroit papers employing dozens more printers than comparable papers. Those negotiated changes cost the publishers $25 million to buy out three hundred to four hundred employees, and $2 million to prepare for a possible strike. Only now are the publishers building the mail room the *Free Press* needed years ago. Only now have they begun to develop subscriber and advertiser databases. "All these things fell by the wayside," a former *News* executive explained, "because we needed the money to keep the war going."

When Joseph Ungaro succeeded Bill Keating at the DNA in March of 1990, he found an operation "at least ten or twenty years behind the times," he said. "There's so much to do and so much catch-up. . . . I don't think [Gannett and Knight-Ridder] were conscious of how far behind we've fallen, or of the changes in the marketplace." When fourteen months later Ungaro was replaced by Frank Vega, a no-necked Neuharth protégé who had been one of the four whiz kids chosen to dream up *USA Today*, Vega found "one of the least efficient operations in America." So focused had the newspapers been on each other that they hadn't seen the world passing them by.

The slow, painful birth of the Detroit JOA was akin to Rip van Winkle waking from his long sleep. When the *Free Press* and the *News* emerged from their war, the world was different. Newspapers were ill-advised to compete solely against each other anymore, with so many nimble new rivals on the scene. Advertisers looked to a diverse array of alternative vehicles before accepting higher rates. Profits didn't come as easily, though Wall Street expected them to grow every year. Subscribers weren't as loyal; indeed, many were bored with newspapers—especially young readers, the generation that will pose newspapers' greatest challenge in the twenty-first century. More than ever, newspapers had to concentrate on business affairs to sustain their journalistic franchise, while resisting temptations to relegate reporting the news to a secondary role. Newspapers were struggling to reinvent the way they presented the news—with new packaging, graphic devices, reader interaction—without devaluing it. Jack Knight's simple formula for success—produce a fairly priced, high-quality newspaper and the money will take care of itself—had become a terribly complicated equation in the 1990s.

In his book, *Read All About It! The Corporate Takeover of America's Newspapers,* former *Chicago Tribune* editor James D. Squires laments the passing of an era in which strong-willed patriarchs and their families ruled the great newspapers. As a newspaper journalist, I can work up some of the same nostalgia, but I don't think I can afford to, because those days—which weren't quite as glorious as Squires chooses to recall—cannot be retrieved. Companies cannot easily go unpublic. Wall Street's understandable hunger for ever-growing profits cannot be wished away. Technological evolution cannot be halted. Whether we like it or not, we must move on, under all the new constraints and pressures that change has brought on.

The Detroit newspapers, though at a lumbering pace, and with a few stumbles along the way, finally seem to be moving on. It remains to be seen whether the JOA is in fact their savior or their curse. For the *Free Press* and the *News* now know that they limped away from one epic battle only to find that the real one—for survival in a new and more demanding era—was just beginning. That war, in Detroit and elsewhere, is far, far from over.

Acknowledgments

At the risk of cliché, I have to say that this book was a labor of love, and not only my own. My wife, Pamela, endured my long travel absences, ungodly early awakenings, weekends at the computer, and occasional periods of distraction as I tried to complete this project while also attending to my duties at the *Detroit News*. No one helped me with this book more—with encouragement, criticism, and faith. I will never be able to thank her enough. Our children, Joel, Kaitlin, and Danielle, tolerated my absences and offered hugs and laughter when I needed them most. I also want to thank my parents, whose unflagging belief in my work has inspired me.

I did some preliminary research while on a summer fellowship at the Woodrow Wilson International Center for Scholars in Washington. Many thanks to Philip Cook and Lawrence Lichty for inviting me to the center and for excusing my failure to deliver the essay they had expected; I hope *Paper Losses* suffices. While at the center, I also made a friend in author Joel Swerdlow, who offered invaluable practical advice for a novice book writer.

My bosses at the *News* were patient and encouraging while respecting my independence and freedom. Thanks to Bob Giles for trusting me enough to offer a paid leave of absence. Also to James P. Gannon and Deb Price of the *News*'s Washington bureau for their tolerance of my extracurricular project. I am especially grateful to Mark Lett, the editor who worked most closely with me on my daily coverage of the JOA for the *News*. All reporters on such an awkward and complicated assignment should have the benefit of Mark's intelligence and sense of humor.

This book wouldn't have been possible without the cooperation of Knight-Ridder, Inc., and the Gannett Company. I am grateful to the many executives and staff who patiently sat for my interviews, especially Messrs. Chapman and Neuharth. I also want to thank Heidi Etzold and Jane Moreau of Knight-Ridder, Sheila Gibbons of Gannett, and Jeanna Copeland of the Freedom Forum for arranging interviews and checking facts. Librarians at both newspapers were extraordinarily helpful. Thanks to Vivian Baulch, Anita Mack, and Pat Zacharias at the *News* and to Chris Kucharski and Bernadine Aubert at the *Free Press*. Librarian Yvonne Egertson of the Newspaper Association of America also was a great help.

Warren Wilkinson, the former director of the Evening News Association, opened his voluminous history of the company to me. Michael W. R. Davis of the ENA contributed a box of his files and a collection of relevant audio- and videotapes. Robert Pisor of WDIV-TV gave me several helpful videotapes and the use of his station's equipment for an afternoon. Michael Schroeder, formerly of the *News* and currently of *Business Week* magazine, and Bernie Shellum of the *Free Press* shared their files on the takeover of the ENA. Neal Rubin of the *Free Press* offered material he had gathered for an academic project on the Newspaper Preservation Act. Ric Bohy, a former *News* reporter now writing for *Detroit Monthly* magazine, helped me research the death of Elton Schade. Barbara Petersen shared her dissertation on the JOA's effects on the *Free Press*. My good friend Andrew Price loaned me a computer when I was in need. I thank them all.

Many other friends and colleagues offered support and encouragement, none more than Brian Egan and David Kocieniewski. Richard Willing lent his intelligence and passion for storytelling to some of the most difficult portions of the book; he also gave it its title. Richard Ryan and Gregory Gordon offered useful criticisms and suggestions.

This book was not an easy sell, but my agent, Suzanne Gluck of International Creative Management, is a tough, smart, persistent professional. I am indebted to her for believing in me. That goes as well for Walter Bode, former editor in chief of Grove Press, who early on saw potential in this story despite my clumsy attempts to articulate it. His colleague Allison Draper was always courteous and helpful. I am grateful to Morgan Entrekin, Anton Mueller, and the others at Atlantic Monthly Press who embraced this book after their company merged with Grove. Also to Ed Sedarbaum, whose careful editing saved me from myself countless times.

Space is too limited to name the dozens of other people who helped make this book possible. I am nevertheless grateful to all of them. I must, however, single out the staffs of the *Free Press* and the *News,* current and past. Whatever passion I have brought to the telling of this tale was inspired in great measure by them.

BRYAN GRULEY
April 1993

Notes

This story derives in part from interviews I did with more than 220 people, including virtually all of the major participants. Only a few significant characters declined to be interviewed. Many individuals, including Alvah Chapman, Peter Clark, and Al Neuharth, sat for several lengthy interviews. I also relied on tens of thousands of pages of court documents and documents filed by Gannett and Knight-Ridder with their JOA application to the Justice Department. In addition, I drew on my coverage of the newspapers' effort to obtain the JOA, including my stories, contemporaneous notes, and firsthand observations. I was present for many of the scenes described in the narrative.

I borrowed heavily from the excellent work of many colleagues, especially *Free Press* reporters John Dunphy, Patricia Edmonds, William J. Mitchell, and Bernie Shellum and *News* reporters Diane Katz, Kathleen Kerwin, Keith Naughton, David Sedgwick, and John F. Nehman. Former *News* reporter Ric Bohy, now a senior editor at *Detroit Monthly* magazine, assisted me with reporting on the death of Elton Schade. Because the *Free Press* and *News* articles I borrowed from number in the hundreds, I have not bothered to cite all of them individually.

Reconstructed dialogue frequently is drawn from verbatim court transcripts or meeting minutes. Occasionally I relied on the memory of participants, though I tried to point out where there were sharp disagreements over what was said. In all cases I strove mightily to represent accurately the spirit and tone of what was said. Most references to an unnamed "*News* reporter" mean me. Until the concluding chaper, I chose not to distract the reader with direct references to the author, although I did see fit in one instance to identify myself in a footnote.

Introduction

The phrase "conservatism and restraint" is borrowed from an *amicus curiae* brief filed by Jane Daugherty et al. in *Michigan Citizens for an Independent Press* v. *Thornburgh.*

Chapter 1: The Promise

Much of the detail in the opening scenes is from a lengthy report in the *Detroit News,* August 30, 1985; a videotape of Neuharth's appearance in the newsroom, provided by Michael W. R. Davis; my firsthand observations; and interviews with Clark, Neuharth, Jay Higgins, and others. Written sources include William Lutz's 1973 history of the *News.*

Chapter 2: The Tin Box

The portrait of Peter Clark emerges from interviews with Clark and many of his colleagues, including Robert Nelson, Richard Spitzley, Richard Wallace, Warren Wilkinson, and others. Material concerning the demise of the *Detroit Times* is from interviews with Lee Hills, Robert Kurzawa, Neal Shine, Clark, Nelson, Neuharth, and others, as well as from Louis Ferman's 1963 paper, "Death of a Newspaper: The Story of the *Detroit Times,*" W. E. Upjohn Institute for Employment Research; and from reports in the *Wall Street Journal,* November 8, 1960, and *Time,* November 21, 1960, and October 27, 1961.

Written sources include early issues of the *News,* James Scripps's personal diary, Warren Wilkinson's unpublished history of the ENA, internal ENA reports and memoranda, an unpublished essay by George B. Catlin, and Walker Roberts's master's thesis, "An Organizational and Economic Case Study of the *Detroit News,*" Michigan State University, 1972. Books consulted include Robert Conot's history of Detroit, Lutz's history of the *News,* Frank Angelo's history of the *Free Press,* Arthur Pound's biography of George Gough Booth, David Halberstam's *The Reckoning,* Richard Kluger's *The Paper,* Peter Benjaminson's *Death in the Afternoon,* Sidney Fine's *Violence in the Model City,* Oliver Knight's *I Protest: Selected Disquisitions of E. W. Scripps,* and Negley D. Cochran's biography of E. W. Scripps.

Chapter 3: The Hornet's Nest

The opening section derives primarily from interviews with Robert Vlasic, Dan Martin, the Booth brothers, and Clark. Sketches of John M. Booth and Warren Booth derive from interviews with family members and others familiar with them. Other scenes rely in part on interviews with Porter Bibb, Peter Kizer, Earl McClure, David McKearnan, Guerin Todd, several ENA directors, Clark, Warren Booth's son, Peter Booth, and others.

Written sources include voluminous documents filed in ENA tender offer litigation, U.S. District Court, Eastern District of Michigan, Southern Division; *L.P. Acquisition Co.* v. *Tyson et al.,* same court; and *Kizer* v. *ENA,* Wayne County Circuit Court. I also used documents submitted with the Detroit papers' JOA application to the Justice Department; letters and internal ENA reports and memoranda collected by Warren Wilkinson; and letters collected by Guerin Todd. Chief among other written sources were several reports by Bernie

Shellum and Michael Wagner in the *Free Press,* as well as reports in the *News; Metropolitan Detroit,* November 1986; *Business Week,* April 1, 1985; *U.S. News and World Report,* February 11, 1985, and May 13, 1985; *Broadcast Investor,* June 10, 1985; and the *Wall Street Journal,* July 1, 1985, and August 14, 1986. I also consulted *Down to the Wire: UPI's Fight for Survival,* by Ronald Cohen and Gregory Gordon.

Chapter 4: White Knights

The portrayal of the ENA's final weeks is drawn from interviews with Ed Frederickson, Clark, Higgins, Kizer, Nelson, Neuharth, Todd, Vlasic, and all but one of the ENA directors, as well as sworn testimony, internal ENA and Gannett memoranda, and other documents filed in the ENA tender offer litigation, in *Kizer* v. *ENA,* and with the Justice Department.

Clark's confrontation with Kizer was recalled by all the participants. The sketch of Neuharth derives from interviews with Neuharth; his autobiography, *Confessions of an SOB;* the *Los Angeles Times,* September 7, 1978; *Business Month,* February 1989; and *Lear's,* December 1989. The reconstruction of the ENA auction relies on detailed minutes of the meeting filed in the ENA tender offer litigation, related documents, and interviews with many of the participants, with the exceptions of Jack Kent Cooke and Edward Gaylord, who did not acknowledge my calls.

Other written sources include several reports in the *Free Press* and the *News;* the *New York Times,* July 11 and August 27, 1985; *Variety,* June 19, 1985; *Business Week,* August 12 and December 9; the *Wall Street Journal,* August 12, August 28, and December 20, 1991. I also consulted *Barbarians at the Gate,* by Bryan Burrough and John Helyar, Allan Sloan's *Three Plus One Equals Billions: The Bendix–Martin Marietta War,* and Pound's biography of George Gough Booth.

Chapter 5: Black Knight

Detail on *SoDak Sports* is from *Confessions of an SOB,* Peter Prichard's *The Making of McPaper: The Inside Story of USA Today,* and interviews with Neuharth. Neuharth at the *Free Press* was recalled by Judd Arnett, Tom Nicholson, Hills, Shine, and others. Neuharth's quote on working with Chapman is from *SOB.* Material on Neuharth's first decade at Gannett is drawn from *SOB, McPaper,* Gannett annual reports, a wide variety of newspaper and magazine articles, and interviews with J. Donald Brandt, Jack Heselden, Douglas McCorkindale, John Quinn, Neuharth, and others.

Material on Frank Gannett is from Ben Bagdikian's *The Media Monopoly,* Ellis Cose's *The Press,* Paul Miller's *50 Plus 50,* Oswald Garrison Villard's *The Disappearing Daily: Chapters in American Newspaper Evolution,* Samuel T. Williamson's *Imprint of a Publisher: The Story of Frank Gannett and his Independent Newspapers,* and Richard Polenberg's paper "Frank E. Gannett: A Progressive Publisher in Politics." Newspaper companies going public is discussed by Sam Kuczun in *Journalism Quarterly,* Summer 1978, and Leo Bogart in the book *Press and Public.*

Circulation data are from the Audit Bureau of Circulations. Transcripts of Neuharth's talks at the Detroit Press Club and the Economic Club of Detroit were filed with the Justice Department. Detail on Gannett's takeover of the *News* is from Gannett and *News* memoranda filed with the Justice Department and provided by other sources, as well as interviews with Don Becker, John Curley, Brian Donnelly, Thomas Farrell, Robert Hall, Richard McClennen, Jerome Tilis, Louis A. Weil III, Neuharth, McCorkindale, and others. Neuharth's February meeting with ENA officials was taped by Michael W. R. Davis. Material on early JOA discussions is from documents filed with the Justice Department and interviews with James Batten, Neuharth, Curley, McCorkindale, Chapman, and others.

Written sources include several stories in the *News;* Associated Press Managing Editors's report on *USA Today,* 1983; *Forbes,* October 1, 1969; the *Washington Post,* December 19, 1978; *Esquire,* September 1979; *Dun's Review,* December 1980; *Tropic* magazine, September 5, 1982; the *Wall Street Journal,* November 13, 1974, and September 16, 1987; *Business Week,* September 30, 1985; the *New York Times,* January 7, 1986; and *Florida Today,* January 12, 1986. I also consulted John K. Hartman's *The USA Today Way* and Nixon Smiley's *Knights of the Fourth Estate.*

Chapter 6: JSK

Chapman's wartime experience is from Don Becker's account in *Editor and Publisher,* November 15, 1975, and interviews with Chapman and retired Col. C. M. "Smitty" Smith. The section on young Alvah Chapman derives from a wide variety of newspaper and magazine articles and from interviews with Thomas Coffey, Lester Freeman, Byron Harless, retired Army Lt. Gen. George M. Seignious II, C. M. "Smitty" Smith, Charles Whited, Chapman, and others.

The portrait of Jack Knight relies heavily on Charles Whited's biography, *Knight: A Publisher in the Tumultuous Century,* less so on Nixon Smiley's *Knights of the Fourth Estate.* Knight's remarks to financial analysts were reported in "A Presentation by Knight Newspapers Inc.," New York Society of Security Analysts, February 24, 1970. Material on Chapman and the development of Knight-Ridder is from a variety of newspaper and magazine articles, Ellis Cose's *The Press,* and interviews with Frank Hawkins, Jr., John C. Fontaine, Bernard H. Ridder, Jr., P. Anthony Ridder, Batten, Chapman, Harless, and others.

Other written sources include *The Mass Media: Aspen Institute Guide to Communication Industry Trends; Facts About Newspapers '89,* the American Newspaper Publishers Association; *Business Week,* August 29, 1970; *Columbia Journalism Review,* November/December 1972; *Editor and Publisher,* November 15, 1975, and April 19, 1986; *Forbes,* January 2, 1984, and August 8, 1988; *Detroit Free Press,* January 24, 1988; *Miami Herald,* February 6, 1991.

Chapter 7: Operation Tiger

History of the *Free Press* is from Frank Angelo's *On Guard: A History of the Detroit Free Press,* Whited's biography of Jack Knight, Smiley's biography of the Knight brothers, a letter from Lee Hills, and interviews. Derick Daniels's thoughts on newspapering are from an essay he wrote for the *Quill,* July 1970. The sketch of Kurt Luedtke is from a profile by David A. Markiewicz, *Michigan* magazine, December 15, 1985, several *Free Press* and *News* stories, and interviews with Gary Blonston, Christina Bradford, Batten, Luedtke, Shine, and others. The sketch of David Lawrence, Jr., is from profiles by Patricia Edmonds in the *Free Press* and Laurie Bennett in the *News,* both July 28, 1989; and Marney Rich in *Detroit Monthly,* April 1988; as well as interviews with Joe Distelheim, Robert Hall, Joe Stroud, Batten, Chapman, Lawrence, Shine, and others.

Free Press financial figures are from Administrative Law Judge Morton Needelman's recommended opinion, December 29, 1987; Assistant Attorney General Douglas Ginsburg's report, July 22, 1986; and documents filed with the Justice Department. Some of the thoughts on newspapers' mounting difficulties are from John Morton, "The Shape of Things to Come," *Washington Journalism Review,* April 1983; and Leo Bogart's writings, including "Urban Papers Under Pressure," *Columbia Journalism Review,* September/October 1974; "Newspapers in Transition," the *Wilson Quarterly,* Special Issue 1982; and Bogart's *Press and Public.*

Chapman and Bernie Ridder spoke of Knight-Ridder's efforts to sell the *Free Press.* Material on JOA negotiations between Knight-Ridder and the Evening News Association is from memoranda and notes filed with the Justice Department, Needelman's recommended opinion, sworn testimony given in the administrative hearing on the JOA, and interviews with Clark, Chapman, and others.

The sketch of the competitive battle in Philadelphia relies heavily on Peter Benjaminson's *Death in the Afternoon,* as well as documents filed with the Justice Department and interviews with Richard McClennen, Jerome Tilis, Hall, and others. Detail on Operation Tiger derives primarily from memos, reports, and other documents filed with the Justice Department; hearing testimony; Needelman's opinion; a report by Howard Gold in the *Miami Review,* January 26, 1987; and interviews with Batten, Chapman, Hall, Harless, Lawrence, Bernie Ridder, Tilis, and others.

Knight-Ridder and *Free Press* thinking on the prospect of competing with Gannett is from interviews and from memos and reports filed with the Justice Department, including an October 25, 1985, presentation by Hall, Lawrence, and Tilis to Knight-Ridder executives. The meeting at the Waldorf Towers was reconstructed from memos and interviews with all participants.

Other written sources include numerous stories in the *Free Press* and the *News;* the *Quill,* October 1981; *Detroit Monthly,* June 1982; the *New York Times,* June 6, 1982; *Time,* January 17, 1983; *Editor and Publisher,* January 29, 1983, and January 14, 1984; *Time,* December 12, 1983; *Broward Review,* January 26, 1987; and an unpublished manuscript by *Free Press* reporter Bernie Shellum.

Chapter 8: Sabbath

Material on the JOA negotiations is from voluminous memoranda and other documents filed with the Justice Department and from interviews with all principal participants. I also used transcripts of lengthy interviews conducted by *News* reporter Ric Bohy with several of the participants, including Neuharth and Chapman; and transcripts of *Free Press* reporter Shellum's interviews of Chapman and Harless. Detail on Chapman's trip to Israel is from Celia Dugger's story in the *Miami Herald,* "Power Brokers Form Bonds in Holy Land," February 1, 1988. A videotape of the press conference announcing the JOA was provided by Robert Pisor of WDIV-TV in Detroit. Neuharth's appearance before the analysts in San Francisco is recounted in the Morton Research newsletter.

Other sources include numerous stories in the *Free Press* and the *News,* especially "A Saga of Power, Pride and Fear," William J. Mitchell, the *Free Press,* August 9, 1988; and "The Deal: From Executive Chat, Tidy Plan Evolved," Bryan Gruley, the *News,* August 9, 1988. Also, *Metropolitan Detroit,* June 1986; the *New York Times,* April 15, 1986; Prichard's *The Making of McPaper;* and Neuharth's *Confessions of an SOB.*

Chapter 9: Welfare for the Rich

Material on the JOA application is from the application itself, accompanying documents, and interviews with Lawrence Aldrich, Calvin Collier, and others. The discussion of the passage of the Newspaper Preservation Act relies heavily on Ralph Johnson's exhaustive dissertation, "Blunting the Thrust of Antitrust: A Legal-Historical Study of the Citizen Publishing Case and the Newspaper Preservation Act," University of Wisconsin, 1975. Other sources include John C. Busterna's 1989 monograph, "Daily Newspaper Chains and the Antitrust Laws," *Journalism Monographs;* Douglas Lea's report, "Lobbying Overwhelms Opponents of Newspaper Preservation Act," *National Journal,* July 25, 1970; "Does Newspaper Competition Make a Difference to Readers?" by John C. Schweitzer and Elaine Goldman in *Journalism Quarterly,* Winter 1975; and *America Inc.,* by Morton Mintz and Jerry S. Cohen. Also Stephen Barnett in the *Recorder,* October 23, 1989; Barnett in *Columbia Journalism Review,* November/December 1980; Dennis Holder in the *Washington Journalism Review,* November 1982; and numerous articles in the *New York Times* and *Editor and Publisher.* President Nixon's change of heart is discussed in Ben Bagdikian's *The Media Monopoly.*

The section on the Justice Department's early consideration of the JOA application relies primarily on interviews with Charles F. Rule, Seymour Dussman, Aldrich, Collier, and others. The Reagan administration's views on economics and law are discussed in *Congressional Quarterly,* February 1, 1986; *Barron's,* October 10, 1986; and the *Economist,* September 23, 1986. Material on the development of opposition to the JOA is from numerous stories in the *Free Press* and the *News,* and interviews with William Keating, Hillel Levin, Kurt Luedtke, Lawrence, and others.

Other written sources include *Forbes,* October 1, 1969; *Editor and Publisher,* March 13, 1982; and *Newsweek,* November 9, 1987.

Chapter 10: Fighting Words

The opening scene is from interviews with Donald Kummer, Bruce Miller, Louis Mleczko, Duane Ice, and Keating (John Jaske declined to be interviewed). The sketch of

Keating derives from numerous articles in the *Cincinnati Enquirer, Metro Times,* the *Free Press,* and the *News,* and interviews with Keating and many others.

Material on the Newspaper Guild is from *The Press and America,* a text by Michael Emery and Edwin Emery; Daniel J. Leab's 1970 history; the *Guild Reporter,* December 16, 1983; Albert Scardino's article in the *New York Times,* August 15, 1988; Daniel Lazare's article in *Columbia Journalism Review,* January/February 1989; numerous stories in the *Free Press,* the *News,* and *Editor and Publisher;* and interviews with Charles Dale, David Eisen, Kummer, Mleczko, and others. The 1967–68 strike was recounted by Jack Crellin in the *News,* August 9, 1968; and David C. Smith and Jack Martin in the *Free Press,* August 10, 1968.

The sketch of Elton Schade relies chiefly on interviews with Thomas Brennan, Tom Minielly, Gretchen Schumann, Edgar Scribner, Joel Wilson, Kummer, Mleczko, Nelson, and others, as well as stories in the *Free Press* and the *News.*

Chapter 11: Bean Counters

Discussion of the assistant attorney general's report on the JOA application relies on the report itself and stories in the *Free Press* and the *News.* Detail of Guild Local 22's membership meeting is contained in the minutes and John Dunphy's story in the *Free Press,* September 26, 1986. Jerald F. terHorst's encounter with Edwin Meese was recounted by terHorst and partially disputed by Meese in interviews. The lawyers' expectations of Needelman are drawn from interviews with Philip Lacovara, John Stuart Smith, Aldrich, Chapman, Collier, Lawrence, and others.

Dialogue from the prehearing conference and the administrative hearing is from transcripts of the proceedings. Courtroom scenes also draw on witnesses' written direct testimony, my firsthand observations, interviews with many participants, and numerous stories in the *Free Press* and the *News.* The private exchange at Needelman's bench was related by Aldrich and confirmed by others. The sketch of Duane Ice is from interviews with Ice and others and an article in the *Arizona Republic,* September 20, 1983. The sketch of Gene Driker is from interviews with Andrew Zack, Driker, and others and from *Free Press* and *News* articles.

Chapter 12: Bolt Out of the Blue

Material on BusCapade is from Neuharth's *Confessions of an SOB* and *BusCapade: Plain Talk Across the USA* and from Lloyd Grove's article in the *Washington Post,* April 10, 1987. Details of the *Free Press*'s woes are from internal memoranda filed with the Justice Department, numerous stories in the *Free Press* and the *News,* and interviews with Scott Bosley, Robert Giles, Batten, Chapman, Hall, Lawrence, Tilis, Weil, and others.

Neuharth told me of his plan in Little Rock in an interview. Madelyn Jennings's notes were filed with the Justice Department. Details on the crash of Northwest Flight 255 are from *Free Press* and *News* articles published the week of August 16, 1987. Lawrence's role in the editing of an article about his testimony is from interviews with Jacquelynn Boyle, Stephen Jones, Lawrence, and others, as well as Edmonds's profile of Lawrence in the *Free*

Press, July 28, 1989. Needelman's thought process was gleaned from interviews with the judge (who declined to speak specifically about the JOA case). The final section is from Needelman's recommended opinion.

Chapter 13: Drastic Measures

Chapman described his late-night epiphany in interviews. Material on Knight-Ridder's JOA campaign is from Mitchell's account in the *Free Press,* February 7, 1988; Gruley's "The Deal" in the *News,* August 9, 1988; numerous other *Free Press* and *News* articles; and interviews with James Blanchard, Clark Clifford, Jack Fontaine, Heath Meriwether, Chapman, Neuharth, Lawrence, Batten, Lacovara, and others. Reader letters are excerpted from the *Free Press,* January 17, 1988. Background on William Timmons and Tom Korologos is from *Dun's Business Month,* August 1983; *Congressional Quarterly,* September 12, 1987; and the *News,* January 20, 1988. Korologos declined to be interviewed; the anecdote concerning Lee Iacocca was recounted by *News* reporter Michael Clements, who was told by Korologos himself. The sketch of Clark Clifford is from several written sources, especially Marjorie Williams's profile in the *Washington Post,* May 8, 1991, and Sidney Blumenthal's profile in the *Washington Post Magazine,* February 5, 1989, as well as from interviews with Clifford and many others. The closing scene was reconstructed from interviews with Clifford, Lacovara, Chapman, Fontaine, and others.

Chapter 14: The Falling Leaf

Material on the Knight-Ridder board meeting and press conference is from the minutes of the meeting, coverage in the *Free Press* and the *News,* my firsthand observations, and interviews with Batten, Chapman, Clifford, Fontaine, Lawrence, Bernie Ridder, Tony Ridder, and others. The remembrance of Winston Churchill is from Blumenthal's profile of Clifford in the *Washington Post Magazine,* February 5, 1989. *News* reporter Michael Clements provided his notes of contemporaneous interviews with John Dingell and Shine. Other sources include Ron Dorfman's essay "JOA Terrorism," the *Quill,* February 1988; and *Time,* February 1, 1988.

Chapter 15: Divided They Fall

The opening scene is from interviews with Jane Daugherty, David Everett, Kummer, and Mleczko. The sketch of Coleman Young is from several sources, especially Kirk Cheyfitz in *Detroit Monthly,* February 1981; Allan Lengel in the *News,* January 27, 1985; Edmonds in the *Free Press,* April 5, 1987; Ric Bohy in *Detroit Monthly,* April 1989; and Ze'ev Chafets in the *New York Times Magazine,* July 29, 1990. Young did not agree to be interviewed for this book; the account of his change of heart is from coverage in the *Free Press* and the *News,* especially Barbara Stanton in the *Free Press,* February 12, 1988, and interviews with Joe Stroud, Chapman, and Lawrence. The reconstruction of Guild Local 22's February 15 meeting is from the minutes, *Free Press* and *News* coverage, and interviews with Kate

DeSmet, Rob Musial, Daugherty, Everett, Kummer, Mleczko, and others. Detail on the unions' withdrawal is from news coverage and interviews with Timothy Kelleher, Driker, Hall, Ice, Keating, Kummer, Mleczko, Wilson, and others. Driker's letter to Seymour Dussman and Harry Flickinger's memo to Brad Reynolds were obtained through a Freedom of Information Act request to the Justice Department. Daugherty and DeSmet provided copies of the letters they wrote to each other.

Chapter 16: Pulling Punches

Meese's woes were recounted in the *News,* February 17, April 24, and April 25, 1988; the *New York Times,* March 29, 1988; the *Wall Street Journal,* April 27, 1988; the *Free Press,* May 15, 1988; and *National Journal,* June 18, 1988. Memos by Steve Matthews, Flickinger, and Reynolds and Clifford's reply were obtained through a Freedom of Information Act request.

The account of the cartoon episode is from the *Washington Post,* July 19, 1988; the *Miami Herald,* August 7, 1988; a *Free Press* computer search; coverage in the *Free Press* and the *News;* and interviews with Thomas Bray, Bill Day, James Hampton, Larry Wright, Stroud, and Lawrence. The section on Meese and his colleagues' deliberations relies on Meese's opinion and order, August 8, 1988; and interviews with Frank Atkinson, William Levin, Michael Socarras, Meese, and Reynolds.

Chapter 17: Wishful Thinking

The sketch of Tony Ridder borrows from profiles by Dory Owens in the *Miami Herald,* January 12, 1987, and by Pete Engardio in *Business Week,* November 23, 1987, as well as interviews. Material on the negotiations between Guild Local 22 and Knight-Ridder is from *Free Press* and *News* reports and from interviews with Charles Dale, Keating, Kummer, Mleczko, and Ridder. Detail on the crucial Guild board meeting is from the minutes and from interviews with several participants. Bob Giles's thoughts are from several interviews. Detail concerning Meese's decision is from the attorney general's opinion, *Free Press* and *News* coverage, and interviews with Chapman, Neuharth, and others.

Chapter 18: To Kill the *Free Press*

The sketches of John Kelly and Matt Beer are from several articles in the *News* and interviews with Beer, Kelly, and others. Kelly's letter to Meese was obtained through a Freedom of Information Act request. The sketch of Bill Schultz is from *News* articles and interviews. Material on pre-JOA planning and implementation is from *Free Press* and *News* reports and interviews with Giles, Hall, Keating, Kurzawa, McClennen, Weil, and several other executives and employees. The $35,000-a-day loss figure, later increased, is from the oral argument before Judge Joyce Hens Green. The sketch of Wendover is from *News* stories and interviews with Wendover and others. Wendover recalled Lawrence's quote about killing the *Free Press* in an interview; Lawrence did not dispute it.

Schultz recalled Lacovara's magnanimous gesture in Judge Green's court. Detail on the hearing is from a court transcript and *Free Press* and *News* coverage. Material on the exodus from Hughes Hubbard and Reed is from Eleanor Kerlow's article in *Legal Times,* September 26, 1988, and interviews. The portrayal of the chaotic response to Judge Green's ruling is from *Free Press* and *News* coverage and interviews with Chapman, Giles, Hall, Lawrence, Weil, and others. Weil remembered the exchange with Lawrence.

Chapter 19: Jerking Around

Letters critical of John Kelly were provided by Kelly and published in the *Free Press* and the *News.* Detail on the Little Rock battle is from court briefs filed by Walter Hussman and Gannett, articles in *Editor and Publisher,* the *New York Times,* and the *Washington Post,* as well as interviews with Aldrich, Hussman, Schultz, Vladeck, and others.

The argument before Judge George Revercomb was drawn from a court transcript, Revercomb's opinion and order, *Free Press* and *News* coverage, and interviews with John Stuart Smith, Aldrich, Chapman, Clifford, Schultz, and Vladeck. The September 15 meeting of Gannett and Knight-Ridder was recalled by several participants, including Aldrich, Chapman, Curley, Fontaine, McCorkindale, and John Smith. Clifford, Schultz, and Vladeck told me of their meeting at Clifford and Warnke. The conversation with Warren Buffett is from interviews with Buffett, Schultz, and Vladeck.

Material on the closing of the *Miami News* is from Joel Achenbach's article in *Tropic* magazine, January 29, 1989; reports in the *Miami News* and *Crain's Detroit Business;* and contemporaneous interviews with David Easterly and Frank Hawkins. Detail on the argument before the D.C. Circuit Court of Appeals is from a court transcript, *Free Press* and *News* coverage, and interviews with Douglas Letter, Aldrich, Clifford, Chapman, Curley, Fontaine, Schultz, John Smith, and Vladeck.

Written sources include the *New York Times,* September 11, 1982, and September 20, 1982; *Fortune,* April 11, 1988; and *American Lawyer* supplement, May/June 1988.

Chapter 20: The Big Win

The meeting at Musial's bar was recounted in interviews with Beer, Kelly, Mleczko, Schultz, and Wendover. Material on the meeting at Gannett headquarters is from *Free Press* and *News* coverage and interviews with Aldrich, Batten, Chapman, Curley, Fontaine, McCorkindale, Neuharth, Tony Ridder, John Smith, and others. Detail on Neuharth's retirement party is from my firsthand observations, a tribute to Neuharth published by Gannett, and the *Washington Post,* March 23, 1989. Neuharth's retirement compensation is spelled out in Gannett's proxy statement to shareholders, March 14, 1988. The citation for *Palmore* v. *Sidoti* is 466 U.S. 429, 80 L Ed 2d 421, 104 S Ct 1879. Specifics of the exchange between Clifford and Smith rely more heavily on Smith's recollection, though I read Smith's version to Clifford, who endorsed it as a fair description. Smith provided charts of the court data gathered by his associates. McCorkindale remembered feeling good about winning "the whole thing" in an interview in August 1990. Chapman admitted in an interview in July 1990 that he wouldn't have closed the *Free Press* if the Supreme Court undid a prematurely launched JOA. Weil's encounter with Justice Byron White is from interviews with Weil and Richard Ryan, my firsthand observations, and Keith Naughton's story in the *News*, October 29, 1989. Detail on the Supreme Court's granting of *certiorari* is from *Free Press* and *News* coverage.

Chapter 21: A Matter of Survival

Material on Elton Schade and his death is from 1992 reporting by Ric Bohy, Schade's certificate of death filed with the Wayne County medical examiner, *News* and *Free Press* coverage, and interviews with Wayne County Medical Examiner Bader Cassin, Julie Eberspacher, Minielly, Schumann, and others.

Detail on the departures of Lawrence, Hall, and Shine is from *Free Press* and *News* coverage and interviews with the subjects. The various parties' Supreme Court arguments are spelled out in their written briefs to the court. Jane Daugherty supplied additional detail about her *amicus* brief in interviews. Material on Brian Flanigan and his death is from a videotape of Flanigan's funeral provided by Richard Willing, and *Free Press* stories and interviews with Patricia Chargot, Jack Kresnak, Nancy Ross-Flanigan, Shine, Willing, and others.

Chapter 22: Five Hundred Miles Away

I witnessed the opening scene. Chapman and Fontaine remembered Knight-Ridder's meetings with Thomas Merrill. Detail on the oral argument before the Supreme Court is from my firsthand observations, a court transcript, *Free Press* and *News* coverage, and interviews with Thomas Merrill, Aldrich, Batten, Chapman, Clifford, Curley, Daugherty, Fontaine, Kelly, Lawrence, McCorkindale, Mleczko, Schultz, Vladeck, Wendover, and others. I also consulted Chief Justice William H. Rehnquist's *The Supreme Court: How It Was, How It Is* and David G. Savage's *Turning Right: The Making of the Rehnquist Supreme Court.*

Michigan Citizens' decision to end its effort to stop the JOA was recounted in *Free Press* and *News* stories and interviews with all the participants. Kelly provided his letter to White and White's reply. The conversation between Jaske and Keating was overheard by *News* reporter Keith Naughton. Material on the labor negotiations is from *Free Press* and *News* coverage and interviews with the principals. The gathering at the Metropolitan Club was recalled by Chapman, Clifford, Letter, and others. Clifford provided a copy of the program and Fontaine's verse. Detail on JOA start-up problems is from the *Wall Street Journal*, January 24, 1990, and November 14, 1991; *Free Press* and *News* coverage, and interviews with James Lipson, Joseph Ungaro, Frank Vega, Batten, Chapman, Curley, Hall, Keating, Kurzawa, McClennen, and several other newspaper executives and employees. Jon Pepper related his truncated encounter with Keating. Shine's return was recounted by Barbara Stanton in the *Free Press*, March 29, 1990. Circulation numbers are from the Audit Bureau of Circulations.

Conclusion: Waking Rip van Winkle

Neuharth repeatedly insisted that the *News* should have retained its daily circulation lead in interviews with me and several other journalists. Mark Hass's remark is from an interview in July 1990. The provision for a reduction in profit split is from Clause 7.4 of the Partnership Agreement between Gannett and Knight-Ridder. Seymour Dussman's remark is from a letter to Ronald Lowe, Wendover's attorney. The estimate of *USA Today*'s cumulative losses was supplied by reliable company sources. Other material on Gannett is from *Editor and Publisher,* October 26, 1991; and *Business Week,* December 16, 1991. Neuharth's quote on the newspaper industry's battle with the Baby Bells is from *Editor and Publisher,* March 28, 1992.

The *Free Press* circulation figure is from the Audit Bureau of Circulations. The reference to investment in research and development is from Robert G. Picard's essay in *Editor and Publisher,* December 19, 1992. Batten's remark is from his keynote address to the annual conference of International Newspaper Advertising and Marketing Executives, January 1992. Kenneth T. Berents's seminal report was published by Alex. Brown and Sons in July 1990. For a discussion of sprawling markets, see John Morton's essay in *Washington Journalism Review,* November 1991. Thomas Curley's words are from *Gannetteer,* January 1990. Detail on the newspaper industry's fight with the Baby Bells is from many sources, especially *Editor and Publisher,* February 15, 1992; Bogart's essay in *Presstime,* March 1992; *News Inc.,* June 1992; *Presstime,* August 1992; and John Rodden's essay in *Media Center Journal,* Spring 1992. Thoughts on the anachronistic nature of the Detroit papers' business operations derive in part from interviews with Keating, Ungaro, and Vega and from the *Journal,* the Detroit Newspaper Agency's newsletter, April 1991. The reference to young readers relies partly on a pair of 1990 studies by the Times Mirror Center for the People and the Press: *The Age of Indifference: A Study of Young Americans and How They View the News* and *The American Media: Who Reads, Who Watches, Who Listens, Who Cares.*

Select Bibliography

Angelo, Frank. *On Guard: A History of the Detroit Free Press. Detroit Free Press*, 1981.

Bagdikian, Ben H. *The Media Monopoly*. Beacon Press, 1990.

Benjaminson, Peter. *Death in the Afternoon: America's Newspaper Giants Struggle for Survival*. Andrews, McMeel and Parker, 1984.

Bogart, Leo. *Press and Public*. Lawrence Erlbaum Associates, 1989.

Claiborne, Jack. *The Charlotte Observer: Its Time and Place, 1869–1986*. University of North Carolina Press, 1986.

Cochran, Negley D. *E. W. Scripps*. Harcourt, Brace, 1933.

Conot, Robert. *American Odyssey*. William Morrow, 1974.

Cook, Philip S.; Gomery, Douglas; and Lichty, Lawrence W., eds. *American Media: The Wilson Quarterly Reader*. Wilson Center Press, 1989.

Cose, Ellis. *The Press*. William Morrow, 1989.

Emery, Michael, and Emery, Edwin, *The Press and America*. 2d ed. Prentice Hall, 1988.

Falbaum, Berl. *The Anchor, Leo and Friends*. JDW Publications, 1978.

Fine, Sidney. *Violence in the Model City*. University of Michigan Press, 1989.

The Freedom Forum Media Studies Center (formerly Gannett Center for Media Studies). *The New Media Barons: Ownership, Leadership and Power* (*Gannett Center Journal*, vol. 3, no. 1, Winter 1989).

———. *Media at the Millenium* (*Media Studies Journal*, vol. 5, no. 4, Fall 1991).

Gordon, Gregory, and Cohen, Ronald. *Down to the Wire: UPI's Fight for Survival*. McGraw Hill, 1990.

Halberstam, David. *The Powers That Be.* Alfred A. Knopf, 1979.
———. *The Reckoning.* William Morrow, 1986.
Hartman, John K. *The USA Today Way: A Candid Look at the National Newspaper's First Decade (1982–1992).* Self-published, 1992.
Holli, Melvin G., ed. *Detroit.* New Viewpoints, 1976.
Kiska, Tim. *Detroit's Powers and Personalities.* Momentum Books, 1989.
Kluger, Richard. *The Paper.* Vintage, 1986.
Knight, Oliver, ed. *I Protest: Selected Disquisitions of E. W. Scripps.* University of Wisconsin Press, 1966.
Leab, Daniel J. *A Union of Individualists: The Formation of the American Newspaper Guild, 1933–1936.* Columbia University Press, 1970.
Liebling, A. J. *The Press.* Pantheon Books, 1975.
Lutz, William W. *The News of Detroit.* Little, Brown, 1973.
Mintz, Morton, and Cohen, Jerry S. *America Inc: Who Owns and Operates the United States.* Dial Press, 1971.
Neuharth, Allen. *Confessions of an SOB.* Doubleday, 1989.
Pound, Arthur. *The Only Thing Worth Finding.* Wayne State University Press, 1964.
———. *Detroit: Dynamic City.* D. Appleton-Century, 1940.
Prichard, Peter. *The Making of McPaper: The Inside Story of USA Today.* Andrews, McMeel and Parker, 1987.
Rehnquist, William H. *The Supreme Court: How It Was, How It Is.* William Morrow, 1987.
Savage, David G. *Turning Right: The Making of the Rehnquist Supreme Court.* John Wiley and Sons, 1992.
Smiley, Nixon. *Knights of the Fourth Estate: The Story of the Miami Herald.* E. A. Seemann Publishing, 1974.
Sterling, Christopher H., and Haight, Timothy R. *The Mass Media: Aspen Institute Guide to Communication Industry Trends.* Praeger Publishers, 1978.
Villard, Oswald Garrison. *The Disappearing Daily: Chapters in American Newspaper Evolution.* Alfred A. Knopf, 1944.
Whited, Charles. *Knight: A Publisher in the Tumultuous Century.* E. P. Dutton, 1988.
Williamson, Samuel T. *Imprint of a Publisher: The Story of Frank Gannett and His Independent Newspapers.* Robert M. McBride, 1948.

Scholarly Papers:

Johnson, Ralph H. "Blunting the Thrust of Antitrust: A Legal-Historical Study of the Citizen Publishing Case and the Newspaper Preservation Act." University of Wisconsin, 1975.
Petersen, Barbara Kathryn. "Relentlessly Interesting: The Effect of the Detroit Joint Operating Agreement on the *Detroit Free Press* Newsroom Culture." University of Michigan, 1991.

Polenberg, Richard. "Frank E. Gannett: A Progressive Publisher in Politics." Cornell University, 1987.

Roberts, Walker. "An Organization and Economic Case Study of the *Detroit News*." Michigan State University, 1972.

Index